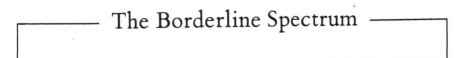

The Borderline Spectrum

THE

BORDERLINE SPECTRUM

Differential Diagnosis and Developmental Issues

W. W. MEISSNER, S.J., M.D.

Jason Aronson, Inc.
New York and London

10 9 8 7 6 5 4 3 2 1

Library of Congress Cataloging in Publication Data

Meissner, W. W. (William Walter), 1931–
The borderline spectrum.

Bibliography: p. 461
Includes index.
1. Mental illness—diagnosis. 2. Psychology, Patho-
logical. I. Title.
RC439.M44 1983   616.89   83-11936
ISBN 0-87668-643-9

Manufactured in the United States of America.

Contents

PART III   ETIOLOGY

Preface

The work which follows has been on my mind for quite some time—years, in fact. When I first came across the concept of the borderline personality, I went through all the confusion and frustration that I have come to recognize and empathize with in residents and other workers in the field who have had the same experience. Part of the difficulty, I decided lies in the complex nature of borderline pathology. That apperception served me well, until my knowledge and experience had grown to the point where I saw that another part of the difficulty might lie in the manner in which the borderline syndrome was conceptualized and diagnosed. This led me down the path that brought me to the writing of the present study.

What was it that bothered me enough to prompt me to re-examine and reassess what there was to be understood about borderlines? Certainly there was dissatisfaction with the state of the therapeutic art. Not only was there controversy, but there was also confusion on how best to treat which borderlines.

This led to the idea that, when I found myself talking about borderline personalities, I might well be referring to more than one clinical phenomenon, despite the prevailing opinion that borderline patients could be considered under a single rubric. My experience said that the tactic was intellectually satisfying, but clinically confusing. I began to look at my borderline patients as reflecting varying degrees and forms of psychopathology, which led to an appreciation that perhaps meaningful diagnostic discriminations were possible. In the process, I began to sense that the range of borderline manifestations was considerably broader than had been thought previously, and that patients seen in acute psychiatric clinics or in the hospital might differ from those seen privately in the presentation, and degree of their pathology and the quality of their lives.

I began to realize that some of my own analytic cases could be characterized as borderline—but only after a significant degree of regression had set in as a result of the analytic process. Moreover, their difficulties, and their manner of dealing with them, was markedly different than those I had seen in the more primitive, disorganized, and flamboyant borderlines in hospital settings. This led to the idea that perhaps there were different kinds and degrees of borderline pathology, which could be meaningfully delineated, and which might call for different kinds of therapeutic intervention.

This monograph is given over to a conceptual and diagnostic reassessment of the range of borderline phenomena as I now understand them. The result will not satisfy everyone—in some areas it does not satisfy me, but my hope is that it will serve the needs of those who will find it helpful.

Boston, Massachusetts

Part I
Background

Chapter 1
Historical and
Conceptual Dilemmas

The concept of borderline psychopathology has only come upon the scene in recent years as a product of increased psychiatric and psychoanalytic understanding of personality organization and functioning. The earliest glimmerings of the idea of borderline conditions or borderline states go back no more than fifty years or so, and a more definitive and specific attempt to focus on the concept has existed for only a score of years. The nature of the pathology and its diagnosis have continued to be matters of uncertainty and debate—largely because of the often obscure and shifting nature of the borderline conditions, and as a reflection of slowly evolving theoretical and clinical resources to deal with them.

Psychoanalytic thinking is currently riding the crest of a wave of intense interest and discussion of the borderline syndrome. Despite the extensive and extremely productive work of Kernberg (1966, 1967, 1970b, 1971, 1975) and others, there remain significant areas of ambiguity, uncertainty, and confusion regarding the diagnosis and treatment of this syndrome.

The term "borderline" has enjoyed wide divergence in use (Rosenfeld and Sprince, 1963) and has been applied rather loosely in a variety of contexts (Maenchen, 1968). Despite Kernberg's clarifications, it is still difficult to know where to establish the borders and how to determine the division between borderline syndromes and other, closely related diagnostic entities. It is generally agreed that borderline psychopathology lies somehow between neurosis and psychosis, but the question remains, in view of the variety of manifestations and the degree to which individual patients manifest both neurotic and psychotic characteristics, whether these borderline conditions can be meaningfully drawn together into a single diagnostic entity.

To some degree, Knight's (1953) observation that the category serves more or less as a wastebasket diagnosis, since it applies to patients who cannot be clearly classified either neurotic or psychotic, seems to be justified. Not only is the diagnosis often made in negative terms (Zetzel, 1971), but it also tends to be applied to those difficult, problematic, and undesirable patients who seem to inhabit the "borderland" of psychiatry, society, and the penal system (Chessick, 1966).

The confusion has been propagated and prolonged by the tensions and ambiguities latent in the diagnostic process, particularly a descriptive emphasis on symptoms and symptom patterns as opposed to more psychodynamic and developmental considerations (Masterson, 1972). Thus, as Mack (1975) notes in his excellent review of the development of the borderline concept, these psychiatric and psychoanalytic areas reflect the influence of many historical factors, particularly the attempt to reach a precise diagnosis with clearly defined features. This attempt reflects the tendency to adhere to a nosological framework, derived ultimately from the tradition of descriptive (Kraepelinian) psychiatry. Counterbalancing this descriptive tradition is the more psychoanalytically derived approach, which emphasizes underlying dynamics, character formation, and character pathology and leads to a more specifically developmental and structural concept of the borderline disorder or disorders.

Some of the conceptual underpinnings that may contribute to such difficulties and to the continuing confusion can be addressed first. These include the terminology and methodology of the diagnostic process, and their implications for the establishment and validation of borderline diagnoses.

TERMINOLOGY

The indeterminateness of the terminology used in referring to borderline psychopathology reflects an underlying ambiguity as to the nature of these syndromes. Borderline psychopathology is alternately described as a syndrome, a state, a condition, or a form of character or personality organization. The question is whether the borderline entity reflects a shifting pattern of symptoms and defenses or whether it is a relatively stable configuration of certain personality characteristics. Related to the first ambiguity is the question of whether the diagnostic description refers to a transient phenomenon as opposed to relatively stable personality characteristics.

The use of the term "syndrome" implies a describable and consistent pattern of symptoms and signs, but all attempts to describe the syndrome have always stumbled on the bizarre quality of the symptoms (Chessick, 1966), the puzzling mixture of neurotic and apparently psychotic symptoms, the pattern of unpredictability, and the dramatic shifts in symptoms and behaviors (Dickes, 1974)—in general, the variability and instability found so frequently in the borderline syndrome (Pine, 1974). Although this fluidity, and the shifting pattern of its expression, is a continual problem for the therapist at all levels of borderline psychopathology, it seems to occur most dramatically in the evaluation of borderline pathology in children (Fintzy, 1971).

Such ambiguities led Zilboorg (cited in Rangell, 1955) to protest that he did not believe that there was any such thing as a borderline case, or that, if one wished to classify such cases, all cases were borderline. In other words, it was impossible to describe the borderline syndrome as such. Dickes (1974) has commented that there is little or no consensus on the diagnosis of the borderline syndrome and that, in fact, we are dealing with a group of diagnostic entities that form a conglomerate of several syndromes of different etiology. We shall return to this question more specifically in discussing the relationship between borderline psychopathology and the more traditional and better-established forms of neurosis and psychosis.

The use of the terms "state" or "condition" in describing borderline psychopathology seems to lean more in the direction of seeing the pathology as essentially transient. These terms emphasize the phenomenology. Knight (1953) has described the borderline state in terms of its proximity to psychosis. But there remains an ambiguity as to whether the borderline state represents regression from neurosis or an expression of psychosis. The attempt was made to describe patients who were neither purely psychotic nor classically psychoneurotic. The description seemed to imply that the neuroses and psychoses were not qualitatively distinct, but rather represented points along a quantitative continuum (Giovacchini, 1973).

Borderline states have been variously described (Knight, 1953; Worden, 1955; Rangell, 1955; Geleerd, 1964). This variety of descriptions led Little (1966) to observe

> "Borderline state" is an imprecise, descriptive term used to label any mental illness which is neither clearly neurotic nor so obviously psychotic that the patient concerned has to be treated as insane. The range of patients is a very wide one. And not only the range of patients, but also the range within any one patient, who may in the course of weeks or months, or even in one analytic hour be neurotic, psychotic, and "normal" by turns. . . . (p. 477)

Similar comments on the heterogeneity of the notion of borderline state have been voiced by Klein (1975), who goes so far as to say that the use of the concept only serves to obscure the uncertainties about the phenomenology, pathophysiology, and course of the borderline illness.

Perhaps the best attempt to differentiate borderline states from borderline personality organization was that of Zetzel (Rangell, 1955; Zetzel, 1971).

She emphasized that the borderline states represent conditions in which the overt clinical picture, whether acute or chronic, represents a group of conditions which the patient presents in the initial interview in a state of regression that immediately challenges the therapist. By way of contrast, the borderline personality initially presents few or no disabling symptoms, but rather shows a variety of disturbances during the course of analysis that require appropriate assessment. In a later elaboration of this position, Zetzel (1971) commented that the borderline states form a group of conditions in which both neurotic and psychotic phenomena are manifested, without fitting unequivocally into either of those diagnostic categories. In fact, the diagnosis is based on an essentially negative evaluation—the patient cannot be described as overtly psychotic or as suffering from any of the generally accepted personality disorders or as manifesting any specific organic disease; the symptoms and character structure are simply not consistent with a diagnosis of neurosis or a neurotic character structure. Consequently, one is left with a borderline diagnosis.

Further, discrimination between borderline states and a borderline personality has important clinical implications. The subsequent history of a patient presenting in a borderline state, including response to appropriate treatment, may lead to a revision of the diagnosis, since the patient may have been seen in an acute regressive crisis. On the other hand, the borderline patient may not always present with initial symptoms that suggest a borderline diagnosis and may, in fact, only reveal such a personality configuration during the course of a psychoanalytic or psychotherapeutic experience. To establish the diagnosis of borderline personality and to differentiate it from such regressive manifestations (borderline states) may require an extended evaluation of the patient's response to therapy and of the nature of the doctor–patient relationship, which may play an essential role. In contrast to the potentially healthy or the neurotic patient in an acute crisis, the borderline patient has great difficulty establishing a secure, confident relationship with the therapist.

Rather, his involvement with the therapist is colored by magical expectations, the failure to distinguish adequately between fantasy and reality, episodes of anger and suspicion, and the predominant fears of rejection. These characteristics of the borderline therapeutic relationship may persist over an extended time, but in a favorable treatment situation, the borderline patient gradually can acknowledge and partially relinquish such unrealistic and magical expectations, fears, and suspicions.

These distinctions become more real and meaningful when applied to real patients. The problem of distinguishing between a borderline regressive state and an authentic psychosis can often be difficult and perplexing. One young man presented in his early twenties with a picture of acute psychosis. He had been serving in the Peace Corps in a primitive, barren region, where he had been relatively isolated from other Peace Corps workers. At the time of his breakdown, he had been living for some weeks under conditions of relative deprivation—subsisting on a rather meager native diet, surrounded by strangers who spoke in a foreign tongue, and under severe physical strain. Then, he had received a letter from his favorite girlfriend at home telling him that she had fallen in love with someone else in his absence, and was breaking off their relationship. Under such circumstances of severe isolation, deprivation, and loss, the patient decompensated and had to be removed from his outpost and returned home. He had apparently panicked, becoming overwhelmed with terror and anxiety and acting in a bizarre and psychotically disorganized fashion.

When he reached our hospital it was only a matter of days after the acute episode, but the residual effects were still quite evident. The patient's behavior was agitated and disorganized; his movements were restless, tense, and jittery. He was unable to sit quietly for more than a few moments, and then would have to jump up, pace about, and sit down again, nervously and anxiously—fidgeting, unable to focus his attention for more than a few seconds and almost completely unable to carry on an intelligible conversation. His mental content was disorganized and marked by ideas of reference and paranoid delusions. His organization of thought and speech was loose, fragmented, tangential, and disconnected, which made it extremely difficult to follow any intelligible content or to make sense out of what he was saying. His affect was mostly fearful, accompanied by tearful outbursts and trembling, which were occasionally interrupted by episodic outbursts of anger and hostility provoked by seemingly trivial occurrences. The patient was, to superficial clinical observation, psychotic, or perhaps more accurately, functioning in a psychotic state.

The patient was started on low doses of phenothiazines, with the intention of gradually increasing the dose until an effect was achieved. But almost immediately he began to show a dramatic improvement. Within a matter of days, his behavior was calm and more organized and directed, his speech became quite coherent, and his thinking seemed to return to a normal pattern of integration and functional organization. The intensity of his emotions, particularly the overwhelming terror he had felt on admission, seemed to disappear completely and was replaced by a compliant, unassuming, respectful, and even deferential attitude. As far as we could see, the patient had returned to his normal mode of personality functioning.

The history revealed that he had had no previous psychiatric disturbance, although from his adolescent years on he had experienced a variety of emotional difficulties that had severely undermined his sense of self-esteem and his own sense of himself as a competent and reasonably effective, autonomous human being. Within a matter of weeks, there was little reason for keeping him in the hospital or for continuing any medication. The

patient was discharged and followed-up in continuing outpatient psychotherapy, and medication was discontinued. During the subsequent therapeutic experience, none of the characteristics of cognitive and affective
disorganization that were so marked during the period of his regressive crisis
could be seen. The ideas of reference and the paranoid thoughts had completely evaporated. The patient's personality remained quite constricted and,
affectively, almost impoverished. This general emotional bleakness was
occasionally interrupted by phobic reactions, particularly in situations in
which he might be called upon to perform or to present himself in some even
minor public manner. At times, he would feel acute anxiety, as though he
were going to fall apart, complaining that his voice would quaver and his
hands shake and being afraid that he would lose complete control of himself
and terrified of what might come out if he were to open his mouth. These
fears served to inhibit any initiative or effective work on his part, so that he
found himself unable to take a job, go to school, or undertake any sort of
meaningful work or endeavor that involved other people. Only gradually, in
the course of the therapeutic work, was he increasingly able to become aware
of and to begin to tolerate gradually the intensity and depth of his rage.
Behind the passive, compliant, bland facade he presented to the world, there
was a towering rage, and bitter resentment. Through all this, the patient's
reality-testing was intact and remained intact through the subsequent years
of his treatment.

The diagnostic problem with such patients is to draw the line between
such regressive crises in an otherwise borderline personality, on the one
hand, and a first psychotic episode in an otherwise psychotically organized
personality, on the other. In this patient, the rapidity of his recompensation
with minimal therapeutic intervention, his maintenance of reality-testing
through a number of years of treatment, the quality of his object relations,
generally, and, particularly, of his capacity for therapeutic alliance, and his
otherwise nonpsychotic history would seem to indicate a borderline diagnosis. Such discrimination on a short-term basis is often impossible, and at
best, extremely difficult. More subtle indices can sometimes be used to
attempt such discrimination, and these will be examined more extensively
in Chapter 4.

If the discrimination between acute psychotic conditions creates diagnostic difficulties, it is also true that the identification of borderline features
in a patient who may present as essentially neurotic also is a matter of
diagnostic challenge. One man, in his late twenties, came for treatment with
a complaint of persistent and moderately disabling anxieties, an inability to
work steadily and committedly in any particular area of intellectual interest,
and difficulties in advancing and completing his Ph.D. thesis. The patient
was judged to be suffering from a variety of neurotic difficulties, motivated

primarily by his castration anxiety and his conflicts with his father, and seemed capable of undertaking psychoanalysis as a treatment of choice.

The patient was able to begin analysis in an unremarkable fashion, but as the analytic experience deepened and became more intense, more of his deeper psychological difficulties became apparent. Not only did the patient have difficulty in establishing a meaningful therapeutic alliance, but he remained guarded, suspicious, and quite distrustful of the analyst. As his history emerged, it became clear that he had been suffering from multiple phobias from as far back as he could remember in his childhood. He frequently experienced terrifying nightmares, and at times when he awoke from such terrifying dreams, he was unsure as to what was real and what was not. His relationships, particularly with women, had a markedly infantile quality, revealing a considerable degree of primitive narcissism and entitlement and a quality of peremptory demandingness that brooked little or no opposition; he expected total acquiescence and responsiveness to his needs from the other person. When these expectations were frustrated, there were repeated outbursts of rage in which he would break furniture, throw objects, and become quite destructive and even assaultive.

His emotional life was a continual turmoil and torment of anxiety, depression, rage, envy, jealousy, guilt, shame, and remorse—all compounded into a picture of inner turmoil and distress that often left him paralyzed and unable to approach even remotely the level of his abilities. The same qualities entered into the analytic relationship, which began to manifest a number of regressive features. Not only was the patient unable to form any meaningfully trusting relationship with the analyst, but he maintained a rather guarded and fearful approach to the analytic situation, which, at times of particular stress, would degenerate into identifiably paranoid reactions. The patient never quite lost his capacity to reassess these intensely emotional reactions and to test them out in realistic terms, but the pattern of emotional reactivity persisted and became more intense as the analytic work advanced. At such times, there would often be some episode of destructive and hostile acting-out, usually aimed at emotionally involved or significant others in the patient's life. These episodes were then followed with intense reactions of shame, remorse, and guilt.

In this case, my impression was that the patient's personality organization was essentially borderline, but that this only became apparent under the regressive strain imposed by the analytic situation. In such cases, even experienced diagnosticians may have difficulty assessing or appreciating the sometimes-subtle indices that would suggest a borderline diagnosis. At other times, such indices are by no means apparent, and the uncovered history and, particularly, the therapeutic experience with the patient come as a surprise.

The distinction between regressive borderline states and borderline personality, to which Zetzel (1971) pointed so clearly a score of years ago, reflects a division between the level of phenomenological description and an evaluation of the organization and integration of personality factors. The distinction was drawn between phenomenological and structural diagnosis. The current trend, particularly following on the work of Frosch (1964, 1970) and Kernberg (1967), is to see the borderline diagnosis more specifically in terms of structural aspects of personality organization. Kernberg (1967) has stated this position quite concisely and clearly:

> There exist an important group of psychopathological constellations which have in common a rather specific and remarkably stable form of pathological ego structure. The ego pathology differs from that found in the neuroses and in the less severe characterological illnesses on the one hand, and the psychoses on the other. These patients must be considered to occupy a borderline area between neurosis and psychosis. The term *borderline personality organization*, rather than "borderline states" or other terms, more accurately describes these patients who do have a specific, stable, pathological personality organization; their personality organization is not a transitory state fluctuating between neurosis and psychosis. (pp. 641–642)

Or again (Kernberg, 1968),

> . . . these patients present a rather specific, quite stable, pathological personality organization rather than transitory states on the road from neurosis to psychosis, or from psychosis to neurosis. The clinical syndromes which reflect such borderline personality organization seem to have in common: (i) typical symptomatic constellations, (ii) typical constellations of defensive operations of the ego, (iii) typical pathology of internalized object relations, and (iv) characteristic instinctual vicissitudes. (p. 600)

Kernberg then supports Zetzel's (1971) observations that under severe stress or the effects of alcohol or drugs these patients may undergo transient psychotic episodes, which usually improve with relatively brief, but well-structured treatment. In psychoanalysis, they may develop a particular form of loss of reality-testing and even delusional ideas related to the transference, possibly even a transference psychosis rather than a transference neurosis.

The shift in point of view from a focus on more or less transient borderline states to that of a stable and perduring personality organization reflected the working-through of underlying issues, having to do with the nature of diagnosis itself, and other ambiguities having to do with understanding both neuroses and psychoses, from which borderline pathology had to be distinguished. Both in the realm of descriptive psychiatry and psychoanalytic formulation, the notions of neurosis and psychosis are clearly delineated and discriminated. It was somewhat disturbing and confusing to think about a set of pathological conditions that may fit neither under the rubric of psychosis nor under that of neurosis, or that may reflect aspects of both. Not only were the diagnostic difficulties confusing and ambiguous, but the conceptual formulations were also cast into turmoil.

DIAGNOSTIC ISSUES

The first important clarification and caution to be made is that, in this discussion, the intention is *not* to resolve diagnostic issues *or* to draw any conclusions having to do with diagnostic discrimination. The purpose here is only to focus the conceptual tensions and ambiguities that enter into the diagnostic process, and to gain some sense of their influence. Reassessment and reformulation of the borderline diagnosis or diagnoses will be attempted later (see Part II).

The latent ambiguities in the use of the concept "borderline" reflect the underlying difficulties in the diagnostic process itself. Diagnostic process implies a procedure for identifying and discriminating between various classes of disorder, specifically in psychiatric diagnoses between forms of mental disorder or illness. In the process, certain signs and symptoms, which are taken to indicate disorder or impaired functioning, are identified. The logic of classifying such disorders implies that, when consistent patterns of signs and symptoms can be identified, they form a syndrome with a determinant etiology, such that the determination of the causes of the syndrome will dictate an effective form of treatment and a correlative prognosis.

METHODOLOGY

The diagnostic premise is the basis for the remarkable progress seen in the medical sciences. The process is generally more successful in medicine, since medical diagnosis rests much more explicitly on objective, observable, or measurable data. Psychiatric diagnosis, however, has few such objective data and requires much more subjective evaluation on the part of the clinical observer. In addition, there are a variety of methodologies available for establishing and validating a diagnostic entity. For example, in the classical Kraepelinian approach, signs and symptoms are observed, and such signs and symptoms are classified as diagnostic categories or syndromes. This general approach has been made more specific and sophisticated by applying more specific forms of evaluation and using sophisticated mathematical techniques in the form of cluster analysis. Consequently, even at the level of descriptive analysis and the establishment of diagnostic categories, there is room for considerable variability.

The most extensive attempt to apply cluster analysis to the borderline categories has resulted in a set of four discriminable borderline conditions (Grinker et al., 1968), but how these categories are related to other descriptive formulations remains uncertain. The question is the extent to which the introduction of such methodologies may select certain factors that alter the descriptive outcome (Gunderson and Singer, 1975). In addition to the multiplicity of methodologies, there is also the question of divergence between clinical diagnosis and research diagnostic concerns. Ideally, a diagnostic category should be sufficiently discrete and specific so that there is a significant degree of agreement among independent observers. Without such specificity and consensus, it becomes difficult, if not impossible, to study the parameters of specific diagnostic entities adequately and to develop effective treatment regimens.

The adequate implementation of scientific resources to the understanding and cure of disease entities rests on the first step of the process, namely the consistency and validity of the diagnosis. Consequently, in an effort to improve diagnostic clarity, specificity, and consensus among observers, research diagnoses tend to be restrictive and to focus on those qualities that are most directly observable, and for which the highest degree of observer agreement is possible. Thus, the research evaluation of any diagnostic entity can be expected to include the majority of those cases that might be clinically so diagnosed, but it can also be expected to exclude many cases that might be included in the clinical evaluation. This problem, for example, has haunted the study of schizophrenia insofar as adherence to the more rigid research criteria for schizophrenia would tend to eliminate from the diagnosis a significant number of patients who show relatively "soft signs" of schizophrenia and who might be so diagnosed in the usual clinical setting.

Needless to say, the efforts to define, classify, and determine the etiology of the borderline conditions have generated a considerable and quite varied literature, with little consensus, however. Regressive borderline states often do not correspond to underlying borderline personality, or conversely, relatively normal or neurotic functioning occurs in patients who prove, on further experience, to have a borderline personality organization. Such diagnostic insecurity undoubtedly contributed to the general disaffection among analysts for diagnostic or classificatory concerns. An extreme example of this reaction was Zilboorg's (Rangell, 1955) attack on attempts to classify the borderline states. He felt that such classifications were Kraepelinian, foreign to concerns of psychoanalysis, and moreover, ineffective, if not misguided. Psychoanalysis, he felt, brought an appreciation of the unitary and indivisible nature of the individual, which was opposed by such attempts.

Even at the level of descriptive phenomenology, establishing the borderline diagnosis is difficult. In a recent review of aspects of differential diagnosis of the borderline syndrome, Guze (1975) has pointed out that there is little agreement on borderline phenomenology and that a great range of clinical features are included in the descriptions of the syndrome without adequate data on their frequency of occurrence or their degree of association with other specifiable features. This is the minimum we require for a diagnostic syndrome. The basic requirement for establishing the borderline diagnosis, namely consistent data on the natural history of the disorder and its delimitation from other conditions, has not been met.

Differential diagnosis from other basic conditions, as for example, sociopathy, alcoholism, drug dependence and addiction, schizophrenia, and hysterical and affective disorders, has not been established. It is impossible to estimate how many patients diagnosed as borderline might also fulfill the criteria for these conditions. Consequently, Guze concludes that borderline conditions are described so vaguely that the differential diagnosis must involve a wide range of related disorders. If the borderline diagnosis in some sense includes all these, then its usefulness is limited, since we would be unable to predict the course, complications, and response to treatment of the illness. If, however, we employ the borderline label to indicate more fundamental features underlying these other diagnostic categories, then we need evidence that these more basic features are independent of the clinical criteria applied to these other categories; that is, those characteristics that point to a borderline disorder over and above the characteristics of hysteria, sociopathy, alcoholism, etc., must be specified, as must the delineations between borderline disorders and affective disorders, schizophrenia, etc. In particular, these diagnoses fail to differentiate between the borderline personality organization and the more closely related character pathologies, such as schizoid personality, latent psychosis, and psychotic character (Blum, 1972) or the more primitive forms of narcissistic personality organization, "as-if" personalities, and the more pathological forms of false self organization and identity diffusion.

In commenting on these difficulties, Mack (1975) has observed that the diagnosis of the borderline personality fails to meet the usual criteria of the diagnosis of personality disorders; it lacks predominant specific behavioral patterns or characterological traits. The tendency to include alcoholism, drug addiction, antisocial behavior, impulsive acting-out, and sexual deviation under this rubric suggests that the borderline diagnosis may, in fact, be used more as a catchall for relatively immature and acting-out patients, rather than as an established diagnostic entity in itself. It seems, then, that despite the rigorous efforts of a score of years and the application of sophisticated diagnostic formulations, the borderline diagnosis may still be serving as a sort of psychiatric wastebasket.

It must be remembered that in all attempts to establish diagnostic categories we are classifying a living process, with its protean manifestations and complex variabilities from patient to patient. The inevitable disparity between the conceptual realm of diagnostic categories and the flux of human personality has been sufficient to turn many analysts against a diagnostic orientation. One is not left, however, to choose between the descriptive categories of classical Kraepelinian psychiatry or no diagnosis at all. Rather, it seems that the choice reflects the problems inherent in any specifically psychoanalytic diagnostic process.

Thus, psychoanalysis seems to generate its own diagnostic orientation. The psychoanalytic diagnostic perspective differs from that of descriptive psychiatry, and it can be characterized by its basic metapsychological perspectives. Rather than the focus on signs and symptoms and their correlative clustering, diagnosis in the psychoanalytic perspective takes topographic, economic, dynamic, structural, genetic, and adaptive concerns into consideration. It is in the complex interweaving and overlapping of these concerns that psychoanalytic assessment is achieved.

This does not by any means imply that the psychoanalyst abhors or does not use diagnostic labels, but rather that the way such labels are utilized and the implications of their use make them considerably different from those generated in a more specifically descriptive context. For example, relatively few of the patients the average practicing analyst might describe as "hysterical" could be fitted under the DSM III category of histrionic personality disorder.

Not only does the inherently descriptive approach on which the DSM III categories are based diverge from and exclude psychodynamic considerations (Frances and Cooper, 1981), but the designated categories cannot be regarded as equivalent. The forms of hysterical neurosis are distributed into various descriptive types. Hysterical neuroses with dissociative manifestations are described in terms of psychogenic amnesia, psychogenic fugue, or multiple personality. Hysterical neuroses that follow the pattern of conversion are described as conversion disorders, in which there is a deficit or an alteration in actual physical functioning, or as psychogenic pain disorders, in which the conversion feature is expressed in terms of pain symptoms. When somatic manifestations of a hysterical neurosis are recurrent and multiple, it is classified as a somatization disorder (Spitzer et al., 1980). As a result, the category of hysterical neurosis, which is essentially a diagnosis based on psychodynamic considerations, is broken up into a series of behavioral and symptomatic syndromes. These categories are of little pertinence and utility for psychoanalytic concerns, however useful they may be for psychiatric classification and for purposes of objective description.

The description of histrionic personality disorder, which is intended to replace the description of a hysterical personality (Spitzer et al., 1980), can be similarly criticized. A histrionic personality is characterized by behavior that tends to be overly reactive, emotionally intense, and turbulent and is often perceived as shallow, superficial, or insincere. Interpersonal relationships are frequently conflicted and sexual adjustment is poor. Behavior tends to be exhibitionistic, with exaggerated emotional expression, as if the individual were playing a dramatic role in order to attract attention and gain admiration. Often, minor stimuli give rise to intense emotional excitability, with irrational or angry outbursts or temper tantrums. Any thwarting of the aims of the individual leads to manipulative behavior that may take the form of suicidal threats, gestures, or attempts. Such individuals, who are superficially warm and charming, are quick to form friendly relationships; once the relationship is established, however, they tend to become demanding and egocentric, inconsiderate of the wishes of others, and frequently seen as vain, selfish, and self-absorbed. At other times they may be clinging, dependent and helpless, constantly seeking support and reassurance. This inconsistent pattern of behavior is often misinterpreted by others.

These individuals are also extremely vulnerable to intense dissatisfactions and dysphoric moods, which tend to be highly reactive to external circumstances and to reflect the vicissitudes of attachment to objects. They tend to be impressionable and susceptible to influence by others, often enthusiastically taking up fads or fashions; vulnerable to the influence of charlatans or faith healers; and in their work, they tend to operate on the basis of intuition or flashes of inspiration and show little capacity for careful, plodding, day-to-day work efforts or for sustained and realistic planning.

If we take this description at face value, we would have to say that it is much closer to the form of primitive hysterical personality or perhaps even the dysphoric personality described later in this work (see Chapter 7) as higher-order forms of borderline pathology. It is, however, a far cry from the portrait of the true analyzable hysteric advanced, for example, by Zetzel (1968). She describes such true hysterics as usually well past adolescence and as having completed a formal education. The patient is usually female, is often a virgin or has been disappointed in sexual experiences, and may have had some periods of promiscuity. She may not be frigid, but she certainly has not been able to make a major sexual investment in a man for whom she cares in a real and meaningful relationship. She may well have been involved with a man to whom she is unable to respond sexually. Even though there is a failure to achieve a mature, heterosexual relationship, such women often are notably successful in areas of work. Most of them have also been able to acquire and keep good friends. There is often a history of a close relationship to the father, who frequently idolized this daughter and took great pride in her academic, personal, and social success. Often, the failure to resolve a well-developed oedipal situation can be attributed partially to external events, for example, the loss of the father at the height of the oedipal involvement. As Zetzel (1968) observes, however, "instead of mastery through neutralization, sublimation and positive identification with the mother, there occurred massive repression, with the oedipal father still unrelinquished and a major barrier to adult heterosexual object choice" (p. 238). In such women, separation or loss of the mother during this same critical period can impair the development of a positive, feminine ego ideal and identification with the mother as a result of oedipal guilt.

Rather than signs and symptoms, the psychoanalytic perspective focuses explicitly on patterns of libidinal fixation and organization, levels and patterns of ego functioning and their integration, the quality of object relations, both in the patient's history and in contemporary experience within and outside of the relationship to the therapist, etc. The psychoanalytic diagnosis, consequently, rests more explicitly on the quality of the therapist's ongoing experience with the patient, rather than on more objectifiable or measurable attributes. The differences have been resolved by some analysts by abandoning classifications or by declaring diagnostic labels useless and pointless.

The most productive strategy may not be to foreclose on the diagnostic concern, even though descriptive categories have only limited utility. Perhaps Kernberg (1967) specified this divergence in diagnostic perspective more clearly than anyone else, in distinguishing between symptomatic description and structural analysis. As Gunderson and Singer (1975) have commented, attempts to evaluate the borderline condition tend to run along parallel tracks. They suggest, for example, that the descriptive accounts tend to cluster into symptomatic and behavioral observations, psychodynamic formulations, and psychological test data. These three areas are claimed, respectively, by the psychiatrist, the psychoanalyst, and the clinical psychologist. Their orientations and methodologies are separate, independent, and often regarded with suspicion by the others. This only adds to the failure to meaningfully integrate the understanding and description of borderline conditions.

There is also the additional concern that divergence in theoretical perspective, even among these groups, gives rise to significant variations in the description and understanding of borderline conditions. Thus, the pathology and symptomatology are differentially emphasized, depending on the observer's theoretical perspectives—as, for example, whether ego functions or defenses, developmental perspectives or aspects of narcissistic integration, and the sense of identity or the vicissitudes of object relations. This dimension is only mentioned here as part of the observer–categorizer variation in the diagnostic process, but it will be discussed extensively in Chapter 2).

In addition to who is doing the describing, the variations in borderline diagnosis also reflect the methods used to collect the descriptive data, the context in which the patients are observed, and the manner in which the patients have been selected (Gunderson and Singer, 1975). Certainly, the amount of structure in the observational setting plays a role in the description of the patient. Psychoanalytically oriented clinicians and Rorschach testers tend to emphasize ego defects, primitive defenses, and disordered thought processes, yet clinicians observing the same patients in structured hospital settings, or by using structured interview techniques, tend to emphasize stable personality features and patterns of interpersonal interaction. There is broad agreement on the tendency of these patients to regress in relatively unstructured settings, but this serves only to emphasize the importance of context in their diagnostic assessment.

Selection factors also are significant. Borderline outpatients, for example, who voluntarily seek treatment as outpatients must be contrasted with hospitalized patients who are brought to treatment on an involuntary basis. In this regard, Gunderson and Singer (1975) contrast the selection procedures in the Grinker study (1968) with those in a similar study by Hoch and Cattell (1959). Both research groups saw the borderline condition as distinct from schizophrenia and selected borderline patients who were then free of schizophrenic symptomatology for study. The Hoch and Cattell sample consisted of patients with severe psychoneurotic symptomatology, but who, on deeper evaluation, revealed signs of schizophrenia. The Grinker group, however, selected their patients on the basis of a relatively good capacity to function between hospitalizations, along with the ego-alien quality of any psychotic manifestations. These patients had relatively good premorbid histories, and hospitalization was not clinically necessary, but rather was only for research purposes. Thus, the Grinker group of patients rarely showed psychotic phenomena and did not develop manifestations of schizophrenia. This contrasted with the Hoch and Cattell group, of which roughly one-quarter developed schizophrenic symptoms later in their course. Consequently, Grinker's conclusion that schizophrenia and the borderline condition represent distinct disorders, and the conclusion of Hoch and Cattell that the borderline diagnosis represented a subgroup of schizophrenia, seem to have been strongly influenced by how the patients studied were selected. The need for hospitalization proved to be a critical variable in comparing samples, in that those patients referred for severe symptomatology seemed to have been a more pathologically disordered group than the outpatients who sought treatment.

As this example suggests, the diagnostic conceptualization of borderline conditions is affected to a significant degree by the ambiguity relating to the separation from and diagnosis of neurosis and psychosis, respectively. This aspect of the problem will now be considered.

BETWEEN NEUROSIS AND PSYCHOSIS

One of the latent problems in the conceptualization of borderline patients involves the conceptual framework for psychoanalytic thinking as it is structured by the polar concepts of neurosis and psychosis. This inherent polarity derives from Freud's original distinction between the transference neuroses and the narcissistic neuroses—the former were based on oedipal dynamics, in which the patient, developmentally, had reached the level of a triangular oedipal involvement, was able to establish a transference neurosis in the analytic situation, and consequently, could be successfully analyzed. The narcissistic neuroses, however, were rooted in earlier and more primitive levels of preoedipal narcissistic development, and the patient had only partially or unsuccessfully gained an oedipal level, was thought to be incapable of establishing a transference neurosis, and consequently was not a suitable candidate for the analytic process. This distinction, translated into terms of neurosis and psychosis, dominated early analytic diagnostic thinking.

The *status questionis* was the critical decision as to which patients were analyzable and which were not, so that the dividing line was between those who could be classified as the classic, analyzable neurotics and those who could not. In such a dichotomous frame of reference, those patients who were not clearly or unequivocally classifiable as analyzable neurotics were easily shunted off into the other category and regarded as either psychotic or as some *forme fruste* of the psychotic, that is, the nonneurotic, category. The question then became whether or not the neuroses and the psychoses were qualitatively different or whether they represented points on a quantitative continuum, which extended from psychosis, at one extreme, through varying states or degrees of neurosis, to normality, at the other extreme.

If Freud could radically dichotomize transference neuroses versus narcissistic neuroses, that does not mean that the notion of a continuum was foreign to him. In addressing himself to the problems in treatment, Freud commented in his *Analysis Terminable and Interminable* (1937):

> As is well known, the analytic situation consists in our allying ourselves with the ego of the person under treatment, in order to subdue portions of his id which are uncontrolled—that is to say to include them in the synthesis of his ego. The fact that a co-operation of this kind habitually fails in the case of psychotics affords us a first solid footing for our judgement. The ego, if we are able to make such a pact with it, must be a normal one. But a normal ego of this sort is, like normality in general, an ideal fiction. The abnormal ego, which is serviceable for our purposes, is unfortunately no fiction. Every normal person, in fact, is only normal on the average. His ego approximates to that of the psychotic in some part or other and to a greater or lesser extent; and the degree of its remoteness from one end of the series and its proximity to the other will furnish us with a provisional measure of what we have so indefinitely termed an "alteration of the ego." (p. 235)

Thus, in this frame of reference, the difference between neurosis and psychosis was not qualitative, but rather quantitative, according to the degree of organization or integration or structuralization of the ego. In the operative model, states of psychopathology can be envisioned as all dealing with the same given drive determinants embedded in the vital stratum of the mind and the id, and that varying levels of psychopathology had to do with the capacity of the ego to restrain, regulate, control, and direct these id derivatives. Similar points of view have been expressed by Zilboorg (Rangell, 1955), Glover (1956), Knight (1953), and Blum (1972).

The continuum concept and the related notion of a quantitative difference between neurosis and psychosis is, in general, adhered to by analytic thinkers with a basically ego psychological orientation. In a somewhat modified sense, this same presumption operates in Kernberg's (1967) analysis of the borderline syndrome. He specifies "splitting" as the characteristic defensive mechanism of the borderline personality, but it is not at all clear that the splitting mechanism adequately distinguishes the borderline from more primitive schizophrenic entities, nor is his argument that the borderline condition is satisfactorily distinguished from the neuroses on this same basis beyond question. It may be that splitting can be found in many neurotics, just as repression may be found in many borderline cases. In any case, the splitting mechanism derives from an underlying defect in the synthetic capacity of the ego. The relative degrees of functionality or impairment of this ego function establish the underlying continuum from psychosis through borderline forms of personality organization to the neurotic and normal. Thus, qualitative and quantitative elements can be readily intermingled.

A strong protest to this quantitative view has been registered by Dickes (1974). He argues that such a consideration of borderline pathology rests on an unproven speculation that health, neurosis, and psychosis form a continuum. But there is no such continuum; rather, these diagnostic entities differ in their respective etiology, course, and outcome, and the neuroses and psychoses cannot be considered to be contiguous. Consequently we are not dealing with a disease spectrum, but rather with a series of illnesses with differing etiology and course that can be traced from their beginnings. In the same way, manic-depressive psychosis and schizophrenia are both psychotic conditions, but they represent different diseases rather than points on a continuum.

The concept of a continuum, he argues, should be applied only to the severity of symptoms within a given disease entity, such as tuberculosis; but, insofar as the neuroses and psychoses do not constitute a single entity, an entity between them does not constitute part of a continuum, and the borderline states cannot be considered as transitional. A point regarding the quantitative-continuum view is that, historically, it extended analytic understanding to more primitive forms of psychopathology, particularly to our knowledge and understanding of the intrapsychic mechanisms underlying schizophrenia. It is largely this orientation that has generated studies of borderline and schizophrenic conditions and consequently has come to hold a predominant position in our current thinking. Thus, the radical dichotomy, in qualitative terms, which was originally propounded by Freud for the transference and the narcissistic neuroses, and which was based on scanty data and a false understanding, seems to have given way to a more comprehensive view. However, this by no means resolves the issue of quantity and quality.

Caught between the neurotic and psychotic polarities, theorists tend to vary in the extent to which they locate the borderline condition in greater or lesser proximity to psychosis. The primary impetus for the study of borderline conditions within the analytic frame of reference came from the difficulties encountered in treating such patients by classic analysis. Thus, conceptually, a hard and fast line was drawn between the classical neuroses and the borderline conditions. Consequently, nowhere does one find in the analytic literature an opinion linking the borderline conditions with the neuroses.

However, as the concept of borderline was developed, particularly as a form of character structure or personality organization, the original discriminations came out of an attempt to define forms of character pathology and to distinguish them over against the symptomatic neuroses. The psychoanalytic elaboration of concepts of character formation, the character neuroses, and the forms of character pathology laid the basis for the developmental and structural conceptualization of the borderline disorders. Mack (1975) has traced this development in detail, but it should be pointed out, for example, that Reich's (1974) early conceptualization of the impulsive personality, which is characterized by ambivalence, the predominance of pregenital hostility, the combined ego and superego defects, and the immature defensive organization, as well as the persistence of primitive narcissistic determinants, was leaning in the direction of a "borderline" category that fell between the neuroses and the psychoses.

A similar emphasis on the nature of the neurotic character was provided by Alexander (1930). In his view, such neurotic characters tended to be impulsive and to carry out an irrational or eccentric style of life rather than to be troubled with neurotic symptoms. In Stern's (1938) early paper on the borderline condition, he pointed out that, in fact, the neurotic characters made up a large portion of the borderline group. Consequently, the concept of character and character neurosis shifted the focus from the formation of symptoms and their connection with neurotic conditions to another level of personality integration, which allowed for a discrimination from the neurotic states, on one hand, and from the psychoses and psychotic-like states, on the other.

Another dimension in the evolving conceptualization of borderline conditions was their separation from psychotic conditions. This effort, in general, has generated a set of conceptualizations of the borderline diagnosis that tends to lean toward the psychotic pole. Other conceptualizations, however, have involved attempts to characterize the borderline diagnosis as a separate and stable entity, which can be conceptualized neither in terms of neurotic nor psychotic dimensions. It may be that the tendency to conceptualize psychopathological states in terms of a continuum, and away from the circumscribed neuroses, as suggested, may contribute to the tendency to link borderline conditions more closely with the psychoses. Correspondingly, the tendency to think in terms of discrete diagnostic entities may serve as a better frame of reference for the definition and clarification of the borderline diagnosis as separate and unique in its pathological characteristics.

The tendency to see borderline condition more in terms of the psychotic frame of reference has been dominant in the early attempts to define the syndrome. In early discussions of the "borderline state," it was viewed more or less as bordering on psychosis (Knight, 1953). But even here, Knight (1953), in his early clarification of the borderline states, focused on specific disturbances of ego defenses and object relationships and emphasized the need for a complete inventory of ego capacities in order to assess the balance between ego strengths and ego weaknesses. His cautions were much to the point, but were too little observed in subsequent discussions. He warned against assuming that the break with reality need be total or that neurotic and psychotic elements must be seen in mutually exclusive terms or that defenses could be correlated with specific points of fixation or regression in libidinal development.

This orientation reflected a general tendency to see the borderline condition as approaching the border of psychosis, but not quite reaching it (Rangell, 1955). In some formulations, it seemed as though the border was not only reached, but also in some degree crossed—such seemed to be the idea behind Zilboorg's notion of "ambulatory schizophrenia" (Rangell, 1955; Zilboorg, 1941, 1956, 1957). This was an effort, on the one hand, to broaden the confines of the diagnosis of schizophrenia, which had been altogether too rigidly constrained in the Kraepelinian framework, and on the other hand, to introduce psychoanalytic concepts into a somewhat obscure area of psychiatric understanding. The reference point, which gave the general orientation to this approach, lies in the psychotic realm, however.

Zilboorg related his ambulatory schizophrenia to attempts both to define the borderline states and to describe "pseudoneurotic schizophrenia." The attempt to describe this category was the work of Paul Hoch and his coworkers (Hoch and Cattell, 1959; Hoch et al., 1962; Hoch and Polatin, 1949). The underlying notion here was that patients manifested a combination of neurotic and psychotic symptoms, in which the neurotic overlay essentially masked an underlying psychotic process, so that these patients were seen as on a continuum with frank schizophrenia. The pseudoneurotic schizophrenics superficially resembled neurotics, but their symptomatology was more diverse, and their anxiety more pervasive and more profound, and they also showed schizophrenic-like thought and affect disturbances (Hoch and Polatin, 1949). Thus, they could be regarded as schizophrenics in disguise. This was demonstrated by eventual deterioration, a more or less autistic life-style, diffuseness of ambivalence and inappropriateness of emotional responsiveness, omnipotence and subtle thought disorders, as well as transient psychotic episodes and chaotic sexuality. A later attempt to delineate the syndrome, based on psychological test data, emphasizes a relatively good social and academic or occupational facade, but with an underlying, relatively ego-syntonic thought disorder and many unintegrated neurotic and psychotic defenses. Pan-anxiety was reflected in fragmentation, blocking, and diffuse perceptual organization. Sexual fantasies and, often, behavioral patterns were chaotic. The alternation of defense mechanisms, reflecting a variety of unintegrated techniques to protect a relatively fragile ego, was a major feature (Weingarten and Korn, 1967). Here again, as Klein (1975) has observed, there are no normative data on the uniformity and incidence of these signs, and the data seem to suggest a heterogeneous collection of treatment-refractory patients rather than a homogeneous grouping. The risk, then, is that many patients who are often labeled schizophrenic or borderline might previously have been regarded as severely neurotic or as having affective or character disorders.

In some descriptions of these syndromes, the line between borderline conditions and frankly psychotic conditions seems rather porous. The distinction is often obscured, such that cases would be described as borderline by some authors and psychotic by others. We have already noted the Kleinian inclination to more psychotic forms of diagnosis. This may also be a tendency among child analysts (Geleerd, 1958; Rosenfeld and Sprince, 1963). Geleerd (1958), for example, delineates a form of borderline psychosis that may never advance to the development of a manifest psychotic state, but the underlying character structure is defined in terms of the helplessness of the ego against inner forces and a fragility of self-object differentiation, which requires omnipotent control.

Geleerd describes the case of an eighteen-year-old girl who had been sent to live with an aunt when the family felt they could no longer cope with her. She had been a problem since infancy; a clinging and dependent baby, who had been highly indulged until the birth of a younger sister. Her hatred for the younger sister was reflected in teasing and merciless torment. At school she was afraid of being teased by other children, and at home she was never able to accept any discipline and reacted to such attempts by violent temper tantrums that terrified the whole household. At nine she was having panic attacks that could only be soothed by a great deal of attention and indulgence. All her emotional reactions were extreme and attention-getting. No one dared cross her or disagree with her because of the scenes that followed. The temper tantrums continued on into adolescence and became extremely disruptive in the family setting.

During her treatment, it emerged that she had a desperate need to maintain power and control over everyone and everything. Often, these needs were linked with sexual fantasies, for example, of raping her younger sister. She had frequent fantasies of seducing men, including her father, which were extremely exciting. Behind the need for power and control were intense feelings of being nothing, hollow inside, and vulnerable. She felt herself to be someone who could be easily humiliated and taken advantage of by anal or sexual rape. Geleerd (1958) comments:

> The patient showed no actual psychotic symptoms, although there was incidence of psychosis in the family. She suffered from no frank delusions, there was no breaking off with reality. Nevertheless, the picture of long-standing disturbance, the intolerance to frustration, the poverty of object relationship, the clinging dependency, the poor social adjustment, the severe "panics," would suggest a maladjustment beyond neurosis. (p. 291)

A continuity from the borderline conditions to the psychoses, in terms of the degree of ego control, is frequently emphasized. Such cases are seen as sharing in a severe developmental failure, with corresponding defects in ego functioning and in the capacity for object relationships. Thus, the borderline condition tends to shade into the psychotic condition, without sharp lines of discrimination (Pine, 1974).

One could argue, of course, that diagnosis and distinctions between borderline and psychotic conditions would be more difficult in children, but it seems that similar difficulties are encountered on the adult level as well. Dickes (1974) has questioned whether the so-called neurotic symptoms in borderline patients can be satisfactorily described as neurotic or whether they are, in fact, closer to being psychotic. Phobic anxiety cannot be presumed to be simply neurotic. Neurotic phobias tend to bind anxiety, whereas in the more psychotic forms, anxiety is generalized, and leads to delusional fears of being killed, maimed, etc. Moreover, he suggests that the ego defects are more consistent with psychosis.

Along this same line, many authors point to the fragility of reality-testing in borderline patients (Worden, 1955; Rangell, 1955) or the presence of a defective sense of reality (Chase and Heyer, 1969, cited in Mack, 1975; Modell, 1963; Frosch, 1964). Emphasizing the impairments in reality-testing or in reality sense would seem to incline the diagnosis significantly in the direction of psychosis. One variant of such a tendency would be to see the potential for psychotic regression and the loss of the capacity to test reality as restricted to the therapeutic context. Such transient psychotic states are rapidly recompensated and do not carry over into the patient's life situation outside of treatment (Kernberg, 1968; Fintzy, 1971; Zetzel, 1971).

Any discussion of reality-testing, however, must be set in the context of quality versus quantity or continuity versus discreteness of the conceptualization of neurosis and psychosis. Reality-testing can be utilized as a unitary, discriminative index, which is either present or absent. Thus, loss of reality-testing definitively would separate psychotic from other conditions and correlatively tend to reinforce the notion of qualitative discreteness. But as Modell (1963) and others have pointed out, reality-testing itself may be conceived in terms of degrees of alteration or impairment. Moreover, the function of reality-testing may be complex, and subject to contextual variation, that is, impaired in special experiences, but not in others.

Another concept that seems to fit in this general frame of reference is the notion of "latent psychosis," as advanced by Bychowski (1953; cited in Robbins, 1956). Bychowski (1953) uses the concept to describe:

> a. Character-neurotic difficulties which, at an appropriate provocation, may burst into psychosis;
> b. Neurotic symptomatology with the same outcome;
> c. Deviant behavior, for instance, delinquency, perversion, addiction;
> d. An arrested psychosis, posing as psychopathy and . . . likely to reveal some day its true nature. Finally . . .
> e. Psychosis provoked by therapeutic or didactic psychoanalysis. (p. 485)

He describes a patient, forty years of age, who sought treatment for his "paranoia," since he feared that the FBI might be after him because of his previous connections with the Communist Party. Besides this paranoid attitude, there were other abnormalities. He had been married for ten years and had fathered a child, but for two years he had been avoiding sexual contacts with his wife, substituting masturbation and peeping through windows. He had become increasingly isolated socially and had adopted asocial behaviors, for example, going for months without taking a bath or shower. He also manifested multiple hypochondriacal complaints, including obdurate constipation and attacks of excruciating gastric pain.

The patient entertained the delusion that he had a penis inside his stomach, a form of identification with the mother who also complained of similar abdominal pain. He felt that his mother had usurped all power in the family by having taken the father's penis inside her. In his fantasy, he would retain the penis in his own stomach by refusing to expel the fecal penis. He would thus outdo the mother in fantasy by keeping the penis in his stomach permanently. Bychowski (1953) comments that one might well regard such manifestations as frankly psychotic if it were not for the fact that they had emerged in the regression-inducing context of analysis:

> We might expect other characteristic reactions from an ego fixated on such a primitive level. Indeed, one cannot help being impressed by the wealth of

manifestations related to the magic omnipotence either in the positive sense or in phobic fear of evil magic of others. Some of these ideas emerge into the system of preconscious and can be elicited under slight pressure, while others belong to the unconscious and require more elaborate analytic work. In a similar way, reactions of primitive rage correlated with the archaic ego remained dissociated from the rest of the personality only to emerge in analysis with great vehemence. In the course of analytic work the introjective love-hate objects may become extrajected and assume the role of persecutors. This happens either in dreams or in the process of analytic working-through. (p. 496)

The symptoms in such patients may represent a form of an abortive or arrested psychosis as a residue of a prior brief acute psychotic phase, which has then stabilized, or patients may present prospective psychoses in the form of a dissociated psychotic core. This psychotic core would be masked or hidden by the defensive efforts of the healthier part of the patient's ego. The adjustment of such patients is precarious and is reflected in frequent acting-out. They preserve areas of primitive ego functioning, which is relatively unmodified and seems to be related to the relatively concretistic preservation of early pathogenic introjects without significant symbolic transformation. The early pathological ambivalence to significant objects is internalized, so that the patient functions in terms of separate ego sectors. At times of stress or regression, the covering defenses deteriorate, with a consequent breakthrough of the dissociated introject, so that the patient begins to function in terms of this pathological sector.

Another important concept in this same frame of reference is the notion of the transitional object relationship as formulated by Modell (1963, 1968). The notion derives from Winnicott's (1953) concept of the transitional object. The transitional object relationship has rich potentialities for illuminating a variety of difficult areas concerning the development and integration of object relationships (Meissner, 1978), but its description tends to link it rather too closely to the borderline and psychotic (schizophrenic) realms, in which the transitional object relationship often operates. Consequently, the concept does not provide a basis for distinguishing between borderline and psychotic manifestations and, in fact, tends to reinforce a sense of their clustering.

Over against the inherent gravitation toward the psychotic ground in our thinking about borderline processes, there has been a consistent and, in recent years, greater attempt to conceptualize borderline entities, in terms that distinguish them from psychotic and/or schizophrenic levels of personality organization, and to define the borderline category, in terms of discrete, stable, and internally consistent forms of psychopathology. This approach tends toward a conceptualization that will effectively allow the inclusion of neurotic and psychotic manifestations in a characterization, which emphasizes the discrete nature of the borderline pathology and adequately distinguishes it from neurotic forms of maladjustment, on the one hand and the psychotic, whether schizophrenic or affective, on the other.

This line of thinking arises out of psychoanalytic conceptualizations of character, character structure, and character pathology. Thus, the borderline entities are increasingly specified in terms of characterological dimensions of their deficits and malfunctioning. This tends to emphasize both the stability of the character structure and the characteristic defensive operations associated with it, as well as to distinguish, clearly and decisively, between borderline pathology and incipient or ambulatory schizophrenia (Knight, 1953; Zilboorg, 1941, 1956, 1957; Hoch and Polatin, 1949; Hoch and Cattell, 1959; Hoch et al., 1962). Thus, Modell (1963), for example, insists on the stable form of the pathology and quality of the object relationships that characterize borderline patients and distinguish them from schizophrenics. Although the borderline may lapse into psychosis, the regressive state remains circumscribed and does not involve the total personality as it might in a psychosis. Borderline patients do not tend to suspend or abandon object relations as psychotics might, but rather the object relationships are maintained, even though they are distorted in the process. The regression, even though it has psychotic-like qualities, is nonetheless circumscribed, time-limited, and readily reversible.

Perhaps the clearest formulations in this line of conceptualization have come from Frosch (1964, 1970) and Kernberg (1967, 1968, 1970b, 1971, 1975). This line of characterological thinking is most clearly emphasized in Frosch's formulation of the "psychotic character." The psychotic character is a counterpart of the neurotic character. Psychotic processes and modes of adaptation play a role in the psychotic character analogous to that of neurotic processes and modes of adaptation in the neurotic character. In this formulation, the issues in the psychotic character as a subgrouping of the borderline category are essentially psychotic issues rather than neurotic, yet they are cast in the form of character pathology, involving specific forms of structuralization, developmental and instinctual vicissitudes, object relations, etc. Psychotic characters will thus show severe impairments in their relationships both to the internal and external environment, as well as disturbances in their relationships with reality, that are quite similar to those of psychotics. The difference, however, is that they retain a relative capacity to test reality, although in relatively primitive ways. Their object relationships are organized at a higher level, even though there is both a push toward objects and a clinging to them, together with the inevitable counter-fear of engulfment. The ability to preserve the capacity for reality-testing and for maintaining object relationships at a need-satisfying level separates this level of character pathology from the more primitive impairment of reality contact and primitive symbiotic object relatedness of psychotics.

The other outstanding formulation of the borderline configuration has been provided by Kernberg (1967). Kernberg's conceptualization of the borderline personality also builds on the line of thinking that directs itself to a stable character configuration. His analysis rests more specifically on structural terms that are embedded in a theory of the internalization of object relationships. Kernberg tries to establish the line between neurotic and borderline conditions by opposing the splitting mechanism characteristic of borderlines to the more advanced form of repression found in neurotics. Similarly, he delineates the borderlines from psychotics in terms of the preservation of reality-testing.

Even in these more advanced and sophisticated attempts to articulate borderline pathology, one can sense the inherent tension and the struggle to preserve the sense of discrete and unique organization from the pull toward a psychotic frame of reference. Frosch (1964, 1970) has difficulty explaining how one can have psychotic symptoms embedded in a stable character configuration at a higher level of organization. By the same token, Kernberg (1967) has difficulty distinguishing clearly between splitting and repression, on the one hand, and on the other, demonstrating how the splitting in borderline conditions differs from that in more primitive conditions. In neither formulation is it clear how the theoretical underpinnings allow for the preservation of reality-testing in one context and not in another.

Perhaps the most thoroughgoing and consistent empirical attempt to approach the borderline conditions from this perspective was made by Grinker et al. (1968). They studied 51 young adults, of both sexes, whom the authors felt were decidedly not schizophrenic. Employing a technique of cluster analysis of a large number of behavioral and observational measures, they were able to delineate four groups of patients: (1) a severely disturbed group bordering on the psychotic; (2) a "core borderline" group, characterized by chaotic interpersonal relations, acting-out, and loneliness; (3) a group, which was comparable to the "as-if" personality, having difficulties in establishing and maintaining an identity; and (4) a somewhat less disturbed group that seemed to border on the neuroses. The follow-up of these patients over a period of three and one-half years only turned up two patients from the most severely disturbed group who had become schizophrenic.

This research seemed to confirm the notion that in the borderline character pathology, considerable internal consistency and internal stability, as a separate and discrete group of diagnostic entities, are maintained. Subsequent follow-up of twenty-eight of these patients seemed to support this conclusion (Werble, 1970). It should be noted, however, that the spread in this patient population runs the gamut from nearly psychotic to hardly distinguishable from neurotic, so that instead of arriving at an internally consistent and unified concept, there seems to be a diagnostic spread, which is pulled in both directions by the latent neurotic-psychotic ambiguity.

IMPLICATIONS

The implicit presence and subtle influence of these conceptual dimensions in psychoanalytic thinking about the borderline diagnosis serve only to pull the notion in a variety of directions simultaneously, so that it undergoes at least a two-way stretch. Attempts at diagnostic clarification must attain reasonable specificity regarding these parameters of the diagnosis and what they imply, so that they can continue to be discussed with some greater degree of consensual meaning and intention. The end product of the diagnostic effort must be to achieve sufficient clarity and definition so that various observers can agree enough to verify the existence and characteristics of the entity. Consequently, those who attempt to define, describe, classify, and explain the borderline classification need to pay greater attention to these aspects of their formulations.

As noted, the inherent tensions and latent ambiguities in conceptualizing borderline pathology have contributed to a certain diagnostic imprecision, if not to say confusion. Attempts to establish borderline pathology as discrete, and distinguishable from the neuroses and psychoses, have generated a formulation of the borderline personality as a stable form of character pathology, with its own characteristic structure, defenses, quality of object relationships, and developmental history. This unifying and integrating trend may be misleading in that it may provide a more or less unified account of an underlying diagnostic heterogeneity. Unless conceptual ambiguities are resolved, diagnostic precision will remain beyond our grasp. And of course, it can be concluded that improving the specificity, effectiveness, and potentiality of therapeutic intervention is a direct by product of diagnostic refinement and its correlative theoretical conceptualization.

The same conclusion can be drawn regarding theoretical formulations which try to explain and understand the manifestations of the borderline condition. It is clear, even within the confines of the present discussion, that leading figures can be found supporting one or the other side of several of the current theories of borderline development and functioning. Frequently enough, the same individual can be found on both sides of an issue—coming at the problem from more than one perspective and becoming unwittingly entangled in the complex conceptual meshwork that we have been trying to untangle here. Clarity and consistency remain an ideal—one that requires considerable conceptual rigor and critical theoretical acumen. Another related dimension of this whole problem is the role of the theoretical assumptions behind different approaches to the conceptualization of borderline pathology. An incursion into that dark thicket awaits us in Chapter 2.

At several points in the present discussion, the difficulties encountered in trying to conceptualize a unified notion of borderline pathology have been obvious. Not only is it difficult to constrain the various manifestations of this condition in a single diagnostic category, but it has proven equally difficult to combine the understanding of the borderline conditions into a single, unified theory. The conceptual tensions and ambiguity latent in our thinking about borderline pathology must be taken into account in charting a meaningful therapeutic course. It is surprising in the light of such diversity of thought that analysts have been able to arrive at a reasonably consistent approach to treatment of borderlines. However, even here, diverging opinions and approaches call for better formulations and clarifications. It is suggested that attention to the latent tensions and ambiguities in our approach to these concepts may help to differentiate more carefully diagnostic aspects and contribute to the more secure and effective elaboration of a therapeutic rationale.

Chapter 2
Theoretical Perspectives

An even more complex and perplexing thicket of problems in our attempts to understand the borderline phenomenon may be found in the bewildering array of theoretical approaches and perspectives. Although thoughtful clinicians can readily come to terms with the idea that borderline pathology may involve multiple defects, it is not always clear how various formulations are related, to what extent they are mutually coherent, and even that they are, in fact, addressing the same data.

The current state of thinking about the borderline personality disorders has been relatively complacent following as it has upon a period of much chaos and confusion. Kernberg (1966, 1967, 1968, 1970b, 1971), in a series of important contributions, finally culminating in a more or less definitive volume (1975), has offered formulations that have a comprehensiveness and a sweep that makes them seem both formidable and definitive. Uncertainties and ambiguities necessarily remain, and a sense of uneasy dissatisfaction has been expressed—having to do not only with diagnostic uncertainties, but also with conceptual difficulties in the understanding of the borderline syndrome (Dickes, 1974; Klein, 1975; Gunderson and Singer, 1975; Guze, 1975), as seen in Chapter 1.

In review, these include terminological ambiguities over whether the borderline entities represent forms of shifting patterns of symptom and defense or more or less stable personality configurations; inconsistent descriptions of borderline syndromes, with dramatic shifts in symptoms and behaviors and general fluidity at all levels of borderline psychopathology; and the need to distinguish between borderline conditions and the more established neuroses and psychoses. Were they *formes frustes* of psychosis, essentially psychoses with a covering neurotic facade, as seen in descriptions of latent schizophrenias, pseudoneurotic schizophrenia (Hoch and Cattell,

1959; Hoch et al., 1962; Hoch and Polatin, 1949), ambulatory schizophrenia (Zilboorg, 1941, 1956, 1957), or even the psychotic character (Frosch, 1964, 1970)? Over against this, other analysts were increasingly forced to confront the question of whether such patients were essentially neurotics and, therefore, in some degree, analyzable (Knight, 1953). Given the dominant dichotomy between neurosis and psychosis, what was not clearly definable as neurosis tended to be regarded as essentially psychosis.

Only gradually did the view emerge that borderline psychopathology was neither neurotic nor psychotic. Since the attempts to describe borderline conditions as both psychotic and neurotic were unsatisfactory, they gave way to a view of such conditions as constituting persistent forms of personality organization or character structure that had to be conceptualized and dealt with in their own terms. Kernberg's work has served to consolidate this perspective.

Other realignments in thinking followed, with the appreciation that transient regressive episodes in such personalities did not necessarily reflect an underlying psychotic process. Zetzel (Rangell, 1955; Zetzel, 1971) delineated borderline states from borderline personality organization, emphasizing that in the borderline states the overt clinical picture, whether acute or chronic, represents a group of conditions in which the patient is initially in a state of regression, which challenges the therapist from the outset. The borderline personality, however, initially presents with few or no disabling symptoms, but rather shows a variety of disturbances during the course of analysis. In a later elaboration, Zetzel (1971) commented that in the borderline states, both neurotic and psychotic phenomena are manifested, but neither fit unequivocally in either of those diagnostic categories. The patient cannot be described as overtly psychotic or as presenting any of the generally accepted personality disorders; no specific organic disease may be manifested, and symptoms and character structure are not consistent simply with a diagnosis of neurosis or neurotic character structure. Consequently, one is left with a borderline diagnosis.

Clinically, the distinction between borderline states and a borderline personality is important. The subsequent history of a patient presenting in a borderline state, including response to appropriate treatment, may lead to a revised diagnosis, since the patient may have been seen in an acute regressive crisis. Borderline patients, however, may not always present initial symptoms that suggest a borderline diagnosis and may, in fact, only reveal such a personality configuration during psychoanalysis or psychotherapy. To establish the diagnosis of borderline personality and to differentiate it from borderline states or other regressive manifestations may require an extended evaluation of the patient's response to therapy, and the evaluation of the nature of the doctor-patient relationship may play an essential role. In contrast to the potentially healthy or the neurotic patient in an acute crisis, the borderline patient has great difficulty establishing a secure and confident therapeutic relationship. Magical expectations, failure to distinguish adequately between fantasy and reality, episodes of anger and suspicion, and fears of rejection characterize a borderline therapeutic relationship, and they may persist over an extended period of time. In a favorable treatment situation, however, the borderline gradually will be able to acknowledge and partially relinquish such unrealistic and magical expectations, fears, and suspicions.

A parallel shift in diagnostic emphasis occurred—from a phenomenological or symptomatic evaluation to an evaluation of the organization and integration of structural aspects of the personality. Kernberg's (1967) perspective, as we have already noted (see Chapter 1), emphasized the specific stable form of pathological ego structure found in borderline patients. The pathology was specifically different from the neuroses and less pathological character structures on one side and from psychoses on the other. He opted for the structural determination of a borderline personality over the symptomatic or phenomenological borderline state. The organization of the personality was itself stable, rather than a form of transitional state, fluctuating between neurosis and psychosis.

The important point here is that these issues and ambiguities still affect our attempts to describe and formulate our understanding of borderline conditions. They also reflect and contribute to diagnostic ambiguities, which raises the possibility that variant theoretical accounts have focused on one or another of the diagnostically heterogeneous entities that form a spectrum of borderline conditions. This diagnostic spectrum has not been well articulated or differentiated. We shall take up the diagnostic issues more extensively in Part II. Although these considerations reflect a certain uneasiness with the current approaches to the borderline pathology, only a minority are dissatisfied; the question remains as to the extent to which the different theoretical formulations can be successfully integrated into a clearer, more encompassing description of this pathological spectrum.

Consequently, in thinking about borderline formulations, the question of the extent to which specific theoretical formulations tend to mask an underlying diagnostic heterogeneity must be addressed. A multitude of theories, each covering only a fragment or subsection of the borderline pathology, cannot explain the whole, although they may have a potential for further integration, casting light on the relationship between such theoretical formulations and the heterogeneous nature of borderline syndromes.

Thus, a first step must be to clarify the theoretical assumptions that serve as the frame of reference for particular theoretical formulations regarding the borderline personality. Psychoanalytic theory is not so much a theory as a collection of models of the mental apparatus, which, taken together, manage to span the range of modalities in which the mental apparatus can function (Gedo and Goldberg, 1973). These various models are not altogether congruent, nor are they reducible to a least common denominator. Rather, they reflect different segments and perspectives of analytic experience and are effectively differentiated by their relative success in explaining one realm of analytic data and by their comparative lack of success in generating understanding of other dimensions of analytic experience. The models can be said to have a limited base and a limited explanatory power, which constrains their usefulness in providing an understanding of the forms of psychopathology. To this perspective can be added the fact that no theory of borderline personality organization gives a satisfactory account of all aspects of the condition, but rather, that each approach tends to formulate, optimally, one or another aspect of the syndrome, while it provides a less than satisfactory account of other aspects.

Our objective in this study is a limited one. An attempt to assess the various theories as contributions to a broader psychoanalytic theory would be a monumental undertaking, quite beyond the scope of this essay and not germane to its intent. These accounts are presented only in reference to their application to borderline conditions, and even then only in a limited perspective. Even within these limitations, it is not possible to convey adequately the rich complexity of content and concept they embody. A basic familiarity and appreciation of these theoretical resources is thus assumed here, so as to avoid oversimplification in applying these formulations to gain an understanding of borderline patients.

THEORIES OF THE BORDERLINE PERSONALITY

Before specific theories are discussed, some initial cautions and clarifications may be useful. First, our primary interest in this discussion is not to criticize or evaluate specific theories, although some points of criticism and comparison will inevitably arise in the course of the discussion. No theory can explain all aspects of a specific syndrome; in some sense, all theories are only partial truths. The emphasis here is rather on the inherent limited explanatory potential of the theoretical orientations under consideration and on the clarification of these in the interest of introducing a note of caution into our use of the available explanatory modalities and clearing away some of the theoretical obfuscations, so that our way to what needs to be understood might be seen more clearly. Not only does the strength or value of any given approach rest on its explanatory power, that is, the range of the borderline personality organization and pathology it explains, it also rests on the strength and validity of its theoretical substructure. Clarification of such theoretical substructures may lead to further specification and integration of the theoretical formulations.

It should also be noted that attempts to formulate the borderline pathology frequently draw on multiple theoretical perspectives, in order to integrate these perspectives into a coherent account (Frosch, 1964, 1970; Kernberg, 1967). Blum (1972, 1974) enlists multiple perspectives, particularly in his reconstruction of the Wolf-Man's childhood. Attempts to integrate preoedipal and oedipal factors touch on complex interactions involving ego structures and defenses, object relations, narcissistic components, etc. This diversity applies particularly in the developmental approach, in which there is a convergence of hypotheses from a number of approaches.

The plan to be followed will not focus on specific theories, but rather on areas of conceptualization of specific deficits on which the understanding of borderline pathology has been based in various theories. Consequently, authors or approaches to borderline pathology may touch on one or more of these areas of defect in their overall accounts. These areas of defective functioning may be considered in a variety of ways in different approaches, and no one approach has incorporated them all. Nonetheless, in varying degrees, specific approaches tend to see one or another of these areas of defect as central to the borderline pathology. The specific areas to be considered tend to relate the central pathology of borderline conditions to (1) instinctual defects, (2) defensive impairments, (3) impairments or defects in other areas of ego functioning and integration, (4) developmental defects, (5) narcissistic defects, (6) defects and impairments in object relations, (7) the organization and pathology of the false self, and finally, (8) forms of identity diffusion.

None of the available accounts of borderline pathology precludes any one of the above aspects; but at the same time, it must be acknowledged that no two theories grant the same place or priority to these aspects. For example, borderline pathology is generally felt to involve significant developmental impediments. Two separate accounts may formulate the developmental deficit in somewhat similar terms, so that their descriptions of the developmental course seem to differ little. However, if one account sees the process as driven by inherent and biologically given determinants whose impact on the developing organism is programmed by a preset timetable of organically determined events, whereas the other account sees the same process as the result of the progressively modulating quality of the infant's object relationships with significant caretaking persons, entirely different theoretical accounts and understanding result. The theories render their accounts of the same developmental progression from opposite sides of the radical, nature-nurture dichotomy. Here the attempt is to delineate the basic theoretical assumptions embedded in accounts of the borderline pathology and to place in some perspective what may be called the "primary defect" and the degree of centrality ascribed to it in various approaches.

Instinctual Defects

Formulations that place the root of borderline pathology in some form of instinctual defect inevitably are caught in the dilemma as to whether the pathology can be basically attributed to an unusual titer of instinctual power or to a relative weakening or impairment of the resources of the ego to regulate, control, and modulate instinctual derivatives. Frequently, the borderline ego is pictured as helpless before the intensity of the onslaught of inner instinctual forces, so that to protect itself, the ego is forced into a position of helpless dependency or of omnipotent control (Geleerd, 1958). Such formulations frequently come out of an instinctual theory background and emphasize the continuity between borderline conditions and psychotic states. The underlying instinctual dynamics, with all their primitive force and primary process integration, seem to be postulated as given, and the ego is helplessly buffeted by these powerful internal forces.[1]

Along the same line, other authors have noted the chaotic and somewhat undifferentiated state of instinctualized energies giving rise to a sense of inner chaos. Particularly noteworthy in the evaluation of borderline patients is the manifestation of material from all phases of libidinal development, which presents a rather confused, mixed picture. This lack of instinctual phase dominance seems to reflect an interference with a normal processing of ego and id influences that allow the emergence of phallic trends in the oedipal situation. The bulk of the libido remains fixed in the oral and anal level, with little evidence of phallic maturation. Rosenfeld and Sprince (1963) have commented on this aspect of the borderline pathology in children:

> There seems to be a faulty relationship between the drives and the ego. At no stage does the ego give direction to the drives; neither does the ego supply the component drives with the special ego characteristics and coloring. It is as if the drives and ego develop independently and as if they belong to two different people. (p. 615)

Thus, the instinctual components remain fixed at a primitive level and seem unable to emerge from the domination of the pleasure principle.

An important question raised by such formulations has to do with the basic reasons for such instinctual impediments. One of the most consistently

---

[1]As an interesting example of this approach, Fisher (1965) speculated that if dreaming serves as a safety valve for the discharge of instinctual drives, one could expect that an increase of the pressure of drives toward discharge would be reflected in increased dreaming time. Thus, the increase of drive pressure and weakened ego defenses in a prepsychotic or borderline character would be manifested in increased dream time. He reports such results in a borderline patient who manifested an abnormally high percentage of dream time and later developed an acute paranoid psychosis. There are obvious diagnostic difficulties in the account, but the focus here is on the theoretical concept of increased drive intensity or pressure as lying at the root of the pathological manifestation.

elaborated attempts to answer that difficult question has taken shape in Kernberg's formulations. A prominent element in his analysis of borderline pathology is the predominance of pregenital and specifically oral conflicts, and primarily, the intensity of pregenital aggressive impulses (Kernberg, 1967). The predominance of primitive pregenital aggression strongly influences the nature of the oedipal conflict. There is a pathological condensation of pregenital and genital aims under the influence of these aggressive needs and, in consequence, a premature development of oedipal strivings (Kernberg, 1967, 1968).

The condensation of pregenital and genital aims under the influence of aggressive impulses sets the stage for primarily oral-aggressive projection, particularly onto the mother, resulting in a paranoid distortion of early parental images. The projection of both oral and anal sadistic impulses turns the mother into a potentially dangerous, persecutory object. The father is also gradually contaminated by this aggressive projection, with a resulting amalgamated image of the father and mother as somehow dangerous and destructive. This leads to a concept of sexual relationships as dangerous, and colored with aggressive and destructive themes. In an attempt to deny oral-dependency needs and to avoid the rage and fear related to them, there is a flight into premature genital strivings, which often miscarries because of the intensity of the aggression that contaminates the entire experience (Kernberg, 1967, 1968). Kernberg comments that these primitive dynamics may serve to discolor transference paradigms as well.

It is frequently difficult to see where or how Kernberg places the primary defect, whether on the level of instinctual organization or in terms of the predominance of splitting defenses or on a defect of ego capacity for synthesis or integration. Nonetheless, some unequivocal statements can be found. He comments, for example, that the ego in its early development has two essential tasks to accomplish: the differentiation of self-images from object-images, and the integration of both self- and object-images, under the influence of libidinal drive derivatives and related affects and under the influence of aggressive drive derivatives and related affects, respectively. The first task is not accomplished in the psychoses, but in the lower level of character organization, for example, the borderline personality organization, self- and object-images are sufficiently differentiated to permit an adequate integration of ego boundaries and a differentiation between self and others. With regard to the second task, however, Kernberg (1970) comments:

> . . . integration of libidinally-determined and aggressively-determined self- and object-images fails to a great extent in borderline patients, mainly because of the pathological predominance of pregenital aggression. The resulting lack of synthesis of contradictory self- and object-images interferes with the integration of the self-concept and with the establishing of "total" object relationships and object constancy. (p. 811)

The need to keep good self- and object-images from being contaminated by primitive aggressive influences leads to a basic defensive division of the ego, which serves as the basis for the defensive splitting, a concept that plays such an important role in Kernberg's thinking about borderline pathology (Wilson, 1971).

The degree to which the balance of constitutional as opposed to environmental factors is unclear in Kernberg's theory. It is clearly not exclusively a theory of nature as opposed to nurture, but one has the impression that constitutional factors play a clear-cut and decisive role. In this sense, Kernberg's developmental theory strikes a somewhat different pose from that of Mahler and her coworkers. The weighting in the direction of constitutional factors, specifically the increased titer of primitive oral-aggressive impulses in Kernberg's theory, has been detailed by Masterson and Rinsley (1975). The presence of such an unneutralized primitive aggression produces a situation in which there is a quantitative predominance of negative introjections, which have further implications for the persistence of splitting and the diminished capacity for constructive ego growth and the integration of self-concepts. Although Kernberg leaves room for the influence of early environmental frustration, the emphasis and the central role seems to be given over to a constitutionally determined heightened aggressive drive, which reflects his predominantly heredo-congenital view. Consequently, in his theory he pays little attention to the importance of maternal or interactional factors within the early mother-child exchange—an emphasis that sets his approach decisively off against the more specifically developmental approach of Mahler. Mahler's approach, by way of contrast, emphasizes the mother's libidinal availability and its role in eliciting the development of the child's intrapsychic structure (Mahler, 1968, 1971; Masterson and Rinsley, 1975).

If this more or less postulated and constitutionally given play of intensified aggression raises a suggestion of a Kleinian motif in Kernberg's thinking, the suspicion is not without substance. Kernberg (1967) has commented

> Pregenital aggression, especially oral aggression, plays a crucial role as part of this psychopathological constellation. The dynamic aspects of the borderline personality organization have been clarified by Melanie Klein and her coworkers. Her description of the intimate relationship between pregenital and especially oral conflicts, on the one hand, and oedipal conflicts, on the other, such as occur under the influence of excessive pregenital aggression, is relevant to the borderline personality organization. (p. 678)

But the Kleinian influence extends beyond the constitutional given of a primary destructiveness, whether related to the postulation of a death instinct or not. Kernberg further postulates that the primitive instincts, libidinal and aggressive, function as the specific organizing principles in the organization of the earliest psychic structures at a point before self-object differentiation has taken place. It is not clear whether these basic instincts or their affective expression serve the organizing function at this level, since Kernberg also suggests that it is the primitive experience of pleasure and unpleasure that serves this basic function. His formulation seems to suppose an early differentiation of aggressive as opposed to libidinal instincts and their primary defusion. It is the combination of this instinctual situation with the emerging experience of part-objects that provides the basis for Klein's paranoid-schizoid position. Thus, the central formulation of Kernberg's theory, the internalized object relation, seems to occur under the influence of these instinctual organizing principles prior to any differentiation between self and object—a formulation that seems to provide its own inherent difficulties.

There is general clinical agreement that aggression plays a primary role in the borderline syndrome, particularly expressed in the ready mobilization of anger and the degree of primitive rage so often seen in such patients (Meza, 1970; Friedman, 1970; Gunderson and Singer, 1975). The clinical facts argue unquestionably to the importance of the role of aggression in understanding the borderline pathology, but they do not argue to the necessity of postulating a primary aggressive instinct or drive, nor do they force on us the theoretical conclusion that aggression is a constitutional given. Such has been the attitude expressed in early Freudian and Kleinian instinctual theory, but it may be that instinctual drives themselves can be conceptualized in terms of developmental process in which certain constitutional givens are shaped and modified by the quality of interaction with significant objects (Loewald, 1971). Nor are we compelled to think of primary aggression as essentially defused and only subsequently modified in a benign direction by fusion with libidinal inputs. It may be, for example, that the destructive and relatively "unneutralized" or "defused" quality of borderline aggression is related to the underlying vicissitudes of injured narcissism, which is threatened on a variety of fronts and for the restitution of which aggression is mobilized (Rochlin, 1973).

The appeal to instinctual factors as basic to the understanding of borderline conditions focuses on essentially economic-energic factors. The key issue then becomes the distribution, channeling, or transformation of basic energies, specifically, aggression. This psycho-economic concern is reflected in a preoccupation with disruptive states of hyperstimulation, modification of aggressive drive stimuli by fusion, and the need to protect nascent structure from overwhelming traumatic forces. This focus may have a useful application during the very early stages of development or in severe psychotic regression, but it is less useful in more evolved contexts of psychic functioning. Its explanatory range is, thus, quite limited (Gedo and Goldberg, 1973).

Defensive Impairment

In the formulation of borderline pathology, the deficits in the defensive structure of the ego are emphasized. Thus, our understanding shifts to the resources of the ego as a system of functions, but the defect in defensive functions, as opposed to other capacities of the ego, are specifically emphasized. The most dramatic failure of the defenses is seen in periods of transient psychotic regression, in which the patient decompensates and presents an apparently psychotic picture complete with helplessness, emotional collapse, and panic. At such points, the patient's vulnerability is most apparent and may provide the basis for difficult psychotic transference distortions (Giovacchini, 1973).

But even on more characterological and less regressed levels of functioning, the borderline tends to manifest relatively primitive defenses, including splitting, projection, projective identification, primitive idealization, and denial (Adler, 1974). Perhaps the strongest emphasis on defensive modalities and their role in borderline pathology is that of Kernberg. He makes adequate room in his description of borderline functioning for other modalities of primitive defensive operations, but splitting is the essential defensive activity that underlies the others, and it is essential to his understanding of borderline pathology. It is the distinction between splitting, as the crucial aspect of defensive organization of the ego at a lower level of character pathology, and repression, as a central mechanism at more advanced levels of defensive organization, that provide the basis for a diagnostic discrimination between borderline conditions and neurotic conditions. Speaking of the splitting process, Kernberg (1967) observes,

> This is an essential defensive operation of the borderline personality organization which underlies all the others which follow. It has to be stressed that I am using the term "splitting" in a restricted and limited sense, referring only to the active process of keeping apart introjections and identifications of opposite quality. . . . Splitting, then, is a fundamental cause of ego weakness, and as splitting also requires less countercathexis than repressions, a weak ego falls back easily on splitting, and a vicious circle is created by which ego weakness and splitting reinforce each other. (p. 667)

Thus the notion of ego weakness, often left unspecified in other approaches, is assigned a specific reference and cause in Kernberg's formulation, namely, the underlying prevalence of the splitting mechanism that is seen as basic to other forms of ego dysfunction (Kernberg, 1967, 1971). The splitting process arises in the primary context of organizing discrete affect states around the libidinal and aggressive drives. This primitive organization is inseparably linked with the internalization of pathological object relationships, which persist in a relatively nonmetabolized condition as a result of the continuing effects of splitting. Kernberg (1966) explicitly relates this conceptualization to the concept of splitting in Fairbairn's account of the schizoid personality.

Kernberg's position has been questioned. Atkin (1974), for example, discusses the apparent splitting in a borderline patient:

> The "cleavage" in the cognitive, thought and linguistic functions that will be demonstrated in my patient can best be understood, in my opinion, as developmental arrest. No anxiety was produced in the analysis of the dysjunction, a proof that it is not a defense (where no knitting into a whole has taken place there can be no "split" in Kernberg's sense). I found that only after some maturity of the ego occurred as a result of the psychoanalysis did anxiety appear when the discrepancies were analyzed. Only then was the dysjunction used as a defense, with resistance against giving it up. (pp. 13–14)

The objection posed here is fundamental in that it focuses on the issue of developmental arrest as opposed to defense. Kernberg appears to assume the differentiation and organization of specific drive states and the internalization of pathogenic internalized object relationships at a developmental stage prior to any differentiation between the infant self and the non-self.

There are inherent difficulties in the term "splitting" even beyond Kernberg's usage. Certainly, Kernberg's effort to narrow the focus of the term so that splitting becomes the fundamental defensive operation in borderline pathology and, thus its clinical touchstone, leaves something to be desired. Splitting is found throughout the broad spectrum of psychopathology. In its most dramatic and intense form, it is identifiable in the psychoses, but it can also be described in relatively healthy neurotics. The effort to focus the differentiation between borderline and neurotic pathology on the presence of splitting in the one and the reliance on repression in the other founders on clinical fact.

In an extensive review of the subject, Pruyser (1975) has pointed out the broad range of pathological expression of so-called "splitting." He also criticizes the ambiguity and confusing connotations associated with use of the term. Kernberg's use of the term has a certain phenomenological or descriptive validity, but it merely describes the disjointed, mutually contradictory, and sudden shifting of patient behaviors, attitudes and emotions, transferences, and relations with important objects that seem to reflect a lack of integration. Pruyser (1975) concludes that

> The word *splitting* is both too slippery and too hard. It does not fit what we know about the mental life and is incommensurate with the temper of modern science, which has moved far and fast in the direction of process conceptions. Whatever psychic structure is, it is not hard and substantial and spatial. Splitting is too spatial, too surgical, and at the same time extremely indefinite. With all these peculiarities, its users, especially when they attempt to reconstruct the

child's mind, run the risk of adultomorphic impositions. Elevated to a psychological concept, the words *splitting* and *split* create more problems than they solve. (p. 44)

If Kernberg's use of "splitting" has some descriptive value, he also relies heavily on the notion of splitting as a defense. "Splitting" thus becomes an active transitive verb denoting a defensive process by which the ego separates psychic contents, particular affects and representations. Dorpat (1979b) has pointed out the lack of empirical evidence to support the notion of splitting as a defense. Kernberg's (1976b) argument that the precipitating of anxiety when a patient is confronted with the unreal quality of his view of the analyst as both idealized and devalued (split representations) suggests that the defensive nature of the splitting is questionable. Dorpat (1979b) points out that anxiety does not necessarily indicate that the behavior is defensive, nor does it follow that, even if it could be shown to be defensive, the defense in question would be splitting rather than, let us say, denial. This point of view is reinforced by Robbins (1976). The linkages with the Kleinian underpinnings of Kernberg's early thinking (later revised by a more developed concept of ego formation) require the postulation of a capacity for psychic differentiation prior to the differentiation of object representations and also assume that splitting serves as a central organizing principle in mental life, a position at variance with current developmental views that the organization of mental life is effected by processes of synthesis and differentiation. All these authors agree that "splitting" can legitimately connote only descriptive divisions in the mental apparatus, and not a specific mechanism of defense.

It can be questioned whether Kernberg's formulations regarding this early developmental stage do not represent a translation of Kleinian motifs into ego psychological terms. The description of this early context has multiple resonances with Klein's description of the paranoid-schizoid position, and the healthy normal or neurotic resolution of this primitive splitting in terms of the fusion of aggressive with libidinal components seems to come very close to Klein's description of the depressive position. Kernberg is quite aware of this derivation, and he takes care to distinguish his position from that of Klein and the Kleinians (Kernberg, 1967).

Other aspects of the defensive configuration in borderlines have received attention. Modell (1961) has discussed the role of denial in borderlines, particularly in relation to separation anxiety. The denial of separation creates the illusion that the object is somehow part of the self and, therefore, cannot be lost. This creates a condition in which individuation cannot be acknowledged, since separation becomes equivalent to loss. Thus, growth to mature autonomy and individuality becomes translated into terms of separation from primary objects. Inherent in this separation is the threat of destruction or annihilation. The borderline differs from the psychotic in that psychotic denial is more severe and leads to the development of restitutional delusions or hallucinations. The psychotic then uses derivatives of internalized objects as the substitute for lost objects, and hallucinations serve as substitutes for painful reality. The borderline, however, does not take this additional step. Modell notes that quantitative factors determine the extent of the denial, particularly in relation to the degree of regression in object relationships. However, Modell's (1961) formulation does not place denial at the root of the borderline pathology, but rather sees it as another manifestation of a defect or a failure in the development of a capacity for object relationship.

The shift to an emphasis on defenses refocuses the borderline pathology in terms of the ego, but it is specifically a defensive ego that is called into play. The description of primitive defenses tends to link the borderline pathology more closely to psychotic levels of functioning. The general tendency is to think in terms of clusters of primitive defensive operations, which can then be explained in terms of some other defect, whether this is seen specifically in developmental terms or not. Thus, the role of primitive defenses in the theory of borderline pathology is generally secondary. This applies also to Kernberg's (1967, 1975) formulations regarding splitting, even though splitting seems to loom large in his general scheme. We cannot forget that it is itself a secondary phenomenon arising out of the primitive organization of internalized object relationships and in response to the predominance of pregenital oral aggression.

A perplexing aspect of borderline pathology has been the curious mixture of postoedipal defensive functions with more primitive pregenital ones, a point noted by Gitelson some years ago (cited in Rangell, 1955). Thus, it can be argued that an emphasis on splitting as a primitive defensive function does not allow for the development of higher defensive capabilities. It can even be questioned whether Kernberg's formulation tends to push out of appropriate perspective the function of higher defenses in borderline personality organization. In general, the tendency to see borderline pathology as closer to the psychotic border than to the neurotic border tends to reinforce this general inclination.

An additional point that demands consideration is the extent to which defensive defects can be read back from a more differentiated and evolved state of intrapsychic organization to early primitive developmental levels. It is by no means clear, for example, how splitting as a defensive activity arises within Kernberg's theory. Its point of departure is from the initial integration of internalized objects and their associated affects, but it is difficult to see how this then moves to the level of defensive functioning. It may be that, in order to make that model of the origin of borderline personality operative, one must postulate initial ego capacities and functions that require a greater degree of developmental maturation and intrapsychic differentiation. This is a fundamental point of divergence between theorists who base their analysis on ego functions, both defensive and otherwise, and developmental theorists.

It is worth reminding ourselves that the theoretical account of the defensive ego represents a more evolved level of ego functioning that has its reference in the topographic model. The topographic model, and later the structural model, which was meant to replace it (Gill, 1963), were derived from clinical data having to do with intrapsychic conflict and were not intended to explain earlier prestructural phenomena.

Ego Defects

Although the focus on defenses as the central aspect of the borderline pathology stems from the point of view that specifically conceptualized the ego in terms of its defensive functions, the emphasis on other nondefensive functions stems from a later and more evolved view of the ego, in which the concept of the ego centers upon notions of autonomy and adaptation. This view was specifically advanced and systematized by Hartmann (1939, 1964) and Rapaport (1958, 1967). In this context, the borderline pathology is viewed as a relatively stable form of ego pathology (Kernberg, 1967). The common denominator is viewed as the ego defect (Blum, 1972), which distinguishes the borderline from the neurotic, and in which the problems of adaptation take precedence over conflicts concerning unacceptable impulses (Giovacchini, 1973). The borderline ego is envisioned as weak, ineffectual, and vulnerable (Ekstein and Wallerstein, 1956; Frosch, 1970).

Kernberg's (1967, 1971) systematic treatment of aspects of ego weakness provides us with a framework for discussing these aspects of defective ego functioning. He lists, besides the predominance of relatively primitive defensive operations related to splitting, a lack of impulse control, a lack of anxiety tolerance, a lack of developed sublimatory channels, a tendency to primary process thinking, and finally, the weakening of the capacity for reality-testing.

The lack of the capacity to delay impulse discharge, normally regarded as a function of the ego, had been previously noted (Rangell, 1955) and related to the general fluidity of borderline cathexes and the inability to establish libidinal object constancy (Frank, cited in Robbins, 1956). But, as Kernberg (1966) points out, the borderline pathology represents a form of selective impulsivity and an acting-out character disorder. The patient may manifest relatively good impulse control in all but one area in which impulse control may be defective. He suggests, however, that rather than diminished impulse control we may be seeing an alternating activation of contradictory aspects of the patient's psychic life, as for example in the switching back and forth between intense sexual fears and impulsive sexual acting-out, both apparently ego syntonic. Borderlines will alternately express complementary sides of a conflict, on the one hand, acting-out a libidinal impulse, and on the other, acting in terms of a specific defensive character formation erected against the impulse. They tend to be conscious of the contradiction, but blandly deny the implications of this contradiction, with a lack of concern over the apparent compartmentalization. Kernberg relates this phenomenon to the underlying defense of splitting, which he sees as lying at the root of ego weakness. Thus, the impulsive behavior may represent the emergence into consciousness of a dissociated identification system, in which the impulses are expressed in impulsive behavior, but have lost contact with the rest of the patient's experience and undergo subsequent denial. He also points out that this pattern of specific loss of impulse control is different from the more nonspecific and erratic dispersion of intrapsychic tension seen in infantile personalities (Kernberg, 1967).

The inability to tolerate frustration, tension, or anxiety to any significant degree has also been frequently noted as a characteristic of borderline patients (Rangell, 1955; Robbins, 1956; Brody, 1960; Worden, 1955; Kernberg, 1967, 1971). As Kernberg notes, the important variable here is not the degree of anxiety in itself, but rather the extent to which any additional anxiety added to the patient's habitual level of anxiety experience tends to induce an increase of symptoms or a pathological regression or other forms of pathological behavior. He regards this as a highly unfavorable prognostic indicator (1971).

Ego weakness is also reflected in a lack of sublimatory channels, specifically expressed in a capacity for work and an enjoyment of living, the capacity for creative achievement, and the ability to invest oneself in activities or in a profession that reach beyond mere narcissistic satisfactions. Although sublimatory capacities are frequently expressed in creative activities and achievement, it should be noted that borderline personalities often are attracted to, and find narcissistically gratifying, enjoyment in creative activities, whereas they find it difficult to deal with and master the day-to-day routine of more humdrum work situations (Fast, 1975).

Similarly, the tendency to primary process thinking, or to regress to levels at which primary process contaminates the secondary process thought processes, is an important index of ego weakness. This particular manifestation of ego weakness plays a particularly telling role, since it is one of the more frequently relied on indices, clinically, for identifying borderline personalities (Kernberg, 1967). Patients rarely manifest a formal thought disorder on clinical examination, but quite regularly, primary process manifestations in the form of primitive fantasies or peculiar verbalizations or other idiosyncratic responses may show up on projective testing. The importance of this indicator as the most important single structural index of borderline organization highlights the importance of the use of projective tests in the diagnosis of such patients. It is not at all clear, however, what a regression in such thought processes may mean, since the evaluation of it as an indicator must be considered in the context of the discrimination from an underlying psychosis.

The most critical index of ego dysfunction is the weakening of reality-testing or the loss of a sense of reality. This is particularly important, since the capacity to maintain reality-testing is one of the most useful discriminatory indices separating borderlines from psychotics (Frijling-Schreuder, 1969). Modell (1963) had noted the loss of a sense of reality in borderlines, but also noted that it was more subtle and less advanced than in schizophrenics. Other authors have noted the weakening in the capacity for reality-testing and in reality sense, noting that the impairment in these capacities may be transient, although in some patients it may be a permanent aspect of their functioning (Adler, 1970; Klein, 1975; Buie and Adler, 1972).

Frosch (1964, 1970) differentiates the quality of the patient's involvement with reality in terms of the relation to reality, the feeling of reality, and finally, the capacity to test reality. All of these aspects of the reality function of the ego are impaired, but the best preserved tends to be reality-testing. It is this relative preservation of the capacity to test reality that distinguishes the borderline syndromes from psychotic states (Frosch, 1964; Giovacchini, 1965). Disturbances in the patient's reality function are usually relatively easily reversible and are facilitated in this by the relative intactness of the capacity to reality test. Even patients who experience hallucinations or depersonalization may still be able to recognize these phenomena as derived from their internal experience, so that their reality-testing remains functional (Frosch, 1970).

Kernberg (1971) reinforces this view by noting that reality-testing involves the capacity to differentiate intrapsychic and external perceptual events. Such reality-testing in borderline patients undergoes transient impairment, particularly under the influence of emotional stress, alcohol, drugs, or when the patient is caught up in a transference psychosis. It is the preservation of reality-testing under ordinary circumstances and in most contexts of ordinary living that differentiates the borderline from the psychotic. A persistent impairment in this capacity in any area of psychological functioning and/or the production of psychotic manifestations must be taken as a manifestation of psychosis. Thus, Kernberg (1971) notes, if these are not present, the patient is not psychotic. He also notes that the frequency or intensity of the loss of reality-testing is not an important prognostic indicator, since the borderline in a regressive transference psychosis usually will respond favorably to treatment and to the increase of structure, either in therapy or in the life situation. This does not hold true for the psychotic loss of reality-testing.

Attention has also been called to the capacity of the ego to control or to regulate inner psychic states as defective in borderline patients. Ekstein and Wallerstein (1954) have compared this function of the ego to that of a thermostat—neurotic patients undergo minimal fluctuations under the control of the secondary process, but in borderline and psychotic patients, the fluctuations are wide-ranging and unpredictable. Thus, the ego is battered back and forth by fantasies and unconscious instinctual derivatives so that the state of the ego fluctuates rapidly and radically from one state to another through the course of the day (Ekstein and Wallerstein, 1954; Dickes, 1974; Klein, 1975; Blum, 1972).

Various authors have focused on the lack of integrative or synthetic function as central to borderline pathology. The defect in this essential function has been related to the incapacity to integrate sensory stimuli (Rosenfeld and Sprince, 1965), the susceptibility to dedifferentiation under stress (Frosch, 1967a,b), the uneven binding of instinctual energies and the failure of neutralization (Rosenfeld and Sprince, 1963), and the failure to coordinate perceptual stimuli, both inner and outer, with executive responses (Giovacchini, 1973). Atkin (1974) has further pointed out that the capacity for integration and synthesis, which normally creates an integrated inner world, is defective in borderline patients and is responsible for lapses and discontinuities in the cognitive sphere, so that primary process influences on language and thinking, as well as predominant pregenital sexual and aggressive responses, may result. The failure to integrate leads to a bland toleration for contradictory states of thought and action in which there is no need to unify or reconcile them. It should be noted that theorists who focus on the lack of capacity for integration and synthesis seem to write out of a background that is more or less developmental.

A latent issue in the discussion of defective ego functions and their relevance to borderline pathology has to do with the question of the degree to which they are considered as discrete, that is to say, the extent to which they are regarded as present or absent or as functional or impaired, as against the extent to which they are seen to function on a continuum, that is, subject to various degrees of operation or levels of functioning. The synthetic function, for example, tends to be conceptualized in terms of gradations of function, whereas reality-testing tends to be seen more in discrete terms. Consequently, reality-testing is often used as a discriminator of the presence of or absence of psychosis.

But reality-testing itself may be conceived in terms of degrees of alteration or impairment (Modell, 1963). Thus, the function of reality-testing may itself be a complex function, which may be subject to contextual variations in the sense that it may be relatively impaired in specific contexts of the patient's experience, but relatively unimpaired in others. The tendency to see these functions operating discretely in the borderline tends to dichotomize thinking and to push the concept of borderline pathology in the direction of linking it with the psychoses. Conceptualizing these functions in terms of gradients offers the opportunity of a more refined conceptualization of the borderline pathology as neither psychotic nor neurotic, while it forces us to a more specific and refined sense of intermediate gradations of functioning within which the borderline pathology occurs. This question is discussed in greater detail in Chapter 6.

In general, the approach to an understanding of the borderline pathology in terms of specific ego defects has only limited explanatory power. The approach, in general, is generated from Hartmann's (1939, 1964) perspective on the relative independence of ego functions, in which he implied that impairment or relative dysfunction could appear in one or another ego function, while other capacities of the ego would be relatively unimpaired. It somehow seems too simplistic, or "neat," that the multiple impairments found in the borderline pathology can be attributed to a single ego defect. Rather, we may be forced to a position that recognizes that ego deviations and defects are a vital and integral part of the understanding of the syndrome, but that we cannot think solely in terms of specific defects. We need to think of multiple deviations in many areas of ego functioning, possibly operating on a different level of disturbance in each area. Such ego functions, which may involve a series of gradations of impairments or levels of functioning, may also be subject to a partial reversibility in their level or integration of functioning, which is particularly labile in the borderline (Rosenfeld and Sprince, 1963).

The conceptualization of impaired, non-defensive ego functions derives from the more evolved concept of the autonomous ego. The defects considered to be central to the borderline pathology take their toll in the diminished autonomy of the patient's ego and its functions and a diminished capacity to relate and adapt to reality. The focus on the ego defects has a certain descriptive validity, although even here the attempt to reduce the multifaceted borderline syndromes to a single defect seems weak. Not only do the specific ego defects not explain all manifestations of the borderline pathology, but they also stand in need of explanation themselves. These defects must be constitutionally given, or they must be explained. Thus, ego defects tend to serve as an intermediate explanatory concept that must give way usually either to a developmental or to a more specifically object relation conceptualization.

Moreover, the frame of reference, the Hartmann-Rapaport ego model, tends to place all capacities for adaptive or autonomous functioning in the ego and sets the ego over against the undisciplined and unmodified id impulses. The function of the ego, therefore, becomes one of regulation and control in the interest of adaptive functioning. The model postulates a radical dichotomy between the undifferentiated energetic and chaotic impulses of the id and the regulating, controlling, modulating, and directing capacities of the ego. The model dictates, then, that the developmental achievement enlarges the capacities of the ego and establishes their jurisdiction over the id. Any defect in this regimen causes the ego to yield to the power of instinctual impulses. It should be noted that this is not the only developmental model that can be envisioned, nor is it the only frame of reference within which the interrelation and integration of id impulses and ego controls can be envisioned (Apfelbaum, 1966). Consequently, just as all healthy and adaptive functioning need not be exclusively a function of ego capacities, so the borderline pathology may not necessarily be a function simply of ego defects as such.

Developmental Defects

Within the developmental perspective, there is a decisive shift away from a reliance on specific defects, whether of an instinctual or a structural nature, to explain the borderline pathology. The basis for understanding rests rather on multiple defects affecting a variety of psychic subsystems and related to the developmental failures involved in a relatively specific phase or level of the child's growing experience. Although the developmental approach rests uneasily on the assumption of constitutional factors, it primarily emphasizes the vicissitudes of the child's object relationships, so that it is, in essence, emphasizing experiential factors over constitutional factors. Further, the explanation depends on the quality of the infant's object relations experience, so that there is a significant degree of overlap between developmental perspectives and specific object relations theories.

To this extent, the developmental approach provides a frame within which multiple perspectives can be organized. It adds a specific and important dimension to other theoretical accounts, namely, progression through time, which allows for the emergence of certain deficits in phase-specific sequence that may undergo a variety of developmental vicissitudes in subsequent phases. As applied to borderline pathology, however, as in any other pathology, the issues of specific and primary defects remain operative. To this extent, current developmental formulations remain usefully eclectic as theoretical commitments. In this degree, then, the developmental orientation shares in and reflects the general theoretical tensions and uncertainties regarding borderline pathologies.

In proposing a developmental approach to borderline pathology a few years ago, Zetzel (1971) envisioned the borderline defect in terms of the developmental failure to achieve adequate one-to-one relationships with the respective parental objects, so that the borderline was prevented from entering into and successfully resolving a triadic oedipal involvement that simultaneously included both parental objects. The borderline may thus show a relative, but not necessarily equal, failure in specific developmental tasks. The affected tasks may include the establishment of a definitive self-object differentiation; a capacity to recognize, tolerate, and master separation, loss, and narcissistic injury; the internalization of ego identifications and self-esteem, which permits genuine autonomous functioning; and the capacity to maintain relatively stable object relationships. The borderline's vulnerability in the differentiation of self and object is illustrated by his difficulty in maintaining the distinction between fantasy and reality, particularly under emotional stress or during a regressive transference reaction. Thus, the borderline's capacity to internalize a stable ego identification and to achieve a genuine autonomy is severely limited and quite vulnerable.

The failure to achieve satisfactory one-to-one relationships points to a relatively early developmental failure. Margaret Mahler (1968, 1971, 1975) has made the most consistent attempt to specify this defect, relating developmental failure to the separation-individuation process. The failure of that process tends to produce a relatively unassimilated bad introject around which the child's inner experience is organized. Specifically, it is the upsurge of aggression in the rapprochement phase of the separation-individuation process that provides the conditions for the organization of the borderline intrapsychic economy (Mahler, 1971).

The rapprochement phase is characterized by increased separation. Development is favorable when the separation reaction is characterized by modulated and ego-regulated affects and where the titer of libido predominates over that of aggression. The child's need to separate is accompanied by a wish for a symbiotic reunion with the mother, but this wish is also attended by a fear of re-engulfment.[2] The child's attempts to ward off maternal impingement on his recently acquired and fragile autonomy tend to mobilize the aggressive response. The two-year-old toddler's autonomy is defended by the vigorous use of the word "No" and the increased aggressiveness and negativity of the anal phase. The rapprochement conflict is brought to an end by the developmental spurt of the relatively conflict-free autonomous ego, which sets the stage for the attainment of libidinal object constancy in the third year (Mahler, 1971).

The upsurge of aggression thus tends to undermine the good self and object representations and to increase ambivalence. The result is a rapid alternation of clinging and negative behavior, reflecting a split in the object world and an attempt to preserve the good object. Mahler emphasizes the

---

[2]The retention of intense symbiotic strivings, in the form of womb fantasies, associated with a dread of merging and a fear of annihilation were identifiable in the Wolf-Man (Blum, 1974) as an expression of borderline pathology.

child's interaction with the mother, particularly the mother's libidinal availability and responsiveness as the determinants of the development of the child's intrapsychic structure. Formation of self and object representations is based on the internalization of the interaction with the mother. Generally, the child's early developmental experience in the symbiotic phase may have been relatively untroubled, but initiation of the attempts to separate and individuate are met by maternal withdrawal of supports. It is this abandonment on the part of the mother that becomes powerfully introjected.

As Masterson and Rinsley (1975) have extended this theory, it is the maternal withdrawal of libidinal availability in the face of the child's efforts to separate, individuate, and achieve some degree of relative autonomy that forms the leitmotif of the borderline child's development. They postulate that the mother herself manifests borderline qualities in that she is excessively gratified by her symbiotic involvement with the child. Thus, the child's separation, especially during the rapprochement phase, creates a crisis in which the mother is unable to tolerate the toddler's ambivalence, assertiveness, and independence. The mother is available to the child only if the child continues to cling and behave in a regressive manner. The borderline child's dilemma is that he needs maternal support in order to continue the process of separating, individuating, and growing, but this very process leads to the withdrawal of that support. Consequently, the child tries to sustain the image of the good, supportive and nurturing mother by splitting it from the image of the bad, rejecting, withdrawing, and abandoning mother of separation.

It should be noted that the "splitting" in this developmental perspective should be distinguished from the notion of splitting advanced by Kernberg as a specific and active defensive function. Splitting here has much more to do with the sense of a failure of developmental integration. The contrast with Kernberg's more defensively oriented view can again be seen in terms of the relative emphasis on the constitutionally determined role of aggression in one approach, as opposed to the emphasis on an environmentally determined reaction to the withdrawal of maternal libidinal availability in the other. The child's intense oral dependence and absolute need for affection and support from the mother result in rage and frustration because of the mother's depriving response. The resulting fear that these intense feelings will destroy both the needed object and the self requires that the image of the mother be split into good and bad portions. Thus, the child constructs the fantasy or illusion of being cared for and loved by a good mother and projects the bad, frustrating, and depriving aspects onto other objects. Since these images remain unintegrated, objects are either good and gratifying or bad and frustrating, without ever being amalgamated into a single object experience. Thus, the child, in Kleinian terms, remains mired in the paranoid-schizoid position and is unable to achieve a more integrated depressive position in which the ambivalence to the object can be tolerated. In these terms, the borderline fails to achieve genuine object constancy (Masterson, 1972). Here again, there is tension between the tendency to view object constancy as a discrete developmental accomplishment and a view of such constancy as relative, involving different degrees or gradients.

It should be noted that although Mahler tends to place the impediments in the separation-individuation process somewhere in the second and third years of life, other authors have placed the developmental defect even further back in the symbiotic phase of development, somewhere in the first year of life (Chessick, 1966; Giovacchini, 1973). As Horner (1975) has noted, the splitting becomes apparent in the separation-individuation phase, but its genetic roots can be traced to earlier levels of the symbiotic merger with an ambivalent object. Moreover, there are some suggestions in Mahler's own formulations that the beginnings of splitting and the forming of good and bad centers of frustration-deprivation or satiation-gratification are taking place even before separation plays its part. Thus, the earliest failures of maternal symbiosis in the hatching phase of separation or before may set the stage for pathological introjections that underlie borderline pathology (Mahler, 1968, 1971).

The developmental approach tends to focus on a particular level of developmental impairment as the specific locus of pathological defect in the borderline syndrome. It must be remembered, however, that the developmental course is subject to a variety of vicissitudes and a sequential elaboration of both progressive and regressive potentialities, which tend to diversify significantly the effects of developmental impediments at any level. Thus, for example, the dilemmas of separation and individuation are critically reworked on the adolescent level, so that the borderline adolescent is again trapped in the conflict between his strivings for autonomy, on the one hand, and his fear of parental abandonment, on the other (Zinner and Shapiro, 1975). Consequently, it must be remembered that whatever deficits can be traced to specific developmental phases, these need to be thought out more carefully in terms of the sequential progression of the developmental achievements and failures as the child moves from, let us say, the conflicts embedded in the rapprochement phase of separation-individuation through subsequent phases of reworking similar issues on into adolescence and young adulthood. It cannot thus be said that a developmental failure at a specific phase, such as the rapprochement phase, can be related, with any consistency or clarity, to a specific configuration or pathological characteristics in the borderline personality on an adolescent or adult level. Mahler (1971) herself has introduced a cautionary note:

> My intention, at first, was to establish in this paper a linking-up, in neat detail, of the described substantive issues with specific aspects of borderline phenomena shown by child and adult patients in the psychoanalytic situation. But I have come to be more and more convinced that there is no "direct line" from the

deductive use of borderline phenomena to one or another substantive findings of observational research. (p. 415)

Thus, the simplistic conceptualization of a link between a phasic developmental failure and a specific form of psychopathology cannot be consistently maintained. Rather, a more careful study of sequential development may suggest meaningful patterns in which sequences of developmental variability can be related more meaningfully to patterns of psychopathology. This demands not only a more intensive and more refined exercise in careful diagnosis, but also more extensive and observational longitudinal data.

It should also be noted that there is a tendency in the developmental literature, particularly in Mahler's work, to relate developmental impediments to a failure of the integrative capacity or synthetic function of the ego. Again, this approach seems to reflect a tendency to organize the complexities of developmental data in terms of a specific ego defect. This reflects a more or less implicit adherence to a Hartmannian frame of reference, in which significant developmental attainments and functional capacities are located in the ego, to the exclusion of other aspects of psychic functioning.

Narcissistic Defects

The emphasis on the role of narcissism in borderline pathology shifts the locus of the pathology to the self. The metapsychological status of the self is still open to considerable question and debate, but the attempt to define borderline pathology in terms of the defects of self-structure leads to a completely new emphasis on pathological impairments and brings the function of narcissism to the center.

Issues of pathological narcissism have often been viewed in terms of narcissistic entitlement (Murray, 1964). Narcissistic entitlement dictates that the patient has a right to life on his own terms. A developmental fixation at narcissistic levels can reflect either excessive gratification or deprivation: either the patient's wishes were always granted, so that he assumes they should be, or they were never satisfied, and he feels the world should make it up to him. Such narcissistic entitlement plays a central role in borderline pathology, since the borderline sees himself as a special person with special rights and entitlements, such that any frustration of these entitled desires tends to undermine and often shatter the patient's self-esteem.

But it must be remembered that there is more than one level of entitlement (Buie and Adler, 1972). The patient's emotional deprivation because of the emotional unresponsiveness and withdrawal of the mother threatens the borderline patient's survival. Such survival entitlement is related to maternal abandonment and its inherent threats of destruction or annihilation and is the basis of the patient's terror and rage. The persistence of such archaic ego states, and their early narcissistic vicissitudes, is often expressed in a sense of fragmentation, confusion between self and object, coexisting or alternating grandiosity and terror, and alternating or tangled states of dread and rage, humiliation and triumph, megalomania and devastation (Moore, 1975).

Much of this approach owes its impetus to the work of Kohut (1971), but the amalgamation of primitive, pregenital object libido and narcissism was appreciated previously. For example, Reich (1953) noted that it is characteristic of early phases of object relations that objects tend to be used primarily for the gratification of the self, and that objects exist only to the degree that they provide such gratification and are destroyed in frustrated rage when such gratification is withheld. The narcissistic omnipotent need to control such objects is often not outgrown and may be regressively revived, so that when the narcissistically invested object fails to provide the needed gratification, problems in self-esteem arise.

The central concept on which Kohut's approach focuses is that of the "cohesive self." The narcissistic personality disorders, as he describes them, have attained a relatively stable and cohesive self, which remains more or less stable, although precariously balanced; but it shows a tendency for transient temporary fragmentation in response to narcissistic injury or loss (Kohut, 1971; Ornstein, 1974). The discrimination between narcissistic personalities and borderline or psychotic patients is cast in terms of the failure of the latter group to attain a cohesive self, so that such patients are unable to mobilize cohesive narcissistic structures to form consistent and analyzable transferences. The borderline patient has a less cohesive self that is subject to fragmentation so that he is unable to maintain the boundaries between self and object. Thus, the central vulnerability of the narcissistic personality is the danger of fragmentation or disintegration when a narcissistic relationship is disrupted, but these individuals possess a resilience that is missing in borderlines, which allows them to repair the shattered narcissism. The threat of disintegration is more central and critical in borderlines, whereas disruption of the narcissistic relationship plays the more prominent role in narcissistic personalities.

It should be remembered that narcissistic vulnerability occurs in the context of the important object relation with the mother. The infant is caught between the threat of symbiotic engulfment, on the one hand, and loss or abandonment, on the other. The usual picture is that of the narcissistic mother who withdraws her love when the child attempts to define himself as somehow separate from her. She becomes emotionally unavailable when he tries to individuate and to establish his own narcissistic equilibrium independently of her. The threat of object loss and abandonment depression leads to a narcissistic oral fixation, which impedes the establishment of a cohesive self (Horner, 1975). It should also be remembered that narcissistic impediments that impinge on the organization and stabilization of the self take place within a more complex family context, in which the child's dependence, and failure to achieve narcissistic differentiation, can be an important function in maintaining the delicate balance of narcissistic equilib rium within the family system (Zinner and Shapiro, 1975).

It should be noted that formulations in terms of the cohesiveness of the self are not very helpful in distinguishing between borderline pathology and psychotic levels of organization. In fact, Kohut's (1971) description of the temporary regressive fragmentation of the self in narcissistic personalities is strikingly similar to the borderline regression as described in other orientations. It is also noteworthy that formulations in terms of the self put the basis of the pathology on an entirely different footing than in other approaches. The potential of this approach is considerable, since it leaves open the possibility of reasonably well integrated functioning in the structural components of the tripartite theory, while the pathology develops and is rooted in the organization and functioning of the self. In most borderline cases, however, such a discrimination cannot be cleanly made, and there is evidence of defects in all the psychic systems.

It should be emphasized that the shift to a narcissistic basis introduces a quite distinct theoretical paradigm. Understanding of the pathology is shifted from a concern with structural integrity or the autonomy of ego/superego function to the organization and stabilization of the self as the significant principle of intrapsychic integration. The shift in emphasis to the centrality of the self follows the lead of the notion of "identity theme," as proposed by Lichtenstein (1964, 1965). Some of the implications in this alteration of basic reference point have been suggested by Gedo (cited in Meissner, 1976a).

However, the shift in perspective raises the question of what defects may be primary, and what defects secondary, as well as the interesting diagnostic question of whether certain borderline categories may involve a pathology of the self, with minimal disruption of ego and superego functions. In addition, the approach through the pathology of the self may link the pathology more specifically to the object relations context, insofar as defects of the self may involve only one side of the self-object differentiation. Within that frame of reference, then, defects in the organization of the self and impairments in object relations may be envisioned as two sides of the same coin. Here again, the emphasis on narcissism seems to focus on an internal frame of reference, which gives rise to a series of economic preoccupations regarding the distribution and stabilization of narcissistic cathexes, rather than an emphasis on the context of interaction, within which narcissistic vicissitudes are worked out vis-à-vis the interaction with objects.

Defective Object-Relations

The contextual framework within which such primitive narcissistic issues are elaborated and worked out is provided by a consideration of object relations. Thus, the object relations theory considerably overlaps and interdigits with the approach to the vicissitudes of early archaic narcissism and the developmental approach. These various approaches tend to be mutually reinforcing and complementary within the confines of their respective emphases. The disturbance and fragility of object relations has frequently been noted (Reich, 1953; Rangell, 1955; Frosch, 1964, 1967a, 1970; Knight, 1953), and perhaps earliest of all by Helene Deutsch (1942), in her description of the "as-if" characteristics. The need-satisfying quality of such relationships, and the intense dependence on objects for the satisfaction of narcissistic oral needs, is characteristic (Keiser, 1958; Blum, 1972; Adler, 1975; Frijling-Schreuder, 1969; Klein, 1975). Thus, borderline patients characteristically feel empty and hungry, demanding to be nurtured by new objects with an overwhelming immediacy and insistence, so that, if these demands are not met, there is an experience of intense rage, which threatens to destroy the needed good object relationship (Adler, 1970). Thus, the libidinal object constancy is fragile and vulnerable, so that object cathexis is maintained poorly and with relative instability (Frijling-Schreuder, 1969; Rosenfeld and Sprince, 1963, 1965). Following a suggestion of Anna Freud, Rosenfeld and Sprince describe borderline children as "constantly on the border between object cathexis and identification" (p. 619). Thus, these children easily revert to identification with the object, which may lead to a sense of merging with the object. The child's incapacity to maintain an object cathexis thus threatens the integrity of the ego, and personality characteristics become merged with those of the object.

It should be noted that Kernberg's theory is explicitly and specifically a theory of pathological internal object relationships. Yet Kernberg's argument concerns itself very little with object relations as such, but rather with the internalized derivatives of object relations, while he designates these internalized derivatives as "internalized object relationships." They seem to come much closer to what has been described, in other contexts, as "introjects" (Schafer, 1968a; Meissner, 1971, 1978). Rather than a theory of object relations as such, it propounds a theory of object representations. Thus, Kernberg's theory addresses itself to the vicissitudes and instability of such internalized objects, with little or no attention to the relationships with objects as such.

One of the most important contributions to the object relations approach to borderline states was based on Winnicott's (1953) formulation of the transitional object. The notion was further elaborated by Modell (1963, 1968) into the concept of transitional object relationships, and then applied to borderline pathology. Although there are remnants of such object relationships in everyone, to some degree, the borderline personality is characterized by an arrest of development at the stage of the transitional object; the healthier neurotic has been able to pass beyond that stage to the experience of the loved object as somehow separate from the self. As Winnicott had already suggested, the remnants of earlier transitional phases can be found in a variety of normal experiences, including creative and imaginative processes, cultural manifestations, and religious experiences. The arrest of object relationship development at this transitional phase is not due to an actual loss of the significant object, but rather to a more subtle failure of mothering in which the mother is unable to make emotional contact with the child and becomes libidinally unavailable. Consequently, there is an absence or a diminished amount of the usual holding and cuddling, so that the mother's attitude toward the child is distorted and she is unable to experience and respond to the child as a separate individual. Modell's formulation does not distinguish adequately between borderline and psychotic forms of transitional relatedness. More recent formulations, however, have enlarged on the potential and utility of the transitional form of object relationship for a more mature capacity for object relations (Coppolillo, 1967). Nonetheless, the dominant concept is Modell's, namely, borderlines suffer from a pathology of object relations based on a developmental fixation in the stage of transitional object relatedness (Fast and Chethik, 1972; Fintzy, 1971; Modell, 1968).

The object relations approach fills an important gap in psychoanalytic theory in focusing on and articulating the early developmental experiences that lie at the root of the child's emerging psychic structure. Consequently, its risk lies in its reductionistic tendency to read the development of later and more differentiated pathology in terms of the primitive vicissitudes of object relatedness. The theory borrows from the developmental perspective in terms of concepts of fixation and developmental deviation or arrest. Although these concepts have their appropriate application and a wide explanatory significance, their application in the more developed and structuralized context of evolved character structure and character pathology involve a radical presumption that demands validation and explanation. Thus, a critical area in this frame of reference that is passed over with only a nod is that of internalization. The theory must explain how object relations become internalized and provide the structural components out of which adult character and its associated pathology is formed and expressed.

The False Self

A brief comment about the false self concept is necessary here. It is another genial contribution of Winnicott (1960), but neither its theoretical underpinnings nor its relationship to the borderline concept have been established. Winnicott's description seems to lie closer to the range of schizoid character pathologies, and forms a schizoid subvariant in which the real or true self is dissociated from the false self that is caught up in compliant submission to the demands of external reality. The false self serves, in part, to protect the true self from affective interactions with other people. The threat to the autonomy of the true self arises from the proximity to objects, which carries with it the risk of engulfment.

The description of the false self is phenomenologically apt and often clinically accurate. The false self configuration is identifiable in some border-lines, or at least in those schizoid characters who fall within the borderline spectrum. Borderline compliance is closely related to the intense clinging dependence and seeking of narcissistic gratification from objects, but the relationship between these conditions needs to be further explored. The "as-if" compliance so often seen in borderlines is another manifestation of this phenomenon.

However, Modell (1975) has recently linked Winnicott's false self or-ganization with Kohut's narcissistic personality. There are striking similari-ties, and the dynamic issues may be closely juxtaposed, particularly the underlying narcissistic dynamics. Unfortunately, the false self concept covers a wide range of psychopathology, all the way from the frankly schizophrenic to the relatively healthy and normal. Modell particularly addresses the illusion of self-sufficiency, by which he characterizes narcissistic personali-ties, and which also seems to be at issue in the guardianship of the false self over the true self. The compliance of the false self insulates the true self from commerce with objects and allows the true self to maintain its relatively grandiose illusion of self-sufficiency. However, similar features are often seen in borderline disorders, and we are left with a need to better define the role of false self characteristics in the borderline personality. Winnicott's formulation has certainly gone further in the direction of offering a basis for understanding borderline compliance than any other.

Identity Diffusion

Loss of identity has frequently been attributed to borderline pathology (Rosenfeld and Sprince, 1963; Frosch, 1970). The loss of ego identity, or its vulnerability, is also an aspect of Kernberg's theory, in that ego identity represents the highest level of integration of internalized object relations. However, the organization of identification systems at a level of ego func-tioning in which splitting is the crucial and central defensive mechanism makes whatever sense of identity has been attained precarious (Kernberg, 1966). Similarly, the loss of identity in borderline patients can precipitate urgent emergency states as reparative maneuvers. The borderline may then feel a sense of inner emptiness, having nothing inside, no individuality or originality. The acute anxiety in this state of identity diffusion can give rise to feelings of depersonalization and derealization. The patient may resort to various forms of acting-out or self inflicted pain or create other emergencies in order to help restore the sense of reality and the sense of self (Collum, 1972).

The original description of acute identity diffusion was given by Erikson (1956) and specifically related to problems in adolescent turmoil and borderline psychopathology. Acute identity diffusion occurs in a context in which experience demands a commitment to adult contexts of physical intimacy, occupational choice, competition, and psychosocial self-delineation. The individual is caught between conflicting identifications, such that every move may establish a binding precedent and a concretization of psychosocial self-definition. Thus, the subject avoids significant choices, with the result that he is left in a situation of outer isolation and inner emptiness. Fast (1974) has spoken of these in terms of the multiplicity of identities, whose identity characteristics stem from the period in development in which the infant is making the transition from narcissism to a commitment to objective reality. The narcissistic sense of unbounded possibility and marked libidinization are characteristic of such partial identities.

In the face of failing identity, there are regressive attempts to delineate identity by a mutual narcissistic mirroring, so that the ego loses its capacity for abandoning itself to a sexual or affectionate relationship with objects. The object thus becomes the guarantee of the continuity of identity and raises the threat of fusion with its inherent risk of engulfment and loss of identity. The subject then often retreats to a position of distantiation, in which he is ready to repudiate, ignore, or destroy any forces that threaten the integrity of self. The need to repudiate lies at the basis of the fanatical embracing of causes or the merging with a "leader" in enthusiastic discipleship. This is an attempt to restitute identity in the face of the inability to gain genuine intimacy because of an incomplete or fragmented sense of identity. The failure of this process may lead to a paralyzing borderline state, in which there is an increasing sense of isolation and withdrawal, a sense of fragmented and diminished identity, a sense of shame and doubt, an inability to derive any sense of gratification or accomplishment from any activity, and a sense of being under the control of powerful forces and lacking the capacity to control or direct, by one's own initiative, the course of one's life. Narcissistic themes of lost opportunities and unfulfilled potentials of greatness are common themes (Erikson, 1956).

The conceptualization in terms of identity seems to be dealing with the outer face of what is dealt with in more internalized terms in the frame of reference of narcissism and the coherence of the self. Thus, although the external frame of reference of the issues of self-cohesion can be articulated in terms of object relations and the psychosocial engagement of the individual, the inner structure of the problems of identity and identity diffusion can be quite adequately spelled out in terms of the structuralization of narcissism and the organization of a stable coherent self-system. It should be noted that the complex of theories having to do with narcissism, object relations, the vicissitudes of false self-organization, and the vicissitudes of identity, in general, tend more in the direction of emphasizing the role of experiential factors over constitutional givens. Each of those approaches seems to be emphasizing aspects or dimensions of the complex developmental experience, particularly its experiential rather than hereditary, or nurture rather than nature, aspects. Thus, the concept of identity diffusion accomplishes little more than to spell out the external implications in terms of the quality of involvement with the environment of the inner fragmentation of the self, which is defined and delineated in narcissistic terms.

Here it would be extremely useful to clarify the quality of organization of self-systems, vis-à-vis the psychosocial environment, and embracing a complex of states reaching, on the one hand, from the forms of identity diffusion described by Erikson and others, through a variety of false self states in which a pseudo-identity consisting of a compliant false self facade is maintained in the interest of protecting the inner autonomy of the true self, to the more mature forms of stable achieved identity, in which the radical split between true and false self has been somehow overcome and integrated. As yet, this complex of ideas involving identity and false self organization remains on a phenomenological level and lacks the theoretical underpinning that would facilitate further integration.

RECAPITULATION

The various theoretical approaches take their point of departure from different reference points within the spectrum of psychoanalytic explanations and models. Consequently, they offer differing theoretical accounts of borderline pathology, so that the different approaches have varying degrees of explanatory power and range. Specific approaches vary in their capacity to explain different aspects of the complex symptomatology, behavior, defensive configurations, and character structure found in the borderline spectrum.

Without being exhaustive, a balance sheet of these relative strengths and weaknesses can be attempted. The approach through instinctual theory provides a good basis for understanding the role of aggression, the lack of libidinal phase dominance, the predominance of primitive oral motifs, the polymorphous-perverse sexual manifestations, the tendency to volatility, the frequently seen hypomanic behavioral patterns, the sense of vulnerability, and the frequently noted, overwhelming traumatic anxiety experience of the borderline. However, instinctual components are not a good basis for understanding the lack of synthetic capacity or regulatory control of inner states, the sense of entitlement and specialness so frequently found in borderlines side by side with a sense of worthlessness and emptiness, or the frequently observed sense of fragmentation and conflictual involvement with objects.

The approach through defenses offers a convincing explanation of the alternation and dissociation of ego states, the tendency to controlling behavior, the role of traumatic anxiety, and the tendency to act-out, as well as the significant role of projection in the borderline clinical picture. This approach, however, is less successful as a basis for understanding the predominance of aggression, the failure of phase dominance, the defects in autonomy, the problems related to narcissism, the fragility of identity and self-cohesion, and, even within the consideration of defenses themselves, the peculiar mixture of pregenital and genital defensive organization.

The approach through ego defects has considerable relevance to understanding ego weakness and the lack of synthesis, the failure of control mechanisms, and the capacity to regulate inner psychic states, as well as the loss of the capacity to test reality. This approach is also useful in understanding regression and the general impediment to autonomous functioning, as well as the pervasive sense of vulnerability. There is little in this approach, however, that allows an understanding of the predominance of aggression and primitive orality, the narcissistc issues of emptiness and worthlessness, side by side with tendencies to idealization, or finally, the characteristic compliance so frequently found in borderline patients.

The emphasis on narcissism deals quite effectively with the concomitant tendencies to idealization and devaluation, the tendency to self-fragmentation and narcissistic vulnerability, the sense of emptiness and worthlessness, as well as the propensity to feelings of grandiosity, specialness, and entitlement. But the narcissistic approach offers little in the direction of understanding the perverse sexuality, typical borderline volatility, and the tendency to acting-out, as well as the impairment of reality-testing and other ego functions.

An approach based on object relations emphasizes the early developmental experience and the more primitive layers of psychic organization. It contributes to our understanding of the disturbances of object relationships and the quality of the patient's experience with objects, particularly the characteristic fear-need dilemma, which pervades the experience with objects. It also helps to articulate the difficulties in self-object discrimination and the tendency to schizoid withdrawal, with its inherent fears of annihilation and engulfment. The object relations approach, however, is less successful in explaining the peculiar dissociation and alternation of ego states, the failures in libidinal phase dominance, the lack of synthetic and regulatory capacity of the ego, and finally, the issues related to narcissism and narcissistic vulnerability.

The approach in terms of a false self organization is perhaps more successful than any in focusing and articulating the issues of submissive compliance in borderline relationships, as well as the fears of impingement and vulnerability. The extent to which these issues overlap with and can be integrated into other approaches remains to be determined, but the false self concept has a limited applicability to the understanding of aggressive and controlling behaviors, the alternation of dissociated ego states, or such commonly observed phenomena as polymorphous-perverse sexuality or hypochondriacal preoccupations.

The conceptualization of borderline states in terms of identity diffusion lends itself well to the consideration of issues of self-fragmentation and the loss of a sense of self, the peculiar borderline emptiness, and the frequent regressive confusion, as well as the tendency to act-out. But the conceptualization in terms of identity offers little for the understanding of aggressive components, the alternation of dissociated ego states, and the tendency to idealization and devaluation.

The developmental approach is less easy to classify or to evaluate in terms of these relative strengths and weaknesses. It overlaps, to a considerable degree, all the other approaches and thus tends to reflect their relative strengths and weaknesses. Its closest ties, however, seem to be to considerations of ego deviations, narcissistic vulnerabilities, and the vicissitudes of object relations. Depending on which aspect it emphasizes, it thereby gains from the explanatory strengths of that theoretical orientation, yet at the same time takes on its inherent weaknesses.

CONCLUSION

Our purpose here has been to cast some faint light on the variety of theoretical underpinnings to approaches to the understanding of borderline psychopathology. In spite of the divergence and variety of these approaches, the question still remains as to the potential integrability of these elements into a consistent and integrated account of greater explanatory power and range. We have noted, at a number of points, that divergent approaches overlap considerably and tend to articulate similar aspects of the borderline pathology from their divergent perspectives. This may offer an initial opportunity for further theoretical integration, but considerably more theoretical effort will be required to advance this integration to any significant degree. The task, for example, of integrating notions of structural formation and formation of ego and superego with the vicissitudes of narcissism and the developmental progression in object relations, has yet to be accomplished.

Our understanding of borderline psychopathology, then, remains somewhat fragmented, limited by our current ability to achieve little more than a low-level, theoretical integration of divergent points of view. The organization of such divergent viewpoints in terms of a particular perspective, most particularly a developmental perspective, does not constitute an integrated theory, but rather a juxtaposition of incomplete points of view, each of which contributes to some fragment of the overall understanding. Even the most comprehensive contemporary attempts to articulate a general theory of borderline pathology can be similarly criticized. The underlying question of considerable significance that this reflection raises is whether, in fact, divergent theoretical approaches are not focusing on subvariants of pathological expression, which may be diagnostically differentiable. Just as we may have to think in terms of a variety of forms of schizophrenia, or a variety of forms of homosexuality, so too we may have to think in terms of a variety of forms of borderline pathology, which resist our attempts at integral theoretical formulation.

Part II
Diagnosis

Chapter 3
General Aspects of Diagnosis

Considerations of theoretical complexities and the conceptual ambiguities involved in any discussion of borderline pathology would seem to lead inexorably toward the problem of diagnosis. A primary consideration must be whether the range and variety of theoretical formulations and the difficulties in conceptual formulation and clarification are not reflecting the fact that we are dealing with an underlying heterogeneity such that borderline pathology cannot be understood in any unified or unitary fashion. If such be the case, it can be better understood why certain theoretical approaches to the understanding of borderline pathology tell us more about some patients than about others, and why our conceptualizations may apply to certain kinds of patients, but not others.

The problem is the ancient conundrum of the one and the many. Are we, in fact, dealing with one form of illness that may have multiple forms of expression, both behaviorally and symptomatically? Or, alternatively, are we dealing with multiple forms of illness, which may share certain underlying general characteristics, but which, nonetheless, require analysis and formulation, each on its own terms? The diagnostic picture is made more complex by the intersection of two trends or diagnostic preoccupations that arose more or less contemporaneously. Clinicians working mainly in a hospital setting approached the diagnostic problem in terms of the differentiation of borderline pathology from the schizophrenic, at first, and later from the affective psychoses. Their patients tended to be severely regressed or otherwise close to a psychotic level of functioning. The characteristics of these more primitively organized borderline patients came to dominate their diagnostic view. In contrast, clinicians in private practice, and largely psychoanalytic in orientation, saw patients who were better organized and who functioned generally more adaptively and displayed borderline features only in transient regressive states. The diagnostic concern here was the differentiation of borderline pathology from a neurotic or higher-level character pathology. The approach here combines both continuity and discontinuity in an attempt to bring some diagnostic order to this confusing scene.

The concept of the borderline spectrum implies a continuous series of disordered functions and underlying pathological structures, extending from the lower border of the psychoses to the higher border of the neuroses, as well as the more integrated forms of character pathology, including narcissistic personalities. In these terms, any variation in levels of functioning and degrees of pathological impairment can be viewed as forming a continuous gradient of varying degrees of intensity and extension. Similarly, it may be possible to carve out of this continuous spectrum of disordered levels of functioning and integration a series of more or less discrete describable syndromes, which may allow us to discriminate more effectively between levels of pathological impairment and offer us a more specific basis both for theoretical understanding and, ultimately, for therapeutic intervention. Pragmatically, the problem concerns itself with discerning the most advantageous strategy available in the current status of our experience and understanding. Does it make sense to think in terms of a more unified diagnostic approach, or does the optimal strategy lie more in the direction of greater diversity, heterogeneity, and multiplicity that call for a greater degree of specificity and differentiation, both descriptively and theoretically?

In order to delineate the approach taken in the present work more effectively, it may be useful to place it in the broader context of current approaches to borderline diagnosis. Early approaches to this problem followed the path of trying to define a variety of clinical syndromes in a significant group of patients who could not simply be diagnosed as psychotic, who seemed to have a variety of features that they shared with healthier forms of personality organization, but who at the same time, seemed to manifest certain characteristics that made investigators think of them as somehow connected with the psychoses, particularly schizophrenia. Such patients might function relatively well, or demonstrate a variety of neurotic conflicts and symptoms, yet they might also possess a quality of eccentricity or bizarreness, or even at times show forms of decompensation that seemed to be closely related to psychosis.

A number of theorists tried to formulate and express these difficult forms of pathology. The literature abounded with such descriptions as "latent psychoses," "ambulatory schizophrenia," "pseudoneurotic schizophrenia," and "borderline schizophrenia." For the most part, authors thought of these entities as variant forms of an underlying schizophrenic process. Even Knight's (1953) description of borderline states seemed to formulate them as closely related to the schizophrenias. Some of the conceptual difficulties in separating out these complex forms of psychopathology from the psychoses have been discussed in Chapter 1. The same may be said about Frosch's (1964, 1970) considerations of the psychotic character, which was defined by its links with an underlying psychotic process.

The result of these efforts was a variety of fragmented clinical descriptions and formulations that seemed to reflect early attempts to deal with parts of the puzzle. Kernberg (1966, 1967) altered this state of affairs radically. He pulled together the various pathological entities that were thought of as somehow occupying a position between frank psychosis, on the one hand, and determinable neurosis, on the other, as the "borderline personality organization." Kernberg not only lumped these various clinical descriptions under a common heading, but he also provided a common structural description, which he felt applied unequivocally to all borderline patients.

Among these structural deficits, he emphasized nonspecific ego weaknesses; a tendency toward primary process thinking, primitive defense mechanisms, and organization; and a particular form of pathology of internalized object relations characterized particularly by defensive splitting. Kernberg's lumping strategy thus effectively reversed the earlier diverse and somewhat disorganized approaches to borderline pathology. The advantages were obvious, in that he provided a coherent and embracing account that linked a variety of descriptive formulations under a common heading and attempted to describe a common underlying structural deficit, which he felt could be identified under the multiple and varying forms of symptomatic and behavioral expression that characterized a variety of descriptive clinical entities. Thus, beneath the variety of phenomenological expressions, he postulated a form of structural defect common to all borderline patients.

The conceptual breakthrough Kernberg thus achieved started a line of thinking that influenced subsequent approaches to borderline diagnosis. It provided the impetus for a series of studies, motivated by the need to consolidate and clarify what was meant by the borderline personality. The basic push in this direction was governed by the research effort to establish a more consistent, reliable, and, one would hope, valid delineation of borderline psychopathology, such that it could be effectively utilized in research study of the syndrome, and clearly and relatively unequivocally delineate it from other forms of psychopathology.

The next significant step was taken by Gunderson and Singer (1975). They surveyed the vast literature on borderline psychopathology and directed their effort toward defining those characteristics of this group of patients that would allow for a greater degree of replicability and lead to further meaningful research. It can be noted, in passing, that the very fact of this concerted effort, following upon Kernberg's contributions, would seem to suggest a dissatisfaction with Kernberg's formulations. The author's assessment is that Kernberg's lumping strategy had, in fact, overreached itself, included too much within its grasp, provided too much of an all-encompassing description of the borderline personality, and led subsequent investigators to seek greater definition, clarity, and a more satisfactory delimitation of the borders of the diagnostic category.

Gunderson and Singer devised a list of six features they believed could be used to characterize the borderline syndrome:

1. The presence of intense affect, usually hostile or depressive;
2. a history of impulsive behavior, comprising episodic acts of self-destructiveness (self-mutilization, drug overdoses, etc.) and more chronic behavior patterns, such as drug dependency or promiscuity;
3. social adaptiveness, reflected in good work or school achievement and, generally, socially appropriate behavior;
4. brief psychotic experiences, often with a paranoid quality, and precipitated in periods of stress or as a result of drug use;
5. psychological testing performance in which performance on structured tests is more or less normal, but performance on unstructured or projective devices reveals bizarre, dereistic, illogical, or primitive responses, which reflect underlying thought disturbances; and
6. interpersonal relationships that vacillate between transient and superficial relationships and relationships that are intense, conflicted, and dependent and reflect varying degrees of manipulation, demandingness, and devaluation.

Gunderson's subsequent work has amplified and extended his perspective on borderline pathology. Using a semi-structured interview approach of his own devising—the Diagnostic Interview for Borderlines (DIB) (Kolb and Gunderson, 1980)[1]—for patients who had been diagnosed clinically as borderline personalities, Gunderson (1977) formulated the characteristics of this borderline sample under five headings: social adaptation, impulse-action patterns, affects, tendency to psychosis, and interpersonal relations. He characterizes borderline patients as being generally aware of social conventions, even though their attitude toward them may be often one of defiance. They tend to lead more or less active social lives, and generally get along reasonably well in social groups. They seem to maintain steady employment,

---

[1]The construct validity and usefulness of the DIB in the diagnosis of borderline patients in terms of the characteristics targeted by Gunderson's criteria has been demonstrated on other clinical populations (Soloff, 1981). Also, its use to distinguish between hospitalized and nonhospitalized borderlines did not reveal much in the way of significant differences (Koenigsberg, 1982). This finding may reflect both the failure of the study to distinguish presently hospitalized from previously hospitalized patients and the selectivity of the DIB for lower-order pathology. Even so, many differences in the expected direction (less severe pathology in the outpatient group) were measured, but they were not statistically significant.

but do not work well under stress, they seem to be able to work well only in relatively structured situations.

Acting-out is a predominant characteristic of the impulse-action patterns, usually in the form of self-destructive acts or hostilely destructive acts directed toward others and a variety of forms of antisocial behavior, including drug and alcohol abuse. The destructive behavior is more frequently directed toward the self than toward others, usually in the form of overdosing, suicidal threats, and self-mutilation (slashing, headbanging, burning, etc.). Although promiscuity is frequently reported among females, there are few reports of deviant sexual habits or preferences. The dominant affects reported by borderlines seem to be depression, anger, and anxiety, although depression is more evident clinically. The depression is frequently related to chronic feelings of loneliness or emptiness.

These patients do not report continuous or severe psychotic experiences, although there are some reports of possible hallucinatory experiences. The commonest forms of psychotic ideation occur in the depressed form of extended periods of feeling worthless or hopeless and in the form of ideas of reference that are decidedly paranoid-like. There is often a feeling of uncertainty or discomfort about such psychotic experiences, suggesting that they may not be completely syntonic. Depersonalization is more common than derealization.

These borderline patients do not withdraw from contacts with other people, but rather feel a need to have people near, and they feel bothered when alone. Such borderlines have friends and keep in touch with them, but are uncomfortable when others try to take care of them. The most intense relationships are frequently troubled and disruptive, characterized by involvements that are strongly dependent, masochistic, manipulative, and characteristically include devaluation of the object.

In summary, we can say that Gunderson effectively condensed and distilled the borderline characteristics as originally proposed by Kernberg. Gunderson's work essentially derives from both Kernberg and Grinker (Grinker et al., 1968) and selects out as borderline practically the same group of patients as does Kernberg. Moreover, despite their differences in orientation and methodology, Kernberg and Grinker arrive at similar diagnostic conclusions (Stone, 1977). The result is more clarity and a better definition of the borderline syndrome, but at the cost of narrowing the focus and the defining boundaries of the borderline category to a smaller and somewhat narrowly defined patient population.

The next step in the progression of this line of thinking was taken by Spitzer and his associates, who further developed and articulated the criteria of borderline pathology as a basis for the categorizations that were finally incorporated into the DSM III. Spitzer's group (Spitzer et al., 1979) attempted to deal with the lack of diagnostic clarity by distinguishing two major ways in which the borderline concept seems to be employed in current usage. The first, which follows the lead of Kernberg and the Gunderson group, refers to a constellation of relatively persistent personality features involving both instability and vulnerability. The second major use of the term borderline, in general psychiatric terms, is to refer to a group of pathological characteristics that generally remain stable over time and are assumed to have a genetic relationship to the schizophrenic spectrum, as developed in the genetic studies of the origin of schizophrenia (Kety et al., 1971; Rosenthal et al., 1971).[2]

A list of behavioral items intended to characterize patients who would fall within the schizophrenic spectrum was used as the basis for developing a list of schizotypal personality items. These included odd communications (e.g., tangential speech, digressions, and vague, circumstantial, metaphorical ideas); ideas of reference; suspiciousness, or paranoid ideation; recurrent illusions; depersonalization or derealization; magical thinking; inadequate social rapport in face-to-face interactions; undue social anxiety or hypersensitivity; and social isolation. A similar list of borderline personality items, based largely, but not exclusively, on the work of the Gunderson group was also formulated. These included a tendency to identity disturbance; a pattern of unstable and intense interpersonal relationships; impulsivity or unpredictability; intense anger that was often inappropriate; physically self-damaging actions, including suicide, self-mutilation, and recurrent accidents; a work history or record of school achievement that was unstable or below expectation; affective instability; chronic feelings of emptiness or boredom; and an inability to tolerate being alone. These lists of characteristics seem to distinguish two identifiable groups of patients adequately (Spitzer et al., 1979), and thus became the basis for the distinction in the DSM III between schizotypal and borderline personality disorders. Features of the respective DSM III descriptions are as follows.

THE BORDERLINE PERSONALITY DISORDER IN DSM III

These patients characteristically show a pattern of instability in a variety of areas, including interpersonal relationships, behavior, mood, and self-image. Interpersonal relationships tend to be intense and unstable with marked shifts of emotion over time. There is frequently impulsive and unpredictable behavior that may become physically self-damaging. Mood is often labile with marked shifts from normal mood to some dysphoric mood

---

[2]See the discussion of the genetic aspects in Chapter 8.

or with intense or inappropriate anger or loss of control. The identity disturbance may be profound, manifested by uncertainty about several issues relating to self-concept, such as self-image, gender identity, long-term goals, or values. There may be problems in tolerating loneliness, and chronic feelings of emptiness or boredom.

The following diagnostic criteria are characteristic of the individual's long-term functioning and are not confined to regressive episodes. At least five of the following are required:

1. Impulsivity or unpredictability in at least two areas that would be regarded as potentially self-damaging, e.g., spending, sex, gambling, drug or alcohol abuse, shoplifting, overeating, physically self-damaging acts.
2. A pattern of unstable and intense relationships, with marked shifts of emotion, idealization, devaluation, manipulation (consistently using/abusing others for one's own purposes).
3. Inappropriate/intense anger or loss of control of aggressive feelings, e.g., frequently loses temper, always angry.
4. Identity instability manifested by uncertainty about several issues relating to identity, such as self-image, gender identity, long-term goals or career choice, friendship patterns, values, and loyalties.
5. Affective instability: marked shifts from normal mood to depression, irritability, or anxiety, often lasting for hours, rarely for more than a few days, with an eventual return to normal mood.
6. Problems tolerating being alone, e.g., frantic efforts to avoid being alone, depressed when alone.
7. Self-punitive or self-damaging behavior, e.g., suicidal gestures, self-mutilation, recurrent accidents, or physical fights.
8. Chronic feelings of emptiness or boredom.

THE SCHIZOTYPAL PERSONALITY DISORDER IN DSM III

These patients manifest various oddities of thinking, perception, communication and behavior, that are never severe enough to qualify as schizophrenic. The disturbance in thinking may take the form of magical thinking, ideas of reference, or paranoid ideation. Perceptual disturbances may include recurrent illusions, depersonalization, or derealization (not associated with panic attacks). Often there are peculiar patterns of communication: ideas may be expressed obscurely or oddly, words may be used deviantly, but never to the point of loosening of associations or incoherence. Frequently, but not invariably, social isolation and constricted or inappropriate affect interferes with rapport in face-to-face interactions.

Characteristics of the individual's long-term functioning (not limited to episodes of illness) include at least four of the following:

1. Magical thinking, e.g., superstitiousness, clairvoyance, telepathy, "sixth sense," "others can feel my feelings."
2. Ideas of reference, self-referential thinking.
3. Social isolation, e.g., no close friends or confidants, social contacts limited to essential everyday task-oriented situations.
4. Recurrent illusions, sensing the presence of a force or person not actually present (e.g., "I felt as if my dead mother were in the room with me"), depersonalization, or derealization not associated with panic attacks.
5. Odd communication (*not* loose associations or incoherence), e.g., speech tangential, digressive, vague, over-elaborate, circumstantial, metaphorical speech.
6. Inadequate rapport in face-to-face interaction because of constricted or inappropriate affect, e.g., aloof, distant, cold.
7. Suspiciousness or paranoid ideation.
8. Excessive social anxiety or hypersensitivity to real or imagined criticism.

None of these patients would be regarded as fulfilling the DSM III criteria for schizophrenia.

In a later article reviewing genetic aspects of the borderline syndrome, Siever and Gunderson (1979) objected that the patients who could be characterized as schizotypal would be assumed to share certain genetic determinants with schizophrenia, since the category was derived from the schizophrenic spectrum of disorders. In reply, Spitzer and Endicott (1979) commented that the genetic relationship between schizotypal features and schizophrenia was suggestive rather than truly demonstrated. They further commented that the schizotypal personality could also be regarded as a subdivision of the schizoid personality disorders. In DSM III, the schizoid disorders are divided into those that are schizotypal, i.e., having odd cognitive and perceptual features, whereas the more straightforward schizoid disorders are marked by a defective capacity to form social relationships, a history of social isolation, and bland or constricted affect.

Some comments can be made regarding the contributions of Spitzer and his group. The first is that there is implicit in the distinction of two groups of borderline disorders an inherent heterogeneity in existing concepts of the borderline pathology. The articulation of the schizotypal pattern formulates a range of borderline pathology that lies closer to psychosis; the borderline personality, however, seems to function at a somewhat higher level. Nonetheless, the point of view presented here would suggest that the line of thinking that derives from Kernberg's formulations, leading to a gradual process of condensation and distillation through the work of Gunderson, and finally to that of Spitzer and his associates, tends to focus on the more primitive levels of borderline functioning. Looking back to the origins of this line of progression in Kernberg's thinking, it seems that the borderline personality has been characterized in terms of its most primitive levels of functioning, or more particularly, in terms of the levels of more primitive pathology usually found only transiently in most borderline personalities, that is, only in phases of acute regressive crisis. There is no account given of the higher-level functioning of patients who may also manifest borderline characteristics, and who rarely, if ever, manifest the regressed functioning or primitive adjustment characterized in the descriptions in question. Thus, we are left with a caricature of the borderline, rather than an adequate clinical characterization.

A similar criticism can be made of the efforts of Masterson and his associates (Masterson, 1976; Masterson and Rinsley, 1975). They follow the trend of basing their approach on Kernberg's methodology, in which the pathology of borderline patients is couched in terms of the more primitive aspects of their functioning. They combine this with a developmental perspective derived from the work of Margaret Mahler. The result is an account of borderline development and functioning that does not lack clarity and definition, but that does not include the broader spectrum of borderline conditions. The borderline condition, in their account, results from a failure of development specifically in the rapprochement phase of separation-individuation due to the failure of libidinal availability in the mother. The patient thus suffers from an abandonment depression, clings to attachments to the mother in an effort to deny the loss of separation, and is afflicted with a split ego and an ego weakness, à la Kernberg. The whole process is set in motion by the pathology of a borderline mother who cannot tolerate the emerging individuation and autonomy of her child. This, then, is a variant of the schizophrenogenic mother and a portrait and theory of borderline pathology that simplifies our understanding, but does not serve us well when our patients cannot be made to fit this procrustean bed. This issue is discussed further in Chapters 6 and 7.

These trends should not be devalued or disparaged, since they have both a purpose and an advantage. The governing consideration is derived from a basic research orientation, which seeks to clarify and further delineate the borderline syndrome, which, however, leads to a narrowing of the limits of the borderline range and the consequent application of this diagnostic label to an increasingly smaller group of better-defined patients; inevitably, a group of patients are thus excluded. The question remains, however, whether such patients may not, in fact, also demonstrate borderline features, but not in the more intense, dramatic, and readily definable form that would satisfy the demands for clarity of definition. The optimal path of clinical utility in the implementation of such diagnostic categories should remain open. Nonetheless, it is, to a certain degree, disturbing and unfortunate that the narrowed and constricted version of the conception of borderline pathology has found its way into the formal definitions of the official diagnostic manual of American psychiatry.

Along with this reductionistic and unifying trend, there have also been contributions that point in a different direction. The early studies of Grinker and his group (Grinker et al., 1968) defined the borderline syndrome in terms of the predominant characteristics of anger, as the dominant affect; defective object relations; failure of self-identity; and the presence of depressive features, usually expressed as loneliness or emptiness. However, using a large number of variables based on observations of large number of patients, Grinker's group found that cluster, discriminate, and factor analyses sorted the patients into various subgroupings that represented different pathological positions. They described four separate groups of borderline patients, ranging from the sickest group, which seemed to be closest to psychotic patients, to a much healthier group, which seemed to be quite similar to neurotic patients in their general characteristics and whose depression seemed to be primarily anaclitic in character (Grinker, 1977).

The concept of the existence of a spectrum of disorders as inhabiting the borderline range has, by no means, been foreign to the psychiatric literature on the subject. Numerous authors have commented on the possibility of thinking about borderline conditions in such terms, and even the work of Kernberg, although directed toward developing a psychoanalytically based classification of character pathology, described levels of the organization of character pathology in terms of instinctual development, superego development, the level of defensive organization, and the vicissitudes of object relationships. This view of the organization of character pathology is discussed in Chapter 6, but it should be emphasized at this juncture that Kernberg's thinking along this line points in a direction more or less opposed to the general drift of his original formulations. However, Kernberg (1976) tends to limit the range of borderline pathology to that of a lower-order character organization. It is with this aspect of Kernberg's formulation that the discussion here will take issue.

The shifting basis of diagnostic criteria for borderlines complicate the problem. As Stone (1979) has noted, when genetic factors play a more direct or identifiable role in the etiology of mental illness, the greater their role in establishing diagnoses; this is most notably the case in the diagnosis of psychosis, whether schizophrenic, manic-depressive, or schizo-affective. When genetic factors play a more obscure or an uncertain role, as in many borderline cases, the diagnostic base shifts to signs and symptoms. Where such indices are not adequate, we may appeal to even more remote criteria, such as response to treatment. The diagnostic criteria shift, depending on what factors seem most reliable. Even within the borderline spectrum, the emphasis on the importance of various criteria shifts. Reality-testing is more central in diagnosing forms of pathology closer to the psychoses and less important in diagnosing the higher-order borderline conditions.

The effort in Part II is directed toward developing the notion of the borderline spectrum as involving a continuum of states of disordered functioning between the realm of the psychoses, on the one hand, and the more functional realm of the narcissistic and neurotic disorders, on the other. The tactic followed will be that of dividing and conquering. An attempt will be made to delineate the borderline conditions, primarily the range of borderline disorders closest to the border of psychosis, from the psychoses. Then, at the opposite end of the continuum, the higher-level borderline conditions will be differentiated from the closely related and often difficult to discriminate narcissistic disorders (Chapter 5).

Having established a spectrum, an exploration of the conditions within the borderline spectrum is in order. Finally, building on the foundations thus achieved, a tentative schema of differential diagnosis for the borderline spectrum will be presented (Chapter 8).

Chapter 4

Differential Diagnosis: The Psychoses

One of the persistent problems in dealing with the borderline syndromes has been their inadequate discrimination from the psychoses. This has been difficult, not only conceptually (Chapter 1) and theoretically (Chapter 2), but also clinically. This discussion will attempt to delineate the clinical discrimination between the functional psychoses and the borderline syndromes. Keeping in mind the larger issues of diagnosis and treatment that remain to be defined for both, discrimination between them is of particular importance, since it serves as the basis for implementing radically different treatment approaches, and also has considerably different prognostic implications.

It is difficult to sharpen the discrimination between psychotic and borderline disorders because diagnostic precision regarding both of them is wanting. There is no universal agreement as to the diagnostic characteristics that would define either the psychoses or the borderline syndromes, and therefore, individual clinicians might draw the line between them with considerable variability. Historically, in fact, it has taken a long time to clarify the borderline syndromes, in order to distinguish them from more clearly psychotic forms of pathology. Early workers in this area tended to see the borderline syndromes much more in terms of their relationship to the psychoses, and not as persistent and stable forms of character pathology. As these areas of relative diagnostic focus gradually emerged and became polarized, the line of discrimination between them was left relatively vague and obscure. Early approaches often saw the borderline conditions as reflecting forms of latent or incipient psychosis, often regarding them as *formes frustes* of more clearly delineated and typical psychoses. Only grad-

ually did the view of borderline syndromes as occupying a position somewhere between the neuroses and the psychoses, and as being characterized by
specific qualities, take shape.

An additional problem here is the fact that the borderline syndromes
are characterized by varying degrees of susceptibility to regression. These
transient regressive "borderline states" are equivalent to short-term transient
psychotic regressions, which look very much like psychotic episodes. The
question then arises whether, clinically, these states represent the breakthrough of underlying psychotic processes or whether they should be regarded as transient stress-related regressions in otherwise nonpsychotic, but
vulnerable personalities. I have argued in support of the latter position
(Meissner, 1978), as have other clinicians (Zetzel, 1971; Kernberg, 1967,
1968, 1975, 1976b). The diagnostic problem is that when one sees a patient
clinically in such a regressed condition, it is often impossible, in the immediate context, to say whether one is seeing a psychotic patient or a
borderline patient in a regressed state. The diagnostic clinical discrimination
must be made on grounds other than the immediate disturbed behavior the
patient manifests in the clinical setting.

MIXED CLINICAL PICTURES

One of the major problems in differential diagnosis of these conditions
is that patients frequently present with a mixed clinical picture of apparently
neurotic and psychotic symptoms and patterns of defense. Because of the
conceptual inclination to separate neurotic from psychotic manifestations,
clinicians will often emphasize one or another aspect of this complex clinical
picture and consequently shift the diagnosis in the direction either of the
neuroses or the psychoses.

It has been questioned, in fact, whether the neurotic manifestations in
these borderline patients can be regarded as simply neurotic symptoms
(Dickes, 1974). The neurotic phobias, for example, tend to be relatively
specific and relatively restricted to a single or narrow range of stimuli. The
phobic symptom binds anxiety, so as to allow the personality reasonably
comfortable and adaptive functioning in other experiential areas. Moreover,
the neurotic phobic has not lost touch with the realities of the situation, that
is, he knows that his fear is unreasonable or unrealistic or that it reflects a
fear of a highly improbable dangerous or destructive event, such as might be
the case in the fear of flying. But in the regressed borderline, the anxiety may
not be successfully bound or constrained to a specific set of stimuli, but
rather tends to become more generalized and may be accompanied by an
almost delusional conviction and fear that the life-threatening event will take
place. In such patients, there may be a diffusely organized and fragmented
clinical picture marked by a pan-anxiety, which is free-floating and diffuse,

and a variety of pan neurotic manifestations, which often alternate with psychotic traits.

Related to this question of mixed syndromes, there is the question of distinguishing between borderline syndromes and masked or latent forms of psychosis. Certainly, neurotic symptoms can mask underlying psychotic processes, as has long been clinically recognized. In fact, Zilboorg (1941, 1956, 1957) felt that such complex syndromes represented modified forms of an underlying schizophrenic process and described them as "ambulatory schizophrenia." A similar problem arises in Bychowski's (1953) description of latent psychotics. These are patients who have a form of abortive or arrested psychosis that may occur as a brief psychotic experience early in life, which is then stabilized so that the patient's current clinical presentation may represent more adaptive and nonpsychotic levels of functioning. Alternatively, they may represent a form of prospective psychosis in which the psychotic core is dissociated from the rest of the functioning ego and is covered by the defensive organization. These patients have a precarious adjustment, with a relatively primitive degree of ego functioning and frequent outbursts of acting-out and relatively concretistic thinking.

As a consequence of such complex and confusing symptomatic pictures, Kernberg (1967) has argued that the diagnosis of borderline conditions cannot be made on merely symptomatic grounds, but rather on structural grounds, that is, by an assessment of the level of integration of personality structures—particularly the ego and its functions, as well as the superego— and the patient's object relationships.

Perhaps the most carefully studied group of patients with mixed symptomatology were the so-called pseudoneurotic schizophrenics (Hoch and Cattell, 1959; Hoch et al., 1962; Hoch and Polatin, 1949). Such patients superficially resemble neurotics and tend to have a good social facade and appropriate behavior, but their symptoms are more diverse and diffuse (pan-neurosis); there is a profusion of unintegrated neurotic and psychotic defenses; anxiety tends to be more pervasive and profound (pan-anxiety), and the patients manifest underlying thought disorders marked by primary process characteristics that mimic schizophrenic-like thought and affect disturbances. Hoch and Polatin concluded that these patients were essentially schizophrenics in disguise. Moreover, a fairly high percentage of these patients later on become frankly schizophrenic.

At the same time, other patients show no psychotic decompensation over time, while still others show the transient psychotic regression with rapid reintegration that is characteristic of borderline states. However, as Klein (1975) has commented, there is no normative data on the uniformity and incidence of the indices of a schizophrenic process in such patients. Rather, the group of patients studied by Hoch and his coworkers seems to represent a heterogeneous collection of patients who are refractory to exploratory psychotherapy. As Klein suggests, the eventual deterioration, the autistic and dereistic approach to life, the diffuse ambivalence, the often inappropriate emotions, the pan-anxiety and pan-neurosis, the omnipotent attitudes, and the subtle, but detectible thought disorders, as well as the tendency to relatively brief and transient psychotic episodes, would tend to reinforce the impression of an operative psychotic process in these patients.

Certainly, if pseudoneurotic schizophrenic patients are not schizophrenic, they have at least one foot in schizophrenia, particularly in that they manifest a more or less persistent, if subtle defect in cognitive processes and a more or less chronic impairment of reality-testing. Consequently, this diagnosis may represent a transitional zone between the psychoses and the borderline syndromes. The pseudoneurotic schizophrenias must thus be regarded as the most primitive form of the borderline spectrum of disorders and mark the transition into the area of the psychoses.

While the waters in this area, in which the lower ranges of borderline disorder merge and mix with psychotic processes, are murky, recent attempts to differentiate them on descriptive grounds have yielded promising results. The work of Gunderson and his associates (Gunderson et al., 1975; Carpenter et al., 1977; Gunderson, 1977; Gunderson and Kolb, 1978; Kolb and Gunderson, 1980) has shown that a fairly good discrimination can be drawn between these groups, even on initial evaluation. Borderline patients generally showed fewer psychotic symptoms (hallucinations, paranoid delusions, depressive delusions) and fewer, if somewhat more severe, dissociative experiences (depersonalization, derealization). Highly significant differences were found in thought disorders, which were rarely seen in the borderline groups. Borderline patients tended to be characterized by a predominance of depression, anxiety, and anger, in contrast to the flatness of affect and withdrawal in schizophrenics.

Even though a percentage of cases can be categorized as psychotic or borderline, the mixed and complex clinical picture makes the task more difficult and more subject to error. It seems unavoidable that there will be a certain residue of patients with mixed symptomatology who will elude secure diagnosis or who will be misdiagnosed. Even after extended evaluation, the diagnostic picture may remain obscure. Nonetheless, in many other cases, effective discrimination can be achieved. Let us consider the factors that provide the basis for such differential diagnosis.

DIFFERENTIATION BETWEEN BORDERLINE SYNDROMES AND PSYCHOSES

Among the indices used to discriminate between the psychoses and the borderline syndromes, perhaps the most important is reality-testing. It is generally felt that borderline patients are able to preserve reality-testing, whereas the loss of this capacity is a specific characteristic of psychotic patients. An exception must be noted to this general rule in that reality-testing may be impaired in varying degrees within the borderline spectrum (Chapter 6); there also may be a significant impairment in the capacity to reality test during transient regressive borderline states (Mack, 1975; Adler, 1973).

Kernberg (1970b) has emphasized that the differential diagnosis of these conditions centers on the persistence of reality-testing in the borderline conditions and its loss in the psychoses, but he notes that the capacity for reality-testing is, in part, dependent on the status of self-object differentiation and on the continuing delimitation of ego boundaries. The persistent impairment in reality-testing in any area of psychological functioning and/or the production of psychotic elements in the form of hallucinations or delusions are the hallmark of psychosis. If these elements are not present, the patient should not be diagnosed as psychotic (Kernberg, 1971).

Kernberg (1975) has suggested that a confrontational technique can be utilized to test the patient's capacity to maintain reality-testing. For the most part, unequivocal schizophrenics will demonstrate the failure of reality-testing in such a confrontation, even during phases of relative compensation. As Stone (1980) notes, this may be due to the tendency of such patients to maintain unrealistic images of themselves and others, even when they are not grossly delusional. In this regard, they differ from primary affective disorders, where there is a greater capacity to recompensate to higher levels of functioning during nonpsychotic intervals. Thus, in Kernberg's schema, confrontation of the psychotic patient tends to worsen the psychotic state and to reinforce primitive defenses. Confrontation of the borderline tends to weaken the delusion and to diminish primitive defenses. Delusional ideas in the borderline have more the quality of overvalued ideas rather than delusions, in the strict sense. The application of this approach to reality-testing in independent patient populations has demonstrated its usefulness, particularly in the discrimination of psychotic from lower-order forms of borderline organization (Bauer et al., 1980).

Although Kernberg feels that the frequency and intensity of the loss of reality-testing is not an important prognostic indicator, it must be pointed out that there is a significant spread within the borderline conditions of a susceptibility to such impairment. In the lower-order borderline conditions (pseudoschizophrenia; psychotic character), such regressive impairment occurs relatively readily and is frequently predominant in the clinical picture. However, in the more highly organized borderline forms, such regressions are considerably less frequent and are usually more restricted to specific emotionally involved contexts. It may be that this difference carries considerable diagnostic and prognostic significance.

A useful set of distinctions in a discussion of the patient's involvement in reality has been provided by Frosch (1970) in his discussion of the psychotic character. The sense of reality is a function of the patient's relationship with reality and his feeling of reality, as well as his capacity to test reality. The relationship with reality involves the capacity to perceive and distinguish the external world and the internal world and to evaluate the appropriateness of one's relationship to them. This capacity relates to the consistency and clear definition of ego boundaries and an adequately developed differentiation between self and object; it is obviously related to the patient's capacity for object relationships and, in part, is a function of it. Disturbances in relationship with reality may be expressed in the form of perceptual distortions, such as hallucinations or illusions, and these may range from barely discernible perceptual distortions to gross hallucinations. Frosch notes that, although such disturbances may occur in the psychotic character, they remain relatively transient and reversible in contrast to the disturbances in the psychoses, which tend to be more enduring and less reversible. This reversibility is facilitated by the relative retention of the capacity to test reality in nonpsychotic patients. Disturbance in the relationship with reality may also be reflected in the diffusion of ego boundaries and the difficulty in distinguishing between self and non-self, between human and non-human objects.

Frosch (1970) summarizes his argument in the following terms:

> . . . with regard to the ego's position vis-à-vis reality, we find that in the psychotic character, as in psychosis, there are impairments in the relationship with reality, the feeling of reality, and the capacity to test reality. In contrast to psychosis, however, these patients' capacity to test reality, while often very defective and manifesting characteristics of earlier developmental states, is nonetheless relatively intact. This factor strongly contributes to their not being psychotic. Although reality may at times be pushed aside and fantasy substituted for it, as in psychosis, these are transient reactions subject to relatively intact reality testing. The psychotic character is most of the time quite able to test reality. It is this element that facilitates the reversibility of disturbances that differentiates the psychotic character from the psychotic. (pp. 38–39)

Consequently, although the aspects of the relationship to reality and the feeling of reality may be significantly impaired in borderline conditions, particularly in the lower-order borderline syndromes, there is a tendency for reality-testing to be relatively intact, even though this, too, may be transiently and regressively impaired. These qualities or aspects of the sense of reality are chronically impaired and malfunctioning in the psychoses. Although these aspects of the involvement in reality contribute to the development of reality constancy (Frosch, 1966), such constancy is lacking in the psychotic's relationship with reality.

In all these cases, the assessment of reality-testing involves evaluating degrees of impairment. Even the loss of the relationship to reality to the point of psychotic productions, such as hallucinations or delusions, may not necessarily be pathognomonic of a psychosis. As Frosch (1970) points out, the disturbance in the relationship to reality must be assessed in terms of the patient's capacity to evaluate such psychic experiences; hallucinations, for example, may not be accompanied by a loss of reality-testing, in that the patient is still able to recognize the phenomenon as unreal or as internally derived. Such a degree of failure of reality-testing is much less than it is in the patient whose hallucinations are regarded as convincing and real. The failure of reality-testing in borderline patients is usually limited to the context of significant emotional relationships, in which the patient misconstrues or misinterprets attitudes and feelings of the significant other. Usually these interpersonal distortions are the product of projections that can be identified and tested with the patient.

The development of a sense of reality and of reality constancy is related to the experience of objects, insofar as the primary objects become the infant's touchstone of and anchor to reality (Frosch, 1966). Impediments in the capacity for object relationships are central to the borderline pathology. Object relationships remain, essentially, on a need-satisfying basis (Brody, 1960; Frijling-Schreuder, 1969). Certain types of borderline patient characteristically develop new and relatively intense clinging relationships quite rapidly, so much so that this is often characteristic of the initial phases of the development of a therapeutic relationship. The intensity of these needs and the tendency to cling to objects as a source of gratification varies considerably in intensity and degree, but nonetheless remains a core disturbance in the borderline group.

The relationship to objects is marked by a general feeling of emptiness and greedy hunger and intense wishes to be nurtured and taken care of, which become insistent and demand immediate satisfaction. If such demands are not satisfactorily met, as they might not be due to the excess of the patient's expectations or the object's inability to respond, then feelings of intense rage are stirred up, along with destructive impulses toward the object. These carry with them not only the fear of retaliatory destruction, but also raise the patient's feelings of vulnerability to abandonment. When the rage reaches a sufficient degree of intensity, it may also result in a defensive regression to a fusion of the self and object representations that give rise to psychotic identification.

This intense hunger and need for objects is expressed in the transference. Kernberg (1968) has observed that borderline patients often reveal an early activation within the transference of highly conflicted derivatives of object relationships, which may be associated with relatively dissociated ego states, each one of which may come to represent a more or less independent transference paradigm. These paradigms usually involve projective mechanisms and reflect the persistence in the borderline character structure of relatively unmetabolized pathogenic introjects. A similar quality of object involvement has been described in borderline children: There are desperate attempts to maintain an illusion of omnipotence; a reliance on projection; and a denied, but nonetheless intense need for dependence on the therapist (Fintzy, 1971). The element of idealization, along with the urgent need to see the therapist as omnipotent and omniscient, is present in children as well as in adults.

This tendency is often seen dramatically in the beginning of therapy. When the therapy is initiated in the context of an acute regressive state, it is frequently the case that borderline patients will make desperate and insistent attempts to establish an intense, needy, clinging, and dependent relationship to the therapist. The initial stages of therapy will be marked by frequent and urgent telephone calls in which the patient, who feels intensely anxious or depressed, is reaching out to the omnipotent therapist, seeking some form of magical relief. Such tactics reflect the needy and regressed state of the patient and present special difficulties in management.

This basic impairment in the capacity for object relations means that the patient is unable to perceive external objects in realistic terms and as complete persons. The characteristics of the object may not only be distorted or misrepresented, but they also may be consistently omitted or selectively perceived, such that only those characteristics are included that fit the predominant feeling tone toward the object at that time. Such an object may be seen as sexually exciting or murderous or despicable without any effort made to include the contradictory qualities of the object into a more comprehensive picture. The subject tends to shift back and forth between the various aspects of the partial object representations—this can be defined in terms of shifting back and forth between aspects of the patient's ambivalence toward the object, during which the object is seen in more or less exclusively good or bad terms. In each instance, the current activated image of the object is taken to be a true representation of the object reality (De Saussure, 1974).

This same discontinuity and shifting of focus takes place in regard to the patient's self-representations, in which there tends to be a series of discontinuous and partial self-images, each of which is regarded as a reflection of the patient's whole self. These images have little connection or continuity and are dealt with in a way similar to that in which the contradictory aspects of objects are handled, that is, by exclusion. The resulting impairment in the self leads to an attempt to stabilize and complete the self-organization by adherence to objects or object-substitutes. The clinical picture is characterized by a continual preoccupation with the self and desperate and constant demands for love from objects, along with an inability to maintain or integrate that love when it is offered. A similar dynamic lies at the core of the borderline's inclination to connect up with groups, causes, or cults, often with fanatic intensity, as a means of gaining a sense of identity or of bolstering a faltering identity (Erikson, 1959).

To the extent that object relations remain on this need-gratifying level, the capacity for object constancy is correspondingly diminished. Object constancy implies the capacity to maintain a meaningful relationship to a specific object, whether one's subjective needs are being satisfied or not. In most borderline conditions, some capacity for object constancy is retained: in varying degrees, object relationships seem capable of reaching beyond the mere level of primitive need-satisfaction. But this object constancy remains extremely fragile and vulnerable, and can be readily threatened by a variety of vicissitudes (Frijling-Schreuder, 1969; Fintzy, 1971). The fragility of object constancy in borderline patients, along with the characteristic shifting of object images back and forth between extreme emotional reactions, has been frequently noted (Kernberg, 1967, 1970b, 1971; Blum, 1972; Masterson, 1972; Meissner, 1978).

The failure to achieve object constancy implies that the patient is unable to relate to significant objects as whole persons, but rather relates to them as parts; that the relationship fluctuates in terms of the patient's need state, and there is poor tolerance for frustration or ambivalence and little capacity to endure frustration of needs; that the individual has difficulty evoking a consistent image of the object when the object is not physically present; and finally, that it carries with it a severe impairment in the individual's capacity to mourn the object, with the result that separation becomes extremely difficult. Such patients often avoid the threat of separation by resorting to primitive forms of defense, including emotional detachment, or acting-out to provoke reinvolvement with the object or to attract the object's attention. This applies particularly to the difficult stages of separation in therapy (Masterson, 1972).

Although the capacity for object constancy and object relationship is impaired in borderline conditions, the incapacity is more severe and extensive in the psychoses. The borderline patient may gain some degree of object constancy, but this remains tenuous and vulnerable, and the patient frequently regresses to the level of need-gratification. The psychotic, however, never gets beyond need-gratification, does not get beyond seeing the objects of his experience in partial and fragmented terms, and is unable to achieve that level of integration of object representations that is the basis for constancy. Object relationships in the psychoses are not based merely on the need to seek gratification from the object, but rather are based on a more primitive form or extension of such a wish, that is, the wish to possess the primary objects or their substitutes through fusion or merging. Such patients resort to primitive forms of internalization, primitive introjective mechanisms, or even oral incorporation, which result in the loss of differentiation between the self and the object, so that the self becomes delusionally identified with the object and the object with the self. The combination of these delusional states of fusion or merger and impairment of reality-testing is the basis for psychotic manifestations. Thus, in the tenuous balance between fragile object cathexis and primary identification, the psychotic patient tends to relate more in terms of such primitive incorporative devices, rather than in terms of the cathexis of objects.

The lack of object constancy, that is, the inability to establish a secure and lasting cathexis of objects, and the corresponding defects in internalization create a situation of intense need for and clinging to objects, which is compounded with an intense fear and distrust of those same objects. This basic dilemma was described some years ago in regard to schizophrenic object relations as the "need-fear dilemma" (Burnham et al., 1969). A similar combination of intense longing and fear is identifiable in borderline patients as well (Blum, 1972). There is a fear of symbiotic fusion, along with an intense ambivalence, so that although the borderline tends to reach out and cling to objects, he is forced to withdraw when the pain or threat of rejection becomes unbearable (Giovacchini, 1973).

Such abandonment may come to mean rejection; a terror of feeling isolated and lonely; or a feeling of inner emptiness, coldness, and deadness. Or it may translate into more profound fears of total destructive abandonment and annihilation. This latter quality is connoted in the psychotic's need-fear dilemma, whereas the more modified and muted forms may find their expression in borderlines. The fear of abandonment stems from an incomplete internalization of maternal caring. The failure of maternal empathy and the threat of abandonment is not only terrifying, but also stirs primitive savage oral wishes to kill, eat, merge, etc. These primitive destructive impulses create a primitive guilt that threatens retaliation and loss of love. In addition, the projection of such rage makes the loved object a source of dread, danger, and persecution, which serves only to reinforce and increase the pattern of withdrawal (Buie and Adler, 1972).

In the psychotic, such fears assume delusional proportions and may achieve a degree of psychotic conviction, which reflects the failure of the capacity to test reality, and may put into operation psychotic mechanisms that distort reality. Such delusional and usually persecutory fears are also seen in the regressive borderline states, but putting them aside for the moment, the analogue of such fears can also be identified in the more primitive, lower-order borderline syndromes, in the psychotic character, and even more predominantly, in pseudoneurotic schizophrenia. In therapy, such patients may have these intense needs and fears stimulated in the transference context. The fears of abandonment can be readily stirred by any rebuke or failure of comprehension on the part of the therapist and, especially, by a variety of countertransference reactions (Kernberg, 1976b). Such fears may easily trigger a transient regression, but usually there is a return to a level of more integrated secondary process functioning after the recovery of a more stable alliance, although the therapy may be pervaded by issues of separation and abandonment. Moreover, the dilemma often tends to have an either/or quality: clinging to one object means abandonment by others, and frequently, the childhood history of such patients reveals a similar theme—that if the child loves one parent, it seems to imply the threat of loss or abandonment by the other.

The intensity and the pathogenic quality of these fears are magnified in the psychotic personality, to the point where they become paralyzing and incapacitating. They also carry with them a delusional and convincing quality, as we have observed. One may also hear the same themes enunciated by borderline patients, but they lack the intensity and the delusional conviction that one hears from the schizophrenic patient. It is not unusual to hear such fears expressed, although the patient maintains an awareness that such feelings arc, in fact, distortions of the reality and that they are expressions of inner fears and fantasies; frequently, then, a sense of conviction is lacking, but nonetheless, the fears persist.

In marginal cases, particularly, the patient's object relationships are predominantly need-gratifying and are intensely ambivalent and conflictual as well. His most meaningful relationships are filled with a diffuse and primitive rage, which at times, seems psychotic in proportions. His self is poorly differentiated and only tenuously maintained, and any object constancy is minimal. In such patients, the need-fear dilemma has a primitive and intense, almost catastrophic quality, which is very like that found in psychotic patients. These patients who are lower-order borderlines are, for all practical purposes, schizophrenic when they are thus functioning, but it is still possible to maintain some distinction in view of the fact that the patients seem to dip in and out of this regressed state easily; thus, the psychotic distortions are not as persistent as they are in authentic psychotic conditions.

In borderline conditions, an inherent fragility and vulnerability of the nuclear narcissistic structures tends to weaken and impair the sense of self-cohesiveness. The potential breakdown of such nuclear structures remains a continual threat, which must be countered by a variety of defensive maneuvers (Kohut, 1972). Kernberg (1970) has described the "lower level" of character pathology as having a poor integration of self-representations, so that the subject's inner world is peopled by caricatures of both the good aspects and the horrible aspects of important objects without effectively integrating them. These residues of object relations or introjects (Meissner, 1971, 1978) create an inner experience of the self as composed of a chaotic amalgamation of shameful, threatened, impotent, and yet, at the same time, exalted and omnipotent images.

This defect in the integration of the inner world of introjects and the failure of a stable self-concept frequently result in a diffusion of identity that

Kernberg regards as characteristic of this lower level of character pathology. Such patients may jump from one isolated and more or less coherent self-image to the next, without any connections to maintain the continuity of the self-image. This is the basis of the phenomenon Kernberg (1967) describes as "splitting." Attempts to assist these patients in developing some capacity for synthesis are often resisted, while the patient continues to rely unconsciously on the fantasied magical powers of the analyst to provide what is missing and to transform the patient into a more integrated, whole person.

Thus, in the borderline conditions, self and object representations may gain some degree of internal integration, but their cohesion is derived from the inclusion of qualities in the respective images derived from external objects of dependence. The resistance to self-integration is often accompanied by unconscious fantasies of more frightening dangers, which are the result of allowing the self to be whole and one, so that many of these patients begin to experience a more severe degree of anxiety only when the capacity for synthesis is, in some degree, achieved (De Saussure, 1974). Achieving a more integrated and individuated self becomes equivalent, for these patients, to separation. When the dependence on objects is of such intensity that the distinction between self and object is blurred or lost, the loss of the object can provoke a severe annihilation anxiety, in which any separation from the object precipitates the fear of loss, which is equivalent to annihilation of the self (Frosch, 1967a).

Although the cohesiveness of the self in borderline conditions remains fragile and vulnerable, at the psychotic level, such cohesiveness is lost or has never been acquired. Borderline patients may show a regressive fragmentation of the self, but this fragmentation is usually transient and is more readily recoverable. In Kohut's (1971) terms, psychotic patients tend toward the chronic abandonment of the cohesive narcissistic configurations and then, in a defensive attempt to escape from the intolerable fragmentation and narcissistic loss, seek restitutive formations in the form of psychotic delusions or hallucinations. In the borderline, even in regressive borderline states, the fragmentation of narcissistic structures is usually only minor and temporary, with only partial fragmentation and no more than a hint of restitutive delusion. In the psychotic, the archaic narcissistic configurations take the form of cold and haughty psychotic delusions of grandeur, which serve to reconstitute, in a primitive and absolute way, the grandiose self, and delusional reconstitutions of the omnipotent object in the form of all-powerful persecuting agencies and powers capable of manipulating and influencing the patient's self.

In view of the fragility and potential vulnerability of the patient's self-organization, it is not surprising that borderline patients sometimes have difficulty maintaining the differentiation between self and objects. Throughout the borderline spectrum generally, differentiation is well maintained, although it is weakened and susceptible to potential regression in the lower borderline forms. In transient regressive episodes, it is usually temporarily and partially lost, but is usually easily and rapidly restored by the provision of structure in the patient's environment. In the psychotic patient, however, the differentiation between self and object is at best unstable and uncertain and may never have been established in any more than fragmentary and partial forms, and it tends to be obliterated for much longer periods. Developmentally, the psychotic patient has not been able to achieve a level of differentiation between self- and object-images that allows for consistent maintenance of this differentiation.

The borderline patient has achieved this level of differentiation and is generally successful in maintaining it. The difficulty comes more in terms of the capacity to integrate various aspects, both good and bad, of self-images, on the one hand, and object-images, on the other. More often than not, borderline regression will lead to the point of self-object differentiation, but not beyond it. Psychotic regression, however, goes beyond self-object differentiation and poses the imminent threat of fusion or merger with the object and the accompanying threat of annihilation. Thus, in Kernberg's (1967, 1970b) terms, borderline patients have achieved a self-object differentiation, but have failed in the integration of both self- and object-images, due to the predominance of pregenital aggression, which results in a decreased capacity for synthesis of contradictory self- and object-images and consequently interferes with integration of the self, of object relations, and achievement of object constancy. These mechanisms fail in the psychoses, in which the essential developmental failure occurs before the differentiation of self and object and thus prevents the adequate integration of ego boundaries.

This difference is seen dramatically in the development of transference psychoses in borderline as opposed to psychotic patients. In all transference psychoses, both borderline and psychotic, reality-testing is impaired, but in borderlines, this comes about by a rapid alternation of projections of self- and object-images, with a resulting blurring of ego boundaries and a transient loss of differentiation of self and object. But in the psychotic, particularly the schizophrenic, there is a fusion between self- and object-images, such that in the transference, the patient experiences a fusion between himself and the therapist. The result is that the patient finds himself in either an "all good" ecstatic fusion with the therapist or in an "all bad," extremely dangerous, threatening fusion with him (Kernberg, cited in Wilson, 1971).

The phenomenon of depersonalization is commonly seen in both borderline syndromes and psychoses. The phenomenon is related to the fragmentation of the self and experientially expresses the result of such fragmentation. Depersonalization is linked with derealization as two phases of an underlying process. Depersonalization represents the loss of the sense of reality as it pertains to the self; derealization represents the loss of the sense of reality as it pertains to the environment (Hunter, 1966). Derealization results from withdrawal of cathexis from an environment that is seen as frustrating, threatening, and dangerous. Depersonalization, however, results from a splitting of the ego, a result of an inability to integrate various self-images or from the regressive breakdown of such integration. Often, depersonalization is seen as a feature of borderline cases and is related to problems of identity diffusion (Kernberg, 1970b; Frosch, 1970). Gunderson (1977) noted in his group of borderlines that depersonalization was more commonly reported than derealization, while in the comparison group of schizophrenics, the opposite pattern obtained, with derealization predominating over depersonalization. Similarly, the phenomenon is seen particularly in incipient stages of psychotic breakdown.

Depersonalization may occur in a wide spectrum of psychopathological disturbances, perhaps more frequently in the schizophrenias and depressions, but may also occur in mild and transient forms, even in relatively normal individuals. It may function defensively and usually is associated with some degree of anxiety. But the connection of depersonalization experiences with disturbances of identity tends to point in the direction of a more severe psychopathology. Disturbance of identity, even to the point of a complete loss of identity correlative to the fragmentation of the self, is usually a predominant feature of psychotic pathology.

Again in borderline conditions, there is neither the persistence nor the severity of the loss of identity that is found in the psychoses, but rather transient confusion and often more subtle and diffuse problems of difficulty in defining and maintaining a consistent identity. It has been suggested (Chapter 7) that such difficulties in establishing and maintaining a sense of identity can be differentially described as one form of borderline disorder. The persistence of feelings of depersonalization in such patients must, therefore, be taken as an index of more serious pathology. It should also be noted that, in the borderline conditions, in general, acting-out may frequently be seen as having a defensive function against the danger of loss of identity. The correlative fear of being merged with or becoming part of the object, being absorbed or devoured by the object, is insufficiently countered by intrapsychic mechanisms, so that acting-out and the corresponding intense affective involvement with the environment becomes a defensive necessity (Angel, 1965).

The defensive configuration in the lower-order borderline syndromes generally reflects the weakened state of ego functioning and impediments of ego strength and ego organization as described by Kernberg (1967). The defenses that Kernberg specifies as characteristic of the borderline personality organization are splitting, primitive idealization, projection and projective identification, omnipotence and devaluation, and denial. The same defense mechanisms, however, are also found operating at a psychotic level, and distinguishing between the psychotic level of defensive organization and a borderline level is, therefore, critical to the differential diagnosis.

In the borderline condition, these defenses are seen in their most primitive and psychotic form in the regressive borderline states, but their operation differs somewhat in the more enduring and better functioning level provided by the characterological organization of borderline personalities. It must be remembered, in discussing defensive organization, that such organization demonstrates a continuum of levels of organization and functioning, reaching from the lowest level of borderline organization, which touches on the schizophrenic, to the highest level of borderline organization, in which these defensive systems are operating in more or less adaptive and/or neurotic ways. They may also be compounded and mixed with a variety of higher-order and mature defenses in higher-level borderline personalities. In fact, clinically, the higher forms of borderline organization may rarely and only exceptionally demonstrate the defenses Kernberg describes, and then only in periods of relative regression and in isolated areas of functioning, usually having to do with conflicts with significant objects.

The presence of such a continuum must be particularly noted with regard to splitting. Kernberg (1967) has described this as the core defensive operation that is fundamental to the understanding of the borderline personality organization and that underlies and influences all the others. It is also a point of differentiation, since he links splitting with the borderline conditions, but rules it out for the neuroses. Thus, where one finds splitting, one finds a borderline; and where one finds repression without splitting, one finds a neurotic. In this study, however, splitting is seen as operating on a continuum of levels of degree of intensity.

Splitting is also found in neurotic subjects, but more often than not, one part of what is split comes to dominate the personality organization, while the rest is repressed. Thus, one frequently finds in depressed neurotics, for example, a view of the self as worthless, valueless, and impotent, but it is only after considerable therapeutic work that the rest of the introjective configuration, which has been equivalently split off and repressed, comes into view. It is only when these patients discover that, behind the more conscious and depressive aspect of their pathology, there lies a narcissistic, entitled, and aggressive side to themselves, which contributes to their pathology, that any effective inroad is made in the pathological organization.

In the borderline continuum, however, the split parts of the personality tend to be less repressed and are more or less available to conscious systems. These tend to operate as the reasonably well defined and articulated, but dissociated, ego states Kernberg describes so well. This is particularly striking in the often extreme and repetitive oscillation of contradictory self-concepts often found in borderline individuals. Moreover, it has been argued whether the phenomenon described clinically actually reflects splitting as a defensive mechanism, as Kernberg would hold, or whether it represents, instead, a developmental failure reflecting a lack of integration of self-images (Atkin, 1974). My own clinical experience suggests that, in the higher level of borderline organization, these various split components are not so readily available as Kernberg suggests. The picture he paints of the typical splitting in borderline patients is much more characteristic of more primitively organized borderlines who may be more highly susceptible to regressive pulls and, consequently, may more easily manifest the results of splitting. In these patients, then, it can be comfortably said that repression operates with considerably less effectiveness than in the higher-level borderline forms.

It should be noted in reference to the discussion of splitting that the levels of the continuum are accompanied by the operation of projective mechanisms that tend to color and often to distort the quality of the individual's object relationships. That aspect of the intrapsychic organization or introjective configuration that is relatively less available to consciousness and that functions at that point in time as the repressed, but still central organizing configuration of the patient's inner world tends to be projected and becomes the qualifying aspect of significant objects in the environment. Thus, the depressed patient will see others around him as superior, more fortunate, better endowed, etc. The borderline patient, in his own fashion, is characteristically caught up in extremely active processes of projection, which serve the essential purpose of externalizing the all-bad aggressive self-image, with the result that the individual creates dangerous, threatening, or retaliatory objects against which he must then defend himself. This can represent the typically paranoid stance found so frequently in borderline patients, in which the patient is seen as the victim of external aggressive persecutory forces. But the projection may go the other way around, and the patient may find it necessary to devalue and demean the object or see himself as powerfully influential and destructive.

These dynamics operate in more intense and extensive ways at the psychotic level. They may be regarded as equivalent to the narcissistic defenses described by Vaillant (1971) and have the effect of altering the perception or interpretation of reality. Psychotic projection becomes delusional, radically distorting reality and tending to create persecutory agencies often bound in a conspiracy that is maintained with psychotic conviction (Frosch, 1967a).

The tendency to idealization is also a continuous quality that spans the spectrum of psychopathology. It is an expression of the archaic narcissistic configuration described by Kohut (1971) in terms of the idealized parental imago. At the borderline level, it operates in a more primitive way than that described by Kohut in the narcissistic character disorders, and leads to the creation of unrealistic, all-good, and powerful object-images, which can protect one against the aggressive and destructive impulses within oneself or those projected onto other objects. In the psychotic form, such idealization becomes delusional and may take the form of a delusional merger or fusion with such an idealized, powerful object.

Denial in the borderline patient may be found operating internally in the form of denial of areas of the patient's conscious experience of self (denial in the service of splitting), or it may operate externally in the form of denial of some sector of subjective experience or of experience of the external world. As Kernberg notes (1967), when patients are pressed about these issues they may acknowledge some awareness of this denied sector of their experience, but they cannot integrate it in any meaningful way with the rest of their emotional experience. Kernberg distinguishes this from a higher form of denial that is implicit in negation. In negation, the patient says that he knows that someone might think that something was true (for example, the therapist might think that the patient was angry at the therapist), but this idea is rejected as irrelevant. Thus, what is denied is never felt or experienced as present in consciousness and remains repressed. In the borderline, however, the denied element is available to some other part of the patient's consciousness, but it is still denied. In psychotic denial, external reality is primarily affected: the perception of external reality is altered and the reality denied or a fantasy substituted for it.

The mechanisms of omnipotence and devaluation reflect the underlying vicissitudes of primitive narcissism and represent the pathological functioning of the residues of the grandiose self. In regard to their operation in the borderline patient, Kernberg (1967) comments:

> These two mechanisms are also intimately linked to splitting and represent at the same time direct manifestations of the defensive use of primitive introjection and identification. Patients using these two mechanisms of defense may shift between the need to establish a demanding, clinging relationship to an idealized "magic" object at some times, and fantasies and behavior betraying a deep feeling of magical omnipotence of their own at other times. Both stages represent their identification with an "all good" object, idealized and powerful as a protection against bad, "persecutory" objects. (p. 671)

Thus, these mechanisms, which link up with primitive idealization, form a variant expression of the same underlying primitive narcissism. On the psychotic level, these mechanisms involve an absolute enshrining of the grandiose self and result in the delusional omnipotence that is required to protect the self from psychotic destruction. The cold withdrawal and omnipotent grandiosity of the paranoid patient are quite characteristic, as well as the megalomanic delusions frequently seen in all forms of psychosis.

It is to be noted in discussing all of these forms of defensive organization that they are subject to degrees of variation and intensity, the psychotic expressions being the most intense and disturbing and the borderline being considerably less so. The critical variable in their assessment is the degree to which they distort the patient's capacity to relate to and maintain a sense of reality. When the defensive configuration gives rise to delusional formations, which are resistant to reality-testing and which are maintained with delusional conviction without responding to therapeutic intervention, it becomes a strong index of psychotic process.

Disturbances in thinking are generally taken to be the hallmark of the psychoses. Nonetheless, there is considerable disagreement over the extent to which thought processes are disturbed in the borderline syndromes. It is generally agreed that thought processes are disturbed and manifest a predominance of primary process in states of transient regressions. In such borderline states, patients may show delusional thought disorders, paranoid distortions, loosening of associations, ideas of reference, delusions, and even evidence of thought disorder on projective tests. However, on the level of nonregressed characterological functioning, the evidence is ambiguous. At this level, borderlines are generally thought to show no impairment of cognitive functioning on structured tests, such as the WAIS, but they reveal deviant and disordered thought processes on less structured and projective tests, such as the Rorschach (Singer, M.T., 1977). Gunderson and Singer (1975) summarize this evidence in the following terms:

> In summary, borderline persons are believed to connect unrelated percepts illogically, overelaborate on the affective meaning of percepts, and give circumstantial and unpleasant associations to the Rorschach ink blots. This disturbed thinking may be more flamboyant and more ego-syntonic than that found among schizophrenic persons. Yet such borderline persons are reported to function adequately on the WAIS, showing few or none of the ideational deviances. (p. 6)

At the same time, Stone (1980) has observed that although the split in test performance described by Gunderson and Singer is frequently found in borderline patients, the criterion is not exclusive, since it may also be found in patients with psychotic structure, particularly those with better intellectual resources.

Clinically one must distinguish between patients who manifest thought disorders in the course of a clinical interview and those patients in whom the thought disorder is considerably more subtle and can be revealed only on projective testing. The presence of disordered thought patterns can be identified clinically in regressed states, as already suggested, as well as in some borderline patients functioning on a nonregressed level. When the evidence of such thought disorganization is available clinically, the observer must think in terms of a psychotic process or of a state of severe ego-regression. More often than not, borderline patients do not manifest disorganized patterns of cognition clinically, but in some patients, the underlying disorder may be picked up on projective testing. This is a feature, particularly of the lower level of borderline psychopathology, and is not characteristic of the higher levels of borderline psychopathology. Consequently, the author differs from the more generally accepted position regarding borderline cognition, namely, that it represents a subtle form of thought disorder that can usually be picked up on projective testing. Rather, it has been my experience that, by and large, borderline patients do not suffer from a thought disorder, even when subjected to projective testing, and they certainly do not manifest it in the clinical interview. However, thought processes may be subtly disordered in the lower levels of borderline pathology, including forms of pseudoschizophrenia and psychotic character. Moreover, disordered thinking may be identified in any of the borderline states during periods of regression.

TRANSIENT PSYCHOTIC REGRESSIONS

In discussing the differential diagnosis between borderline and psychotic conditions, a discussion of transient psychotic states, the so-called borderline states, which form the most difficult area in the differential diagnosis of these patients, has been left until now.

It must be noted that the regressive potential is not uniformly distributed in borderline conditions, but rather that it tends to be more characteristic of the lower-order of borderline pathology, particularly in the pseudoschizophrenics and psychotic characters. Consequently, even though the predominant description and characterization of borderline psychopathology has been based primarily on such regressive phenomena, the fact remains that these regressive states are not uniformly characteristic and constitute the exception more than the rule (Gunderson and Singer, 1975). Frequently enough, however, borderline patients come to clinical attention in such states of regression; and when they are hospitalized, it is frequently on account of such regressive manifestations. This creates an important selective factor in the systematic evaluation of borderline functioning. In Gunderson's studies (1977), for example, the choice of patients diagnosed as borderline in the hospital setting automatically selects for the more primitive and regressed aspects of borderline functioning.

In a regressed state, the borderline patient may look psychotic for all practical purposes. However, certain indices help to distinguish the borderline regression from more authentically psychotic expressions. The regression in borderline patients is usually stress-related and most typically has to do with vicissitudes in significant object relationships. Moreover, the psychotic expressions remain relatively unsystematized and have an ego-alien quality that reflects the persistence, even in the face of psychotic regression, of some degree of reality-testing. At some level, then, the patient may be capable of identifying delusional content or even hallucinations as products of his own inner world. It is as though part of the ego is caught up in the psychotic process, while another part remains objective and capable of testing the psychotic expressions. There are thus no stable delusional systems or persistent hallucinations, although disturbances of states of consciousness are frequently seen in the form of depersonalization, dissociative states, and, to a lesser extent, derealization. Psychotic symptoms are usually only questionably present, or, if present, are transient, readily reversible, circumscribed, and experienced as alien (Gunderson et al., 1975). It should also be noted that borderline regressions are often seen in relation to toxic states, particularly from the hallucinogenic drugs, and less frequently, marijuana.

Often there is a rapid and intense clinging dependence on the important objects who are cast in the role of magical saviors to whom the individual looks for relief from the intense inner pain, but who inevitably and invariably disappoint the patient, which leads to further outbursts of impotent rage. This pattern of behavior is quite characteristic and serves to differentiate these patients, in a striking way, from the schizophrenic withdrawal or often cold hostile grandiosity of the psychotic patient.

In the hospital setting, frequently enough, these patients will actively and intensively engage members of the staff in these magical expectations and demands and precipitate intense struggles and acting-out episodes as the result of their inevitable frustration (Adler, 1973). The easy frustration of such infantile and magical wishes leads quickly to an intense narcissistic rage, which may often express itself in destructive acting-out, in the form of self-laceration or mutilation, window-breaking, and verbal and physical abuse. Frequently, there is a quality of turning the rage on and off at will, or of controlling assaultive behavior—either in terms of its most effective timing or of its direction to objects—that is, assaultive behavior may be directed against the staff, but never against fellow patients—points that distinguish it from the less differentiating loss of control in schizophrenic patients.

Acting-out in such hospital settings may take place as a result of specific disappointments or dissatisfactions or as a manifestation of envy of sicker patients who get special management and attention. It is as though the special management given to regressed or suicidal patients were regarded as special gifts or privileges. Destructive behavior on the part of such patients may be more devastating than that of psychotic patients because it may be aimed at particular staff members and may take the form of undermining the relationship of staff members to other patients, often encouraging these more seriously disturbed patients to use drugs or to attempt to escape or even to commit suicide (Friedman, 1969).

The setting of limits is extremely important in the management of such patients, even more so than in the treatment of psychotic patients. An atmosphere of intense caring and concern for the individual needs of patients may limit the regression and respond to the needs of schizophrenics, but at the same time, such attitudes may induce or reinforce regressive behavior in borderline patients. The same patterns of acting-out behavior have been noted in the abuse of medication by these patients. They tend to use alcohol excessively, characteristically overuse medicines, taking pills of all sorts and manipulatively getting medication from more than one source. Attempts by the therapist to wean them from such medication often constitute an invitation to open warfare, which is generally unsuccessful. This contrast with the typical pattern of schizophrenic behavior, which follows a pattern of outer obedience and acceptance with inner rebellion and resistance—the typical master-slave interaction (Havens, 1968).

In the psychoanalytic or psychotherapeutic setting, borderline patients are prone to form psychotic transferences as a manifestation of their more general regressive tendency. In such psychotic transferences, the therapist is recreated as the evil or persecuting objects of the patient's childhood. Thus, in delusional transference, the distinction between the reality of the present relationship with the therapist and the infantile fantasy is lost. The primitive fears of annihilation such regression carries with it may lead to fantasies of fusion with the therapist and tendencies to incorporative identification with the psychotic object.

Even in such regressions within the transference, however, there is less tendency toward fusion with the therapist and a more likely pattern of rapid alternating projection of self- and object-images, with rapid alternation between the inside and the outside, the partial blurring of ego boundaries, and the correlative loss of self-object differentiation. This contrasts with the psychotic tendency to fusion between the self and the therapist, which, as noted, is either all-good or all-bad (Wilson, 1971).

An important differentiating point with regard to the transference psychosis is that it tends to be confined to the therapeutic setting and does not extend generally beyond the confines of the relationship to the therapist or the therapeutic hour (Modell, 1963; Atkins, 1967; Frosch, 1967b). It has also been noted, particularly by Zetzel (1971), that a characteristic of borderline regression is that it tends to be rather readily reversed in a good therapeutic situation, a point of important differentiation from the psychoses. Thus, an important diagnostic feature becomes the quality of the patient's interaction with the therapist over time and the extent to which the patient responds to appropriate management and adequate structuring of the environment (Kernberg, 1971). The psychotic regression in borderline states must be characterized as partial and transient and, also, as sensitive to the structuring aspects of the environment (Frosch, 1970).

Psychotic patients do not demonstrate this degree of environmental responsiveness; rather, psychotic manifestations tend to persist over longer periods of time, despite environmental structuring and appropriate management. To this it can be added that regressive potential and sensitivity to environmental structure are not uniformly distributed among borderline conditions. These aspects tend to be notably more severe in more primitive borderline conditions, but are less frequently, even exceptionally, seen in higher-order forms of borderline pathology.

Some discrimination may be possible on the basis of drug responses, particularly when the discrimination is between frank psychosis and psychotic-like regressive states. Psychotic patients require the use of adequate antipsychotic doses of neuroleptics, usually the phenothiazines, for any effective drug response. When such drugs are used in an acute regressive crisis with such patients, the first effects are usually seen as moderating the patient's agitation and emotional turmoil, but any change in the patient's delusions or disordered thought processes may take longer, and then only when adequate antipsychotic, therapeutic drug levels have been maintained. Thus, in treating the typical disturbed schizophrenic patient, the clinician can expect to see a quieting down and a greater degree of control over the patient's disorganized behavior within the first few days or weeks, but the more typically psychotic delusional or cognitive difficulties may well continue to be in evidence for a period of weeks to months. Under the same circumstances, the borderline patient can be expected to respond relatively rapidly to medication. The patient's recompensation may take place quite dramatically, even on low doses of phenothiazines. The behavioral disorganization and affective turmoil responds quickly, and the entire clinical picture may return to normal within a matter of days. Moreover, the borderline patient does not require continued medication in order to maintain this reconstituted level of functioning.

In fact, borderline patients may not require neuroleptics to achieve such recompensation. Some patients may respond well to antidepressant medication, for example, imipramine or amitriptyline, and other patients do reasonably well even on such tranquilizing drugs as Valium. The effectiveness of neuroleptics, by way of comparison to less potent drugs like the antidepressants or minor tranquilizers, may reflect the extent to which the patient's personality organization approaches the psychotic border. Patients whose characterological level of functioning is not far removed from the psychotic may respond better to neuroleptics. Even here, however, there is good evidence that such patients, who occupy the lowest stratum of the borderline spectrum, may do better on antidepressants, whether of the tricyclic or MAO inhibitor type, than on phenothiazines (Klein, 1977). Beyond the question of the use of drugs in the differentiation between psychosis and borderline states, the question of the usefulness of psychopharmacological agents in the treatment of borderline patients and the differential diagnostic implications of drug response is a complicated subject to which we will return later (see Chapter 7).

SUMMARY AND CONCLUSION

Discrimination of borderline syndromes from the psychoses is often difficult, clinically. The problem most often arises in the acute setting in which a crisis has arisen—the typical example being that of acute hospitalization. The clinician's task is to assess the patient's apparently psychotic symptoms and behavior to determine whether they are the manifestations of an underlying psychotic process or whether they reflect a more or less transient regression from a somewhat higher level of habitual functioning. Some discrimination between these categories is possible, even in the acute presentation, since borderline patients only exceptionally demonstrate Schneiderian first-rank symptoms or any other discriminating indices of psychosis (Gunderson et al., 1975; Carpenter et al., 1973).

Although differentiation may be clear-cut between the psychotic and the higher-order, better-functioning borderline, the discrimination between the lower-order borderline forms or transient borderline states and psychoses is less precise. The focus in this study has been on this area of differentiation.

Discriminating indices are both short and long term. Differentiation can only be adequately made with a longer-term evaluation of the patient. Nonetheless, on a short-term basis, evaluation of the patient's behavior can point the diagnosis in one direction or other. The presence of a clear precipitant; the presence of intense (often verbalized) anger; the patient's attempts to engage the therapist in an intense, dependent, clinging, and demanding relationship, usually in a manipulative fashion; the partial, fragmentary, often circumscribed, ego-alien quality of the patient's psychotic productions; the marked tendency to act-out feelings, particularly anger, in a way to obtain increased attention and concern from doctors, family, friends, or hospital staff; the persistence of some degree of reality-testing and areas of significant realistic functioning; the transient nature of regressive manifestations and the ready reversal of regression in structured environments and with appropriate therapeutic management, particularly, adequate limit-setting—all point toward a borderline diagnosis. Moreover, these factors carry an accumulative weight, so that the more of these factors that can be validated, the more secure the diagnosis of borderline psychopathology.

On a longer-term basis (beyond a few days), one would expect the above indices to be better discriminated. In addition, there is more opportunity to study patterns of patient behavior—both interaction with staff and other patients and with the therapist. Important areas include tolerance for frustration and the tendency to act-out as a means of relieving tension and frustration. The tendency to interact with the staff in manipulative or divisive ways is also important. These contrast with patterns of psychotic withdrawal or diffuse unfocused hostility and destructiveness. Most important in long-term evaluation, however, is the therapeutic relationship in which a more adequate assessment of the patient's thought processes and capacity for object relatedness is possible.

In many cases, differentiation is not clear-cut. Often, a long-term outcome will suggest that an apparently borderline patient was actually pre-psychotic. Other patients, however, may seem severely regressed and have a relatively benign outcome. Systematic studies have only begun to explore this area, and there is much to be learned. The question remains open whether borderline patients can become schizophrenic or manic or psychotically depressed, or whether psychotic patients can become borderline. The author's experience suggests that both are possible, but that the transition from borderline to psychotic is exceptional. The borderline's defenses and psychic organization seem adequate to prevent the transition to psychosis. More frequently, apparently schizophrenic or manic-depressive patients may be seen who have progressed significantly in therapy so that they could be said to be functioning on a borderline level—even a high level of borderline organization (Meissner, 1978).

Chapter 5
Differential Diagnosis:
The Narcissistic Disorders

One of the basic sources of confusion and difficulty in attempts to understand the lower-order forms of character pathology has been the lack of clarity in discriminating between forms of borderline disorder and the so-called narcissistic personalities. The primary contenders for recognition in this area are the notion of borderline personality provided by Kernberg (1967, 1968, 1971, 1975, 1976a) and Kohut's (1971, 1972) approach to the narcissistic personality disorders.

The Kernberg description of borderline personality organization arose out of a context in which the borderline conditions were a poorly defined and poorly conceptualized spectrum of disorders that were neither clearly psychotic nor classically neurotic. The major contribution of Kernberg's analysis is his definition of the distinguishing characteristics of this intermediate range of pathology, which established certain specific and definable characteristics. The emphasis in his approach was to delimit the boundaries of the borderline range and to distinguish it from the psychoses at the lower level of pathological organization and from the more clearly established neuroses at the higher level. Consequently, his description of the borderline conditions tends to lump them into one category, which, in effect, groups together a number of pathological conditions that occupy the space between the higher forms of neurosis and neurotic character, on the one hand, and psychotic conditions, on the other.

Obviously, a problem arises from the fact that the narcissistic personalities fall somewhere within this spectrum. In an attempt to classify these conditions, the narcissistic personalities would have to fall somewhere between the neurotic character disorders, such as the hysterical or obsessive-compulsive characters, and the borderline conditions. On the one hand, a problem arises from the attempt to extend the analysis of borderline personality structure to include the narcissistic personalities. Kernberg, for example, sees narcissistic personalities in terms of underlying borderline features (1967); tends to emphasize the similarities of defensive organization, including the use of primitive defenses of splitting, denial, omnipotence, and idealization (1970a); and in general, emphasizes the common denominators, particularly in terms of narcissistic character traits and narcissistic deficits in both types of personality organization (1971).

On the other hand, Kohut (1971), in his discussion of the narcissistic personality disorders, describes them essentially as cohesive self-organizations manifesting specific archaic narcissistic configurations. He leaves open the question of vulnerability to regression, so that the actual delineation from borderline conditions is somewhat obscured, even though he differentiates them from borderline states. Kohut (1971) writes:

> The central psychopathology of the narcissistic personality disturbances, on the other hand, concerns primarily the self and the archaic narcissistic objects. These narcissistic configurations are related to the causative nexus of psychopathology in the narcissistic realm in the following two ways: (1) they may be insufficiently cathected and are thus liable to temporary fragmentation; and (2) even if they are sufficiently cathected or hypercathected and thus retain their cohesiveness, they are not integrated with the rest of the personality, and the mature self and other aspects of the mature personality are deprived of a sufficient or reliable supply of narcissistic investments. (p. 19)

Consequently, the relative descriptions of borderline and narcissistic personalities leave a considerable overlap both in the narcissistic characteristics and in the tendency to regression, particularly to transient and partial regressions. Kernberg also remarks on the regressive potential of narcissistic personalities (1970a, 1974) and makes no attempt to distinguish between them on this basis. One way to summarize this problem is to say that Kernberg writes as though the diagnostic spectrum stretching between the psychoses and the neuroses were occupied by nothing but forms of borderline personality. At the same time, Kohut writes as though the same diagnostic vacuum were occupied by nothing but forms of narcissistic personality.

Kohut does attempt to differentiate these conditions on the basis of the relative cohesion of nuclear narcissistic structure. As he sees it, the narcissistic personalities are characterized by an insecure cohesiveness of the nuclear self and self-objects and only fleeting fragmentation. He contrasts this with borderline conditions in which the symptomatology hides the fragmentation of nuclear narcissistic structures or in which the break-up of such structures remains an everpresent potential, which can be prevented by avoiding the regression-inducing narcissistic injuries—as in schizoid personalities. These intermediate conditions are again distinguished from the frank psychoses in which there is a permanent and protracted fragmentation of narcissistic

structures and in which the symptoms openly reflect their decompensation
The discrimination between the fleeting fragmentation of the narcissistic
personality and the hidden or potential breakdown of nuclear narcissistic
structures in the borderline (including schizoid) conditions is difficult to
grasp, if not tenuous in conceptualization.

The upshot of the ambiguities in these approaches is that there is
considerable diagnostic confusion and difficulty in discriminating appropriately between these various forms of psychopathology. In fact, Ornstein
(1974) has argued that Kohut's classification of the narcissistic personality
disorders has now come to encompass those conditions previously considered
to be borderline or psychotic characters, and may even include some of those
previously diagnosed as neurotic characters or psychoneuroses.

This differential emphasis in approach to narcissistic personality disorders has given rise to differences in therapeutic approach as well. Based on
his concept of archaic narcissistic configurations, such as the grandiose self
as part of a normal developmental progression, Kohut emphasizes the need
for empathic responsiveness and acceptance of the patient's grandiosity and
need to idealize the analyst. Kernberg, however, sees these archaic narcissistic
formations as forms of developmental arrest or of pathological development.
Consequently, rather than empathic acceptance, Kernberg insists on the
interpretation of narcissistic structures consistently as defensive elaborations
both against more primitive and against more mature object-relationships.
His emphasis is on the defensive aspects of the narcissistic configuration and
on the need to work through narcissistic issues in terms of the related
aggressive and libidinal concerns (Ornstein, 1974).

Ornstein's suggestion that the argument may founder on the fact that it
is concerned with essentially different patient populations is a cogent one
and points in the further direction of the possibility that part of the difficulty
arises from ambiguities in diagnosis. The present discussion is an attempt to
bring some greater degree of differentiation to this problem in differential
diagnosis. The strategy will be to try to define the essentials of the narcissistic
personality organization and then clarify the differentiating aspects of the
borderline conditions.

ASPECTS OF NARCISSISTIC PERSONALITY ORGANIZATION

Certainly it is clear that all forms of personality organization have their
narcissistic elements that influence the form of the pathology. However, we
are discussing here forms of character pathology in which the narcissistic
disorder forms the central or core dimension of the patient's pathology. The
wide spectrum of narcissistic pathology is not equivalent to the more restric-

tive diagnosis of narcissistic personality. An essential note on which that diagnosis rests is the capacity for forming stable and at least potentially analyzable narcissistic transferences. We need also to remind ourselves that these narcissistic disorders will cover a pathological spectrum that will include those personalities whose level of functioning is quite good, as well as those whose functioning may be relatively impaired.

In trying to order the narcissistic personality types, Bursten (1973) has suggested that the highest level of narcissistic personality organization is found in the phallic narcissistic personality. The exhibitionism, pride in prowess, and show-offishness and the often counterphobic competitiveness and risk-taking in the service of narcissistic exhibitionism are quite familiar. Such individuals tend to be self-centered and have an exorbitant need for approval and admiration from others—particularly admiration. There is often a quality of arrogance or contempt in their relationship with others, which is defensive in tone and tends to mask underlying and often repressed feelings of inadequacy or inferiority.

This inner sense of inferiority often stems from a sense of shame from an underlying identification with a weak father figure compensated by the arrogant, assertive, aggressively competitive, often hypermasculine and self-glorifying facade. In other words, the unconscious shame over the fear of castration is continually denied by phallic assertiveness. This may even be accompanied by a sense of omnipotence and a feeling of invulnerability, which allows such individuals to continually take risks, feeling that some miraculous fate of good luck will carry them through. Such individuals tend to have a firmly established, cohesive sense of self, which shows little tendency to regression or fragmentation.

Such individuals often seem to have strong inner resources for maintaining their independence and express little need for others beyond the sort of admiration and acknowledgment we have described. The intense attachment to narcissistically invested objects that may be found in other forms of narcissistic pathology is not usually apparent in these patients, or is concealed behind a facade of hyperadequacy. The extent of their real dependency becomes apparent only when the love or support of such objects is lost. These personalities may have elements of grandiosity and omnipotence that reflect the persistence of the grandiose self, in Kohut's terms, and there may, at times, be an idealization of objects, which then serve as models for imitation or identification. The vulnerabilities of such personalities are generally well concealed by counterphobic and counterdependency mechanisms.

Nonetheless, they remain susceptible to the ravages of time and diminishing capacity and potency. The diminished capacity to perform with advancing age, whether sexually, physically, or intellectually, can constitute a narcissistic trauma with rather severe pathological results. The outcome is usually a depression.

Such individuals do not generally show a dramatic regressive crisis, but rather, under conditions of severe stress, the regression may be severe and, at times, irreparable. One wonders whether the cases of war neurosis in which individuals seemed to suffer from little or no fear or anxiety about danger prior to the traumatic event, but who seemed incapable of reconstituting in the usual way to pretraumatic levels of functioning, were not, in fact, phallic narcissistic characters. In such cases, the assault on the individual's self-image created by the traumatic event would have so damaged the individual's self-image and self-esteem that it proved relatively incapable of reconstitution.[1] That self-image had been based on a view of themselves as fearless and as able to withstand any amount of stress or danger. The exprience of severe anxiety would have destroyed that image, and created an impediment to its reconstitution or effective treatment (Zetzel and Meissner, 1973).

A more subtle variant of this form of narcissistic pathology was described by Tartakoff (1966) several years ago as a variant of an apparently well-adjusted, sociologically "healthy" personality. These were often academically or professionally successful individuals who were able and ambitious, who often had achieved significant degrees of professional respect and recognition, but who found themselves dissatisfied with their life situation. Difficulties arose in connection with competitive feelings or in competitive situations or in their inability to gratify the needs of others in intimate human relations, with family, close friends, etc. Some of these individuals could recognize their symptoms, usually reactive depressions, anxiety attacks under stress, or a variety of psychosomatic symptoms. Others were essentially asymptomatic, recognized no underlying motivation for treatment, but sought analysis essentially as a way of broadening their professional training. They shared the conviction that their exceptional abilities, talents, or virtues would win them success if they worked properly at it. Achieving these goals or life expectations had become essential to their psychic harmony. They often experienced little difficulty in life, since their abilities and endowments usually allowed them to gain some measure of narcissistic gratification and recognition from the environment or at least to maintain the hope of fulfilling their narcissistic expectations—a facet of their experience that can receive considerable cultural and social reinforcement from prevailing attitudes in our society. It is when the reinforcements begin to fail or the expectations begin not to be met that narcissistic imbalance and symptomatic manifestations may arise.

---

[1] A striking literary portrayal of just this form of narcissistic pathology is provided in the character of Marrow, the "hero" of John Hersey's *The War Lover* (1959).

In analysis, success in therapy was seen as a means to this end. Active mastery of the analytic situation and the conflicts it mobilized was a first line of defense for these patients. They treated the analysis as an adaptive task that carried the unspoken assumption that they would gain acceptance or acclaim from the analyst as a reward for their efforts. Their behavior was defensive, often competitive with the analyst, with an implicit expectation of gaining a special relation with the analyst. This may be expressed in the fantasy of being a special patient, especially interesting or especially difficult, preferred to other patients, even loved—exclusively—by the analyst.

When the adaptive function of the patient's attempts to master the analytic situation are seen and understood as repetitions of previously successful endeavors, a second line of preoedipal transference emerges in the idealization of the analyst. This externalization of the ego-ideal comes closer to Kohut's (1971) notion of the idealizing parental imago. Conformity to the analyst's expectations holds the promise that the patient will be rewarded by success in the analysis and will thereby be endowed with the qualities of omnipotence and omniscience he attributes to the analyst. Such fantasies may continue to be unspoken and become a secret source of resistance. Insofar as the analyst fails to meet these narcissistic expectations, the patient's disillusionment and narcissistic rage can become intense. In describing these patients, Tartakoff (1966) refers to the "Nobel Prize complex," which embraces two predominant fantasies: (1) an active grandiose fantasy of being powerful and omnipotent and (2) a more passive fantasy of being special, selected for special recognition by reason of exceptional talents, abilities, virtues, etc.

Some of these aspects of the narcissistic personality are exemplified in the case of a young physician who came into analysis because of a recurrent depression. He complained not only of long-standing depressive issues, but also of a more acute depressive reaction following the break-up of a love relationship. His dominant complaint on entering treatment was that he seemed to continually get into relationships with women in which he would feel intensely involved and the relationship would develop at a rapid pace, but soon he would find himself feeling bored and resentful and the relationship would turn sour and come to an end. At the time I first saw him, the patient had successfully completed medical school, had finished a year of internship, and was beginning his residency in internal medicine. Throughout his professional career, he had continued to work at a high level of competence and professional attainment.

The significant elements in the patient's history focus around two major sequences of events: the first, his childhood illnesses, the second, his father's death. In the second year of life, the patient had been treated for an infection by an antibiotic to which he developed a severe reaction, resulting in severe kidney damage and a persistent chronic glomerulonephritis. The illness was a cause for considerable anxiety in his early years, and the basis for frequent hospitalizations. The stigma of this disease process in young adulthood was a moderately elevated blood pressure, which was generally effectively treated with mild diuretics. During periods of stress, there was a tendency for the blood pressure to rise to significantly higher levels, occasioning significant anxiety and a series of panicky visits to his physician.

The second important event in the history was the death of the patient's father when the patient was ten. The father died suddenly of a massive heart attack, an event that marked a significant turning point in the patient's life, from which he never fully recovered. The mobilization of his capacity to mourn the death of his father adequately was an important aspect of the analytic work. But not only had he suffered a loss of his father, but the consequences of his father's sudden death reverberated throughout the rest of his family. Particularly important was the effect on his mother, who became severely depressed, was unable to mourn the loss of her husband effectively, and consequently became a complaining, demanding, bitter, resentful, and hostile woman. Even at the time of his beginning treatment, in his mid-twenties, the patient still carried on an unremitting, hostile war with the mother, marked by continual arguments, bitterness, recrimination, mutual accusations, and charges that each did not care about the other and were exclusively absorbed in their own needs and demands.

I would like to focus here, for purposes of diagnosis, on the narcissistic aspects of the patient's pathology. The narcissistic preoccupations were pervasive and permeated nearly all aspects of the patient's clinical material. Along with his predominantly depressive affect, there was a pervasive sense of narcissistic inferiority and vulnerability. He often felt inadequate and incompetent, unable to measure up to the expectations of those around him, particularly his superiors, as well as inadequate and unable to compete successfully with his fellow residents. His self-esteem was constantly in question and under stress, and was pervaded by a sense of worthlessness.

Along with these feelings of inadequacy and worthlessness, but emerging more slowly and in a relatively more masked fashion, there were sentiments of narcissistic superiority as well. From time to time, he would express sentiments of superiority, feeling that he was better than the people with whom he worked and against whom he found himself in competition. His thoughts of himself as a snob were related to his feelings about his own Jewishness and the connotations of superiority and specialness he attached to being a Jew. But he also felt the need to be perfect and above any question, criticism, or reproach for anything he turned his hand to. Since this perfectionistic goal constantly eluded him, he was left with a chronic sense of inadequacy and failure.

Along with these feelings, there was an underlying sense of his own specialness, which constantly led to repeated disappointments and resentment that others would not recognize this special quality in him. He wanted desperately and urgently to be number one, whether that meant being the number one son in his mother's eyes or number one with his father, with his girlfriends, or in his work or wherever he turned. Much of this material having to do with his specialness in the eyes of his parents was tied in with intense sibling rivalry with a much older brother who was an outstanding student, and with whom the patient constantly strove to find ways to compete successfully and to win out over him. With his mother, he constantly complained about her seemingly greater interest and involvement with his brother and his academic success and complained bitterly that she never complimented or praised him.

In his work situation, he was constantly plagued by the wish to outdo all the other residents in his training group, and whenever any other resident would stand out or receive some acknowledgment or praise, he would be consumed with envy and resentment. He was constantly making comparisons, seeking to find some way in which he could feel superior to the people around him, constantly criticizing and putting them down, and feeling cheated, deprived, and resentful whenever they seemed to beat him out.

There were also significant exhibitionistic themes, which expressed themselves in terms of his wishes to show everyone else up and his wanting to be admired for his superior intelligence, knowledge, and ability. The exhibitionism also found expression in frankly genital terms, in which he balanced his preoccupation and doubts about his own genital size and adequacy by wishes to show his penis, particularly to his girlfriends, and feeling pleased and elated when they would admire it.

Another important narcissistic motif that played itself out in this case was the patient's sense of himself as an "exception." Freud (1916) originally described the exceptions as claiming privileges over everyone else because they had endured some suffering or depriving experience early in their lives for which they felt guiltless and which allowed them to feel that they had been unjustly treated by fate. My patient regarded himself as an exception not only because of his childhood illnesses and the subsequent stigma of chronic kidney disease, but also because he had been deprived and cheated by fate when his father died at such an early age. His life had been radically changed by that event, and he saw himself as deprived of the resources that would have allowed him to grow to a mature and productive manhood. He would repeatedly and tearfully bemoan his fate, feeling very sorry for himself and seeing himself as a poor, helpless child, deprived of the chance for an effective and productive life, the victim of a sad fate.

There was also a deep and pervasive sense of entitlement, which expressed itself in terms of wanting to be loved for himself rather than for any accomplishment or action, but also feeling entitled to such acceptance, love, recognition, and admiration simply because he was who he was. He felt that no demands should be placed on him to perform or produce, that he should not have to work, that he should not be subjected to pressures and demands, but rather that he should receive the recognition, acceptance, and love he expected automatically, without having to earn it. The demands were at times peremptory and absolute. He wanted what he wanted, when he wanted it, and on his terms. The demands had an all-or-none quality: if they were not completely and instantaneously fulfilled, it was as though he had been completely denied and rebuffed.

Life became a series of unremitting demands placed upon him in the face of which he felt overwhelmed and burdened. Everywhere he turned, people made demands on him that he felt were unjust impositions on his time and energy, so that he felt drained, exhausted, and constantly burdened. He constantly was forced to meet demands from his patients, from the nursing staff, from his mother, from his wife, even from the analyst.

The narcissistic dimension also found its way into the transference. The primary expression there took the form of an idealization in which the patient saw me as a strong, steady, and magically powerful figure. He would constantly compare his own level of professional competence with mine. Issues of envy and competition were evident, along with the powerful wish to be like me, or at least to be like the idealized image he held of me. He basked in the reflected glory of this narcissistically enhanced and idealized image, and it fed into his powerful wishes to be the special patient, the favorite son of a powerful and idealized father. Such an analyst-father would possess unusual powers, an extraordinary degree of skill and competence, which would allow him to effect a magical cure. Such a cure, in the patient's fantasies, would be realized without any effort, involvement, pain, or anxiety on his part. He could play the part of the pleasing, accepting, conforming, favorite son; and I would deign to exercise my omnipotent power and relieve him of all his burdens.

While the patient saw me as big, powerful, important, and endowed with wizard-like and magical powers, the reciprocal aspect of this illusory vision was to portray himself in the relationship as small, powerless, helpless, dependent, insignificant, and worthless. Although the idealizing and self-devaluing configuration dominated the analytic transference, the reciprocal configuration also came into play. From time to time, the patient found himself defensively needing to devalue me, needing to see me in diminished terms as a vehicle for defending his own sense of threatened self-esteem. In short, both aspects of his narcissistic pathology, the superior, entitled, and special side of himself as well as the inferior, inadequate, and worthless side, came to play an important role in the transference.

It would be important to note in this case material that the patient was able to form an effective therapeutic alliance and to engage in the analytic relationship and in the work of the analysis quite consistently and effectively, that there was little or no suggestion of ego regression in the course of the analytic work, that he was able to form and maintain relatively stable narcissistic transference configurations, that developmentally he had been able to form and maintain a consistent and coherent sense of self, that there was no hint of fragmentation or loss of his sense of cohesive self anywhere in the history or the analytic work, and finally, that the focus of the narcissistic issues fell predominantly on issues of self-esteem and self-worth. Any one of these features might present quite differently if borderline psychopathology were in question. For these reasons, the patient could be judged to be a narcissistic personality, showing many features similar to the Nobel Prize complex described by Tartakoff, and in no sense could he be regarded as borderline.

At a somewhat more pathological level, the narcissistic need expresses itself not simply in terms of the drive to gain recognition and admiration, but also in the entitlement to use, manipulate, or exploit others for the purposes of self-enhancement or aggrandisement. Bursten (1973) described such personalities as "manipulative." His description of these personalities comes close to the description of psychopathic or antisocial personalities, and it is undeniable that the pathology may frequently take this form in a more or less flagrant degree. However, the antisocial or psychopathic quality of such personalities cuts across the discrimination we are attempting to make between narcissistic and borderline personalities.

Nonetheless, the contempt for others, the implicit devaluation of others as having potential value only in terms of their exploitability or manipulability in the service of self-enhancement, the high value often placed on putting something over on others or getting away with something, even though that involves suspect practices that may be deceptive or even dishonest, all carry the narcissistic stamp of this sort of personality and reflect the persistence of residues of the grandiose self. The exploitative form of narcissistic repair covers an underlying narcissistic vulnerability in which the self feels vulnerable to exploitation or manipulation by others and is constantly turning the tables, as it were. The inherent sense of shame, vulnerability, and worthlessness attached to this narcissistically vulnerable self-image is equivalently projected onto the victim of the subject's exploitation, so that the denial and reassurance that one's self is not really entrapped in this impoverished self-image is gained through the projection onto and subsequent exploitation of the victim. It should be noted that, in these circumstances, the victim is of vital importance to the subject as a means of maintaining the subject's narcissistic equilibrium, but that the victim is in no sense valued or idealized, but rather held in a devalued posture or even regarded with contempt. This contrasts with the more phallic form of narcissism described above, in which there is little pressure to seek favor or support from, or *a fortiori*, to manipulate or exploit, objects. Rather, their exceptional endowment and precocity has led them to expect success and admiration, so that the need to gain or extort such narcissistic feedback from others is less. Their dependence is focused on evidence for such success and the related narcissistic gratification, with a related impairment in the capacity for meaningful love relationships.

The sense of self in more exploitative patients is relatively well established and subject to little regression, as long as the resources for continuing narcissistic repair are available. These patients maintain a sense of separateness in their relations with others and have considerable difficulty in developing meaningful or mutually gratifying relationships, since the premise of any meaningful relationship rests on the underlying narcissism, which requires that the other be put in the service of the self. When the means of narcissistic repair fail or become unavailable, such patients generally fall prey to depression. Depending on the severity of the pathology, the depression can be quite severe and even suicidal. Something similar can be seen even more dramatically in the effects of inpatient confinement and restricted mobility on criminal psychopaths (Vaillant, 1975). When such patients are confined, and control is established over their behavior so that flight is impossible and they are relatively immobilized, the underlying depression becomes much more clinically apparent. Such psychopathic personalities are more primitive than exploitative narcissistic personalities and would fall within the borderline spectrum.

At even more pathological levels, however, the narcissism becomes even more needy, clinging, and demanding. There is a heightened need to be given to, supported, and taken care of that reflects a sense of peremptory and uncompromising entitlement. The neediness for such input from others may be so profound as to take on a symbiotic quality so that these individuals often become involved in intensely dependent and needy involvements with the significant others in their lives. Frequently such involvements have a highly ambivalent, hostile-dependent quality, since the object is never quite capable of satisfying the patient's narcissistic demand and expectation. Consequently, such individuals are constantly exposed to the threat of disappointment and frustration, feeling deprived and often desperate. In such states they can become sullen and pouting, even whining and complaining, in their attempts to wheedle the necessary response from the important other.

As with all narcissistic personalities, there is in these individuals as well, a capacity for charm, the ability to entertain, flatter, and influence others. But the quality of this activity is quite different from that in the phallic narcissist for whom the objective is gaining admiration, or from the more exploitative narcissistic personality for whom the objective is putting the other in the service of his own narcissistic objectives. In these more severely disturbed narcissistic patients, the objectives are much more in the line of drawing others into the position of giving, supporting, taking care of, or otherwise filling up the intense neediness and deprived emptiness that characterize the narcissistic vulnerability of these patients. Consequently, the quality of behavior in such individuals is intensely oral and has been aptly characterized by Bursten (1973) as "craving."

At all levels of narcissistic pathology there are degrees of both narcissistic vulnerability and grandiosity. It should be noted that these qualities are inherently linked and are never found in isolation. Frequently one or the other dimension may be found as a more explicit or conscious manifestation of the narcissistic aspects of a given personality, but even in such cases, the correlative aspect of the narcissistic pathology can also be found on further clinical investigation. Thus, the phallic or exploitative narcissistic character who displays his vanity and grandiosity in a variety of more or less public ways can be found to carry a concealed core of narcissistic vulnerability and feelings of inferiority, shame, weakness, and susceptibility. Similarly, the clinging, dependent, needy, and demanding type of more primitive narcissistic character will be found, on closer evaluation and more extensive investigation, to be concealing a core of grandiosity that underlies the infantile expectations and extreme sense of entitlement that makes them feel that they have a right to demand concern, care, and attention from others often to the point of considerable self-sacrifice and disadvantage or detriment to the other. This same grandiosity also expresses itself in the sulking, pouting, whining, and demanding quality of the efforts to gain narcissistic supplies.

There is often an implicit supposition that others owe it to the subject to make up for the deprivation and deficits the subject feels he has suffered at the hands of depriving others, which he feels are owed to him. The obligation falls upon others, therefore, to make up this deficit and to exercise themselves to undo the wrongs that have been done to the subject rather than on the subject to take upon himself the responsibility for dealing with his own difficulties. This goes along with a general blaming tendency in such individuals, which tends to lay the responsibility for the individual's difficulties at someone else's door—frequently, parents or other caretakers, but not infrequently other family members, friends, employers, coworkers, etc. This tendency, in its more extreme forms, may take a paranoid expression. As we have noted elsewhere (Meissner, 1977b, 1978b), such narcissistic pathology forms a substantial part of the core of paranoia.

Actually Kernberg's (1967) early description of narcissistic characters is quite apt and it may be useful at this point. He writes:

> These patients present an unusual degree of self-reference in their interactions with other people, a great need to be loved and admired by others, and a curious apparent contradiction between a very inflated concept of themselves and an inordinate need for tribute from others. Their emotional life is shallow. They experience little empathy for the feelings of others, they obtain very little enjoyment from life other than from the tributes they receive from others or

from their own grandiose fantasies, and they feel restless and bored when external glitter wears off and no new sources feed their self-regard. They envy others, tend to idealize some people from whom they expect narcissistic supplies, and to depreciate and treat with contempt those from whom they do not expect anything (often their former idols). In general, their relationships with other people are clearly exploitative and sometimes parasitic. It is as if they feel they have the right to control and possess others and to exploit them without guilt feelings—and behind a surface which very often is charming and engaging, one senses coldness and ruthlessness. Very often such patients are considered to be "dependent" because they need so much tribute and adoration from others, but on a deeper level they are completely unable to really depend on anybody because of their deep distrust and depreciation of others. (p. 655)

It is easy to see that it is but a short step from this description to the borderline characteristics that Kernberg has described so well. In fact, he does take this step, consistent with the inclusive methodology he uses in defining the borderline syndrome.

The primary and most discriminating locus of narcissistic pathology is in the patient's object-relationships. Here, the need to be loved and the investment in and use of objects as a means of redressing and maintaining narcissistic equilibrium are the predominant aspects. Over one-quarter of a century ago, Reich (1953) described some varieties of narcissistic object choice in women, which she ascribed to a repressive resolution of the oedipal-castration trauma by regression to a pregenital level of narcissistic passivity and demandingness. In these women, the feelings of shame and inferiority were resolved by a narcissistic object choice that was seen as undoing the trauma of castration and re-establishing the narcissistic balance.

She described two predominant patterns, one in which a dependent and subservient attachment was established with one man who became the admired and indispensable idealized object; a second pattern was characterized by brief, intense infatuations, in which there was an admiring idealization accompanied by a transient imitative mirroring of the man's characteristics. These idealizing infatuations would quickly burn out and turn to devaluing rejection, which then would lead to a recreation of the cycle with another object. Reich drew a comparison of this type of object choice with Deutsch's (1942) "as-if" personality. To this latter type of narcissistic object involvement can be added the more or less exploitative use of objects for sexual and narcissistic gratification, which runs into deeper and more troublesome narcissistic threats when faced with the prospect of more long-lasting involvement and commitment. For such women, the prospect of giving or sharing in an enduring relationship is seen as a narcissistic loss rather than a gain.

These early characterizations are quite consistent with Kohut's (1971) formulations. Kohut has emphasized, as the predominant characteristic of narcissistic personalities, the formation of cohesive narcissistic configurations around which personality organization takes shape. These configurations, on the objective side, involve the idealized parent imago, on the subjective side, the grandiose self. These relatively stable configurations are cathected with narcissistic libido, either idealizing or grandiose-exhibitionistic, and manifest themselves in various forms of object-relations and in analytic transferences.

The therapeutic activation of the omnipotent and idealized object leads to the formation of an idealizing transference in which residues of the lost infantile experience of narcissistic perfection are restored by assigning it to a transitional self-object, the idealized parent imago. Thus, all power and strength are attributed to this idealized object, so that the subject feels empty and powerless when separated from it. Consequently, he must bend every effort to maintain contact and union with this object. Thus, the continuing contact and union with an idealized self-object seems to characterize one of Reich's (1953) forms quite adequately. The second form, however, is unable to sustain a consistent object-attachment and vacillates quickly between narcissistic configurations, between infatuation and contempt, idealization and devaluation. This instability and the defects of object constancy give rise to an "as-if" quality and suggest that such narcissistic attachments are essentially borderline.

Such idealizing transferences can reactivate archaic narcissistic states that stem from one or other multiple levels of development. This may include primitive mergings of the self with an idealized maternal imago or may reflect later developmental traumata, which produce specific narcissistic fixations. Such traumata or narcissistic disappointments may create impediments in the development of the child's idealization or may contaminate or undo insecurely established idealizations, which may interfere with the idealizations of objects. This may result, by failure of internalizations, in insufficient idealization of the superego and secondary structural deficits resulting from fixations on the narcissistic aspects of preoedipal and oedipal objects. Kohut (1971) notes:

> Persons who have suffered such traumas are (as adolescents and adults) forever attempting to achieve a union with the idealized object since, in view of their specific structural defect (the insufficient idealization of their superego), their narcissistic equilibrium is safeguarded only through the interest, the responses, and the approval of present-day (i.e. currently active) replicas of the traumatically lost self-object. (p. 55)

These varieties of pathogenic narcissistic fixation give rise to differentiable transferences. Certain varieties of idealizing transference reflect the disturbances of later stages of the development of the idealized parent imago, particularly at the time of introjection of the idealized object in the formation of the ego ideal. More archaic forms of narcissistic idealization may reflect themselves in the expression of global mystical or even religious concerns associated with awe-inspiring qualities that do not seem to emanate from a clearly delimited, single admired figure. Although such primitive idealizing elements tend to be more diffuse and vague, particularly when merged with elements of the grandiose self, the special bond and the idealizing attachment to the analyst is never in doubt. In such cases, the restored narcissistic equilibrium is experienced as a sense of omnipotence and omniscience along with feelings of esthetic and moral perfection. These feelings are maintained as long as the patient can feel that he is united and sustained by the idealized analyst. Along with this, there is a diminution of the symptomatology due to the narcissistic imbalance, particularly affecting the diffused depression, disturbed work capacity, irritability, feelings of shame or inferiority, hypochondriacal preoccupations, etc. The establishment of union with the idealized object also minimizes the threat of further narcissistic regression, perhaps to even more archaic precursors of the idealized parent imago (Kohut, 1971). The narcissistic dynamics in the Wolf-Man's case seem to have followed such a pattern (Meissner, 1977b).

In some individuals, the narcissistic fixation leads to the development of the grandiose self. The reactivation in analysis of the grandiose self provides the basis for the formation of mirror transferences. Kohut (1971) has described three forms of these:

> The cohesive therapeutic reactivation of the grandiose self in analysis occurs in three forms; these relate to specific stages of development of this psychological structure to which pathognomonic therapeutic regression has led: (1) the archaic *merger through the extension of the grandiose self*; (2) a less archaic form which will be called *alter-ego transference* or *twinship*; and (3) a still less archaic form which will be referred to as *mirror transference* in the narrower sense. (p. 114)

In the most primitive merger form of mirror transference, the analyst is experienced only as an extension of the subject's grandiose self. Consequently, he becomes the repository of the grandiosity and exhibitionism of the patient's grandiose self. Kohut uses such terms as merger or symbiosis to describe this extension, but reminds us that what is at issue here is not merger with an idealized object, but rather that the merger is achieved by a regressive diffusion of the borders of the self to embrace the analyst, who is then experienced as united to the grandiose self. The analogy to the adult experience of cathexis of one's own body or mind reflects the kind of unquestioned control or dominance that the grandiose self expects to exert over the invested object. The analyst may find himself forced to resist the oppressive tyranny with which the patient seeks to control him (Kohut, 1971). The quality of this merging and extension of the grandiose self seems to eliminate the object as such and to make it simply a reflection of the self.

Consequently, merging of this nature must be regarded as severely regressive and comes closer to the modalities of incorporation that I have described elsewhere (Meissner, 1971, 1979). To this extent they may be regarded as psychotic in character, or at least regressively borderline.

At a somewhat less primitive level of organization, the activation of the grandiose self leads to the narcissistic object being experienced as similar to and, to that extent, a reflection of the grandiose self. In this variant, the object as such is preserved, but is modified by the subject's perception of it to suit the subject's narcissistic needs. This form of transference is referred to as alter-ego or twinship transference. Clinically, dreams or fantasies referring to such an alter-ego or twinship relationship with the analyst may be explicit. As Kohut (1971) notes:

> The pathognomonic therapeutic regression is characterized by the fact that the patient assumes that the analyst is either like him or similar to him, or that the analyst's psychological makeup is like, or is similar to that of the patient. (p. 115)

In this type of transference then, the reality of the analyst is preserved, but it is modified after the fashion of a transitional object by a projection of some aspects of the patient's grandiose self onto the analyst.

In the most mature and most developed form of the mirror transference, the analyst is experienced as a separate person, but nonetheless one who becomes important to the patient and is accepted by him only to the degree that he is responsive to the narcissistic needs of the reactivated grandiose self. Kohut appeals here to the model of the gleam in the mother's eye, which responds to and mirrors the child's exhibitionism. In this way the mother participates in and reinforces the child's narcissistic pleasure in himself. Thus, in this strictest sense of the mirror transference, the analyst's function becomes one of admiring and reflecting the grandiosity and exhibitionism of the patient. This need on the part of the patient may also take a more subtle form in which the patient seeks such admiration and confirmation from the analyst, but constantly acts in such a way that reflects the fear of not getting it. Consequently, the patient becomes extremely resistant out of a continuing fear that the revelation of less than ideal impulses, fantasies, or wishes may deprive him of the analyst's admiring eye. For such patients, the grandiose self is not so much confirmed as maintained intact behind a highly defensive facade. The analyst runs the risk, in such cases, of becoming a threat to the vulnerability of the grandiose self and may even be seen in persecutory or paranoid forms of transferential distortion.

There is an assumption in the Kohut argument that where the "archaic" narcissistic configurations or their transferential expressions are identifiable, one is dealing, by definition, with narcissistic personality disorders as such. This may be one source of diagnostic confusion, since both narcissistic configurations can be found expressed in varying degrees and modalities, not only in the lower levels of pathological organization, even the psychotic, but also at higher levels of organization, in relatively well-organized, more or less neurotic personalities. Such an assumption would presume that wherever the idealized imago or grandiose self are identifiable, one is dealing with a narcissistic personality. It seems more reasonable, from the perspective taken in this study, to view the formulations Kohut has provided as fundamental forms of pathological narcissistic organization that can be found expressed at many different levels of pathology and character structure. Consequently, one can view the narcissistic personality as having one or other or both of these configurations as a predominant part of the personality structure, but the diagnostic formulation does not simply rest on the identification of these configurations. It must include other factors as well.

One of the primary aspects of narcissistic personality organization and a significant dimension of its diagnosis is the element of self-cohesion. Kohut has emphasized that these patients have developmentally attained the stage of cohesive self-organization and that it is by reason of the attainment of such stable and cohesive psychic organization that these patients can establish stable narcissistic transferences. Moreover, Ornstein (1974) has emphasized that the establishment and maintenance of a cohesive self is a *sine qua non* for psychoanalysis and lays the ground of possibility for the formation of narcissistic transferences. Bursten (1978) marks this relatively greater degree of self-cohesion as a central characteristic of the narcissistic personality organization. He writes:

> People with narcissistic personality types have a firmer sense of self. Generally, they confirm their sense of self more easily. Kohut (1971) indicates that they have a more cohesive self and are less vulnerable to fragmentation. However, the confirmers utilized in the maintenance of this cohesive sense of self give them their typical narcissistic stamp; they are self-oriented. Self-esteem and the use of omnipotent others to bolster themselves are characteristic. (p. 18)

Not only has Kohut (1971) emphasized this cohesiveness of the structure and functioning of the self in such narcissistic personalities, he has also emphasized this as a discriminating factor from primitive borderline or psychotic forms of organization. He comments:

> Disturbing as their psychopathology may be, it is important to realize that these patients have specific assets which differentiate them from the psychoses and borderline states. Unlike the patients who suffer from these latter disorders, patients with narcissistic personality disturbances have in essence attained a cohesive self and have constructed cohesive idealized archaic objects. And, unlike the conditions which prevail in the psychoses and borderline states, these patients are not seriously threatened by the possibility of an irreversible disintegration of the archaic self or of the narcissistically cathected archaic objects. In consequence of the attainment of these cohesive and stable psychic configura-

tions, these patients are able to establish specific, stable narcissistic transferences, which allow the therapeutic reactivation of the archaic structures without the danger of their fragmentation through further regression: they are thus analyzable. (p. 4)

DISCRIMINATIVE ASPECTS
OF THE BORDERLINE CONDITIONS

I would like to turn at this point to those aspects of borderline conditions that may serve as potential points of differentiation from the narcissistic personality disorders as delineated above. An important point to note in the context of an attempt to more carefully delineate these syndromes is that the extant descriptions of the borderline conditions, dominated of course by Kernberg's (1967) delineation of the borderline personality organization, embrace a fairly wide spectrum of pathological conditions and forms of characterological deficit. Certain aspects of the description of borderline disorders apply to some borderline patients and not to others, whereas other aspects of the description apply to a different subgrouping and not to others.

One would have to conclude that the borderline conditions constitute a heterogeneous group of diagnostic entities within which further diagnostic specification and refinement are required in order to make sense out of the total clinical picture. The diagnostic reach of such borderline conditions stretches all the way from the schizophrenia-like conditions described as "pseudoneurotic schizophrenia" (Hoch and Cattell, 1959; Hoch and Polatin, 1949; Hoch et al., 1962) to the forms of borderline personality that seem to present a relatively well-organized and well-functioning neurotic facade, and only under conditions of regressive inducement, such as the analytic situation, do the underlying borderline features begin to be manifested. There is a radical clinical distinction between such patients whose borderline features are activated only under conditions of regressive inducement, and then only gradually and in relatively minor degree, and those patients who come to clinical attention under conditions of acute regressive crisis usually requiring hospitalization. I would maintain that there is a real clinical and diagnostic differentiation to be made between these groups of patients and that the quality of transient regressive psychotic-like states and the marked borderline propensity for acting-out, often in self-destructive ways, are characteristic of the lower-order borderline pathologies, such as the psychotic characters and the pseudoschizophrenias. A fairly large proportion of borderline patients, however, have much better organized and better functioning personality structure and may show little or none of the regressive qualities that have become classically attributed to borderline personality structure. If such patients show any indications of such propensities, it is often in very subtle or minor degrees, or they may become more apparent in periods of transient regressive stress.

In attempting to distinguish between the narcissistic personalities and the borderline conditions, Kohut (1971, 1972) has emphasized the relatively greater propensity for regression and regressive disorganization in borderline personalities as compared to the narcissistic. That discriminating point retains its validity in reference to forms of borderline personality in which such regressive potential is a marked feature, but it is of considerably less use in distinguishing between, let us say, the analyzable borderline and the analyzable narcissistic personality.

Other points of discrimination relative to regression may have some validity. Adler (1975) has noted that borderline patients are more likely to regress from a variant of narcissistic transference to a hungry, demanding, clinging stage when the narcissistic longings or needs are not met. Additional hints may be taken from the quality of anxiety in such regressive states, remembering that severe or structural regressions are much less likely to be seen in narcissistic than in borderline patients. The narcissistic emphasis falls much more heavily on the maintenance of narcissistic equilibrium, and it reveals the loss of such equilibrium in the typical narcissistic signal affects of shame and depression. Anxiety is much less likely to appear in such personalities. Anxiety is much more available to the borderline, however, and it frequently has a dramatic life or death quality connected with separation or even survival anxiety (Corwin, 1974). For diagnostic purposes, when such severe separation or survival anxiety related to the fear of inner fragmentation or dissolution of the self are found in patients whose transferences have a markedly narcissistic quality, these patients must be regarded as falling within the borderline range.

The quality of regressive borderline involvement with objects, that is, the more or less chronically regressed quality of object-relationships in lower-order borderlines and the quality of object-relationships in higher-order borderlines in transient regressive states, has been often and well described (Kernberg, 1967; Masterson, 1972; Blum, 1972; Adler, 1974; Corwin, 1974). Kernberg (1974) has particularly emphasized, in the therapeutic context, the expressions of ego weakness, the proneness to transference psychosis, and the repetitive and chronic activation of intense rage reactions with a quality of ruthless demandingness or depreciating attacks on the therapist in borderline patients. These reflect the alternate activation, in Kernberg's terms, of all-good or all-bad internalized object-relations in the transference, the increase of pathogenic splitting reflected in mutually dissociative ego states (such as haughty grandiosity coexisting with feelings of inferiority), the forms of pathological idealization and omnipotent control alternating with narcissistic withdrawal and devaluation. Along with the pathological influence of pregenital and oral aggression, these seem to be quite characteristic of such regressive borderline states.

Kernberg regards personalities on this level as forms of narcissistic personality that function on a borderline level, so that the category of narcissistic personality is used by him inclusively, as opposed to Kohut's exclusive usage which opposes narcissistic personalities to borderline and psychotic categories. Kernberg (1974), however, also recognizes that the presence of a coherent narcissistic configuration characterizes the narcissistic personality in opposition to the borderline. This can give rise to differences in patterns of primitive idealization. The pattern of intense attachment with forms of primitive idealization, found most frequently in women with infantile or borderline personalities who cling desperately and unrealistically to idealized men, may form nonetheless a more enduring pattern than the transitory involvements of narcissistic personalities. The primitive idealization in such borderline patients of the all-good object acts as a defense against the projection of aggression onto the all-bad object and, in Kernberg's view, may even have positive implications as a first step in the direction of establishing a love relationship different from the intolerably ambivalent love-hate relationship to the primary objects. In such patients, when the splitting is modified, the relationship with the love object may be able to begin to tolerate and resolve the primitive pregenital conflicts against which the idealization provides a defense (Kernberg, 1974).

On the other hand, the regressive activation of the grandiose self may serve as the basis for a narcissistic withdrawal and isolation, which gives rise to a schizoid picture. The role of such schizoid withdrawal as a defense against affects, and particularly as a defense against affective involvement with the analyst and the narcissistic quality of the illusion of self-sufficiency that accompanies it, has been clearly delineated by Modell (1973, 1975).

Although the organization of defenses and the patterns of functioning in such patients can be recognized as specifically narcissistic, we are suggesting here that this recognition may not be an adequate basis for diagnostic discrimination. Rather than simply extending the narcissistic categories to more primitive levels, it may be more useful in the long run to regard these more primitive forms as variants of the borderline syndrome, regarding the variants of schizoid psychopathology as one subsection of borderline pathology (Meissner, 1978a). As Kohut (1971) notes:

> The first modification of the dynamic consequences of a specific weakness in the basic narcissistic configurations of the personality concerns a particular mode of defense against the dangerous regressive potential that is associated with the central defect, a defense which usually results in what is referred to as the *schizoid personality*. This defensive organization (which should be included among the borderline states) is characteristically encountered in personalities

whose basic pathological propensity is toward the development of psychosis; it is, however, not encountered in patients with analyzable narcissistic personality disturbances. The schizoid defensive organization is the result of a person's (pre)conscious awareness not only of his narcissistic vulnerability, but also, and specifically, of the danger that a narcissistic injury could initiate an uncontrollable regression which would pull him irreversibly beyond the stage of the nuclear, cohesive, narcissistic configurations. (p. 12)

Horner (1975) has noted the oscillatory patterns of object-relations in borderline patients. She notes, for example, the double approach-avoidance conflict involving, on the one hand, object loss as the consequence of continuing separation and individuation, and on the other hand, the danger of the loss of self connected with regressive attempts at restitution of the union with the symbiotic object through merger. Driven by separation anxiety and depression, on the one hand, and the fear of loss of self, on the other, the borderline patient is seen as chronically oscillating between two object-relational positions without being able to gain any stabilization at either position. Similarly, she sees the borderline patient as alternating between the position of the narcissistic personality, in which the object is seen as existing for or to meet the demands of the self, and the schizoid position, in which the individual flees from any sense of attachment or dependence on the object.

The description of such oscillatory patterns is reminiscent of Kernberg's emphasis on splitting and the maintenance of alternating or often coexistent, yet contradictory ego states. Although such patterns are frequently identifiable in the more labile and more primitively organized borderlines, at the lower range of the borderline conditions, they are not at all characteristic of higher-order borderline personality configurations. Such patterns may also be seen in higher-order borderline personalities under conditions of transient regressive disorganization. But they are by no means characteristic, nor do they present a predominant or often even identifiable aspect of the day-by-day functioning of such personalities.

The alternation of omnipotence and devaluation frequently seen in such borderline states is a case in point (Kernberg, 1968). Such highly narcissistic extremes serve as a defense against threatening needs and narcissistic vulnerabilities connected with the involvement with others. As Kernberg notes:

Such "self-idealization" usually implies magical fantasies of omnipotence, the conviction that he, the patient, will eventually receive all the gratification that he is entitled to, and that he cannot be touched by frustration, illness, death, or the passage of time. A corollary of this fantasy is the devaluation of other people, the patient's conviction of his superiority over them, including the therapist. The projection of that magical omnipotence onto the therapist, and the patient's feeling magically united with or submissive to that omnipotent therapist, are other forms which this defensive operation can take. (p. 615)

It is quite correct clinically that the more one finds the pattern of such alternation or oscillation present in a patient, the more likely it is that the underlying personality organization is borderline. In the more primitively organized borderline, this may become quite readily apparent insofar as the contradictory ego states and their corresponding transferential paradigms may be quickly mobilized and projected onto the analyst. In the more highly organized borderline patients, however, such oscillatory patterns are by no means immediately evident and may only begin to express themselves after quite long periods of analytic experience and after some significant effects of the analytic regression have taken place. It is only then that the underlying borderline features become apparent, whereas initially such patients may present looking very neurotic or, at times, even normal. At that unregressed level of functioning, one of these polar positions is usually more or less stabilized, while the other is repressed. In contrast, in the narcissistic personality, one is much more likely to find a consistent and coherent, although narcissistically impregnated and vulnerable configuration, around which the patient's personality is organized and functions.

At this juncture, I would like to introduce material from a case that I would regard as falling within the borderline spectrum and as qualifying as analyzable. In discussing this case, I would like to compare it with the previous case of the more clear-cut narcissistic personality already described (pp. 202–208).

The patient, a young man who had just turned thirty, came with the complaint that his life was stagnating and seemed to be going nowhere for reasons that he was unable to discern. He had obtained a degree in architecture from a rather prestigious school, but did not seem to be effectively advancing his career in any sense. He had been able to get jobs with prestigious firms, but had squandered the opportunity, coming late for work, spending hours in his office staring out of the window or reading the newspaper, rather than working on the projects assigned to him, and generally wasting time in either making no effort or in quite unproductive effort. Under these circumstances, it was not long before he was informed by his employers that his services were no longer required.

The last such firing took place while the patient was still in analysis, and he subsequently spent the succeeding year doing little or nothing, spending long hours fiddling away time in his apartment, dreaming of projects that he would undertake, but actually doing nothing. He would spend most of the morning browsing through the newspaper, and spent most of the rest of the day wandering around aimlessly and nonproductively. He continued to pay for his analysis through his savings. When these savings began to run out, he started looking for work again and was able to land another job with a somewhat less distinguished firm than the one he had previously been with. Partly as a result of the work in the analysis, he was able to engage in this job more effectively and kept it for a significantly longer period of time.

Not only was there stagnation on the career front, but he also found himself unable to engage in any meaningful or enduring relationship with a woman. He was afraid of committing himself to any single woman, since this meant he would have to give up the opportunity to be involved with all the other women who crossed his path. Each relationship that he developed with a woman proved to be less than satisfactory even before it had gotten off the ground. They were not beautiful enough, not intelligent enough, not entertaining enough—and worst of all, they might have had sexual relations with another man. And beyond the horizon loomed all the constraints, responsibilities, and burdens of marriage, family, and children. He saw all this in exclusively negative terms.

The patient's other major complaint was of an inability to urinate in public bathrooms. He would only feel comfortable and be able to urinate successfully in the privacy and security of his own bathroom. Whenever he was in any public place and found himself having to urinate, he would go to the men's room but would stand ineffectually at the urinal, unable to pass water. He had a similar problem with defecating in any public toilet, constantly afraid that someone would come into the bathroom and would see his feet under the stall door. He imagined that people would be attentively listening to the sounds he made or the smell that came from his feces.

Similar concerns would even invade the privacy of his own bathroom. At times when he would have friends or relatives visiting in his apartment, he would be fearful of urinating within earshot, again feeling that they would be listening to the sounds he made or the smells that might come from the bathroom. He was never able to explain the basis for his conviction that people would be so fixated on his bodily productions, nor was he able to define, in any way, what their reactions or thoughts about it might have been, what they might have thought of him as a consequence, or what the implications of such hyperinterest on their part might be. His preoccupation was carried to such an extent, however, that, if people would stay with him in his apartment for several days, he would only enter the bathroom to urinate surreptitiously when he was sure that they were not within earshot, and would refrain from defecating for periods of several days as long as they were around.

These urinary and anal preoccupations were connected with a variety of phobias that included the fear of heights; the fear of crowded places; and even a touch of agoraphobia, which took the form of panicked feelings that he could lose control of himself and, like an epileptic or someone having a stroke, fall on the sidewalk and lose control of his bodily functions, and thus, urinate or defecate. These fears were associated with severe anxieties about loss of control and an overwhelming feeling of shame.

These symptoms, needless to say, had a severely inhibiting and paralyzing effect on his life. Because of his inability to urinate or defecate outside his own home, the range of his social activities was severely limited. He could not go out to a bar with his friends of an evening drinking, because inevitably he would have to urinate and be confronted with his difficulty. By the same token, other fears, particularly of being in crowded public places, limited the capacity to join his friends in dining, concert-going, or any other public activity.

The patient was brought up as the oldest son of a rather large Catholic family. He had one older sister and several younger siblings. His relationship to his mother was affectionate and supportive, although she instilled in him a strong sense of Catholic morality and virtue. His relationship with his father was, on the contrary, distant and fearful. He found any communication with his father to be difficult and troubled. His father always seemed distant and unavailable, and my patient never felt that he could measure up to his father's expectations of him or that he could, in any way, equal the father's standard of achievement.

Like the previous narcissistic patient, this patient's father also died suddenly of a heart attack when the patient was fifteen years old. Much of the analytic material was marked by a sense of frustrated longing for closeness and acceptance from this unavailable and disapproving father, and was taken up with the mourning of the loss of the father—something that the patient had never been able to accomplish. Even so, there was a strong sense of identification with the father that expressed itself in incidental ways. The father had been a successful architect, and my patient, denying that he had ever wanted to follow in his father's footsteps, claimed that he had decided to go to architectural school "because there didn't seem to be anything else to do."

My patient seemed to have had a more or less normal upbringing, but described himself, even in his latent years, as a somewhat shy and socially awkward lad, who was an extremely talented student and modestly successful in athletic endeavors, but who had a constant sense of embarrassment and self-consciousness, particularly when any attention was called to him on account of his accomplishments. Despite his successful school record, he constantly felt that he could not understand things and that other people must understand them better than he did. He could never understand why it was that he got better marks than they did. This was true even in his graduate work, where he constantly had the feeling that he had not been able to master the rudimentary principles, so that when more advanced applications were in question he would be swimming in uncertainty and doubt. Even in his later work as a functioning architect, he would never feel sure of himself, would be constantly plagued by feelings of uncertainty about his ideas or his approaches to problems, and seemed constantly to look to his older colleagues for direction and guidance, never feeling that he could follow through on his own ideas unless someone he felt knew more or had better judgment approved them.

The difficulties in urinating linked up with a general sense of genital inadequacy. He experienced considerable difficulty in meeting young women and in engaging them in any but the most superficial conversation. When he found himself involved with any young woman, things went reasonably well until the relationship began to deepen and the prospect of a sexual encounter began to present itself. At that point, he would typically become increasingly anxious, increasingly diffident about the relationship, and would find ways to frustrate or interrupt it. When he finally got to the point of being able to tolerate a more intimate and sexual relationship with one of his girlfriends, the sexual activity itself became a source of considerable concern and anxiety. At times, he would be impotent; at other times, he would be able to gain an erection of some degree, but was convinced that his penis was too soft or too short to allow for effective penetration. He developed a conviction that his penis was bent in some abnormal manner that would not permit effective penetration and would prevent his partner from experiencing orgasm. Only after some time in analysis was he able to uncover fantasies of castration, of having his penis bitten off in the woman's vagina as part of his castration fears. It became clear that any assertion, any aggressiveness, any phallic striving or success carried with it in his mind the threat of oedipal retaliation, castration, and inevitable defeat.

The narcissistic problems loomed largely in the patient's psychopathology. The patient was convinced that it was his destiny to do some great or noble work, to achieve some important and memorable goal. He was never sure what form this great accomplishment might take—whether it would be to build an architectural masterpiece or to become a saintly hero or to write an important, famous literary work. Anything less than this level of accomplishment seemed trivial and unimportant in his eyes. The jobs he obtained and the projects he worked on in no way seemed to give promise of the kind of greatness and importance he ambitioned. When he went to work, nothing seemed to catch his imagination or to elicit his interest. It all seemed trivial and boring. It was only by dint of the greatest effort and self-discipline that he could force himself to do any work at all.

When he was finally fired, the patient retreated to his apartment with a sigh of relief to spend endless hours in dreaming dreams of glory. He would think of projects to keep his mind busy or to improve himself, but they would come to naught. He thought he should brush up on calculus, and would open the books on the desk before him, only to spend the next hour or two staring out the window. When he thought about taking a job and going back to work, he could not envision himself accepting any kind of work that he felt to be beneath his standards, or in any sense demeaning. If the prospect of work did not open before him the opportunity for the stimulus, challenge, and performance of great deeds, he was simply not interested.

Although these narcissistic embroilments seemed to paralyze him, the situation was more complex. It was as though the patient resisted and shied away from every avenue that opened itself before him and invited him to plunge into the ongoing stream of life. But the invitation was not one that he found gratifying or stimulating. Rather, engagement in life meant for him that he would have to accept the limitations and constraints of reality, that he would have to undergo change, and that he would put his feet on the path leading inexorably toward death. His father, an energetic and enterprising man, had been extremely successful in setting up his own architectural firm and in making a significant mark on the world. But his father had died in his mid-fifties of a massive coronary. The patient's underlying identification with the father dictated that he, too, ran the risk of following the same course, that if he were to engage himself with energy and commitment to any course of career development or life progression, it meant that he was following the same path that his father had trod—a path that led inexorably to death.

It is interesting to compare the position of this patient with the previous, more purely narcissistic patient previously described (pp. 202–208). Although narcissistic issues play a predominant role in the pathology of both cases, in the previous patient the symptomatic expression was limited more or less to the patient's depression. He complained bitterly about the burdens placed on him by the demands of others, but he was nonetheless able to maintain a vigorous and demanding work schedule and to move forward in the pursuit of career goals. In the present patient, however, the symptoms took the form of multiple phobias that proved to be severely limiting and incapacitating to the patient's social and effective work involvement.

The fear generated by the underlying introjection of the father as victim was operating in both cases, but in the narcissistic patient the aggressive derivatives were sufficiently modulated to allow him to continue along a career path toward some meaningful goals and fulfillment. He was afraid that because of his illness and the pressure of demands put on him that he would meet the same fate as his father. But the fear did not prevent him from continuing along that path. In the present patient, however, the fear comes closer to a delusional conviction that he was somehow doomed to the same fate as the father. The fear becomes paralyzing, is displaced into a variety of phobic expressions, and prevents the patient from effectively committing himself to any life-course, to any career pattern, or even to a meaningful heterosexual relationship that would hold out the prospect of marriage and family.

This reflects the disturbance in the sense of self that is operative in the borderline case, but that plays an insignificant part in the narcissistic personality. The narcissistic physician is entangled in issues of entitlement and self-esteem; the more borderline architect is dealing with an underlying disturbance in his sense of self that impedes and distorts his sense of identity.

He is unable to complete the developmental work that would allow him to establish himself in some meaningful and definitive way as an adult, engaged in and committed to certain role tasks and functions that would define him in terms of adult capacities and functions. The realization of an adult identity is staved off and frustrated, and in its place the patient clings to adolescent dreams of glory, being unwilling to surrender any of the highly narcissistically invested potentialities that might give meaning and sustenance to the residues of the grandiose self for the dull constraints and limitations of a real identity and a real adult status.

It is also interesting to compare these patients in terms of their capacity to engage in the analytic situation and the analytic work. As I have already noted, the narcissistic patient was able to form a reasonably stable and effective therapeutic alliance and a relatively stable idealizing transference. For the present patient, however, engagement in the analytic situation was considerably more problematic. He found it extremely difficult to engage in the analytic relationship because of a powerful negative distortion based on elements of a negative father transference.

The patient felt that he could not trust me and held me in constant suspicion, questioning my motives and intentions. He found himself on the couch being unable and unwilling to speak for long periods of time. He felt resistant and hostile, unwilling to communicate anything to me, and unwilling to give me the satisfaction of knowing that my interpretations were in any way meaningful or correct. At times, he would find himself spending long periods of time in total silence, feeling that there was nothing for him to say, or at least nothing worthwhile. At other times he would find himself experiencing a stubborn, unyielding silence, which he was more readily able to connect with his difficulties in communicating with his father. Along with these stubborn silences, he was frequently late and frequently missed appointments. It was clear that the patient was terrified of the analytic relationship and insecure, fearful, and hostile in his relationship to me and that the analytic involvement mobilized all his fears of fragility and vulnerability that underlay so much of his symptomatology and pathological character traits.

The therapeutic alliance, in this case, was hardly satisfactory, but rather was more of a misalliance. It was highly impregnated with narcissistic elements in the form of magical expectations that somehow the analytic process would allow him to obtain the fantasied narcissistic objectives of greatness, specialness, and importance that he cherished and craved, but without any effort or change on his part. But not only was the alliance contaminated by these narcissistic elements, it was also distorted by the intrusion of aggressive derivatives that derived from his introjective configuration in the form of powerful aggressive derivatives.

Here, the distinction from the previous narcissistic case was most striking. The patient's capacity to relate to me as an independent object was contaminated by aspects of the victim-posture to which he clung so assiduously, in part as a defense against underlying aggressive and destructive impulses. These were the same impulses that, genetically speaking, were at play in the patient's maintaining a passive and immobilized victim-stance as a defense against aggressive and destructive wishes against his father. Any attempt on his part to be assertive and aggressive, particularly if they should lead in the direction of successful competition with the father, would threaten with the same punishment that his wishes had inflicted on the father—death by a fatal heart attack. *Vivit lex talionis*!

The contrasts in these cases highlight the sometimes subtle differences in the capability for and quality of object-relations in narcissistic, as opposed to borderline personalities. These differences can express themselves in the transference. There is a constant tendency within therapy for the borderline patient to distort the relationship with the therapist by projections that tend to undermine an often tenuous therapeutic alliance. These distortions may project upon the therapist magical expectations of omniscience and omnipotence, while they subject him to devaluations and counterattacks that reflect the patient's own inner fears of vulnerability and impotence (Adler, 1970). The assigning of omnipotence to the therapist is accompanied by an assumption of impotence, need, and dependence in the patient. His only course is to submit in compliant acceptance and hope thereby to induce the therapist to use his omnipotence on the patient's behalf. Such patients tend to set unrealistic and grandiose goals so that change, or progress, in therapy gives little satisfaction, since it does not approach the fantasied grandiose goal.

For many borderline patients, for much of the time, the transference manifestations may remain relatively stable and be indistinguishable from transferences of narcissistic personalities. But for the more primitive forms of borderline character pathology or for borderline patients functioning under the duress of transient regressive stress, the transference may become relatively unstable, becoming permeated by pathogenic relationships from the past, which are then lived out in the present as if the distortion is the only form of reality the patient can know. These more regressive transferences thus reflect the failure of the capacity of the patient at that phase of the treatment to maintain the distinction between reality and fantasy. The therapist will become aware of the increasing intensity of affective responses, which may elicit correspondingly intense countertransference feelings.

The patient may become confused, may begin to distort the meaning and purpose of the therapy as well as the therapist's intent, and may experience an escalating intensification of feelings of hopelessness and despair. At such times, as Friedman (1979) has noted, the patient becomes like an angry child who thinks that the therapist-parent has complete power to provide relief and sustenance, but willfully refuses to help the patient.

In the treatment of the borderline patient, there will be periods of improved functioning, more meaningful involvement in the therapeutic relationship, and seemingly more effective therapeutic work, but this apparent gain will be reversed and nullified by an apparently uncaused emergence of more regressive and negative transference feelings. At such times, the patient's affective response is inappropriate, and its intensity quite out of proportion to the stimulus situation. This form of negative transference reaction has many of the earmarks of the negative therapeutic response (Asch, 1976).

In more severely disturbed borderlines, there can be a rapid oscillation of projections and introjections that affect the organization of self- and object-representations, creating a fragmentary and shifting configuration of elements of both the self and the perception of objects. Consequently, the perception of other people becomes grossly inconsistent and variable, showing a lack of awareness of contradictions from state to state, a rapid fluctuation between contradictory states, and a volatility of behavior that seems to parallel the perceptual fluctuations. The capacity to perceive others as separate, to relate to them realistically in terms of a variety of traits and qualities, then, gives way to a relationship based on the projection of parts of the self that must then be controlled by possessing or destroying the object.

Such projective turmoil is found only in the more primitive forms of borderline pathology or in borderline regressive states. By and large, in the general run of borderline patients, one does not see this sort of chaotic and fragmentary projective distortion. Nonetheless, there is a tendency for significant relationships to be discolored by projective expectations and interpretations. Such projective distortions may take place in reasonably healthy or neurotic individuals just as easily, but they present more of a problem for the borderlines, since they tend to dominate his perception of the object more pervasively as well as being less available to correction by other qualifying or contradictory pieces of evidence.

These characteristic and often shifting projective transference distortions are quite different in character from the transference paradigms associated with the narcissistic personality. The narcissistic personalities tend to present relatively stable narcissistic transference paradigms, in which the analyst is related to as one or other form of narcissistically invested object. Although the constitution of such objects requires a projective aspect (Meissner, 1978), the quality of it is quite different, since it is put in the service of maintaining narcissistic equilibrium. Certainly it does not show the shifting and fragmentary pattern frequently seen in the borderline patient.

As Ross (1976) has observed, borderline pathology has more directly to do with failures in the cohesiveness of the self than with specifiable ego defects. Certainly some distinction is necessary here, since ego defects related to specific developmental impediments can be found in the lower-order borderline conditions, although less so in the higher-order borderline conditions. In this latter realm of borderline pathology, ego functions and their correlative structures seem relatively well integrated, whereas the impairments have more to do with the integration and cohesiveness of the self (Meissner, 1981b). Consequently, attempts to describe borderline pathology in terms of pervasive ego defects has run afoul of this basic differentiation in the forms of borderline pathology.

Thus, a common impairment in the borderline conditions is the inherent fragility and vulnerability of nuclear narcissistic structures, which result in impaired cohesiveness of the self. The potential disruption of such nuclear structures is a continual threat that must be countered by a variety of defensive and avoidance measures. Kernberg has observed with regard to his "lower level" of character pathology that these individuals have a poor integration of self-representations, so that caricatures of both the good and the bad aspects of important objects come to dominate the inner world without any effective integration of these aspects. These residues of object-relations, the introjects (Meissner, 1979), serve as the basis for the integration of the self.

In the borderline, the self is thus composed of a chaotic amalgamation of shameful, threatened, impotent, and yet at the same time exalted and omnipotent images. Such patients may leap from one isolated or more or less coherent self-image to the next, without any intervening connections to maintain the continuity of self-experience. Such patients resist attempts to help them gain a measure of synthesis and rely unconsciously on the fantasied magical power of the analyst to provide what is missing and to transform the patient into a more integrated whole person. As Frances et al. (1977) have noted:

> The borderline patient has integrative deficits in self-constancy which are manifested by persistent fragmentation and splits in his self-structure, occurring in time both cross-sectionally and longitudinally. As a result, his present self-experience is not securely placed within a context of past and future selves. Instead, his ongoing experience of himself contains continual potential newness, unfamiliarity and dissonance—more than the usual discontinuity in the self over time. (p. 328)

An important discrimination in terms of the capacity to maintain self-cohesiveness must be made between narcissistic personalities and the borderline conditions. In general, narcissistic personalities have been able to establish a relatively cohesive sense of self that is firmer, more consistent, and more stable than the borderline self. Although the narcissistic concerns of grandiosity and the need for an omnipotent other are prominent in the pathology of narcissistic characters, the narcissistic structures remain somewhat vulnerable to transient regression as a consequence of disruption of essential self-supporting relationships. But the danger of fragmentation or disintegration is relatively minor and is buffered by the relatively good resilience of such character structures and the maintenance of well-integrated ego capacities and functioning.

The borderline, however, has a generally less cohesive self that is more readily subject to regression and fragmentation, in which the boundaries between self and object are less securely established.

The threat of inner fragmentation is relatively more central in borderline conditions, whereas the threat of disruption of a narcissistic relationship plays a more central role in the narcissistic personalities. Bursten (1978) has noted that borderline personality types have to deal with a central difficulty of maintaining a firm sense of self. Self-integration is unstable and is at constant risk of dissolution. The narcissistic self is firmer, less at risk, and less in danger of fragmentation, but nonetheless needs continual confirmation. The characteristic devices of narcissistic personalities, including narcissistic object-choices and the archaic narcissistic configurations described by Kohut, may be seen, in this perspective, as ways of confirming a threatened or unstable sense of self. Another way of putting it is that the borderline issues are more concerned with self-cohesion than with self-esteem, the narcissistic issues are more concerned with self-esteem than with self-cohesion. In both diagnostic areas, both aspects remain problematic, but the emphasis differs.

Closely related to the issues of self-esteem and self-cohesion is the experience of emptiness, which can express itself in various forms in both narcissistic and borderline personalities. For the narcissistic personality, the experience of emptiness translates more into terms of a sense of shame or worthlessness, the feeling that one is nothing or amounts to nothing, related to the perceived discrepancy between the achievements of the realistic self when measured against the internalized aspirations of the idealized self or idealized objects. In Kohut's (1971) terms, if the narcissistic cathexis of the realistic self is deficient and the archaic narcissism embedded in or invested in repressed vestiges of the grandiose self or idealized parent imagos, the individual's experience of himself and his sense of self are permeated with a sense of emptiness and depressive lack. The emptiness is based on a failure to accept and invest appropriate realistic goals and aspirations related to more realistic self-representations, on the one hand, and on the failure to moderate and integrate effectively the exaggerated and unrealistic demands of the grandiose self with the demands of reality, on the other.

Kernberg (1975), in his turn, attributes the experience of emptiness in narcissistic personalities to a defensively formed pathological grandiose self, together with a deterioration of the inner world of objects. Thus, such narcissistic individuals have little empathic capacity toward other human beings and tend to lead a withdrawn and impoverished social life, which serves to confirm, in fantasy or reality, their pressing need for admiration and narcissistic satisfaction. The emptiness is due to the deterioration of connections between the grandiose self and object-representations because of the narcissistic frustration and disappointment involved in such object-relations.

The emptiness in borderline personalities is much more closely related to the integration of the sense of self. Mild disturbances in the sense of self may be experienced in terms of a feeling of vagueness about one's self, a frustrated search for meaning of one's existence, or even may be manifested in the inability of the patient to establish any line of progression that would lead toward a form of more or less definitive identity. In its more severe forms of expression, the failure of self-integration may express itself in a chronic state of emptiness or nothingness, which may lead ultimately in the direction of psychotic delusions of personal extinction or annihilation or, acutely and dramatically, to an impulsive suicide attempt (Singer, M.,1977).

The vulnerability of the borderline sense of self and its fragile cohesiveness give rise to attempts on the part of these patients to regain or stabilize the self. This may be accomplished at times by fanatical dedication or infatuation with causes, religious movements, or other sources of dedication, which allow the borderline to gain some sense of definition of self and a corresponding sense of identity. However, these commitments tend to remain inconstant and often are subject to sudden shifts of conviction in quite different directions. Such involvement in extrinsic çauses tends not to be characteristic of narcissistic personalities.

SUMMARY

I have attempted a diagnostic differentiation between narcissistic personality disorders and the borderline conditions, based on descriptive clinical and structural considerations. I have argued that the narcissistic personality disorders constitute a group of higher-order character pathologies with stable narcissistic transferences and achieved self-cohesion, stable characterological traits, a minimal regressive tendency, and a stability of functioning, all characterized by the predominance of narcissistic needs and the seeking of narcissistic stability through narcissistic supplies and supports from narcissistically invested objects.

More primitive forms of narcissistic pathology, with more severe degrees of impairments in self-cohesion and heightened regressive tendencies, should not be regarded as forms of narcissistic personality, but rather fall more appropriately in the borderline category. The fact that more primitive forms of narcissistic pathology also manifest archaic narcissistic formations, typically the grandiose self and the idealized parent imago, should not argue to the diagnosis of narcissistic personality disorder, but simply reflect more primitive forms of narcissistic pathology existing in other, developmentally earlier, more severe forms of psychopathology. The borderline conditions, on the other hand, form a spectrum of forms of psychopathology, extending from higher-order borderline conditions (primitive hysteric, dysphoric personality) in which the more typical borderline features emerge only after significant regression, whether induced analytically or precipitated by stress, to more primitive forms of borderline organization, characterized by tendencies to regression, emotional lability, instability, tendencies to act-out, more subtle forms of thought disorder, and other indices of more primitive personality functioning and organization.

Chapter 6
Degrees of Variation
in the Borderline Spectrum

As we have commented in our previous discussion, there is considerable confusion and ambiguity regarding the definition and diagnosis of the borderline condition. More often than not, the borderline terminology is used in a general way to refer to patients who manifest basically neurotic symptomatology, but who somehow also convey an impression of more serious psychopathology. Such patients may manifest transient psychotic fragmentation; pathological narcissistic phenomena; character distortions; quasi-addictions and addictions; massive and bizarre, as well as multiple symptoms; a history of behavior disorders and difficult interpersonal relationships; and a pattern of atypical reactions early in the experience of therapy, including extreme rigidity, the emergence of early archaic material, the manifestation of primitive transference reactions, and frequently enough, a rapid if not euphoric improvement (Stone, 1954). There is a lack of diagnostic precision and a failure to differentiate the borderline syndrome from closely related forms of pathology, such as the schizoid personality, latent psychosis, or psychotic character (Blum, 1972).

Guze (1975) has noted that there is little agreement on borderline phenomenology. Current descriptions include a wide range of clinical features without adequate data on the frequency of their occurrence, either by themselves or in combination with other features, which are required to determine whether we are dealing with a syndrome or not. Establishing the diagnosis requires systematic data on the natural history of the disorder and its delimitation from other conditions. This has not been accomplished for the borderline diagnoses. Moreover, the connection of borderline syndromes with psychopathy, alcoholism and drug dependence, schizophrenia, hysteria, and the affective disorders remains to be established. In other words, the borderline description is so nonspecific that it embraces an as yet unspecified differential diagnosis covering a wide range of disorders.

Moreover, the defining characteristics are so general or abstract that it is difficult to know if they refer consistently to the same kinds of patients. It is impossible to know how many of the patients defined as borderline might also meet criteria for psychopathy, alcoholism, drug dependence, hysteria, etc. If the diagnosis is extended to include all these various entities that somehow fall between the established borders of the psychoses, on one hand, and the neuroses, on the other, its usefulness is restricted, particularly in relation to predictions of the course, complications, and response to particular treatments.

Guze (1975) argues further that if the diagnosis is meant to be supplemental and to reflect more fundamental pathological features, then there should be evidence to show that these basic features are independent of the clinical criteria of, let us say, hysteria (i.e., that one can be borderline and not hysterical) and must be compared to the clinical criteria of other conditions, such as affective disorders or schizophrenia. In some settings, the diagnosis is used as a more or less wastebasket term for cases that do not fit neatly into other categories (Knight, 1953a; Zetzel, 1971). Thus in the prison setting, antisocial personalities who engage in criminal acts are rarely diagnosed as borderline; the diagnosis is reserved for cases without a predominant pattern of either deep social deviance or addiction or antisocial behavior. As long as the tension is discharged and conflict avoided through various forms of acting-out (addiction, alcoholism, delinquency, etc.) many of these antisocial individuals are able to maintain a stable character pattern and avoid regression, but when placed in isolation in the prison setting they undergo a transient decompensation with a loss of reality-testing, overwhelming anxiety, and self-destructive behavior (Jacobs, 1975; Vaillant, 1975).

Both Kernberg (1967) and, subsequently, Gunderson and Singer (1975) set forth detailed lists of characteristics of borderline patients (see discussion pp. 69–72). The argument has been raised that the inclusion of such diverse manifestations under a single heading of borderline state or borderline personality organization only serves to obscure the uncertainties about their phenomenology, pathophysiology, and the course (Klein, 1975). Klein concludes that the borderline syndrome is, in fact, an extremely heterogeneous mixture and that the phenomenological dissection of this mixture is impeded by emphasizing structural elements and ego functions. He argues that the more useful strategy would be to focus on the patient's longitudinal affective status, with particular emphasis on the reactivity or lack of reactivity associated with affective swings and the particular nature of the stimuli engendering them. Insofar as the borderline disorders lack the usual characteristics of personality disorders, that is, a predominant behavioral pattern and personality traits, there is a risk of its being regarded as a form of character disorder without a behavioral specialty. Kernberg, in fact, relates it to a variety of behavioral disorders, including alcoholism, addiction, antisocial behavior, impulsive acting-out, and sexual deviance. The resulting risk is that the diagnosis becomes a catchall or wastebasket for immature or acting-out patients (Mack, 1975). Thus, the Gunderson-Singer criteria would seem to provide a general description that cannot be applied univocally to all borderline patients. Some characteristics apply to some patients, other characteristics to others. Nonetheless, these criteria seem to narrow the range of borderline characteristics more than do the criteria set up by Kernberg.

Zetzel (in Rangell, 1955; Zetzel, 1971) had distinguished borderline states from the borderline personality. The borderline state is a condition of mixed neurotic and psychotic symptomatology, which reflects a transient regressive condition. When we see a patient in such a regressive state, a diagnosis of borderline personality is not justified, since only the subsequent history, including the patient's response to appropriate therapeutic management, will indicate whether such a diagnosis is justified. Zetzel also noted that frequently enough the borderline personality does not always initially present with symptoms that would suggest a borderline diagnosis; rather, many apparently normal or neurotic individuals may only reveal borderline characteristics during the course of psychoanalytic or psychotherapeutic treatment or other regression-inducing circumstances.

This distinction involves an important point in the evaluation of patients in the borderline range, a point that has been emphasized by Gunderson and Singer (1975). What one sees in the evaluation of borderline patients and what indications of psychopathology are available for observation and assessment depends on both the amount of structure in the setting in which the phenomena are observed and the circumstances in which the patient and the clinical observer meet. When patients are evaluated in the more regressive context of psychoanalytic treatment or on projective test devices, there tends to be an emphasis on ego defects, primitive defenses, and latent thought disorders. Yet when the same patients are observed by competent clinicians in structured hospital settings or in the context of a structured interview, there tends to be an emphasis on more stable personality features and capacities for adaptation. Thus, the sensitivity of borderline conditions to external conditions and the tendency to regress in unstructured settings emphasizes the importance of the context of observation and study and suggests that such regressive potential may be pathognomonic for any definition of the range of borderline conditions (Gunderson and Singer, 1975).

In clinical situations in which the mixture of neurotic and psychotic symptoms is found, attempts to conceptualize borderline psychopathology have, at times, stressed the psychotic features, at other times, the neurotic. The assumption that neurotic manifestations in these syndromes are equivalent to neurotic mechanisms as known in the classic neuroses is questionable (Dickes, 1974). Thus, a neurotic phobia would tend to bind anxiety and leave the patient with an anticipatory fear that he might be killed; the psychotic symptom, however, tends to spread the anxiety, leaving the patient with the delusional conviction that he will be killed. The problem of assessing such mechanisms can be seen in relation to the problem of anxiety. Such patients may frequently enough reveal castration fears, or even fears of the loss of object love or of object loss, but in periods of regression, there may emerge also a primitive annihilation anxiety in which the preoccupation and fear with issues of survival and nonsurvival reach delusional intensity (Frosch, 1966). The emergence of such annihilation anxiety is related to the psychotic regression associated with transient borderline states. It is easy to see why theorists have argued for the existence of an underlying psychotic process in these patients.

It was only gradually, and with the persistence of these underlying conceptual ambiguities (see Chapter 1), that the concept of the borderline personality as a persistent and enduring personality configuration was achieved (Kernberg, 1967). Although empirical discrimination can be made between borderline and schizophrenic conditions (Gunderson et al., 1975), the question remains whether selection criteria are not drawing from a pool of borderline patients that, in fact, represents a spectrum of disorders with a wide variation in regressive potential. Thus, borderline and psychotic groups can clearly be discriminated, for example, on Schneiderian first-ranked symptoms; yet, three of these borderline patients did manifest these symptoms (Gunderson et al., 1975). Correspondingly, the range of borderline pathology in the Grinker et al. (1968) study extended from the apparently neurotic to the near psychotic. Such findings argue to an internal heterogeneity within the borderline group.

The concept of a borderline spectrum of heterogeneous diagnoses is not particularly new. Even in his early formulation of borderline conditions, Knight (1953a) commented, "The term borderline case is not recommended as a diagnostic term, for a much more precise diagnosis should be made which identifies the type and degree of psychotic pathology" (p. 108). Similarly, Fenichel (1945) suggested that the most practical concern was the capacity to distinguish between patients who are in danger of becoming psychotic and those who are buffered from psychosis by the development of certain eccentricities. A number of authors have, in fact, emphasized that the borderline group is constituted by an aggregate of more than one syndrome of differing etiology (Dickes, 1974; Masterson, 1972; Giovacchini, 1973). Modell (1963), for example, regards the borderline category as a heterogeneous grouping of patients that can be formed into a single nosological entity because of the particular quality of the transference relationships the patients manifest. Consequently, the notion of a spectrum of differentiable diagnoses constituting the borderline spectrum of disorders cannot be regarded as an unfamiliar concept.

In a recent review of this question, Perry and Klerman (1978) reassessed the criteria for the borderline diagnosis with an eye to its validity. The diversity and lack of consensus regarding diagnostic criteria led them to conclude that (1) either the diagnosis itself was illusory, (2) there is a valid core entity adequately described by common criteria so that other differentiating criteria are neither significant nor essential, or (3) there are, in fact, definable, differentiable subtypes within the borderline group. The first alternative is regressive and hardly satisfactory. The second reflects the predominant current view. The third alternative, also supported by these authors, is congruent with the approach taken in this study.

In addition we can suggest that, as we have noted, the more generic attempts to describe the borderline conditions themselves and to distinguish them from the neuroses or psychoses are really considering the borderline conditions under a single rubric. Such considerations may lump together heterogeneous symptomatology and diagnostic considerations that can be usefully differentiated regardless of the diagnostic criteria established. It should be added that, in the wake of Kohut's (1971) analysis of the narcissistic disorders, in which a cohesive self is attained along with the capacity for forming cohesive narcissistic transferences (Ornstein, 1974), the extent of the borderline spectrum must be set, on the one hand, by the border with the psychoses, but on the other hand, by the border with the narcissistic character disorders, rather than the neuroses as such.

COMMON FEATURES

In the assessment of the spectrum of borderline disorders, the first elements we wish to focus on are those that are found throughout the borderline spectrum in varying degrees. In other words, the spectrum of borderline conditions reveals the following defects, in one or another degree, such that may vary considerably from entity to entity. The assessment of degrees of impairment is greatly facilitated by Kernberg's (1971) analysis of prognostic factors relating to the borderline group.

Two points need to be noted. First, the question arises whether the relative degrees of impairment suggested by these common dimensions of borderline pathology suggest a continuum of degrees of pathological intensity as we move from the level of narcissistic character disorders in the direction of conditions more closely linked with the psychoses. As a general rule, this view can probably be maintained, but there also may be exceptions. For example, the level of anxiety experienced by a pseudoneurotic schizophrenic may not be as intense or as disruptive as that being experienced by a usually well-functioning borderline in a period of extreme stress or crisis. Similarly, the apparently well-functioning facade of a false-self personality may appear to reveal a minimum of pathology, until the false self is undermined and a regression may take place, even to psychotic levels.

Related to this issue of the assessment of degrees of pathology, we must re-emphasize that this assessment addresses potential differential diagnoses to the level of consistent characterological functioning that is identifiable in these various entities. The regressive borderline states, which remain a potential in all these cases, are not being considered here. That regressive potential is, itself, a matter of relative degree, but the essential nature of the character pathology cannot be judged from its transient regressive and often psychotically appearing crisis manifestations.

Object-Relationships

Perhaps the most critical dimension of borderline pathology is the quality of object-relationships it embodies. These patients are generally described as capable of rapidly developing new relationships that tend to reflect primitive object-relationships (Kernberg, 1973). Modell (1963), for example, distinguishes between patients who show unstable defenses, fluctuating ego states, and a capacity to suspend or readily abandon object-relationships and a second group whose defenses are more stable, but who seem unable to suspend or abandon their involvement with objects. Consequently, their relationships tend to be distorted, but nonetheless are maintained.

This quick and clinging involvement with objects is often generated by an intense need in which the objects are related to on a need-satisfying basis, rather than on any mature or reciprocal terms (Brody, 1960; Frijling-Schreuder, 1969). The intensity of such needs and the clinging to objects as a source of satisfaction can vary considerably in intensity and degree. Nonetheless, all these patients share a core disturbance in their capacity for object-relationships. There is a general feeling of emptiness and greedy hunger, intense wishes to be nurtured and taken care of, which are insistent and demand immediate satisfaction; if such demands are not satisfactorily met, as they might well not be because of the excessive expectations or through the inability of the object to respond, massive feelings of intense rage are mobilized, along with destructive impulses toward the object, which not only carry with them the fears of retaliatory destructiveness, but also raise the level of vulnerability to abandonment when and if the object encounters this rage. When the rage reaches sufficient intensity, it may also trigger a defensive regression to an incorporative level resulting in the fusion of self- and object-representations and psychotic manifestations.

This intense hunger and need for satisfaction from objects manifests itself in the transference as well. As Kernberg (1968) has noted, borderline patients often reveal an early activation within the transference of highly conflictual derivatives of object-relationships, which may be associated with relatively dissociated ego states, each one of which seems to represent independent transference paradigms. These paradigms more often than not have a projective quality and reflect the persistence in the character structure of relatively unmetabolized pathogenic introjects.

Modell (1963) has emphasized the transitional quality of object-relations in the borderline group. A similar quality of object-involvement is observable in borderline children, along with intense attempts to maintain an illusion of omnipotence, reliance on projection, and a denied, but nonetheless obviously intense need for dependence on the therapist (Fintzy, 1971). The urgent need to see the therapist as omnipotent and infallibly omniscient is present, as it is in adults.

Although the desperate and dependent need for the object may manifest itself in an intense, clinging and rapid emergence of highly emotional involvement with the therapist in some patients, there are others in whom the threat of closeness and the fears of dependency on the object give rise to a defensively motivated distancing and withdrawal. In such patients, a more or less schizoid posture impedes the development of the therapeutic relation, while it essentially defends against similar wishes for closeness and dependence that underlie the need for rapid involvement in the previously described cases.

There is a curious heterogeneity to the borderline individual's experience of objects. The sensitivity of borderline patients to latent and even unconscious impulses and motives has often been remarked. They seem unusually responsive to unconscious fantasies or impulses, as well as to more primitive superego elements in others. But more positive aspects of the ego functioning of the other seem to be held in distrust, so that there is no integration of the consistent and enduring aspects of the ego in the patient's image of objects. The primitive and drive-related aspects of the object are taken as somehow genuine and valid, but the persistent and positive aspects of character, self, and ego are treated as fake or untrustworthy. Thus, the involvement with objects remains on the level of relatively primitive and undeveloped attachment in which objects are responded to only as need-gratifying and as fluid and interchangeable, whether idealized or degraded (Krohn, 1974).

The borderline's experience of objects seems to bypass the essential qualities of the object's own consistent self-representation, that is, the enduring personality traits, character, and other ego attributes. Thus, the borderline subject maintains only a partial and impoverished contact with important aspects of the object. As Keiser (1958) has remarked, for such patients, such uncertain and suspect objects can never become parts of the patient's ego, but must be retained only as uncertain sources of narcissistic supply. There is never an accumulation of memory residues of object relationships that might give rise to any convictions about meaningful identity, empathy, or self-love, no basis for the memories of human kindnesses that might lead to the conclusion that objects may be counted on to be persistently generous and loving, or that having once given, they might conceivably give again.

The upshot of this impairment is that the patient is unable to perceive external objects as realistic and as complete persons. Characteristics of the object may not only be distorted or misrepresented, but also may be consistently omitted, or characteristics may only be included that fit with the predominant feeling toward the object at that time. Thus, the object may be seen as sexually exciting or murderous or despicable, without any attempt to include the contradictory qualities into a more comprehensive picture of the object. The result is that the current image of the object is destroyed and a new picture created internally, which is then taken to be the true representation of the object (De Saussure, 1974). The same discontinuity and shifting of focus takes place in reference to the patient's self-representations in which there tends to be a series of discontinuous partial self-images, each of which is accepted as reflecting the patient's whole self. These various images seem to have little connection or continuity and are dealt with in the same way as the contradictory aspects of objects were, by excluding them from the current image. Consequently, the clinical picture is marked by continuing preoccupation with the self and desperate and constant demands for love from objects, along with an inability to maintain or integrate that love when it is offered.

Object-Constancy

As long as object-relations remain on this need-gratifying level, the capacity for object-constancy is significantly diminished. Object-constancy implies the capacity to maintain a meaningful relationship to a specific object, whether one's subjective needs are being satisfied or not, or even when they are being frustrated. In most of the borderline conditions, there is some capacity for object-constancy, insofar as object-relationships, in varying degrees, seem capable of moving beyond the level of mere primitive need-satisfaction; but that object-constancy is extremely fragile and vulnerable and can be readily threatened by a variety of vicissitudes (Frijling-Schreuder, 1969; Fintzy, 1971). The fragility of object-constancy, that is, the diminished capacity for tolerating and integrating the ambivalent aspects of involvement with objects without shifting back and forth between extreme emotional reactions, has been noted on many occasions (Kernberg, 1967, 1970b, 1971; Blum, 1972; Masterson, 1972; Meissner, 1978).

In sum, then, the failure to achieve object-constancy implies that the patient is unable to relate to significant objects in his experience as whole persons, but rather only as parts; that the relationship fluctuates in terms of the patient's need state and that he has a poor tolerance for frustration or ambivalence, or a poor capacity to endure frustration of needs; that the individual has difficulty in evoking a consistent image of the object when the object is not physically present; and finally, that it carries with it a severe impairment in the individual's capacity to mourn the object, so that separation is extremely difficult. Such patients often avoid the threat of separation by forms of emotional detachment or acting-out to provoke reinvolvement with the object or to attract the object's attention. This is particularly the case in the difficult stages of separation in therapy (Masterson, 1972).

Borderlines carry with them an impaired capacity for internalization, which relates to the inability to establish object-constancy. The instability of object-representations and the impaired capacity to maintain the cathexis of objects increases not only the clinging dependence on external objects, but also tends to create, in the face of the precariousness of object cathexis and object-constancy, a regressive tendency to retreat to more primitive forms of introjection or, on more primitive and psychotic levels, incorporation (Meissner, 1971). This seems to be the sense of Anna Freud's comment that in such borderline conditions, particularly in children, the subject lives on the border between a tenuous and fragile object cathexis and primary identification (Maenchen, 1968).

The upshot of the lack of object-constancy, the inability to establish a secure and lasting cathexis of objects, and the corresponding defects in internalization, is that there is created a situation of intense need for and clinging to objects, which is compounded with an intense fear and distrust of those same objects. This dilemma was described some years ago in schizophrenic object-relations as the "need-fear dilemma" (Burnham et al., 1969). Despite this intense longing for object contact and support, involvement with objects is also feared in borderline patients (Blum, 1972). There is a fear of symbiotic fusion, along with intense ambivalence so that although the borderline tends to reach out and cling to objects, he is forced to withdraw when the pain or threat of rejection becomes unbearable (Giovacchini, 1973).

Abandonment Fears

The need for the object may vary across a wide range of degrees of intensity, just as the fear of abandoment may take various forms. Such abandonment may mean rejection; it may mean the terror of a feeling of isolation and loneliness; it may connote a feeling of inner emptiness, coldness, and deadness; or it may translate into fears of total destructive abandonment and annihilation. The fear of abandonment stems from an incomplete internalization of maternal caring. The failure of maternal empathy and the threat of abandonment is not only terrifying, but also stirs primitive savage oral wishes to kill, eat, merge, etc. These primitive destructive impulses create a primitive guilt, which threatens retaliation and loss of love. In addition, the projection of such rage makes the loved object a source of dread, danger, and persecution, which serves only to reinforce and increase the pattern of withdrawal (Buie and Adler, 1972).

Such intense object-needs and fears can also be stimulated in the transference context. The fears of abandonment can easily be stirred by any rebuke or failure of comprehension on the part of the therapist and, especially, by a variety of countertransference reactions (Kernberg, 1975). As we shall see, these may easily trigger a transient regression, but often return to a level of more integrated secondary process functioning after recovery of a more stable alliance. The therapy may become pervaded by issues of separation and abandonment. Moreover, the dilemma often tends to have an either/or quality. Clinging to one object means abandonment by others, and frequently in the childhood history of such patients the therapist hears the same theme: that if the child loves one parent, this seems to imply the loss of or abandonment by the other.

The quality of such object involvement, the combination of need and fear, and the conflicts over dependence and abandonment reflect a developmental failure of the process of separation and individuation. The dilemma of separation threatens the child with symbolic engulfment if it clings to the object; and at the same time, it threatens loss or abandonment if it moves away from dependence on the object. Horner (1975) notes that in such situations one often finds a mother who tends to withdraw emotional support when the child first attempts to separate from her and to define himself as individual. The mother's emotional unavailability prevents the achievement of a secure object-constancy that would ensure the child's capacity to maintain narcissistic equilibrium on its own terms. Thus, abandonment depression and a narcissistic oral fixation, which are the hallmarks of borderline pathology, are consolidated (Masterson, 1972).

The establishing of object-constancy is secondary to the emergence of a cohesive self, which depends on the gradual internalization of equilibrium-maintaining maternal functions. The development of this capacity, that is, the ability to recognize and tolerate both hostile and loving feelings toward the same object and to value the object for qualities other than those having to do with need satisfaction, are both essential to the capacity for object-constancy and form a critical developmental step in the direction of more mature and stable object relationships (Horner, 1975). In the borderline conditions, the need-fear dilemma remains a pervasive problem that expresses itself in varying degrees of intensity—both of the need to cling to objects as well as the fear of abandonment by objects. Moreover, the respective forms of borderline pathology can be seen as qualitatively different ways of dealing with, defending against, and resolving this underlying and central dilemma.

Self-Cohesiveness

A common impairment for these borderline conditions is the inherent fragility and vulnerability of nuclear narcissistic structures that result in impaired self-cohesiveness. The potential breakdown of such nuclear structures poses a continual threat, which must be countered by a variety of defensive and avoidance maneuvers (Kohut, 1972). As Kernberg (1970b) has pointed out in regard to his "lower level" of character pathology, such individuals have a poor integration of self-representations so that the inner world is peopled by caricatures of both the good and the horrible aspects of important objects without effective integration of these aspects. Such residues of object relations or introjects (Meissner, 1978) create an inner experience of the self as composed of a chaotic amalgamation of shameful, threatened, impotent, yet at the same time exalted and omnipotent images.

This defect in the integration of the inner world of introjects and the failure of a stable self-concept frequently result in a diffusion of identity, which Kernberg regards as characteristic of this lower level of character pathology. In fact, an acute identity diffusion is typical of the transient regression of the borderline states. But even on the characterological level, such patients may jump from one isolated and more or less coherent self-image to the next without any intervening connections to maintain the continuity of the self-image. Moreover, attempts to assist the patient to develop some capacity for synthesis are often resisted, while the patient relies unconsciously on the fantasied magical powers of the analyst to provide what is missing and to transform the patient into a more integrated whole person.

The impairment of narcissistic structures, and the corresponding failure of integration of self-representations, is reflected in a variety of pathological expressions in borderline conditions. Besides the deficits in the maintenance of a sense of identity, there are a variety of states of inner self-organization in which partial or fragmented self-integration is achieved. The more or less discontinuous shifting from one introjective configuration to another in borderlines has been variously described (Kernberg, 1967; Meissner, 1978). In addition, however, other patients may resolve the problem of inner instability by a mimetic imitative-introjective shaping of a transient self-integration that remains dependent on involvement with or attachment to a particular object

(Meissner, 1974b). This is the classic "as-if" pattern described by Deutsch (1942). Other forms may achieve relative stabilization and narcissistic equilibrium by a more persistent inner splitting of persistent fragmentary self-integrations [e.g., Winnicott's false-self organization (1960)].

Thus self- and object-representations may gain some degree of internal integration, but their cohesion is derived from inclusion of qualities in the respective images derived from external objects of dependence. The resistance to self-integration is often accompanied by unconscious fantasies of more frightening dangers that result from allowing the self to be whole and one, so that many patients begin to experience a more severe anxiety only when the capacity for synthesis is in some degree achieved (De Saussure, 1974). Where the dependence on objects is of such intensity that the distinction between self and object is blurred or lost, the loss of the object can provoke a severe annihilation anxiety, in which any separation from the object precipitates a fear of loss that is equivalent to annihilation of the self (Frosch, 1967a, b).

Less serious disturbances in the sense of self may fall short of the sort of identity diffusion or fragmentation of self-representations that is often found in more primitively organized borderline personalities or in regressive borderline states. In better-integrated forms of borderline pathology, one may find states of diffusion or lack of definition in the sense of self; a seemingly endless and frustrated search for meaning or purpose to one's existence; or even a holding back or an inability to commit oneself to an adult course of life, to a specific job or occupation or career, or to a single, specific woman and the implications of intimacy, marriage, family, and children and all the burdens and responsibilities such commitment would entail.

An important discrimination in terms of the capacity to maintain self-cohesiveness must be made between narcissistic personalities and the borderline conditions. In general, narcissistic personalities have been able to establish a relatively cohesive sense of self, which is firmer, more consistent, and stable than the borderline self. Although the narcissistic concerns of grandiosity and the need for an omnipotent other are prominent in the pathology of narcissistic characters, with the corresponding defects in the quality of object relationships, the narcissistic structures remain somewhat vulnerable to transient regression as a consequence of disruption of essential self-supporting relationships. But the danger of fragmentation or disintegration is relatively minor and is buffered by the relatively good resilience of such character structures and the maintenance of well-integrated ego capacities and ego-functioning.

The borderline, however, has a generally less cohesive self, which is more readily subject to regression and fragmentation and in which the boundaries between self and object are less securely established. As Bursten

(1973) has noted, the threat of inner fragmentation is relatively more central in borderline conditions, whereas the threat of disruption of a narcissistic relationship plays a more central role in the narcissistic personalities. He thus places the narcissistic personalities as an intermediate form of pathology between the more severe dysfunction of the borderlines and the healthier range of complementary types of personality, in whom the capacity for real, reciprocal, and relatively non-narcissistic object-relations obtain. Although individuals in the complementary or neurotic range have the resolution of conflicts of the oedipal phase as a primary task, the borderline and narcissistic disorders have as their primary task the resolution of conflicts related more centrally to the oral phase of development. Thus, the integration of the narcissistic personality reflects a more successful negotiation of the separation-individuation issues and the achievement of a relatively more cohesive and individuated self, even though the need for the narcissistic object persists. In the borderline range of personality disorders, however, the negotiation of separation and individuation is more difficult, and is significantly less successful in attaining an adequate degree of separation to allow for cohesive self-formation (Horner, 1975).

REGRESSIVE POTENTIAL

The potential for disintegration of narcissistic structures and the vulnerability of self-cohesiveness, along with the ambivalent, highly conflicted, and precarious cathexis of objects, set the stage for the regressive potential that is generally held to be characteristic of borderline patients. The regressive tendency is often linked with defective ego structure and is associated with the general fluidity of the borderline personality, the regression often being transient and relatively readily reversible and reaching, in a limited way, psychotic or near-psychotic levels (Blum, 1972; Giovacchini, 1973; Kernberg, 1967). It is important to emphasize that, in the present consideration, the focus is not on the characteristics of such regressive crisis states, but rather on the inherent regressive potential that characterizes the personality structure itself. As Zetzel (1971) emphasized, little of predictive or diagnostic value can be based on such regressive states, since one must wait for information based on the subsequent history, including the patient's response to appropriate therapy and an evaluation of the patient-therapist relationship, before any secure evaluation can be made. Nonetheless, borderline conditions vary in the degree of regressive potential, and this may serve as a differential diagnostic point.

Borderline regression is typically met in the context of a long-term, relatively intense therapeutic relationship. The pace and the depth of the regression exceeds that normally expected in the therapeutic context and often precipitously reaches a depth that seems nearly psychotic. The regressive pulls seem to exceed the capacity of the ego to control or to modulate them. Such regressions can be severely disruptive of the therapeutic work, have a radical all-or-none quality, and can often be frightening in that they impinge on issues of life and death. There is a failure of the differentiation between self and object and between inner and outer reality, and an emergence of primitive defenses as described by Kernberg (1967), which include splitting, projection, primitive idealization, and denial; there is also an intensification of the dilemmas of need and fear in relation to the therapist, with periods of apparent fusion and a loss of the distinction between fantasy and reality, between the patient's projections and the real qualities of the therapist. Unresolved feelings of abandonment and neglect are stirred up, together with an emergence of primitive rage with an intensification of destructive clinging and, at the same time, tendencies to destructive acting-out, suicide, or depressive withdrawal and schizoid isolation (Adler, 1974).

The regressive potential is often difficult to evaluate and frequently requires a trial of analysis or an intensive, analytically oriented therapy to mobilize regressive pressures in the patient. Some suggestions toward the evaluation of regressive potential have been advanced by Kernberg's description of intermediate and lower levels of character pathology (1970b).

· The evaluation of regressive potential depends in critical ways on the context in which such patients are seen and on the selective factors that might have brought them to seek therapy. Friedman (1969), for example, describes the regressive behavior, including enraged acting-out and destructiveness; self-destructive behavior; verbal and physical abuse; disruptive and assaultive behavior, generally toward staff, but rarely toward patients; and the involvement of the staff in intense and highly conflictual relationships. Such patients manifest a much more severe regressive potential with a much higher propensity for destructive acting-out, as well as the casting of a broad net to ensnare others in their intensely dependent and destructively ambivalent involvement. These hospitalized patients very likely function at a lower level of the borderline spectrum and should be contrasted with patients whose regression is relatively slow in developing, often only after months or more of intensive therapy or analysis, and whose regression remains more or less confined to the therapeutic setting. In the latter patients, the emergence of a borderline state is usually a function of some breakdown in the therapeutic relationship, whether a lack of empathic understanding on the part of the therapist or some other form of countertransference vicissitude. In any case, the transference distortions do not generalize to other individuals in the patient's life and do not become a form of self-perpetuating psychosis outside the therapy (Ekstein and Wallerstein, 1954; Fintzy, 1971).

Reality Testing

Thus, the borderline ego does not bridge over into psychosis, either in terms of the loss of reality-testing or in terms of the development of delusional thought systems. The loss of reality-testing, for example, is usually relatively limited to one area of the patient's experience and can be more or less readily regained by effective therapeutic intervention (Frijling-Schreuder, 1969). The borderline regression can be further distinguished from psychotic regression by reason of the fact that it is usually reversible, transient, related to a vicissitude of object relations (implying the persistence of attachment to objects), and ego-alien and unsystematized (Gunderson and Singer, 1975). A valid and moot question remains, therefore, as to whether the transient regressive episodes observed in some forms of the borderline spectrum are indeed psychotic.

Projection

A number of authors have noted the propensity for projection in borderline conditions (Blum, 1972; Rosenfeld and Sprince, 1963; Buie and Adler, 1972; Robbins, 1976). Kernberg has also indicated projection as one of the major characteristic defense mechanisms of borderline pathology (1967, 1973). Moreover, as Giovacchini (1972) noted, the general tendency of these patients to externalize is consistent with the pattern of acting-out. There is a general tendency to transpose inner problems into terms of the external world so that there is a more or less exclusive preoccupation with reality without any consideration of contributions from the self. This results in a constant tendency to blame forces outside the self for difficulties and problems, without assuming any responsibility on one's own part.

Moreover, a constant tendency within therapy is to distort the relationship with the therapist by projections that prevent the patient from establishing contact with the real personality of the therapist and that tend to undermine an often tenuous therapeutic alliance. Thus, these projective distortions may thrust upon the therapist magical expectations of omniscience and omnipotence, while they may subject him to devaluations and attacks that reflect the patient's own inner fears of vulnerability and impotence (Adler, 1970). The tendency to assign omnipotence to the therapist is paralleled by the assumption of impotence, need, and dependence, on the part of the patient. It is the powerful others who have influence and strength, and it is the function of the patient only to submit in compliant and puppetlike manner and, thus, to induce the therapist to exercise his all-powerful capacity on the patient's behalf. A similar mode of adapting to the requirements of the work situation has been described by Fast (1975). Such patients tend to set unrealistic and grandiose goals so that the achievement of a goal or progress in treatment gives little satisfaction because it does not measure up to the fantasied goal. Consequently, it is difficult to establish and work through any meaningful sequence of step-by-step progression of means toward an anticipated goal.

In some patients, particularly the more severely disturbed borderlines, a rapid oscillation of processes of projection and introjection affects the organization of self- and object-representations to create a fragmentary and constantly shifting configuration of both elements of the self and the perception of objects. Thus, the perception of people becomes grossly inconsistent and variable, there is a lack of awareness of contradictions from state to state, a rapid fluctuation between apparently contradictory ego states, and a volatility of behavior that parallels the perceptual fluctuations. The capacity to perceive others as separate and to relate to them realistically in terms of a variety of traits and capacities gives way to a relationship based on a projection of parts of the self, which then must be controlled by possessing or destroying the object.

Such projective turmoil is to be found only in the more primitive forms of borderline pathology or in borderline regressive states. By and large, in the general run of borderline patients, one does not see this form of more or less chaotic and fragmentary projective distortion. On a more characterological and less regressed level, however, there is a tendency for significant relationships to be discolored by projective expectations and interpretations. Such projective distortions can be identified in reasonably healthy and in neurotic individuals as well, but they become a problem for the borderline insofar as they tend to dominate the perception of the object more pervasively and are also less available to correction by other qualifying or contradictory pieces of evidence. Such projective distortions are usually testable and correctable in the therapeutic work, in contrast to psychotic paranoid distortions that maintain an intensity and a delusional fixity that resists modification.

Ego- and Superego-Defects

The last of the common elements of the borderline spectrum we shall discuss are the defects in ego and superego structure and function. A number of authors have pointed to ego defects, particularly, as central to the borderline pathology (Kernberg, 1967, 1973; Blum, 1972; Giovacchini, 1973; Ekstein and Wallerstein, 1954, 1956; Frosch, 1970; Frijling-Schreuder, 1969; Buie and Adler, 1972; Klein, 1975; Rosenfeld and Sprince, 1963, 1965; Atkin, 1974). An important issue in the evaluation of ego defects is the extent to which they have relevance for borderline states as opposed to the more stable

conditions of borderline personality organization. Here again, the evaluation of the severity of ego defects depends critically on selective and contextual factors under which patients are evaluated.

The ego-functions that are usually discussed include a variety of primitive defense mechanisms such as projection, denial, splitting and primitive
idealization (Kernberg, 1967; Rosenfeld and Sprince, 1963), defects in reality-
testing or the sense of reality (Frosch, 1970; Gunderson and Singer, 1975),
and impairments of the synthetic function (Rosenfeld and Sprince, 1963,
1965; Giovacchini, 1973; Atkin, 1974). In terms of the focus of this discussion, it should be noted that all forms of ego weakness are subject to varying
degrees of intensity, ranging from very minor and incidental impairments to
the severe disorganization and dysfunction characteristic of psychosis. For
example, if we look at the indices of ego weakness provided by Kernberg
(1967, 1971), it is clear that each of these indices is subject to a wide range of
variation and degree of impairment. He lists the predominance of primitive
defensive operations, a lack of impulse control, a lack of anxiety tolerance, a
lack of developed sublimatory channels, a tendency to primary process
thinking, and a weakening of reality-testing.

It is correct to say that the prominence or greater evidence of any or all
of these indices would suggest borderline pathology, since in a severe degree
of manifestation they all point in the direction of psychosis and away from
neurosis. But the primitive defenses can be found in modified form, even in
neurotic and classically analyzable patients. In such patients, projection does
not take the form of delusional distortion of reality, but rather may manifest
itself in misinterpretation, suspiciousness, guardedness, misguided convictions, misinterpretations of contexts and meanings, etc.—what I have taken
to calling the "soft signs" of paranoia (Meissner, 1978). Even splitting, which
Kernberg makes the hallmark of borderline pathology, can be seen in milder
and less pervasive degrees in healthier, better-organized patients (see Chapter 1). The point of my argument is, not that such primitive defenses cannot
be characteristically identified in the borderline pathologies, but rather that
they are subject to considerable degrees of variation and that one must
choose carefully what one classifies as primitive or not so primitive. Such
primitive defenses can be identified in the personality functioning of the
lower-order borderline conditions, but would be less apparent and considerably less disturbed in the higher-order borderlines.

Deficits in the control of impulses also vary considerably. In the higher-
order borderline who regresses only gradually under the influence of a more
or less controlled analytic regression, impulse control is not a serious problem
and becomes so only when the patient reaches more regressed levels of
functioning. Even then, the lack of impulse control is usually related to
specific vicissitudes of object-relationships—often precipitated by alliance
failures or countertransference difficulties within the therapy. This is a far

cry from the flamboyant and ill-controlled tendency to the expression of impulses, frequently in the form of destructive acting-out, that is seen in the more primitive organization of lower-order borderline pathology, and frequently in the hospital setting. A similar observation can be made about the lack of anxiety tolerance, insofar as many treatable patients who turn out to be borderline demonstrate a considerable capacity for the tolerance of anxiety, and even in the face of increasing regression, retreat only to a level of separation anxiety, frequently without any need to intensify symptoms or to act-out in self-destructive ways.

Kernberg (1971) describes the capacity for sublimated activity in terms of the enjoyment of work and life, a capacity for creative achievement, the ability to invest oneself in activities or a profession that reaches beyond mere narcissistic needs, as well as a degree of satisfaction from such activity and an abiding concern for the intrinsic values inherent in such activity or professional work. He also notes that the evaluation of such sublimatory potential is extremely difficult, particularly since, as Fast (1975) has noted, it is not uncharacteristic of many borderline personalities to achieve considerable degrees of creative expression and accomplishment in areas of creative work, such as art, music, and poetry, whereas their capacity to apply themselves with the same energy and industry to areas of everyday work or to the holding down of a job are severely compromised. There is, thus, a considerable gradation from the severe constriction of sublimatory potentials and the susceptibility to drive derivatives and narcissistic needs found in more primitive forms of borderline organization and the often highly developed capacity for creative expression found in some higher-order borderline personalities.

The tendency to primary process thinking is often made a central touchstone and a major characteristic pathognomonic of borderline conditions (Gunderson and Singer, 1975; Kernberg, 1967, 1971). It is said that borderlines do not generally reveal evidence of a formal thought disorder on mental status examination or in the context of an ordinary relatively structured interview, but that on projective testing, they reveal primitive fantasies, a diminished capacity to adjust to the formal givens of the testing situation, peculiar verbalizations, fabulizing, combinatory and confabulated thinking, reasoning that is often odd or circumstantial rather than logical, a mingling of separate perceptions simply because they occur together temporally or spatially, an overelaboration of affective meaning of perceptions, etc. Although these observations may have relevance as global indices of borderline psychopathology, it must also be recognized that such manifestations may not be characteristic of the total range of borderline conditions. Consequently, the conclusion that projective testing is of considerable significance in the evaluation of borderline pathology remains valid, but it can also be argued that a significant number of borderline personalities need not show such cognitive disorganization. My tendency at the moment is to expect such latent disorganization of thought processes in the lower levels of borderline pathology, but to suggest that it may not be at all evident in a significant number of higher-order borderlines.

The role of reality-testing in the borderline pathology has been viewed contradictorily, partly because of the variability of the capacity for reality-testing in these patients and partly because of the inherent ambiguity of the borderline concept. Reality-testing has become the touchstone of the tension between the need to discriminate between the borderline conditions and the neuroses and the need to keep the borderline condition clearly discriminated from the psychoses. The former concern leads to a tendency to emphasize the vulnerability of borderline reality-testing, the latter, emphasize its preservation as a distinguishing feature from the psychoses.

The argument is compounded by the difficulties connected with the assessment of ego-functions like reality-testing in the context of regressive states as opposed to more characteristic personality functioning. In general, reality-testing and reality-contact is well established and well maintained by borderlines in their general run of functioning, but it is jeopardized under circumstances in which regression takes place, i.e., under the influence of emotional stress, alcohol, or drugs, or the emergence of a transference psychosis (Kernberg, 1967, 1971). The preservation of reality-testing under normal circumstances, and the ready reversibility of the loss of reality-testing in regressive states, is characteristic of the borderline pathology and discriminates it from the psychoses (Kernberg, 1967, 1971). As with other parameters of ego functioning, it can be said that the vulnerability of reality-testing is correlated with the level of regression, as a general rule, but that the susceptibility to such regressive influence is more marked in the lower forms of borderline personality integration. Further, where defects in reality-testing are relatively stable and permanent, they have the character of the projective distortions or illusions we have previously described.

Ego and superego integration are interrelated, so that where one finds severe ego defects, one may also expect to find impediments in the structure and functioning of the superego. Good quality superego integration cannot be achieved without good ego integration, but there can be severe superego defects along with a reasonably, well-integrated ego-functioning. Defective superego integration, based on relatively archaic and destructive introjective elements and marked by severity and primitive functioning, as well as a susceptibility to projection, has frequently been commented on (Blum, 1972; Buie and Adler, 1972; Kernberg, 1967, 1973; Kramer, 1958). Tendencies to projection can be seen in the overidealization and magical expectations that are put upon helping and caring persons, as well as the punitive, demanding, rejecting quality injected into object-relations. This gives rise to a frequent alternating pattern of overvaluation and devaluation (Adler, 1970), as well as the intense and highly conflictual relationships established with staff members in the hospital setting (Adler, 1973; Friedman, 1969).

The levels of superego integration have been delineated by Kernberg (1967, 1970b, 1971). He points out that the combination of guilt, remorse, and concern about the self points in the direction of greater superego integration, whereas the prevalence of impotent rage, helplessness, and hopelessness points in the direction of poorer superego integration and a lower level of character pathology. He also cautions against the use of depression as an index of levels of pathology, since both excessive depression or its absence, in terms of schizoid withdrawal, may indicate a lower level of character organization (Kernberg, 1967).

In general, on both the intermediate and the lower level of character pathology, there is a lack of superego integration, but on the intermediate level this is reflected in the tendency for projection of superego components (reflected in a lessened capacity for guilt and a tendency to paranoia), contradictions in value systems, and severity of mood swings. At the lower level of character organization, superego integration fails because the intensity of the pregenital aggression prevents the adequate synthesis of contradictory self- and object-images. I have described this failure of integration elsewhere (Meissner, 1971, 1978) in terms of the failure of internalization and the maintenance of relatively primitive introjective configurations as derivatives of object-relationships.

In Kernberg's terms (1970b), the split between good and bad images interferes with superego integration. This results in an overidealization of self- and object-images, leading to fantasied ideals of power and perfection. The projection of bad self- and object-images, which are subsequently re-introjected primarily as distorted experiences of frustrating or punitive aspects of the parents, leads to the reinforcement and the pathological predominance of sadistic superego precursors and a diminished capacity to integrate these with narcissistically impregnated and idealized components of the ego-ideal. This pathological mechanism is maximally true in lower levels of character pathology, but can also be detected in more moderate degree at the intermediate level. Where there is sufficient integration of good and bad internalized object-relationships or object-images, the central core of the ego is protected by a more stable repressive barrier, thus creating the conditions for the progressive integration of sadistic superego precursors with the ego-ideal.

On the higher level of character organization, sadistic superego precursors may be expressed in terms of a harsh, punitive, or demanding superego. The actual level of functioning may depend not only on the quality of pathological character traits and on the interpersonal environment, but also on the degree of pathological superego pressures on the ego. Thus, a sadistic, relatively well-integrated superego in a depressive-masochistic character may produce a severe depression sufficiently disorganizing so that nonspecific manifestations of ego weakness appear, making the patient's functioning seem worse than the actual level of the character pathology (Kernberg, 1970b).

Other indicators of levels of pathological organization, which serve as prognostic indicators as well (Kernberg, 1971), are the extent to which pathological introjections are enacted by character traits and the extent to which such introjects are tolerated by the patient's ego; the greater the degree of self-destructiveness expressed in such traits, the lower the level of character functioning and the worse the prognosis. A punitive superego may have an inhibitory effect on ego functions, but the more primitive integration of the aggressor-introject into sadistic character traits defends the ego from superego pressures by a sort of pathological freedom and arrogance through identification with the omnipotent, sadistic superego figure. The more the primitive superego introject dominates the organization of the personality, the more there may be a crude expression of aggression, which can be socially inappropriate, and the abdication of reality-testing by the ego in certain social settings in order to accommodate the demands of this pathological introject. Kernberg (1971) comments on superego integration as follows:

> In spite of the usual predominance of splitting operations in the superego, reprojection of superego nuclei in the form of paranoid trends, tolerance on the superego's part of contradictory value systems, of contradictory ego states and of identifications embedded in pathological character traits that are in striking contrast to superego values, quite a variation exists in borderline patients regarding the degree to which abstracted, depersonified, integrated superego values are present. Some patients with borderline personality organization, i.e., patients with narcissistic personality structures (Kernberg, 1970) have much more serious superego pathology than their ego functioning would indicate. (p. 622)

The factors connected with the relatively higher-order abstraction and depersonalization of the superego include awareness of the values of others, awareness of the interpersonal implications of values, and internalized and consistent value systems. Indications to the contrary would include antisocial trends that are ego-syntonic and integrated into the individual's pathological character structure.

Such individuals lack a set of internalized and coherent values and are relatively unaware of the values of others or the implications of such values. They often lack a capacity for reality-testing in interpersonal relationships and a capacity for meaningful insight. There is no concern for regulating behavior relative to moral values and a relative incapacity to experience guilt and depression. Such indices reflect the failure of superego integration and serve as an index of a lower level of character organization; they are a less optimistic prognostic indicator. Severe failure of superego development may also manifest itself in the failure of signal guilt, which, instead of activating self-observant and integrative functions of the ego as it might in a higher-order character organization, results in a tendency to trigger paranoid distortions of an all-or-none quality, rather than compensatory and adaptive mechanisms. The failure of integration may also be reflected in the extent to which the pathological superego tolerates contradictory value orientations or ego states.

CONCLUSION

We have surveyed some of the aspects of borderline psychopathology that lend themselves to degrees of differentiation. These gradations in aspects of pathological organization and functioning provide a possible basis for more careful differentiation of forms of borderline pathology. Although the current conceptualization of borderline conditions tends to treat them in a more or less global manner, we would suggest, on the basis of this differentiating analysis, that the borderline conditions may be more usefully regarded as a complex of intermediate forms of character pathology. These conditions in the aggregate form a spectrum of potentially differentiable borderline diagnoses.

Chapter 7
Borderline Diagnoses

As the preceding discussion has suggested, the borderline conditions have consistently been a source of ambiguity, uncertainty, and difficulty. The history of the concept has been marked by considerable conceptual ambiguity and terminological confusion (see Chapter 1), finally evolving in the direction of Kernberg's (1966, 1967) descriptive and theoretical clarification. Despite this progress, a significant degree of theoretical diversity and lack of specificity tends to characterize contemporary approaches to the borderline problem (see Chapter 2).

I have argued earlier in this study that a basic prior difficulty, which lends confusion and ambiguity to our attempts to clarify and understand borderline pathology, is that we may, in fact, be dealing with a heterogeneous group of forms of character pathology. Thus, a given description or theoretical account of borderline pathology may refer to one segment of this grouping, but be less pertinent to other segments. Other clinical formulations and theoretical accounts may have greater relevance to other forms within the borderline grouping. Perry and Klerman's (1978) review of the criteria for borderline diagnoses emphasizes the lack of agreement over diagnostic criteria and concludes (1) that the borderline concept is an illusion, (2) that the borderline concept is adequately defined by common criteria that would apply across the borderline spectrum, such that other distinguishing criteria are nonessential, or (3) that there are, in fact, definable subtypes within the borderline group. The first alternative seems regressive, the second reflects current trends in the approach to borderline diagnoses (as exemplified in the efforts of Kernberg, Gunderson, and Spitzer), and the third (favored by these authors) is congruent with the intentions of the present study. The present effort aims at some initial diagnostic discriminations that may suggest directions of further differentiation and empirical validation of diagnostic categories.

It has already been argued here that the borderline conditions offer a heterogeneous continuum of levels and degrees of pathological personality functioning that can be traced along several important parameters, including the quality of object-relations, the degree of object-constancy, the level of achieved and maintained self-cohesion, the regressive potential, the degree of projective tendency, and levels of ego and superego structuralization (see Chapter 6). Qualitative and quantitative degrees of difference that can be described for these parameters potentially provide the basis for a hopefully meaningful diagnostic discrimination. This approach suggests that the borderline conditions form a complex group of differentiable forms of psychopathology consisting of a spectrum of borderline character disorders. Any effort to scan the already extant formulations of borderline personality must thus begin the process by mapping out areas of potential diagnostic differentiation.

Three outstanding difficulties counter such an effort. The first is the predominant position of Kernberg's (1967, 1975) immense contribution to the understanding of borderline pathology. His formulation tends to follow a lumping strategy: it provides a general description that embraces, without differentiating, most of the borderline spectrum [Perry and Klerman's (1978) second option]. The success of this contribution makes one feel that to venture beyond it is risky, or that further differentiation is unwise or clinically unfruitful. At the same time, Kernberg's work makes a further clarifying step possible, and he has provided a useful initiative in that very direction by his description of levels of character pathology.

A similar point can be made for Frosch's (1964, 1970) formulations on the psychotic character. Frosch (1982) makes it clear that he intended his description of the psychotic character to be inclusive and to cover the full range of the borderline spectrum.

The second difficulty stems from the traditional analytic aversion to diagnosis. Historically, this reflects a long-standing reaction to the classifying obsession of Kraepelinian descriptive psychiatry and the counteremphasis on psychodynamic and motivational considerations. At one extreme, this takes the form of Zilboorg's (in Rangell, 1955) allegation that there is no such thing as a borderline condition or else that it is useless to try to make such categories [essentially, Perry and Klerman's (1978) first option]. Nonetheless, analysts do diagnose and in quite sophisticated ways. The assessment of analyzability is, however, a complex diagnostic process. Moreover, the current active controversy over the approaches to narcissistic disorders hinges, in large measure, on a diagnostic discrimination between borderline pathology and narcissistic personality disorder. I would only argue here that analytic diagnosis has been too long neglected and that it provides an important area of significant analytic study and reflection. Excessive classification and the rigidity and reification of classificatory schemata, however, must be avoided.

The third difficulty is perhaps the most perplexing and is inherent in the methodology used in this initial attempt to sort out potential differential diagnostic categories. The problem arises from the fact that we are attempting to integrate, into an overall spectral perspective, descriptions and diagnostic labels that have arisen from quite independent sources, each with a prior conceptual and methodological commitment. None of the descriptions and approaches taken by students of borderline psychopathology has had the problem of differential diagnosis in mind. Rather, these approaches have been intent on providing a meaningful and clinically inclusive description and categorization that would serve to establish the pathology they were dealing with as a discrete realm of psychopathology.

Thus, the Hoch and Polatin (1949) description of pseudoneurotic schizophrenia is intended to cover those cases that seem to combine neurotic levels of personality organization and functioning with psychotic manifestations. Frosch's (1964, 1970) description of the psychotic character was intended to embrace a broad range of pathological expressions characterized by the persistence, in various subtle and minor ways, of the affinity of these individuals' personality structures to psychosis and the ease with which these patients regressed to more primitive levels of functioning. But the description was meant to be inclusive and embraced even patients who showed an increased potential for such regression, regardless of whether or not such regressive episodes ever actually occurred in the course of their life history. By the same token, as we have noted, Kernberg's (1967) definition of the borderline personality organization deliberately set out to sweep all forms of less than neurotic character dysfunction into a diagnostic rubber bag that seemed to have infinite expansibility. Thus, the borderline personality organization came to represent all forms of character dysfunction from the upper level bordering on neurotic character organization to the upper border of the psychoses.

The difficulty here arises from the fact that these same descriptions will be utilized in the interest of narrowing the focus of diagnostic applicability, thereby reducing the range of application of these descriptive categories, and, one hopes, increasing their diagnostic specificity and limiting the range of application within the borderline spectrum. Consequently, in the ensuing description of the psychotic character, although it is based on Frosch's work and leans heavily on this descriptive phenomenology, the use and application of the diagnostic label does not have the same range and connotation as Frosch would give it. It does not cover the broad range of borderline psychopathology, but rather is applied here to a limited subsegment of the borderline continuum and is characterized by specific notes, which distinguish it from the less severely disturbed borderline categories above it and from the more severely disturbed, near-psychotic pseudoschizophrenias below it. At each step of our discussion, then, the author has had to remind himself, and the reader should be constantly aware, that we are putting old wine into new wineskins. The attempt places these pre-existent categories into a new frame of reference and alters their perspective and original intention. Thus, there is a constant tension between the diagnostic validity emerging from this procedure and the original intentions of the authors of these categories.

With these cautions in mind, I would like to undertake a tentative reassessment of the borderline conditions to determine the extent to which meaningful diagnostic differentiations can be attempted. Rather than treating these groupings as discrete entities, I would envision them as descriptive groupings or clusters that show a certain general clinical consistency, even though there may be a degree of overlap in the concrete cases and a number of cases may show characteristics of more than one grouping. The groupings thus represent differentiable patterns of borderline character structure formed in the attempt to deal with a variety of developmental and object-related vicissitudes, more or less common to this intermediate range of personality development and function.

THE HYSTERICAL CONTINUUM

Pseudoschizophrenias

The first group includes a variety of disorders variously described as pseudoneurotic schizophrenia, borderline schizophrenia, ambulatory schizophrenia, or even latent schizophrenia. These patients have been described most extensively by Hoch and his associates (Hoch and Cattell, 1959; Hoch and Polatin, 1949; Hoch et al., 1962). They emphasize that these patients reveal primary symptoms, which they share with schizophrenia, even though they may be less striking and intense; they include thought and association disorders both of process and content, disorders of affective regulation, and disorders of sensorimotor and autonomic functioning. They regard this disorder as a form of schizophrenia, distinguished by its prominent secondary symptoms that include pan-anxiety, pan-neurosis, and pan-sexuality. The anxiety is diffuse, chronic, intense, and pervasive. The neurotic symptoms are usually multiple, shifting, and confusing; they include obsessions and compulsions, phobias, hysterical manifestations, hypochondriasis, depression, and depersonalization and a variety of apparently neurotic defense mechanisms that occur simultaneously or successively. The obsessions and phobias may often reach delusional proportions. This pan-neurotic picture may include tendencies to acting-out, dramatic or histrionic behavior, or antisocial and drug-dependent behavior. Sexual organization and functioning is chaotic, both in fact and in fantasy (Hoch and Cattell, 1959; Weingarten and Korn, 1967).

It should be noted that the thought disorder is a persistent and characteristic feature of pseudoschizophrenia. On clinical contact, the disorder may be more or less evident, but it usually can be found on careful observation and mental testing. Rather than clear-cut delusions or hallucinations, such as one might find in frank psychoses, there are overvalued ideas or unreasonable beliefs maintained with less conviction or consistency than delusions. Primary process and schizophrenic-like thought processes are almost unexceptionally revealed under the influence of sodium amytal and in the use of unstructured projective tests like the Rorschach (Deniker and Quintart, 1961). Moreover, the thought disorder is relatively ego-syntonic. It persists even though patients may present a reasonably good social facade and appropriate behavior and even have considerable academic or occupational achievement. The record of achievement is often somewhat erratic, however (Weingarten and Korn, 1967). Similar features have been described by Zilboorg (1941, 1956, 1957) regarding what he called "ambulatory schizophrenia."

There has been some argument whether the pseudoschizophrenic group should be regarded as essentially psychotic. Hoch and Zilboorg seemed to feel that they were dealing with a form of schizophrenia (Dickes, 1974; Kernberg, 1967), but Kernberg (1967) clearly opts for including these patients in the borderline spectrum. It can be presumed that borderline patients who show schizophrenic symptoms or have a schizophrenic outcome would fall in this category (Gunderson et al., 1975). Even in the Hoch group, there was considerable heterogeneity regarding long-term outcome, but there was a high incidence of life-long illness, with nearly 40 percent requiring rehospitalization, often many times, with 10 percent attempting suicide, and with 20 percent developing overt schizophrenic symptomatology. One-half of these (10 percent) developed chronic forms of schizophrenia with typical catatonic, paranoid, and even hebephrenic symptomatology.

Thus, we must conclude that these patients, if not basically schizophrenic, live on the very border of psychosis. The fragility and vulnerability of the ego in these patients is reflected in the constant susceptibility to drive influences, the intolerance of and the inability to bind anxiety, which teeters on the brink of traumatic and even catastrophic anxiety. Although the defensive organization and symptom-patterning can often look neurotic, the symptomatology is generally more severe than would be expected in a neurotic pattern of organization (Dickes, 1974) and is not at all effective in binding the underlying anxiety. Thus, an anxiety persists, which is often incapacitating, and elicits a multiplicity of relatively unsuccessful defensive maneuvers. Nonetheless, these patients are not simply schizophrenic, since they retain sufficient ego capacity to organize a variety of neurotic defenses and to channel drive expression into neurotic symptom formation—even though these attempts are inadequate and fail to achieve their objectives.

In addition to the ego defects, it must be presumed that the constantly shifting pattern of defense and symptomatology reflects not merely shifting configurations of such aspects of functioning, but in addition, corresponds to the fragmentation, inner disorganization, and shifting configuration of the patient's self. There is little cohesiveness or stability in the organization of the self, so that whatever tentative configurations are achieved cannot be maintained or stabilized over a significant period of time. Correspondingly, these patients have considerable difficulties in object-relationships, which tend to be intensely ambivalent and cover a diffuse and intense primitive rage; they are chaotically caught up in the flux of the dilemma of intense need and paralyzing fear.

It is well to note that selective factors undoubtedly operated in the Hoch and Cattell studies in which the pathology of pseudoneurotic schizophrenia was determined: They limited their study to patients with severe psychoneurotic symptomatology, who revealed signs of schizophrenic activity on deeper evaluation (Gunderson and Singer, 1975). It is little wonder, then, that a significant number of these patients were later to develop frank schizophrenia and that the authors would conclude that they were dealing with a subgroup of schizophrenia.

In sum, then, pseudoschizophrenics represent the lowest order of character pathology within the borderline spectrum, bordering on and sharing some characteristics with the psychoses. Essential to the diagnosis are the failure of reality-testing, a diffuse intense and chronic anxiety, the multiplicity and shifting variety of symptomatology and defense organization, and chaotic sexual functioning. These patients have a high potential for regression, but the emergence of primary process and psychotic-like symptoms need not wait upon such regression, since they remain a constant, if often subtle part of the syndrome. The evidence of primary process thinking and failure of reality-testing are usually identifiable on clinical examination.

Such patients generally run a difficult and chaotic clinical course. Medication is absolutely essential in their treatment. The intermittent use of neuroleptics may often be helpful, but usually at lower doses than required for psychotic patients and for less extended periods of time. Caution in the long-term usage of neuroleptics with such patients should be taken, in view of the obvious, long-term side effects of these drugs. Frequently, antidepressant drugs, the tricyclics or MAO inhibitors, may be particularly useful in treating panic attacks in such patients. Panic attacks tend to occur in the context of the relatively severe phobic anxieties that plague these patients, and these antidepressants seem to be relatively specific in blocking such attacks. Minor tranquilizers may be useful for more diffuse anxiety, but often prove to be of little, if any help.

Pseudoschizophrenic patients require long-term, relatively intensive psychotherapy. It should be largely supportive and directed toward gaining deeper insight only when the patient is functioning sufficiently well to permit such work to proceed and to allow the patient to tolerate the associated anxiety without regression. The therapist's participation should be a relatively active structuring, with a considerable amount of surrogate ego work and an appropriate setting of limits on the patient's propensity for acting-out and for self-destructive behavior. At times, particularly in regressive crises, hospitalization is unavoidable. This is particularly the case in the face of severely destructive acting-out and the threat of suicide (see Table 7-1).

Psychotic Character

The psychotic character was described in some detail by Frosch (1964, 1970). These patients may never actually develop psychotic symptoms, but they have a high capacity for psychotic decompensation under certain circumstances. Their transient regressions may be accompanied by a loss of reality-testing, but they retain the capacity to reverse the regression readily, so that the psychotic episodes tend to be transient. Here, the issues remain psychotic, but unlike pseudoschizophrenics, these patients are better able to maintain their functioning on a more or less consistent level during non-regressed periods, and they thus remain in reasonably good contact with reality and are relatively more able to function adaptively. However, the propensity for transient regression, even though such episodes are relatively brief and reversible, remains a marked aspect of this form of character pathology.

These patients generally have a vulnerable ego, but are in a relatively stronger position than the pseudoschizophrenics, who have little capacity to organize, in any stable fashion, a consistent pattern of defensive organization or neurotic symptomatology. Psychotic characters can achieve this level of organization, but it is susceptible to regressive pulls. The maintenance of an integrated and cohesive sense of self is a constant difficulty, in that the self is continually threatened with dissolution and disintegration and plagued by the need to cling to objects, as well as by the fear of fusing with them. The need-fear dilemma is thus pitched at a near-psychotic level, and the implicit threat is psychic death. As a general rule, self-object differentiation is preserved, but remains problematic and tenuous, and is frequently blurred or even lost in regressive episodes. Where such ego boundaries become porous and uncertain, there is often a preoccupation with identity problems;

TABLE 7-1
Pseudoschizophrenic Characteristics

Self-cohesion	Tentative, partial, easily fragmented, identity problems prominent; frequent identity diffusion
Self-object differentiation	Poor differentiation, poorly maintained
Object-relations	Intensely ambivalent, need-fear dilemma severe; object-constancy lacking; relations essentially need-satisfying; poor tolerance for ambivalence; relations transitional
Internalization	Predominantly introjective; regress to incorporation; little capacity for identification
Ego organization	Fragile, multiple defects; ego weakness; poor synthetic capacity, defenses immature/narcissistic; areas of autonomous functioning poorly maintained; minimal subliminatory capacity
Reality-testing	Poor, often loses capacity to distinguish reality from fantasy; sense of reality and relation to reality defective
Impulse control	Poor, marked tendency to relieve tension by acting-out
Anxiety	Diffuse, chronic, pervasive pan-anxiety, often traumatic/catastrophic; little capacity for signal anxiety
Superego	Defective, destructive archaic superego precursors; predominance of aggressor/victim-introjects
Primary process	Thought disorder clinically evident, marked on projective tests; delusions often remain available in non-regressive phases
Regressive potential	High, frequent, rapid regressions to psychotic levels; high potential for paranoid projection; perceptual distortions; distortions of object-relations; paranoid reactions, usually not organized into systematic delusions
Treatment	Medication: neuroleptics (low dose), antidepressants for panic attacks, tranquilizers for anxiety Psychotherapy: supportive > expressive Hospitalization: often necessary

this is often the case in analysis, where regressive pulls tend to increase the dedifferentiation and defusion of ego boundaries. As Frosch (1970) notes, in the analytic situation this may result in tenuous identifications with the analyst that have an "as-if" quality, as well as attempts to increase the sense of differentiation and separation from the analyst, which may take the form of negativism or even of paranoid distortion. In the regressive phases, the intensity of these fears is buffered by a variety of primitive defenses, which are psychotic in nature, but even at levels of better functioning, the object involvement of these individuals is highly qualified by the active use of projective and introjective mechanisms, which tend to lend a paranoid discoloration to object-relationships and to intensify the inner feeling of vulnerability and victimization.

In this connection, an important area for the evaluation of ego functioning is that of the patient's involvement in reality. In general, the capacity to relate to the environment, which Frosch breaks down into functions of the relation to reality, the feeling of reality, and the capacity to test reality, is relatively intact, but susceptible to regressive distortion. It is the relative preservation of the capacity to test reality and the ready reversibility of the loss of these functions that distinguishes the psychotic character from the psychoses proper.

One young woman came to therapy because of her unstable and often chaotic emotional life, characterized by precipitous depressive episodes that often brought her to the brink of catastrophic panic and suicide. In such phases, her world was colored by projective distortions that were transparently derived from her brutalizing, sadistic, and probably paranoid father and her passive, depressed, and withdrawn mother. In therapy, the extent to which her view of the world and the people around her was a direct reflection of old painful and disappointing relations with the important objects in her life became quickly apparent. Also apparent was a pervasive looseness of thought patterns and associations that gave her descriptions a confusing and highly tangential quality. It was never clear whether the context of her material was related to ongoing present time or whether she was, at that point, addressing herself to old objects, infantile feelings and terrors, old hurts and losses, etc. These would appear and disappear in her discourse without warning—in a fashion reminiscent of Breuer's (Breuer and Freud, 1893–5) description of Anna O's shifts into her *condition seconde*. Nonetheless, the patient retained the capacity—at times with some therapeutic clarification after I had caught on to the subtle shifts that seemed so ego-syntonic for her—to focus back on the reality and to put her self in realistic contact with it.

The combination of an impaired sense of reality with relatively intact reality-testing can result in experiences of depersonalization and derealization

(Arlow, 1966), not unfamiliar states in the psychotic character. Even where hallucinations or illusions result from regressive states, the psychotic character may maintain a greater distance from the psychotic experience, regard it as ego-alien, and even be aware that the hallucinatory experience is internally derived.

The same patient lived in two worlds simultaneously, or rather would shift back and forth between the world of reality, where she lived most of the time, and the world of fantasy, to which she retreated at times of stress when the world of reality seemed too fearful or too disappointing. The second world was peopled with animal characters to whom she had given affectionate pet names and to whom she attributed definite personalities. They were her friends who came to comfort and protect her in times of trouble.

The animal friends, in fact, came from a period of her childhood when the animals, who were her pets and her special friends, were killed by her sadistic father. One was a favorite dog the father had shot. Another was a pet pig the father had ordered killed and served at the family dinner table. The refusal of my patient to eat her pet pig became the occasion for a violent family scene in which the enraged and tyrannical father was threatening to kill his rebellious daughter or otherwise severely punish her for this refusal, while the impotent and ineffectual mother wailed in helpless distress. She cherished these friends, seeing them as the objects of persecution and murder on the part of her father, and preserved them in a special delusional realm where she would never lose them again.

It was only after many years of therapeutic work that the details of this second delusional realm began to emerge and to become available for discussion. The patient had held me in considerable distrust, fearing that if she should share the details of this second world with me I would somehow condemn her for it or force her to give them up. This delusional system, however, served her as a desperate resource. At times of stress, she would describe herself as "going away," meaning that she could retreat from the world of reality and enter the second world, where she would be entertained and consoled by her friends. The going away usually took place at times of depression, which was the typically pathological form of this patient's regressive crises. The going away could last for a matter of seconds, hours, days, or even, at times, weeks. During severe regressive crises, the patient tended to isolate herself from all human contacts and would remain in bed for days at a time.

Much of my experience with this patient reflected what has become familiar to clinicians as the caricature of a borderline presentation. When I first saw the patient she had been through a period of several chaotic years in which there were multiple suicide gestures by way of slashing and overdosing, multiple hospitalizations, and a generally difficult and chaotic clinical course. The beginning of our clinical relationship was also tempestuous—

marked by the all-too-familiar onslaught of desperate and needful clinging, urgent telephone calls, tearful threats and recriminations, and a series of readily mobilized transference distortions that were largely paranoid in character.

I have remarked on the high level of regressive potential in these patients and the extreme affective lability. This case also demonstrates an important aspect of the psychotic characters, as we are using the term here; that is, in addition to the marked regressive potential and affective lability, these patients never quite seem to remove themselves from the taint of psychotic-like processes even at their more integrated and better reconstituted levels of functioning. This patient had a remarkable reconstitutive capacity, contributed to undoubtedly by her considerable ego strengths. During the course of the therapy, she was able to graduate from college, to engage in a series of increasingly demanding jobs, and after several years of homosexual experimentation, to develop finally a meaningful and satisfying relationship with a man, finally marrying him. Despite this steady progression, which reflected the success of therapeutic efforts, the patient continued to manifest signs of a minor degree of thought disorder, with tangential thinking, loosening of associations, and at times, concreteness. At the same time, her delusional second world remained a constant feature of her psychic organization. The patient maintained this delusional system even though she could sometimes acknowledge that it was a product of her imagination, and not a part of the world of real experience. It is the persistence of such psychotic-like symptoms in the psychotic character that differentiates between this level of borderline organization and the dysphoric personality disorder, which may show similar psychotic-like features in regressive episodes, but during periods of reconstitution and more functional integration tends not to show features that might suggest minimal or latent psychosis.

It may be useful to compare the preceding case with another case, which also falls under the category of psychotic character. This was a young man who came to see me in his mid-twenties, after a history marked by a severe phobic regressive reaction in adolescence and a subsequent period of decompensation that had been diagnosed as psychotic and treated by hospitalization. When I first saw the patient, he was suffering from a severely inhibiting and paralyzing paranoid existence. He lived alone, but could hardly maintain himself and meet his day-to-day necessities. He had no friends. He spent most of his time hiding in his apartment and reading. He was terrified of going out in the streets, being delusionally convinced that the people who walked by him on the sidewalks were watching him hostilely and threateningly, and fearing that, at any moment, when he least expected it, they would turn on him and gun him down or stab him to death.

He had difficulty even going out to buy food for himself. He would go to the grocery store in a sweat of anxiety. He would grab a loaf of bread and run up to the counter and quickly put the money down and run out, not even waiting for his change. If he had to wait, he would become terrified that the clerk would suddenly reach under the counter, pull out a gun, and shoot him. After some time in therapy, the patient was gradually able to tolerate the stress involved in looking for work and in taking a job. His ability to maintain himself in the work situation was severely limited, however, since it was not long before he was paralyzed by fears that the people with whom he worked were harboring hostile and destructive intentions toward himself. He would quickly get himself into a state of paranoid anxiety and flee in terror from the situation. Even as the patient struggled with these considerable difficulties, it was not difficult for him to appreciate that his convictions about the hostile intentions of others were largely the product of his own imagination—of his own disordered thinking and fears rather than real threats. The emotional power of the fears, however, was overpowering.

It is important to note that in both these patients, ego-functions otherwise remained remarkably intact and adaptively functional. Beyond the limits of the delusional system, reality-testing was intact, and the capacity to deal adaptively and effectively with the environment was unimpaired. But even in phases of relatively non-regressed functioning, i.e., at levels of more adaptive functioning, delusional processes and cognitive dysfunction remained part of the clinical picture.

Even outside of regressive episodes, there is a basic orientation to the world based on distrust and tendencies to project and externalize. Such patients will use action or antisocial behavior to deal with intolerable and painful affects and projection to reinforce their sense of entitlement to manipulate, exploit, or destroy an environment that does not respond to their intense needs (Adler, 1970). Moreover, as Modell (1961) has pointed out, the maintenance of a belief in reality assumes a degree of separation and differentiation between self and object. If the inner reality is denied and externalized, that is, treated as though it were an aspect of external reality, this would imply a partial regression of the ego, with a loss of the differentiation and distinction between what is internal and what is external. The blurring of the distinction between self and object, between inside and outside, results in a loss of separateness that may intensify the underlying object-related conflicts. The denial of separateness can thus create an illusion of merging with the object with the corresponding threat of engulfment.

The object relations in such patients are generally on an intense need-gratifying basis, which often leads to unrealistic demands. The frustration of these demands leads to intense rage, which often expresses itself in a paranoid form. Thus, relationships with objects are often highly conflictual and intensely ambivalent. Moreover, the superego remains poorly integrated, its components having undergone little depersonification or abstraction. Rather, superego functioning is carried out in terms of often regressed and archaic superego precursors, which remain highly susceptible to forms of externalization and projection. Thus, superego integration is highly irregular and reflects multiple lacunae, so that there is a propensity for impulsive acting-out behavior side by side with hypercritical and harshly punitive superego attitudes. There is a capacity for guilt and depression, but this seems to be fragmentary and inconsistent.

We can wonder whether many of the clinical descriptions given of borderline patients in the literature are not more suitable or more specifically congruent with the characteristics of the psychotic character. For example, we can wonder whether Adler's (1970) description of the more primitive aspects of patients who overvalue or devalue in therapy, Greenson's (Rangell, 1955) description of chronic borderline states, Bychowski's (Bychowski, 1953; Robbins, 1956) discussion of latent psychosis, or the descriptions of borderline disorders in terms of relatively primitive character organization (Kernberg, 1970) or in terms of intense, stormy and quickly mobilized transference distortions (Brody, 1960; Kernberg, 1967) are not more appropriate to the description of the psychotic character. Thus, Kernberg's (1967) delineation of borderline personality functioning and deficits can be more suitably applied to these more primitively organized, regression-prone patients than to the better-organized, better-functioning borderline patients described in the following sections.

I would like to contrast this primitive characterological organization and the propensity for regression with the description of the dysphoric personality, which follows. Certainly, the regressive potential can be found at all diagnostic levels, but susceptibility to regression is a marked characteristic of borderline and psychotic conditions. Discriminatory lines are difficult to draw, but I would tend to feel that patients who quickly manifest a tendency to regression in therapy, or whose regression does not remain within the limits of the therapeutic situation, but tends to generalize outside of it, should be seen as functioning on the level of the psychotic character. Similarly, we can wonder, as Frosch (1967b) suggests, whether there may not be important differences between patients who continue in or return to the analytic work despite the regression and those who leave the analysis on account of it. The former may represent higher levels of borderline organization with sufficient ego strength to maintain the relationship in the face of regressive vicissitudes, whereas the latter may reflect a lower order of borderline organization that lacks these basic capacities.

These regressive phenomena are in contrast with the more gradual and paced regression that one might often see in the borderline personality whose regressive proclivities require considerably more analytic work and therapeutic regression (Zetzel and Meissner, 1973) in order to become manifest. Again, this runs counter to the prevailing trend to amalgamate descriptions of borderline pathology. Frosch himself tends to minimize the differences between his own description of the psychotic character and Kernberg's description of borderline personality organization. Although Kernberg's description may embrace the psychotic character, it tends to override important discriminations that are worth preserving and clinically significant. The psychotic character demonstrates a regressive fragility that many better-integrated borderline personalities do not.

The young woman described above presented characteristically in the early part of her therapy with frequent and severe regressive episodes, usually depressive in character. The rapidity with which these episodes would develop out of relatively innocuous precipitants, and the rapidity with which they were resolved, following relatively minor therapeutic intervention and clarification or interpretation, was striking. The rapid alternation of such intensely disturbing emotional states revealing both a high degree of regressive potential and a ready capacity for reconstitution would point to a diagnosis of psychotic character. The dysphoric personality as described below would not manifest this pattern. In addition, the psychotic character continues to manifest psychotic-like symptoms or features in cognitive or affective functioning even in non-regressive phases. This was the primary implication of describing these patients as characterologically having psychotic features (Frosch, 1964, 1970). The dysphoric personality manifests such features only in regressive phases, not in non-regressive phases.

The regressive propensity of the psychotic character typically reflects early experiences of a survival-threatening kind that have an impact on psychic development. The ego may be left fragmented, poorly integrated, and vulnerable and thus prone to dedifferentiation under stress of various kinds, particularly those having to do with threat to object-relationships. It may be that such tendencies to severe regression may be suspected in the initial contact with the patient, particularly if slips of tongue occur with more than the usual frequency and reflect the invasion of id impulses and a defensive weakening (Frosch, 1967a).

Such lapses and discontinuities in the cognitive sphere, resulting in the emergence of primary process in language and thinking, particularly with a more or less bland tolerance for contradictions in thought and action without any need to reconcile or unify them, are characteristic of borderline pathology (Atkin, 1974). Kernberg (1967) relates these observations to early mental conflict and the role of splitting as basic to the diagnosis of borderline. Margaret Little (1966) has also commented in this regard:

> The first appearance of any illness, or the first thing that may lead an analyst to regard a patient as being a borderline psychotic may be a faulty perception, an inaccurate inference or deduction, a failure to use symbols or analogy, the presence of symbolic equation, or other evidence of concrete thinking; or a piece of totally irrational, often irresponsible, behaviour in a person whose ways of perceiving, thinking, and behaving are otherwise quite ordinary, though he may

have other symptoms of neurosis. Areas of primary and secondary process thinking can exist side by side, and will be present or absent according to the predominance of survival, pleasure, or reality principles. (p. 479)

The difficulty in the initial stages of evaluation of such patients, however, as Zetzel (1971) has noted, is that we cannot tell whether we are dealing with a patient who is presenting symptoms from a regressive borderline state or whether we are seeing the manifestations of a more or less consistent personality functioning. Time and experience with the patient, particularly an assessment of the patient's response to effective therapeutic management, and the evolution of the object-relations aspects in the transference and alliance will provide more solid ground for evaluation.

To summarize the psychotic character, then, we are dealing with a condition in which the ego capacities are significantly stronger than those in the pseudoschizophrenic group, since they allow the patient, over significant stretches of his experience, to maintain a reasonably effective adjustment to his work and social environment and permit him to achieve a relatively good degree of effective ego-functioning in other areas. However, the underlying issues, particularly those having to do with the relationship with objects, are pitched at a more or less psychotic level and share in the psychotic intensity and life-and-death extremes of psychotic anxiety. What distinguishes the psychotic character is the relative instability of the organization of the self and the ready regression of narcissistic structures to the level of primitive archaic narcissistic formations characterized by grandiosity and excessive idealization. More specifically, the psychotic character, in its fragile and still highly vulnerable organization, has a ready potential for regression, which affects the effectiveness of ego-functioning and precipitates the utilization of psychotic defenses. Moreover, we can suggest that this differentiated picture of the psychotic character comes closest to the more familiar description of the classic regressive disorganized acting-out and intensely tempestuous borderline patient, particularly those assessed and treated in the hospital setting.

It is possible to suggest some conjunction of the present attempt to categorize borderline disorders with previous attempts. The psychotic characters are closely related to the Borderline Personality Disorder as described in DSM-III (see Chapter 3, pp. 72–73). By the same token, there are also overlapping characteristics with Rifkin and coworkers' (1972) description of emotionally unstable character disorders. The pseudoschizophrenics thus manifest a number of features that are described for the Schizotypal Personality Disorder. These categories encompass what are being designated in this study as lower-order borderline disorders. The line of discrimination between these lower-order disorders and subsequent higher-order disorders has to do with the fact that the lower-order disorders tend to show the basic picture of emotional lability and more or less regressive functioning as a chronic or characterological feature of their personality organization. In higher-order borderlines, these features emerge only in regressive crises and borderline states, and are not an aspect of the patient's more usual, better-integrated states.

Treatment of the psychotic characters is easily the most problematic and difficult and poses the near-impossible dilemmas that challenge our best therapeutic efforts. Medication is not often very useful, except for sedation or transient relief of anxiety. The patients who show extreme emotional lability, and particularly mood swings, may respond to lithium—possibly related to a connection with manic-depressive features. At times of regressive crisis, I have found Valium to be helpful on a transient basis to ease the patient through the crisis. Otherwise, drugs can be used for specific target symptoms as indicated.

Psychotherapy is indicated and essential for these patients. It must be long term and intensive, directed to exploratory and expressive channels when the patient is capable of such an effort. Otherwise, the therapeutic effort remains supportive, intervening more actively and controllingly in regressive phases. Hospitalization may often be necessary to gain control of regressive crises, but more often than not patients can be managed through such crises by medication, limit-setting, and more frequent visits if necessary. Psychoanalysis is generally not advisable for these patients (see Table 7-2).

Dysphoric Personality

To put the dysphoric personality in perspective relative to the previously described entities, we are dealing with progressively less severe, better-integrated, organized forms of character pathology. The dysphoric personality, then, represents a step up in the consistency of organization and capacity for functioning from the psychotic character, even as the psychotic character also represented a step up from the level of the pseudoschizophrenias. In general, then, the expression of the common borderline elements previously described will be on a higher level of differentiation and integration in the dysphoric personality than that seen in the previously described forms.

A number of parameters can be used to characterize the dysphoric personality. Perhaps the most general category has to do with the quality of life-style found in such patients. These patients, in general, share with the other borderlines the difficulties in carrying on their daily lives and relating to other human beings. Thus, there is a bizarre and often alienated quality to their life-style (Giovacchini, 1965; Blum, 1972). Also in common with other

TABLE 7-2
Characteristics of the Psychotic Character

Self-cohesion	Fragile, obtained episodically; identity diffusion in regressions; poor boundaries; depersonalization in regressions
Self-object differentiation	Generally preserved but tenuous, lost in regressive states
Object-relations	Need-fear dilemma at near-psychotic levels; frequent distortion by projection, primarily need-satisfying; poor object-constancy, relations usually highly ambivalent, conflictual
Internalization	Predominantly introjective, can become incorporative in regressive states; poor capacity for identification, may be "as-if" in quality
Ego organization	Vulnerable; defenses neurotic/immature; can regress to narcissistic
Reality-testing	Lost in regressive crises; reasonably well-maintained in nonregressive phases; sense of reality often impaired; at times difficulty distinguishing between fantasy and reality
Impulse control	Affective lability; frequent/rapid shifts, strong tendency to act-out
Anxiety	Separation anxiety > castration anxiety; some capacity for signal anxiety, becomes traumatic or annihilative under regressive pressures
Superego	Poorly integrated; archaic precursors predominate, more dramatically in regressions; multiple lacunae
Primary process	Usually subtle in nonregressed phases; may or may not be clinically detectable; clearly detectable on projective tests; may be persistent delusions, even hallucinations, in nonregressed phases
Regressive potential	Capacity for regression to transient psychosis, readily reversible; regressions affect all functions: ego, superego, high potential for paranoid distortion
Treatment	Medication: lithium; tranquilizers Psychotherapy: long-term, intensive, supportive/expressive; psychoanalysis not advisable Hospitalization: necessary in severe crises, especially if suicidal

borderline conditions, the dysphoric personality has a sense of inner emptiness and deep loneliness (Collum, 1972; Chessick, 1974).

Moreover, there is a peculiar quality to these patients' subjective experience of interpersonal situations. They seem extraordinarily sensitive and
responsive to their unconscious fantasies and impulses, as well as to the
primitive superego contents in the significant objects around them. The
conscious and intentional ego activity of people around them is held in
abiding suspicion and mistrust, as though they were somehow deceptions or
malicious tricks, whereas the id and superego elements seem somehow more
genuine. These patients also tend to feel that the elements of enduring
character style, self-organization, and ego-functioning in themselves are
somehow unreal or phony (Krohn, 1974).

Correspondingly, the dominance of the oedipal phase is not so clearly
seen in these patients (Frijling-Schreuder, 1969), with the result that, like
Kernberg's (1967) infantile personalities, there is a mixture of pseudohypersexuality with sexual inhibition and sexual provocativeness, which is rather
direct or crude or inappropriate, mixed with orally determined exhibitionism
and demandingness. The sexual promiscuity in infantile women has a more
drifting quality, with little stability in object-relationships, along with more
or less conscious, primitive or polymorphous-perverse fantasies. Moreover,
there seem to be multiple deviations in all areas of personality functioning,
which may be on a different level of disturbance in different areas (Rosenfeld
and Sprince, 1963). The failure to achieve oedipal phase dominance means
that in the pathology of these patients, libidinal material can be detected
from all phases of libidinal development, which leads to an often confused
and disturbed picture. Phallic trends are interfered with, so that there is a
faulty relationship between the operation of the drives and the ego, and the
bulk of the libido remains fixed in the oral and anal phase.

The fluidity and variability may express itself in shifting levels of ego
organization, which fluctuate between reality orientation and contact with
painful aspects of the environment and a preoccupation with idiosyncratic
fantasies. The ability of the therapist to establish and maintain contact with
these patients seems to mitigate the influence of fantasy; but when the
alliance weakens or the therapeutic contact is lost, inner stimuli seem to play
a more prominent role (Pine, 1974).

The general fluidity and lack of phase dominance is related to the
propensity to acting-out in borderline conditions. The more flamboyant and
particularly destructive forms of acting-out are found in borderline states
and may represent an attempt to restore a sense of reality by creating a
situation of intense feeling or pain to counter the emptiness and feeling of
unreality related to the acute diffusion of identity in the regressive state
(Collum, 1972). This regressive form of acting-out is more closely related to
the functioning of the psychotic character than to that of the dysphoric

personality. On a more general level of adjustment, however, acting-out in the dysphoric personality may take the form of externalization, in which the patient transposes his inner conflict and difficulties to the outer world and becomes more or less exclusively preoccupied with dealing with them in that external realm. Consequently, there is a constant tendency to blame forces outside the self for one's problems, and assuming little or no responsibility for them. This externalization and blaming often takes the form of subtle projections, particularly in the therapeutic setting (Giovacchini, 1972).

We have already noted the tendency to regression in the dysphoric personality, but it should be noted that this tendency is neither so intense nor as marked as in the psychotic character. Dysphoric personalities do undergo brief psychotic experiences, which frequently have a paranoid quality (Gunderson and Singer, 1975); although these regressive episodes may be provoked by drugs or severe developmental or emotional crises, they are most frequently seen in the dysphoric personality as a result of developments in the psychotherapeutic relationship. Because of the peculiar sensitivity of borderline object-relationships, these patients' function often improves rapidly in response to good therapeutic handling. This is true not only of borderline children (Frijling-Schreuder, 1969), but also of borderline adults (Zetzel, 1971).

When seen in a regressive crisis, dysphoric personality patients, unlike potentially healthy neurotics, are unable to establish a confident relationship with the therapist easily. Rather, magical expectations, diminished capacity to distinguish between fantasy and reality, episodes of anger and suspicion, and fears of rejection dominate the therapy for an extended period. Gradually, however, such patients are able to respond to good therapeutic management and, at least partially, to relinquish their unrealistic and magical expectations, as well as their fears and suspicions, and establish an, at least workable therapeutic alliance (Zetzel, 1971). Even so, as Blum (1972) has noted, these patients retain the capacity to control and reverse their regression, turning it to adaptive use.

The difficulties in therapy with these borderline patients may often lie less in transference vicissitudes than in the therapeutic alliance. Even when the transference neurosis develops unexceptionally, there often remains a tentative, insecure quality to the alliance, with an underlying basic mistrust and an inability to relate to the therapist as a reliably helpful, benignly well-intentioned object. Subtle misalliances can develop and persist through long stretches of the therapy. One young man came to analysis because of his fragile self-esteem, depressive concerns, and his general dissatisfaction with his life. His analysis unfolded unremarkably with uncovering of much important genetic material and a fairly intense, but workable transference neurosis. But as time went on, real therapeutic gains seemed incommensurate with the level and extent of insight he had gained—as though we were caught up in a subtle, pervasive, low-grade negative therapeutic response. Gradually it became clear that a faulty alliance permeated the analysis. Only then did the degree of guardedness and suspicion, the abiding conviction that, despite his years of experience in the analysis, somehow I would turn on him, hurt him, reject him, put him down, and make him feel worthless and impotent, become apparent. Only as these issues came into focus did the more border-line qualities of the patient's manner of relating and his involvement in the analysis appear.

Nonetheless, the dysphoric personality is able to retain a relatively good level of functioning and adaptation to reality. Regression in these patients is more typically seen either as the result of progressive involvement in the therapeutic relationship and increasing susceptibility to regressive pulls, usually in analysis, but also frequently enough in psychotherapy, or in particularly intense relationships with significant objects outside therapy. Thus, the dysphoric personality may be able to retain relatively good, well-functioning relationships with a wide spectrum of other people in his environment, but may regress to relatively infantile and destructive, if not maladaptive, involvements with particular objects. This pattern is not uncommon between husbands and wives. It should be noted that the stress that precipitates such regressive states is characteristically one having to do with the vicissitudes of object involvement.

It is in these regressive states that intense affects, usually hostile and destructive or depressed, are often unleashed (Gunderson and Singer, 1975; Kernberg, 1967). The destructive impulses may be turned against the self in forms of self-destructive cutting, self-mutilation, or impulsive suicidal gestures. Such regressive destructive manifestations reflect the organization at a primitive level of the themes of victimization and aggressive destructiveness, which reflect the inner organization of the victim-introject and the corresponding aggressor-introject (Meissner, 1978; Robbins, 1976). Although Kernberg relates such self-destructive tendencies to the predominance of pregenital and oral aggression, these self-destructive tendencies can be manifested or organized into pathological character traits that reflect a more or less self-destructive etiology (Kernberg, 1971).

In these cases, a more or less structured, self-directed aggression can be reflected in the tendency for negative therapeutic reaction or a tendency to draw pleasure and pride from their self-destructive power, enjoying the defeat of those closest to them, including the therapist. This may be rationalized as a submission to a harsh and demanding value system, often religious, but not exclusively so. Kernberg stresses the need to distinguish between unconscious self-defeat as a submission to a sadistic superego and a more conscious affirmation of self-destruction as an ego-ideal, which calls for the sacrifice of any happiness, success, satisfaction, or rewarding relationships to this ideal. The motif of suffering (victimization) thus plays a prominent role in such patients. This tendency may also reflect a need to defeat oneself as the price for defeating an unconsciously hated or envied helper. The self-destruction, therefore, becomes a triumph over the envied object, and this obviously plays itself out in the negative therapeutic response as a triumph over the therapist. The need to defeat the therapist may also be related to elements of oral envy and the revengeful destruction of a potential, but not fully satisfying source of love and gratification. It should be noted as well that even at more adaptive levels of functioning, in the ways in which the dysphoric personality patient goes about carrying out his daily life, ample evidence can be found to identify the elements of victimization and destructive aggressiveness (Meissner, 1978).

Perhaps at this point it would be useful to consider some case material to help focus the clinical characteristics of this group of patients. I would like to discuss several cases, the first of which is a woman who came into treatment in her middle-fifties after a series of losses and disappointments that had plummeted her into a rather severe depression, with suicidal thoughts that had persisted for several years. Despite her suicidal ideation, the patient had resisted treatment and had gradually spent most of her life savings, drifting from one part of the country to another in an aimless search for relief from her depression.

The immediate precipitant for her difficulties was the firing of her boss. She worked as an executive secretary for a highly placed corporate executive who, toward the end of an outstanding career, became increasingly depressed and turned to alcohol. The deterioration in his performance led to his being relieved of a very responsible position. At this time, my patient had been offered another comparable position with the company, but, because of her intense feelings about the discharge of her own boss, she refused to accept any other position and retired from the company. Her relationship to this man had in fact been a form of office marriage, in which she had been, for nearly one-quarter of a century, his devoted helper, confidante, friend, soulmate, and even, from time to time, sexual partner. He had been for her the form of narcissistically invested sustaining object (Levine, 1979), or the kind of "significant other," the loss of whom is so frequently the precipitant for depression in more primitively organized character structures.

The origin of these difficulties could be plainly traced in the patient's life history. She had been the only child of somewhat eccentric parents, who were able to live quite comfortably on inherited wealth. When she was still quite young, the parents of her first cousin were killed in an automobile accident, and the first cousin then came to live with her and her family. This cousin, apparently a very needy and manipulative young woman, capitalized on the sympathetic feelings of her new family, so that gradually a family myth was evolved that the cousin needed all the help she could get in order to face the rigors of life, whereas my patient could fend for herself.

My patient, previously the one and only child, suffered all the pangs of sibling rivalry, and in addition, was equivalently put in second place to this presumably more needy, unfortunate cousin. All through her growing-up years, as a consequence, she would be asked to sacrifice things for her cousin's benefit, to give up opportunities and advantages so that her cousin would not feel hurt, rejected, etc. The final upshot of this was that, when the father passed away and the final disposition of the family inheritance was made, the mother decided that my patient was well able to take care of herself and earn her own living, and so signed over the rest of the family fortune to the cousin. My patient compliantly agreed with this arrangement—but, obviously, as the years went by and began to take their toll, the resentment and anger at this state of affairs became more potent and troubling.

In her growing-up years, my patient had a rather poor relationship with her mother, never feeling very close or affectionate, and never feeling that her mother basically loved her in any real or meaningful sense. However, she doted on and felt close affectionate ties with her father. Her father, a peculiar man, was quite intelligent and well-read, but had never worked a day in his life and had a rather eccentric life-style. When the father passed away—my patient was in her early twenties—she felt as though she had lost the one person in the world who was close to her and meant anything to her and the only one who had ever been her friend. It was not long after this, however, that she was able to replace the lost father by her attachment to the young executive, who became the significant other, the sustaining object, to whom she devotedly attached herself, and in relation to whom her life took on meaning and substance.

It was not difficult to guess what was in store for my patient when this important object was removed from her life. She plunged into a severe depression, and for years afterwards wallowed in feelings of helplessness and self-pity. For years, she lived on a thin edge, constantly preoccupied with suicidal thoughts and fantasies, but never having the courage or conviction to attempt suicide. The patient remained chronically suicidal through most of the period of psychotherapy, which lasted over a number of years. At times, the suicidal impulses would be more acute and pressing and consequently more worrisome. A number of medications were tried, but never with any marked effect. Usually, the patient's reaction to side effects outweighed the minimal benefits of the drug. Several antidepressants were used and for a time, Valium. The most effective drug seemed to be a combination of an antidepressant and a neuroleptic, Triavil.

At one point, during a particularly intense regressive crisis, we agreed upon hospitalization. However, within a day or two after entering the hospital, the patient seemed to be feeling quite well, had recompensated to her usually effective level of functioning, and was making herself useful on the inpatient unit, talking with other patients about their problems. The ward staff was quick to point out that she no longer seemed to need the ward, and the therapist was left scratching his head, wondering whether the admission had been necessary.

In between these regressive periods of suicidal preoccupation and intense feelings of helplessness and hopelessness, the patient would return to apparently effective levels of functioning in which her native resources of good intelligence, efficiency, and executive abilities clearly manifested themselves. At such points, the patient would be able to gain employment and, by way of her efficiency and effectiveness, would get a considerable amount of positive feedback from her employers, who usually felt that she was capable of a much higher level of work than that for which she had been hired. She would then collapse into one of her regressive states, in which she became totally ineffectual, apathetic, depressed, and suicidal, so that her work would deteriorate and they would have to let her go.

Over the years I worked with her, there were countless such cycles; but gradually the patient succeeded in diminishing her resources so that she was reduced to more and more humble living circumstances and increasingly menial jobs, none of which she seemed to be able to hold for any length of time. After too long a period of proud resistance, she finally agreed to accept welfare payments; and since she was unable to continue her therapy, it was terminated. It seems likely that what this patient sought and was unable to find was the same kind of sustaining object-relationship she had formed with her former boss. Without such a relationship, she was unable to maintain the sense of inner autonomy and self-cohesion that would have buffered the effects of her depression and allowed her to function more adaptively and productively in her life situation. In such a relationship, self-cohesion and libidinal object-constancy remain contingent on the continuity of the relation to the object. The loss of the sustaining object leaves these patients vulnerable to a sense of inner fragmentation and a loss of cathexis of the world of objects. They feel that it is not worth the effort to survive in such a world.

In the regressive phases of her pathology, the sense of victimization, and its helplessness and hopelessness, and the feelings of inferiority and worthlessness reflecting the residues of inferior narcissistic pathology came to dominate the clinical picture. It was particularly the quality of this patient's capacity for object-relationships, the recurrent regressive episodes marked by a failure of usual defensive capacities, and a loss of autonomous self-structure, as well as the capacity to function more adaptively and effectively during non-regressive phases, that would stamp this patient as a dysphoric personality.

The second patient is a young man who began his analysis just before his thirtieth year. He had graduated from a prestigious university with highest honors and then had spent several years in a graduate program. However, he felt diffident, even indifferent about his work, feeling that it was not sufficiently involving and that it did not offer the promise of significant achievement or reward even if he were to obtain his degree. His feelings persisted even though his performance was exemplary and earned him the highest recognition and acknowledgment from his peers and professors. He felt generally dissatisfied with himself and his life and where he saw it heading.

The patient felt highly ambivalent about his attainments. He was constantly playing down or discounting any of his many accomplishments. In talking about his academic achievements and the praise and recognition they had brought him, he had a sense of embarrassment or shame, feeling he did not deserve such acknowledgment and praise, that there was something fraudulent or deceptive about it. After his graduation, the school library had put up a special display of outstanding senior theses for that year. He felt overwhelmed with shame and humiliation at the sight of this display and found it necessary to purloin the copy of his thesis from the display; he then went to the catalog and removed all cards there that had any reference to his work.

The patient's personal life also bore definite stigmata. His relationships with women tended to be tempestuous and tortuous, marked by frequent fights, a chaotic course of up-and-down feelings, including swings of depression and anxiety, bouncing back and forth between rage and desperate need, but somehow never being able to find any middle ground in which the relationship could be carried on reasonably. If there were such periods, they seemed to be small islands in a vast raging sea—transient episodes that did not seem to last very long, but rather were immediately swallowed up by the turmoil of affects.

When he first began the analysis, the patient could maintain only very poor control over his affective responsiveness. His feelings tended to be somewhat disorganized and chaotic, highly labile, and quick to lead to explosive outbursts. Any least frustration or stress would make the patient feel desperate and helpless, feeling the intense rage within him welling up in uncontrollable fashion and making him want to lash out destructively and vindictively at any object within range.

His tolerance for any frustration was mininal. If he broke the point on his pencil, he would become furious and smash the pencil to smithereens. If his car ran out of gas, he would become enraged at the vehicle; and with a sense of impotent rage and frustration, he would kick it and hit it with his fist, even to the point, at times, of hurting himself. On one occasion, his car, which was rather old and rundown, would not start because of a transmission failure. The patient became so enraged that he seized a crowbar and smashed the car with repeated blows so that it became a shamble of dents, broken windows, and smashed headlights. When arguments arose between himself and the woman he lived with, the same rage would overwhelm him, but he would usually take out his rage on some inanimate object—smashing a window or a lamp or throwing dishes, etc. On very rare occasions he would actually strike her, and at these times he would then be overwhelmed with guilt, remorse, and self-recrimination.

The patient came by these borderline attributes honestly enough, since he seemed to manifest many borderline characteristics even as a child. His father had been a minister—the pastor of a rather large congregation in an Eastern metropolis. The father was a widely respected man in his community and looked up to by many people in the congregation, and even beyond, as a wise man and a moral teacher. However, the patient's relationship with the father was rather distant and troubled. He remembers his father as a big, burly man with a violent temper. He recalled that his father would quickly and easily lose his temper and become enraged and violent—although there is no indication that the father was ever abusive or violent to his son. However, in the quick-temperedness and easily mobilized, violent aggressive feelings, father and son were much alike.

The patient recalls his feelings of terror of his father, even from very early years. He remembers as a very small child, for example, coming into the bathroom in the morning to watch his father shave—consumed by the usual childish curiosity. But he would suddenly get the idea that his father would turn on him and attack him with the razor, and he would run in terror from the bathroom. He lived in constant terror of his father's rages and the threat of violent physical abuse that seemed always to hover in the background.

The patient's mother, a farmer's daughter from the Midwest, did not have very much education, certainly not as much as the patient's father. She was withall a somewhat passive and depressed woman, who would only cower and cry when the father would carry on in one of his rages. The patient could never remember a time when he felt that his mother could be a source of protection or comfort for him. He constantly painted her in terms of ineptitude and inadequacy.

One of his earliest memories was of his being put in a playpen in the backyard when suddenly a large snake began to approach him. He was terrified and screamed and cried loudly, but it was some time—seemingly an eternity—before his mother came to pick him up and comfort him. But the patient's primary indictment against his mother was that she had been so ineffectual in protecting him from his father's potential brutality.

For as far back as the patient could remember, he was plagued with a variety of phobic anxieties. These made a torture of his life, not only when he was very young, but even through latency and adolescence. His capacity for phobic reaction would fasten on almost anything. He recalled, as a small child of three or four years of age, hearing his parents talk about an epidemic of sleeping sickness caused by the tsetse fly. Not realizing that there was no sleeping sickness and no tsetse flies in his part of the world, he spent several nights cowering in terror in his room, fearing that flies would come in and somehow attack him in his sleep. Similarly, he heard his father talk about bacteria in the water of the swimming place where his family would spend their summer vacation. He became terrified of the water, refused ever to go into it, and was constantly afraid that if he were to enter it he would somehow become infected and die. There seemed to be an almost endless and inexhaustable series of such phobic concerns that permeated his life and made almost everything that he undertook an agony of fear and anxiety.

Despite these fears, he continued to do well in school and became an excellent student, usually at the top of his class. However, socially life was considerably more difficult for him. He had few friends, was always very shy, and found it difficult to engage in play with other children his own age. He was constantly afraid of getting hurt or somehow suffering some terrible accident that would maim him for life. His relationships with girls were similarly distant and awkward. He found it almost impossible to talk in the presence of girls, he was constantly ashamed of himself and felt that they were critical of him or that they would laugh at him for his shyness and awkwardness. These feelings persisted on through adolescence, so that he was unable to have any meaningful contact with members of the opposite sex until well into college. Even then, he dated little and preoccupied himself almost exclusively with his studies and in excelling, academically.

Despite his academic success, his phobias and anxieties came back to haunt him. Pursuing his fantasies of following some career in which he imagined he could become rich, powerful, and famous, he decided to go to medical school. He was accepted at one of the most prestigious medical schools in the country. His experience there was a horror. In the face of the intense competition, the overwhelming amount of material, the pressure to perform, he seemed unable to concentrate and had great difficulty studying —something he had never experienced before—and seemed unable to keep up with his courses. He found himself obsessively preoccupied with the diseases and illnesses he heard and read about, and developed severe hypochondriacal anxieties. He was paralyzed by a variety of phobic concerns in the dissecting lab, terrified of the corpse, fearful that he would cut himself, become infected and die, and morbidly and increasingly preoccupied with thoughts of death. He could no longer tolerate the strain and resigned in shame and humiliation. He frequently appealed to this experience as proof of his inadequacy and inferiority. It was a festering sore that continued to plague him, even years later.

Like the previous patient, this patient also possessed considerable personal resources and ego strengths. At no point in the turmoil of the affective storms that plagued his life was there any suggestion of psychotic decompensation. But at times of regressive crisis, in the face of particular stresses or disappointments, he would be precipitated into intense feelings of depression marked by a sense of shame, inadequacy, and worthlessness. He would at times be plagued by suicidal thoughts, which had a desperate and helplessly pleading quality, and at such times, there would even come into the picture a certain paranoid quality to his thinking in which he would begin to feel that people were laughing at him or that they were thinking bad or derogatory things about him. At such times, when things did not go as he wished, he would even begin to entertain the possibility that people were putting obstructions in his way just to frustrate him and to make him feel impotent and helpless.

Despite all these fears and anxieties and emotional turmoil, the patient continued to be able to function in the world, and carried on his program of studies quite successfully. During the course of our analytic work together, the patient gradually was able to achieve some greater degree of emotional stability and was finally able to face and work through the decision about what career course he wished to follow, deciding on a program of studies quite different from the one he had been following for several years. He was able to undertake the graduate program he had chosen and continued to work effectively and successfully in it during the remainder of his analysis.

In this patient, then, we can see a lifelong history of somewhat marginal emotional functioning, which extended from the phobically overwhelmed features of his childhood to the emotional turmoil and phobic anxieties of adulthood. The quality of his object-relationships was, on the one hand, needful and clinging, again in the typical borderline fashion of desperately searching for a sustaining object, but on the other hand, tended to be distrustful, cold, demanding, rejecting, and fearful. At times, when regression would get the better of him and would become relatively severe—episodes that happened rarely, perhaps once or twice during the several years of our analytic work together—the patient would become almost delusionally fearful, a little paranoid, and would begin to experience a sense of inner confusion and disorganization that seemed to suggest some degree of inner fragmentation and loss of self-cohesion. At such times, he would become terrified of dying or of losing his mind. In retrospect, it seems that he must have experienced such a relatively severe regressive crisis with loss of inner self-cohesion in his medical-school experience. All these characteristics, including the regressive swings, the capacity for integral non-regressive functioning, and the relative paucity of any psychotic-like manifestations, would be consistent with the diagnosis of dysphoric personality.

The third patient I would like to discuss was really quite similar to the second case, but with some minor variations. The patient was in his early thirties when he came to analysis. His complaint centered primarily around his considerable difficulties in getting his life going in any consistent direction. He had been an undistinguished and barely adequate student in college, largely because of his emotional difficulties. Despite his obvious gifts and high level of intelligence, he had always found it difficult to engage himself in any consistent and effective way in studying, never being able to perform very well or consistently unless he found the material of the course to his liking and unless he was able to feel comfortable with his professor. Since this was rarely the case, his performance tended to suffer accordingly; but under the right circumstances, his performance could be brilliant.

After college, he had spent several desolatory years, being unable to make up his mind what he wanted to do and trying a variety of odd jobs, none of which seemed to satisfy or interest him. He then tried a series of graduate programs, feeling that he ought to use his intelligence in some more productive way and having the conviction that he was destined to perform some noble, significant, intellectual accomplishment. The only possible path he saw to such a goal was through a graduate degree. But he tried several paths, none of which seemed to be satisfactory. He first chose medical school, but his undergraduate record closed that door to him. He then tried other related fields in the biomedical area, was accepted in several programs, and in each one would do creditable work in the beginning of his program, but soon would become entangled in arguments and recriminations with his professors. Before long, the quality of his work began to suffer; and before the semester was out, he would be asked to leave the program.

Similarly, the patient's relationships with women left a great deal to be desired. He would find himself repeatedly becoming attracted to some woman with whom he would fall madly in love and then try to pursue her with an intensity and demandingness that, whether she found him attractive or not, would soon result in angry rejection. At times he would become infatuated and obsessed with women he hardly knew. He would constantly be devising ways of meeting them, talking to them, running into them in the lunchroom, etc., in the hopes that he would be able to gain some response from them that would bring him closer to his cherished fantasy of a meaningful and satisfying relationship. But his dealings with women were always awkward and rarely satisfactory. He would, for example, invite a girl for dinner and a show, and then expect her to pay her own way, claiming that he was only a poor graduate student and could not afford such dates. There seemed to be little capacity on his part to take into account the feelings or expectations of his companions.

The patient was born when his parents were middle-aged—his mother in her middle forties and his father over fifty. He was an only child. The patient's mother was a quiet, submissive, depressed, rather masochistic woman, who tended to view life in terms of the burdens and sorrows that it brought her. The myth grew up in the family, partly on the basis of fact and partly as a function of the mother's psychological need, that the patient's birth had been extremely difficult and traumatic for her and that in the course of it she had nearly died. The patient had assimilated this story to mean that in the process of birth he had so damaged his mother that she was forever after unable to have any more children. Thus, even from the beginning of his life, there was embedded in his psychological experience an image of himself as somehow evil and destructive.

The patient's father was a man of some education and considerable intelligence, who had at one point in his career been a rather distinguished writer and editor. Later in his life, however, he had been unable to sustain the level of output that had marked his earlier career and had been forced to gradually take less and less prestigious and financially rewarding jobs. He wound up in a rather menial position in a local publishing house. The father at home, however was something of a martinet. He was demanding and perfectionistic of both his wife and his son. If things were not done as he demanded, he would fly into rages and become violent and abusive. When the patient was still very young, even two or three years of age, his father would undertake to teach him how to count, how to read, how to add and subtract, etc. The father would set a rather high, demanding, and perfectionistic standard for his little son's performance; and when the child would make mistakes and not meet his expectations, he would fly into one of his rages. My patient remembers feeling terrified and helpless in the face of his father's onslaught. He remembers even as a small child feeling stupid and that he would never be able to measure up to his father's expectations.

At the same time, my patient had a very high regard for his father's intellectual abilities and talents. His father knew several languages, could write well with good literary style, and was something of an amateur painter. My patient could remember the skill with which his father would sit down at a drawing board and sketch some scene. Trying to emulate his father, my patient would try to do the same thing, expecting that he should be able, with consummate ease as had his father, to sit down and immediately sketch something that would be comparable in quality to his father's work. When what turned out on the paper was nothing but childish scribbling, he would go into a rage, tear up the paper and throw it away, break the pencils, and run into his room crying in a fit of frustrated rage.

The same expectation that things should somehow be easy for him, that he should not have to make an extraordinary effort to accomplish his goals, no matter how high he might set them, plagued his existence even into his analysis. He was convinced that, if he were gifted with superior intelligence and if a given field were the right one for him to follow, everything should come easily and successfully to him and that he should not have any difficulty in understanding concepts and in performing the tasks that were set for him, with ease and aplomb. When this so often proved not to be the case, he would become easily frustrated, begin to feel helpless and desperate, and become almost completely incapable of further work.

Like the previous patient, the regressive crises in this patient did not take on a psychotic character in any sense. However, unlike the previous patient, the regressions did not take the form of severely paralyzing terror or rage attacks. Rather, this patient tended to become depressed, feeling desperate, impotent, and helpless. He would wallow in feelings of inferiority, inadequacy, humiliation, and worthlessness. He would think of suicide as the only way out of his seemingly endless difficulties and frustrations.

Although he never became paranoid, he would, nonetheless, rail in impotent rage at the figures who seemed to deny him what he sought, especially the professors who would make such excessive demands on him, yet would not give him adequate help so that he could feel that it was possible for him to satisfy these demands. They all served as transferential substitutes for his intolerant, demanding, unhelpful, quick-tempered father.

Gradually, over several years of analysis, this patient was able to gain some insight into the dynamics of his feelings and reactions, managing to achieve some greater degree of tolerance for his own limitations and for the restrictions and demands of reality. Finally, he was able to decide on a definite career, and he was accepted into a graduate program in another part of the country, and so terminated the analysis. In sum, the overall dynamic and diagnostic picture for this patient was very nearly identical to the preceding case.

Another point to keep in mind in reference to the regressive episodes, both in reference to the dysphoric personality, and even more particularly in reference to the psychotic character, is the quality of the emergent transient psychosis. The regression in some of these patients is characterized by the emergence of schizophrenic symptoms, but in other cases, the regression seems to point in the direction of a more manic-depressive configuration. The existence of such cyclothymic characteristics in at least some borderline personalities (Robbins, 1976; Stone, 1980) raises the question of differential symptomatology that might be expressed on a more characterological level as well. A clinical description of such early subtle signs of a "protomanic personality" has been offered by Stone (1976).

It is customary, in the descriptions of borderline pathology, to refer to ego defects (Blum, 1972; Maenchen, 1968; Masterson, 1972; Brody, 1960) or to ego weakness (Kernberg, 1967). Such defects are quite evident in regressive borderline states, but we wish to focus the question of ego-functioning at a more specifically characterological level. At that level, the dysphoric personality is capable of maintaining a quite adequate functional capacity, but ego apparatuses remain vulnerable and reveal a characteristic instability (Rosenfeld and Sprince, 1963). The terminology of defect and weakness, I would prefer to reserve for the lower orders of borderline pathology.

The ego of the dysphoric personality reflects a certain passivity, which is manifested in more or less passive or masochistic behaviors, a sense of ego helplessness, and difficulty in maintaining a sense of control or capacity to achieve goals. Such individuals often anticipate defeat and may adopt a posture of passivity as a form of a minor, often quite subtle role in their more characterological level of adjustment; this passivity is a marked characteristic of borderline states in periods of regression. Thus, the primitive defenses (Rosenfeld and Sprince, 1963; Kernberg, 1967) are identifiable, but cannot be said, at this level of organization, to be distinguishable from the use of similar defenses in neurotic personalities or in the higher-order character disorders. More specific comments about the interplay of introjection and projection, particularly in reference to object relationships, will be made later. But in general, the mobilization of defensive operations has a neurotic quality, so that these patients are capable not only of using higher-order defenses, including repression, but in their use of lower-order defenses, they remain essentially within the neurotic range. It is only in regressive crises that the full flowering of the primitive defenses, including splitting, primitive idealization, projection, denial, omnipotence, and devaluation, as they have been described, for example, by Kernberg (1967), are in evidence. In general, dysphoric personalities tend to function with fairly high level defenses during non-regressive periods. The defenses tend to be of a neurotic or near-neurotic level. During regressive states, however, they tend to shift to the level of immature or narcissistic defenses (Meissner, 1980b).

A specific comment can be made about the defensive operation of splitting. The role of splitting in Kernberg's theory is central, since it underlies the factors of ego weakness and the inability to achieve adequate integration of both good and bad self-images and good and bad object-images. This affects the quality of the patient's object-relationships, as well as the failure of internal integration, which leaves the patient vulnerable to regression. Moreover, Kernberg cites splitting as characteristic of borderline pathology and uses it to discriminate between borderline and neurotic forms of organization, the latter having repression as the central defense mechanism.

Although the description of splitting seems, from the point of view of this review, to have a valid application to the lower orders of borderline pathology and to the organization of psychic experience in regressive states, its applicability to the borderline personality must be taken in a more subtle and refined sense. It has more to do with the characteristic organization of aspects of introjective configurations, particularly the component elements of the victim-introject and the aggressor-introject (Meissner, 1978). In terms of the characterological organization of the borderline personality, it must be said that both these configurations are operative, along with others that are better expressed in terms of narcissistic components.

Each configuration can be found to operate alternately in different contexts of the subject's experience without the accompanying tendency for one or the other configuration to be more completely repressed, as is the case with neurotics. In the neurotic personality, and particularly in forms of character pathology, one can identify these configurations, but usually only after a considerable amount of analytic work and in the context of increasing analytic regression. One or the other of the introjective configurations may be more or less available to the patient's conscious awareness, but the others tend to be correspondingly repressed. In the borderline personalities, however, these configurations remain relatively unrepressed and are generally much more available and more readily expressed, along with the contradictory ego states that accompany them.

Thus, a view from the vantage point of introjective organization makes the discrimination between splitting and repression less polar and places the diagnostic discrimination between the borderline and neurotic forms of personality organization, more on the manner in which splitting and repression are utilized, rather than on an all-or-none presence or absence of these mechanisms. Nonetheless, Kernberg's statement to the effect that the more these primitive mechanisms of splitting, primitive idealization, projection and projective identification, denial, omnipotence, and devaluation dominate the clinical picture, the more the diagnosis of a borderline is warranted, retains its validity, since these mechanisms are characteristically found in the lower-order forms of the borderline spectrum. Where they do, in fact, come to dominate the clinical picture in the present perspective, one would infer that the patient's pathology represented one of the forms of lower-level borderline pathology or that the patient was functioning in a regressive state. At the same time, it must be said that in many borderline personalities, as here described, there may be little indication of the operation of such mechanisms, in clinical terms, and that they may become operative only under special conditions of induced regression.

Something similar can be said about the manifestations of ego weakness. On the characterological level, the lack is relative and results only in a tendency toward more or less direct expression of impulses and a pattern of nonspecific diminishing of impulse control. This relates to the general variability and tendency toward acting-out as reactions to the building-up of psychic tension. Depending on the degree of diminished control, this suggests the necessity for setting limits within the therapy and a general need for the therapist to maintain a more active structuring approach. In general, the impulsivity of relatively non-regressed, dysphoric personality patients is easily managed and responds readily to effective therapeutic intervention. If the loss of control is more severe, however, this may reflect a regressive state. The diminution of ego control in such patients has been compared to an unreliable thermostat; rather than a breakdown in thermostatic control, there is relative unpredictability and variability of functioning (Ekstein and Wallerstein, 1954).

Anxiety tolerance is compromised in the dysphoric personality, but not to the degree found in the psychotic character and, even more extremely, in the pseudoschizophrenic. In the latter entities, the level of anxiety tends to be pitched at a level of severe separation anxiety or even a catastrophic or an annihilation anxiety level. The issues for these entities, then, tend to be psychotic in proportion; an extreme anxiety is then pitched at a life-and-death level. In the dysphoric personality, the issues tend to be generated more on the level of castration and separation anxiety. Such patients may express castration fears and castration motifs, but, particularly in a meaningfully productive and gradually regressive therapeutic context, the issues rapidly become those of loss of love and fear of loss of the object. The description of intense, traumatic, overwhelming fears of disintegration, annihilation, the panicky fear of merging or engulfment, and the fears of inner disintegration and loss of identity (Maenchen, 1968; Rosenfeld and Sprince, 1963; Frijling-Schreuder, 1969) are more closely related to lower levels of borderline pathology or are found more explicitly in transient regressive borderline states even in the dysphoric personality.

Nonetheless, on the characterological level, there tends to be a free-floating and diffuse anxiety, which exceeds the capacity of multiple symptoms and character structures to bind (Kernberg, 1967). The crucial issue is not the degree of anxiety experienced, but rather the extent to which any additional anxiety may lead to an increase in symptoms or acting-out or may precipitate an ego regression (Kernberg, 1967, 1971). In other words, the dysphoric personality retains a capacity for signal anxiety, even though that anxiety may be pitched at a level of separation concerns; only when one retreats does it reach a traumatic level or a level of annihilation anxiety in which the relationship to the potentially lost object is based on incorporation in regressive states (Little, 1966). In these terms, then, the presence and capacity for signal anxiety, even though it be diffuse and chronic, can be an optimisitic prognostic indicator (Kernberg, 1971).

The lack of sublimatory channels should be regarded less as a lack than as a variably expressed capacity that depends very much on circumstances. Kernberg (1967, 1971) has noted the difficulty in evaluating this capacity, particularly in relation to the capacity for creative achievement and the ability to invest oneself in an activity or a profession beyond the mere satisfaction of narcissistic needs. The dysphoric personality patient often seems compromised in this regard; but where such creativity or artistic expressivity can be tapped, these patients often prove capable of high degrees of productive effort and creativity. It is extremely difficult, however, to tease out of such forms of self-expression the satisfaction of narcissistic needs that may be inherently related to such activities. Taken in themselves, however, as objective activities wihout considering the underlying narcissistic components, it would seem that the dysphoric personality often enjoys considerable capacity for sublimatory activity.

The synthetic function undergoes severe regression in borderline states, but in the dysphoric personality, it maintains a fairly well integrated level. Most descriptions of the failures of synthesis have to do with this regressed level of functioning (Rosenfeld and Sprince, 1963; Masterson, 1972; Kernberg, 1967, 1970b). However, the synthetic function is also more characterologically and chronically impaired to the extent that there is a failure to integrate various contradictory components of the introjective alignments around which the organization of the self is constructed (Meissner, 1978). The extent of the failure of synthesis is thus reflected in the splitting of the internal self-organization and self-representations and the tendency to alternate between various introjective configurations and corresponding ego states. Thus, the dysphoric personality's self-cohesiveness is rather tenuously maintained and is constantly jeopardized by the tendency to retreat to and to respond in terms of the respective introjective configurations.

In the same vein, reality-testing is generally well maintained in the dysphoric personality and is placed in jeopardy only in the context of a regressive borderline state (Rosenfeld and Sprince, 1963; Frijling-Schreuder, 1969; Kernberg, 1967; Masterson, 1972). The maintenance of reality-testing under ordinary circumstances distinguishes the borderline conditions from the psychoses (Kernberg, 1970b, 1971); in the dysphoric personality, this weakening or loss of the capacity to test reality is seen only in regressive crises (Gunderson and Singer, 1975). In contrast to the psychotic character, the dysphoric personality is less susceptible to regressive pulls and therefore has a more solid footing in reality. By way of contrast, in the psychotic character, reality may be pushed aside and fantasy substituted for it with relative ease, even though these patients retain an intact capacity to test reality so that the psychotic reactions are brief and transient. Dysphoric personalities, however, retain a relatively firm sense of their relationship to reality and the feeling of reality, along with a maintained capacity to test that reality.

We have discussed the tendency to primary process thinking in relationship to regressive potential. Here also, it can be said that the indices for primary process organization and cognition reflect the regressive functioning of the borderline state and are intimately connected with the reactivation of carly pathological introjects and primitive defensive operations, as well as the partial refusion of self- and object-images (Kernberg, 1967). Consequently, it can be said that, on a general characterological level of functioning, the dysphoric personality shows little greater inclination to primary process organization than higher-order forms of character organization and functioning.

It is to be understood that some degree of primary process is found in even the best functioning, well-adapted personalities. The dysphoric personality may give no greater indication than that expected of average neurotic patients of thought disorganization or of a formal thought disorder on clinical examination. Similarly, these patients do not provide evidence on unstructured projective tests of disorganization of thinking either. Such evidence would suggest that the patient was functioning in a regressive modality, or that the diagnosis should be changed in the direction of a lower order of character pathology. The presence of subtle indicators of less than totally logical or fully consistent thinking or combination of precepts may be entirely consistent with the dysphoric personality diagnosis, but similar findings can be found in the Rorschach protocols, for example, of neurotics or higher-level forms of character pathology. A higher incidence of these more subtle signs, however, may reflect a primary process tendency, but does not suggest a formal thought disorder or psychotic cognitive organization.

The object-relations of dysphoric personalities require careful delineation. As we have already observed, the dysphoric personality shares in the need-gratifying quality of object-relationships, in general. Object relationships also tend to reflect the influence of relatively intense narcissistic needs. These aspects of the quality of object-relationships are evident in the three cases of dysphoric personality presented above. However, in the therapeutic context, the more typical picture in the dysphoric personality is for these needs to emerge gradually over time as the therapeutic relationship develops and as the more regressive aspects of the relationship mature and emerge. The rapid, precipitous, and intensely ambivalent involvement with objects is not characteristic of the dysphoric personality, as it might be of the psychotic character or the pseudoschizophrenic.

When that form of intensely ambivalent and clingingly dependent involvement with the therapist is observed in the dysphoric personality, it is usually in the context of at least a partial regression. It is not altogether uncommon for such patients to come to the therapeutic situation propelled by the distress and turmoil associated with a regressive borderline state, so that such behavior may be seen; but it cannot serve diagnostic differentiation until the further evolution of the developing therapeutic relationship brings more adequate data for assessment.

In addition, object-constancy is relatively well maintained, but remains vulnerable (Rosenfeld and Sprince, 1963; Frijling-Schreuder, 1969; Kernberg, 1970b, 1971). Generally, as the intensity of the involvement with a given object increases, the dysphoric personality's capacity to tolerate and integrate aspects of increasingly intense ambivalent feelings becomes more and more tenuous. Thus, even at levels of characterological functioning, there is a certain instability in object-relations, a diminished capacity for empathy (Kernberg, 1970b), or a peculiar quality of the experience of meaningful relationships in which the subject is considerably more responsive to the instinctually derived aspects of the object rather than the more enduring and consistent character traits or ego qualities (Krohn, 1974). The need-fear dilemma in patients on this level of characterological functioning remains an unexplicit, but subtly pervasive concern that runs as a constant countermelody under the more predominant themes and day-to-day concerns; when there is a significant involvement with objects, the entire tenor of the relationship is pervaded by a subtle and often implicit, but also often relatively conscious and explicit fear of abandonment.

There is a constant seeking and a tendency to cling to available objects as a means of allaying or filling up the sense of inner emptiness, but no object seems to satiate that deep and inner craving, and the patient is left with an unfulfilled sense of need that may reach even desperate proportions, and an intensified sense of frustrated and disappointed longing. Under these circumstances, the dysphoric personality is quite capable of provoking struggles and turmoil in a frantic attempt to gain concern, attention, and caring from objects that are seen as, in part, frustrating or rejecting. The tenuous capacity to maintain libidinal constancy and the difficulty in integrating aspects of the ambivalence remain a constant source of difficulty. In general, these patients tend to feel needy and unsatisfied in their relationships (Adler, 1975), but the motifs are expressed in a muted, more or less chronic fashion, with occasional exacerbations, which tend to be relatively transient and labile and create brief periods of turmoil and conflict in the patient's life, but then quickly return to a more day-to-day level.

The components of this dilemma in relationship to objects may frequently enough be solved, particularly in women, by a certain clinging dependency and compliant submissiveness. The issue of borderline compliance has been focused recently by Robbins (1976). If borderline aggression and attempts to control are frequently striking aspects of this syndrome, it is no less true that borderline compliance and victimization are important and frequently observed components (Robbins, 1976; Meissner, 1978). This form of object choice has been described by Reich (1953) as a form of narcissistic object choice in women. This form of object involvement and relatedness tends to teeter on the brink between object-relationship and introjection and comes close to the descriptions of "as-if" personalities and false-self configurations. However closely the issues may be related among these various expressions of borderline compliance and object-need, the patterns are significantly different to sustain differentiation. The compliance in the dysphoric personality is primarily an expression of the victim-introject and lacks the plasticity and imitativeness of the "as-if" personality or the quality of schizoid protectiveness in the false-self organization. Nonetheless, it seems clear that the tendency for such compliance can be a source of difficulty that must be consistently and cautiously sounded out in the therapy of such patients.

Difficulties in object-relationships are themselves reflected in transference dynamics. Although rapid involvement in intense clinging and demanding involvements with the therapist makes a shambles of the therapeutic alliance and impairs the utility of transference interpretations (Little, 1958; Adler, 1975), this transference behavior is not, by and large, characteristic of the dysphoric personality in its non-regressive phases. Kernberg (1968, 1976b) characterizes the borderline transference by a premature activation of conflict-ladened object-relationships, along with mutually dissociated ego states. This premature activation of regressive ego states is much more characteristic of the psychotic character, or even in a more fragmented way of the pseudo-schizophrenic, but it is exceptional in the dysphoric personality. Such reactions may be seen in these patients in the early stages of therapy, when the patient is seen in a regressive crisis, but it cannot be said to be characteristic of the general run of transference reactions characterizing the dysphoric personality. The descriptions of transference disturbances tend to focus on the regressive manifestations that accompany borderline states (Little, 1966; Adler, 1970). These patients may show tendencies to transference acting-out, to projective distortions of the therapeutic relationship, to valuing and devaluing, but these tendencies are often muted, may be quite subtle, and do not have the disruptive, chaotic, or severely disturbed aspects that are associated with more regressed states. In fact, it can be safely said that such transference reactions, if less frequent, are not difficult to identify, even in relatively healthy and non-regressed neurotic patients.

Perhaps the most helpful discrimination in understanding the borderline transference is Modell's (1963, 1968) analysis of the "transitional object-relationship." Although there is a tendency to read the transitional object-relationship as akin to that of the schizophrenic, it must be maintained that the quality of the transitional object-relationship found in the dysphoric personality is distinct from a transference psychosis. As a transitional object, the object is perceived as outside the subject, as a separately existing individual, but is perceived or interpreted in terms of elements that are attributed to the object from the subject's own self. These transference distortions, although they are based on the operation and interplay of projections and introjections (Meissner, 1978), do not reach delusional proportions and are not marked by the loss of boundaries, the sense of fusion, and merger that may be found in a frankly psychotic transference.

Such manifestations may be found in regressive states, but more typically, the transference relationship is increasingly contaminated and distorted by the patient's conviction of certain attitudes, judgments, opinions, feelings, or other states of mind that he has attributed to the analyst, which tend to undermine the precarious alliance and the patient's capacity to engage meaningfully and productively in the analytic work. Generally, such distortions are corrigible, however, since the patient's sense of reality and capacity to test reality remain intact. This tendency is one, as previously stressed, that can also be found in relatively neurotic or even normal individuals, and it differs in the dysphoric personality only in the degree to which it reflects the underlying introjective configurations. Thus, the predominance of the transitional object-relationship within the transference requires that in the therapy of these patients, considerably greater attention and greater activity be mobilized in the interest of establishing and sustaining a therapeutic alliance. This remains a valid rule of thumb, even when such patients are in an analytic situation.

These factors point to what appears to be the predominant area of pathology in the borderline personality, the pathogenic organization of introjects. That is to say, the primary defect in the dysphoric personality is not regarded as a defect in the structure of the ego, as might be the case in lower-order borderline forms. Rather, the impediment is in the organization of constituents of the self. The identifiable pathogenic configurations of introjects in borderline personality include the victim-introject and the aggressor-introject, as well as the narcissistically determined and impregnated configurations of grandiosity and inferiority. It should be noted that these pathogenic configurations can be found across a broad range of forms of psychopathology, but what is characteristic about the borderline personality is the manner in which these configurations are organized and maintained relatively available to consciousness without adequate communication between the dissociated ego states or a capacity to integrate elements from the respective introjective organizations. It is this phenomenon, in part, that has been addressed by Kernberg in terms of "splitting." Within each configuration, however, the introjective alignment is maintained with relative consistency and often with considerable investment and resistance to change. It is these introjective configurations and their relative availability and variability that underlie, I believe, the multiplicity of identities often seen in the borderline personality (Fast, 1974). However, the multiplicity of identities is not unlimited in my experience, but relates rather to different underlying introjective configurations. Moreover, it is this variability and capacity to shift relatively easily from one narcissistic configuration to another, as well as the greater susceptibility to regression, that distinguishes the borderline personality in its narcissistic aspects from the narcissistic personality. By way of contrast, the narcissistic personality tends to develop relatively consistent narcissistic transferences, either of the mirroring or idealizing form described by Kohut (1971).

To summarize the dysphoric personality, then, it is a form of character disorder that represents a distinct step up the developmental scale from the psychotic character. The borderline issues are no longer substantially psychotic, the level of anxiety is pervasive, but of a signal variety dealing primarily with issues of separation, dependency, and loss or loss of love. The propensity for regression is limited to more or less special circumstances as opposed to the more general, marked and readily expressed regressive potential of the psychotic character. The particular vulnerability of the dysphoric personality is on the level of object-relations and, particularly, the characteristic quality of the interplay of projections and introjections, which continually color and, to a certain extent, distort the patient's experience of the interpersonal environment. These patients, in general, maintain a consistent relationship to reality, an integral sense of reality, and an intact capacity to test reality. These capacities are diminished only during periods of crisis and in regressive states. The quality of object-relations and transference are subject to a characteristic variability, which reflects the internally organized configuration of introjective elements. These patients are able to maintain relatively good ego-functioning, in general, and reveal ego weakness only in regressive crises—a characteristic that distinguishes them from lower-order borderline conditions. Thus, Kernberg's description of ego weakness is more pertinent to these lower-order disorders (pseudoschizophrenias, psychotic characters) than to the dysphoric personality as such. Rather, the locus of pathology in the dysphoric personality seems to reside more in the organization of the self and its correlative introjective configurations.

The dysphoric personality represents a transitional form of character pathology between the lower-order borderline conditions and higher-order borderline conditions. Medications are of little use in the long-term management of such patients. Medication, however, may help with target symptoms. Neuroleptics in low doses may help manage regressive crises, especially where self-fragmentation and delusions enter the picture. Valium or other tranquilizers on an intermittent basis can, at times, ease patients through difficult periods. My own experience does not suggest that antidepressants are ever of much help. My own preference is to work through crises, as much as possible, in psychotherapy. Hospitalization is not often indicated for these patients, but may be necessary in a malignant crisis, especially when suicidal impulses are prominent.

Psychotherapy is essential for the dysphoric personality. A supportive approach only will do little for these patients. The approach should be expressive, exploratory, intensive psychoanalytically oriented psychotherapy, at the least. Most of these patients can tolerate more than once-weekly sessions. Some dysphoric personalities may be able to undertake psychoanalysis; some may need it. The safer approach is to undertake a period of psychotherapy, and only after gaining a better sense of the patient's capacities, his ability to involve himself productively in the treatment process, and particularly his capacity to form a therapeutic alliance, would the therapist consider the possibility of analysis (see Table 7-3).

TABLE 7-3
Characteristics of the Dysphoric Personality

Self-cohesion	Usually good in nonregressive phases, but vulnerable and tenuous
Self-object differentiation	Usually maintained; weakened in regressive states
Object-relations	Maintains good relationships, generally; need-satisfying, generally; often narcissistic difficulties in more intimate relationships; object-constancy obtained, but fragile; capacity to tolerate ambivalence tenuous, need-fear dilemma subtle, becomes more acute in regressions
Internalization	Basically introjective; introjects become more primitive and destructive in regression; capacity for identification present, but not well developed
Ego organization	Adequate ego integration in non-regressive phases; vulnerable to regression in borderline states; defenses shift from normal/neurotic to immature/narcissistic
Reality-testing	Well maintained except in regressive crises; maintains capacity to test reality
Impulse control	Tendency to externalize conflicts; intense affects in regression; anger; impotent rage; may become self-destructive; pregenital aggression
Anxiety	Primary separation and castration anxiety, traumatic only in regressive phases; capacity for signal anxiety in non-regressive phases
Superego	Integration irregular, tends to be severe/punitive; often contradictory value systems; in regression, punitive aspect can become self-destructive
Primary process	Usually not apparent clinically; may not appear on unstructured tests; appears only in regressive phases
Regressive potential	Less marked, occasional regressive episodes; frequently paranoid; may be result of therapeutic regression
Treatment	Medication: target symptoms, neuroleptics in crises, tranquilizers Psychotherapy: expressive; psychoanalytically oriented > supportive; psychoanalysis for selected patients Hospitalization: rarely necessary

Primitive (Oral) Hysteric

In approaching this next borderline entity, the primitive hysteric, we are dealing with a form of character pathology that presents with a more or less flamboyant hysterical symptomatology, but in which the character organization tends to be somewhat more infantile. The role of more infantile factors in the hysterical personality was noted by Marmor (1953), particularly in regard to more primitive oral characteristics. The presence of such infantile characteristics in the hysterical personality may reflect the organization of the personality on a more infantile borderline level; it may also suggest that discrimination between this level of personality organization and the higher level of hysterical personality functioning was not adequately made.

The prominent hysterical characteristics included in the description of the hysterical personality might also be included in a list of characteristics of the borderline personality, particularly, emotional lability, strong suggestibility, easy disappointment, alternating idealization and devaluation of objects of dependence, compulsive needs for love and admiration, intense feelings of inadequacy, strong dependence on others, approval for maintenance of self-esteem, and a tendency to dramatize or to act-out feelings. The discriminating differences that distinguish the primitive hysteric from the hysterical personality are the level of pregenital (particularly oral) libidinal elements, the prominence of narcissistic elements in the personality organization, the lesser degree of cohesiveness in self-organization, the greater degree of regressive potential, and the relatively less mature level of defensive organization.

The hysteroid patients of Easser and Lesser (1965) also fall in this part of the borderline range. They described these patients as more deeply disturbed than classically neurotic hysterics. The role of pregenital (primarily oral) fixation in their personality organization produced a caricature of the hysteric, marked by emotional instability, irresponsibility, poor work history, chaotic and transient love relationships, early childhood emotional problems, and markedly disturbed sexuality often involving combinations of promiscuity and frigidity.

Reich (1933) noted the tendency of the hysteric to genitalize the mouth and the anus, so that these always come to represent the female genital and may be accompanied by perverse tendencies. He also remarks on the tendency of hysterics to oral regression and that oral fixation is accompanied by a tendency to depressive reactions. Marmor (1953) emphasizes the predominance of oral elements in the more primitively organized hysterics and raises an important question regarding their susceptibility to regression. It is suggested that this picture of the more regressive aspects of the hysterical personality is more applicable to the present category of primitive hysteric than to our current understanding of the hysterical character as such.

A discrimination along these same lines has been made by Kernberg (1967) in his attempt to distinguish hysterical personality from infantile personality. The infantile personality shares the features of hysteria, but these are organized on a lower level of character pathology than they are in the hysterical personality. Thus, emotional lability in the infantile personality is more generalized and diffuse, so that there are few conflict-free areas in the life experience and a higher degree of social inappropriateness. Although the hysteric lacks impulse control in specific areas and during periods of intense conflict, the infantile personality lacks impulse control in a much more diffuse way. Hysterical overinvolvement becomes, in the infantile personality, a much more childlike overidentification, with a more desperate and inappropriate clinging. The motives and inner experience of others is often grossly misread, even if there remains a capacity for good social interaction and adaptation.

Long-lasting or significant involvement with objects frequently shows a progressively more regressed, childlike, oral, demanding, and frustrated aggressive quality, which is not characteristic of the hysteric. The need to be loved, to be the center of attention and attraction, functions on a less specifically sexualized level and has a quality of greater helplessness and inappropriate demanding, and reflects more primitive narcissistic trends. The hysterical tendency to pseudohypersexuality, in combination with sexual inhibition turns into a sexual provocativeness, which is often more crude and inappropriate and reflects more orally determined exhibitionism and demandingness than in the sexualized hysterical approach. When this takes the form of promiscuity, it has a more drifting quality, with little stability of object-relationships. There may also be a tendency to conscious sexual fantasies or a primitive polymorphous-perverse character in the infantile personality, which is generally missing in the more diffuse repression of the hysteric.

The infantile character is generally less competitive either toward men or women, but there is often a rapid shifting between positive and negative feelings, between submission and childlike imitation, and stubborn resentful negativism. Pregenital and specifically oral problems predominate, so that there is a reduced capacity for stable object-relationships and a weakening of the capacity to maintain object-constancy. Involvement with objects tends to have a more childlike dependency, which is oral and demanding as well as aggressive. These characteristics seem quite consistent with the primitive hysteric as we are describing it here. As Kernberg (1970b) further notes, these patients may present as predominantly hysterical, but careful examination and particularly extended experience of the development of the transference may be necessary to reveal the underlying infantile structure.

The careful discrimination of these patients from the more usual neurotic hysteric is important, particularly for the practical implications for therapy. An example came to my attention in the form of an attractive and intelligent young woman who came with a history of recurrent depression, repeated episodes of impulsive acting-out sexually, and a strong tendency to erotize previous therapeutic relationships. This included successful seduction of two previous therapists. The patient presented, more or less, as a classic, if somewhat flamboyant hysterical personality. The early phases of the analysis were marked by rapid, but conflictual transference involvement. Her tendency was to seek to establish a somewhat clinging and idealizing relationship with me, this alternating with angry denunciations and devaluations when I failed to respond or tried to interpret or even to examine her need to idealize me.

As the transference evolved, it became more specifically and intensely erotized. The patient became involved in a continuing attempt at seduction, which was never blatant, but was intensely felt by her. There was difficulty in keeping the analytic work going; her motivation seemed to shrink to nothing but the wish to get gratification from me. Her fantasies were explicit, erotic to the point of perversion, and were accompanied by powerful impulses to give up the analysis and make our relationship as sexual as she wished. Along with this erotization of the analytic relationship, there was a continuing tendency to act-out her sexual frustrations in the form of depressive episodes that had a highly labile and intense quality (although never to the point of suicide) and expressed themselves in repeated masochistic interchanges with important male figures, especially her somewhat paranoid and sadistic husband.

There was also a strong current of narcissism in this patient's personality structure. At levels of better functioning in the analysis, her performance would be largely indistinguishable from that of a narcissistic personality. It was primarily during more regressive phases of the analytic process that more borderline characteristics were evident. The narcissistic features included an overweening sense of entitlement, a powerful need for attention and admiration, and a certain exhibitionistic quality. The narcissistic element played itself out in her relationship with men. She tended to be physically attracted to large, strong, egotistical, self-centered men, whom she saw in idealized terms as powerful and phallic. Attaching herself to these men, who somehow make up for the lack she felt in herself—translated at times into terms of acquiring a powerful penis, but, by and large, more poignantly and centrally as corresponding to a sense of narcissistic compensation and as filling up an emptiness or defect she experienced in herself. Her needful attachment to these powerful phallic objects cost her untold suffering that took the form of masochistic surrender and repeated victimization.

It was noteworthy that, in this young woman, whose capacity to function and to deal effectively with her environment was in other areas outstanding, her ability to test reality in the therapeutic relationship seemed so tenuous. Her wishes were so powerful that she chose to ignore any of the aspects of the reality of our relationship that did not fit the requirements of the fantasy.

Much of the analytic work fell on establishing and maintaining the therapeutic alliance. This remained fragile and uncertain for much of the early period of the analytic work. As it became more stable and consolidated, the analysis settled into a form more consistent with the basically hysterical organization of the patient's personality. During the early phases of working through these more tempestuous transference vicissitudes, however, the issues were to a significant degree borderline in character.

Particularly useful in discriminating the levels of hysterical pathology is Zetzel's (1968) categorization. The first group represents the more classically described hysterical character, whose conflicts are essentially genital, who has been able to reach an effective level of oedipal involvement, and who is able to tolerate a triangular conflict. Such patients are able to maintain significant object-relationships with both parents, even though postoedipal relationships are often more ambivalent than the preoedipal. They can easily recognize and tolerate internal conflicts and distinguish between internal reality and external reality. In contrast, the second group of potentially good hysterics usually present a wider range of symptoms, are generally younger and less mature, and are generally less successful and consistent in their work achievement and in the maintenance of relationships. They are less consistent and more passive, and often fearful of dependent wishes, which are closer to the surface than in the good hysteric. Zetzel notes that these patients generally have difficulty in establishing a stable analytic situation (therapeutic alliance) and may react by a flight into health or a plunge into a regressive transference neurosis before an effective alliance can be established. This group of potentially good hysterics seems to belong to the primitive hysterical group.

The third group Zetzel described are hysterical women who have an underlying depressive character structure. These women generally reveal an impoverished sense of self-esteem and tend to devalue their own femininity. They may have experienced a genuine triangular conflict, but usually with an excessive idealization of the father and an accompanying devaluation of the mother. They may have the capacity to tolerate considerable depressive affect, but they fail significantly in the area of positive mastery, so that they tend to see and experience themselves as passive, helpless, and vulnerable. They can easily develop passive and dependent transference reactions, which interfere with their capacity to distinguish between transference neurosis and alliance. They present serious problems in the terminal phases of analysis and may drift into relatively interminable situations. This group, also, seems to belong within the primitive hysterical category.

The last group, Zetzel's "so-called good hysterics," presents a floridly hysterical symptomatic picture and in treatment proves incapable of tolerating a genuine triangular conflict. They have intensely sexualized transference fantasies and tend to regard such fantasies as areas of potential real gratification. They are incapable of distinguishing between internal and external reality, have considerable difficulty in maintaining a distinction between alliance and transference neurosis, and, thus, are poor candidates for analysis. These patients reflect a basic developmental failure in ego-functioning, which results in an impaired capacity for reality-testing. This last group would seem to be more primitively organized than the primitive hysterics and would be more consistently categorized with the psychotic characters. Finally, it can be observed that the characteristics of the primitive hysteric are quite consistent with the group described in Grinker and co-workers' (1968) study as closest to the border with neurosis.

It may be useful at this point to note Klein's description of hysteroid dysphoria, since it seems to show many characteristics that overlap with those of the primitive hysterics, but may also show characteristics that are more severely disruptive, akin to those seen in dysphoric personalities. The diagnostic criteria for hysteroid dysphoria are listed in Table 7-4.

Hysteroid dysphoria, as its name suggests, may represent a relatively disruptive form of primitive hysteria, a form of dysphoric personality, or may occupy some intermediate ground between these categories. It is a form of borderline disorder with a specific behavioral component, namely, over-eating or oversleeping. Depressions in such patients may be of short duration, but tend to recur frequently and tend to be excessively disruptive. Serious rejection or abandonment by the object of attachment may produce more prolonged or severe depressions. Narcissistic elements also play a significant role. The maintenance of self-esteem seems excessively dependent on a continual flow of external approval. Also, physical appearance and attractiveness is a matter of great moment. The normal level of personality functioning is decidedly hysterical in character, showing characteristics that are histrionic, flamboyant, highly emotional, seductive, intrusive, and often self-centered or demanding. Love objects and attachments tend to reflect poor social judgment, insofar as they are usually inappropriate and almost always overidealized. Stone (1980) regards these patients as essentially borderline.

The primitive hysterical personality, then, shares in the basic borderline issues that are common to the rest of the borderline conditions and also has some distinguishing characteristics. The transient attachment and involvement with objects and the alternation between idealization and disparagement is reminiscent of the "as-if" personality, but the primitive hysteric maintains a better integrated and more cohesive sense of self without the "as-if" characteristics. At a more primitive level of organization, the primitive hysteric can look like the dysphoric personality, but here again the dysphoric personality is distinguished by the inability to maintain a cohesive sense of self and the tendency to alternate between a variety of introjective configurations. Primitive hysterics rather, even at the lowest level of character organization, tends to articulate themselves around the victim-introject, thus assuming some of the qualities of a depressive structure. Moreover, it must be

---

TABLE 7-4
Diagnostic Criteria for Hysteroid Dysphoria[1]

---

1. Intolerance of personal rejection with particularly severe vulnerability to loss of romantic attachment, as manifest by more than usual difficulty seeking or maintaining intimate relationships or work

2. A depressive, painful, crash-like reaction to interpersonal rejection. Episodes are usually brief, lasting only hours to days; however, they can last longer, particularly in the event of continued rejection

3. The dysphoric response to rejection is usually associated with either a, b, or c:
   a. Overeating any food or a craving for sweets
   b. Oversleeping or spending more time in bed
   c. A sense of extreme fatigue, leaden paralysis, or inertia

4. During any two-year period after age 18 has had at least four periods of depressed mood in response to feeling rejected that were associated with some impairment of daily functioning (i.e., social withdrawal, missing a day of work, neglect of home or appearance, self-medication with drugs or alcohol)

5. Self-esteem depends on constant external approval and is markedly diminished by loss of that approval

6. The rejection-precipitated depressions are usually non-autonomous in that the patient can be brought out of them by well-meaning attention and applause. In an occasional extreme state, patient will be rejecting of help, and self-isolating

7. Normal state is at least one of the following: histrionic, flamboyant, intrusive, seductive, self-centered, demanding, or greatly concerned with appearance (use of observational data as well)

8. At least three of the following:
   a. Abuses alcohol, marijuana or sedatives episodically when depressed
   b. Abuses stimulants on occasion when depressed; may become habituated to them
   c. Normal mood is expansive and active
   d. Chronic dieting is necessary to maintain normal weight
   e. Poor social judgments with overidealization of love objects
   f. Applause is usually highly stimulating and rewarding
   g. Usually withdraws socially when depressed
   h. Makes suicide gestures or threats
   i. Is often physically self-mutilating when depressed

9. Above symptoms are not due to any other mental disorder, such as somatization disorder, schizoaffective disorder, or cyclothymic disorder

---

[1]From Liebowitz and Klein (1981); all nine criteria must be met.

remembered that the primitive hysteric retains the capacity to mobilize hysterical defenses and a hysterical style to defend against underlying conflict.

The treatment indicated for primitive hysterics is long-term, intensive, psychoanalytically oriented psychotherapy or psychoanalysis. Drug management is generally not very productive, but may be called for and useful for certain target symptoms, particularly anxiety. Klein (1977); and Liebowitz and Klein (1981) have presented evidence that patients who fit the description of hysteroid dysphoria can be effectively treated by MAO inhibitors. The drug seems to modify the emotional reactivity of such patients effectively, thus leaving room for more rational judgment and planning, less vulnerability to depression in reaction to loss or rejection, a modified quest for romantic involvement, and less symptomatic use of alcohol and drugs. Klein also notes that the tricyclic antidepressants do not have the same effect and apparently are of no greater help than a placebo, and may, in fact, make some patients worse (see Table 7-5).

This consideration of the primitive hysteric rounds off an important subsegment of the borderline spectrum. The sequence from the pseudoschizophrenic group through the psychotic characters and the dysphoric personality to the primitive hysteric represents a progression in levels of pathological disorganization from the more severe to the less severe. The sequence might be envisioned as an extension of basically hysterical features to progressively lower levels of character organization and functioning. The parameters that characterize this sequence are increasing affective lability, diminishing anxiety tolerance, increasing intolerance to frustration, increasing tendencies to externalization and acting-out for the release of tension, increasing signs of ego weakness, increasing signs of the instability or fragmentation of introjective configurations and a corresponding failure in self-cohesion, an increasing titer or primitive pregenital aggression, increasingly primitive organization of defenses, increasing susceptibility to regressive pulls and the tendency to regressive states and, most importantly, the quality of object-relations, which is marked by an increasing clingingly dependent and ambivalent involvement with significant objects, constantly threatened by fears of abandonment and loss. I would like to characterize this sequence as the hysterical continuum; it can be contrasted with the schizoid continuum to which we can now turn our attention.

THE SCHIZOID CONTINUUM

The Schizoid Personality

The schizoid continuum is a rather loosely organized group of character pathologies, which represent a variety of resolutions of the basic schizoid dilemma. That dilemma is an expression of the need-fear dilemma, in which

TABLE 7-5
Characteristics of Primitive Hysterics

Self-cohesion	Reasonably well maintained; vulnerable to fragmentation only rarely and in most severe regressions; more consistently organized around victim-introject
Self-object differentiation	Well maintained, usually even in regressive crises
Object-relations	Marked tendency to idealization/devaluation; compulsive needs for love/admiration; strong dependency needs; tendency to sexualize relations; strong narcissistic component; good capacity for object-constancy
Internalization	Predominantly introjective, never incorporative; identificatory capacity limited by defensive needs, but can be mobilized
Ego organization	Usually well-functioning; defenses normal/neurotic; become more immature under regressive stress; reasonably good subliminatory capacity
Reality-testing	Intact, usually not lost even in regression
Impulse control	Emotional lability, oral needs, tends to dramatize/act-out needs, anxiety tolerance weak
Anxiety	Chiefly separation mixed with castration themes; maintains capacity for signal anxiety; traumatic only in severe regression
Superego	Well integrated usually; tendency to guilt/depression, rather than projective distortion/blaming; tends to be punitive, but may be lacunae
Primary process	Not characteristic, even on projective testing
Regressive potential	Moderate; may regress readily, but usually only for brief periods; tends to become depressed and infantile; rarely psychotic
Treatment	Medication: tranquilizers, MAO inhibitors for hysterical dysphoria Psychotherapy: psychoanalytically oriented psychotherapy or psychoanalysis Hospitalization: rarely needed

the intense need for objects is countered by the fear of closeness or intimacy with the same objects. The schizoid defense counters this fear of involvement (which in its more severe manifestations becomes a fear of engulfment) by withdrawal from or minimization of the need for objects. For purposes of this discussion, we will include in the schizoid continuum the schizoid personality, the "as-if" personality, the false-self organization, and finally, the condition of identity-stasis.

The schizoid dilemma and defense are seen most characteristically in the schizoid personality. The schizoid personality has been the object of study of a small group of object-relations theorists, particularly Guntrip (1969). The schizoid patient complains of feeling isolated, cut off, shut out, out of touch, apart, and strange or he complains of life seeming futile and meaningless, empty, leading nowhere, and accomplishing nothing. External relationships seem to be affectively empty and are characterized by an emotional withdrawal. Vital and effective mental activity has disappeared into a hidden inner world, so that the patient's conscious self is emptied of vital feeling and capacity for action and seems to have become unreal. Glimpses of an intense activity in this inner world can be captured in fragments of dreams or fantasies, but the patient merely reports these as if he were a dispassionate and neutral observer and not involved in this inner drama and turmoil. The attitude to the outer world is one of noninvolvement and mere observation, without any feeling, attachment, or sense of participation. Such an individual often lives by himself, characteristically has few or no friends, has few meaningful interactions in the community of his fellows, is withdrawn, is usually hypersensitive and shy, and often is eccentric. He is unable to express any feeling or to show any anger, and he responds to conflict with relative detachment. These patients may also show paranoid characteristics manifested in extreme sensitivity, suspiciousness, and guardedness. They may often complain of depression and of a diminishing interest in things, events, and people around them, feeling that life is futile and meaningless, and they often express suicidal ideation. This "depression" is not typical, in that it lacks the inner sense of anger and guilt often found in clinical depressions. Real depression tends to be more a struggle in which the patient tries to avoid turning his aggression outward into overt angry and destructive behavior against a cathected object. Such depression is essentially object-related. But the schizoid personality has effectively withdrawn his cathexis from objects and has renounced them. However, the schizoid state may alternate with depression and be confusingly mixed with it.

The schizoid's primary defense against anxiety is to remain emotionally isolated, inaccessible, and remote. The schizoid condition, then, is a relative cancellation of external object-relations and an attempt to live in a detached, withdrawn manner. Whereas the depressive dilemma is that of anger directed toward a love object, such that the expression of that anger would destroy the object and the anger must consequently be turned against the self, the schizoid dilemma is that of destructive love, in which the anxiety arises from the fear of destroying and losing the love object through the intensity of devouring, hungry, greedy, needy dependency. The schizoid personality cannot exist in a relationship with another person, nor can it exist out of it without risking the loss of both the object and himself. Love relationships consequently are seen as mutually devouring and destructive. The dilemma of the need and fear of objects in the schizoid is particularly intense.

Although the position of schizoid withdrawal may be regarded as a regressed posture (Guntrip, 1969), it is nonetheless a protective, highly defended position that buffers the ego against disruptive regression at the cost of maladaptive external effects (Giovacchini, 1973). In both children and adults, there is a constricted and underdeveloped affective life, a quality of emotional distance, and preoccupation with inner thoughts and a fantasy life. Despite a turning inward, the integrity of other functions is maintained without the characteristic shifting ego organization seen in psychotic characters, or even in the dysphoric personality, in its shifting back and forth between dissociated ego states. Thus, the schizoid personality is able to maintain a position of reasonably good functioning in the real world, even as he holds himself emotionally aloof. Consequently, the defenses are so rigidly maintained that the character structure is quite stable, and disruptive states are relatively uncharacteristic of this entity (Pine, 1974).

The stability of character functioning, and the emotional withdrawal and lack of affect, distinguishes the schizoid personality effectively from all other borderline conditions, including the "as-if" personality and the false-self organization. The "as-if" personality does become attached to objects and does show emotional responsiveness, even if they are of the "as-if" quality described. The false-self organization is often and regularly involved with objects, even apparently meaningfully involved with objects, but this involvement itself is utilized for defensive purposes.

A young man who started and remained in analysis for a period of several years demonstrated schizoid personality characteristics. He originally complained of no particular inner distress, except that he did not feel that his relationship with his wife was particularly satisfying. The reason for seeking treatment was the development of some cardiac irregularity that his physicians related to stress and for which psychoanalytic treatment was recommended. Psychiatric evaluation suggested that he was so well defended that only analysis would reach the underlying conflicts. The assumption was probably correct, but one might more accurately guess that not even analysis could reach behind the rigid schizoid shell this patient erected around himself.

He was quite successful in a responsible and demanding job, but he had little to do with his fellow workers beyond the bare superficialities related to work tasks. He did not leave his office to socialize with other employees, he would not eat lunch in the company cafeteria, nor would he ever attend any of the frequent office parties. He was a loner—held in respect for his efficiency and ability, but friends or intimates with none. His marriage was little better. It was a marriage of convenience in which there was little affect, rare sex, which usually took the form of his wife masturbating him, and little or no sense of giving or sharing. When they would go out to dinner, for example, he would insist that his wife pay her half of the check. He refused to have children, feeling that the idea of giving or sharing with them was intolerable. It was a marriage, indeed, that was no marriage.

In the analysis, the patient's severe obsessionalism became apparent; it included the keeping of detailed lists, even to the number of times he wore articles of clothing, preoccupations with anal matters and functioning, his penchant for efficiency and punctiliousness, his punctuality (never late for an hour), and his generally obsessional demeanor. In the analysis, he would relate trivial details at great length; and when I commented on the defensive aspect of this behavior, he would become indignant and pose the classic obsessional dilemma—Wasn't he saying what came to his mind? Was that what I wanted or not?

For a long time, the work of the analysis focused on diminishing the level of his obsessional defenses—with some success, but with continuing difficulty. Little by little, the nature of the transference difficulties became clear. He was an only son, born nearly a decade after his parents' marriage. He saw his father as a weak, petty, selfish man, who was basically a failure in life and who functioned more or less as his mother's man-in-waiting. His mother was dedicated to her career and put that before any consideration for him. She had not wanted a child, and after he was born, turned her attention back to her work, putting him in a secondary position. As he was growing up, his parents had sent him away to camp in the summers, and from secondary school on, had put him in boarding schools—obvious proof to him that they did not want him, did not love or care about him, and were only involved with him to the extent that he could be drawn into the service of their narcissism.

All these elements came into play in the transference. He saw me as only interested in him as a patient, as a case to study, and only worth the money he paid me. He saw me as more interested in what I could learn by studying his case, and only concerned to the degree that I could use him as material for writing an article. He wanted me to care about him, take a deep interest in him, and do things for him. He particularly clung to a magical conviction that, if I so wished, I could explain all his difficulties to him and do something magical to make things better in his life. Regardless of my attempts to modify or challenge this conviction, he clung stubbornly to it. The analysis became for him a stubborn effort to get me to do for him what he wished from me. If he did the analysis correctly, if he came, talked (no matter about what!), paid his bills, didn't get angry at me for denying him what he wanted, eventually he would win out and I would work the magic.

There were, in addition, other preoccupations that suggested that he was functioning on less than a neurotic level. His generally schizoid life-style suggested more severe pathology. His narcissism was quite pathological and pervasive, reflecting pathological residues of the grandiose self, along with correlative inner feelings of worthlessness and inadequacy, which were usually related to bitter complaints about how his parents had treated him. The analysis turned into a stubborn holdout for the fulfillment of his infantile and highly narcissistic wishes. His rage mounted over my refusal to comply with those wishes. His effort became an attempt to defeat me, to prove the analysis worthless, to make me admit my inadequacy and defeat in the face of his impervious defenses and impossible demands. The underlying border-line issues remained impervious to analytic influence, and the analysis was finally terminated on the patient's initiative—after a long exploration of the motives and reasons behind his need to end the analysis prematurely.

In retrospect, this patient presented with a well-functioning and obsessional facade, but the basic issues were of a borderline order. It was on these issues that the analysis foundered. The threat posed by the analysis was too great, particularly the need to give up his schizoid defense and to allow himself to relate, in a meaningful and dependent way, to another human being. At no point in the analysis was there ever a meaningful therapeutic alliance. The issues were narcissistic and were caught up in the intense conflicts over the need to be accepted and loved against the fears of dependency and the threatening involvement with the analyst. His realization that he would never have it on his terms, and that further progress in the analysis meant exposure of his schizoid vulnerability, was more than he could tolerate.

These conditions all depend on the central problem, namely, that of the potential dissolution of nuclear narcissistic structures, which is an ever-present potentiality and danger. In these terms, the narcissistic vulnerability of the schizoid stands in marked contrast to that of the narcissistic character (Kohut, 1971). The schizoid withdrawal results from intense narcissistic vulnerability and the fear that narcissistic injury will initiate an uncontrollable regression. The retreat from real objects, then, does not serve to protect what is vital in the self against unappreciative or threatening objects, but occurs because of the danger inherent in the frustration of narcissistic needs. By way of contrast, the narcissistic character seeks out and is involved with objects as sources of needed and sought-for narcissistic sustenance.

The quality of emotional withdrawal, in any case, should not mislead us into a belief that the schizoid individual is uninvolved or withdrawn from object-relationships. Indeed, his contact with objects is intense, highly ambivalent, and subject to the torments of the schizoid dilemma as described His commerce with objects, which is intensely colored and distorted by projections, turns these objects into threatening, persecuting, engulfing, devouring objects. The basic organization of the schizoid self, then, is formed around an internal victim-introject that provides the core of the personality organization. Protection of this vulnerable and victimized core of his self-organization then is effected by schizoid withdrawal. The basic defect of the schizoid character lies at an extremely early level of the introjection of primary objects. The schizoid condition is based on the internalization of hostile, destructive introjects. These internalized unconscious objects are locked away within the psyche, where they remain as rejecting, indifferent, or hostile. The result of this negative introject is that it becomes a focus for feelings of inner worthlessness, vileness, inner destructiveness, evil, and malicious power. We have already come to recognize these introjective configurations as the victim-introject and its correlative aggressor-introject (Meissner, 1978).

To summarize this differential focusing of the schizoid personality, then, it can be said that the schizoid is confronting the same basic issues that underlie other borderline conditions, particularly the closely related conditions of identity-stasis, the "as-if" personality, and the false-self organization. The primary differentiating characteristic, however, is the quality of emotional withdrawal and isolation, which serves as the characteristic defense against these underlying needs.

There is little room for drug management in the treatment of such schizoid patients. There is usually little or no anxiety, and the depression is not of a sort that will respond to antidepressants. There is also little by way of tendency to regression, since the schizoid facade is usually maintained with ironclad solidity. Extensive exploratory or expressive psychotherapy or psychoanalysis is the indicated treatment. In either case, the treatment must be long term and relatively intense, since the schizoid defense will not yield easily or quickly to any therapeutic intervention (see Table 7-6).

The False-Self Organization

The false self is essentially a schizoid condition marked by a form of turning away from interpersonal relationships that is motivated more by the need to preserve a sense of inner autonomy and individuation than by a specific anxiety about intimate contact with objects. The idea was originally introduced by Winnicott (1960), who described a split between the false self, that part of the personality that is related to and involved with the external environment and real objects, and the true self, that part that inhabits the inner core of the personality and is hidden away from the

TABLE 7-6
Characteristics of the Schizoid Personality

Self-cohesion	Vulnerable; fear of narcissistic injury; potential for regressive fragmentation variable; grandiose self-sufficiency
Self-object differentiation	Rigidly maintained; regressive fear of merger/engulfment
Object-relations	Need-fear dilemma intense; emotionally isolated/noninvolved, schizoid dilemma (destructive love); projective distortions (often aggressive); essentially need-satisfying; poor tolerance for ambivalence
Internalization	Primarily introjective; more pathogenic in regression; never incorporative; capacity for identification limited, but only when fear/distrust lessened
Ego organization	Generally well maintained; rigid, often obsessional defenses
Reality-testing	Well preserved
Impulse control	Rigid; regressions rare; little emotional variability; no acting-out
Anxiety	Rarely felt or expressed; separation issues predominate; can become traumatic in severe regressive crises
Superego	Well integrated around archaic precursors; moral and value systems well-organized and consistent; tends to be severe/rigid
Primary process	Rare, even in regressed states
Regressive potential	Rare; often fear of uncontrollable regression, defended against by rigid structure
Treatment	Medication: none Psychotherapy: intensive psychoanalytically oriented psychotherapy or psychoanalysis Hospitalization: rarely needed, only in severe regressive crisis, if suicidal

scrutiny of observers. The self equivalently regards itself as the true self and correspondingly regards that part of the personality related to external objects or to the physical body as the false self.

The false self is essentially erected to protect and preserve the true self and to guard it against losing its sense of subjectivity, vitality, and inner autonomy. Thus, the dilemma is essentially a schizoid dilemma, in that the inner autonomy and authenticity of the true self is threatened by engulfment in its relationships to objects. The reality of these objects and the relatedness to them is an impingement, similar to the infantile impingement of the "not-good-enough-mother," which may threaten to overwhelm or obliterate the self.

The narcissistic vulnerability underlying the false-self organization relates to the persistence of an infantile grandiose ego-ideal or grandiose self. The false-self individual feels that his early caretakers and later significant objects do not appreciate or accept his grandiose attempts to preserve a sense of inner spontaneity and integrity, and he thus retreats to an inner world to preserve this sense of vitality and spontaneity. It is a retreat to a kind of grandiose self-sufficiency that is characteristic of schizoid states (Modell, 1975). This same grandiose self-sufficiency is often what motivates these patients to seek treatment. The goal of the treatment for them is to be able to achieve and maintain such isolation and self-sufficiency without the stigmata of loss or abandonment.

However, the need to retain spontaneity and vitality is somewhat different from the schizoid dilemma in which the fear of disorganization and engulfment is attached to attempts to relate with any intensity to real objects, so that the schizoid retreats primarily to avoid the outcomes of this disastrous object-involvement.

The other important component of the false self Winnicott delineates is the element of compliance. There is a compliant aspect to the true self in any healthy personality, which derives from the ability of the infant to comply without fear or danger or the risk of exposure or vulnerability. Thus, the socialization of the child involves compliance and adaptability, but even here Winnicott notes the capacity to override this compliance at crucial points or periods, for example, adolescence. The compliance of the false self, however, is a substitute way of relating to objects and dealing with the external environment, which is fallacious, unreal, and fragile. The operations of the false self seem false, often empty, and lacking in vitality or significance and may be a source of inner desperation and hopelessness.

The false self may, to all intents and purposes, appear quite normal and adaptive. It may even provide the individual with at least a partial sense of "identity." The observations that were relevant to identity diffusion regarding the tendency to adhere to causes, groups, leaders, etc., may also apply to the false-self organization. Nonetheless, trouble arises where authenticity and real object involvement are called for. When the false self cannot measure up to or sustain itself in the face of such pressures or demands, the outcome may be a severe regression into a borderline state. At its pathological worst, the false-self organization may cover an underlying schizophrenic process, so that when the false self begins to fragment, the schizophrenia emerges, often in the form of acute disorganization and decompensation.

The false-self organization, then, represents another form of adaptation to or defense against an underlying schizoid dilemma. In this case, rather than adopting a form of "as-if" involvement or schizoid withdrawal, there is a split within the organization of the personality, which allows the true self to retreat to an inner world colored with narcissistic isolation and self-sufficiency, while there is constructed another self-organization based on compliance and the need to protect and buffer the true self from the impingements of the outside world. The false-self organization may thus carry on at a high level of adjustment and involvement with reality, but the true self remains hidden and withdrawn. Consequently, the pathology takes the form of the internal organization of the self, which is motivated by underlying narcissistic and object-related conflicts.

As with the schizoid personality, drugs have little place in the clinical management of such patients. The treatment of choice is long-term, intensive, expressive psychotherapy or psychoanalysis. Such patients must develop a basis in adequate trust in the therapeutic relationship, which may require years of therapeutic effort. Analysis would be indicated or preferred for those patients who would seem to be capable of tolerating the regressive pulls and the intensity of the analytic relationship without unduly precipitous fragmentation of the false self and regression (see Table 7-7).

The "As-If" Personality

Deutsch's (1942) original description of the "as-if" personality focused on the patient's impoverished emotional relationships. Such patients may be unaware of their lack of normal affective involvements and responses, in which case the disturbance may be perceived by others or first detected in treatment, or they may be keenly distressed by their emotional defect, which may be experienced as transitory and fleeting or recurring in specific situations, or may persist as an enduring distressing symptom. Deutsch explains

> that every attempt to understand the way of feeling and manner of life of this type forces upon the observer the inescapable impression that the individual's whole relationship to life has something about it which is lacking in genuineness and yet outwardly runs along "as if" it were complete. Even the layman sooner or later inquires, after meeting such an "as if" patient: what *is* wrong with him, or her? outwardly the person seems normal. There is nothing to suggest any kind of disorder, behavior is not unusual, intellectual abilities appear unimpaired, emotional expressions are well ordered and appropriate. But despite all this, something intangible and indefinable obtrudes between the person and his fellows and invariably gives rise to the question, "What is wrong?" (p. 263)

The patient's relationships are devoid of warmth; expressions of emotion are formal; the inner experience is excluded. Deutsch compares it to the performance of an actor who is well trained to play the role, but who lacks

TABLE 7-7
Characteristics of the False-Self Organization

Self-cohesion	Well maintained around the true-false self split; narcissistically vulnerable; tendency to grandiose self-sufficiency
Self-object differentiation	Well-maintained
Object-relations	Schizoid dilemma; relates through false self; compliance; may often appear normal; limited capacity for real object love
Internalization	Introjective; capacity for identification poor; may take place when false self resolved
Ego organization	Well preserved; defenses generally higher order
Reality-testing	Well maintained
Impulse control	Good, generally within normal limits
Anxiety	Mobilized in the face of challenge to false-self; separation issues predominate, signal anxiety; can become traumatic in regression
Superego	Consistent; reasonably well-integrated; capacity for guilt/depression
Primary process	Not characteristic
Regressive potential	May regress when false-self undermined; variable regressive potential
Treatment	Medication: little place Psychotherapy: intensive psychoanalytically oriented psychotherapy or psychoanalysis Hospitalization: rare

the necessary spark to make his enactment of the role true to life. She takes pains to distinguish this inner emptiness from the coldness and distance of a more schizoid adjustment: in one, there is a flight from reality or defense against forbidden instinctual drives; in the other, external reality is sought in order to avoid anxiety-ladened fantasies. In the "as-if" personality, it is the loss of object cathexis that is involved, rather than repression. The relationship to the world is maintained on a level of childlike imitation, which expresses an identification with the environment and results in ostensibly good adaptation to reality, despite the absence of object cathexis.

The result is passivity to the demands of the environment and the highly plastic capacity to mold oneself and one's behavior to external expectations. Attachment to objects can be adhesive, but there is a lack of real warmth and affection in the relationship that creates such emptiness and dullness that the partner often breaks off the relationship precipitously. When the "as-if" person is thus abandoned, he may display a spurious ("as-if") affective reaction or a total absence of affective reaction. The object is soon replaced with a new one, and the process repeated.

It may be useful at this juncture to examine some of the cases Deutsch (1942) describes as manifesting "as-if" characteristics. The first was a woman who had been raised as an only child of noble Europeans. As was the custom in such circles, the care and training of the child was given over to nursemaids and tutors. Only on certain specified days would the child be brought to her parents for a formal evaluation of her progress and educational achievement. Such occasions were cool, distant, and ceremonious; and when the business was done, she would be returned to the care of her tutors. From the parents she received no warmth, no tenderness, not even punishment. At the same time, part of the patient's program of development was a strong emphasis on the importance of the parents and a constant drilling in love, honor, and obedience toward them—emotions that she never had the opportunity to experience directly and truly.

Under such conditions, one could hardly expect much by way of authentic emotional growth. To make matters worse, there was little opportunity for emotional attachment to her caretakers, who worked under the directives given by the parents and who, also, frequently changed. To compensate for these deficiencies, the patient developed a vivid and active fantasy life about the parents. She developed an elaborate myth in which the parents possessed divine powers through which the patient was able to gain anything her heart would desire. All the stories and fairybook legends she read were absorbed into this elaborate myth in which narcissistic gain reigned supreme, and there was little room for expression of the frustrated yearning for love that permeated her real existence. The narcissistic regression into fantasy was thus a compensation for the deprivation she felt with her parents and for the absence of any substitute libidinal ties. The patient's early outbreaks of rage and resentment were gradually disciplined and brought under control and replaced by a completely compliant obedience.

By the age of eight, when she entered a convent school, the "as-if" condition was already well established. There was no difference between her and any of the other pupils, superficially. She developed the usual attachment to one of the nuns, had apparently tender friendships with other girls, and went devoutly through the practices of religion, and even was seduced into masturbatory practices with apparent feelings of guilt. All of this was without real feeling, without significance, without real belief, and even without real guilt. They were all carried out as a kind of imitation, so that she would be able to be like her comrades. For this patient, there was never any real or meaningful attachment or libidinal involvement with real objects. Identifications remained vacillating and transitory, more in the order of imitation than, in any sense, real internalizations.

The second patient was a woman whose father had had a severe mental illness and whose mother was neurotic. Her memories of her father were limited to thinking of him as "a man with a black beard." He was largely absent from her life, and she only remembered times when he would come home from the sanitorium, yet still have to be nursed in an isolated room. The myth that she created about her father replaced him with a fantasied man of mystery with whom she had many different kinds of experiences that served to make her a superhuman being. This child again was largely raised by nurses, but despite this she was able to establish a relatively strong libidinal attachment to her neurotic mother. Her later object-relationships reflected some capacity for object libido, especially in homosexual relationships, but never substantially altered the "as-if" quality. An impediment to her more meaningful attachment to the mother was created by the birth of a younger brother, which stimulated intense feelings of rivalry and aggressive envy.

One avenue of compensating for these losses was her attempt to imitate her brother, whom she almost completely mirrored not only in fantasy, but also in real behavior. Unfortunately, this brother also showed signs of childhood psychosis. The sister thus imitated her brother's bizarre behavior and lived with him in a world of fantasy. These imitative behaviors averted her intense hatred and aggressive feelings toward the brother and transformed them into compliant passivity in the form of submissive imitation. There were no other meaningful object-relationships that might have mitigated this pathological picture.

A third patient had been born into a family in which the father was alcoholic, and also brutally mistreated her mother. Early on, she sided with her victimized mother and created fantasies of rescuing her mother from her misery, so that they could live happily together. When she finally discovered that her mother was not simply a passive victim, but rather took pleasure in such brutalization, her disappointment turned to a severe devaluation of her mother, and this deprived her of her only love object. Her subsequent efforts were turned to trying to make up for this loss by creating a series of imitative relationships of an "as-if" sort. Her libidinal instincts remained relatively primitive, with vacillations between giving them free reign and strongly inhibiting them. She became promiscuous and indulged in a variety of sexual perversions. She would retreat from such periods of acting-out by an imitative relationship with some conventional person to whom she became attached. The result was a frequent shifting of interests and occupations, depending on whom she was connected with. All of this occurred with a marked lack of affect.

The stream of interests was extraordinarily superficial and unrealistic. She seemed indefatigably active in following them out, but her engagement in so many concurrent activities gave her behavior a hypomanic quality. In the analysis, the analytic work seemed to be unusually successful. The patient began to understand many things about herself, and as she did, the eccentric behavior seemed to fall away. In part, her hidden agenda had been to become an analyst, in imitation of Deutsch. When she realized that this was impossible, she collapsed into a state of total lack of affect and inner emptiness, gradually becoming increasingly negativistic and resistant to the analytic process as a result.

Deutsch also comments on the moral character of these patients, which generally seems to be weak or lacking. Their moral standards, ideals, and convictions simply reflect those of the individuals to whom they attach themselves, whether for good or evil. They easily become involved with social, ethical, or religious groups and thus seek to give content and reality to the experience of inner emptiness that characterizes their sense of self. Their adherence to one point of view after another may be overenthusiastic and easily shifted, even from one contradictory view to another. They are also quite suggestible, as a result of their passivity and automaton-like identification. Deutsch also notes that the passivity tends to mask aggressive tendencies so that there is an air of goodness and amiability, which may easily turn to their opposites, badness and irritability. The failure of superego formation is related to the failure to achieve a strong enough oedipal involvement and the resulting impairment of a failure of identifications. Thus, the superego precursors are not effectively internalized and remain dependent on external objects. The organization of the internal world in these patients is based primarily on the interplay of imitation and introjection, and fails to reach a higher level of more autonomous identifications (Meissner, 1974b).

Ross (1967) has reviewed the literature on "as-if" phenomena and suggests that, although the "as-if" personality was rare in clinical experience, there also existed a wide spectrum of "as-if" states that range from the apparently normal to the definitely psychotic. In fact, "as-if" qualities may be found in varying degree and at various times in many borderline patients, presumably as a secondary aspect of the failure to establish and maintain a cohesive self-organization and its associated sense of personal identity. There are also affinities with states of depersonalization.

Reich (1953) described a type of "as-if" narcissistic object choice in women. Greenson (1958) also described patients with what he has called a "screen identity," who resemble "as-if" personalities. Like "as-ifs," they constantly seek the company of others, searching for need-satisfying objects, ceaselessly looking for new experiences and objects, all these patients, however, were well oriented to reality and usually socially successful. They were also often sensitive, perceptive, empathic, narcissistic, orally fixated, and exhibitionistic and possessed an eminently corruptible superego. Katan (1959) also distinguished between true "as-if" personalities in which identifications tended to be of the primary type and "pseudo-as-if" states in which identifications were secondary and the personality contained an hysterical core. Similarly, Masud Khan (1960) pointed to the possible connections between "as-if" states and Winnicott's notion of the false self. Ross (1967) also explores the relationship between "as-if" characteristics and states, on the one hand, and the psychopathology of the impostor and the psychology of acting as a profession, on the other. Both the "as-if" personality and the impostor reflect a failure of identity as "doer" insofar as they easily acquire roles without any inherent interest or need for a sense of real accomplishment within them (Fast, 1975).

The literature has frequently associated "as-if" characteristics with borderline conditions. Modell (1963) regarded the "as-if" syndrome as part of the borderline spectrum, and Kernberg (1967) also included the "as-if" disorder, as described by Deutsch, within the borderline psychopathology. Others, however, have pointed to the intensity of affect and the particularly destructive hostility and anger in the borderline conditions and discriminate between these conditions and the "as-if" personality and schizoid personality on these grounds (Gunderson and Singer, 1975).

Object relations in the borderline conditions have often been described as superficial and transient. Knight (1953) observed that the borderline's conventional, although superficial adaptation to the environment and the maintenance of relatively superficial object-relationships revealed varying degrees of intactness. It has, in fact, been thought that the borderline's capacity for adequate social functioning may depend on maintaining such a superficial involvement (Gunderson and Singer, 1975). It may be, however, that this quality of superficiality and transiency of relationships is related more to the "as-if" characteristics of borderline conditions, as typified in the "as-if" personality, and is relatively less applicable to other borderline entities. In Deutsch's description of the "as-if" personality, interpersonal relationships are described as plastic and are based on imitation, reflecting the weakness of object cathexis. The lack of any real emotional responsiveness or involvement leads to repeated dissolutions of relationships and reflects the disparity between more or less adequate superficial relatedness and the conflicts embedded in more meaningful or emotionally involved object contexts.

It should be noted that, in the Grinker et al. (1968) study, one of the defined groups (group III), is more or less congruent with the description of the "as-if" personality and is empirically distinguished from the more characteristic borderline group (group II). This "as-if" group is described as having bland and more or less adaptive behavior, with little evidence of negative affect or negative behavior. Affective behavior is generally appropriate, but little positive affect is manifested. These patients reveal no evidence of a capability for loving anybody or anything, and no indications of any well-developed sense of identity. Their relationships remain complementary ("as-if"), and their demeanor is generally isolated and withdrawn. They wait for cues from others in the environment and attempt to relate to them by assuming complementary roles. They are equivalently "as-if" characters who behave as they are expected to behave and often appear to be involved in the contexts and situations in which they find themselves, yet their role continually vacillates, depending on the important other to whom they must relate and adapt. They have given up the search for identity and have settled for an imitative substitute. They repress all individuality and relate, by passive compliance and mimicry, as a way of defending against the threatening pain of abandonment. Individuation and individuality for them imply separation and abandonment.

The "as-if" personality reflects a certain quality of borderline compliance, which reflects the underlying dynamics associated with the victim-introject (Robbins, 1976; Meissner, 1976b, 1978). It represents a resolution of the problem related to the victim-introject, as well as the dilemmas of narcissistic peril and object-relations conflicts through the vehicle of transitory and superficial "as-if" involvements, and their associated internalizations. The issues of compliance are shared with other borderline conditions, particularly cases of identity-stasis, schizoid personality, and false-self organization. The discrimination between them on this level lies in the manner in which these conflicts are dealt with—whether by diffusion of identity, by "as-if" imitative attachments, by schizoid withdrawal, or by the organization of the false self. Similarly, the "as-if" involvement with love objects must be differentiated from the hysterical identifications that result from powerful libidinal object cathexes. Hysterical repression is used to alleviate this essentially neurotic anxiety, whereas the inner conflict in the "as-if" patient is reduced by a defect in the development of affect, which leads to an impoverishment of the total personality (Deutsch, 1942).

To sum up this discussion, then, we can say that, although "as-if" states may be found in a variety of pathological conditions, either in conjunction with or as a defense against depersonalization, the "as-if" personality may also be identifiable as a distinct clinical pattern within the borderline spectrum. The disturbance in narcissism, the capacity for object-relations, and the internal organization of the self in the "as-if" disturbance may function at a number of levels of pathological intensity, and in this range of expression, roughly parallel disturbances in identity-stasis, schizoid character organization, and the false-self organization. The "as-if" personality resolves these underlying conflicts by a transient, often superficial, imitative and idealizing attachment to an object. This attachment is paralleled by a modification of the self in terms of imitative and introjective mechanisms, which, because of their defensive vicissistudes, lead to no further or more meaningful internalizations (Meissner, 1974b). Thus, these patients do not present with a significant deficit in ego-functioning as a general rule, but rather the pathology lies in the realm of the organization of the self, which achieves a transient cohesiveness through such "as-if" mechanisms. Deficits in structural organization not only of the ego, but also more particularly of the superego are thus secondary to this basic dynamic.

Treatment of such patients is almost entirely a matter of psychotherapy, either in the form of an analytically oriented psychotherapy, or psychoanalysis, when possible. Medication has little or no place in the management of such patients, except occasionally and intermittently for specific target symptoms (see Table 7-8).

Identity-Stasis

We are indebted to Erik Erikson for the notion of identity diffusion, which he described as a problem that presented itself in borderline or adolescent patients, frequently as a life crisis (Erikson, 1956). Erikson, in fact, describes a condition of "acute identity diffusion," which is familiar enough in the context of borderline regression; our attempt here is to focus on a condition akin to identity diffusion as a chronic enduring modality of personality organization. Erikson envisions the state of acute identity diffusion as arising when developmental experiences, particularly in adolescence, demand a commitment to physical intimacy, occupational choice, competition of various sorts, and in general, to a specific form of psychosocial self-definition. The necessity of choice and commitment gives rise to conflicting identifications each of which narrows the inventory of further choice; movement in any direction may establish binding precedents for psychosocial self-definition. The result is an avoidance of choice, a lack of inner definition of self, and an external avoidance, isolation, and alienation.

For the adolescent caught in this turmoil, there is a regressive reattachment to old libidinal objects, a reemergence of primitive introjections, along with their associated, more or less archaic conflicts. Engagement, whether it be in terms of friendship, competition, sex, or love, becomes a test of self-delineation. Engagement carries with it the constant threat of fusion and loss of identity, which may result in various forms of social isolation, stereotyped or formalized interpersonal relationships, or even the frantic seeking of intimacy with improbable or inappropriate partners. Such attachments, whether as friendships or as affairs, become simply attempts to delineate identity by a form of mutual narcissistic mirroring. Such patients have a characteristic difficulty in committing themselves to any line of action or

TABLE 7-8
Characteristics of the "As-If" Personality

Self-cohesion	Poorly integrated; dependent on object attachments; poor sense of identity; assumes complementory roles; cohesiveness maintained by "as-if" mechanisms; identity diffusion with loss of attachment
Self-object differentiation	Usually well maintained, but weakened in intense attachments
Object-relations	Emotional relationships impoverished; lack genuineness; lack of capacity for object cathexis; need-satisfying, object-constancy poor; relations superficial/transient; passive compliance; narcissistic attachments
Internalization	Imitative; introjective; little capacity for identification
Ego organization	Well maintained; tendency to regression when "as-if" attachment lost
Reality-testing	Well maintained
Impulse control	Good; may appear normal
Anxiety	Separation predominates; fear of abandonment
Superego	Moral standards/ideals tend to be imitative; shift easily from one contradictory view to another; dependent on external objects
Primary process	Not characteristic
Regressive potential	Usually mild with loss of object attachment; generally easily reversed by new attachment
Treatment	Medication: none Psychotherapy: psychoanalytically oriented psychotherapy or psychoanalysis Hospitalization: rarely; only in severe regressions

career choice. Particularly difficult is a commitment in the areas of work and love: they find themselves unwilling or unable to make a definitive choice of life partner, just as they may find it extremely difficult to decide upon and commit themselves to any line of life endeavor, such as a profession or other career. All the difficulties in work identification, which we have noted in other contexts, can also be found in this group of patients (Fast, 1975). At times, these difficulties in self-definition and commitment are found in one area, but not in others. The patient may have a well-defined work life or career, but be unable to make the defining commitment in an intimate love relationship.

Such issues may arise in the context of other borderline disorders, most strikingly in dysphoric personalities. The young men described above as dysphoric personalities experienced identity-stasis in varying degrees, but there were other features that seemed to suggest a somewhat greater degree of pathogenicity, for example, the tendency to regression and greater affective lability. In those patients, identity-stasis tended to shade over into identity diffusion, reflecting a somewhat greater vulnerability of self-cohesion.

The best example I have of identity-stasis as such is the case of the young man presented above (see pp. 231–241) as an example of the differentiation of borderline pathology and narcissistic personality. Patients with identity-stasis are very close to narcissistic personalities in terms of structural organization and level of ego integration. They are both potentially analyzable, so that meaningful diagnostic discrimination is often difficult. In the case of the young man in question, total paralysis of any capacity to achieve any definition or progression in his life-course dominated the clinical picture. He avoided or frustrated any opportunities for development of his career as an architect. He cut off and negated any other avenue of work or life engagement. He repeatedly and consistently avoided any involvement with a woman that might have led toward marriage and a family.

Erikson has also described a variety of reactions to this underlying diffusion or stasis of identity. A variety of forms of distantiation may result in a readiness to repudiate or ignore or even destroy forces that are seen as somehow dangerous to the self. They may resort to intense and devoted attachment to a set of ideas or an ideology, a group, a cause, or even a leader—all of which, by implication, involve repudiation of other causes, groups, leaders, etc. Attachment to such causes or groups may take on some of the "as-if" characteristics or even evolve into a false-self configuration. The attachment to and repudiation of groups, leaders, causes, and ideologies may attain an almost paranoid flavor, even as these processes always involve identifiable paranoid mechanisms, particularly the interplay of projections and more or less primitive introjections (Meissner, 1978). The failure of these devices, however, may lead such individuals in a position of withdrawal to a position of constant self-questioning and introspective uncertainty, a need for constant and doubtful self-testing, which can result in an almost paralyzing borderline state in which there is an increasing sense of isolation, a loss of a sense of identity, a deep sense of inner uncertainty and shame, an inability to derive any sense of accomplishment from external activities, and a feeling that one is the victim of circumstances and forces beyond one's control without any sense of initiative or responsibility for the direction of one's own fate.

There may, in fact, be a retreat to an identification with the victim-introject as a convenient escape from the uncertainties and emptiness of identity diffusion. Moreover, the narcissistic aspects of this configuration should not be missed. There are protests of potential greatness, missed opportunities, a need to cling omnipotently to a sense of the availability of all possibilities, and an unwillingness to sacrifice any possibilities or limit any potentialities in the inevitable determination and self-limitation of specific choice. There is a fear of engagement, a reluctance to compete or to assert oneself as separate and individual, a fear of time and its passage, a constant vacillating, doubt and uncertainty, and an unwillingness to choose that often looks obsessional, but is, in fact, driven by motivations of a different order.

Such conflicts may also express themselves in the form of adolescent or late-adolescent crises; these patients may be willing enough and reasonably successful in playing the role of the student, the one who is only learning and preparing in some tentative and uncommitted way for a possible future career, or that of the diligent apprentice or graduate assistant; yet, when the issues of choice and self-direction emerge, as they inevitably must, there is considerable difficulty in making that commitment, whether it be to write a thesis, to apply for a job, to marry, to father a child, etc. It should be noted that identity diffusion and the accompanying chaos in the sense of self reflects an inability to establish a stable self-concept and, correlatively, a lack of integration of internalized object derivatives (Kernberg, 1967, 1970b). The emergence, establishment, and consolidation of a consistent and coherent sense of identity is related to the integrity and cohesiveness of the self and depends upon the capacity for positive and constructive identifications. To the extent that the sense of identity is vulnerable and lacks cohesion, as in these patients, this reflects the internal organization of introjects, which are sufficiently embedded in issues of conflict and defense to prevent meaningful or substantial integration. The diffusion of identity is not to be regarded as equivalent to the loss of identity, which occurs in psychotic fusions or in delusional states of merger with the object. Such severe psychotic regressive states of merger and fusion entail primitive operations of incorporation (Meissner, 1971).

An important question is the extent to which identity diffusion, or identity-stasis, is an aspect of all the borderline conditions, particularly in regressive borderline states. It is undoubtedly a prominent feature of such regressions and must be regarded as correlative to the acute disorganization and loss of cohesion in the organization of the self. However, we are suggesting here that identity diffusion can take a more characterological form and may represent a more or less persistent personality configuration that can be given a separate and differential diagnosis. It should also be considered, however, that under the impetus of developmental pressures, or external pressures stemming from environmental situations or life conditions or other possible modifying influences, the configuration may evolve into other forms of borderline adjustment. The availability to the patient afflicted with identity-stasis of resolutions of the "as-if" or false-self variety are considerably greater than resolutions of the dysphoric or schizoid type. Although these latter forms of resolution are less available and less frequently observed, they remain nonetheless possible. Similarly, identity-stasis rarely, if ever, shifts into the configuration of the psychotic character or the pseudo-schizophrenic.

In sum, then, identity-stasis represents a form of character pathology that involves an impairment of meaningful identifications and an inability in self-definition. The pathology does not reside in the ego or even in the superego, as much as in the organization and delineation of the self. There is a defect in what Federn called "ego feeling" (Krohn, 1974). There is a complex interplay with object-relations conflicts related to the incapacity to define or commit oneself. On a primitive genetic level, however, the underlying fears have to do with the threat imposed in separation and individuation and the surrender of infantile objects and one's dependence on them. Ultimately, commitment to a life, whether of work or of love, means to accept limitations and change, the surrender of infantile omnipotence and narcissistic entitlement, and the ultimate acceptance of the finitude of human existence and death. Maintaining the self in a posture of persistent uncertainty and lack of definition and commitment is to maintain a condition of continuing possibility and a denial of the necessity to ultimately come to terms with the demands and expectations of reality.

Again, the treatment of choice for conditions of identity-stasis is psychoanalytically oriented psychotherapy or psychoanalysis, preferably the latter. It has been my experience with patients in this group that psychotherapeutic efforts rarely are able to penetrate to a level where the underlying issues and conflicts can be effectively addressed and resolved. Other contingencies and external circumstances may not allow for engagement in the analytic process, in which case psychotherapy becomes a meaningful alternative. As in other areas of the schizoid continuum, drugs have little or no place in the treatment of these patients (see Table 7-9).

The four categories of personality disturbance in the schizoid continuum can be regarded as variant modalities of dealing with the same underlying problem, namely, the incapacity to establish and maintain a coherent and individuated sense of self in the face of a powerful need for and dependence on objects, which is accompanied by a fear of loss or dissolution of self posed by attachment to that object. Thus, the respective entities—identity-stasis, "as-if" personality, schizoid personality, and false-self organization—are all struggling with a form of need-fear dilemma, all suffer from impediments of libidinal object-constancy, and thus all represent variant modalities of the attempt to come to terms with this underlying set of object-related conflicts.

The schizoid personality resolves the conflict by affective withdrawal and the preservation of self by defensive avoidance of object involvement.

TABLE 7-9
Characteristics of Identity-Stasis

Self-cohesion	Lack of self-definition in terms of social roles/commitments; often conflicting identifications; self-organization cohesive, but lacks sense of determinate identity/stability
Self-object differentiation	Usually well maintained
Object-relations	Tend to be formalized, sometimes alienated; attempts to achieve identity by mirroring; narcissistic; tend to be need-satisfying; fear of engagement/commitment paralleled by fear of separation
Internalization	Introjective; poor capacity for constructive identification; more impeded than lacking
Ego organization	Well maintained
Reality-testing	Well maintained
Impulse control	Generally good; tendency to anxiety/depression
Anxiety	Tends to chronic/diffuse; separation/castration; signal anxiety; rarely traumatic
Superego	Superego conflicts; tends to be punitive, values tend to be at variance with social and cultural norms
Primary process	Not characteristic
Regressive potential	Slight; regressions rare; tend to be extremely brief; marked by identity diffusion, increased anxiety, or depression
Treatment	Medication: none Psychotherapy: psychoanalytically oriented psychotherapy or psychoanalysis, preferably the latter Hospitalization: none

The false-self personality resolves the conflict by a protective withdrawal of the true self in a truly schizoid manner and a compliant compromise with reality through the false-self facade. The "as-if" personality resolves the conflict by adopting a superficial, transient, imitative involvement with objects that equivalently minimizes real, meaningful, or enduring commitment to an object-relationship. "As-if" adjustment can be taken as a more fragmentary, transient and superficial version of the false-self organization.

Finally, the resolution of the conflict in identity stasis is achieved by maintaining an inner ambiguity and avoiding self-definition.

The schizoid continuum therefore shares certain characteristics that offer some differentiation from the hysterical continuum, although considerable overlap—or even shifting—within the continuum is clinically evident. There is, generally, besides the sense of withdrawal and isolation, a rigidity of defenses and a resistance to regression that is quite different from the hysterical continuum. This is more true of the schizoid personality and the false-self organization, whose defensive organization is well-maintained in the face of regressive pressures. The "as-if" personality is more likely to show regressive features, but these are easily absorbed in a new "as-if" configuration. Regression, in cases of identity-stasis, may be countered by increased schizoid withdrawal or by retreat to a negative or pseudo-identity (as, for example, in fanatic adherence to a "cause"). These patients tend to show a much higher titer of what has been described as borderline compliance (Robbins, 1976).

In the treatment of such patients, the relatively rapid mobilization of transference paradigms seen so characteristically in patients from the hysterical continuum is more exceptional in the schizoid continuum. The difficulty with these patients lies much more in the direction of obtaining any degree of meaningful object involvement. Although they are dealing with the same borderline issues, these patients tend to respond with varying degrees of withdrawal or lack of involvement, even though this may at times be marked by or mixed with superficial compliance. The analyst is forced to wait a long time before meaningful contact with the patient's inner self becomes possible. Thus, although the problem with patients in the hysterical continuum tends to be that the analytic relationship and the therapeutic alliance tend to be inundated by transference distortions driven by an intense clinging need and dependence, the problem with the schizoid continuum tends to take the opposite forms of withdrawal from any meaningful transference involvement. The result is that not only the therapeutic alliance, but the transference as well are difficult to establish and maintain. Thus, we can infer that the therapeutic problem and approach will differ considerably for these respective dimensions of borderline pathology.

SUMMARY AND CONCLUSIONS

This differential diagnosis of the borderline conditions is an attempt to impose a greater degree of order on a sometimes chaotic and confusing picture. The differentiation has its weakness insofar as it is based on a narrow range of experience, and primarily on clinical impressions. There is a need for systematic study and evaluation of such differentiations on much larger patient populations in order to establish the validity of these groupings. The difficulties inherent in finding sufficiently large numbers of patients and of subjecting them to adequate diagnostic scrutiny should not be underestimated. Many of the differentiations involved here require long-term experience with the patient and a reasonably intense setting to allow for the important discriminators to emerge, particularly those having to do with the experience within the transference.

If this differentiation proves supportable, there would seem to be important implications for our understanding of borderline pathology. There are certainly theoretical implications, since the nature and degree and location of the pathology in various categories differs and is subject to a considerable range of variation. Thus, the understanding of the pathology involved in the "as-if" personality must be considerably different from that involved in our understanding of the dysphoric personality or the psychotic character. Previous theoretical attempts have tried to span too wide a clinical gulf and consequently, to that extent, have had only limited success and limited explanatory power (see Chapter 2).

There is also the question of levels of psychopathology. Although we can describe a rough organization in terms of levels of psychopathology, it must be remembered that we are describing differentiations within a common grouping of disorders, all of which share certain characteristics and each of which may operate at a more or less integrated level of personality functioning. In the differentiation presented here, within the hysterical continuum, clearly the pseudoschizophrenic group is the most primitively organized. The primitive hysteric may generally be the best organized and best functioning of all, although even here we have noted the presence of borderline characteristics that may carry poor prognostic and therapeutic implications nonetheless.

There is also a broad discrimination related to forms of pathology. Those conditions marked by affective lability and availability in which the affect becomes more intense, conflicted, and disorganized with increasing pathology, leading toward increasing disorganization and destructuring of personality functions, can be distinguished from those conditions that are marked by affective restraint and control in which affect becomes increasingly withdrawn and isolated with greater pathology, leading in the direction of increasing retreat from object involvement and a rigidity and hyperstructuralization of personality organization. The dichotomy runs between a basically hysterical continuum and the schizoid continuum. The former continuum, characterized by affective lability and increasing disorganization, leads from the hysterical character at the highest level (Zetzel's true hysteric) through the primitive hysteric to the dysphoric personality, and at even lower levels of character pathology, to the psychotic character and the pseudoschizophrenic. The latter continuum follows the obsessional line from the obsessional character neurosis toward increasing degrees of withdrawal and rigidity of structure in the schizoid grouping, through the "as-if" personality, the false-self organization, and finally the schizoid personality in which withdrawal and rigidity are most pronounced and pervasive.

A relevant question is whether, in the decompensation or therapeutic progression of the borderline conditions, they may not follow along the lines of these respective continuua. Does the primitive hysteric regress in the direction of the dysphoric personality? Does the psychotic character make therapeutic progress through a phase in which he resembles the dysphoric personality and moves further in the direction of a primitive hysterical integration? Does the severely isolated, withdrawn schizoid evolve toward healthier functioning in the direction of a potential false-self configuration? Adler (1981) has suggested something similar, namely, that the therapeutic progression of borderline patients generally follows a course along a continuum leading toward the narcissistic personality. In other words, as borderline patients improve, they become more like narcissistic personalities. A similar progression may obtain within the borderline spectrum. These suggestions are questionable speculations only.

In any case, we cannot take for granted that any progression in levels of organization carries with it direct implications for prognosis without taking other factors into account; these include those spelled out in considerable detail by Kernberg (1971). The prognostic indicators are also closely related to indications of optimal therapeutic approach, but it must be stressed that such indications require more subtle and detailed diagnostic considerations for each individual patient and cannot rest simply on diagnostic categorization.

APPENDIX

The tables in this appendix cross-reference the previous tables of descriptive diagnostic characteristics in terms of specific characteristics as they appear over the spectrum of borderline diagnoses so that these differentiations are more easily available to the reader.

TABLE A-1
Self-Cohesion in Borderline Syndromes

Pseudoschizophrenia	Tentative; partial; easily fragmented; identity problems prominent; frequent identity diffusion
Psychotic character	Fragile; obtained episodically; identity diffusion in regressions; poor boundaries; depersonalization in regressions
Dysphoric personality	Usually good in nonregressive phases, but vulnerable and tenuous
Primitive hysterics	Reasonably well maintained; vulnerable to fragmentation only rarely; in most severe regressions, more consistently organized around victim-introject
Schizoid personality	Vulnerable; fear of narcissistic injury; potential for regressive fragmentation variable; grandiose self-sufficiency
False-self organization	Well maintained around the true-false self split; narcissistically vulnerable; tendency to grandiose self-sufficiency
"As-If" personality	Poorly integrated; dependent on object attachments; poor sense of identity; assumes complementory roles; cohesiveness maintained by "as-if" mechanisms; identity diffusion with loss of attachment
Identity-stasis	Lack of self-definition in terms of social roles/commitments; often conflicting identifications; self-organization cohesive, but lacks sense of determinate identity/stability

TABLE A-2
Self-Object Differentiation in Borderline Syndromes

Pseudoschizophrenia	Poor differentiation; poorly maintained
Psychotic character	Generally preserved, but tenuous; lost in regressive states
Dysphoric personality	Usually maintained; weakened in regressive states
Primitive hysterics	Well maintained, usually even in regressive crises
Schizoid personality	Rigidly maintained; regressive fear of merger/engulfment
False-self organization	Well maintained
"As-if" personality	Usually well maintained, but weakened in intense attachments
Identity-stasis	Usually well maintained

TABLE A-3
Object-Relations in Borderline Syndromes

Pseudoschizophrenia	Intensely ambivalent; need-fear dilemma severe; object-constancy lacking; relations essentially need-satisfying; poor tolerance for ambivalence; relations transitional
Psychotic character	Need-fear dilemma at near-psychotic levels; frequent distortion by projection; primarily need-satisfying; poor object-constancy; relations usually highly ambivalent, conflictual
Dysphoric personality	Maintains good relationships generally; need-satisfying generally; often narcissistic difficulties in more intimate relationships; object-constancy obtained, but fragile; capacity to tolerate ambivalence tenuous; need-fear dilemma subtle, becomes more acute in regressions
Primitive hysterics	Marked tendency to idealization/devaluation; compulsive needs for love/admiration; strong dependency needs; tendency to sexualize relations; strong narcissistic component; good capacity for object-constancy
Schizoid personality	Need-fear dilemma intense; emotionally isolated/noninvolved; schizoid dilemma (destructive love); projective distortions (often aggressive); essentially need-satisfying; poor tolerance for ambivalence
False-self organization	Schizoid dilemma; relates through false self; compliance; may often appear normal; limited capacity for real object love
"As-if" personality	Emotional relationships impoverished; lack genuineness; lack of capacity for object cathexis; need-satisfying; object-constancy poor; relations superficial/transient; passive compliance; narcissistic attachments
Identity-stasis	Tend to be formalized, sometimes alienated; attempts to achieve identity by mirroring; narcissistic; tend to be need-satisfying; fear of engagement/commitment paralleled by fear of separation

TABLE A-4
Internalization in Borderline Syndromes

Pseudoschizophrenia	Predominantly introjective; regress to incorporation; little capacity for identification
Psychotic character	Predominantly introjective; can become incorporative in regressive states; poor capacity for identification; may be "as-if" in quality
Dysphoric personality	Basically introjective; introjects become more primitive and destructive in regression; capacity for identification present, but not well developed
Primitive hysterics	Predominantly introjective; never incorporative; identificatory capacity limited by defensive needs, but can be mobilized
Schizoid personality	Primarily introjective; more pathogenic in regression; never incorporative; capacity for identification limited, but only when fear/distrust lessened
False-self organization	Introjective; capacity for identification poor; may take place when false self resolved
"As-if" personality	Imitative; introjective; little capacity for identification
Identity-stasis	Introjective; poor capacity for constructive identification; more impeded than lacking

TABLE A-5
Ego Organization in Borderline Syndromes

Pseudoschizophrenia	Fragile; multiple defects; ego weakness; poor synthetic capacity; defenses immature/narcissistic; areas of autonomous functioning poorly maintained; minimal subliminatory capacity
Psychotic character	Vulnerable; defenses neurotic/immature; can regress to narcissistic
Dysphoric personality	Adequate ego integration in nonregressive phases; vulnerable to regression in borderline states; defenses shift from normal/neurotic to immature/narcissistic
Primitive hysterics	Usually well-functioning; defenses normal/neurotic, become more immature under regressive stress; reasonably good subliminatory capacity
Schizoid personality	Generally well maintained; rigid; often obsessional defenses
False-self organization	Well preserved; defenses generally higher order
"As-if" personality	Well maintained; tendency to regression when "as-if" attachment lost
Identity-stasis	Well maintained

TABLE A-6
Reality-Testing in Borderline Syndromes

Pseudoschizophrenia	Poor; often loses capacity to distinguish reality from fantasy; sense of reality and relation to reality defective
Psychotic character	Lost in regressive crises; reasonably well-maintained in non-regressive phases; sense of reality often impaired; at times difficulty distinguishing between fantasy and reality
Dysphoric personality	Well maintained, except in regressive crises; maintains capacity to test reality
Primitive hysterics	Intact; usually not lost even in regression
Schizoid personality	Well preserved
False-self organization	Well maintained
"As-if" personality	Well maintained
Identity-stasis	Well maintained

TABLE A-7
Impulse Control in Borderline Syndromes

Pseudoschizophrenia	Poor; marked tendency to relieve tension by acting-out
Psychotic character	Affective lability; frequent/rapid shifts; strong tendency to act-out
Dysphoric personality	Tendency to externalize conflicts; intense affects in regression, anger, impotent rage; may become self-destructive; pregenital aggression
Primitive hysterics	Emotional lability; oral needs; tends to dramatize/act-out needs; anxiety tolerance weak
Schizoid personality	Rigid; regressions rare; little emotional variability; no acting-out
False-self organization	Good; generally within normal limits
"As-if" personality	Good; may appear normal
Identity-stasis	Generally good; tendency to anxiety/depression

TABLE A-8
Anxiety in Borderline Syndromes

Pseudoschizophrenia	Diffuse; chronic; pervasive; pan-anxiety; often traumatic/catastrophic; little capacity for signal anxiety
Psychotic character	Separation anxiety > castration anxiety; some capacity for signal anxiety; becomes traumatic or annihilative under regressive pressures
Dysphoric personality	Primary separation and castration anxiety; traumatic only in regressive phases; capacity for signal anxiety in nonregressive phases
Primitive hysterics	Chiefly separation mixed with castration themes; maintains capacity for signal anxiety; traumatic only in severe regression
Schizoid personality	Rarely felt or expressed; separation issues predominate; can become traumatic in severe regressive crises
False-self organization	Mobilized in the face of challenge to false-self; separation issues predominate; signal anxiety; can become traumatic in regression
"As-if" personality	Separation predominates; fear of abandonment
Identity-stasis	Tends to chronic/diffuse; separation/castration; signal anxiety; rarely traumatic

TABLE A-9
Superego in Borderline Syndromes

Pseudoschizophrenia	Defective; destructive archaic superego precursors; predominance of aggressor/victim-introjects
Psychotic character	Poorly integrated; archaic precursors predominate; more dramatically in regressions; multiple lacunae
Dysphoric personality	Integration irregular; tends to be severe/punitive; often contradictory value systems; in regression punitive
Primitive hysterics	Well integrated usually; tendency to guilt/depression rather than projective distortion/blaming; tends to be punitive, but may be lacunae
Schizoid personality	Well-integrated around archaic precursors; moral and value systems well organized and consistent; tends to be severe/rigid
False-self organization	Consistent; reasonably well integrated; capacity for guilt/depression
"As-if" personality	Moral standards/ideals tend to be imitative; shift easily from one contradictory view to another; dependent on external objects
Identity-stasis	Superego conflicts; tends to be punitive; values tend to be at variance with social and cultural norms

TABLE A-10
Primary Process in Borderline Syndromes

Pseudoschizophrenia	Thought disorder clinically evident; marked on projective tests; frequent delusions; remain available in nonregressive phases
Psychotic character	Usually subtle in non-regressed phases; may or may not be clinically detectable; clearly detectable on projective tests; may be persistent delusions, even hallucinations, in non-regressed phases
Dysphoric personality	Usually not apparent clinically; may not appear on unstructured tests; appears only in regressive phases
Primitive hysterics	Not characteristic, even on projective testing
Schizoid personality	Rare, even in regressed states
False-self organization	Not characteristic
"As-if" personality	Not characteristic
Identity-stasis	Not characteristic

TABLE A-11
Regressive Potential in Borderline Syndromes

Pseudoschizophrenia	High, frequent, rapid regressions to psychotic levels; high potential for paranoid projection; perceptual distortions; distortions of object relations; paranoid reactions usually not organized into systematic delusions
Psychotic character	Capacity for regression to transient psychosis; readily reversible; regressions affect all functions (ego; superego) high potential for paranoid distortion
Dysphoric personality	Less marked; occasional regressive episodes; frequently paranoid; may be result of therapeutic regression
Primitive hysterics	Moderate; may regress readily, but usually only for brief periods; tends to become depressed and infantile; rarely psychotic
Schizoid personality	Rare; often fear of uncontrollable regression, defended against by rigid structure
False-self organization	May regress when false self undermined; variable regressive potential
"As-if" personality	Usually mild with loss of object attachment; generally easily reversed by new attachment
Identity-stasis	Slight; regressions rare; tend to be extremely brief; marked by identity diffusion, increased anxiety, or depression

TABLE A-12
Treatment in Borderline Syndromes

Pseudoschizophrenia	Medication: neuroleptics (low dose), antidepressants for panic attacks, tranquilizers for anxiety Psychotherapy: supportive > expressive Hospitalization: often necessary
Psychotic character	Medication: lithium, tranquilizers Psychotherapy: long-term, intensive, supportive/expressive, psychoanalysis not advisable Hospitalization: necessary in severe crises, especially if suicidal
Dysphoric personality	Medication: target symptoms, neuroleptics in crises, tranquilizers Psychotherapy: expressive, psychoanalytically oriented > supportive, psychoanalysis for selected patients Hospitalization: rarely necessary
Primitive hysterics	Medication: tranquilizers, MAO inhibitors for hysterical dysphoria Psychotherapy: psychoanalytically oriented psychotherapy or psychoanalysis Hospitalization: rarely needed
Schizoid personality	Medication: none Psychotherapy: intensive, psychoanalytically oriented psychotherapy or psychoanalysis Hospitalization: rarely needed; only in severe regressive crisis if suicidal
False-self organization	Medication: little place Psychotherapy: intensive, psychoanalytically oriented psychotherapy or psychoanalysis Hospitalization: rare
"As-if" personality	Medication: none Psychotherapy: psychoanalytically oriented psychotherapy or psychoanalysis Hospitalization: rarely, only in severe regressions
Identity-stasis	Medication: none Psychotherapy: psychoanalytically oriented psychotherapy or psychoanalysis, preferably the latter Hospitalization: rare, if ever

—————— Chapter 8 ——————
Borderline Diagnosis:
Childhood and Adolescence

Up to this point in our discussion, we have been primarily concerned with the borderline conditions as they are found in adult patients. However, borderline conditions or their analogues can occur in younger patients as well. The recognition and diagnosis of borderline conditions during the course of childhood and adolescent development have their own peculiar difficulties, which merit separate consideration. The material in this chapter is not based on direct clinical experience, however, but rather depends heavily on the findings and views of clinicians and researchers who have dealt more intimately with borderline conditions in younger patients.

The point of view here is an extension of that developed earlier. The central point regarding borderline conditions in younger age groups will be similar to the point articulated throughout the earlier parts of this monograph, namely, that the spectrum of borderline disorders represents a heterogeneous grouping of forms of psychopathology that may take a variety of forms or levels of pathological disturbance and that these forms can be successfully discriminated. Thus as will be seen, at the adolescent level, the borderline disorders show a heterogeneity that approximates the levels of organization and diagnostic differentiation identified in adult patients. Although the picture may be somewhat more obscure and the level of diagnostic differentiation less developed, the situation is analogous to the so-called childhood borderline disorders.

THE BORDERLINE SYNDROMES IN CHILDHOOD

It is by no means surprising that the diagnosis of borderline conditions in children has emerged only in recent years and that, in general, it has tended to parallel the development of thinking about borderline conditions in adults. Diagnostic criteria based on borderline patients, however, cannot be simply used for children, precisely insofar as the child is, in fact, still developing. Thus, the interweaving of developmental and pathological aspects in borderline conditions in children is difficult and controversial. It has even been questioned whether a borderline condition can even be diagnosed before puberty (Rosenfeld and Sprince, 1963). Efforts in this area are plagued by the question as to how much of the apparently disorganized or disturbed behavior and functioning can be attributed to developmental vicissitudes and how much must be regarded as pathological.

Earlier attempts to delineate the borderline syndromes in children reflected the prevailing views of borderline pathology in adults. These were dominated by an emphasis on the proximity to or connection with psychosis. Borderline conditions tended to be described in terms resembling those used for the psychoses. Levels of neurotic achievement in such children were regarded as tenuous, intermittent, fragile, and easily regressing to more primitive levels. The fragility of neurotic defenses left the child vulnerable to an imminent threat of psychotic breakthrough.

Ekstein and Wallerstein (1954) emphasize the use of neurotic and psychotic mechanisms in children whose presentations seemed variously borderline, schizophrenic-like, or severely neurotic. They found marked, frequent fluctuations in ego states, alternating between psychotic and neurotic ego organization. This produced a pattern of marked variability and unpredictability, which seemed to be a primary characteristic in such cases. Often, the therapist would be misled into thinking that he was dealing with a relatively intact ego, but suddenly and without warning there would be a dramatic shift in which neurotic defenses crumbled as archaic mechanisms and primary process thinking erupted. Subsequently, the neurotic defenses would reappear again almost as rapidly. Ekstein and Wallerstein felt that an important distinction between the ego of the neurotic child and that of the borderline was the potentiality for regression, which seemed to occur under lesser degrees of stress and more rapidly in the borderline child. Often, such precipitous regressions were associated with a failure of empathy or comprehension in the child's therapist. Ego control mechanisms were seen as either badly damaged or inadequately developed. The continuity between different and often opposing ego stages was perceived as tenuous and easily disrupted, and the patients lacked the capacity to modulate such transitions.

Subsequent investigators, following the lead of thinking about adult borderline conditions, which increasingly tended to separate such conditions from the psychoses, also were inclined to differentiate borderline childhood psychopathology from that which was more identifiably psychotic. Frijling-Schreuder (1969) observed that the psychotic child seemed to be constantly flooded by external stimuli, which produced a continuous state of traumatic anxiety. Such children attempt to regulate this state of excessive excitation by resorting to primitive forms of projection and introjection, which lead, ultimately, to the formation of delusions.

Childhood psychoses, consequently, were found to be characterized by extremes of overstimulation, an absence of a capacity for social adaptation, and a lack of reality contact. In contrast, the borderline states may also be characterized by a flight from reality, but in these cases, reality-testing remains relatively intact or at least, it is not impaired to the same degree. The ego is more able to utilize secondary process resources and to maintain the anxiety within manageable bounds so that it is more likely to be experienced as a form of signal anxiety. Although there is still the threat of being overwhelmed and engulfed by the object, the child nonetheless can attempt to master such primitive fears. Anxiety is a constant feature of the clinical picture; it tends to take the form of separation or disintegration anxiety, rather than castration anxiety. In the psychotic child, the anxiety is so overwhelming that it interferes with reality-testing and leads to a regressive dissolution of psychic structure, whereas in the borderline child, the anxiety is of the same quality, but is susceptible to management and defensive reaction by the ego.

Object-relationships also differ in significant ways in the psychotic child and the borderline child. The psychotic child does not get beyond the stage of need-satisfying object-relationships. The borderline patient can move beyond this level to develop some degree of object-constancy, although the relationships to objects remains highly dependent and ambivalent, and the object-constancy thus achieved remains highly vulnerable to regressive strain (Frijling-Schreuder, 1969). Fast and Chethik (1972) have also emphasized the pathology in object-relationships, arguing that in borderline children both self-representations and object-representations have not attained a level of integration as coherent and stable wholes. A constant feature of the borderline child's object-relationships is the projection of self-fragments onto external objects, such that the child then interacts with the object largely in terms of the projection, rather than in terms of the other individual's actual characteristics. These authors argue that such impediments in the integration of object-representations represents a failure to complete the transition out of narcissism and into the stable experience of external reality. Thus, object-relationships tend to be transitional (Modell, 1963, 1968; Meissner, 1978).

Borderline children tend to experience relatively limited, transient psychotic regressions. Frijling-Schreuder (1969) calls such a regression a "micro-psychosis." In the borderline condition, there remains a core of ego functions, however, which is relatively intact; in an actual psychosis, the ego, and its capacity for reality-testing, are completely overwhelmed. Childhood psychosis is also marked by a markedly low degree of frustration and tolerance for anxiety; impulses are acted-out without any capacity for delay or translation. Although the capacity to tolerate frustration and anxiety may be impaired in borderline children, in many cases there may also be a relatively high degree of frustration tolerance and the means for coping with this handicap.

The borderline child has achieved some level of differentiation between ego and id, and a level of ego development that allows for the utilization of secondary process resources and of somewhat more mature defenses. This allows intersystemic conflicts (e.g., between ego and id, between ego and superego, between superego and id) to develop. Although basically libidinal conflicts, having to do with masculinity-feminity, activity-passivity, and libidinal-aggressive tendencies, may be resolved in the psychotic child only by resorting to delusions or to a complete regressive disintegration, in the borderline child, they may take the form of intersystemic conflicts and thus give rise to a mixture of phobic, conversion, and obsessional symptoms. Borderline anxiety may be diffuse and relatively encompassing, similar to the pan-anxiety described in more primitive adult borderline cases, but this reflects the capacity of the ego to be more aware of the threat to its own integrity and its capacity to produce signal anxiety.

Object-relationships are contaminated by strong dependency needs, which often become conflictual and impede the development of more mature relationships. Often, the resolution of such conflicts takes the form of excessive compliance or rigid conformity, again similar to the configurations seen in adult patients. Internal integration remains unstable and vulnerable to sudden and severe regressions; but at the same time, it is also characteristic of such borderline organization that, under conditions of appropriate stimulus and structure, reintegration is readily mobilized and achieved. In addition, every step forward in development is accompanied by severe anxiety, which may precipitate a regression; but in spite of such regression, the patient often can reintegrate at the higher developmental level. Table 8-1 shows various aspects of the differential diagnosis between childhood psychosis, childhood borderline states, and the neuroses.

A somewhat different approach was taken by Pine (1974). He emphasized the presence in such disturbed children of severe developmental failure or aberration in ego-functioning and in the capacity for object-relationships. Thus, borderline children are distinguished from neurotics, who are characterized by unconscious drive-defense conflict and symptom formation that takes place in a more or less normal context of development. In its more extreme and pathological forms, he suggests that the borderline conditions, in fact, shade into the realm of psychosis, so that frequently there is no sharp distinction between the borderline child and the psychotic child. There are, in fact, different groups of children who can be regarded under the borderline rubric. They would include groups showing chronic ego deviance, shifting levels of ego organization, internal disorganization that is reactive to external disorganization, incompletely internalized psychosis, severe ego

TABLE 8-1
Some Provisional Differential Diagnostic Criteria[1]

	CHILDHOOD PSYCHOSIS	CHILDHOOD BORDERLINE STATES	NEUROSIS
Reason of referral	Unmanageable at home	Behavior ununderstandable	All kinds of difficulties
Description of child	Strange	Strange	All kinds of descriptions
Environmental influences	Overstimulation Lack of contact or abnormal contact	Overstimulation Lack of contact or abnormal contact	Neurotic family relationship (less intense than in psychosis or borderline cases)
Drive development of the child	No real phase dominance of any developmental phase Many traits of early phases, all phases overlap and merge Great difficulties at the transition from one phase to the next Abnormal libido distribution, with lack of object cathexis or objects cathected with narcissistic libido Preference for lifeless objects. Too intense cathexis of the self. Chronic excitation	No real phase dominance Developmental phases overlap and merge. Difficult transition from one phase to the next. Less disturbance of libido distribution than in psychosis. Great dependency on a few objects. Symbiotic relationships. Too much cathexis of the self, but less chronic excitation. Less vitality. Often fetishistic traits. The fetish may represent a transitional object or a primitive identification with a person by means of something associated to that person.	Phase dominance Conflicts stemming from the oedipal phase, with regression Object cathexis Self-esteem may be disturbed by neurotic conflicts

(Continued on pp. 248–249)

TABLE 8-1 (*Continued*)

	CHILDHOOD PSYCHOSIS	CHILDHOOD BORDERLINE STATES	NEUROSIS
Aggression	High impulsivity. Dangerous to themselves and to the environment	Open aggression lacking, with impulsive outbursts	Difficulties in aggression regulation, but as a rule not dangerous to others. Only dangerous to themselves in suicidal impulses or accident proneness
Conflicts	Severe intrasystemic conflicts Masculinity–femininity active–passive libidinal–aggressive Lack of intersystemic conflict	Intersystemic and intrasystemic conflicts	Intersystemic and intrasystemic conflicts
Ego development	Specific disturbances of integration and of reality-testing. No distinction between self- and object-representation. Active warding off of this distinction and of the perception of the object. Speech is not used as a means of contact with the object. Concretisms and neologisms. The need for	Specific disturbances of integration. Less disturbance of reality-testing than in psychosis. Differentiation between self- and object-representation, but with tendency to regression to nondifferentiation. Disturbance of the use of speech as a means of contact, often with a strong need for	Disturbance of integration and reality testing only in symptom formation Speech is used as a means of contact Secondary process is used extensively

	human contact may persist, and this may lead to restitutive processes. Secondary process mainly lacking	contact. Unrealistic ideas of grandeur, but no constant delusions. Secondary process thinking is used defensively. "Star and moon boys"	All kinds of defense mechanisms are combined in the defense organization. This may lead to deadlock within the structure
Defense	Mainly by primitive projection and introjection. In addition, ritualized and stereotyped behavior is used as a defense against disintegration. Open anxiety may be lacking, but there are outbursts of panic and impulsive behavior	All kinds of defense mechanisms are used. More primitive projection and identification than in neurosis. Phobic displacement and obsessional symptoms. Defense is very ineffective. Pananxiety	
Superego	No structured superego, but archaic anxiety projected into the outer world	Primitive superego structure very dependent on outer objects. Some internalization with a tendency to regression and to re-externalization	More internalization of conflicts with structured superego
Frustration tolerance	Very low	May be high apart from specific traumatic situations	May be high or low
Progressive tendencies	Great opposition to change. Every developmental step may lead to severe regression	Much anxiety at every step in development. Danger of psychosis if pushed to take such a step. Especially attempts at adult object relations and at sexual contact may lead to psychotic decompensation	If adult object-relationship and sexual contact are reached, this may be of help in recovery

[1]From Frijling-Schreuder, 1969.

limitation, and schizoid character. Pine's formulation thus comes close to acknowledging the inherent heterogeneity of borderline conditions, even in children, ranging from the border of psychosis, in which discrimination from frank psychosis is exceedingly difficult, up to the higher neurotic border at which borderline children approximate, but do not quite achieve a level of neurotic adjustment.

More recently, the status of borderline syndromes in childhood was reviewed by Bemporad et al. (1982). They emphasize that the age of the child is a significant factor in the diagnosis. In their view it is difficult, if not impossible, to diagnose a borderline condition in a preschool child, since borderline children often manifest behavior that would be considered normal for younger children, but becomes inappropriate at a later chronological age. The developmental impediments are seen as reflecting a failure to master the developmental tasks of latency, rather than as failures of earlier developmental periods. They also comment on the rather high incidence of neurological soft signs in these children, suggesting that organic pathology of the central nervous system may be significant in the etiology of borderline conditions. This question is taken up more in detail in Chapter 11.

The first area of pathological involvement is that of fluctuation of functioning, following the earlier observations of Ekstein and Wallerstein (1954, 1956). The borderline child seems to shift rapidly back and forth from a neurotic to a more psychotic-like state relative to the level of external stress or support. Such shifts tend to be time-limited and can be quickly terminated by reassurance and support. The second characteristic is the relative inability of borderline children to deal with anxiety, either through the formation of neurotic defenses or by regression to psychotic distortion or delusion. The capacity to utilize signal anxiety is limited, so that the signal anxiety tends to become a threat in itself, escalating to panic and terror. The anxiety, in contrast to neurotic anxieties, is rooted in fears of self-annihilation, mutilation, or even world catastrophe. These anxieties often seem similar to those found in schizophrenia, so that the pan-anxiety of these children seems to resemble the description of pseudoneurotic schizophrenics by Hoch and Polatin (1949).

Cognitive idiosyncracies are also found in borderline children, particularly an excessive fluidity of thought and a failure to discriminate between fantasy and reality. Thus, fantasy themes may often intrude on their day-to-day experience. Here again, there may be a variety of cognitive defects that are not easily categoried, but that may point to some underlying organic difficulties. Learning disabilities, including problems in maintaining attention focus, and poor perceptual motor skills are frequent.

The area of object-relationships reflects the fundamental pathology of the borderline child in the assessment of these authors, as well. The range of interpretations of these impaired object-relations includes fixation at a symbiotic level of development, need satisfying object-relationships, conflicts over the wish to merge and the fear of the loss of self, and recurrent withdrawal. Some children can make socially appropriate and friendly contacts on an initial or a superficial level, but become confused and conflicted if the contact continues over a prolonged period. Other children seem to be able to substitute one object for another without regard for the individuating characteristics of the object, as long as their needs are gratified. Others seem to adopt an "as-if" mode of adaptation, assuming a role for the sake of gaining acceptance, approval, or other forms of emotional reward. With their childhood peers, they bully smaller children, but are more fearful and shy with children their own age. In group situations, they tend to withdraw or fly into rages in which they may harm themselves or others.

Lack of control, as noted, is a general difficulty. These children have difficulty in controlling anger, delaying gratification, controlling their response to frightening or threatening fantasies, and appropriately directing motoric impulses. Frustration quickly leads to temper tantrums or frantic hyperactivity. States of rage or panic can escalate with little provocation. The authors feel that this incapacity to dampen both inner and external excitation may point toward an underlying organic defect.

In general, these children demonstrate an unevenness in development, with precocious attainment in some areas, age-appropriate capacity in other areas, and marked retardation in still others. The fluctuation between high and low levels of capacity is almost pathognomonic, but is difficult to generalize, since the mix is so variable. Bemporad and coworkers (1982) comment:

> This last characteristic may be taken as paradigmatic of the clinical picture of borderline children. There is such variation in superficial symptoms that the total Gestalt must be considered when making the diagnosis. While children vary in the degree of disturbance in the areas we have specified, every child is deviant to some degree in each area. (p. 600)

A point that should be emphasized in observations of this nature is that borderline expressions and symptomatology are characterized by a wide range of pathological involvement and intensity, even at the level of the early developmental organization found in children. The same observations that can be made in adults regarding the levels and degrees of pathological impairment in the various areas of impairment (see Chapter 6) can also be made in the clinical borderline syndrome in childhood. What is striking about the expression of the borderline condition in childhood is its marked variability and fluctuation, which distinguishes it, to a degree, from more adult forms of borderline pathology in which levels of functioning seem to be more clearly differentiated and, at the same time, less fluid and variable. Even in this regard, however, borderline pathology in childhood seems to approximate the characteristics we have already observed in more primitively organized adult borderlines, particularly the pseudoschizophrenics and, to some degree, the psychotic characters.

In any case, the diagnosis of childhood borderline condition is neither a simple nor a homogeneous entity, but rather spans a range of pathological conditions with a marked degree of variable expression corresponding to the fluidity and lack of structure inherent in psychic formations that are in the process of development and structuralization.

THE BORDERLINE SYNDROMES IN ADOLESCENCE

At the level of adolescent development, the difficulties of diagnosis are again compounded by the issues of the interweaving of parameters of development and pathology, with further difficulties involving the assessment of adolescence itself as a developmental period. The diagnostician is repeatedly challenged regarding the extent to which behavioral difficulties, difficulties in achieving and maintaining a stable sense of identity, questions of emotional lability and reactivity, and the general question of adolescent turmoil are to be regarded as part of a normal developmental pattern, on the one hand, or as forms of pathological deviance, on the other.

Kernberg (1979), for example, has commented on the tendency to confuse normal and neurotic identity crises in adolescence with the more severe and pathological syndrome of identity diffusion characteristic of borderline organization. These characteristics consist of identity diffusion, severe object-relationship pathology, and defects in superego integration (marked by an incapacity to assume responsibility, a lack of concern, defective investment in values, and failures in basic honesty) and are found in borderline conditions; they are not normal characteristics of adolescent development.

THE ADOLESCENT PERIOD

It may be useful, in this context, to review briefly aspects of adolescent development, particularly with an eye to elucidating those aspects of adolescent development that can create difficulties in the diagnostic process. The transition to the adolescent phase of development is marked by some highly significant processes that contribute to the definition of individual personality. If the latency period can be described as a period of relatively instinctual quiescence, the transition to adolescence must be described as a period of recrudescence of instinctual pressures. A variety of developmental changes are thus instigated, which open up areas of basic conflict that remain as residuals of earlier levels of development and offer the opportunity for a reworking of those conflicts and their fashioning into a new and emergent sense of identity. This regression in adolescent development serves to reactivate and intensify the functioning of basic mechanisms of introjection and projection. These are, in large measure, responsible for the reworking of personality configurations that characterizes this period.

The different use of projection, from latency to early-adolescent, has been described by Sarnoff (1972). He describes this use as a shift from projection associated with repression, in the earlier phase, to a use of projection associated with denial, in the later phase. Sarnoff emphasizes that the latter form of projection, namely, that associated with denial, is equivalent to the form of projection and displacement frequently involved in paranoid conditions. Conversely, projection associated with repression, which is a characteristic of latency manifestations, closely follows the pattern of phobia formation.

This shift in projection parallels a transition of the primary role of defense from fantasy and symptom formation to a role in the testing of fantasy against reality in establishing object-relations, along with the partial dissolution and opening up of the superego to cultural influences. In other terms, a shift from id projections to superego projections can be identified. As Sarnoff (1972) notes:

> Through projection the superego is externalized. The child who attributes her formerly internalized commands to a peer or teacher stands the chance of acquiring an externalized ego ideal, with characteristics of the ego ideal of the new object. With reinternalization of the ego ideal (the projection-reinternalization is a dynamic, ongoing series of events) modifications of the superego take place. (p. 521)

The transition to adolescence is marked by changes in bodily growth and increased hormone secretion. The onset of such changes is associated with greater instinctual pressures, so that adolescence is characterized by a reopening and a reworking of earlier developmental conflicts and fixations. The more marked upheaval of adolescence is, to a certain degree, anticipated in the closing stages of the latency period by more subtle and transient cathectic shifts. The preadolescent typically forms close and somewhat idealized friendships with same sex peers, which reflects an intensification of already established latency patterns. The capacity, which is often developed in the latency period, for sustaining sublimated interests and work habits seems to become more fluid and variable. There is a confused and somewhat conflicted searching for different interests, goals, and sources of involvement, which reflect an underlying dissatisfaction. These transitional shifts signal the onset of a developmental phase that promises to be considerably more active and tumultuous than the relative quiescence of the latency period (Blos, 1962).

The upsurge of instinctual drive intensity at the onset of adolescence obviously presents the ego with a problem. Mastery of these instinctual drives and their derivatives is one of the major developmental tasks of adolescence. As a result of these increased drive pressures, a regression in ego-functioning is induced, which serves to reactivate basic unresolved conflicts from earlier developmental levels. The developing ego is thus presented with the necessity and the opportunity of reworking some of these underlying conflicts in a more thoroughgoing, definitive way. There is thus the opportunity to undo earlier developmental defects and consequently to model the psychic apparatus more effectively. Thus, adolescence presents the opportunity for new and more meaningful identifications that can provide a major direction and organization for the remodeling processes.

IDENTITY-FORMATION

Increasingly in recent years, the attitude toward the adolescent period has shifted from seeing it as a period of upheaval or developmental disorganization to seeing it more in terms of a normative crisis. The view that adolescence is a normal growth experience, marked not only by conflict and regression, but also a remarkable growth potential, is one that is increasingly accepted. Thus, infantile conflicts and fixations can be reworked so as to reorganize the personality. Reworking is accomplished by an exposure to and a complex interaction with social and cultural influences stemming from the larger society, into which the adolescent is gradually introduced and in terms of which he must seek a definitive place. The potential resolution of these basic conflicts is twofold. They may be resolved in terms of more effective forms of structural and characterological organization or, conversely, they may be resolved in terms of a solidification into more stable symptom patterns of characterological defects.

A significant part of the adolescent development is what Blos (1967) calls "second individuation." The first individuation takes place in the first two years of life in the achievement of self-object differentiation. The individuation of adolescence, however, is considerably more complex and leads, ultimately, to the establishment of a sense of identity. The adolescent process is one of increasing self-definition.

In normal adolescents, self-awareness is at first fragmented and disjointed. The adolescent must struggle to achieve some sense of self by opposition to what he wishes himself not to be. Thus, the rejecting, opposing, contradicting, resisting, and rebelling of the adolescent are driven by this need. The issue of separation, along with the companion issue of individuation, however, is a primary concern of the adolescent's vicissitudes. He must also test himself in a variety of roles and functions—often finding it necessary to push experimentation to the limits of excess in order to clarify his sense of inner functions and uncertainty. These strivings and testing of the limits have a positive value in contributing to the adolescent's emerging sense of self-awareness and self-definition. The negative delineation of self, however, fosters an essential individuation that is required for the building of a more mature sense of identity and, at the same time, contributes to the adolescent's increasing sense of relative autonomy.

The working through of such a process of individuation will encounter multiple difficulties. Becoming more of an individual by way of separation from significant objects places the adolescent more and more at risk. He may be overwhelmed by feelings of isolation, loneliness, and confusion and confronted with the futility and the unreality of childhood (narcissistic) dreams and fantasies. He becomes increasingly aware of his own inherent limits, as well as the need for more mature involvements and commitments. Faced with inevitability and the decisive finality of the end of childhood, he must increasingly become independent of significant adults and gradually assume responsibility for himself and the direction of his life. It is no surprise, consequently, that many adolescents find the vicissitudes of development threatening and seek ways to prolong the adolescent posture by remaining in more regressed and dependent positions.

One of the primary adjustment problems of the adolescent period involves object-relations. In the child's earlier experience, development was closely linked with objects; in the earliest stages, there was the crucial capacity for self-object differentiation. His optimal development in the first two years of life depended vitally on the quality of his relationship with his mother—on his trusting reliance on her mothering activities and on his emerging capacity to tolerate her absence for increasing periods of time. Object-relations for the preoedipal child are concerned with establishing meaningful and mutually rewarding relationships, on a one-to-one basis, with both parents. If the child has attained these adaptive goals in the preoedipal years, when he comes to the triangular oedipal involvements in which he must relate to both parents simultaneously in the oedipal situation, his capacity to resolve these relationships and their accompanying conflicts is improved. He can establish less threatening and more comfortable relationships with both parents by a patterning of identifications based on the relative strengths of both parents. Even through the postoedipal and latency years, the parents remain the predominant objects in the child's life—although the broadening of the child's object-relation involvement has already begun. Teachers and other significant adults begin to play a significant role in the child's development.

In adolescence, however, object choice and object involvement take a decisive turn away from the parental objects. The major developmental task becomes the establishment of a capacity for heterosexual object choice on a genital level. An essential part of this process is the renunciation of the primary objects—the parents or parental substitutes. The child must surrender the parents as his love objects. Changes in the quality of parental relationships that were brought about in the resolution of the oedipal situation and the subsequent modifications of the latency involvement with parents must be relinquished, but the relinquishing of these important objects leaves the adolescent with a marked object hunger. The abandonment of parental objects and the seeking of new and appropriate objects gives rise to important inner shifts of cathexis, which strongly influence both object-representations and self-representation. There arises an inner lability of cathexis, which makes the adolescent's sense of self all the more uncertain and confused. The adolescent's capacity to carry through this important developmental step rests on the extent to which he is capable of tolerating the insecurity and loss that is implicit in the separation from and renunciation of the parents as love objects. That capacity reflects earlier developmental achievements.

During adolescence, the libidinal economy becomes organized around genital impulses. Preoedipal and oedipal attachments to parental objects are replaced by nonincestuous attachments to heterosexual objects. The translation from one phase to the other is attended by other shifts in instinctual alignments. The quality of object-relations shifts subtly and gradually from a need to be loved and taken care of to a progressively manifest need to love and take care of. The child's dependence on parental objects and relative passivity is gradually translated into a relatively more independent self-direction and activity. The polarity of activity and passivity that was elaborated in earlier interactions with the parents reemerges in adolescence as a crucial issue that must be decisively resolved. Struggles over relinquishing and finding objects, as well as the crisis of activity and passivity, leads to a recrudescence of ambivalence. The adolescent becomes overly sensitive to the currents of love and hate stirred up within him, and he may often vacillate confusingly and confusedly back and forth between them. He does this both with his relationships with his parents, who he both rejects and clings to, and with his new-found objects, who he both hungers for and reviles. The resolution of these conflicts culminates, in the normal course of development, in relatively nonambivalent object-relations and in an ego-syntonic balance of activity and passivity that becomes a characteristic pattern.

The intensification and reactivation of basic ambivalences regressively activates defensive processes for managing these conflicting impulses. Thus, basic processes of projection and introjection come into play and are potentially brought into the service of reworking the emerging sense of adolescent identity. This developmental potentiality, however, is both progressive and regressive. Defensively motivated operations of the paranoid process (Meissner, 1978) may be pulled by the intensity of defensive needs and the underlying conflicts into more regressive forms of resolution that leave the resulting identity more susceptible to oedipal and preoedipal instinctual pressures.

The renunciation of parental objects and the attendant loss of object libido has a number of important consequences. The loss of parental objects leads to a transitional narcissistic phase that is intermediate between attachment to parents and a more definitive heterosexual object involvement. Libido is withdrawn not simply from the external parent or parental object-representations, but from the internalized parent as well. The superego arose from the internalization of parental representations in the resolution of the oedipal situation. The superego, together with the ego-ideal, thus became the primary agency for intrapsychic regulation and for the maintenance of self-esteem. The shifts in cathexis weaken superego functions so that the adolescent is left with less effective inner controls and feels the directives of conscience as less compelling. Many social and cultural influences reinforce this weakening of the superego. In renouncing the parents, the adolescent also withdraws from the internalized parental equivalents that reside in the moral evaluative standards of the superego. This has its risks for future development and for the adolescent's adaptation to the world around him, but as Erikson has pointed out so clearly, these inner developmental shifts provide the potential for reformulation and revivification of the values and beliefs not only of youth, but also of the community at large.

The adolescent's withdrawal from the familiar objects of childhood leads to a narcissistic overvaluation of the self and is increasingly aware of an inner process, becoming self-absorbed, self-centered, and self-concerned. This may lead to a narcissistic withdrawal and disturbances of reality-testing. The adolescent often uses narcissistic defenses to defend against the disappointment and disillusionment of his meager position in reality and may find it difficult to give up the gratifying parent on whom he has come to depend—especially if that parent has been overly protective and solicitous— and face his own limitations and inadequacies. He may be afraid to take responsibility for his own abilities and their consequences, as well as afraid to face the demands of adult responsibility.

With this narcissistic regression, the intensity of narcissistic needs is heightened. This leaves the adolescent self more susceptible to narcissistic injury and disillusionment. This provides another important source of the mobilization of introjection-projection, specifically as narcissistic defenses.

Introjection and projection thus come into operation in specific ways to sustain the threatened sense of self and to jeopardize its integrity. The regressive activation of introjection-projection tends to regressively intensify cathexis of and attachment to parental objects.

In this way, adolescent conflicts can be considerably prolonged. It is easy to understand that the reluctance to renounce dependence on and love of parents often is not simply an adolescent issue, but that it also has its roots in the child's earlier developmental history. The process of detachment from parental objects or their substitutes can go on for a very long time—and even in the normal course of development, it continues through adolescence into the postadolescent period. Only when the individual enters upon and can accept responsibility for adult tasks and commitments is the relationship to the primary objects finally decided and resolved.

The withdrawal of libido from parental objects disqualifies the parents as sources of libidinal gratification, and the adolescent as a result hungers for objects. The hunger is reflected in the marked adolescent propensity for shifting, labile, superficial, and transient attachments and identifications. This is the adolescent's way of preserving his ties to the outside world and avoiding a complete libidinal withdrawal. The lability of this internal situation makes the ego susceptible to regressive pulls. The relatively stable identifications acquired in the preceding developmental phases lose their stability and consolidation, to some extent. They are subject to regressive influences, and the pattern of the relationship to parental objects involves more primitive forms of internalization. The relations to the parents are based more on the interaction of introjection and projection. As was the case in earlier levels of development, the real parents are confused with "good" and "bad" introjects. The pattern of adolescent vacillation between rejecting and clinging to parents reflects the influence of these introjective components in the relationships. The introjects had been more or less dormant during the latency period, but are again revivified in adolescent regression. The attachment to new objects serves a twofold purpose here. It facilitates the decathexis of the old introjects, and at the same time—particularly in regard to the "bad" introjects—it offers the possibility of modifying and neutralizing these potentially dangerous introjects by acquiring new "good" introjects. Ultimately, the inner vicissitudes of the infantile introjects must be resolved through a definitive identification—preferably with the parent of the same sex.

The critical achievement of adolescent development is the sense of identity. The definition of self that emerges in late adolescence is a work of synthetic processes in the ego. Erikson has described the establishment of a sense of identity as a phase-specific achievement involving the formation of a qualitatively new psychic formation. The formation of a sense of identity is more than a sum of childhood identifications. As Erikson (1959) describes it:

The sense of ego identity, then, is the accrued confidence that one's ability to maintain inner sameness and continuity (one's ego in the psychological sense) is matched by the sameness and continuity of one's meaning for others. Thus, self-esteem, confirmed at the end of each major crisis, grows to be a conviction that one is learning effective steps toward a tangible future, that one is developing a defined personality within a social reality which one understands. (p. 89)

Identity develops out of a gradual integration of identifications, but the resulting whole forms an integrated totality that exceeds the sum of its parts. Childhood identifications are newly integrated in the adolescent remodeling that issues in a more final self-definition and irreversible role-patterns that set the young person on his life-course.

In the elaboration of these inner processes, it is essential that the emerging adolescent self be recognized and responded to in meaningful ways by the adult community into which he is growing and within which he seeks a place. Such a reciprocal response—an extrapolation of the mutual regulation or earlier phases of development—supports the adolescent emergent self and allows him to sustain vital defenses in the face of the growing intensity of instinctual impulses, to consolidate areas of growing capacity and achievement with social roles and work opportunities, and finally, to reorganize earlier patterns of identification in a consistent fashion and to integrate the new configuration with the patterns of role and value available within the society.

In summary, adolescent development marks an advance in instinctual drive organization toward a genital heterosexual position. The genital position becomes relatively definitive and irreversible. The libido is directed outward and the ego gains a new investment in objects. The turning to new love objects reactivates oedipal fixations that must be renounced and resolved. Adolescents thereby can elaborate more mature and adult positions of masculinity and femininity. The ego gains in its capacity to organize more effective defenses and sublimations, to attain restitutive solutions and adaptive accommodations. These become aligned in highly individual and unique patterns, which are gradually consolidated into an emerging character structure. Thus, adolescent development translates the idiosyncratic constellation of drives and conflicts into more unified and integrated patterns of personality organization. The normal developmental process of adolescence is finally integrated when the emerging pattern is subjectively grasped and more or less accepted as belonging to an inherently identifiable sense of self.

The formation of a sense of identity is a significant developmental achievement. It provides the developing personality with a coherent sense of its own individuality as well as a sense of both what it is in itself and in its relationships with the significant objects in its world. It is obvious that, in a sense, the issue of identity pervades all phases of the developmental process, specifically in terms of its relationship to the emergence and shaping of the self. But, as Erikson (1959) so clearly said, the issue of identity rises to a characteristic crescendo in the adolescent period. This is understandable, insofar as it is specifically within the adolescent context that the individual must define and delineate his identity in broader and more complex terms that extend to the broader stage of social interaction and cultural involvement. It is through an emergent sense of identity, then, that the adolescent achieves a sense of belonging and participating and sharing in the concerns and directions of the human community of which he is a responsible and responsive part.

NORMAL ADOLESCENCE

Given such multiple developmental vicissitudes, the question remains whether the patterns of deviance and turmoil so often seen in adolescence are, in fact, a form of disturbance or not. Psychoanalysts have generally characterized the adolescent period as one of turmoil and rebellion. Even Anna Freud (1969) described adolescence as a "developmental disturbance." The profound reorganization that takes place in the adolescent years, which is frequently accompanied by upheaval and relative chaos, is emphasized (Blos, 1962). Even the process of identity formation may bring the adolescent into conflict with parents and other authority figures and precipitate a rebellion, which is necessary to establish his own unique sense of self. The process may be accompanied by anger, anxiety, poor communication with adults, and even depression. In this view, the so-called identity crisis is often viewed as a normative aspect of adolescent development.

The question can reasonably be asked in the light of these formulations whether there is such a thing as normal adolescence. At least one answer to the question has come from the extensive work of Offer (1969; Offer and Offer, 1969). The picture of adolescent development that emerges from this study of relatively normal adolescent males presents a somewhat different picture of the adolescent period than that based on clinical impression.

Many observers have felt that it is in the area of the management of drives and affects that much of the turmoil and chaos of adolescence takes place. But very few of Offer's subjects experienced any difficulty in control of impulses. They manifested no frank clinical syndromes and no deviant behavior. In fact, variations of mood were modest and certainly not dramatic —quite different from the clinical adolescent population. These relatively normal adolescents experienced periods of depression, but these were usually related to some external precipitant, rather than to something internal. Moreover, the depressions were limited in time, and the subjects seemed to be able to work themselves out of these depressions by engaging in a variety of activities.

Generally, anger was not a problem for these young people, and when it occurred they seemed readily able to master and sublimate it in forms of physical activity. They were often critical of parents, but rarely angry, and never manifested the forms of chronic rage so often seen in borderline adolescents. Rarely were such affective states acted-out in any form of antisocial behavior.

Generally, conflicts were in the area of sexual behavior and experienced as discomfort over sexual impulses, feeling anxious and ill at ease with girls, and feeling awkward in communicating with parents about such subjects. Dating was infrequent in the early teen years, but by the senior year of high school, most boys were dating and enjoying relationships with girls. For many of these boys, sports and physical activity provided a controlled and socially approved channel for the expression of physical aggression. Most of the subjects of this study carried on a busy round of activities and seemed to manage internal tensions by sublimation through activity rather than by destructive acting-out or fantasy.

When rebellion manifested itself, it was generally mild in character and was never expressed antisocially or illegally. Generally, rebellion was experienced in the early teen years, from about twelve to fourteen. It took the form of disagreeing with parents or teachers, breaking rules set by the parents, and arguing over such episodes and other minor points of conflict. Offer made the point that rebellion in these adolescents almost never involved significant issues of value or life-style. Rather, he felt that such behavior served to initiate or reinforce a process of emancipation from the parents without actually disrupting the parental relationships. By and large, such negative behavior gradually diminished as the adolescent moved into the later years of high school and became more invested and involved in social activities outside the home. Offer concluded that one important reason why these adolescents were able to negotiate the developmental tasks of adolescence relatively successfully and without the turmoil of the disturbed adolescent lay in their rather high degree of ego strength that allowed them to withstand and master the pressures and conflicts of their adolescent experience.

King (1971) has surveyed a number of such studies of relatively normal adolescents and reached the following significant conclusions:

1. The identity crisis is not a common occurrence among normally developing adolescents, nor do these adolescents experience excessive degrees of turmoil or conflict. Such findings would tend to weaken support for the view that some form of developmental crisis or disturbance is an integral part of adolescent growth to adulthood.
2. Relationships between these adolescents and their parents tend to be relatively untroubled and unconflicted. Evidence of a generation gap is weak. Most adolescents tend to absorb and follow the parental value system

and life-style. If there is any rebellion, it is typically found in early adolescence and is clearly in the service of emerging autonomy. It is generally limited in scope, confined to minor issues, and does not extend to delinquency or destructive acting-out.

3. As a rule, relationships with peers are comfortable and adaptive. Relatively healthy adolescents usually have enough friends with whom they feel comfortable sharing their feelings. The withdrawn, painfully shy teenager does not belong in this group.

4. These adolescents have a good sense of their own competence and have a high level of self-esteem. They occasionally have self-doubts, but these feelings are usually balanced by the feeling that they can cope and have the capacity to learn from their experience. Guilt and depression rarely occur, and almost never with a sense of hopelessness or giving up.

5. These adolescents have good capacities for coping and adapting to life and its demands. They can deal with painful feelings, talk about them, share them, and communicate with others about them. They tend not to block such feelings or to turn them into fear or depression. They are able to deal with them by shifting the focus of their interest or by emerging themselves in various forms of physical activity; sports is an especially important vehicle for sublimating both aggressive and sexual energies. They also can make good use of humor to help keep their problems in perspective, and often employ anticipatory planning and role rehearsal as an adaptive strategy.

The question remains whether the outcome of these studies of so-called normal adolescents provide us with an authentic model that can serve a normative function in assessing adolescent progression. It seems clear that the vast majority of adolescents pass through the developmental crisis of that period without the tumult and turmoil that is often associated with adolescence. Adolescent turmoil may serve developmental objectives insofar as it contributes to the liberation of the child from his earlier object ties, facilitates his disengagement from dependence on parents and family, and helps to transform his involvement with the adult world into one of greater maturity and independence. But these same objectives can, and often are, achieved without undue deviance or disruption. In this connection, Zellermeyer (1974) has argued that when such turmoil develops it is on the basis of a prior deviation in the preadolescent period. In other words, such behavioral deviations and disorders are not exclusively adolescent, but rather are superimposed on a preadolescent maturational failure. He writes:

> It is now felt that we are dealing with a metadisorder, which superimposes itself on pre-adolescent maturational failures of various degrees and/or also results from external forces either in the family or the sociocultural environment at large, which inhibit, disrupt or distort the forward thrust of the growing young person and thereby interfere with his undisturbed passage through adolescence.

Only in rare instance without pathological antecedents or adverse circumstances, does adolescence as a strictly individual process produce a major behavioral crisis. (p. 262)

At the same time, other investigators have found a considerable degree of variation in the occurrence and expression of adolescent turmoil that makes its evaluation, independent of other factors, difficult. Thomas and Chess (1976), for example, studied a group of adolescent subjects longitudinally, only some of whom manifested behavior disorders. Many of these adolescents showed the usual manifestations of adolescent turmoil, including rebelliousness, conflict with parents and authority figures, negativism, impulsivity, tension, mood swings, and vacillation in plans and ambitions. In some cases, the manifestations of turmoil were associated with identifiable behavior disorders. In other cases, there seemed to be no associated clinical pathology. And in still other cases, when the behavioral problems were expressed in terms of passivity and inhibited functioning, there was little turmoil evident, despite clear-cut pathological indices. The authors concluded, on the basis of these findings, that no inference can be made regarding the significance of the presence or absence of adolescent turmoil in any specific case.

DIAGNOSTIC COMPLICATIONS

Needless to say, in the light of these findings, any evaluation of adolescent patients is faced with a number of difficulties. For one thing, symptom formation and other neurotic expressions occurring in adolescence, such as anxiety or depression, may affect the adolescent's capacity to function to such an extent that the disruption might suggest underlying ego weaknesses and a defective capacity for control that might indicate a borderline diagnosis. Also, adolescents are vulnerable to so-called identity crises, manifested by rapidly shifting identifications with various ideologies or social groupings, which may, at times, suggest the presence of identity diffusion. By the same token, a relatively severe impairment in the capacity for object-relationships may be interpreted as occurring at a more neurotic level and involving issues of dependency and rebellion, which would thus underestimate the degree of pathology involved in conflicts with authorities and in other social areas. Conversely, essentially neurotic conflicts with parents and other authority figures may activate a more primitive defensive potential so that the adolescent's efforts at omnipotent control, projection, and devaluation may begin to look somewhat borderline (Kernberg, 1978).

In addition, antisocial behavior may be a form of normal or neurotic adaptation to an antisocial cultural subgrouping or may reflect a more severe form of character pathology. The narcissistic reactions so frequently observed in adolescents may mask more primitive narcissistic features, particularly when there may not be any frank antisocial behavior to alert the diagnostician. Further, in the sexual areas, the emergence of relatively more perverse sexual trends in adolescence may mimic features found more typically in borderline personalities. There is always the additional risk that the adolescent who manifests certain borderline features may, in fact, be suffering from an evolving psychotic condition in which the psychotic expressions are more insidious. As Kernberg (1978) notes, in such cases insidious delusion formation may be mistaken for hypochondriacal tendencies or an excessive preoccupation with physical appearance.

Kernberg (1978) also notes that not infrequently, narcissistic character pathlogy tends to be reinforced by narcissistic features within the family context, so that the diagnostician is presented with the problem of disentangling the patient's pathology from the family's pathology. When truly narcissistic pathology exists, it should be regarded as reflecting an impairment of or deficit in earlier childhood development, rather than a by-product of current family dynamics and interactions.

An additional problem is that the successful negotiation of the adolescent crisis never reaches completion or closure. Even under the most favorable circumstances, its resolution remains relatively incomplete. Thus, adolescent conflicts, in one form or another or in varying degrees, can remain operative throughout the life-course. A definitive identity is not yet firmly established, only a foundation has been laid for further progress. Occupational choice has not become definitive and irreversible, but rather has been limited to a range of possible alternatives. Even heterosexuality has not as yet reached its mature form of expression. The achievement of a post-ambivalent, less narcissistic, more object-concerned attitude toward the sexual object is a late acquisition (Zellermeyer, 1974).

BORDERLINE DIAGNOSIS IN ADOLESCENCE

Given these difficulties and uncertainties, the diagnosis of borderline conditions in adolescence remains problematic and uncertain. Kernberg's (1979) paradigmatic view suggests that the syndrome of identity diffusion, a severe pathology of object-relations with part-object transferences, a lack of superego integration, and a predominance of primitive defensive operations characterize the borderline personality in adolescence. Consequently in his view, late-adolescent borderline patients have not accomplished the normal developmental tasks of adolescence. They have not achieved an integrated self-concept or ego identity; they have not consolidated normal sexual identity with the proper subordination of pregenital to genital strivings, and an emerging capacity for tender and erotic feelings in a capacity for stable object-relationships; they have not loosened parental ties, nor adopted adult social roles and relationships; and finally, they have not replaced infantile superego regulations with more abstract and depersonified, yet flexible and adaptive moral values.

The borderline adolescent's attitude toward his parents usually shows excessive involvement with them, violent rebelliousness, hostile dependency, and generally, chaotic interpersonal relations. Moreover, in psychotherapy, borderline adolescents tend to overidentify the therapist with parental images or react defensively and hostilely, often with a chaotic alternation of mutually split-off parental or combined father-mother images and a defensive rejection of the therapist as different from the imposed parental images. In this complex of symptoms, Kernberg (1978) emphasizes the importance of identity diffusion as fundamental to the borderline diagnosis. Others (Aarkrog, 1977) have emphasized the presence of transient psychotic states in a personality marked by intact areas of functioning and varying patterns and changing levels of functioning. Such cases often have a manifest history of borderline disorder in earlier childhood or may have developed an inherent vulnerability, which the onset of adolescence seems to have precipitated into a more frankly borderline condition. Aarkrog (1977) comments that many of these borderline adolescents live in a fantasy world of figures derived from fairy tales—a world of witches, demons, princes, and princesses—that defend against the threatening aspects of reality and involvement with real objects. The maintenance of such inner fantasy worlds may be analogous to that seen in more adult patients, for example, in the psychotic characters.

At this point we can usefully consider some of the diagnostic impressions in the literature. Kernberg (1975, 1978) discusses patients who present with predominantly narcissistic difficulties and a narcissistic personality organization. Although he regards all such patients as possessing an under-iying borderline structure, he admits that they often function at a higher level than is usual in borderline cases. He regards their pathology as centered on the pathological grandiose self, and manifesting primitive defensive operations of grandiosity, omnipotent control, and devaluation. Conflicts tend to center around envy, emotional shallowness, overdependency on external sources of admiration, and a combination of feelings of superiority and inferiority. Many adolescents with narcissistic personalities do not get into difficulties during adolescence, but may become relatively dysfunctional later in life.

When a diagnosis of narcissistic personality can be made in adolescence, the disorder may be relatively severe. Such cases often manifest characteristic narcissistic features. There may be a form of contradictory school performance marked by intense ambitiousness and perfectionism, on the one hand, and a sense of failure and withdrawal from activities, on the other.

There may be symptomatic depressions reflecting feelings of defeat, inadequacy, and shame at not having achieved a narcissistic triumph and a tendency to devalue what does not come easily or is not immediately rewarding. There may be a socially engaging facade, with a considerable amount of charm and superficial friendliness. The combination of this facade with multiple talents and good intelligence may obscure the underlying incapacity to a commitment to life goals or to deep personal relationships. There may be feelings of sexual inferiority, as well as sexual inhibition, which at times, combine with sexual promiscuity.

Tendencies to omnipotent control, grandiosity, and devaluation may express themselves in violent rebelliousness against the parents, but this must be differentiated from more normal forms of adolescent turmoil. The normal or neurotic adolescent may have conflictual relationships with his parents, and tend to criticize or devalue them, but this is usually accompanied by a capacity to appreciate and value other aspects of his parents and by a capacity for other meaningful relationships that he does not devalue. The normal or neurotic adolescent can express guilt and concern and maintain enduring and nonexploitative relationships with others (friends, teachers, etc.) without the degree of conflict and of alternating devaluation and idealization that may be found in the borderline.

Rosenfeld and Sprince (1963) noted that their adolescent borderline boys seemed to present analytic material that was as confused as that of latency children. There were features derived from all phases of libidinal development, with a lack of phallic phase development. The puberty spurt seemed to suggest a leap to the phallic level reflected in physical maturity and sexual fantasies. But the material had an "as-if" quality, a reflecting unstable phallic primacy that readily regressed to oral or anal levels. They attributed the lack of oedipal development and the failure to achieve phallic phase dominance to adolescent borderline development.

Often, borderline adolescents will manifest pathological symptoms that may include anxiety, depression, hypomanic behavior, stealing, drug or alcohol abuse, confused and perverse sexuality, and even temporary breaks with reality. These symptoms often do not fit the familiar pattern of other emotional disorders, but instead seem to be mixed together in a confusing and inconsistent fashion. Usually in such cases, the combination of anxiety and depression expresses and to a certain extent masks an underlying identity diffusion. This differs from a more normal discontent with oneself and the world that may express itself in cynicism and bitterness, but continues nonetheless, in normal adolescent development, to be a functional part of it. It must also be distinguished from the more ominous delusional and dissociative reaction associated with a schizophrenic process.

Breaks with reality may suggest a diagnosis of schizophrenia, but usually in borderline cases, they are similar to transient psychotic episodes in adult patients and remain time-limited and relatively readily reversible. The developmental and other adjustment stresses associated with adolescence create a need in such patients to withdraw from the reality of the adult world, which they are expected to confront and deal with, and to retreat into a fantasy world where they can still entertain visions of themselves as effective, capable, and strong. Thus, the normal adolescent weakening of the barrier between conscious and unconscious thought systems is carried, in these cases, to a retreat into fantasy that impedes the adolescent's capacity to deal with real problems and real challenges. At times, this escape into fantasy may become relatively chronic, yet remain sufficiently encapsulated so that the normal life-course is not significantly disrupted. The patient will maintain such a delusional system alongside his conscious everyday experience.

The diagnosis of psychosis in an adolescent and the differentiation between a psychotic process and a transient borderline state is particularly difficult. This is especially true when the young patient first experiences a psychotic-like regression. The degree to which the regressive episode becomes actually disabling may be helpful in some cases: if the impairment in the ability to continue in school or work is of such a degree that the individual's adaptive mechanisms are overwhelmed and totally impaired, a diagnosis of psychosis may be warranted. In addition, when there are recurrences of such episodes, or when the regressive episodes last longer, this may reinforce the impression of psychosis. The general criteria that apply to the differentiation of psychosis from borderline conditions in adults apply equally well here (see Chapter 4).

Acting-out is almost always a problem in borderline adolescents. This reflects not only the decreased tolerance for frustration and inner tension that may characterize adolescents more generally, but also factors that may be associated with borderline vulnerability. In many cases, there may be sociopathic tendencies. Chwast (1977) associates these tendencies with what he calls the "malevolent transformation." Such a transformation occurs in an individual who has felt rejected and hated throughout his life, who then turns this feeling around into a rejection and hatred of others.

The individual loses a capacity for empathic feelings toward others, so that antisocial acting-out and its consequences become more tolerable. The process is reinforced when the youngster feels alienated from or rejected by people in his environment. Feelings of anxiety and depression arise in connection with dependency needs and the threat of disapproval from significant others. The depression reflects the sense of lost love from these important others, which is accompanied by a loss of self-esteem and an increase of self-hate. The acting-out may become a vehicle for avoiding these difficult and painful feelings. By the same token, guilt may also be an important factor in acting-out behavior. But more typically in borderline adolescents, the tendency to act-out involves a failure of inner controls that

reflect the underlying ego weakness and the failure of sufficient ego integration at earlier levels of preadolescent development.

Kernberg (1975, 1978) has pointed out that, in assessing antisocial
behavior in adolescence, some important discriminations must be made. One
must discriminate among a labeling of behavior as antisocial in merely
conventional or legalistic terms, rather than in strictly clinical terms; antisocial behavior that is within the range of normal reaction to an abnormal
antisocial subgroup; antisocial behavior that reflects a neurotic reaction,
usually in the form of struggles over adolescent dependency and rebelliousness; antisocial behavior that is part of a severe character pathology (particularly narcissistic); and finally, the diagnosis of antisocial personality itself.
When the diagnosis of antisocial personality can be made, the patient can be
taken as having an underlying borderline personality structure. Most of
these cases are characterized by poor impulse control, poor capacity to
handle and tolerate frustration and anxiety, a limited capacity for guilt,
inadequate resources for effective sublimation of drives and impulses,
manipulative and exploitative behavior, and chronic hostility and aggression
(Chwast, 1977).

The pathology of identity in borderline adolescence may be affected by
the relative instability and disorganization of the relationships among psychic
systems and is reflected in the inevitable impairment of object-relationships.
The expected destabilization caused by adolescent developmental vicissitudes
as such are often aggravated by the failure of family and society to contain
adequately the inner confusion and dissociation connected with this form of
regressive crisis, with the result that varying degrees of depersonalization are
experienced; the adolescent then attempts to counter this depersonalization
by desperately assuming a given identity or by an attachment to an ideologi-
cal group or a cult. In such cases of depersonalization, there may also be
distorted perceptions of reality, in which patients are overwhelmed by
feelings of strangeness and derealization. There may also be a confusion and
defusion of body boundaries. In other cases, a severe schizoid picture can
evolve, with the typical schizoid characteristics of isolation, loneliness, and a
lack of communication with the outside world. The adolescent seems to be
withdrawn and to care for nothing or no one and is often easily offended
and suspicious. Schizoid withdrawal is often accompanied by a high degree
of narcissistic self-investment reflected in feelings of self-sufficiency, omnipotence, and a contemptuous devaluation of objects, usually as a defense
against feelings of dependency.

The pathology of identity may occasionally take on the dimensions of a
psychopathic character, with apparent lack of guilt and responsibility and
the peremptory seeking of an immediate fulfillment of wishes, without any
consideration of delay or consequences. The underlying ego weakness and
the incapacity to tolerate frustration leaves these adolescents unable to deal
effectively with tension and delay of gratification. Impulsiveness becomes

ego-syntonic and is a desperate attempt to confirm the illusion of omnipotence and to deny underlying fears of rejection or punishment.

Failure in adolescent identity formation may also express itself in terms of an "as-if" resolution, similar to that seen in more adult cases. The adolescent often appears normal, with normal intellectual and emotional capacities, but with the same lack of authenticity and with the imitative compliance that is seen in his adult counterpart. There is little authentic experience of affects, and one can sense the lack of authenticity in their behavior. They are unable to experience feelings deeply or to grasp, empathically, the experience of others. When they attach themselves to ideologies, their beliefs are not genuinely internalized, but rather are based on imitative attitudes and compliance with the expectations of the group. They generally tend to be passive, easily influenced, often suggestible and are often rapidly and radically variable, depending on the input from significant others to whom they may be then attached (Grinberg and Grinberg, 1974).

In a somewhat more systematic fashion, Goldstein and Jones (1977), reporting on research on high-risk samples from the UCLA Family Project, defined four groups of disturbed adolescents that would seem to fall within the borderline range:

Group I. Aggressive–Antisocial
This group is characterized by poorly controlled, impulsive, acting-out behavior. Some degree of inner tension or subjective distress may be present, but it is clearly subordinate to the aggressive patterns which appear in many areas of functioning, i.e., family, school, peer relations, the law.

Group II. Active Family Conflict
These adolescents are characterized by a defiant, disrespectful stance toward their parents and belligerence and antagonism in the family setting. They often exhibit signs of inner distress and turmoil, such as tension, anxiety, and somatic complaints. Few manifestations of aggression or rebelliousness appear outside of the family.

Group III. Passive–Negative
These teenagers are characterized by negativism, sullenness, and indirect forms of hostility or defiance toward parents and other authorities. In contrast to Group II, overt defiance and temper outbursts are infrequent and there is a superficial compliance to adults' wishes. School difficulties are frequent, typically described as underachievement, although there is little evidence of disruptive behavior.

Group IV. Withdrawn-Socially Isolated
These adolescents are characterized by marked isolation, general uncommunicativeness, few, if any, friends, and excessive dependence on one or both parents. Gross fears or signs of marked anxiety and tension are often present. Much of their unstructured time is spent in solitary pursuits.

Other indices of potential borderline disorder may come from behavioral syndromes that are more frequently associated with borderline personality structure. When one observes such a behavioral syndrome in an adolescent, the index of suspicion for one of the borderline diagnoses must be increased. Such behavioral syndromes include:

1. Suicide (Gunderson and Singer, 1975; Meissner, 1977a): This usually takes the form of a manipulative suicide gesture, but may prove fatal. Repeated attempts raise the index of suspicion. Such attempts can be made in regressive crises by borderline adolescents at any level of personality organization, but are more frequent and more likely in cases of marked ego weakness.
2. Addiction and Alcoholism (Kernberg, 1967; Meissner, 1981a; Wurmser, 1978): The level of addictive potential is generally higher in borderline patients, especially in lower-order forms. What is in question is not merely drug usage, but rather the psychological vulnerability that underlies compulsive addiction.
3. Antisocial Personality (Kernberg, 1975, 1978): The antisocial potential is often a vehicle for paranoid tendencies that can reflect underlying borderline deficits and vulnerabilities.
4. Homosexuality/Transsexuality (Socarides, 1968, 1980; Meyer, 1982): This is particularly relevant for the developmentally arrested homosexual in whom phallic-oedipal conflicts derive from deeper preoedipal nuclear conflicts. The homosexuality reflects a basic disturbance of gender identity that may mask deeper-lying identity problems of a borderline sort. The transsexual disturbance is a more extreme expression of gender dysphoria consistent with borderline pathology.

These diverse observations allow us to draw several important conclusions. The onset of puberty introduces a fundamental biological and developmental stress, which impinges on already existing borderline vulnerabilities. Thus, the child who has manifested borderline features in childhood will continue his borderline career into adolescent years. In many cases, however, difficulties in behavior and adjustment are first seen in this early stage of adolescence, which suggests that the basically borderline character of the young person's psychic structure was not previously evident and that the stress induced by the onset of puberty and its vicissitudes created a situation in which the underlying borderline features became manifest.

In terms of diagnostic evaluation, it is not at all clear that in the transition out of childhood and in the early phases of adolescence, sufficient discrimination can be made among various borderline syndromes. At the early-adolescent level, we may have to be content with relatively gross discriminations that reflect fundamental problems in ego integration and the capacity of the developing ego to handle the stresses of the adolescent period. When such capacities have failed to develop or are seriously impeded, we may be dealing with a relatively severe form of borderline dysfunction. However, there may also be cases in which the underlying borderline impediments do not manifest themselves directly as disruptions in behavior or adaptive functioning, but rather become apparent only when developmental problems are not resolved in the later phases of the adolescent developmental period, on into late adolescence and even early adulthood. Such individuals may be capable of adequate, even high levels of adaptive achievement and social orientation, but they ultimately run aground in the more definitive tasks of adult orientation and adjustment, particularly in the establishment of a definitive sense of identity and in the commitment to a life-course of definite career or work achievement and object involvement. We have previously characterized such individuals as higher-order borderlines, in some of whom the underlying borderline features would not become evident in the ordinary run of day-to-day experience and would appear only under the highly specific and specialized regressive conditions of the analytic couch.

To conclude this discussion, then, I would suggest that, in the early phases of adolescent development, the articulation and definition of syndromes is relatively imprecise and vague and must remain so, at least for the time being, as a function of the degree of rapid and uncertain change that is taking place in that early phase of adolescence. However, as we move toward the later phases of adolescent development, the configurations toward which adolescent borderline structures tend to evolve begin to approximate, in more meaningful ways, to categories identifiable in more adult patients. Although the adolescent process heightens the degree of liability and fluidity in these formations, this lessens with time, and as the adolescent approaches adulthood, he may tend to settle into one or other of the more recognizable borderline categories, as previously described.

As Rinsley (1980b) observed:

> Clinical experience with these adolescent patients attests to the borderline early adolescent's symptomatic similarity to the borderline latency child, hence to the latter's more protean, psychotic-like clinical appearance. As the borderline adolescent traverses middle and late adolescence, the clinical picture in many cases comes increasingly to resemble that of the borderline adult. (p. 160)

There may well be cases, however, in which borderline features escape detection for a considerable period of time and become manifest only in the light of the progressive failure of the individual to complete the developmental tasks of adolescence and to enter the effective world of adult adaptation.

Chapter 9

Analyzability of Borderline Syndromes

The analyzability of patients who fall within the borderline spectrum has been too little addressed in psychoanalytic literature. Questions, however, assume added significance in the context of this monograph, since the major conclusions drawn earlier are that the borderline spectrum involves a heterogeneous grouping of subdiagnoses that reflect varying degrees of psychopathology and that call for correspondingly different forms of psychotherapeutic intervention, ranging from more purely supportive interventions to psychoanalysis. The questions inevitably loom large—To what extent are some borderlines analyzable? And, how can we reasonably determine those patients within the borderline range who might have a reasonable expectation of a productive outcome from psychoanalytic treatment?

The criteria for the analyzability of patients in classical psychoanalysis are more or less generally accepted and well established. Freud's own criteria were certainly rather general. He felt that analyzable patients would be under fifty years of age (feeling that psychic rigidity was a correlate of advanced age); have reasonably good intelligence and reliability; have a character that was neither worthless nor degenerate; not require any urgent removal of symptoms; and be capable of forming a transference neurosis. Fenichel (1945) specified certain obvious constraints, namely, mental deficiency, speech impediments, along with a predominance of secondary gain or the lack of a reasonable and cooperative ego. Other authors (Zetzel, 1968) have added the requirement of the developmental achievement of a genuine triangular-oedipal conflict. There is general agreement that psychoanalysis is most appropriately restricted to cases of psychoneurosis. There is also general agreement that the diagnoses more accessible to psychoanalytic intervention include the hysterias, both conversion and anxiety; mixed hysterical-obsessional syndromes; obsessive compulsive neurosis; psychosexual inhibitions; facultative bisexuality; neurotic (reactive) depressions;

certain character neuroses; and with limitations, certain psychosomatic illnesses (Glover, 1955; Greenson, 1967).

Yet the criteria for analyzability remain, to some degree, problematic and uncertain. There is grudging admission that the determination of analyzability cannot depend on assessment of symptoms alone, since many cases with apparently florid and incapacitating symptoms prove to be successfully analyzable. By the same token, other patients whose symptomatology seems to be of a relatively benign order and either hysterical or obsessional in quality, prove to have underlying character structures that are considerably more primitive and unanalyzable.

In addition, there is a general awareness that any attempt to determine analyzability simply in terms of diagnostic categories has usually been unsuccessful. When such categorical assessments are attempted, they must be regarded in terms of a more or less typical case organization or with the implicit stipulation that other things are indeed equal. Thus, although the criteria for classical psychoanalysis are generally stated as applicable to the psychoneuroses, there is also a view, more recent in origin and linked to the widening of the scope of psychoanalysis (Stone, 1954), that some of the more severe forms of character disorder, including certain borderline cases, may, in fact, be analyzable.

Certainly significant problems are inherent in any attempt to assess the analyzability of borderline patients. In the first place, the literature on borderline assessment and diagnosis deals primarily with what we have already described (see Chapter 6) as lower-order borderline conditions. This is true of both the early literature on borderline psychopathology, which associated borderline states with the psychoses and tended to regard borderline pathology primarily as a modified form of schizophrenia, and the later formulations that have been so strongly influenced by Kernberg. As we have noted, Kernberg's assessment of borderline personality organization presents more or less a caricature of borderline conditions, in emphasizing the more regressive or primitive aspects of borderline organization and functioning. As long as that assessment of borderline conditions obtains, there is little room for an analytic approach to such conditions.

The argument in this chapter contends that the criteria of analyzability as applied to cases within the borderline spectrum must be significantly modified from those described in traditional psychoanalytic terms. Correlative to this, however, it would seem to be quite rare or unusual that the classical psychoanalytic technique could be carried out with borderline patients of any description without the introduction of significant parameters. Thus, the following discussion shares in the basic conundrum common to all approaches to the widening scope of psychoanalysis, namely, to what extent can the parameters necessary for adapting psychoanalytic technique to more primitive forms of character pathology be consistent with the basic requirements of the psychoanalytic modality? And, to what extent can such modified forms of psychoanalytic treatment continue to be regarded as authentically psychoanalytic?

A difficult question that such considerations generate is: To what extent can the procedures indicated for patients in the borderline spectrum be regarded as essentially forms of psychoanalysis rather than psychotherapy? Related to this procedural question, there is still the basic question at the root of the issue of analyzability: Does the patient have the resources to utilize and respond to the psychoanalytic modality, however modified by parameters, with the anticipation of a better therapeutic result than might be undertaken in a more explicitly psychotherapeutic approach? Thus, the traditionally problematic question as to what constitutes the essence of psychoanalysis and what separates it from psychotherapeutic modalities continues to plague us.

CRITERIA OF ANALYZABILITY FOR CLASSICAL PSYCHOANALYSIS

The criteria for analyzability for the classical psychoanalytic technique have achieved a fair degree of consensus. There is general agreement that one major requirement is a sufficient degree of ego strength, including both the capacity for autonomous ego-functioning and the maintenance of firm reality-testing (Guttman, 1960; Waldhorn, 1960). Greenson (1967) has also noted that engagement in the psychoanalytic process requires the capacity for contradictory ego-functions, insofar as, on the one hand, the patient must regress to a position of relative passivity, free associate, and suspend reality-testing, while, on the other hand, he must exercise a relatively high order of ego-functioning in maintaining ego controls, taking initiative and responsibility within the analytic context, working to understand the analytic productions, and maintaining a definitive contact with reality as an essential aspect of his capacity to distinguish between fantasy and reality.

Perhaps the clearest statement of the importance of ego strength for the psychoanalytic modality was made in the findings of the Menninger Research Project on Psychotherapy (Kernberg et al., 1972). In that study, ego strength was defined in terms of (1) the degree of integration, stability, and flexibility of intrapsychic structures (this included the defense organization, the capacity for anxiety tolerance, and implicitly, the capacity for impulse control, thought organization, and subliminatory channel capacity); (2) the degree to which object-relations were adaptive, deep, and gratifying of normal instinctual needs; and finally, (3) the degree to which psychic malfunctioning was manifested directly by symptoms. The study concluded that, although patients with high ego strengths seem to improve regardless of the therapeutic modality or the level of the therapist's skill, the greatest improvement seemed to come through psychoanalysis. By the same token, poor ego strength seemed to be a contraindication for either psychoanalysis or even supportive therapy.

The capacity for involvement in meaningful object-relations is also an important contributing factor in the patient's ability to enter a therapeutic alliance, as well as to permit the development of a transference neurosis. The character of the patient's capacity to form object-relations must be determined from the longitudinal history of such relationships in the course of the life history, particularly significant object ties and most notably those developed in the family context, with special emphasis on oedipal object ties and their resolution.

The patient's capacity for anxiety and for the toleration of frustration and anxiety loom large in the consideration for analysis, since the analytic process places such intense demands on these capacities. The patient must have the capacity for signal anxiety, rather than a tendency to the overwhelming and regressive effects of traumatic anxiety. By the same token, Anna Freud's (1936) distinction of superego and objective anxiety relates to analytic prognosis insofar as the former anxiety creates a purely endopsychic conflict, which is easier to modify through analysis of the underlying introjective configurations than is objective anxiety. Similarly, castration anxiety, which tends to develop later and to reflect intrapsychic conflict, has a better prognosis than the earlier, more catastrophic separation anxiety. If patients are unable to withstand the onslaughts of such anxiety without excessive regression or the mobilization of primitive defenses, the analytic work is seriously impeded. Such patients often need reassurance and narcissistic support and constantly seek evidence from the analyst of affection, power, and prestige. Other patients are terrified of their own affective responses; become rigidly controlled or withdrawn in the analytic situation; and tend to retreat behind intellectualizations, rationalizations, or abstractions (Waldhorn, 1960).

Motivation also plays a significant role. Here the strength of the patient's motivation, as manifested in the wish for recovery or for deeper self-understanding, augers a good prognosis as opposed to the neurotic compulsion to confess or to dispel anxiety or symptoms or to gain narcissistic gratification. Kuiper (1968) even goes so far as to postulate that the wish for self-understanding is a powerful prognostic indicator, which can effectively outweigh other negative indicators. Thus, if the wish for self-understanding is strong enough, it may serve to counterbalance other contraindications or even serious psychopathology. In this same vein, one important finding of the Menninger Study (Kernberg et al., 1972) was that the combination of good ego strength with a high level of motivation, in the form of a mature wish for change in the direction of better functioning by means of a collaborative venture with a therapist, proved to be an extremely positive prognostic indicator for psychoanalysis, but not necessarily for other therapeutic modalities. By the same token, the study demonstrated that an increase in the level of motivation at the time of termination of the treatment or subsequent follow-up reflected a more immature wish to be taken care of that tended to activate idealization, longing, and dependency wishes that seemed to form a part of the mourning process associated with the termination of therapy.

Others have focused on the requirement that, developmentally, the patient must have achieved a level of genuine triangular conflict to undertake analytic work. Thus, Zetzel (1968) points out that the capacity for triangular conflict involves the development of ego-functions, a capacity for tolerating anxiety, as well as the development of the capacity for signal anxiety, and implies that the individual has retained significant object-relationships with both parents, although the postoedipal relationships tend to be more ambivalent and less satisfying than the preoedipal relationships. But a decade and one-half of broadened clinical experience, and the deepening of our understanding of the interplay between oedipal and preoedipal determinants developmentally, has shifted the ground of opinion somewhat, so that analysts are increasingly tolerant of preoedipal or pregenital fixations and components in the organization of personality structure.

In addition, the patient who undertakes analysis must be able to assume and tolerate a relatively passive role and position. This may particularly be a problem for patients with homosexual, paranoid, or sadomasochistic conflicts. Such patients often develop defensive needs for activity in one form or another, which can lead to obscure, obfuscating, nonverbal behavior or acting-out or to a view of the analytic hour as a dissociated and unreal experience.

In recent years, there have also been more systematic attempts to assess the factors that enter into decisions regarding analyzability. Lower et al. (1972) studied the selection process in a series of forty applicants to the Philadelphia Psychoanalytic Institute for supervised analyses. The qualities associated by the judges with a positive decision for analyzability were:

1. Psychological mindedness: This should include "a capacity for insight, introspection, intuition, verbality, remembering dreams and fantasies; awareness of transference, of internal conflict; sensitivity to own feelings and curiosity about drives."
2. Motivation: Positive motivation includes aspects of hope, realistic expectations, the desire for self-understanding, and the desire to change. The desire to change was clearly differentiated from the more magical wish for relief or magical cure.
3. Favorable subjective responses: This includes the impression made on the interviewer insofar as the patient made a favorable impression, seemed to

relate well, and presented himself as pleasant, friendly, attractive, or interesting.

4. Good social adaptation: Included here are object-relationships of good quality and the capacity to sustain heterosexual relationships, particularly in the marriage relationship.

5. Ego strength: This includes such features as good adaptive ability, the capacity to tolerate frustration and anxiety, the capacity for sublimation, and other related characteristics such as responsibility, cooperativeness, and sophistication.

6. Lack of defensiveness: This includes the availability of affect and the degree to which the individual was open, frank, honest, sincere, sensitive, and reactive.

7. Good work performance: Both school and job accomplishments are included here.

8. Oedipal pathology: This refers specifically to the capacity for triangular conflict, but also includes the availability of "hysterical features."

The factors associated with a decision for poor analyzability were:

1. Poor ego strength: This includes a limited capacity for the toleration of frustration and anxiety, poor instinctual control, a limited capacity for sublimation, poor judgment, faulty reality-testing, the clinicity of symptoms, vulnerability to regression, and the presence of ideas of reference (suggesting underlying paranoid traits).

2. Poor social adaptation: Included here are poor quality of object-relationships, which tend to have an infantile or a narcissistic component, lack of trust, problems with authority, and tendencies to dependence, loneliness, and isolation.

3. Preoedipal pathology: Oral and anal characteristics and a history of early deprivation or loss are included here. The presence of addictive or perverse features were also reflected, along with varying degrees of narcissistic pathology.

4. Defensiveness: This includes the unavailability of affect, tendencies to intellectualization, easy rationalization, rigidity, excessive denial, and a lack of access to unconscious material through dreams or early memories.

About a decade ago, Greenspan and Cullander (1973) provided an even more systematic assessment profile, constructed along metapsychological lines. They suggested twelve categories:

1. Ego intactness: This refers to the assessment of the basic integrity of the ego, including perceptual and motor apparatuses and such related functions as memory, the basic ego-functions, particularly reality-testing, the capacity for secondary process thinking, and the presence of adequate ego boundaries.

2. Ego flexibility: This reflects the ego's capacity to utilize a repertoire of finely discriminated operations, in contrast to ego rigidity, in which the operations are sparse and poorly discriminated.

3. Affects: This indicates the extent to which affects are multiple, flexible, and developmentally advanced, in contrast to their less desirable sparsity, rigidity, or developmental limitations. Attention is directed to the predominant affects, particularly those emerging under stress, their level of developmental maturity, and their flexibility and selectivity.

4. Defenses: This category concerns the extent to which defenses are developmentally mature, stable, flexible, selective, and effective, as opposed to the degree in which they would be developmentally limited, unstable, rigid, and overly generalized or ineffective.

5. Capacity for relatively conflict-free and autonomous ego functioning: This category specifically pertains to the capacity of the ego to observe and to experience simultaneously, the capacity to regress in the service of the ego, the ability to learn, the ability to grasp psychological connections, creativity, curiosity, intelligence, and the capacity for synthesis, integration, and further differentiation.

6. Superego functioning: Measured here is the extent to which the superego is maturely and realistically organized, adequately internalized, predominantly benevolent, and self-esteem enhancing, as opposed to the less desirable immaturity of superego organization, the tendency for externalization, and the degree to which superego functions are punitive, guilt-producing, or depressive.

7. Drive organization: This includes assessment of the extent to which drives are adequately fused and integrated at a genital level of organization, and the extent of pregenital fixation.

8. Relationship potential: This category involves an assessment of the capacity for object-relationships, including the degree of transference potential.

9. Motivation for treatment: Included here is the degree to which motivation is thoughtful, realistic, and related to inner tensions or conflict the individual wishes to explore and understand. A negative aspect of this dimension would reflect the degree to which motivation is based on external pressures outside the patient, or the extent to which the individual's expectation are based on magical or external factors.

10. Reality considerations: Included are issues of availability and financial resources and the stability of work, family, and social situations.

11. Intuitive impressions: Here are included special assets or liabilities of the patient, or hunches based on intuition or experience.

12. Reasonable goals and special problems: This includes an assessment of the capacity for internal structural change, symptomatic change, and change in areas of conflicts or in ego-syntonic character traits.

Such systematic assessments are generally congruent with more traditional views of the qualities desirable in potentially analyzable patients. At the same time, it must be kept in mind that such assessments are directed toward the selection of more or less ideal potential analysands for the classical, unadulterated psychoanalytic process. Although these indices may require modification in the assessment of borderline patients for analysis, these studies nonetheless provide meaningful categories in terms of which that assessment can be made.

THE ASSESSMENT OF BORDERLINE PATIENTS FOR PSYCHOANALYSIS

The presence of borderline features or a borderline diagnosis has generally, in the traditional view, been regarded as a major contradiction to psychoanalysis (Knapp et al., 1960; Waldhorn, 1960). However, as we have already noted, these assessments of borderline pathology have been made within a context in which the borderline label connoted serious psychopathology akin to the psychoses—predominantly the group we have called lower-order borderline conditions. Given this diagnostic context and its implications, there would be little room for argument as to whether such patients would be suitable for analysis. However, in terms of the argument we have been developing here, such a conclusion would leave out of consideration the entire group of higher-order borderline cases we have been at pains to describe (see Chapter 7).

There are clearly a number of borderline features that, when seen in their more acute and regressive forms, would not be helped by psychoanalysis. Primary among these are the ego deficits that have been noted in relatively regressive borderline conditions. The implied levels of fixation and developmental failure and the necessity for the ego to expend excessive energy in the defense against regression would contraindicate analysis (Glover, 1955). In addition, lapses in reality-testing that result in magical feelings and a failure to discriminate between fantasy and reality in the analytic setting are contraindications (Waldhorn, 1960). Such patients may readily resort to more primitive defenses, including denial, projection, magical thinking, hypomanic defenses, and acting-out (Guttmann, 1960). In addition, one of the significant findings of the Menninger study (Kernberg et al., 1972) was that patients with a significant degree of ego weakness (the equivalent of Kernberg's borderlines) tended to do very poorly in psychoanalysis, primarily because they tolerated regression poorly and were susceptible to transference psychosis.

The tendency for transference reactions in borderline patients to remain unstable, and the vulnerability to transference psychosis, has been frequently noted in the literature (Guttman, 1960; Waldhorn, 1960; Kernberg, 1974; Goldberg, 1974). The emergence of a transference psychosis is generally regarded as destructive of the analytic situation, and thus a major contraindication. Along similar lines, the incapacity of some borderline patients to form an effective therapeutic alliance, and the lack of availability in some borderline patients of a reasonably cooperative ego capable of engaging with the analyst in a collaborative and exploratory venture, was seen as an essential impediment. Adler (1979) has even questioned the capacity of borderline patients to form a therapeutic alliance. Adler clearly has in mind the more primitive, lower-order forms of borderline pathology to whom he attributes the incapacity to achieve stable, evocative memories. Such individuals would be unable to sustain the memory of an object in the absence of that object. Such a marked cognitive deficit would certainly interfere with the capacity for forming stable object-relations, or even entering into a meaningful therapeutic alliance.

The analytic requirement that the patient be able to tolerate a reasonable degree of frustration and anxiety is also one that tends to eliminate certain borderline patients. The analytic situation places a considerable demand on the patient for delay of gratification and for frustration of a variety of wishes and desires and tends to stimulate a significant degree of anxiety—all of which must be tolerated and worked through for the analytic process to have an effect. Patients whose personalities are organized along infantile and more primitively narcissistic lines have great difficulty in sustaining this degree of frustration and anxiety (Waldhorn, 1960).

We have already noted the frequency with which paranoid attitudes or persecutory anxieties are found in borderline patients. Such attitudes may be reflected in an intense degree of persecutory anxiety in relationship to the analyst, or they may be manifested more subtly, in terms of antisocial attitudes or rebellious attitudes toward authority figures that may be expressed indirectly, derivatively, and in muted fashion (Meissner, 1978).

The quality of anxiety in borderline patients also often contraindicates analysis, since the anxiety is frequently of a more primitive and more destructive form than signal anxiety. In borderline patients, the anxiety is frequently traumatic and overwhelming and stems from relatively primitive developmental levels, expressing itself as a fear of separation, a fear of loss of love or the loved object, and even more primitively, at times, in psychotic-like fears of annihilation. In addition, because of the relatively infantile and often highly narcissistic quality of the borderline patient's structure, the motivation for analytic work leaves much to be desired and reflects the instinctual push for gratification or narcissistic completion that expresses itself in magical expectations for a cure by means of a symbiotic attachment to a powerful, sustaining analyst-object (Levine, 1979).

Despite this catalogue of characteristics that would exclude borderline patients from the analytic couch, the literature, even in terms of the some-what slanted view of borderline pathology that pervaded the earlier literature, has still left room for the possibility that some borderline patients would, in fact, be analyzable. Such was the impact of Stone's (1954) comments on the widening scope of psychoanalysis. He questioned whether the presumed inability of such patients to develop an effective transference might have more to do with the intensity and ambivalence of transference reactions than with any underlying incapacity. Reflecting the views of the Kris Study Group on Analyzability, Waldhorn (1960) included some questionable bor-derline states under those patients who were generally agreed to be suitable for psychoanalysis. Similarly, Greenson (1967) included certain borderline conditions under those patients he saw as questionably analyzable, along with impulse neuroses, perversions, addictions, and delinquencies. Diatkine (1968) would even go so far as to say that, despite the relative intensity and acuteness of symptomatology, some borderline patients may, in fact, be easier to analyze than some more rigid, resistant neurotics.

The question remains, then, as to what specific criteria can be used to identify the analyzable borderline. There is general agreement that such an assessment cannot be made on the basis of the intensity or acuteness of symptomatology. Some patients may show little or no symptomatic disturb-ance, yet possess an underlying borderline structure. Again, patients who may develop severe and disturbing symptoms, even symptoms that may appear for a time psychotic, in an acute regressive state, may prove on further experience to have a sufficient degree of stability of inner psychic structure and capacity to permit them to undertake analytic work with considerable success. It is for this reason that Kernberg's (1976a) emphasis on structural diagnosis has been both illuminating and helpful.

For the sake of clarity, I will expand on some of the criteria of border-line analyzability in terms of the categories provided by Greenspan and Cullander (1973).

Ego Intactness

The basic ego apparatus is not often in question in borderline patients, insofar as perceptual and motor functions are generally intact and functional. A particular question, however, in this regard has been raised by Adler (1979), who has described the failure of the capacity for evocative memory as a major developmental impediment in borderline psychopathology. The failure to achieve solid, evocative memory with regard to affective object-relationships causes these patients to regress to a level of merely recognitional memory in the face of certain forms of stress. These usually involve the loss of important people in their lives or even the real or fantasied loss of love or support from them. This deficit is reflected typically in the incapacity of such borderline patients to recover positive images or fantasies regarding the helpful, loving, or sustaining people in the patient's present or past life, but instead an overwhelming vulnerability to negative images of a painful, hurtful, or destructive sort is seen. The view here is that the disturbed memory functioning in such patients is less likely to be a matter of developmental ego defect than a question of selective regressive functioning in the face of particular stresses, as related to a borderline regressive state. More often than not in such patients, memory capacities remain intact in other, nonaffectively involved areas of their functioning.

Although the ego apparatus is generally intact in borderline patients, these functions are vulnerable to regression, and the whole question of the level of functioning of various aspects of the patient's ego is a matter of primary importance. Of particular importance is the capacity for reality-testing, which generally remains relatively intact. Remembering that even reality-testing is not a matter of presence or absence, but rather is subject to wide variations in degree, the patient's capacity to test reality should be carefully assessed. Total absence of such a capacity is the hallmark of psychosis. But this capacity is often vulnerable in borderline patients, particularly those close to the psychotic range.

Patients whose reality-testing seems fragile, and is frequently subject to regressive crises, would not seem suitable for analysis, particularly since the regressive pulls of the analytic situation would create particular difficulties. But there are certainly borderline patients in whom the capacity to test reality shows no such vulnerability, nor has it been lost to any significant degree, even in regressive crises. Such patients would have a more optimistic prognosis. Other borderline patients may show very infrequent or rare weakening of this capacity or may reveal some vulnerability in this area only in certain selected areas of their experience, usually those having to do with significant object-relationships. In such cases, the disturbance is mild, and although it is not an optimistic indicator for the patient's capacity for psychoanalytic work, it would not be a forthright contraindication, either.

The other ego-function to be assessed is the patient's cognitive organization. When the patient shows a frank thought disorder and a tendency to primary process thinking on clinical examination, the likelihood is that this deficit is accompanied by other severe problems concerning the organization of psychic structure and that such patients are probably not suitable for analysis. Frequently enough, however, borderline patients will not reveal any suggestion of a thought disorder clinically, but rather may manifest mild thought disturbances on projective testing. In such cases, an assessment of the extent and degree of such disorganization is important: if the disturbance seems relatively mild in degree and does not otherwise interfere with the ego's capacity to function, this need not contraindicate analysis.

Ego Flexibility

Here the question has to do with the degree to which the ego can tolerate internal conflict without significantly disrupting ego-functioning. If the ego tends to be excessively rigid in its neurotic formations and defensive organization, this does not auger well for analysis. The stress in borderline patients may frequently lead to breakdowns of ego-functioning in the form of temporary loss of reality-testing, a fragmentation of the sense of self, a loss of the synthetic capacity to integrate thought and affect, or even severe states of inhibition or alteration of drive gratification. A retreat to severe restriction or relatively primitive defense organization probably reflects underlying structural defects and would suggest a relatively primitive borderline organization. Assessment of the degree of such loss of function and the ease of rapidity of recovery is central.

Of particular importance is the question of vulnerability to regression. When the capacity to maintain adequate ego-functioning is too easily or too frequently lost or when the extent of regression is relatively severe, that is, when the regression precipitates a reaction of psychotic or near-psychotic proportions, this would serve to contraindicate analysis. More often than not, many borderline patients, particularly those in the higher order of the borderline range, show only mild regressive episodes that are infrequent or rare in their life experience and do not necessarily serve to contraindicate analysis. It is also critically important to assess such patients at their more or less general and characterological level of functioning, rather than in their relatively infrequent, regressive phases.

Autonomous Ego-Functions

In the view being developed here, not all borderline patients show the signs of ego weakness that Kernberg attributes to his more caricatured version of borderline psychopathology. In fact, through most of their life experience, many borderline patients show few or no signs of ego weakness or may show them only on rare occasions under conditions of regressive stress. In the assessment of autonomous ego-functions, some sense of the relative capacity of the patient to function in a conflict-free manner must be gained. This may be the case in many areas of the patient's life, or it may manifest a relative inability to function in a conflict-free manner in certain isolated contexts. When such is the case, it augers well for the analytic process; but when the degree and extent of conflict-ridden functioning is excessive, it augers poorly.

The patient's ability to regress in the service of the ego is also of considerable importance, since this is essential to the psychoanalytic process.

The crucial issue is the extent to which the patient can undergo a therapeutic regression without losing or disrupting ego-functioning. The more such autonomous functions are interfered with by conflict, the less optimistic the prognosis.

Superego Functioning

Although the neurotic patient suffers from a relatively severe and punitive superego, the superego is sufficiently integrated so that the outcome is cast on the level of intrapsychic conflict. At the borderline level, however, the superego tends to be even more highly punitive and destructive, but at the same time, less well integrated. The result is often contradictory superego demands that may be sadistic, prohibitive, or self-devaluing, on the one hand, while primitive ego-ideal demands that seek omnipotence, power, and perfection persist, on the other. There may also be contradictions in value systems and severe mood swings (Kernberg, 1976a).

Of critical importance to the assessment of analyzability, and reflecting the lack of ego-superego integration, is the propensity of patients to project superego components, thus externalizing the essential conflict. This tendency undermines the patient's capacity for concern for others and for guilt. When this tendency is severe, as it often is in lower-order borderline patients, the patient will manifest a variety of paranoid traits, utilizing relative primitive forms of projection and externalization. The critical variable is the extent to which such projective distortions are transient and remain under the control of the patient's capacity to test reality and to integrate his projective distortions with other sources of information. If that capacity is impaired or lacking, analysis would be contraindicated.

Affects

Here the important elements are the assessment of the patient's capacity for meaningful affective expression and the extent to which affects can become disruptive or disorganizing. The predominant affects are anxiety and depression. Their prognostic relevance hinges on the extent to which these affects are both meaningful, in their relation to a suitable context, and the extent to which they can be tolerated by the patient without undue regression. When such affects are essentially related to intrapsychic conflicts and are not unduly incapacitating (that is, producing a regressive loss of ego-functioning), the prognosis is relatively optimistic. Affects may be more immature, developmentally, as for example, severe emotional hunger, fear, rage, jealousy, and envy. Such feelings are characteristically borderline, but again there is the question of the degree to which they pervade the patient's inner world and the extent to which they can be modified. If some degree of flexibility and selectivity can be demonstrated, particularly in connection with appropriate stimulus contexts (rage in one context, empathy in another), the prognosis would be more optimistic than if the patient's range of affects were more constricted and used indiscriminately.

It is important to assess both the depth and the intensity of anxiety and depression. The anxiety should be primarily signal anxiety, that is, the patient should have the capacity to tolerate a significant degree of anxiety without regression. If the anxiety becomes too quickly traumatic, and the patient resorts to regression or to more primitive defenses, this is not a good indicator. If the anxiety is predominantly related to intrapsychic conflict, this would seem to be a more optimistic indicator than if the anxiety were externally related, as, for example, to fears of separation, loss of love, object loss, or even annihilation.

By the same token, the intensity and depth of depression should be assessed. If the depression is primarily reactive, and appropriate to the stimulus context, this would indicate a good prognosis. The patient's capacity to mourn important losses is an important index of the potential success of the analytic process. The extent to which the tendency to depression overrides the capacity for mourning would be less optimistic, prognostically (Goldberg, 1974). In addition, if the depression tends to be long in duration and/or relatively severe (to the point of suicidal impulses), the prognosis is less optimistic. However, even the presence of suicidal impulses must be put into context and cannot be assessed independently. Many borderline patients may be vulnerable to suicidal impulses in regressive states; but if such states are relatively rare in their experience, and if at the level of their normal characterological functioning the depressive impulses are muted and suicidal intentions are foreign to their experience, the exceptional suicidal element is of less prognostic significance.

Drive Organization

The typical configuration in borderline patients is some integration of both pregenital and genital drive components. Even where the drive components have reached a level of more or less stable genital organization, pregenital elements, particularly oral and anal derivatives, will characteristically be found to contaminate the drive organization. The predominance of primitive oral aggression to which Kernberg ascribes much of borderline pathology is relatively rare. When such primitive aggressive drives come to dominate the drive organization, this would contraindicate psychoanalytic work.

However, it is also important to assess whether the apparent fixations represent actual developmental stopping points beyond which the patient has not been able to move effectively in his developmental progression or whether they represent regressive retreats to such fixation points from a higher level of developmental achievement. In these terms, the assessment of patients in regressive phases is not sufficient, but must wait for a characterological assessment of the patient's best level of achieved functioning. When the drive organization is predominantly pregenital and reflects either major fixations or arrested development, this would not be a good indicator. When the pregenital elements are primarily regressive, much again depends on the frequency, intensity, and depth of the regression. For many borderline patients, particularly those of the higher-order type, such regressions are not characteristic.

Defensive Organization

The extent to which the borderline patient resorts to primitive narcissistic defenses, particularly projection, denial, and distortion, would suggest a degree of ego weakness that would preclude successful analytic work. Borderline patients, generally, combine immature and neurotic defenses (Meissner, 1980b). In regressive crises, it can be expected that the drive organization will shift toward a more immature and narcissistic level. Consequently, the adequate assessment of the defense organization in any patient requires an assessment of the patient's capacity for defensive functioning at more typically characterological levels of functioning as well. As with all such assessments of regressive crises, duration and ready reversibility are important features. In many borderline patients, such regressive shifts in defensive organization are relatively rare and, consequently, may not contraindicate psychoanalysis. The relatively primitive defenses described by Kernberg, that is, projection, primitive idealization, omnipotent control, omnipotence, and devaluation, are more frequently manifested in regressive states or in more primitively organized borderline personalities who would not be suitable for analytic work.

Relationship Potential

The patient's capacity for object-relationships is a direct index of the transference potential, which affects the capacity for therapeutic alliance. The Menninger Study (Kernberg et al., 1972) concluded that patients with a poor history of object-relations tended to do poorly in psychoanalysis and that patients with a more optimistic history of object-relationships did comparably better. Poor object-relations were a particularly important prognostic indicator, espccially when accompanying a significant degree of ego weakness. Of central concern is the patient's capacity for enduring, meaningful, and intimate relationships with significant figures around him. The lack of such a capacity does not augur well for psychoanalysis. An important aspect of this assessment is the degree of ambivalence or outright sadism or hostility in preoedipal object-relationships. The more troubled, disruptive, or traumatic such relationships have been, the less optimistic the prognosis. If the patient has, in some degree, achieved preoedipal developmental tasks, particularly the capacity to accept the limitations of one-to-one relationships without feeling either rejected or devalued, along with a capacity to tolerate separation from important objects of dependence, this would tend to support a more positive prognosis.

Particularly useful and important in the assessment of the patient's relationship potential is the evaluation of the capacity to enter into a meaningful therapeutic alliance. The extent to which the patient can enter into a reasonable and cooperative collaboration with the analyst would go a long way toward contributing to a more optimistic prognosis. When such a capacity is clearly lacking, this is a strong contraindication to psychoanalysis. Often in the assessment of some patients, a trial interpretation is useful as a measure of the extent to which the patient can actually engage in collaborative reflection with the therapist.

Motivation

The nature of the patient's motivation undoubtedly plays a central role in the assessment of borderline patients, as it does in the assessment of any patient for analysis. The basic issue in the assessment of borderline patients is the extent to which the patient's motivation for treatment reflects a sincere and honest wish for self-understanding and a commitment to the prospect of intrapsychic change through a collaborative effort with the analyst. If the patient's motivation is serious and realistic, and relates to the need to explore and understand his own inner tensions and conflicts, the possibilities for a successful analytic undertaking are considerably enhanced. Such motivation in borderline patients must be contrasted with the more or less infantile, narcissistically tinged, magical expectation on the part of the patient that the analyst will work some powerful and magical cure that will alleviate all difficulties in the patient's life without any serious effort or need for work and understanding by the patient himself. If the patient does not really seek treatment by his own volition, does not understand what he is getting into, or actually wants something else that would satisfy his needs or alleviate his pain, it is better that he not undertake analysis.

Self-Organization

This reflects the patient's psychic integration and functioning. One of the central, discriminating factors separating borderline psychopathology from narcissistic personality disorders is the achievement in the latter of self-cohesion and the capacity to maintain a cohesive sense of self in the face of regressive strain. This capacity is found in the more highly developed narcissistic personality, whereas it is more highly vulnerable and susceptible to regressive pulls in borderline psychopathology. The failures of self-cohesion in borderline patients may be seen in terms of failures of identity formation; in the relative incapacity to maintain a firmly delineated and secure sense of identity; in states of depersonalization; in intense feelings of emptiness, loneliness, or nothingness relative to the inner sense of self; or even, particularly in regressive crises, in a sense of inner fragmentation and loss of self. Patients who are unable to maintain a relatively stable sense of self or whose self-organization is vulnerable to fragmentation are usually borderlines whose pathology is at a near psychotic level. Such patients should not be psychoanalyzed. Patients whose identity crisis is of an acute and severe nature or who are subject to severe states of identity diffusion or depersonalization are also probably not analyzable. However, other patients whose difficulties in establishing a firm sense of identity are more peripheral, that is, have more to do with the integration of significant life roles and commitments, rather than in an underlying sense of inner psychic integrity or self-organization, may be potentially analyzable.

The quality of emptiness in borderline patients should be carefully evaluated in terms of the depth and quality of the experience and the developmental level it seems to reflect. The experience of intense inner emptiness, accompanied by feelings of panic and despair, seems to reflect critical early developmental failings and characterizes borderline patients who live close to the border of psychosis (Adler and Buie, 1979). In an effort to alleviate or to avoid such intense feelings of painful aloneness and emptiness, such patients develop intense needs to be held, fed, and touched and ultimately seek to assuage the pain of abandonment by merging with a significant object.

Such feelings are intensely mobilized in the intimate dyadic relationship characteristic of analysis. When these needs are not adequately fulfilled, there is an intense reaction of disillusionment, disappointment, and rage. Such patients are frequently unable to maintain positive images or fantasies of sustaining objects, either past or present. This basic inability would impede the capacity for a consistent and meaningful therapeutic alliance.

However, in better organized and better functioning borderlines, the fear of abandonment may take a less malignant form, expressing itself more explicitly in terms of loss, separation, and abandonment. Such fears, although they reflect early developmental vicissitudes, do not necessarily imply the depth and severity of the inner emptiness and loss of self seen in more primitive personality structures. Such difficulties, however, may reflect a basic incapacity for meaningful and constructive internalization in such patients, which deserves careful consideration with regard to the assessment of analyzability. Such patients may indeed be capable of undertaking the analytic process, but may, however, have considerable difficulties in the termination phase, particularly with the inevitable mourning process and its attendant internalizations.

Something can be gained, regarding the assessment of borderline analyzability, from a consideration of diagnostic formulations. In discussing the analyzability of hysterics, Zetzel (1968) describes four groups of hysterical patients with increasing degrees of severity of psychopathology. The first group are the good hysterics who have achieved a level of genuine triangular conflict and who are able to retain significant object-relationships with both parents, even though postoedipal involvements may be more ambivalent or less satisfactory than preoedipal. Such patients have achieved the major developmental tasks of the preoedipal years, including the acceptance of the limitations of one-to-one relationships and the tolerance of increasing separation from important objects, as well as the capacity for deriving pleasure from active mastery and learning. Such patients are clearly analyzable.

The next group of potentially good hysterics have an analyzable hysterical character structure, but they are less ready to make the serious commitment required in the analytic situation. They are less mature than the true hysterics, and are usually youngest or only children. They are more passive and less consistent in achieving important life goals. Their friendships are less stable and more openly ambivalent, and they have difficulty with dependency wishes, which are frequently more available than is typically the case in neurotic hysterics. Such patients have considerable difficulty in establishing a stable analytic situation and in entering a meaningful and consistent therapeutic alliance. They seem to be authentically neurotic, but with a more immature character structure, and their unresolved dependency conflicts often reflect unresolved oedipal issues. They would be analyzable, but with somewhat greater difficulty than the first group.

The third and fourth groups, which Zetzel calls "so-called good hysterics," probably fall within the borderline spectrum. The third group consists of patients with an hysterical facade, which masks an underlying depressive character structure. This group may be analyzable, but a long and difficult analysis would be required. Such patients have generally failed to mobilize active resources during important developmental crises. Their self-esteem is basically low, and they tend to devalue their own femininity. They often idealize their fathers to an excessive degree, but have highly ambivalent relationships with their mothers. Although they are able to tolerate considerable degrees of depression, they are deficient in the capacity to master the depression actively and tend to become mired in feelings of helplessness and inadequacy. They tend to develop passive dependent transference reactions, which interfere with the adequate discrimination between therapeutic alliance and transference neurosis. They generally present serious problems in the terminal phase of analysis, particularly the process of separation, mourning, and internalization. Zetzel cautions that they may be analyzable, but traditional analysis should not be attempted without careful assessment. This group of hysterics falls within the range of primitive hysterics (see Chapter 7).

The fourth group is composed of patients whose hysterical symptomatology fails to achieve a meaningful level of oedipal or genital conflict. These so-called good hysterics are characterized by hysterical symptomatology, which tends to be florid and acutely disruptive. They are incapable of tolerating a genuine triangular situation. They tend to express intense sexualized transference fantasies and often fail to maintain the discrimination between fantasy and reality, responding to such sexualized fantasies as if they were potential areas for real gratification. Their inability to maintain a distinction between internal and external reality undermines their capacity for therapeutic alliance and for the emergence of an analyzable transference neurosis. Zetzel felt that such patients did not meet the criteria for traditional psychoanalysis and that the major area of pathology lay in the developmental failure affecting basic ego-functions.

Such patients are close to Kernberg's form of borderline personality organization or to the hysteric dysphoric forms of pathology described by Klein (Liebowitz and Klein, 1981). They also resemble the hysteroid personality described by Easser and Lesser (1965), and would seem to fall into the category of dysphoric personality or psychotic character. The more primitively organized psychotic characters would presumably not be capable of analytic work. However, those hysterical patients who might fall within the range of the dysphoric personality organization may, in fact, have the capacity for meaningful analytic work.

Assessment should be made carefully and over an extended period of time. Evaluation of the patient's potential analyzability should not be made in periods of relative regressive strain, but rather should focus on the more general and characterological level of the patient's functioning. Consequently, an extended period of face-to-face, analytically oriented psychotherapy is probably the optimal approach. Thus, the analyst benefits from an extended period of observation and experience with the patient, which allows for a more extensive evaluation of the important aspects of the patient's psychic structure, and can then serve as a basis for the assessment of analyzability. When such patients can maintain reasonable levels of ego-functioning, do not seem excessively vulnerable to frequent or intense regressive pulls, are able to maintain a consistent and realistic level of motivation, and show a capacity in the course of therapeutic experience for forming and maintaining a reasonably stable therapeutic alliance, they may be capable of sustaining and profiting from analysis.

Perhaps the most exhaustive categorizing of analytic accessibility in terms of diagnostic formulations was provided by Glover (1955). It will be of interest to examine Glover's distribution of cases, primarily from the point of view of determining the extent to which the cases that we would see as falling within the borderline spectrum might be regarded as potentially analyzable, in his assessment. Glover's contribution has been criticized on the ground that it seems to imply that the degree of accessibility is presumed to be uniform for all cases under a particular diagnostic heading (Waldhorn, 1960). But obviously, there is a wide degree of variability in the extent to which patients who might fall within the same diagnostic category might possess qualities and capacities that would affect assessment of analyzability. Consequently, it is a useful caveat that the determination of analyzability does not hinge on diagnostic labeling in a simplistic or one-to-one fashion.

The most accessible cases in Glover's appraisal are the psychoneuroses, under which he includes the hysterias, both anxiety and conversion types, the mixed hysterical and obsessional syndromes, psychosexual inhibitions of a relatively mild type, facultative bisexuality, the reactive depressions, the so-called mild crises, and forms of social and work inhibition. Among the crises, Glover includes uncontrollable transference neuroses, acute work inhibitions, or even analytic stagnations that may be clinically unobtrusive, but that interrupt the therapeutic work. Although such regressive crises are not entirely foreign to authentically psychoneurotic cases, they are common stuff within the borderline spectrum. Moreover, Glover notes that work inhibitions tend to be more difficult to resolve than corresponding sexual inhibitions, reflecting, to a greater degree, the involvement of the ego and the underlying difficulties in ego formation. This is suggestive, particularly in view of the fact that, as we have seen (Chapter 7), the condition of identity-stasis can often express itself in forms of work inhibition that stem not merely from conflicts over work achievement or issues of oedipal victory and defeat, but may also involve more profound issues related to self-integration and identity formation. In such cases, according to Glover, as well as in cases of mild perversion or depression, there is a faulty degree of ego-functioning that mitigates analytic accessibility.

Cases that are only moderately accessible would include the obsessional neuroses, fetishism, alcoholism or drug addiction, what Glover called chronic maladjustment, and psychopathic delinquency. Major obsessional neuroses often prove to be relatively severe and intractable, particularly when they cover or defend against an underlying depressive or paranoid substructure. The relevant question here is whether Glover is, in fact, addressing cases in which there may be an obsessional overlay with an essentially borderline substructure. By the same token, he notes that there may be some cases of hysteria in which there is an underlying psychotic level of fixation.

In our view, such vulnerable substructures would be regarded as more characteristically borderline than psychotic, keeping in mind that in the conceptual framework within which Glover worked, the dichotomy between psychosis and neurosis was still dominant, and an adequate conceptualization of borderline psychopathology had not yet been attempted. The overlying symptomatic formations were thus protected against the underlying vulnerability to regression and defective ego formation that may have reflected the essentially borderline qualities of the patient's psychic structure.

In most of these cases, Glover tends to refer to an underlying depressive or paranoid substructure. This is true with regard to fetishism, where the dichotomy is drawn between ego distortion, on the one hand, and a disorder in sexual organization, on the other. In the latter type of fetishism, psychoanalysis can be undertaken, but spontaneous transference reactions may not coalesce into a transference neurosis. Although castration anxiety predominates, it may be contaminated by pregenital factors similar to those contributing to homosexual fixations; thus, heterosexual interest is preserved from homosexual contamination at the cost of limiting both sexual object choice and gratification. But when ego distortion is in question as, for example, in cases where there may be inhibition and sensitiveness in social relationships, work difficulties, addictive problems, or larval systems of depression or paranoia, the analysis must take a more actively intervening and directive course, rather than the more expectant approach characteristic of classic psychoanalysis.

By the same token, cases of alcoholism or drug addiction are also characterized by a similar symptomatic defense against underlying and localized systems of a depressive or paranoid type. The difference between the more severe fetishistic mechanisms and the addictive mechanisms is that one uses a sexual organization, the other, a nonsexual organization, for such defensive purposes. The common element is the displacement to a symbolic object. In view of the fact that underlying borderline psychic structure may be found in many cases of addictive personality, we can wonder again whether the underlying depressive or paranoid systems to which Glover refers may not, in fact, reflect the essentially borderline structure in such patients.

The group of chronic maladjustment disorders would include prepsychotic or larval psychotic states, which Glover regards as extremely intractable, but in some degree, nonetheless accessible to psychoanalytic treatment. The pathogenesis in such cases of severe character disorder is essentially in the ego, in his view, and would include forms of psychopathy as, for example, sexual psychopathy, in which the symptoms are primarily sexual, but reflect a degree of ego disorder; "benign" psychopathy, marked by social incapacity along with psychosexual disorder; and finally, antisocial psychopathy, in which delinquent behavior may be associated with sexual maladjustment and ego instability. Such cases would more than likely fall under the category of either a primitive hysteric or a dysphoric personality. In Glover's terms, they would be moderately accessible to psychoanalytic treatment, but not in a straightforward classical form. Rather, they would require some significant modification of psychoanalytic technique so that the underlying structural deficits could be dealt with. Glover particularly notes the tendency of such cases of maladjustment, particularly early in the analytic work, to use projection as a first line of defense.

The last group of moderately accessible cases are the psychopathic delinquents. In chronic maladjustment, the psychopathy is essentially private, in the sense that the basic conflict, unhappiness, and frustration are borne primarily by the patient himself. In cases of psychopathic delinquency, however, the psychopathy becomes extrinsic and social, or rather, antisocial. Such cases occur midway between normal and prepsychotic or psychotic groups. The two groups are distinguished by the higher quantity of externally directed aggression, whether sexual or social, in the latter group. Projective defenses are prominent, in addition to a callousness toward objects and an apparent indifference to the consequences of deviant behavior. This would seem to reflect an atrophy of guilt mechanisms and a weakness in the capacity for reality-testing, particularly in the area of object-relations. This suggests the early tenuousness of primary object-relationships. Fantasy formations and conflicts are characteristically acted-out, rather than channeled into symptom formation or forms of neurotic inhibition (as in the case of the psychoneurotic). To a much greater degree than the "private psychopath," the delinquent psychopath enters the analytic situation in a state of projective defense and readiness, which markedly distorts the initial transference reactions, so that they are characterized by a high degree of suspicion and hostility. As Glover notes, such patients are prone to create frequent crises in the course of the analytic work, frequently involving interruption of the analysis. More frequently than not, the analytic work is not resumed, but resumption on a voluntary basis can be taken as a sign of progress. In the analysis of cases of psychopathy, as well as cases of addiction, Glover remarks that we often come too close for comfort to the psychotic border. But in many such cases, the capacity for the patient to maintain reality-testing, even though this may occasionally be seriously diminished, is sufficient to protect the patient from psychotic regression.

In discussing intractable cases, Glover comments on psychotic and severely psychopathic characters. Such cases often use predominantly alloplastic systems of defense, attempting to modify the environment to suit the instinctual needs and demands of the patient. In contrast to the psychotic, such patients do not abandon object-relations and substitute fantasy for reality, but rather they tend to maintain a rather tenuous system of object-relationships continuing in efforts to modify such objects to suit their needs and thereby to maintain their hold on reality. The more regressive forms of psychotic character manifest a variety of regressive features, including a reduction of tenuous reality contacts and an exaggeration of idiosyncratic thought and behavior. The underlying structure varies from extremes of regressive and introjective disorder to extremes of projective reaction, thus reflecting, in a more or less larval manner, the forms of pathological expression that can be found in more intense and extreme forms in the psychoses.

Thus, it seems clear from the tenor of Glover's discussion that he would maintain the possibility of meaningful analytic intervention, more likely in a modified form, with patients we would describe as falling within the borderline spectrum. Although such an approach inevitably raises serious questions regarding technique and management, our emphasis here falls more particularly on the diagnostic implications. Allowing for the differences in terminology and perspective, however, we would conclude that at least one outcome of Glover's assessment is that some cases of what we would regard as essentially borderline psychopathology are indeed accessible to psychoanalytic treatment. The critical question remains as to the extent the traditional psychoanalytic technique can be applied, and to the extent, depending on the assessment of the accessibility of the patient, the technique requires adaptation and modification.

An additional indication as to potential analyzability of patients whose underlying structure may be borderline, can be drawn from types of character pathology that may be superimposed on the underlying psychic structure. As Stone (1979) has suggested, character typology may form another index of accessibility to analytically based treatment. In Figure 9-1, the more accessible forms of character formation are located to the left, and less accessible to the right. Such character formations may be superimposed on an underlying borderline structure.

In these terms, patients who manifest hysterical or obsessive forms of character structure or those who are predominantly depressive-masochistic or phobically anxious would be most amenable to a classical psychoanalytic approach. Such forms of character organization tend to cluster toward the higher end of the borderline continuum and would typically be found in greater or lesser degree among primitive hysterics or dysphoric personalities. Character forms that have a more infantile, passive-dependent, narcissistic, or schizoid organization tend to be relatively more poorly organized, and reflect deeper levels of psychic dysfunction and structural liability. Such character forms tend to cluster in the middle range of borderline structural impairment; they would more typically characterize the dysphoric personality or schizoid variants. The last group of character types, the paranoid, hypomanic, inadequate, explosive, and antisocial, would tend to characterize more primitive

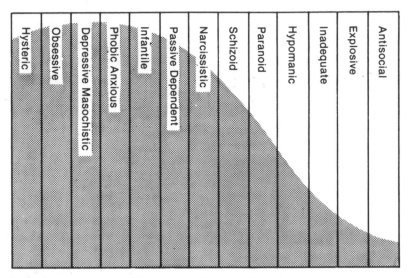

Characterological Types

FIGURE 9-1. Character types. The shaded area designates the area of greatest applicability of the psychoanalytic method. The curve reflects the impressions of Stone and of Kernberg that patients in whom certain characterologic types predominate (those on the left) do better with psychoanalytic therapy than do those in whom other types (those on the right) predominate. (From Stone, 1979, p. 9)

levels of borderline organization, predominantly the psychotic characters and pseudoschizophrenics. Thus, we can postulate a rough correspondence between forms of character organization and levels of borderline integration, although obviously this parallel is extremely rough and many variations in degree, as well as possible exceptions, would have to be taken into account.

The following conclusions can be drawn from a summary of our impressions of borderline analyzability:

1. Some borderline patients are potentially analyzable, but these cases would seem to fall in the group of higher-order borderlines.

2. The extent of ego defect, the capacity for object-relations, and the vulnerability to regression must be carefully assessed. Significant impediments in any of these areas would contraindicate analysis.

3. The capacity to form a meaningful therapeutic alliance and the quality of motivation are particularly important areas.

4. An adequate assessment cannot be made on an acute basis or in terms of the nature or intensity of symptoms. The assessment of analyzability requires enough time to evaluate the patient's usual level of characterological functioning rather than acute regressive phases.

5. Most borderline cases require a lengthy period of preparatory, psychoanalytically oriented psychotherapy as both a context of assessment and a propaedeutic to entering the psychoanalytic situation.

6. For many cases, a period of trial analysis is advisable.

Part III
Etiology

Chapter 10
Biological Genetics

Although the possibility of genetic influences on schizophrenic and other psychotic syndromes has been intensively studied and documented, the role of such basic biological factors in the borderline conditions has not been. This survey will address itself, specifically and exclusively to those genetic influences that derive by way of inheritance and that contribute the biological substratum, whether in terms of factors, qualities, or specific vulnerabilities, which in some combination with environmental and developmental influences result in the forms of borderline pathology. Consequently, we are addressing the implications of the science of genetics itself, and not "psychogenetics," which is concerned with nongenetic environmental influences.

The contribution of such biological and genetic components to the borderline syndromes is infrequently discussed, but it seems to remain as a persistent, generally vague underlying assumption. Whereas such an assumption may be stated in nonspecific terms, it is also an unstated assumption in theoretical approaches to borderline conditions. For example, Kernberg's reconstruction of the borderline personality emphasizes the high titer of pregenital aggression, particularly related to oral conflicts, as basic to borderline psychopathology. The origin of such aggression is not explored except as a presupposition of biological and genetic determinants. A similar case can be made for other specifiable defects, which are taken as basic to borderline defects, whether they are considered in terms of ego defects, narcissism, etc.

The more common attitude among contemporary theorists is that genetic and environmental factors complement each other, in varying degrees, to bring about a variety of developmental and/or pathological outcomes. This attitude tends to focus on how these factors interact, rather than on how they may be set off against each other, in a form of either/or dichotomizing. As

Stone (1980) has noted, we may discover cases with significant genetic loading who have been protected in the course of development by optimal home environments. We may also find cases with less of a genetic diathesis who were reared in mildly pathogenic environments. A child with a modest genetic disposition may escape the stigma of borderline organization by virtue of benign developmental experiences. The same blending of heredity and environment in varying degrees of pathogenicity presumably underlies the heterogeneity of borderline cases. By the same token, the borderline structure of some cases may be the result of a hereditary predisposition that the best environment cannot overcome.

Perhaps the most useful approach is one that was indicated some years ago by Freud (1905) in his description of a "complemental series" of degrees of interaction between constitutional and accidental (environmental) factors.

In this chapter, the complemental series will be evaluated in terms of its relevance to the borderline conditions. The extent to which this is possible is nonetheless limited by the degree to which genetic studies of the major psychoses provide a useful base for evaluating the contribution of genetic components, as well as by the limitations imposed by diagnostic difficulties and ambiguities regarding the borderline conditions themselves.

There are conceptual (see Chapter 1) and diagnostic (Kernberg, 1967; Stone, 1980; see also Chapter 7) difficulties in delineating the borderline conditions. There is even terminological confusion regarding the use of the term "borderline," since it has different connotations in different investigative contexts. In most genetic research, it represents a milder form of schizophrenia, as part of the schizophrenic spectrum; for many clinicians, it is a clinical condition showing some aspects of a schizophrenic or an affective process; for Kernberg, it is a particular form of psychostructural character organization; for Grinker, it is a phenomenologically described entity that differs from both the neuroses and the psychoses. As Stone (1979) observed, the conception cuts across etiological lines: patients who appear to have a borderline personality structure may later prove to have a schizophrenic or an affective psychosis.

It is necessary to distinguish transient borderline states, transient regressive states that may manifest more or less psychotic aspects, but that generally resolve so that the patient returns to a normal level of functioning in a relatively short time or under proper therapeutic management. Such states may be found in a wide range of personality disorders, and their clinical significance has been widely discussed. Transient regressive states have been noted in patients in psychoanalysis, but the implications of their presence are not clear, diagnostically (Frosch, 1967a,b). The borderline states or transient conditions must be distinguished from the more stable character pathology or personality organization found in the borderline personality organization. This more enduring personality configuration has been described in considerable detail by Kernberg (1967), but there remains

room for discussion of the psychopathological range that it should include
It should be noted that in borderline states or conditions, the emphasis is on
phenomenology whereas in the borderline personality, as such, there is
greater concern with the structural organization of the personality.

The spectrum of borderline conditions represents a continuum of degrees
of psychopathology, ranging from the healthier, more differentiated, and
integrated border, represented by the narcissistic character disorders, to the
less mature, less differentiated, and less well-integrated border, represented
by the defined psychoses. As we shall see, the direction of genetic research in
schizophrenia has been toward the definition and study of schizophrenic
spectrum disorders—a cluster or spectrum of psychopathological states,
only some of which may be characterized by psychoses, although they share
a genetic etiology with schizophrenia. The notion of a schizophrenic spectrum
arose in the context of the study of families of schizophrenic patients. A
certain number of relatives of the schizophrenics studied seemed to be somewhat eccentric, having some minor degree of schizophrenic-like symptoms
without a full psychotic picture. Such individuals were regarded as "schizoid,"
but more recently, they have been labeled as representing "borderline states"
(Kety et al., 1971; Rosenthal et al., 1971). The question, then, has to do with
the extent to which the genetically defined schizophrenic spectrum overlaps
with the otherwise identifiable spectrum of borderline conditions. To the
extent that this is possible, it can be argued that the borderline conditions
that fall within the schizophrenic spectrum share the same genetic etiology as
the entities within that spectrum. In addition, there is a fair amount of
evidence that suggests the influence of affective genetic factors as well.

The role of genetic factors has important implications, both diagnostically and therapeutically. Genetic factors speak to a biological substratum
for the disease process. The etiology, however, is both biological and psychological. Thus, the clinician who emphasizes the biological runs the risk of
overemphasizing symptoms to the exclusion of psychological structure. He
might prescribe medication for the symptoms and ignore the persistent
psychostructural impediment. His psychologically oriented colleague, who is
often psychoanalytically trained, might readily recognize the signs of a
borderline personality structure, but neglect heredity, and, thus, might be
slow to add the appropriate medication to the treatment regimen. Optimal
diagnosis and treatment require attention to both factors, biological and
psychological.

THE GENETICS OF SCHIZOPHRENIA

Support for a genetic hypothesis in the etiology of schizophrenia has
come from the epidemiological study of the incidence of schizophrenia as
correlated with degree of consanguinity in relatives of known schizophrenics.

The incidence of schizophrenia in families of schizophrenic patients is higher than the general population, with a higher incidence in the siblings and children of schizophrenics than in parents (Kety, 1976a; Rosenthal, 1971). Thus, the greater the degree of consanguinity to the schizophrenic patient, the higher the incidence of the disorder in the relatives.

Such data, however, must be questioned, since they do not provide solid evidence for the operation of genetic factors—families share not only in the same genetic endowment, but are also subjected to similar environmental influences; this is discussed later. But as Wender (1971) has observed, the problem is undoubtedly more extensive than the incidence figures indicate. This is compounded by the fact that the boundaries of the syndrome remain unclear. A series of conditions that resemble schizophrenia phenomenologically may result from the operation of similar genetic factors. Thus, if the same genetic factors operate in conditions such as the schizoid disorders or the borderline conditions, then they may be affecting a significant portion of the psychiatrically disturbed population.

More specific and convincing evidence comes from studies of the rates of concordance and discordance in monozygotic and dizygotic twins. Since monozygotic twins are, for all practical purposes, genetically identical, and since dizygotic twins share no more of their genetic constitution than do ordinary siblings, when genetic factors are thought to play an important role, we would expect a high concordance rate in monozygotic twins and a concordance rate in dizygotic twins that differed little from the coincidence of schizophrenia in non-twin siblings. As expected, these studies report markedly higher concordance rates among monozygotic than dizygotic twins (Kety, 1976a; Rosenbaum, 1968), although there is a tendency for concordance rates to increase modestly as a result of more careful selection and more sophisticated statistical evaluation. Gottesman and Shields (1972) reported a monozygotic concordance rate of 50 percent and a dizygotic rate of 9 percent. However, diagnosis plays a role here. If a narrow definition of schizophrenia is used, restricted to a core chronic or process form, monozygotic rates tend to be lower, dizygotic higher. If the concept is broadened to include cases from the schizophrenic spectrum, both monozygotic and dizygotic rates tend to rise (to 58 and 24 percent, respectively). This could be interpreted as reflecting the less specific schizophrenic genetic disposition among borderline cases.

Although such studies seem to provide convincing evidence of a genetic influence, since they support a strong relationship between closeness of biological relationship and incidence of the disease, the operation of contaminating factors continues to play a role.

Additional questions can be posed, however, from the point of view of studies of twins that are discordant for schizophrenia. Pollin et al. (1965) studied a group of such discordant monozygotic twins and found significant dlffeiences between the schizophrenic twin and the non-schizophrenic co-twin. In general, they found that the schizophrenic twin weighed less at birth, was seen as vulnerable by the parents, and particularly by the mother who thought that his survival was imperiled; he was the recipient of a greater degree of worry, involvement, and attention from the parents; and his early development was slower. He was seen as the weaker and the less competent twin; he was more docile and compliant, less independent and autonomous; and finally, these relative differences between the two twins tended to persist. Similar findings were reported in an extensive study of twin pairs by Kringlen (1964), in addition to generally lower concordance rates. His general conclusion was that genetic factors do not seem to play as great a role as had been assumed in the etiology of schizophrenia.

Similar trends are observable in borderline twin pairs, suggesting that the organic disparity and the biological advantage of the discordant twin was less in borderline families than in schizophrenic (Pollin et al., 1965). Discordance may be the result of environmental rather than genetic influences, with the genetic element in the borderline group simply being more sensitive to environmental influence. Also, borderline probands had more significant affective disturbances in childhood than their schizophrenic peers (Siever and Gunderson, 1979).

Rosenthal (1971), in his review of twin studies in schizophrenia, pointed out that there is an almost total absence of schizophrenia in the families of discordant twin pairs, whereas there is an incidence of about 60% in the families of concordant twin pairs. The affected discordant twin tends to have a later age of onset and a more favorable outcome than his concordant counterpart. The unaffected discordant twin tends to have a better premorbid social and sexual history; the affected discordant twin tends to have a better premorbid adjustment than either of the concordant twins. Rosenthal concludes that, in biological terms, we are dealing with at least two broad groups of schizophrenia; in one, the genetic contribution is minimal, in the other, the genetic contribution is probably considerable.

However, Siever and Gunderson (1979) have concluded that twin studies, in general, do not contribute much to our understanding of the genetic relationship between borderline and schizophrenic pathology. Explicit or homogeneous diagnostic criteria and appropriate controls are lacking. Even so, the borderline syndrome is identifiable more frequently in the cotwins of chronic schizophrenics than of any other group. They conclude that other genetic factors, not necessarily connected with schizophrenia, and a combination of environmental influences may play a more determining role in borderline pathology than in classic chronic schizophrenia.

Another attempt to disentangle genetic and environmental influences has been by comparing individuals at risk for schizophrenia who were raised in adopted families with those raised in their biological families. The adopted individual presumably shares his genetic factors with his biological parents, but his developmental environment with his adopted parents. Not only do the phenotypic sequelae of various hereditary factors stand out more clearly, but the more dilute forms composing the schizophrenic spectrum can be more carefully evaluated and their connection with the core condition determined more precisely (Stone, 1980). Among genetically related, but reared-apart subjects (Karlsson, 1966), and among patients born of schizophrenic mothers, but reared separately (Heston, 1966), the incidence of schizophrenia was consistently higher than among control groups who were similarly reared, but who were not related to schizophrenics.

The gradations of illness in the biological and adoptive families of adopted schizophrenics led Kety and his group (1968) to formulate a set of diagnostic categories to reflect degrees of schizophrenic illness (see Table 10-1). Their results indicated that chronic schizophrenics (B1) and borderlines (B3) seem to be genetically related and could be counted as part of the schizophrenic spectrum. By the same token, acute schizophrenic reactions (B2) and schizoid personalities (C) did not show any such relation. There are more borderlines and schizophrenics in the families of index cases than in the controls, suggesting that specific schizophrenic factors are shared by the two groups, but that their etiological role is greater in the schizophrenic group. Conversely, no chronic schizophrenics (B1) were found in the families of index borderlines (B3), consistent with less genetic loading among border-lines. As Siever and Gunderson (1979) note, this finding is also consistent with the possibility that one borderline subgroup only may be genetically related to chronic schizophrenia.

Summarizing the Heston (1966) data along with results of the studies of his own group, Wender (1969) notes that about 9 percent of the offspring of schizophrenic parents become schizophrenic when they are raised in adoptive or foster homes—as opposed to none of the offspring of non-schizophrenic mothers so reared. This percentage is quite close to that of offspring of schizophrenics who become schizophrenic when reared by their own parents. Counting cases in the borderline or schizoid range of the spectrum, more than 30 percent of the index group showed psychopathology as opposed to only 6 percent of the control group.

Additional data are provided by the adoption studies of the NIMH group on a Danish population. Comparing the biological families of adopted schizophrenics with adoptive families, they found a significantly greater prevalence of schizophrenia-related (schizophrenia spectrum) disorders in the biological families than in the adoptive families of thirty-three schizophrenic index cases. Not only was the prevalence lower in adoptive families, but it was also randomly distributed between index and control cases (Kety et al., 1971). Further, comparison of the children of schizophrenic parents, put out for adoption, with children of parents with no known psychiatric history, also put out for adoption, revealed nearly twice the rate of spectrum disorders in the index group (31.6 percent) as in the control group (17.8 percent) (Rosenthal et al., 1971).[1]

More recent data from the Wender-Kety-Rosenthal group (Wender et al., 1976) reports on a study of 216 adoptees identified on the basis of Danish population records. Addressing themselves particularly to the question of whether genetic factors play a role in the incidence of borderline schizophrenia, they found more borderline schizophrenia in the index group (20 percent) than in the control group (10 percent). This finding would tend to support a theory of genetic transmission. The investigators also realized that the amount of psychopathology in the control group suggested that the biological parents of these subjects might also have had undetected psychiatric illness. Wender (1971), in reviewing the Rosenthal data, had earlier commented that the severity of psychopathology in the parent is not closely correlated with the severity of psychopathology in the offspring. In other words, borderline schizophrenic patients are just as likely to have children in the schizophrenic spectrum as are chronically schizophrenic parents. Consequently, the degree of psychiatric disturbance in children of the control group may also be due to genetic transmission from mildly disturbed, undiagnosed control group parents.

In addition, cross-fostering studies have helped to separate the role of genetic and experiential factors. Wender et al. (1974) compared four groups:

1. An index group: Offspring of biological schizophrenic parents adopted and raised by normal parents
2. Normal controls: Offspring of normal biological parents adopted and raised by normal parents
3. The cross-fostered group: Offspring of normal biological parents adopted and raised by parents with schizophrenic spectrum diagnoses
4. Nonadoptees: Offspring of schizophrenic parents raised by their own parents

The results indicate a higher degree of probable schizophrenic or borderline psychopathology in the index group compared to the controls, but no significant difference between the controls and the cross-fostered group. The authors (Wender et al., 1974, 1976; 1977) conclude that these results support the hypothesis of genetic factors in the etiology of borderline conditions, but

---

[1]These studies (Kety et al., 1971; Rosenthal et al., 1971; Rosenthal and Kety, 1968) have been strongly criticized (Benjamin, 1976). Statistical criticisms are advanced, particularly, regarding sample size and failure to observe assumptions of independence. Benjamin argues that proper statistical analysis shows that significant differences between index and control groups occur among half-siblings, a conclusion that runs counter to the assumption that genetic effects are proportional to the degree of consanguinity. Kety (1976b) refutes these objections, arguing particularly that the finding regarding half-siblings does not contradict genetic hypotheses, since such genetic influences are always affected by socioenvironmental selective factors.

TABLE 10-1.
Diagnostic Classification System used in Adoptive Studies[1]

A. Definitely not schizophrenia (specify diagnosis)

B. Chronic schizophrenia (chronic undifferentiated schizophrenia, true schizophrenia, process schizophrenia)

   Characteristics: (1) Poor prepsychotic adjustment; introverted; schizoid; shut-in; few peer contacts; few heterosexual contacts; usually unmarried; poor occupational adjustment. (2) Onset: gradual and without clear-cut psychological precipitant. (3) Presenting picture: presence of primary Bleulerian characteristics; presence of clear rather than confused sensorium. (4) Posthospital course: failure to reach previous level of adjustment. (5) Tendency to chronicity

B2. Acute schizophrenic reaction (acute undifferentiated schizophrenic reaction, schizo-affective psychosis possible schizophreniform psychosis, [acute] paranoid reaction, homosexual panic)

   Characteristics: (1) Relatively good premorbid adjustment. (2) Relatively rapid onset of illness with clear-cut psychological precipitant. (3) Presenting picture: presence of secondary symptoms and comparatively lesser evidence of primary ones; presence of affect (manic-depressive symptoms, feelings of guilt); cloudy rather than clear sensorium. (4) Posthospital course good. (5) Tendency to relatively brief episode(s) responding to drugs, electroshock therapy, etc.

B3. Borderline state (pseudoneurotic schizophrenia, borderline, ambulatory schizophrenia, questionable simple schizophrenia, "psychotic character," severe schizoid individual)

[1]Reprinted with permission from S. S. Kety, D. Rosenthal, P. H. Wender, and F. Schulsinger. The types and prevalence of mental illness in the biological and adoptive families of adopted schizophrenics. In: D. Rosenthal and S. S. Kety, eds. *The Transmission of Schizophrenia.* Oxford: Pergamon Press Ltd., 1968. pp. 345–352.

do not support the role of family psychopathology, since there was no increase in borderline pathology in the cross-fostering group.

One of the early findings in the adoption study was the identification of more non-schizophrenic psychopathology among the relatives of schizophrenic patients. The design of these studies suggested that the increased incidence could be attributed to genetic factors, so that not only do certain identifiable forms of schizophrenia have a genetic basis, but the same might also be said of other phenomenologically non-schizophrenic syndromes. Thus, Rosenthal and Kety (1968) found that the biological offspring of schizophrenic parents who were reared in adoptive homes exhibited a higher rate of such non-schizophrenic disorders than did controls who were similarly

TABLE 10-1. (*Continued*)

Characteristics: (1) Thinking: strange or atypical mentation; thought shows tendency to ignore reality, logic, and experience (to an excessive degree) resulting in poor adaptation to life experience (despite the presence of a normal IQ); fuzzy, murky, vague speech. (2) Experience: brief episodes of cognitive distortion (the patient can, and does, snap back, but during the episode the idea has more the character of a delusion than an ego-alien obsessive thought); feelings of depersonalization, of strangeness, or of unfamiliarity with or toward the familiar; micropsychosis. (3) Affective: anhedonia—never experiences intense pleasure—never happy; no deep or intense involvement with anyone or anybody. (4) Interpersonal behavior: may appear poised, but lacking in depth ("as-if" personality); sexual adjustment—chaotic fluctuation, mixture of heterosexuality and homosexuality. (5) Psychopathology: multiple neurotic manifestations that shift frequently (obsessive concerns, phobias, conversion, psychosomatic symptoms, etc.); severe widespread anxiety

C. Inadequate personality
Characteristics: A somewhat heterogeneous group consisting of individuals who would be classified as either inadequate or schizoid by DSM-III. Persons so classified often had many of the characteristics of the B3 category, but to a considerably milder degree

D 1, 2, or 3. Uncertain B1, 2, or 3 either because information is lacking or because even if enough information is available, the case does not fit clearly into an appropriate B category

---

reared in adoptive homes. They postulated a "schizophrenic spectrum" to describe a series of disorders that would encompass not only the schizophrenias, but also the borderline conditions, certain paranoid disorders, schizoid disorders, and the more general category of inadequate personality.

The notion of the schizophrenic spectrum designates a theory of a cluster or spectrum of psychopathological states that share a genetic etiology with schizophrenia. It embraces a diathesis-stress theory, which postulates the genetic diathesis as required for the development of a spectrum illness (Rosenthal, 1963). As Reich (1976) has noted, the notion of a genetically determined schizophrenic spectrum does not preclude the possibility of several discrete genetic continua, each with its own spectrum of disorders; or that, if such spectra exist, they might not be phenotypically similar. The possibility of phenotypical behavioral states, which mimic spectral entities, but without the genetic basis, may prove difficult to differentiate. Nonetheless, the spectrum approach assumes that a majority of cases of schizophrenia represent a single genetic continuum based on a single defective gene or on a defective polygenic system. The value of the spectrum approach is that it provides at least partial answers to both nosological and etiological questions. It offers the possibility of documenting genetic continuity among groups of identified and carefully described nosological entities. Reich (1976) comments on the theoretical advantages in the following terms:

> Although it supposes a biological diathesis, it specifies neither a particular deficit nor a specific relationship between such a deficit and environmental stress or developmental patterns. Consequently, it is not only consistent with, but can also provide the conceptual groundwork for, a number of diverse biological and psychological theories. In short, it enables separate approaches, which have been seen, in the past, as mutually exclusive, to facilitate rather than vie with each other. (p. 10)

The high incidence of such disorders among the relatives of schizophrenics was recognized even in the nineteenth century, and these disabilities were described as "schizoid," in the sense of being schizophrenia-like. Heston (1970) follows this usage in his analysis of spectrum disorders, so that we can usefully follow it here, noting as we do that the term "schizoid" does not have the same connotation as in "schizoid personality."

Such schizoid disorders have been associated with antisocial behavior, thus leading to the designation "schizoid psychopath." In Heston's (1966) earlier study, schizoid psychopaths were found to have police records involving impulsive crimes, unreasoning assaults, and poorly planned thefts. Other characteristics include social isolation, alcoholism, sexual deviation, and other eccentric and suspicion-ridden reclusive behavior. Other characteristics are more closely related to schizophrenic manifestations. Among these, Heston (1970) lists rigidity of thinking, blunting of affect, anhedonia, sensitivity, and suspiciousness—all of which are characteristic of both schizoid and schizophrenic disorders. Although schizoid individuals do not show the characteristic thought disorder, delusions, or hallucinations that schizophrenics do, nonetheless, descriptions of behavioral or regressive lapses seem to suggest a comparable psychotic quality.

Re-analysis of the Kety et al. data showed that the borderline diagnosis was made more frequently than any other for relatives of borderline (B3) probands (Siever and Gunderson, 1979). Relatives of borderlines also manifested slightly more affective disorders than the schizophrenic or control groups. Thus, the borderline group, of itself, does not demonstrate a genetic relation simply to schizophrenia, but may also be related to affective disorders. The genetic relation is based on data from chronic schizophrenic probands (B1). The results suggest that some, but not all, borderlines carry such genetic factors, that some borderlines may share other genetic factors unrelated to schizophrenia, and that borderlines, generally, may form a more genetically diverse group than chronic schizophrenics.

Returning to the data of twin studies, although the concordance rate in monozygotic twins is about 46 percent, there is evidence that most of the remaining 54 percent were abnormal and that nearly all these non-schizophrenic cotwins were schizoid. Only about 13 percent could be regarded as normal or near normal; and since the inherent errors of such research tend to increase the proportion of apparent normals, this figure is very likely inflated. The conclusion seems clear: namely, that the monozygotic cotwin of a schizophrenic is about as likely to be schizoid as schizophrenic and that the inherited trait is a more basic schizoid disposition. At the least, it can be said that a case has been made for regarding the spectrum of schizoid and schizophrenic disorders as alternative expressions of a single genotype (Heston, 1970).

Similar supporting data derive from adoption studies. The concentration of spectrum disorders in biological relatives of index cases is much higher than among control cases not genetically related to a schizophrenic. The pattern of spectrum disorders in cases diagnosed as chronic schizophrenia was the same as for cases diagnosed as borderline schizophrenia. This would tend to support the inclusion of borderline schizophrenia in the schizophrenic spectrum (Kety et al., 1971; Rosenthal et al., 1971; Rosenthal and Kety, 1968). Kety (1976b) notes two exceptions: first, the schizoid or inadequate personality did not show this concentration; and second, there was little evidence for such spectrum disorders in the biological relatives of probands with "acute schizophrenic reaction." Cases designated as "acute schizophrenic reaction" showed no schizophrenia-related disorders among biological relatives (Kety et al., 1971). Thus, there is reason to question the genetic relationship of both acute schizophrenic reactions and schizoid personality to schizophrenia, but there is also reason to question the homogeneity of the schizophrenic syndrome, particularly in reference to the notion of the schizophrenic spectrum.

The conclusion is reinforced by Rosenthal's (1975) findings regarding assortative mating. He found a tendency for index parents to mate selectively with spouses also having a spectrum disorder. When this happens, the incidence of spectrum disorders in the offspring is three to five times higher than when the other parent does not have a spectrum disorder. Again, the genetic relation of spectrum disorders to process schizophrenia is supported, consistent with the hypothesis that the softer spectrum disorders (including some borderlines) have a less specific genetic vulnerability than the core schizophrenic disorder.

THE ROLE OF AFFECTIVE GENETIC FACTORS

Following a somewhat different line of research, recent evidence suggests that borderline conditions may have some genetic relation to the affective psychoses, in addition to their genetic loading for schizophrenia. The offspring of manic-depressive parents also have a higher percentage of schizophrenic spectrum diagnoses than controls, suggesting that borderline disorders and affective disorders may be related, genetically. As Siever and Gunderson (1979) observe, as we go from process schizophrenia to softer spectrum diagnoses, the schizophrenic genetic factors become less specific and less determining, and the possibility of the interplay of affective genetic factors increases.

A revealing piece of work was contributed in this respect by Stone (1977). Comparing eighteen hospitalized borderline cases with twenty-three psychotic inpatients, he found that none of the borderline group's psychiatrically ill relatives were schizophrenic, but 11 percent were schizoaffective, and 89 percent manic-depressive. In contrast, of affected relatives of the psychotic group, 32 percent had schizophrenic spectrum disorders, 11 percent were schizoaffective, and 54 percent were manic-depressive. These results support the conclusion that borderlines share familial factors with the major psychoses and that affective factors play a major role. Thus, the impression from studies of extended families of schizophrenics and adoption studies that the borderline diathesis may reflect genetic heterogeneity is reinforced.

Siever and Gunderson (1979) are careful to note, however, that the striking relation to affective disorders may be related to different diagnostic criteria. The use of psychostructural criteria (à la Kernberg) may tend to include patients with more affective features. Nonetheless, Stone's findings point in the direction of a much more complex genetic picture than might be envisioned on the basis of schizophrenic studies. Regardless of the basis for diagnosis, borderline patients (or at least some subset of borderlines) will have a high number of relatives with major psychoses, both affective and schizophrenic.

In his excellent summary of genetic data, Stone (1980) argued for a continuum of psychotic disorders running from the purely schizophrenic pole to the affective pole. Many schizoaffective patients have a strong affective component that shifts the balance of factors away from the schizophrenic side toward the affective side. Earlier views of schizoaffective disease, much like the early history of the borderline category, tended to view schizoaffective disorders as variant forms of schizophrenia. Currently, affective factors are emphasized. The genetic continuum thus can be envisioned as a series of reciprocally related genetic loadings for schizophrenia and manic-depressive psychosis (see Figure 10-1).

By the same token, the role of genetic factors in the borderline syndromes can be viewed analogously. The genetic diathesis to borderline illness may derive from a schizophrenic vulnerability, an affective vulnerability, or some combination of the two. Stone (1980) visualizes these relations by a phenotypic continuum (see Figure 10-2). Borderline patients may share the genetic diathesis anywhere along this continuum. Stone's estimate of current diagnostic usages in this regard are shown in Figure 10-3.

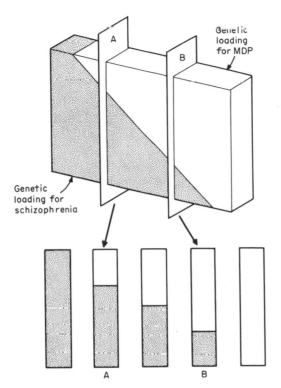

FIGURE 10-1. Hypothetical complementary series of genotypes related to schizoaffective disorders (Stone, 1980)

The borderline diathesis can be viewed as involving some loading of schizophrenic and affective genetic factors, thus reflecting varying degrees of schizophrenia-like stigmata and/or less than psychotic affective disturbances. Stone (1980) diagrams this view (Figure 10-4).

It is well to keep in mind, in all this, that diagnosis, even of well-established entities like schizophrenia or manic-depressive psychosis, is generous both in pitfalls and lack of consensus. Recent trends, however, have led in the direction of increasing rigor and restriction in the diagnosis of schizophrenia, and research efforts to define the syndrome more consistently and reliably have led the way. More of what was earlier called schizophrenic is now diagnosed as affective disorder. The trend must affect our view of related borderline disorders. Thus, the earlier trends that overestimated schizophrenic genetic loading in borderlines are now countered by an increase in affective factors.

The implications of such loading may have not only diagnostic, but prognostic implications as well. Borderline cases near the schizophrenic end of the spectrum tend to have a poor prognosis, whereas patients with a

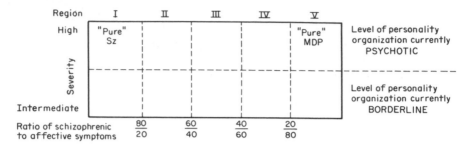

KEY: *Region I:* Schizophrenic syndromes without any features of affective disorder. At this (as at the opposite) end of the continuum, the clinical picture is distinctive, permitting the notion of a separate category.

Region II: A region of apparently schizophrenic disorders, where there are sufficient degrees of affective (manic, depressive) symptoms to incline one away from the diagnosis of unequivocal schizophrenia and toward a schizoaffective disorder.

Region III: Schizophrenic and affective stigmata are here rather evenly divided. This region comprises the conditions which are most justifiably labeled *schizoaffective* without qualifying adjectives.

Region IV: A region of disorders with predominantly affective (manic and/or depressive) symptoms, but where there are signs and symptoms usually associated with schizophrenia sufficient to incline one away from a purely manic-depressive diagnosis.

Region V: The pure affective disorders, free of any schizophenic symptoms. Unipolar depression, bipolar-I and -II disorders, and so on, would be placed here. Severity may range from psychotic (manic-depressive psychoses proper) to borderline (spectrum MDP conditions).

FIGURE 10-2. Phenotypic continuum of schizophrenic and manic–depressive (primary affective) disorders (Stone, 1980)

higher affective loading may have a better prognosis. It may also be that patients with predominantly affective loading may prove to be less severely disturbed. These patients, in effect, may represent forms of nonpsychotic affective disorders (Stone, 1980).

Many borderline patients can be meaningfully described as schizoaffective, but do not meet the criteria for psychosis. These patients may reflect the influence of dual hereditary factors. There also seems to be a strong female representation among such disorders, which include the depressions, anorexia nervosa, and certain premenstrual disorders. Thus, genetic factors may interact with hormonal factors to produce a borderline picture. Stone (1980) observes that premenstrual symptom outbreak is more the rule than the exception. Premenstrual tension may be a complaint even for well-integrated women who function on a normal or neurotic level otherwise. The premenstrual syndrome may induce a transient regression, the "borderline-for-a-day" phenomenon. Diagnostic evaluation at such times would see a different picture than at other times of the cycle.

Along this line, Rinsley (1980c) has conducted an interesting *Denkexperiment*. Taking Rosenthal's (1970) hypothesis that schizophrenia is transmitted by two genes S and Z, Rinsley calculates the distribution ratios of the various alleles. According to the hypothesis, Ss influences socialization such that the dominant S produces a tendency to gregariousness and the recessive s a tendency to withdrawal. In the same fashion, Zz influences thought patterns, such that Z produces a tendency to well-organized, logical thinking, whereas z tends toward the opposite. The combinatorial possibilities are (1) sociable/coherent thought, (2) social/disorganized thought, (3) asocial/coherent thought, and (4) asocial/disorganized thought. The genotypes for (1) are SSZZ, SSZz, SsZZ, and SsZz; for (2), SSzz and Sszz; for (3), ssZZ and ssZz; and for (4), sszz. These distributed in the Mendelian ratios 9:3::3:1.

The double recessive genotype sszz would lead to schizophrenia, the double homozygous dominant genotype SSZZ to normality. The possible genotypes are listed in Table 10-2. The distribution turns out as follows: less than 10 percent of offspring will be normal; less than 10 percent schizophrenic; 50 percent will suffer from some form of neurotic syndrome, 25 percent will be psychotic. A little less than 20 percent would be borderline (in Rinsley's terms), but an additional 33 percent would have some form of "atypical

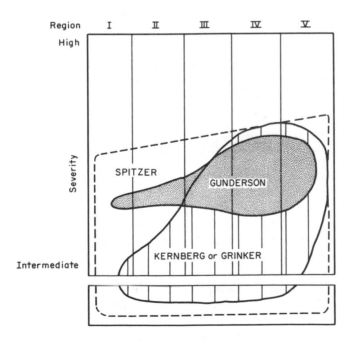

FIGURE 10-3. Mappings of some recent borderline domains onto the Sz-MDP diagram (Stone, 1980, p. 43)

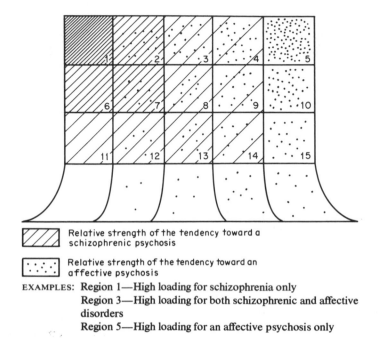

Relative strength of the tendency toward a
schizophrenic psychosis

Relative strength of the tendency toward an
affective psychosis

EXAMPLES: Region 1—High loading for schizophrenia only
Region 3—High loading for both schizophrenic and affective
disorders
Region 5—High loading for an affective psychosis only

FIGURE 10-4. A hypothetical genotypic continuum of tendencies to schizophrenic and affective psychoses (Stone, 1980)

dysphoric disorder" (with borderline, manic-depressive, and schizoaffective features). Interestingly enough, this thought experiment at least points in the direction of more empirically derived results.

GENETIC MODELS

A variety of genetic hypotheses have been proposed to account for data of this sort. The most commonly accepted and perhaps most parsimonious explanation is that a single autosomal gene accounts for the common genetic contribution to both schizoid and schizophrenic disease. This so-called dominance hypothesis is supported and virtually required by the fact that the spectrum disorders occur with equal probability in the monozygotic twins of schizophrenics. The support data are represented in Figure 10-5; the proportions of first-degree relatives showing the disease fit reasonably well with the theoretical proportions predicted by the dominance hypothesis (Heston, 1970).

There is considerable debate about the weight of genetic factors and their interplay with environmental-experiential factors in the etiology of schizophrenia. Similarly, the appropriateness of various genetic models and

TABLE 10-2
Genotypes of Schizophrenic Genes S and Z[1]

SSzz.   Dominant-recessive genotype. Phenotype characterized by extraversion and autistic thinking (thought disorder). Outgoing or other-directed, but presenting with confused, disordered ideation illustrative of significantly impaired abstract-categorical reasoning, hence unable to "make sense" of self and environment. *A manic-depressive phenotype*

Sszz.   Mixed dominant-recessive genotype. Phenotype characterized by thought disorder and predominant, but variable extraversion and socialization. Ambivalent concerning interpersonal relations and often pervasively confused. *A schizo-affective phenotype*

SsZz.   Full heterozygote. Phenotype characterized by predominant, but variable extraversion and relatively coherent ideation. Degree of penetrance of recessive alleles (s,z) will determine degree of ambivalence and conflict in interpersonal relations and of autistic tendency, the latter compensated for or corrected, with some effort. *A neurotic phenotype*, close to the "borderline" border, hence presenting with various borderline symptoms and features

ssZZ.   Dominant-recessive genotype. Phenotype characterized by marked introversion and coherent thinking. These schizoid individuals prefer their own company and think clearly and logically about themselves and their environment. Possessed of sufficient intelligence, a scholar, artist, scientist, philosopher, or inventor considered peculiar, odd, or strange. *A borderline phenotype*, close to the "neurotic" border (Grinker et al., 1968)

ssZz.   Mixed dominant-recessive genotype. Phenotype characterized by marked introversion and various degrees of autistic thinking, compensated for or corrected with some effort. Paranoid symptoms and features are often prominent. *A borderline phenotype*, close to the "psychotic" border (Grinker et al., 1968)

sszz.   Full homozygous recessive genotype. Phenotype characterized by marked introversion and incoherent ideation (thought disorder). *The schizophrenic phenotype*

[1]From Rinsley, 1980c, p. 633.

their implications for schizophrenia research have been debated (Matthysse and Kidd, 1976; Reich, 1976). Clearly, the data indicate that genetic factors do play a role in schizophrenic etiology, but that there is a significant degree of heterogeneity relative to different conditions within the schizophrenic spectrum.

With regard to affective genetic factors, two major models have been proposed; in one, the unipolar and bipolar varieties are treated as genetically

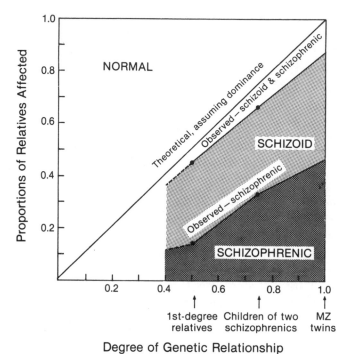

FIGURE 10-5. Observed and expected proportion of schizoids and schizophrenics (Heston, 1970, p. 253)

distinct, in the other, the threshold model is governed by a single major locus. The higher concordance rate between monozygotic twins for bipolar rather than unipolar illness suggests genetic disparity and a greater role for genetic factors in bipolar disorders. Bipolar disease would be seen as transmitted by a single major dominant gene, with early onset, better lithium response, and a higher degree of mania in first-degree relatives. Unipolar disease, on the contrary, would have polygenic transmission, later onset, poor lithium response, and less mania in first-degree relatives. This model is depicted in Figure 10-6.

The second model represents a variable liability from genetic and other factors. When a threshold of liability is reached, pathological expression follows. The genetic component is hypothesized as a single major gene. According to the model, the liability of homozygous normals is below the threshold for affective disorder. Heterozygotes would have a higher liability and would occupy the region between the threshold for affective disorder and that for bipolar disease. Liability in this region would be associated with recurrent depression and other forms of unipolar disease. Bipolar disorders would tend to have a homozygous recessive liability and would exceed the threshold for bipolar disease. The model also allows areas of overlap (e.g., heterozygotes below the threshold for affective disorder or above the threshold for bipolar disease). See Figure 10-7. Both models, whether treating the genetic basis of affective disease as genetically heterogeneous or as homogeneous, are as yet equally viable alternative explanations.

Given these genetic findings and their implications, we can consider the implications of these genetic findings and theories for the borderline conditions.

THE GENETIC DIATHESIS IN
BORDERLINE CONDITIONS

It is necessary to consider the extent to which the borderline conditions form a diagnostic spectrum that overlaps with the schizophrenic spectrum, on one hand, and with the spectrum of affective disorders, on the other, and to that degree, would support the conclusion that the spectrum of borderline disorders shares in the etiology attributable to these independent

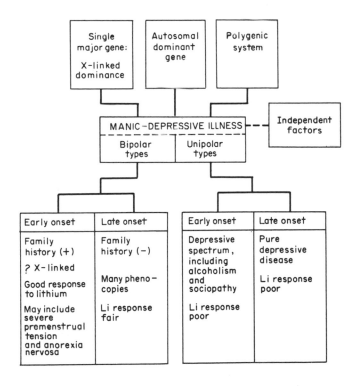

FIGURE 10-6. A model for the transmission of affective disorders in which unipolar and bipolar forms are genetically distinct (Stone, 1980, p. 147. Based in part on Cadoret and Winokur (Sperber and Jarvik. 1976, pp. 67, 69).

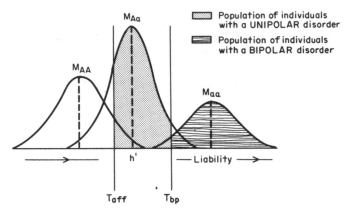

M_{AA} = mean liability value for the homozygous normal
M_{Aa} = mean liability value for the heterozygote
M_{aa} = mean liability value for the homozygous affected
T_{aff} = threshold for all affective disorder (i.e., least amount of liability that will still induce manifest affective disorder)
T_{bp} = threshold for bipolar disorders (i.e., liability at or above this level will induce an affective disorder of the bipolar type)
h' = the liability value associated with the mean of the heterozygote group

FIGURE 10-7. Parameters of a single-major locus model of affective-disorder transmission (Stone, 1980, p. 149. Adapted from the modification of Kidd's model by Gershon et al., 1975)

genetic systems. The conceptual conflict lies between the nosological approach and the etiological approach. In nosological terms, there has always been a problem in establishing a dividing line between schizophrenic and non-schizophrenic disorders. That diagnostic discrimination, however, has always been, and remains, a matter of clinical description of signs and symptoms. At the same time, the spectrum concept proposes that some proportion of non-schizophrenic disorders have the same genetic etiology as schizophrenia. This poses an even more difficult diagnostic problem of determining which of the spectrum of non-schizophrenic disorders can be reasonably included within the schizophrenic spectrum and, thus, by inference, owe part of their etiology to determinable genetic factors. A parallel argument applies to the affective psychoses and their place relative to the broader spectrum of affective disorders. In other words, in the diathesis-stress/learning model, in what illnesses among the borderline conditions can we posit such a genetic diathesis?

In both diagnostic and conceptual terms, the history of the borderline concept has been taken up with the problem of disengaging the area of borderline conditions from the psychoses (see Chapter 4). Early attempts to delineate borderline diagnoses saw them as mitigated expressions of the schizophrenic process, rather than as independent diagnostic categories with certain qualities and characteristics independent of either the psychoses or the neuroses.

It may be useful at this point to look at some of the diagnostic descriptions applied in schizophrenia spectrum research. One of the inherent problems in genetic research is that a genotype must be identified through phenotypical descriptions, which must necessarily be clinical. Not only are there multiple phenotypical descriptions that may relate to the single genotype, but there may also be quite similar phenotypical behavioral states that may mimic the phenotypical states that are genetically related, so as to make differentiation extremely difficult.

In Kallmann's (1938) investigations, his notion of "schizoidia" seems to lean heavily on the clinical resemblance of such patients to schizophrenics; in fact, he regarded the distinguishing features of the schizoid to be precisely those fundamental symptoms that characterize schizophrenia, but appeared in these patients as a milder form of a characterological abnormality. The group working with Rosenthal and Kety (1968) included in the schizophrenic spectrum certain disorders seen among biological relatives of schizophrenics, namely, schizophrenia, possible schizophrenia, borderline states, certain paranoid disorders, schizoid disorders, and inadequate personalities (see Table 10-1).

Similarly, Grinker and Holzman (1973) included in the schizophrenic syndrome the nonpsychotic manifestations of the schizophrenias, embracing the so-called latent schizophrenias, preschizophrenias, incipient schizophrenias, ambulatory schizophrenias, and remitted schizophrenias, as well as schizophrenic characters. Within this group of disorders, they delimited five qualities they believed to be distinctive of the schizophrenic process: (1) the presence of a thought disorder, even though subtle; (2) a striking quality of diminished capacity to experience pleasure, particularly in interpersonal relationships; (3) a strong characterological dependency; (4) a severe impairment in competence; and (5) an exquisitely vulnerable sense of self-esteem. They go on to note that the disorder, the basic genetic diathesis, need not lead to psychosis, but rather that the looseness of organizational coherence so often found in these individuals may sometimes lead to a reorganization of reality that might have a certain social, artistic, or scientific value. Frequently among genetic researchers, there has been a tendency to lump these various nonpsychotic entities into a single category, similar to Kallmann's (1938) use of "schizoidia." Thus, Heston (1970) combined the various entities into a single category of "schizoid disease." However, as Reich (1976) notes, although such an approach may help to indicate how extensive the area of spectrum psychopathology is and may illuminate its prevalence and even mode of transmission, it is of little help in determining well-defined diagnostic entities.

I would like to shift ground at this point and attempt to describe certain levels of psychopathology within the general group of diagnostic entities encompassed by the borderline conditions as previously delineated (see Chapter 7).

It should be remembered that, in discussing the borderline spectrum, our point of origin is quite different in context from that of the genetic studies. These diagnoses arise primarily out of a clinical context and reflect a wide range of clinical experience with patients in a variety of settings and in contexts that usually involve one-to-one, long-term therapeutic involvements or small group therapy contexts.

Latent and Incipient Schizophrenias

Starting at the psychotic border of the borderline spectrum, the first group of disorders to be discussed are those that can be regarded as equivalently schizophrenic, lying close to or on the border of schizophrenia—but decidedly in schizophrenic territory. Here I would include the latent schizophrenias and the conditions called incipient schizophrenia. These patients are described as having clear symptoms of schizophrenia, including thought disorder and excessive dependency, but as not necessarily having had an acute psychotic episode. Latent schizophrenics may be mistaken for schizoid personalities and may occasionally show behavioral peculiarities and thought disorders without acute decompensation or more obvious psychotic pathology. Incipient schizophrenia can be regarded as an early stage of schizophrenic disorganization preceding a schizophrenic breakdown. These diagnostic categories are clearly schizophrenic and would presumably form a significant part of the schizophrenic spectrum. By inference, they would therefore reflect a significant genetic component. Nonetheless, clarity and consistency require that they be differentiated from the borderline spectrum. Differential diagnosis is no easy matter and the risk of misdiagnosis high (see the extended discussion in Chapter 4).

Pseudoschizophrenias

The first group of disorders within the borderline spectrum comprise those that can be described as pseudoschizophrenia (see the diagnostic reformulation in Chapter 7). This category was originally described by Hoch and his coworkers (Hoch and Cattell, 1959; Hoch et al., 1962; Hoch and Polatin, 1949). Such patients were taken to manifest a combination of neurotic and psychotic symptoms, in which a neurotic overlay masked an underlying psychotic process. These patients were thus seen as on a continuum with frank schizophrenia. Superficially, they resembled neurotics, but their symptomatology was more diversified, their anxiety more pervasive and profound, and schizophrenic-like thought and affect disturbances were apparent (Hoch and Polatin, 1949). The schizophrenic component was demonstrated by an eventual psychotic deterioration, the more or less autistic life-style, the diffuseness of ambivalence and the inappropriateness of emotional responses, the omnipotence and related thought disorders, and the presence of transient psychotic episodes and relatively chaotic sexuality. A subsequent evaluation of the syndrome, based on psychological test data, emphasized that such patients may retain a relatively good social, academic, or occupational facade, but there is an underlying thought disorder that is relatively ego-syntonic, and a profusion of unintegrated neurotic and psychotic defenses (Weingarten and Korn, 1967). The distinction drawn here rests on the descriptive aspect of pseudoschizophrenias in which the neurotic symptomatology seems to predominate in the clinical picture, and the schizophrenic dimensions are identified either on more intensive exploration or over time. Presumably, the psychotic manifestations in the incipient or latent types of schizophrenia are more clinically apparent and available and less masked by neurotic formations. In any case, we would suggest that the pseudoschizophrenias reflect, in fact, the stigmata of the schizophrenic process and thus form part of the schizophrenic spectrum disorders. The evidence in support of borderline schizophrenia as part of the schizophrenic spectrum has been described; to the extent that the pseudoschizophrenias overlap with Kety et al.'s (1968) borderline state (B3, see Table 10-1 above), they would share the same genetic diathesis.

The Psychotic Character

The next rung up the diagnostic ladder is represented by the psychotic character, as described by Frosch (1964, 1970), although it does not have the inclusiveness or scope Frosch intended. In the present diagnostic schema, the term has a more limited and specific application (see Chapter 7). The issues that dominate the pathology in the psychotic character so defined are essentially psychotic rather than neurotic, yet they are cast in the form of a character pathology that represents a persistent personality configuration involving specific forms of structuralization, developmental and instinctual vicissitudes, object relations, etc. The psychotic character has a severe impairment relating to both internal and external environments, and the disturbances in his relationship with reality are similar to those of the psychotic. Unlike the psychotic, however, he retains some capacity to test reality, although in relatively primitive ways. His object-relationships are organized at a higher level, although they are still caught up in the need-fear dilemma.

The ability to preserve the precarious capacity for testing reality and for maintaining object-relationships, even at a need-satisfying level, distinguishes this level of character pathology from the more primitive impairment of reality contact and primitive symbiotic relatedness of the psychotic.

In trying to define the pathology of the psychotic character and relate it to the schizophrenic spectrum, we enter an area where very little is known. The foremost question is "How much weight are we to give the schizophrenia-like manifestations that are found in these forms of character pathology?" Opinions vary, but the predominance of psychotic manifestations and the intensity of psychotic issues in these patients would seem to suggest that they belong within the schizophrenic spectrum, even though these manifestations are embedded in characterological formations. It should be noted that the capacity for characterological formations in these patients suggests that if a schizophrenic genetic etiology is involved, it may be mitigated by a combination of other genetic (decreased penetrance, modifying factors) and environmental factors. Thus, the operation of the psychotic process does not influence development in ways that impede or fragment the formation of some kind of characterological structures, yet what is embedded in those structures is essentially psychotic.

At the same time, the psychotic character manifests an emotional lability, a tendency to extremes of mood and mood swings that suggest affective disorder. We can guess that the more primitively organized borderlines, in whom Stone (1977) identified affective symptoms and a significant genetic loading for affective disorder, were psychotic characters. We would suggest that more often than not the regressive phases of the psychotic character have a schizoaffective quality, reflecting a combined genetic diathesis. It may also be that some psychotic characters come to clinical attention in a regressed state, and are thus misdiagnosed as schizoaffective. To the extent that the psychotic character may overlap with Spitzer's "unstable borderline personality," it may reflect similar affective components. Stone (1980) has observed that unstable personalities seem to occupy the border of the primary affective disorders.

The Dysphoric Personality

The next category in our progression is the dysphoric personality. As noted, this form of personality organization describes only one segment of the further-reaching spectrum of borderline conditions and represents a stable personality configuration.

Other attempts have been made to refine the notion of borderline personality and to make it more specific. In the study by Grinker et al. (1968), in which the statistical approach of cluster analysis is based on a large number of behavioral and observational measures, four groups of patients were delineated: (1) a more severely disturbed group that seemed to border on the psychotic, (2) a "core borderline" group that was characterized by relatively chaotic interpersonal relationships, a tendency to act-out, and severe loneliness, (3) a group with difficulty in establishing and maintaining an identity, regarded as comparable to the "as-if" personality, and finally, (4) a somewhat less disturbed group that seemed to border on the neuroses.

These findings seem to lend support to the idea that in borderline pathology a considerable internal consistency and stability is maintained and thus it could be regarded as a separate and discrete group of diagnostic entities. Follow-up of twenty-eight of these patients further supported this conclusion (Werble, 1970). But the diagnostic breakdown, however, extends from the nearly psychotic range to a neurotic one, which is hardly distinguishable from that of any of the neuroses. Consequently, an internally consistent and unified concept was never found, but rather a considerable diagnostic spread was demonstrated. In terms of the present discussion, only the second or core group of borderline patients would fit the characteristics of the dysphoric personality. The Grinker study underlines the inherent difficulty of the differential diagnosis of the borderline conditions and the ease with which conditions that lie closer to the border of psychosis can be amalgamated or confused with the borderline personality organization.

More recently, Gunderson and Singer (1975) have analyzed studies of the borderline conditions, methodologically, to identify the features that seemed to approach a consensus of what constitutes the borderline personality. They focused on the following aspects: (1) the presence of an intense affect, usually strongly hostile or depressed; (2) a history of impulsive (acting-out) behavior, including both episodic acts (self-mutilation, overdosing) or more chronic behavior patterns (drug dependency, promiscuity), which are usually self-destructive; (3) a usually well-maintained social adaptiveness in areas of achievement, such as school or work, along with appropriate appearance and behavior; (4) brief psychotic experiences, which are usually transient and tend to have a paranoid quality or may be activated by the use of drugs, or in stressful or unstructured situations; (5) psychological test performance, in which often bizarre, dereistic, illogical, or primitive responses are given on unstructured and projective tests, but not on more structured test materials; and (6) interpersonal relationships, which vacillate between transient, superficial relationships and intense, highly dependent relationships characterized by devaluation, manipulation, and demandingness.

Such a consensus description is a helpful clarification, but it needs to be qualified in terms of our current discussion. In the strict sense of a borderline personality organization being utilized here in the context of delineating a spectrum of borderline disorders, the borderline characteristics (ascribed to borderline disorders as a unified group) may not be found to the same extent in all diagnostic subgroupings. Many borderline personalities are generally capable of secondary process thinking and adaptive ego-functioning in the normal course of relatively structured and familiar contexts of social living. In periods of crisis or transient regression, however, such patients may show an increase in primary process manifestations. In poorly organized border-lines, such primary process thinking may show up on unstructured test mate-rials; but frequently enough, it will not. The regressive pull in such unstruc-tured situations may, for some of the better organized borderlines, not be sufficiently strong to affect the level and organization of their functioning. The same patients, on the other hand, in periods of crisis or regression, may show considerable primary process disorganization.

The point of view suggested here is that the dysphoric personality organization forms a stable personality configuration, which, as opposed to the psychotic character, for example, is basically nonpsychotic. Thus, differ-entiation between the psychotic character and the dysphoric personality should be made on the basis that in the psychotic character the patterns of personality organization and the basic issues remain psychotic, whereas in the dysphoric personality, they are only psychotic in periods of transient regression. Even when the psychotic character is functioning at a relatively good level of adjustment, the psychotic manifestations are still diagnostically available; in the dysphoric personality, however, these are relatively less available and only become available in regression. The question can also be posed whether, in the diagnosis of such patients, many of the apparently psychotic-like manifestations that have been attributed to the borderline personality as such may not, in fact, reflect material gathered from diagnostic categories further down the borderline spectrum, such as the psychotic character or the pseudoschizophrenic.

Consequently, it can be argued that the dysphoric personality has a problematic cut-off point within the borderline spectrum for the extension of schizophrenic genetic etiology. One can argue the case on any one of a variety of footings. One might argue, for example, that any form of person-ality functioning in which schizophrenic-like or psychotic symptoms are expressed is evidence enough to include that entity within the schizophrenic spectrum. But from a different point of view, the fact that such manifestations occur only transiently and regressively in these patients rules against the assumption of genetic etiology and for the interplay of environmental factors. Or at least, whatever schizophrenic diathesis operates in such cases, its influ-ence is nonspecific, dilute, and highly interactive with environmental factors. We can remind ourselves, in this regard, that there was little evidence for the presence of schizophrenic spectrum disorders among biological relatives of patients with "acute schizophrenic reaction" (Kety et al., 1971). It would appear *a fortiori* that acute borderline regressive states are even less likely to yield supportive evidence of a genetic etiology. Moreover, the capacity these patients have to reconstitute and quickly reverse the regressive trend when they again find themselves in structured and supportive contexts would seem good evidence for the importance of environmental factors in this form of pathology. Thus, transient regressive episodes may form one of the phenocopies or mimicking of phenotypes, which may not necessarily relate to the genotype.

By the same token, the argument for the operation of affective genetic factors runs along similar lines. The dysphoric personality manifests a degree of emotional lability, but markedly less than that seen in the psychotic character. Nonetheless, there is a marked vulnerability to depression. Depression is liable to be a marked aspect of regressive episodes. We can suggest, therefore, a significant affective genetic diathesis for these patients, but one that is less marked and more subject to environmental influences than in the more severely disturbed psychotic character.

The "As-If" Personality

The next category of the borderline spectrum is the "as-if" personality, a category first described by Helene Deutsch (1942). Such patients give an initial impression of normality, but on closer inspection, they seem to lack all originality in their thought and work and any real warmth in their personal relationships. They seem to lack an inner subjective experience of affect; it is as though they are actors in life who perform the socially expected behaviors with technical skill, but have no sense of inner meaning, purpose, or conviction. Their method of adaptation is essentially imitation, rather than any more meaningful or enduring internalization (Meissner, 1974b). These patients are not subject to the intensity of feelings and the rapid swings of emotional state that so vividly characterize the dysphoric personality, but nonetheless they represent a form of character pathology that resembles the schizoid personality. Here, the failure of capacities for meaningful internalization and the resulting inner emptiness are resolved by a chameleon-like imitative responsiveness to external sources of influence that seem to point in the direction of schizoid compliance. Similarly, there is much less tendency to regression than in the dysphoric personality or, for that matter, in the more susceptible psychotic characters. Consequently, there would seem to be little justification for including the "as-if" character disorders in the schizophrenic spectrum. The tendency of emotional factors to depend so exclusively on external factors would also argue against any endogenous affective disorder, and thus, against any significant role for an affective genetic diathesis.

The Schizoid Personality and the Schizoid Character Disorder

The next group of disorders present more of a diagnostic problem in that they represent a considerable spread or range of psychopathology. The schizoid personality is usually described in terms of affective withdrawal and the withholding of object libido. There is a sense of withdrawal, of observing the world from a position of non-involvement, and of mere observation rather than participation. The major defense against anxiety is to keep emotionally out of touch, inaccessible, and isolated.

The schizoid character disorder, however, may occur at any number of levels of intensity of the pathology, ranging from relatively mild schizoid conditions to extremely severe and therapeutically unavailable schizoid withdrawal and entrenchment. For the most part, schizoid personality organization represents a rigid, staunchly defended position, which reflects relatively primitive developmental difficulties. However, the tendency to regress to psychotic levels of functioning is markedly diminished in these cases, even as their accessibility to therapeutic intervention can be very little. Relatively mild forms of the schizoid condition, which are usually related to some degree of obsessional symptomatology, however, may be more accessible to therapeutic intervention, and in some cases, even analysis.

In view of the lack of schizophrenic symptoms and the minimal susceptibility to regression in these patients, they can be regarded as forms of relatively severe character pathology, which represent a staunchly defended characterological defect, but which give no grounds for including them in the schizophrenic spectrum. These patients are generally less susceptible to regression than the dysphoric personality, and certainly less than the psychotic character. One might usefully regard these disorders, especially in their more severe and pathological forms, as a likely outcome of a stressful schizophrenogenic environment without the accompanying genetic diathesis that would tip the balance in the direction of a more specifically schizophrenic disorder. Similarly, there is little or no basis for the role of affective genetic factors in such cases.

Hysteroid Dysphorics

The remainder of the borderline diagnosis—identity-stasis and the primitive hysteric—offers no basis for any significant genetic input from the schizophrenic-affective genetic continuum. Consideration should be given, however, to Klein's (1975) "hysteroid dysphoria" (see Chapter 7).

A high percentage of the relatives of hysteroid dysphoric probands proved to have serious unipolar or bipolar affective disorders (Stone, 1980), which suggests a strong relation of affective genetic determinants to this disorder. It has been suggested (see Chapter 7) that hysteroid dysphoria may well form a subvariant of the dysphoric personality or psychotic character. The affective diathesis may be a significant factor in the etiology of these disorders.

A point that should also be stressed in considering the borderline spectrum and its relationship to the major psychotic spectra is that all these disorders are subject to states of transient regression, in which the potentiality for the emergence of psychotic-like manifestations is inherent. One of the ranking characteristics of these states is their relative susceptibility to such regressive episodes. This consideration marks the importance of distinguishing between borderline conditions or disorders and borderline states. In the borderline states, which represent transient regressive psychotic episodes, patients may look much sicker than they, in fact, are, and their rapid recompensation under appropriate conditions of structure and therapeutic management gives the clue to the fact that one is dealing with a borderline state rather than a borderline condition. Borderline states may mimic schizophrenic manifestations or affective psychoses and can be mistaken for them; but insofar as they represent transient, situationally induced states, they must be regarded as phenocopies rather than authentic phenotypes of the schizophrenic or affective diathesis. Consequently, the occurrence of such borderline states cannot be taken as convincing evidence of an inherent relationship to the schizophrenic or affective genotype. In this respect, the failure to demonstrate a higher incidence of spectrum disorders among the biological relatives of patients with acute schizophrenic reactions would tend to support this.

The importance of distinguishing such states that mimic the psychotic spectrum phenotypes cannot be overestimated. The risks of overdiagnosing schizophrenia in relationship to the schizophrenic spectrum concept and its implications for the treatment of the personality disorders has been thoroughly discussed by Reich (1975).

CONCLUSIONS

If we ask ourselves what is inherited in the schizophrenic or affective spectrum, what is it that constitutes the genetic diathesis in the etiological model, we can only answer that what seems to be inherited is some form of schizophrenic or affective vulnerability or predisposition. Only when that vulnerability is operative does the interplay of genetic and environmental factors result in a schizophrenic or psychotic outcome. However, that genetically transmitted vulnerability is subject to varying degrees of penetrance, or expression, and can be modified by a variety of factors. Heston (1970), for example, lists among such modifying factors environmental events themselves, as well as complex traits that have been empirically linked to schizophrenia (such as somatotype, intelligence, autonomic reactivity).

Thus, we are dealing with the equivalent of a complemental series in the sense so aptly described by Freud. At the pathological extreme of this series, genetic factors play a predominant role and express themselves in the most severe forms of process or childhood schizophrenia or, alternatively, in the affective diathesis, in the classic form of psychotic depression, or in manic-depressive psychosis—although even here environmental factors play a role. Within the wider range of schizophrenic disorders, the role of environmental factors is expanded, but again the complex of influences stemming from the patient's familial and social environment are not sufficient to cause the schizophrenic disorder, but rather impinge on an underlying genetically transmitted diathesis, the combination of factors brings about the schizophrenic outcome. One can also argue that in these more ordinary forms of the expression of the disorder, the impact of the genetic component may be mitigated by a lessened degree of penetrance or by the presence of polygenetically determined, modifying traits. This modification of the genetic impact allows greater room for the play of environmental influences. The same conclusion also applies to the affective factors.

By the time we reach the lower strata of the borderline spectrum, the expression of genetic factors is considerably muted, and the play of environmental factors becomes more important. In the pseudoschizophrenias, the schizophrenic process is in evidence, but the expression of the genetic components is sufficiently mitigated so that there is more of environmental impact, with a more or less neurotic overlay. This process is similarly extended to the level of the psychotic character organization, although here, too, the presence of genetic factors, however mitigated, and their effects structuralized in characterological formations seem to remain operative. From this point on in the borderline spectrum, however, there is little evidence of the presence or the operation of schizophrenic genetic factors. Rather, we are dealing with stable forms of character organization, with varying degrees of inner cohesiveness and structuralization, that can be adequately accounted for by environmental and developmental influences. These patients do not become psychotic, but may undergo transient regressive states that look psychotic, and must be regarded as phenocopies.

It is also suggested that some borderline conditions reflect the influence of an affective genetic diathesis that would relate them to the primary affective disorders. We have found a basis for such an affective component in the psychotic character and dysphoric personality. These categories together may represent the predominant forms of borderline psychopathology.

Although our purpose here has been to delineate the overlap between the schizophrenic spectrum, the spectrum of affective disorders, and the borderline spectrum, we must remind ourselves that the point of view advanced is tentative and open to question in view of the uncertainty and lack of careful diagnostic substantiation for these various levels of personality description (Guze, 1975). Moreover, our argument can be regarded as little more than a tentative hypothesis. The discriminative criteria suggested here are derived from a clinical base of observation and do not directly involve the genetic hypothesis. Substantiation of the genetic argument rests on epidemiological grounds, for example, the number of schizophrenic spectrum disorders and affective disorders in the biological relatives of schizophrenic and affective disorder patients. Confirmation of the role of genetic factors must await not only more careful diagnostic studies of entities in both the borderline and schizophrenic spectra and the spectrum of affective disorders, but also a more careful study of genetic factors, their substantiation, and their discrimination from interacting environmental influences throughout the whole spectrum of schizophrenic and non-schizophrenic disorders.

Chapter 11
Organic Factors

The basic issue of diagnostic heterogeneity in the borderline spectrum we have tried to articulate (see Part II) poses questions regarding the possibilities of a comparable etiological heterogeneity. The complex of causal factors that may contribute in varying degrees to the disturbances within the borderline spectrum embraces a broad range, extending from the biogenetic, at one extreme, to complex interpersonal, social, and even cultural factors, at the other.

In this chapter, we will discuss a particular set of factors that may interact with both genetic and environmental factors to influence the etiology of borderline syndromes. Organic factors may contribute to borderline pathology, but to the extent that they do, they play a complex and variable role. Organic factors may operate in conjunction with genetic influences and may, in fact, represent one pattern of their expression. By the same token, organic factors may arise and play a role in the final common path of borderline pathological expression, quite independently of genetic factors. These may take the form of congenital defects (as opposed to genetic) or of later trauma to or disruption of the functioning of the organism, particularly and specifically the central nervous system.

We have already discussed the diversity of the genetic factors that contribute to the borderline spectrum. Such diversity is a matter not only of divergent gene components, but also of varying degrees of genetic expression or penetrance. At the same time, genetic influences do not operate in a vacuum, but are involved in a complex interplay with environmental influences that operate in various ways and to various degrees to determine or to modify the genetic outcome. The extent to which genetic factors respond to and are influenced by environmental factors can vary considerably. Again, there is a continuum of degrees of genetic and environmental interaction. Genetic factors may play a direct and decisive role in the outcome, as in the case of genetically determined biological defects. The genetic links between certain forms of central nervous system disorder or conditions of enzyme deficiency have been well studied and clearly established. The organic outcome in terms of structural or functional deficits would represent one type of pattern of hereditary/environmental interaction in which the hereditary factors play a predominant and determining role.

At the other extreme, environmental factors may play a predominant and vitally determining role. Here one would have to think of the variety of factors that contribute to the normal progression of organic development, without which such development is impaired. Thus, there is evidence that nutrition plays a vital role in the laying down of the basic components of the central nervous system and thus may influence the development of cognitive abilities. Trauma, in association with difficult births, may also play a significant role in a variety of forms of central nervous system damage that affect later development and behavior. The phenomenon of hippocampal sclerosis and its connection with birth traumata have been recognized for some time.

Other forms of organic impairment may reflect a higher degree of environmental input, though still in conjunction with genetic components. The ingenious experiments of Hubel and Wiesel (1965, 1970) have clearly demonstrated the role of appropriate and critically timed environmental stimulus in the development of central nervous system functions. The animals they studied were genetically endowed with the normal mechanisms for reception and processing of visual stimuli, but when these stimuli were withheld during crucial periods of development, the corresponding functions and their sustaining structures failed to develop. Here the integration of genetically determined structures was impeded by a lack of appropriate environmental interaction, with resultant neuroanatomical and neurophysiological deficits.

Keeping in mind the spectrum of genetic/environmental influences, it seems entirely reasonable to suppose that psychological or psychodynamic factors may also play an etiological role that can be seen as expressing another variant pattern in the overall schema of genetic/environmental interaction. Psychological influences affect genetically determined structures in the central nervous system and may influence, to varying degrees, the pattern of their development. If specific visual input is required for the normal expression of genetic and physiological capacities in the organization of the visual apparatus, we can also argue that other specific and perhaps more complex forms of stimulus input are equally important in the organization and functioning not only of specific sensory systems, but also in the more complex and variable integration of higher-order functions of the human central nervous system, functions that contribute to the capacity for cognitive, behavioral, and personality functioning.

In all these cases, we are arguing for a complex balance of organic and psychological factors that contribute to and shape the development of the individual personality. Within a more specifically psychological and developmental approach, there is a tendency to emphasize the role of psychological factors, giving them a primacy and predominance that tends to override and even overlook organic factors that may also be operating in the same developmental context. By the same token, in the emphasis on organic factors, there is the tendency to see them as playing a predominant, determining role, to the disadvantage and devaluation of the role of concomitant psychological inputs. In fact, we are dealing with continua in which heredity interacts in some form or some degree with environmental factors, even though the selective patterns of the interaction may vary considerably in form and degree. We have then also to consider the continuum of psychological and organic factors entering into a complex interaction that may vary greatly in the form of their relative expression, which is uniquely determined in the individual's developmental history.

Consequently, in considering the role of organic factors in the forms of impairment found in the borderline spectrum, there is never a context in which there is the possibility of organic factors operating independently of other complex etiological factors. Where an individual case may be placed in the spectrum of borderline conditions will be determined by the complex interaction of multiple factors, with biological and organic components in complex interplay with the psychological—both cognitive and affective—aspects of the individual's unique developmental history.

Although the developmental context provides a unique laboratory for the study of the interplay of complex etiological influences, organic factors may also affect complex behavioral capacities exclusive of developmental considerations. The concern here is particularly with toxic influences that may impair or disturb central nervous system function both acutely and chronically. The theoretical implications of the possibility that certain forms of borderline psychopathology may indeed be the effect of toxic substances acting on the central nervous system and thus contributing to the pathological picture are immense. That excessive or chronic drug use may produce such an effect must be taken seriously. We will focus, particularly, on the toxic effects of alcohol and its possible role in the production of borderline-like syndromes.

THE RELATIONSHIP OF BORDERLINE CONDITIONS TO ORGANIC SYNDROMES

The coincidence of borderline diagnoses with a high incidence of neurological signs has been frequently noted. This is probably an outcome of earlier studies of neurological deficits in schizophrenic patients as, for example, in the incidence of selective brain atrophy and reversals of normal asymmetry in the brains of schizophrenics as detected by computed tomography (Luchins et al., 1982). Bemporad and his group (1982) have observed a striking incidence of organic impairment in a group of children diagnosed as borderline. This most often took the form of poor coordination, perceptual motor difficulties, hyperactivity, poor concentration, some learning disabilities, soft neurological signs, and nonspecific abnormalities on the EEG. They suggest that these impairments may contribute to, but not necessarily cause the problems these children have in motor control, in their inability to contain anxiety effectively, and in their chronic difficulties engaging and responding to reality.

By the same token, others (Andrulonis et al., 1980b) have observed an increased incidence of such organic factors in adult borderline patients. A subcategory of borderline patients seem to have a history suggestive of minimal brain dysfunction in childhood or to be concurrently suffering from a form of episodic dyscontrol syndrome (Andrulonis et al., 1980b; M. Murray, 1979). Complex behavioral dysfunction and regressive patterns of behavior have also been found in connection with complex partial seizures, variously described as psychical seizures or psychomotor seizures or temporal lobe seizures (G. Murray, 1981).

Based on such findings, the group at the Institute of Living (Andrulonis et al., 1980b) have suggested several subgroupings for borderline patients. Patients who show little or no organic involvement may be regarded as having a purely psychogenic form of the disorder. In terms of this discussion, such patients would be in a group with a minimal degree of organic involvement. A second group of patients suffer from various forms of learning disability, attention deficit, and/or minimal brain dysfunction (MBD). A third group demonstrated aspects of the episodic dyscontrol syndrome characterized by frequent episodes of violent or self-destructive behavior. Such patients usually have a history of some form of birth trauma, febrile seizures, head injury, loss of consciousness, hyperactivity, learning disorders, enuresis, firesetting, cruelty to animals, antisocial behavior, drug or alcohol abuse, traffic violations, serious automobile accidents, arrests, suicidal gestures, and pathological intoxication from minor amounts of alcohol. They experience frequent failures in significant areas of life—in work, school, and marriage—and are often resistant to psychotherapy or psychotropic medication. Andrulonis et al. (1980b) conclude that the borderline syndrome may represent a recognizable entity in its own right and can be clearly differentiated from episodic dyscontrol or other forms of minimal brain dysfunction or that it may also coexist with one or both of these more neurologically relevant categories.

MINIMAL BRAIN DYSFUNCTION

In recent studies, a connection between a borderline personality diagnosis in adults and a history of MBD in childhood has been sought. Often abnormal character traits and an inadequate adjustment can be traced back in the history of borderline patients to very early childhood. Many such borderline or pre-borderline children show typical patterns of impulsivity, developmental deficits, hyperactivity, learning disabilities, and attention deficits. Most MBD children have an average or even an above-average IQ, but their learning and behavioral difficulties range from mild to severe. Deviations may express themselves to varying degrees and in combinations of impairment in perception, conceptualization, language, memory, and motor control.

Most such children do not have a history suggesting central nervous system trauma, although there may be such problems. The prenatal history may include factors of threatened miscarriage, toxemia, maternal hypertension, diabetes, rubella, trauma, infection, and alcohol or drug abuse. The delivery is often characterized by prematurity, neonatal jaundice, and/or anoxia, raising a suspicion of brain damage. In infancy and early childhood, there may be a history of cranial trauma, viral or bacterial encephalitis, poisoning, cerebral vascular accidents or severe episodes of childhood illness, such as mumps, chicken pox, or rubella or severe systemic illnesses that produce dehydration and high fever, resulting in seizures.

Learning disorders are common, even in the face of normal intelligence and adequate educational opportunity. A close examination of cognitive capacities may reveal specific deficits that interfere with the acquisition of linguistic and symbolic skills. This may be reflected in difficulties in reading, speaking, handwriting, and arithmetic computation. The school problems may be complicated by attentional deficits and hyperactivity. The hyperactive behavior often has a driven and disorganized quality, and the child has difficulty in both focusing and sustaining attention. Projects fatigue the child readily, and he is easily distracted. There may be overcompensation in the form of rigidity and perseveration of tasks or some difficulty in switching sets. The attention span is not only subject to temporal limitation, but also has a relatively narrow processing capacity. The memory is limited in the amount of information it can retain at any given time.

In addition to attentional and learning difficulties, the child often has soft neurological signs, which interfere with his capacity to function effectively. There are often problems in motor integration and coordination, which may be confined to fine motor movements of the hands, fingers, mouth, and tongue. Directional confusion is frequently found: confusion may arise between concepts of right/left, front/behind, and before/after.

Problems that require analysis, organization, and planning generally reveal poor performance levels. Electroencephalogram irregularities are frequently observed.

A number of aspects of the MBD child's behavior suggests immature ego functioning. Behavior is generally impulsive and shows a lack of capacity for planning, organization, judgment, and reasoning. The child is unable to stop talking or moving about. Even though he can foresee the consequences of certain behaviors, he rarely trys to control them. There seems to be a lack of internal controls, and activity is almost completely controlled by external stimuli; the behavior is basically reactive. At the same time, the child shows poor frustration tolerance, such that any delay in gratification may give rise to a temper tantrum or to verbal abuse. The demanding, controlling, bullying quality of the child's behavior strains his relationships with his peers and causes endless interpersonal difficulties. Often such children fail to grasp the subtleties and implications of the social interactions they engage in, in an impulsive and narcissistically demanding fashion (M. Murray, 1979).

Given this configuration of deficits, particularly the immaturity of ego-functions and their correlative deficits, it is not difficult to envision the negative impact of such constitutionally or organically based factors on personality development. The inherent intolerance of frustration creates a continual experience of frustration, which can effectively distort the child's experience of his environment, particularly the interpersonal environment. More specific difficulties in perception, memory functioning, and attention can distort what might otherwise be an ordinary context of development into one that is frustrating and correspondingly unresponsive to the child's needs. It is not surprising to hear a young mother, who is otherwise sensitive and capable, express her concern that no matter how hard she has tried, everything she did for and with the child turned out wrong. Such children are often "difficult" in that they are highly labile emotionally, caught up in the conflict between the need for clinging dependence at one moment and rejecting independence at another. Not only do they have difficulty in taking pleasure from normal interpersonal interactions, but the pattern of rejecting, demanding, and uneven behavior may be discouraging to the mother who then becomes inconsistent and ambivalent in her mothering. She may vacillate between withdrawal and rejection, in the face of the child's frustration and demands, on the one hand, and oversolicitude and overprotection, in response to the child's clinging dependency and her own guilt, on the other. Such mothers are often plagued with guilt, uncertainty, confusion, and ambivalence.

The lack of neurological integrity also gives rise to difficulties in dealing with impulses, particularly those of an aggressive nature. Such aggressive impulsivity is difficult to control at best, but when mixed with a relatively poor degree of frustration tolerance and a chronically negative experience in important object-relations, it leads to an intense degree of intrapsychic rage and impotent frustration. Insofar as the child lacks inhibitory controls over these enraged impulses, his angry outbursts and frustrated resentment serve only to disrupt further his relationships with important others and frustrate any real sense of satisfaction or reciprocity.

Minimal brain dysfunction children often have speech and language difficulties as well. Acquisition of speech is often delayed, and the capacity to grasp language interaction with any degree of proficiency strongly inhibited. The language difficulties may interfere with the capacity to process information through auditory channels, so that the child comes more and more to depend on visual and/or kinesthetic sensory modalities to establish contact with the world. Tangential thinking and difficulties in logical cognition are often found in this context. As the child matures, this basic confusion and language disability may be interpreted as a thought disorder, with corresponding diagnostic consequences. As M. Murray (1979) comments:

> The cognitive slippage and distortions of the reasoning and interpretive processes which use language as a base further exacerbate the MBD child's already poor psychological development, and the feeling of confusion, illogic, alienation, and aggression eventually fuse into a fairly cohesive personality organization which is diagnosed as borderline ego structure. (p. 396)

There seems to be little doubt that MBD children are significantly more at risk for developing a variety of personality disorders as they grow up; they often manifest antisocial behavior, depression, and episodic violence as adolescents (Anderson and Playmate, 1962; Mendelson et al., 1971). They are more likely to be institutionalized as delinquents or psychiatric patients (Huessy et al., 1974) and also are at greater risk for developing impulsive personality disorders (Hartocollis, 1968). It also seems that MBD children who manifest impulsive, aggressive, or antisocial behaviors have a generally poorer prognosis than more immature hyperactive children (Weiss et al., 1979; Andrulonis et al., 1980b).

As adults, such patients often manifest behaviors that are characterized by impulsivity, depression, anxiety, aggressive outbursts and temper tantrums, drug abuse, emotional lability and hyperreactivity, mood swings, distractibility, antisocial behavior, suicidal gestures, nervousness, eating problems, alcoholism, and hyperactivity (Bellak, 1979). Male adults are more sociopathic and assaultive and are comparatively unable to keep jobs. In females with MBD, there is a higher incidence of suicidal gesture, promiscuity, and depression. Relief of tension may be sought in violent acting-out or in the use of drugs. There is a need for constant stimulation, without which these patients suffer intense feelings of emptiness and depersonalization. Under excessive stimulation or stress, however, they become disorganized and regress. Similarly, Hartocollis (1968) found a readiness for anger, low frustration tolerance, irritability, free-floating anxiety, low self-esteem, identity diffusion, and feelings of emptiness and loneliness in MBD adults. There may also be EEG abnormalities that correlate with impulsivity, lability of mood, depersonalization, and dyscontrol (Bellak, 1979).

In addition, retrospective studies have determined the incidence of childhood MBD in patients with various forms of adult psychopathology. A childhood history of MBD has been found in withdrawn, schizoid, or schizophrenic adults (Quitkin and Klein, 1969), in impulsive/destructive or emotionally unstable character disorders, in explosive and aggressive personalities (Morrison and Minkoff, 1975), and in adults who are antisocial and assaultive (O'Neal and Robbins, 1958; Morris et al., 1956).

EPISODIC DYSCONTROL SYNDROME

The second large group of organic-related disorders is that of the so-called episodic dyscontrol syndrome. The syndrome has been variously noted in patients with aggressive personality disorders (Mark and Ervin, 1980; Monroe, 1970, 1978; Tunks and Dermer, 1977). Such patients often show borderline characteristics. Similar to MBD patients, the histories of these individuals include birth trauma, febrile seizures, head injuries with loss of consciousness, hyperactivity, learning disabilities, enuresis, firesetting, cruelty to animals, antisocial behavior, drug or alcohol abuse, frequent traffic violations and serious automobile accidents, frequent arrests, suicidal gestures, and pathological intoxication with small amounts of alcohol. Failures in the areas of work, school achievement, and marriage are frequent. Often enough, the family history also includes alcoholism, depression, and sociopathic and violent behavior (Andrulonis et al., 1980b).

Monroe (1970), whose discussion of episodic syndromes is quite comprehensive, divides so-called episodic behavioral disorders into forms of disordered action (episodic dyscontrol) and other intermittent periodic or remitting complex disorders that may have a psychotic, sociopathic, neurotic, or even physiological manifestation (episodic reactions).

Such episodic disorders refer to "any precipitiously appearing maladaptive behavior which is usually intermittent and recurrent, and which interrupts the 'life-style' or 'life-flow' of the individual" (Monroe, 1970, p. 2). Such interruptions can be either inhibitory or disinhibitory. Episodic inhibitions would include such phenomena as narcolepsy, catalepsy, akinetic mutism, periodic catatonia, and petit mal. These are obviously of less relevance in our current discussion than are episodic disinhibitions that interrupt the life-flow of the individual. When such disruptive behaviors are out of character for the individual and do not fit the immediate context or situation, they would seem to be forms of episodic dyscontrol. When the interruption is more or less sustained, yet characterized by precipitous onset and equally abrupt termination, they are more likely forms of episodic reaction. Such episodes of disordered behavior may last from minutes to hours to years, and be characterized by complex forms of personality disorder and dysfunction.

Monroe (1970) arranges the forms of episodic dyscontrol into a hierarchy in terms of the intensity and quality of drive components, the integration and complexity of motor patterns, and the specificity of motivational components. The lowest level of the hierarchy is *seizure dyscontrol*. Here the action is characterized by an explosive affect and a relatively chaotic motor behavior, which seems to be diffuse and uncoordinated, as well as object-less. The affect is relatively undifferentiated, with mixed components of rage, fear, and sexuality expressed in turbulent or rapidly vacillating fashion. The intention of the action is diffuse, nonspecific, and multidirectional and lacks intention or direction toward any specific object. Its pattern suggests an ictal component and is often associated with widespread neuronal discharges, which are often centrencephalic.

The next level of hierarchical organization of dyscontrol is *instinct dyscontrol*. Here, the motor response is abrupt and uninhibited, with little or no delay between impulse and action. The affects, however, tend to be more differentiated and responsive to specific needs. Although the action is primitive in character, it is better coordinated, linked with specific needs, and generally directed toward a specific object.

The next level of dyscontrol is *impulse dyscontrol*. Acts of impulse dyscontrol take the form of abrupt explosive expressions of relatively primitive affects, usually rage and aggression, and are characterized by overt homicidal, suicidal, or sexually aggressive behavior. There is little difference between the actual behavior of impulse dyscontrol and that of instinct dyscontrol, but in impulse dyscontrol, the impulsive act follows a period characterized by mounting tension and conflict as to whether the urge should be responded to or whether control should be maintained. When the tension becomes intolerable and overpowering, the explosive act occurs. The act is followed by a tremendous sense of relief, both because of the gratification of the basic urge and because of the release from tension and brooding doubt of the earlier indecision. This pattern of urge and conflict is often experienced in conditions of kleptomania, pyromania, exhibitionism, scoptophilia, and other fetishes. In such cases, however, the repression of unconscious needs and the minimizing of conscious premeditation would tend to shift such behaviors to acting-out rather than impulse dyscontrol.

The highest level of episodic dyscontrol is *acting-out*. Monroe (1970) defines acting-out, in this context, as

> a circumscribed, yet complex and significant act (or short series of acts) with a common intention carried through to completion and resulting in at least

partial or substitute gratification of a need. The act is so patently inappropriate to the situation, so out-of-character for the actor and so inadequately explained by the person committing the act that one can only conclude the act is determined by unconscious motives and is an attempt to resolve repressive conflicts. (p. 20)

Acting-out has frequently been associated with borderline conditions, particularly as an aspect of efforts to prevent or counter the loss or diffusion of identity (Angel, 1965). It has also been associated with other forms of psychopathology, particularly antisocial behavior. These various forms overlap, to a certain degree, with acting-out as a form of episodic dyscontrol, but there may also be noteworthy differences. Such behaviors may not manifest the quality of precipitous interruption in the individual's life-style or life-flow and, consequently, would not be characterized as episodic dyscontrol. The degree of coordination of the activity and the relevance of the apparent intention makes the evaluation of such disruptive behaviors difficult, so that interruption of a life-style may be difficult to evaluate. Nonetheless, in such forms of acting-out, the behavior usually comes as a surprise to the actor or even to an informed observer.

At times, the pattern of dyscontrol can become so frequent that it forms a more or less impulsive life-style, a form of "alloplastic readiness to act," that may be elaborated into a form of personality organization. Such patients are described as emotionally unstable, hysterical, or sociopathic, but insofar as the behavior has come to form a way of life and a personality style, it has a different character and a different quality than that found in the acting-out that is a form of episodic dyscontrol. In the dyscontrol syndrome, the precipitous and maladaptive acts occur after varying periods of predominantly unconscious premeditation.

In episodic reactions, we are dealing with more complex states that are often accompanied by intense affects or impulses and lead to dyscontrol acts that often have a homicidal, suicidal, or sexual intent. Conditions of episodic dyscontrol and episodic reaction seem to share common features: the overwhelming of control mechanisms by drive pressures and the altered state or level of consciousness. They differ from episodic dyscontrol primarily in duration, the episodic dyscontrol taking the form of a single act or a short series of acts, the episodic reaction being more sustained. Associated behavioral deviations may be regarded as psychotic, neurotic, sociopathic, or physiological. Often, the episodic behavior is superimposed on a pre-existing psychopathology.

Patients who manifest *episodic psychotic reactions* often have associated schizophrenic symptoms that run a remitting, intermittent, or atypical course. These episodic reactions often manifest acts of dyscontrol based on the patient's delusional preoccupations, as well as primary process thinking and other schizophrenic manifestations. These include perceptual or conceptual distortions, hallucinations, delusions, hypochondriacal preoccupations, somatic delusions, and tangential and bizarre concrete thinking. These patients also experience states of altered consciousness that often have a dreamlike quality and at least a partial memory loss for the period of the episode. During periods of remission, the patient may regain a relatively normal level of adjustment or may return to an identifiable base line of pathological adjustment. The precipitous onset of such states suggests a connection with ictal phenomena, particularly when the intervals are relatively brief. Such behaviors may be connected with complex psychic seizures, and such patients have often been described as suffering from a form of reactive schizophrenia. The behavior is certainly reminiscent of forms of borderline psychopathology in which the episodic and psychotic-like quality of acute regressive states is remarkably similar.

In *episodic sociopathic reactions*, the dyscontrol acts tend to have an antisocial quality, but they must be distinguished carefully from other forms of antisocial behavior. Such behaviors may be considered psychotic when there is evidence of a defect in central integrative capacities, or neurotic when the behavior reflects a rebellion against excessive and inappropriate conscience mechanisms. Many patients with this form of episodic behavioral disorder give a history of other organic involvement of the central nervous system, which are often the characteristics noted in MBD children; these include hyperkinetic activity, motor incoordination, brief attention span, distractibility, and a certain explosiveness, even in normal motor movement.

Episodic neurotic reactions may occur in a variety of forms, but Monroe (1970) notes the most common forms as diffuse anxiety, phobic symptoms, depressions, hypochondriacal reactions, clusters of conversion symptoms, and finally, dissociative states. The reactions may last only a matter of minutes or hours or days.

Because episodic dyscontrol is intermittent does not mean that the intervening periods will necessarily be normal. Rather, it is more frequently the case that the episodic behavior is superimposed on an underlying personality disorder. The episodic dyscontrol may be the presenting difficulty, and often be serious enough to require hospitalization, and then it may be found to be only one aspect of a more general psychopathology. In such cases, it is important to distinguish between the dynamics and etiology of the underlying nonepisodic psychopathology and the superimposed episodic behavior. This would be consistent with the need to distinguish, in borderline patients, between acute and intermittent regressive phenomena and the more enduring characterological level of psychological functioning and organization.

In terms of the role of organic factors, acting-out, as it is defined in this context, is more likely to be due to psychodynamic or experiential factors, whereas the lower levels of dyscontrol—seizure dyscontrol, instinct dyscontrol, and impulse dyscontrol—probably reflect impaired central nervous system functioning. Certainly, the precipitous onset and sudden remission of episodic behavioral disorders, and the patient's experiencing them as in some sense ego-alien, as though they were "spells" or "attacks," underlines this ictal quality.

One of the major difficulties in linking episodic dyscontrol and impaired functioning of the central nervous system is the fact that seizure activity can take place in subcortical structures without any indication of dysrhythmic EEG activity at the cortical level. The limbic system structures, including the hippocampus and the amygdala, are known to have low convulsive thresholds, but stimulation of such deep temporal lobe structures may or may not induce typical seizure patterns for a given patient. Studies of patients with chronically implanted electrodes in temporal lobe structures support the view that ictal disturbances are associated with episodic behavioral difficulties.

The assumption behind the differentiation between ictal and nonictal phenomenon, namely, that ictal behavior reflects a massive and excessive neuronal discharge, and that such related phenomena as prodromal symptoms, aura, and postictal and interictal behavior do not result from such a discharge, may be an oversimplification. Seizure discharges in the septal/hippocampal/amygdala circuits of the limbic system may occur in connection with symptoms originally thought to be prodromal (irritability, tension, insomnia, or excessive sensitivity). The problem of determining which episodic behavioral disorders can be attributed to epileptic phenomena and which cannot remains unresolved.

If the behavior begins and ends abruptly without obvious cause or explanation, if the patient's memory of the period of the attack is fragmentary or lacking, if there is a family or personal history of epileptic seizures, if there is an abnormal EEG, and if the patient responds to anticonvulsant medication, we might make a strong case for an epileptic etiology. But these indications do not absolutely assure the diagnosis. In fact, it is not at all clear, in clinical terms, when a patient is in an ictal, postictal, or interictal state. If a patient is having a simple partial seizure, manifested only in the affective experience of fear, he may not look at all like the textbook description of a temporal lobe patient; but implanted electrodes might detect spiking in the frontal or rhinencephalic regions. Symptoms in such patients are more often diagnosed as psychiatric and referral made on that basis.

In fact, ictal expressions in psychomotor or temporal lobe epilepsy tend to be much more complex and variable and much less stereotyped and repeatable than in other forms of epilepsy. The symptoms of such ictal discharges closely mimic symptoms seen in a variety of psychiatric patients. Differential diagnosis is still possible on the basis of the abrupt onset and remission of symptoms and the ego-alien quality of the seizure experience. There is also a qualitative difference between the hallucinations, depersonalizations, or delusions accompanying a psychomotor attack and those found in schizophrenia. The psychomotor symptoms tend to be simple or fragmentary; they are often brief and repetitive with comparatively little conceptual elaboration or complexity. There is usually an altered state of consciousness, although amnesia is seldom total. Monroe (1970) assumes that at least some of the behavioral disturbances associated with temporal lobe epilepsy that are supposedly nonictal are, in fact, due to seizure activity, particularly when they are marked by a precipitous onset and remission. Moreover, the ictal expression is not necessarily brief, but may persist for hours, weeks, and at times even months; but whatever the duration, the onset tends to be precipitous and the remission equally so.

There is good evidence that many explosive rage or fear reactions have an ictal basis. The aggressive acts found in cases of instinct and impulse dyscontrol are probably ictal and not simply due to post-seizural confusion or interictal disturbances. The dyscontrol behavior in such cases is usually poorly coordinated and diffusely directed, and usually of short duration. The disorganization is such that the primitive homicidal, suicidal, or sexual intentions are rarely successfully completed. Nonetheless, at the higher levels of episodic dyscontrol, where the behaviors are better organized and more socially effective, there may also be epileptoid phenomena at work, that are related to undetected neuronal discharges.

Certain patients with selective epileptic foci may manifest forms of "subclinical psychosis" that closely mimic borderline syndromes. Monroe (1970) cites several cases of patients with temporal lobe foci who presented with syndromes of an episodic character that mimicked aspects of Hoch's pseudoneurotic schizophrenia or other atypical psychoses. Centrencephalic discharges would be responsible for patterns of episodic inhibition with torpor, apathy, diminished initiative, and dulled affect. On the contrary, dyscontrol patterns with an intense affect, impulsive behavior, and psychotic symptoms may be due to a rhinencephalic disturbance. Monroe suggests that centrencephalic seizures are often accompanied by a confusional apathetic state and that rhinencephalic seizures would mimic a "productive psychosis." When centrencephalic and rhinencephalic activity occur together, symptoms not found in either state may be produced. An excessive neuronal discharge in rhinencephalic structures might be responsible for intense affects, particularly, dysphoric affects, and the combination lead to the relatively uninhibited expression of these affects. These are the patients who would be prone to impulsive acting-out of homicidal, suicidal, or sexual impulses. In syndromes of episodic dyscontrol, there is either an excessive intensity of instinctual drives or a defect in inhibitory controls or some combination of the two. This may reflect an inhibition of higher central nervous system control mechanisms (centrencephalic seizures) or the production of intense dysphoric affects (rhinencephalic seizures).

One can conclude that ictal discharges are a possible mechanism for many of the episodic behavioral disorders and that many behavioral abnormalities not previously regarded as epileptic in origin may well be manifestations of partial epileptic discharges that may be limited to subcortical structures, particularly those of the limbic system. Andrulonis et al. (1980a) have argued that the episodic dyscontrol syndrome reflects an underlying disorder of the subcortical temporal lobe/limbic system, characterized by stimulus overinclusion or stimulus flooding and violence related to subictal events. These patients may be regarded as forming a subcategory of the borderline syndrome, marked by the presence of dyscontrol episodes and abnormal EEG findings, as well as a history suggestive of organicity. Such patients may be considerably helped by ethosuximide.

Organic dysfunction may be expressed by complex forms of impulsive behavior, rather than by a more apparent seizure activity. Other investigators have also postulated a major role for the temporal lobe/limbic system in the etiology of aggressive behavior disturbances (Fields and Sweet, 1975; Flor-Henry, 1969, 1972; Glaser et al., 1963; Goldensohn and Gold, 1960). Patients with abnormal EEG activity in the temporal lobes manifest a wide variety of episodic behavioral disturbances, including depersonalization, free-floating anxiety, depression, impulsive behavior, destructive rages, and schizophrenic-like psychotic episodes (Slater and Beard, 1963). Certain patients may have abnormal EEGs, including nonspecific temporal and frontal lobe abnormalities (Andrulonis et al., 1980b) and fourteen- and six-second positive spiking in the temporal lobes (Boelhouwer et al., 1968) that may be associated with hyperreactivity or the abnormal persistence of autonomic responses to external stimuli. The episodic dyscontrol may not accompany an excessive discharge, since the manifest behavior is usually highly organized and skillfully carried through to completion, thus representing higher hierarchical levels of episodic dyscontrol (Monroe, 1970).

In childhood behavioral disorders, there may be a detectible maturational lag that can be identified by EEG abnormalities and that correlates with a psychological maturational defect. When such EEG maturational delay occurs, there seems to be a high incidence of behavioral disorders, often with symptoms similar to forms of episodic dyscontrol or episodic reactions. It is also possible that the EEG abnormalities in such behaviorally disturbed children simply reflect more diffuse brain pathology. The behavior patterns, then, similar to those found in MBD children with outbursts of unprovoked and destructive aggressive behavior, may not be specifically related to the EEG abnormalities.

As children with behavioral disorders grow up, the behavior disorders tend to be recategorized as psychopathic or sociopathic. The rate of EEG abnormalities among sociopathic patients is relatively high—more than 50 percent in some studies—suggesting that the antisocial behavior in such patients may reflect an underlying form of episodic dyscontrol. In episodic dyscontrol, the balance between primitive urges and higher control mechanisms is disturbed. If the loss of impulse control becomes a way of life, then the stage is set for a pattern of behavior that may be characterized as psychopathic or criminal. Hill and Wetterson (1942) long ago distinguished an aggressive group of psychopaths from a more inadequate group. The aggressive group was characterized by suicide attempts, violence toward others regardless of consequences, repeated destructive acts, and aggressive and impulsive behavior. The incidence of EEG abnormalities in this group was 65 percent, as compared to 32 percent in the inadequate group. In a similar study of delinquent adolescents, Jenkins and Pacella (1943) found that abnormal EEGs were more characteristic when delinquent behavior was characterized by assaultive tendencies with emotional instability, irritability, and poor self-control. More recent studies (Wolff et al., 1982; Lewis et al., 1982) have tended to reinforce and refine these impressions. Not only is psychomotor epilepsy more frequent in delinquent populations, but the severity of the delinquency also seems to be related to the degree of psychomotor symptomatology.

By the same token, it is clear that such EEG abnormalities are found in individuals who do not show psychopathic behavior. In addition, studies of psychopathic personalities with abnormal EEG findings also reveal a background of severely disturbed family and social relationships during the individual's early life experience. Family histories are often marked by parental dissension, separation, emotional deprivation, etc. Consequently, it seems more than likely that aggressive and antisocial behavior might reflect both organic and experiential factors. It may require not only disturbances in central nervous system functioning, but also developmental influences that instill and reinforce tendencies toward aggressive and destructive acting-out.

TOXIC INFLUENCES

In any discussion of the role of organic factors relative to borderline syndromes, one of the central questions to be considered is the relationship between possible toxic influences, in the form of exogenous substances, and such syndromes. It has commonly been observed that borderline personalities tend to have a higher addictive potential and are often more apt to abuse substances, whether drugs or alcohol. Conversely, addict populations, both drug abusers and alcoholics, have been found to possess borderline personality characteristics. An obviously critical question is whether the borderline personality structure carries with it a vulnerability to drug or alcohol abuse, in other words, an inherent addictive potentiality or whether, in certain settings, the abuse of drugs or alcohol can, in fact, modify central nervous system function so as to produce a borderline-like picture.

The tendency to abuse drugs or alcohol has been a frequent finding in studies of borderline populations (Kernberg, 1967; Gunderson and Singer, 1975). Hard-core addicts tend to show a common set of personality characteristics. They are often almost totally and compulsively preoccupied with the use of the drug and the life-style that accompanies it. Because of their addiction, they see themselves as rebellious deviants with little connection with or regard for the straight world. Their images of themselves seem to involve antisocial activities, rebellious attitudes, aggression against established aspects of society, and their own intense sense of victimization. Their sense of self and their self-esteem seem to depend on a negative identity.

Their beliefs, often directly related to the drug and its usage, are often magical, but may include other areas of their experience as well. Often, there is a suggestion of primary process thinking that expresses itself in the form of distorted or overvalued ideas. The capacity to discriminate reality from fantasy is often impaired. The defenses of projection, introjection, and denial are prominent. Superego functioning often shows severe deterioration, such that they cannot be trusted to follow the normally accepted rules, ethics, and codes of social behavior. Their general psychological functioning often has a paranoid cast. At the same time, these individuals are clearly not schizophrenic or psychotic. Much of their functioning reflects a deterioration in ego autonomy and, more generally, in the adaptive functioning of the ego (Zinberg, 1975).

The prevailing view would place greater emphasis, in the case of compulsive drug users, on the role of psychological factors in substance abuse, particularly on the vulnerabilities that are inherent in the addictive personality, prior to drug abuse, that stem from early developmental influences (Wurmser, 1978). In his extensive work on such addictive populations, Wurmser emphasizes the elements of narcissistic vulnerability and the role of a "narcissistic crisis" in the addictive phenomenon.

A somewhat divergent view has been taken by Zinberg (1974, 1975). He argues, essentially, that a combination of extrinsic circumstances and factors can lead an individual to drug abuse and that the toxic effects of the drug, once they begin to take hold, draw the individual into a set of socially determined circumstances that, together with the pharmacological effects of the drug, create a picture of personality disturbance that may be diagnosed as severe psychopathology. In such cases, the psychopathology cannot be determined to have preceded the drug affects, but rather seems to be a consequence of drug abuse. Zinberg (1974) comments:

> The most important single concept about drug-induced states to emerge in the last decade is this—to understand the subject's response one must consider drug, set, and setting as a basic whole. "Set" refers to the person's attitude toward the experience and includes his personality structure. "Setting" refers to the influence of the physical and social environment in which the drug use takes place. . . . My insistence on the set-setting interaction means that I place less emphasis on the irremediable basic influence of early psychic development. While I do not ignore this early aspect of set, I see the effects of persistent social attitudes, particularly when magnified by the mass media and accepted by the public as a social crisis, as a factor influencing the continuing personality development of the individual. (p. 2)

He then continues his argument:

> Once defined as deviant, removed from usual social supports, thrust into an increasingly less diverse group for social stimuli, drawn into constant, real and imagined conflict with the police and the law, personality changes occur. When all this is aided by the persistent use of a drug that, at least in the United States of 1974, furthers this social process, is it a surprise that heroin users can be diagnosed as severe narcissistic character disorders? (p. 35)

Apparently, the "severe narcissistic character disorders" would be diagnostically equivalent to the borderline syndromes as described in this study.

Similar problems arise in a discussion of the relation between alcoholism and borderline syndromes. Certainly, not all alcoholics are borderline personalities, but it seems likely that many alcoholics, and even possibly most, could be so considered, especially when the history involves the abuse of alcohol from an early age, rapid addiction, and heavy drinking over a period of years. Alcoholics also tend to utilize more primitive defenses, including denial, projection, and rationalization. They are also often characterized by deep dependency needs, avoidance of conflicts, pathological narcissism, grandiosity, and a marked use of splitting. These lower-level defenses are also found in borderline personality functioning, so that a reasonable conclusion can be drawn, namely, that the area of overlap between borderline syndromes and vulnerability to the addictive use of alcohol must be considerable (Hellman, 1981). From a clinical standpoint, then, it would seem reasonable that the clinician should assume, in trying to treat alcoholic patients, that he is dealing with an underlying borderline personality structure, unless evidence to the contrary is clearly established. In such cases, the clinician should be alert, particularly, to the pathological degree of narcissism, elements of grandiosity, and the use of more primitive defense mechanisms.

The same chicken-and-egg conundrum regarding etiology that has arisen with regard to the relationship between the use of addictive substances more generally and borderline personality characteristics has also arisen with regard to the connection between borderline structure and alcoholism. The argument has been presented quite forcefully by Bean and her coworkers (Bean and Zinberg, 1981) that the so-called "alcoholic personality" is, in fact, a complication of alcoholism, produced by the toxic effects of the alcohol itself and the social and psychological sequelae of its abuse. The syndrome produces obvious distortion in personality function, involving such characteristics as impulsivity, narcissism and self-centeredness, self-destructiveness, a lack of responsibility and stable values, poor judgment, regressive behavior, mood lability, and irritability and a more primitive defensive organization, involving denial, rationalization, projection, and minimization. The picture that emerges is again quite similar to that often seen in borderline personalities.

The problem of etiological sequence must, at this point, remain unresolved. In the face of our ignorance, and in view of the conflicting findings on both sides of this issue, it is perhaps wisest to suggest that both paradigms have their inherent validity and that they may be variably expressed in different patient populations. Thus, certain addictive personalities may have inherent defects in their psychic structure that bring them to the use of certain substances to compensate for such defects or to alleviate the dysphoric affects associated with them. By the same token, other populations of drug or alcohol abusers may initiate substance use in socially accepted and reinforced contexts, but are then adversely affected by the toxic effects of these substances and their social sequelae and thus induce conditions of distorted psychological functioning that may appear borderline—and, indeed, effectively may be borderline. The important point here is that possible toxic influences form another potential realm in which organic, nonpsychological factors may enter into the complex etiology of the borderline picture.

RELATION TO BORDERLINE SYNDROMES

We are left, then, with the question as to the relevance of these findings to the borderline syndrome: To what extent do such organic factors contribute to the borderline picture in given patient populations? Some data are available from the Hartford study (Andrulonis et al., 1980b). These authors have visualized the relationship between borderline syndromes and the organic conditions of minimal brain dysfunction and episodic dyscontrol in terms of the accompanying Venn diagram (Figure 11-1). The borderline diagnostic criteria were based on a combination of the DSM-III and the Gunderson and Spitzer criteria. In terms of our earlier discussion (see

Borderline Syndrome   Minimal Brain Dysfunction Syndrome

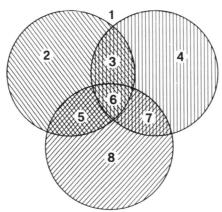

Episodic Dyscontrol Syndrome

Key: 1. Not borderline syndrome, nor episodic dyscontrol syndrome, nor minimal brain dysfunction syndrome; 2. Borderline syndrome, but not minimal brain dysfunction syndrome, nor episodic dyscontrol syndrome; 3. Borderline syndrome and minimal brain dysfunction syndrome, but not episodic dyscontrol syndrome; 4. Minimal brain dysfunction, but not borderline syndrome, nor episodic dyscontrol syndrome; 5. Borderline syndrome and episodic dyscontrol syndrome, but not minimal brain dysfunction syndrome; 6. Borderline syndrome, episodic dyscontrol syndrome, and minimal brain dysfunction syndrome; 7. Episodic dyscontrol syndrome and minimal brain dysfunction syndrome, but not borderline syndrome; 8. Episodic dyscontrol syndrome, but not minimal brain dysfunction syndrome, nor borderline syndrome.

FIGURE 11-1. Venn diagram of relationship between the borderline, minimal brain dysfunction, and episodic dyscontrol syndromes (Andrulonis et al., 1980b, p. 55)

Part II), we can presume that the population in question was diagnostically selected for the more primitive and less organized end of the borderline spectrum.

In this patient population, 62 percent of the total borderline population had no history of organicity; this group would include 44 percent of the male patients and 71 percent of the female. But 11 percent of the total sample had a past history of brain trauma, encephalitis, or epilepsy (nine females and only one male), and 27 percent of the total sample had a positive history of MBD or learning disability. Also, 53 percent of the males had a positive history of MBD or learning disability as against only 13.5 percent of females. Thus, the subcategory of the borderline syndrome, which also includes MBD or learning disability, is represented predominantly by male patients. Patients with such organic brain dysfunction, both male and female, tend to have an earlier-onset psychiatric illness and are admitted to the hospital at younger ages than are nonorganic borderline patients. In this patient sample, the mean age of admission for nonorganic patients was twenty-four, whereas the mean age for borderline females with organic brain dysfunction (MBD) was twenty-one, and the comparable age for males eighteen.

Males and females also differed significantly in their patterns of symptomatic expression: borderline males manifested higher degrees of antisocial acting-out and abuse of alcohol and/or other drugs, whereas females were found to be more frequently depressed. The females also showed a much higher percentage of mini-psychotic episodes than did male borderlines (78 percent versus 50 percent). The mini-psychotic episodes were usually time-limited and related to stress, taking the form of depersonalization, derealization, or paranoid distortions. Females also led in having a history of significant eating disturbances—both obesity and/or anorexia (females about 50 percent; males about 16 percent).

Data of this nature suggest that there are important areas and significant degrees of overlap between pathogenic and organic factors and the borderline syndromes. The authors of the Hartford Study (Andrulonis et al., 1980b) summarize their findings in the following terms:

> Overall, the organic brain dysfunction borderline patients, in particular those in the minimal brain dysfunction-learning disability subcategory, appear significantly distinct from the nonorganic borderline patients. The borderline patient with organic brain dysfunction is more often male with an early onset of his illness, beginning with symptoms of the minimal brain dysfunction syndrome. In grade school and high school years, this individual often demonstrates academic difficulties and acting-out behavior. His family history is most commonly positive for alcohol and/or drug abuse. The nonorganic borderline patient is more often female with an adolescent onset of psychiatric difficulties. This patient tends to do better during grade school years, but then acts out during the late high school years. This female patient is also more likely to become seriously depressed, to have a family history of an affective disorder, and to experience more frequent mini-psychotic episodes. (pp. 62–63)

At this point, I would like to offer a tentative assessment of the potential role of organic factors relative to the diagnostic subdivisions suggested within the borderline spectrum (see Chapter 7). In this connection, it would seem that certain clear-cut distinctions can be enunciated. The entities that compose the borderline spectrum have been divided into two general groupings, forming two relatively discrete subcontinua within the borderline spectrum, namely, the hysterical continuum and the schizoid continuum. Apparently, there is no basis for ascribing organic components to the component entities of the schizoid continuum. That ascription is based on the nature of the entities involved and the characteristics of respective entities. All are more or less chronic conditions that clearly reflect the influence of psychological developmental parameters and are characterized by none of the behavioral disturbances connected with neurological dysfunction.

The condition of identity-stasis is clearly related to a developmental crisis in the psychological integration of the personality, having to do almost exclusively with higher-order functions. One does not find, at this level of the borderline spectrum, any of the abrupt discontinuities in conceptual, affective, or behavioral realms that might suggest organic dysfunction.

Similarly, in the case of "as-if" personalities, the "as-if" condition is a chronic disability in the area, particularly, of self-organization and object-relations. The underlying motivational components are constantly present, and not subject to disruptive discontinuity. Regressions in "as-if" personalities would seem to reflect clearly the vicissitudes in object-relationships and the underlying vulnerability due to fragile self-organization.

By the same token, the false-self organization reflects long-term developmental difficulties and constitutes a relatively constant and chronic psychological condition based almost exlcusively on motivational and developmental parameters. The same can be said even more decisively of schizoid personalities, which generally reflect a life-long pattern of interaction with objects that is clearly caught on the horns of the schizoid dilemma, between the need for and the fear of objects.

Some qualifications might be useful to keep in mind with regard to the assessment of these entities and the possible influence of organic factors in their etiology. It would seem obvious that in any one of these diagnostic entities, a given patient might also have some form of organic disability. For example, there is nothing contradictory about an individual with a basically schizoid personality as his characteristic modality of personality functioning also suffering from episodic dyscontrol. The more critical question here is whether such underlying neurological factors might contribute to the diagnostic syndrome itself. The essence of the argument is that there is no room for the influence of such factors in the etiology of the borderline entities within the schizoid subcontinuum.

The case may be somewhat different when we turn to the entities within the hysterical subcontinuum. It is within this realm of the borderline spectrum that the elements of regressive crises, emotional instability and lability, and disruptive behaviors play a much more considerable role. As we move from the higher-order forms of borderline organization within this subcontinuum to the lower-order forms, the possible role of disruptive organic factors in contributing to the symptomatology and etiology of the disorder increases.

In the higher-order forms of borderline dysfunction, the primitive hysterics and the dysphoric personalities, organic factors are considerably less likely or might conceivably be restricted to relatively rare and special cases.

The dynamics of the primitive hysteric would seem to be fully intelligible on psychological grounds alone. Periods of regressive crisis are more or less clearly associated with periods of psychological stress; however, underlying and subtle dysfunctions at a subcortical level cannot be completely ruled out, particularly when there is the possibility that such neurologically disruptive states may be responsive to emotional stress.

When such regressive and emotionally disruptive states in their most extreme forms involve intensely aggressive responses, particularly suicidal or homicidal urges, such an underlying neurological dysfunction is more likely. This would most likely be the case, as already observed, when such disruptive states seem to have an abrupt beginning and end, which suggests a possible seizure focus. Other rare conditions that may be associated with primitive hysterical personality organization, such as acute dissociative states, forms of multiple personality organization, and fugue states, may also be connected with epileptic-like dysfunction—again most tellingly when the onset of such conditions is relatively abrupt, seems to have little in the way of precipitating stress, and ends abruptly.

In the case of the dysphoric personality, the situation is much the same. The question of a possible influence of organic factors would be relevant only within periods of regressive crisis. The likelihood of organic influences in such regressive states is somewhat diminished, since such regressive crises in both primitive hysterics and dysphoric personalities do not tend to occur with the same quality of abrupt disruptiveness that one associates with seizure phenomena. In dysphoric personalities, regressive states are relatively rare and occur only under regressive pressures, which might be created, for example, in the analytic situation.

With due respect for the mysteries and complexities of the interaction between personality variables and underlying neurological substrates, the possibility that the regressive strains experienced in terms of the level of psychological interaction might not, in fact, induce or stimulate some manner of disruptive dysfunction at the neurological level should not be eliminated. The regressive characteristics of irritability, expressions of rage, emotional lability and instability, and the general unruliness and disruptiveness of drives, both libidinal and aggressive, would be consistent with an underlying subcortical, presumably limbic, neuronal discharge.

When we remind ourselves that such subtle subcortical seizure foci are, by and large, undetectable by an ordinary EEG, and that such subcortical foci tend to mimic psychiatric symptoms, in any case, the situation is by no means clear and we are left with little more than hunches and hypotheses. It can be noted at this higher-level of borderline organization that, if such organic factors did come into play, their role would be restricted to periods of regressive crisis and the nature of the organic disruption would be essentially episodic and epileptic in some form.

When we move to the lower level of borderline organization, to the psychotic characters and the pseudoschizophrenics, the likelihood of organic disruption as an important part of the contributing etiology of these conditions is considerably greater. In such lower-order cases, the more characterological base of psychological functioning seems to reflect a higher degree of vulnerability to organic disruption. It is more often these patients who will have some history of organic impairment in childhood, as, for example, borderline patients with a history suggestive of MBD.

Moreover, the general characteristics of these entities, particularly the emotional instability and lability, the irritability, the high titer of aggressive impulses, the quality of behavioral impulsivity, and the intolerance of frustration and anxiety, would tend to tip the balance in favor of more chronic forms of neurological impairment or dysfunction, rather than the more episodic forms. As in the higher-order forms of borderline organization, here, too, vulnerability to regression may also reflect episodic disruptive influences, but the susceptibility to the influence of more chronic forms of neurological impairment must be countered with greater weight in this group than in the higher-order borderlines. To the extent that regressive crises reflect more acute neurological dysfunction, these lower-order borderlines must be regarded as being considerably more vulnerable to such regressive influences, presumably reflecting a higher degree of neurological instability. The potentiality for such regressive disruption would be more marked and severe in the pseudoschizophrenics than in the psychotic characters.

To return for a moment to Monroe's (1970) hierarchy of the organization of dyscontrol acts, the more primitive forms of dyscontrol can be found at this level of borderline disorganization. When the regressive disorganization has the qualities of explosive affect, diffuse and uncoordinated motor behavior, and relatively undifferentiated affects and seems to lack specific intentionality or object direction, we may be dealing with a form of seizure dyscontrol. When the behavior seems to reflect little capacity for delay between impulse and action and is better coordinated, more linked with specific needs, and directed toward specific objects, these may be episodes of instinct dyscontrol. When the affective expression is abrupt and explosive— usually expressing rage and destructive aggressive feelings—and often homicidal, suicidal, or sexually aggressive and when the disruptive activity seems to follow a period of mounting tension and conflictual urges, we may have an instance of Monroe's impulse dyscontrol. These more primitive forms of episodic dyscontrol can be found at any level of the hysterical subcontinuum, but only in acute regressive crises. The more primitive the episode, that is, when it occurs in the form of seizure or instinct dyscontrol, the more an underlying epileptic phenomena must be taken into account.

At the highest level of episodic dyscontrol, acting-out may be found throughout the hysterical subcontinuum; we can also note that it is relatively uncharacteristic in the schizoid subcontinuum. Acting-out, in fact, is a highly complex and organized form of behavior. The extent to which any piece of acting-out may reflect unconscious psychological motivational factors, or may correspondingly reflect the influence of conditions of episodic dyscontrol, is difficult to evaluate in any given instance. Monroe (1970) had, probably correctly, insisted that if the behavior does not reflect the characteristics of episodic dyscontrol, that is, the precipitous interruption of the individual's life-style or life-flow, then it should not be regarded as reflecting the influence of organic factors. In actual fact, many episodes of acting-out may not reflect these basic dyscontrol characteristics, so that the etiological foundation would have to be ascribed to psychological rather than to organic factors.

To summarize, then, the conclusions of this discussion, it would seem that there is little or no basis for an organic etiology in the schizoid subcontinuum, although even here room must be left for the inductive implication of possible neurological dysfunctioning, but not in a primary role. Within the hysterical subcontinuum, however, the role of organic factors in the etiology of these conditions is greater. In the higher-order groups, organic factors may operate in a limited fashion, episodically, that is, through disruptive epileptic foci presumably operating at a subcortical, primarily limbic level. These factors operate restrictively within regressive states and do not contribute directly to the basic personality organization. At the lower levels of borderline organization, however, organic factors may play both a chronic and episodic role, contributing to a basic instability and chronically dysfunctional incapacity of the central nervous system structures, which affects not only the overall level of personality organization and functioning, but also may operate, episodically, contributing to the disruptive and often destructive quality of regressive episodes.

Chapter 12
Developmental Aspects

The preceding discussion of etiological factors contributing to the borderline syndromes focused on nonpsychological factors, namely, genetic and organic elements that can contribute, in varying degrees, to at least some borderline conditions. Those factors, of necessity, affected the ongoing psychological development of each patient. Whether such nonpsychological organic factors were at work or not, every borderline patient, as every human being, passed through the vicissitudes of the developmental process, which is here conceived in specifically psychological terms. It is to a consideration of that process and its impact on the development of borderline pathology that we now turn our attention.

THE NATURE OF THE DEVELOPMENTAL PROCESS

Before we consider the influence of the variety of aspects of the developmental process on borderline pathology specifically, it may be useful to look at the nature of the developmental process itself. From the very beginning, neonatal behavior is organized into distinct and recurrent forms of action. The implicit psychological structure at this earliest level of development takes the form of reflex schemata that ensure that behavior will be repeated in a relatively stable form. Ongoing experience elicits new schemata that advance the infant another step along the path of increasing adaptation and interaction with his environment (Wolff, 1963), and the emergence and consolidation of these schemata progress to further development and differentiation. Anna Freud (1980) has suggested that when the appropriate constitutional and environmental ingredients are available to an optimal degree, development emerges along three lines, leading to a gradual distinction between soma and psyche, between the infant's own body and the mother's body, and between self and object.

The effects of early perceptual and sensori-motor development (Sander et al., 1971) may not be limited to these dimensions, but may also be concerned with establishing overall regulatory mechanisms that pertain to the activity of the infant relative to his environment and fundamental to his emerging capacity for adaptive functioning. In this sense, the early action patterns, which are regulated only by reflex schemata, are enlarged upon by the repetition of specific contingencies that arise between various states of the infant and the sequence of caretaking activities. Even in the first days of life, there is the opportunity to establish certain stable patterns in the interaction between infant and caretaker (Sander et al., 1971).

But the path of development is variable, and there are considerable individual differences. Different infants will respond to similar or nearly identical stimulus conditions quite differently. The same developmental transitions may be achieved through different routes as a function of the infant's achieved action patterns, at any given point, and the way the mother responds to the child's activity (Escalona, 1963). In general, the course of development follows an epigenetic sequence, which is marked by the progressive emergence and differentiation of various aspects of the infant's capacity to function and interact. Although general patterns of such sequential development can be described, individual infants vary markedly even within the range of normal developmental potentialities. Pathological deviations from the normal program also increase the spectrum of variability considerably.

A major conceptual difficulty encountered in the assessment of early behavior and its relevance to development arises in connection with our understanding of object-relations at this early phase. Much of the developmental literature takes its lead from object-relations theorists who insist that the infant has a relationship with the mothering object from the very beginning. The difficulty comes in connecting this view with our more evolved and developed notions of object-relationships. As pointed out elsewhere (Meissner, 1979), there can be little doubt that the interaction between mother and child is real. But the question of whether, in the child's mind, there is any differentiation between his own sense of himself and the representation of the object-mother is quite a different matter. Although no observational resources allow us to infer such an intrapsychic distinction in the neonate, it also seems to be a mistake to infer the existence of an intrapsychic relationship on the basis of a real, observed external relationship. An important distinction, therefore, in our discussion is that between object-relatedness, which refers to the real, external, observable relation between mother and infant, and object-relationship, which implies a further stage of intrapsychic development involving the formation of self- and object-representations.

The problem reflects a more general difficulty in psychoanalytic research, namely, the integration of reconstructive data based on information and experience gained from the later context of the analytic situation and direct observational data gained in the study of infant and child behavior. The effort to understand the developmental vicissitudes of the borderline syndromes must ultimately depend on the integration of data from both sources, by way of mutual clarification and refinement.

Any reconstruction of the developmental experience of any given patient on the basis of data gathered from the psychoanalytic or psychotherapeutic situation is fraught with peril and particularly vulnerable to the reconstructive fallacy—that is, the tendency to see prior events as causally related to subsequent outcomes. Ultimately, the view of development as generated within such a perspective must be checked against and integrated with more immediate and direct observations at earlier levels of development. The case has been stated admirably by Settlage (1977):

> Invaluable as it is, the genetic, reconstructive approach has limitations with regard to those aspects of development, particularly infantile development, that are subsequently condensed, telescoped, integrated, synthesized, or transformed so as to be difficult to perceive in the analysis of the older child or adult. The lack of capacity during the preverbal and preoedipal phases for conscious memory and full verbal symbolization tends to preclude the clear representation of earliest psychic experience in the analytic situation, thus seriously handicapping reconstruction of those phases. Psychoanalytically-based empathic observation of interpersonal behavior during this developmental period, along with a study of its determinants, is thus essential to a complete and accurate psychoanalytic understanding of the initial development of object relations and of psychic structure, and to the process of reconstruction in the treatment of disorders whose psychopathology involves these areas of development. (p. 810)

Our concern here is with the early patterns of mental organization by which the infant integrates his experience and comes to organize it into meaningful patterns. Particularly important is the organization of the self and the corresponding self-representations, along with that of the object and object-representations. These patterns are normally integrated during the first three or four years of life and form the basis for relatively stable and enduring mental configurations. In pathological development, however, they assume a relatively rigid and distorted configuration that brings about various fixations at infantile and pathogenic levels of development. We would expect that the failure of the developing infant to acquire or complete any of the developmental tasks at any given level of developmental organization would result in faulty structural configurations that would serve as the basis for various forms of psychopathology.

PHASE-SPECIFIC DEFICITS

One of the critical questions with regard to borderline psychopathology is whether the borderline deficits and the failures of developmental integration can be attributed to a single phase of development or whether they are more usefully regarded as stemming from a number of developmental phases. Perhaps the earliest important contribution to this question came from Margaret Mahler (1971). Following Kernberg's (1967) characterization of borderline psychopathology, Mahler emphasized the characteristics of splitting; the role of separation anxiety; the narcissistic fixations; the condensation of oedipal with preoedipal determinants, particularly unresolved preoedipal aggression; and the severe conflicts in object-relations; she concluded that these characteristics seem to reflect a failure to resolve the developmental tasks of the rapprochement period and the so-called "rapprochement crisis."

The outcome was a somewhat stereotyped unitary view, which linked the more or less caricatured view of the borderline provided by Kernberg (see Chapter 3) with a single preoedipal developmental period from the sequence of separation and individuation, namely, the crucial rapprochement phase. It would have provided a neat package, linking developmental failures and defects with the adult form of psychopathology.

But Mahler was cautious, and perhaps rightly so. She (1972) commented:

> My intention, at first, was to establish in this paper a linking up, in neat detail, of the described substantive issues with specific aspects of borderline phenomena shown by the child and adult patients in the psychoanalytic situation. But I have come to be more and more convinced that there is no "direct line" from the deductive use of borderline phenomena to one or another substantive finding of observational research. (p. 415)

Subsequently, Mahler (Mahler and Kaplan, 1977) seems to move away from a unitary view. She observed:

> In our assessments of the personality organization of narcissistic and borderline child and adult patients, the overriding dominance of one subphase distortion or fixation must not obscure the fact that there are always corrective or pathogenic influences from the other subphases to be considered. (p. 84)

An alternative view would regard the pathological outcome in any given individual as the result of developmental deficiencies and conflicts occurring at multiple developmental levels. The developmental derivatives thus may have some impact on the final pathological outcome, but if particular and major deficits can be traced to the developmental vicissitudes of a given developmental period, it is equally important, in the overall evaluation, to assess the extent to which prior developmental phases may have set the stage and contributed to the pathogenic outcome of a particular later stage as well as to how patterns of subsequent influences come to affect and are modified by the developmental process in later developmental phases. Thus, there is no reason why borderline patients may not manifest significant oedipal level conflicts, just as there is no reason why patients with neurotic disorders may not reflect the effect of significant preoedipal defects.

Thus, a pattern of pathological expression may reflect conflicts and deficits at multiple developmental levels. Dorpat (1979a), for example, cites the case of an obsessive scientist who came to treatment because of his inability to complete scientific papers. The symptom reflected the usual defensive inhibition related to structural conflicts over oedipal aggression and competition, but in addition, the inhibition of initiative also reflected a partial developmental defect at the level of separation-individuation. Such initiative here carried with it the implications of threatening separation and independence from his early caretakers, particularly his mother. Such layering of developmental influences is frequently seen in borderline patients, for whom symptomatic conflict at a more superficial layer may, concurrently, reflect the persistence and influence of underlying structural deficits.

Consequently, although developmental paradigms may be useful in providing a framework of explanation and clinical understanding, a more thorough exploration is needed of the way structural deficits, both in the integration of self and the experience of objects, in the respective developmental stages, are affected. In this respect, Horner (1979) observes:

> Only then can we detect certain defects in the organization and integration of the self in the earliest stages of its evolution, defects that will reveal themselves later on when the thrust of development will be impeded by their existence. This is particularly true of the borderline patient. Because of a defective early organization, the symbiotic partner continues to be needed, as a kind of prosthetic device, if the self is to be kept in any semblance of organization. The awareness of separateness that is inevitable in the separation-individuation process evokes severe separation anxiety with restitutive efforts aimed at eliminating the psychic danger—the danger of dissolution of self. (pp. 8–9)

Consistent with this view, Horner believes that the so-called "rapprochement crisis" (Mahler et al., 1975) is the point in development where the pathology of borderline structural deficits becomes apparent, rather than being the source of origin of these deficits. She views the conceptualization of borderline defects as a result of maternal failures associated primarily with the rapprochement phase as seriously oversimplistic and reductionistic. The borderline failure to resolve the rapprochement crisis, then, can be seen as due to the influence of pre-existing structural deficits that are already in place as the child enters the rapprochement period.

In terms of developmental etiology, disruption of developmental organization and integration can be due to a wide variety of causes, although damage to the organization of the psychic structure is the final outcome. Such causes, and their attendant failures, impinge on the developmental process at any point. Generally, we presume that the earlier the failure in terms of the infant's developmental experience, the more severe the impact on structural integration, and the more malignant the pathology. In terms of the epigenetic perspective, such deficits have their precedents in developmental influences, and their consequent effects on the ensuing developmental resolutions. The achievement of subsequent developmental tasks is inevitably compromised by the residues of unresolved primitive fears, anxieties, and structural impediments.

By the same token, growth does not take place as a unitary process, but rather it emerges progressively along certain developmental lines. The concept of developmental lines was suggested by Anna Freud (1965) to conceptualize the complexities of both normal and pathological development. She commented:

> there are similar lines of development which can be shown to be valid for almost every other area of the individual's personality. In every instance they trace the child's gradual outgrowing of dependent, irrational, id- and object-determined attitudes to an increasing ego mastery of his internal and external world. Such lines—always contributed to from the side of both id and ego development— lead, for example, from the infant's suckling and weaning experiences to the adult's rational rather than emotional attitude to food intake; from cleanliness training enforced on the child by environment pressure to the adult's more or less ingrained and unshakable bladder and bowel control; from the child's sharing possession of his body with his mother to the adolescent's claim for dependence and self-determination in body management; from the young child's egocentric view of the world and his fellow beings to empathy, mutuality, and companionship with his contemporaries; from the first erotic play on his own and his mother's body by way of transitional objects to the toys, games, hobbies, and finally to work, etc.
>
> Whatever level has been reached by any given child in any of these respects represents the results of interaction between drive and ego-superego development and their reaction to environmental influences, i.e., between maturation, adaptation, and structuralization. Far from being theoretical abstractions, developmental lines in the sense here used, are historical realities which, when assembled, convey a convincing picture of an individual child's personal achievements or, on the other hand, of his failures in personality development. (pp. 63–64)

The framework of analysis provided by the concept of developmental lines has subsequently been extended to a systematic evaluation of personality development in childhood (Greenspan et al., 1976), to the assessment of analyzability (Greenspan and Cullander, 1973), and even to the assessment of the analytic process itself (Greenspan and Cullander, 1975). In general, we do not expect to find homogeneity in levels of development among the various segments of the personality. It is not infrequently the case in border-line patients, for example, that we find a marked heterogeneity in developmental attainments, with a high level of development in cognitive, intellectual, social, esthetic, or other skills, along with relatively primitive levels of development in terms of object-relations or self-integration.

An interesting application of the concept of developmental lines in the understanding of developmental levels has been provided by Stolorow and Lachmann (1978). They argue that in the assessment of borderline conditions it is particularly important to distinguish between levels of structural conflict and pathological expressions that are rooted in arrests in ego development. They argue further that each of the defense mechanisms represents an end point of a series of developmental achievements in a developmental line that itself reflects levels of developmental organization. The use of a particular defense, therefore, has important implications for understanding not only related instinctual conflicts, but also determining whether specific developmental tasks were accomplished.

Thus, the conflict-based use of denial can be distinguished from a developmental inability to register and affirm the reality of events. Idealizations based on the developmental inability to register and affirm the real qualities of self or objects are quite distinct from more evolved idealizations that connote a defensive denial of such real qualities of self or objects. By the same token, projection can be viewed as a defense, for example, by which painful or undesirable elements related to the self-representation are translated into terms of object-representations to deal with intrapsychic conflict. The correlative process of introjection can also function in a similar defensive fashion, particularly in dealing with issues of separation or object loss. The defensive function serves to avoid anxiety and other painful affects involved in the instinctual conflict.

The prestages of both projection and introjection can be identified in early developmental phases in which self- and object-representations tend to merge or in which stages of partial self-object differentiation or confusion are at issue. They distinguish, usefully it would appear, between the role of projection, precisely as a defense against structural conflict, and projective identification, as a remnant or regressive revival of an early arrested prestage of defense, reflecting a developmental deficiency in the maintenance of self-object differentiation and boundaries.

Stolorow and Lachmann (1978) also apply the same distinction to Kernberg's analysis of splitting in borderline patients. They argue that in those cases in which contrasting, all-good and all-bad object-images are rigidly attributed to two or more separate external objects, as in the case of split transferences, the operation is most likely one of defensive splitting, to ward off intense ambivalent conflicts. When the alternation of contradictory images occurs relative to the same external object, however, they propose that this can be viewed more reasonably as an arrest in ego development at a stage prior to the integration of opposing representations, and reflects the failure to accomplish this developmental task. They argue, in addition, that these developmental distinctions would seem to play a central role in the assessment of borderline functioning and that they also have important therapeutic implications.

ORIGINS OF BORDERLINE PATHOLOGY
IN THE SEPARATION-INDIVIDUATION PROCESS

The framework of developmental phases provided by Margaret Mahler and her coworkers (Mahler, 1963, 1968; Mahler et al., 1975) is generally used in discussing the evolution of object-relationships and their role in development. It is also a convenient paradigm to assess the specific phase-related deficits that may play a role, to some degree, in the development of forms of borderline psychopathology.

The first developmental phase encompasses the first two or three months of life and constitutes the *autistic phase*. During this stage, awareness of surroundings is limited, except for brief episodes of alert awareness prompted more or less by biological needs in which the infant is in contact with caretaking figures. The developmental task during this period is the initial attachment to the mothering figure. An association may be built up between the mother's face and pleasurable sensations and relief from internal distress. The failure of this developmental stage results in a fixation in which the child makes no move toward attachment to the mothering or caretaking figure, and the pathological outcome is a form of infantile autism (Horner, 1975).

The appearance of social smiling in the second or third months marks the shift to the second phase, the *symbiotic phase*, during which the infant, coming from the predominantly coenesthetic and inner-directed organization of the autistic phase, is increasingly interested in the external world and, particularly, in the perceptual Gestalt provided by the mother. This Gestalt is gradually incorporated into the infant's own emerging body-image and self-representation. Normally a period of increasing interest in the external environment is marked by an increase in eye-to-eye contact and smiling and cooing, as well as increasing curiosity and exploratory activity.

During this phase, the infant becomes dimly aware of the presence of a need-satisfying object. In normal symbiosis, the infant behaves and functions as though he and his mother formed an omnipotent system, a dual unity with a single common boundary (Mahler et al., 1975). The essential feature of such symbiosis is the quasi-hallucinatory fusion with the maternal representation and, particularly, the delusion of the common boundary between these two separate individuals. In instances of severe disruption of individuation and psychotic disorganization, the ego can regress to this primitive delusion in what Mahler describes as the "symbiotic child psychosis." It is within this symbiotic orbit, which involves both physiological and socio-biological dependency on the mother, that the structural differentiation that leads to the formation of a functioning ego takes place.

With optimal mothering, the symbiotic phase is comfortable and secure for both mother and child. Within the security of the symbiotic orbit, early elements of an emerging self-representation are gradually acquired. Mahler (1963) observes:

> Certain action and ministration schemes of the mother, which are evident in the symbiotic phase, seem to be assimilated by the infant. This is an imitation without mental content, a complex individual patterning acquired within the symbiotic community. The patterns are too complex to be regarded as inborn, yet they seem to be irreversibly established at an age at which they could not have been the outcome of ego identifications. (p. 311)

Through good-enough mothering, the mother, at this stage of development, senses and responds to her infant's needs and thus helps create the illusion within him that he is the source of his own nurture. Thus, at this primitive stage the infant can be said to assimilate or internalize the mother's nurturing function.

After several months of intense social interaction, particularly with the mother, the infant enters the process of separation-individuation itself and begins to "hatch" from the symbiotic orbit. This subphase of *differentiation* is characterized by a shift from the illusion of permanent, inner-directed, symbiotic fusion with the mother to a more outward-directed, differentiated, exploratory interest in the external environment. Sometime in the fourth to the sixth month, the infant has a sufficient degree of differentiation between self and object so that he will cry or reach out for the mother when she leaves the room, but he will also develop an intense interest in strangers, frequently making a busy comparison between the mother's and the stranger's face. This interest in the stranger tends to become increasingly negative, leading to a pattern of frowning, fussing, or crying in the presence of strangers around the seventh to the ninth month.

Spitz, (1965) in his early studies of the so-called "eighth-month anxiety," recognized it as a function of the development of sufficient self-object differentiation to allow for an emerging fear of the mother's loss. He concluded that stranger anxiety was a necessary feature of normal development. However, there is considerable variation in its occurrence. When the developmental progression has been positive and has served to establish an adequate foundation in basic trust, and particularly when exposure to other caretaking persons besides the mother has been a feature of early experience, stranger anxiety may be relatively mild (Mahler et al., 1975).

Attachment is a fundamental issue in the formation of the symbiotic bond and the hatching from it. The failure of attachment may have severe implications for the early organization and development of the self. The degree of anxiety or distress experienced by the child is a function of the accessibility and responsiveness of the principal object of attachment. The separation from or loss of the object may be a matter of actual physical separation or it may be the result of the object's emotional absence or withdrawal.

Bowlby (1973) has described a sequence of reactions to separation in children at this early stage. Children who had formed an attachment bond after the age of six months showed a sequence of reactions to separation involving first protest, second despair, and finally detachment. The protesting child screams, cries, and cannot be comforted. This gives way to despair, in which the child is preoccupied with his mother's absence and constantly looks for her return. At the same time, he alternately clings to and rejects his special transitional object—the substitute object of attachment for the missing mother. His feelings toward substitute caretakers are clearly mixed and ambivalent. In the final stage of detachment, the child seems to have settled down and to have accepted the separation, but when the mother returns he may act as though he does not recognize her or will retreat from her in tears. He may turn his affection to a substitute object. The longer the separation, the longer the period of detachment. Even after the detachment is resolved, there is usually a phase of marked ambivalence toward the mother, and behavioral difficulties.

If the separation is prolonged excessively or is repeated too frequently during the first three years of life, Bowlby suggests that the detachment can become indefinitely prolonged. Spitz (1945, 1946), in his studies of anaclitic depression and hospitalism following separation from the mother, observed that children who had had a satisfying relationship with the mother for the first six months experienced a profound depression after separation, accompanied by a severe retardation in developmental parameters. These children would recover from the anaclitic depression after the return of the love object, but if the separation continued beyond five months, there was an increasing deterioration into the more severe and seemingly irreversible condition of hospitalism.

As the symbiotic phase begins to be resolved, the child gradually comes to recognize his dependence on external sources. When the symbiotic phase has been adequate and the pattern of mothering sufficiently responsive and supportive, this dependency maintains its elements of comfort and security. As the child hatches from the symbiotic influence, he is increasingly able to utilize the expanding range of his experience in a way that does not excessively stress or threaten his strivings for self-differentiation and integration. Under such circumstances, the titration of displeasure or discomfort remains minimal, and the infant can formulate an attitude of basic trust relative to what emerges now as the first partial representations of the good object.

But when the mothering experience is not adequate or is inconstant or depriving or reflects, in one or other degree, significant elements of maternal ambivalence, the capacity of the child to synthesize these discordant elements is exceeded, and these elements are synthesized into the emerging experience of a configuration or Gestalt of bad-object–related experiences. As Horner (1975) observed, a merger of self-with-good-object, based on the good-mothering experiences, and a corresponding self-with-bad-object merger, based on unsatisfactory mothering experiences, occur during the symbiotic stage. Such an inherent disparity of experience is not within the capacity of the child's rudimentary ego to harmonize or integrate.

Where the child in the differentiation phase seeks to separate from the symbiotic merger with the bad object, this may reinforce or confirm the merger with the good object, which subsequently becomes the basis for establishing symbiotic relationships with idealized others. This is accomplished by a more or less paranoid view of the now separated and rejected bad object-world. If differentiation takes place from the good object only, there may be a naively idealized view of the external world, together with a tendency to seek symbiotic involvement with bad or hurtful objects. Horner suggests that this vicissitude of early cognitive organization may be a more parsimonious way of understanding the splitting of the object, and derivatively, the self-organization. In this respect, her view differs from the views of Mahler and Kernberg, since the effects of splitting become apparent later in the separation-individuation process, although splitting occurs during the very beginning of separation-individuation, in the phase of symbiotic merger with the ambivalent object. Horner (1975) comments:

> In the symbiotic stage, the mother is experienced as part of the self. Since the experience of both self and other must emerge from this stage through the process of separation and individuation, it is logical to assume that the disturbance of the symbiotic relationship will lay the groundwork for difficulties in the process of separation-individuation. (p. 100)

Thus, the mother who cannot tolerate the child's individuation in the later phase of rapprochement may have found his earlier attempts at self-assertion as, for example, his efforts to feed himself at five months, equally unsatisfactory (Horner, 1979).

The differentiation subphase, then, is marked by a continuing, yet diminishing attachment to the symbiotic union with the mother, and a gradual and emerging differentiation between the self and the mothering object. When the residues of the symbiotic phase persist into the differentiation subphase, they tend to interfere with and contaminate the structural achievements of the subsequent practicing and rapprochement phases.

Mahler and Kaplan's (1977) description of the case of Sy provides a good example. Sy was the victim of his mother's suffocating envelopment and intrusiveness. From his sixth month on, he was caught up in a continual attempt to extricate himself from her engulfing seductiveness by pulling, crawling, and turning away from her insistent embraces. The capacity for locomotion at seventeen months raised the possibility of object loss and precipitated Sy into an intensely stormy and conflicted rapprochement phase. He entered this phase of development without adequate ego preparation for separate functioning, a normal attainment of the practicing subphase. The absence of an effective practicing subphase deprived him of the capacity to modulate the impact of pregenital instinctual drives and also interfered with the development of internal sources of narcissistic satisfaction, which would have been derived from the emergence of autonomous ego functions and the normal aggressive spurt associated with practicing. Sy's symbiotic involvement with his mother was extended up to his twentieth month, at which point he was precipitously launched into the rapprochement phase of separation-individuation with only nominal experience of differentiation and practicing. Evaluating this child's later development, Mahler and Kaplan (1977) comment:

> In his eleventh year, Sy's good basic endowment has allowed him to extricate himself and create distance, analogous to the way he actively pushed, crawled, and turned away from the engulfing mother-child symbiosis—and thereby escaped outright psychosis. Nevertheless, the prolonged symbiosis has cast its shadow over all future subphases of separation-individuation. It continues as the grossly erotic, overly aggressivized, out-of-phase oedipal constellation which has left an indelible stamp on Sy's body representations. (p. 79)

In the last few months of the first year, the next subphase of separation-individuation, namely, the *practicing period*, begins. This is marked by an intense degree of curiosity and interest in exploring the environment, while retaining the mother as a base of security from which the infant can venture out and to which he can return when necessary. The emergence of locomotor capacities, at first crawling and then walking, combine with this burgeoning curiosity to form the basis for the exercise of increasingly independent ego capacities that draw the child away from the maternal orbit. This facilitates the hatching process and propels the toddler into a "love affair with the world" (Mahler, 1972).

It is also a period of increasing awareness of the degree of separation from the mother, and marks the beginnings of the child's individuation out of the representational fusion between mother and self to a more independent and autonomous functional sense of self. Separation brings with it the threat of object loss. Awareness of the mother's absence often induces a low-keyed response at this stage—a sort of mini-anaclitic depression. Mahler et al.

(1975) infer a concentration of the image of the absent mother in an effort to ward off the sense of loss, separation anxiety, and depression. This is also the period, as Winnicott (1953) observed, in which transitional objects develop and transitional phenomena occur, as a consolation to the infant in the face of separation, and as a way of restoring, to a degree, the illusion of union with the mother.

As has been frequently observed, the infant's early relationship with the mother is marked by the capacity of the mother to satisfy the infant's internal needs (Hartmann, 1952; Hoffer, 1952). At the earliest stage of development, the drives and inner need-states are imperative and are dominated by the pleasure principle, such that there is an inherent demand for immediate satisfaction and relief. Anna Freud (1952) has pointed out that these demands have to be modulated and brought under control before the infant develops the capacity to maintain cathexis of the object, even under conditions in which satisfaction is not forthcoming. The development of this capacity allows for an increasing degree of separation from the mother. In her view, it is possible to exchange objects in the very earliest months of life, provided the necessary need-satisfaction is maintained, but by about five months, the degree of specific and focal attachment to the object increases so that any separation from the object may lead to acute distress.

As the relationship with the mother is transformed from one of primary need-satisfaction to one of increasing attachment, the mother image ceases to be associated only with states of need-dependency and with conditions of need-satisfaction; the infant becomes capable of a more consistent and permanent level of libidinal cathexis in which the maternal representation is maintained regardless of need-satisfying conditions (A. Freud, 1953). Although experiences of need-satisfaction lead to the development of a good object-representation, the experience of need-frustration lays the basis for the formation of a bad object-representation. An adequate degree of frustration, along with adequate levels of satisfaction in the relationship with objects, serves to stimulate appropriate degrees of separation. In addition, without a measure of frustration and delay, the stimulus may be lacking for the development of ego-functions and for the increasing differentiation of self and object.

The capacity to discharge aggression against the object may be compromised, which turns aggression against the self. Consequently, where need-satisfaction is inadequate, there may be a premature differentiation of the aggressive drive, resulting in a hypercathexis of perception with aggressive derivatives, premature separation from the object, and excessive formation of frustrating and bad object-representations. The infant's emerging psychic structure, in such instances, may be overburdened with conflict and not allow need-satisfaction and tension discharge to be achieved. This can result in a severe disturbance in the infant's relationship with the mothering object, even in the first six months, and would similarly tend to intensify subsequent separation and stranger anxiety (Rubenfine, 1962).

Particularly during the symbiotic phase, the relationship to the mother is predominantly need-satisfying. The mother is equivalently seen as an extension of the self. As the stage of need-satisfaction progresses, the object is only transiently recognized as, in some degree, separate only at moments of increased need, as when the infant is feeling the pangs of hunger; but when satisfaction of the need occurs, the object again becomes fused and ceases to exist until the need arises once again. In this sense, the need-satisfying function takes precedence, and predominates over the role of the object (Edgcumbe and Burgner, 1972).

The transition out of total need-dependency toward object-constancy is a vital aspect of the "hatching" process that begins separation-individuation out of the symbiotic maternal relationship. An important aspect of this developmental step is the emergence of transitional objects and transitional phenomena, as originally described by Winnicott (1953). As later suggested by Tolpin (1971), the transitional object becomes the vehicle for the gradual process by which certain characteristics and functions originally provided for the child by the external caretaking object become internalized, that is, they are transformed by an emerging internal psychic structure that carries out the same function in the service of maintaining internal homeostasis. For Tolpin (1971), following Kohut, the basis of the process is narcissistic, but in fact, it may have broader and more far-reaching implications.

A significant aspect of this emerging developmental paradigm is that the infant begins to use an object (in Winnicott's sense, to "create" an object), that is, to endow some object in the external world with a similar capacity to that originally experienced in the relationship with the mother. The mother's original role of soothing and quieting the child is transferred to the blanket or the cuddly toy so that it begins to possess the soothing and tension-relieving qualities that were originally the mother's. The child creates such an object usually when he has sufficiently emerged from the symbiotic orbit and begins to perceive the mother as the increasingly separate, but important vehicle for his comfort and relief from distress. The transferral facilitates the child's increasing independence from the mother insofar as, in virtue of his partial replacement of the mother by the soothing, tension-relieving blanket or toy, he has gained a means of calming and soothing himself that does not require the presence or participation of the mother. This developmental progression also shifts the basis of his involvement in the world from relative passivity to increasing activity and control. The dependence and the often addictive attachment to such transitional objects may gradually disappear, as the child develops an increasingly internalized capacity for self-soothing and internal regulation.

The process of separation from the mother is a gradual one that involves a series of minute losses through separation and surrender of symbiotic dependence, through gradual degrees of transitional dependence toward increasing self-dependence and emerging individuality. Tolpin (1971) writes:

> By preserving the mental organization associated with the "good-enough" mother who mediates structure while it is lacking "inside," the blanket eases the stress of transition to object constancy. . . . At the same time, it promotes internalization of the mental structure on which object constancy depends—the inner structure now performs for the self some of the equilibrium-maintaining regulations which depended at first on the need-satisfying object. Circumscribed losses of the mother in her role as need-satisfying (structure-mediating) soother or regulator not only are inevitable and unavoidable during infancy; they are also necessary in optimal doses if mastery of separation from her and individuation of the psyche are to occur. (p. 328)

By the same token, a parallel process of assimilation and internalization of the mother's anxiety-relieving functions also contributes to the elaboration of ego-functions that facilitate internal regulatory capacities and subserve the emerging function of signal anxiety in the service of the organization of appropriate defenses and the preservation of self.

The internalization of these functions proceeds smoothly and effectively in the context of good-enough mothering and an appropriate titration of degrees of frustration-gratification and separation-dependence. The mother's failure to support or facilitate this process can prove traumatic and frustrate developmental objectives, leaving the child excessively dependent, threateningly isolated, or vulnerable to overwhelming and disruptive anxiety.

The practicing phase is also critical for the development of narcissism. In the earlier differentiating phase, the child is often surrounded by admiring and approving adults and he basks in this admiration. These early narcissistic supplies are an important source of the child's narcissistic investment of his own body. This form of narcissistic refueling begins in the symbiotic phase and continues through the differentiation and early practicing subphases. Each phase contributes to the organization of narcissism and its degree of healthy integration or pathological distortion.

But in the practicing subphase, a source of internal narcissistic enhancement is added by means of the child's first autonomous achievements. In different ways and in different degrees, the toddler's self-love, his primitive overvaluation of his accomplishments, and his sense of omnipotence contribute to the infant's burgeoning sense of narcissistic enhancement. When the interaction with the mother is excessively frustrating or rejecting, or when the titration of separation or abandonment is excessive, the child's narcissistic invulnerability may be precociously and precipitously depleted, with consequent traumatic effect (Mahler and Kaplan, 1977).

If the practicing period provides a sense of exhilaration in the exercise of autonomous functions and a complementary feeling of magical omnipotence—what Joffe and Sandler (1965) call the "ideal state of self"— it is invariably followed by a period of retrenchment in which the child's increasing experience of reality impinges on and modifies this ideal state. The practicing phase thus gives way to the rapprochement phase, and the child's sense of narcissistic enhancement gives way to a period of narcissistic vulnerability. The basic issue at this phase of development is whether the child will be able to surrender and modify some of his narcissistic self-investment and omnipotence without suffering an excessive sense of diminution or defeat.

The farther the toddler moves out of the protective maternal orbit, the more readily he begins to learn that there are obstacles in the world that stand in the way of his omnipotent domination. In the face of frustration, pain, and limitation, his need for the protective and powerful mother increases, and his separation anxiety grows apace. Behaviorally, there is an increasing concern with the whereabouts of the mother and a more intense need for the mother to share in each new experience and each new acquisition. The earlier "refueling" of the practicing phase is replaced by a constant seeking of an interaction with the mother, and increasingly as the exploratory range increases, with the mother and other significant adults.

Settlage (1977) has concisely summarized the developmental agenda of the rapprochement phase as follows:

> *In summary*, the main intrapsychic phase-specific developmental tasks of the rapprochement subphase, which also constitute the areas of vulnerability in the rapprochement crisis, are: (1) mastery of the cognitively intensified separation anxiety; (2) affirmation of the sense of basic trust; (3) gradual deflation and relinquishment of the sense of omnipotence experienced in the symbiotic dual unity with the mother; (4) gradual compensation for the deflated sense of omnipotence through development of the child's burgeoning ego capacities and sense of autonomy; (5) a firming up of the core sense of self; (6) establishment of a sense of capability for ego control and modulation of strong libidinal and aggressive urges and affects (e.g., infantile rage); (7) healing the developmentally normal tendency to maintain the relation with the love object by splitting it into a "good" and a "bad" object, thus also healing the corresponding intrapsychic split; and (8) supplanting the splitting defense with repression as the later defensive means of curbing unacceptable affects and impulses toward the love objects. (p. 817)

This catalogue of developmental tasks makes us more acutely aware that the borderline patient experiences failure or compromise in the accomplishment of each and all of these items. Borderlines vary in the degree of severity of the respective failure, in the degree of unresolved contamination from prior developmental phases, and in the extent to which subsequent developmental experience can undo, rework, or compensate for these critical developmental fixations.

As autonomous functions become more elaborated and developed, the interaction occurs at progressively higher levels of functional organization and symbolization. Physical contact is replaced by the use of language and symbolic gesture. Basically, the toddler is confronted with the realization that the world is not his to have on his own terms, but rather that he must increasingly cope with it on his own and without the protective support and intervention of his parents. In the face of these obstacles and frustrations, his sense of omnipotence begins to wither away and he begins to feel small and helpless, becoming increasingly aware of the fragility of his capacities and the limitations of his strength (Mahler, 1972a).

The separation from powerful protecting figures becomes a more critical issue in the rapprochement phase, and the child does what he can to resist it. Increasingly, he comes to realize that the objects of his love and dependence are, in fact, separate individuals, even as he himself has increasingly become a separate individual. The conflictual struggles in which the child involves both parents are very much concerned not only with the stabilization of autonomy and resistance to symbiotic re-engulfment, but also have to do with the child's unwillingness to recognize and tolerate the separateness and individuality of his parents. The threat, then, is not simply that of object loss, but more specifically, it is the loss of object love. The child experiences separation and periods of maternal absence or unavailability as rejections. The separation anxiety reflects an underlying sense of impotence and vulnerability, along with the inherent threats of the child's continuing dependence on powerful, yet separate parents.

The child has to struggle with the conflicting wish for reunion with the love object and the fear of re-engulfment. Any impingement on his recently achieved autonomy is warded-off. The increased negativism and aggression of the anal phase also serve this purpose. Separation may lead to a variety of frustrating, unpleasurable, or even frightening experiences in the interaction with the mother, particularly, that give rise to the experience of a bad object and may become assimilated and internalized as a bad introject. An increased titration of aggressive drives may also come into play and bring about an identification between the child's emerging sense of self and the bad introject. In the rapprochement subphase, this aggression may be unleashed so as to sweep away the good object and any corresponding good sense of self. Thus, in cases when the realization of impotence and helplessness is too sudden or too painful, there may be a too precipitous deflation of the sense of narcissistic omnipotence, which may result in angry outbursts and temper tantrums (Mahler, 1972).

The child's behavior, in such cases, may be motivated by a fear of re-engulfment by the "mother of separation," who has now become dangerous and threatening insofar as she is still experienced as omnipotent, yet as sufficiently separate from the child so that he no longer participates in that omnipotence. In less than optimal development, the ambivalent conflicts of the rapprochement subphase can be seen in rapidly alternating clinging and negativistic behaviors. This can reflect the underlying split of the child's object world into good and bad objects, providing a means by which the good object can be protected against derivatives of the aggressive drive.

The view of Mahler and her coworkers (Mahler, 1972; Mahler and Kaplan, 1977; Mahler et al., 1975; Settlage, 1977), locating the arena of borderline developmental arrest or fixation in the later practicing and rapprochement subphases of separation and individuation, has been extended and elaborated by Masterson (1976), Rinsley (1980a,b, 1981), and Masterson and Rinsley (1975), into a somewhat stereotyped theory of borderline development. In their view, the borderline outcome is the result of a particular mode of interaction between mother and infant during the separation-individuation process. Here the mother relates to the infant so as to reward or to reinforce the child's dependency and to threaten, by withdrawal of libidinal supplies (loss of love, rejection, abandonment), any attempts on the part of the child to move in the direction of increasing aggressiveness, assertiveness, or separation. This process represents a failure to resolve the mother-infant symbiosis and results in the formation of only partly differentiated self- and object-representations and a failure of object-constancy.

This pattern of mother-child interaction represents a failure of "good-enough mothering," and reflects an inability on the part of the mother to perceive and respond to the child in terms of the child's own actual individuality. Rather, the mother's interaction with the child is governed by her own projections onto the child, a process Rinsley (1971) calls depersonification. Rinsley (1980b) describes the process in the following terms:

> Depersonification reflects a breakdown of the otherwise finely tuned mutual cueing and communicative matching between mother and infant that is essential for the latter's healthy development. Rather than traversing the normal course of ego development, the depersonified infant proceeds to develop what Winnicott calls a *false self*; this false self evolves as expression of the child's pathological, pseudocomplementary response, in terms of self-image and later self-identity, to the mother's misperception and mishandling of him; instead of a self-image reflective of increasing separation-individuation vis-à-vis the mother, the child proceeds to develop a self-image based upon the depersonifying mother's projections onto him and responds accordingly. Thus, what emerges as the growing child's self-identity actually reflects a pseudoidentity based upon and developing in relation to the mother's own pseudoidentity. (p. 151)

One important achievement of the rapprochement subphase is the organization of a more or less unified self-system and a corresponding self-representation clearly differentiated from object-representations (Mahler et al., 1975). An important aspect of this self-integration (individuation) and the separation out of the symbiotic maternal orbit is the assimilation of maternal functions into the emerging self. This represents an evolution from the prior assimilation of the omnipotence of the object into a grandiose self-structure that takes place during the narcissistic peak of the practicing period. The assimilation of the rapprochement phase, however, is based, to a considerably greater degree, upon real experiences with a good-enough mother rather than on infantile illusions of omnipotence. The process by which these internalizations are achieved has already been described (see pp. 685–687) in terms of the transmuting internalization of elements of the transitional object experience (Tolpin, 1971).

One way of viewing developmental progression at this stage is to see it in terms of the vicissitudes of the child's relationship to transitional objects. Borderline patients, in general, do not experience this integration of transitional phenomena completely or successfully. The borderline's defective use of transitional objects interferes with a capacity for the integration between inner and outer reality and reflects the exceptional difficulties in separation often experienced by these patients.

Rather than the soothing and nurturing function of the more normal transitional object experience, the borderline experience is contaminated with a higher degree of anxiety, particularly separation anxiety, and the transmuting function of such objects is interfered with so that the structural internalization is also interfered with. For most infants caught in this predicament, transitional objects have little more than temporary comforting capacity. The child's capacity to form and to utilize such transitional objects in the service of optimal psychic growth, effective separation-individuation, and increasing autonomy can be compromised, at times severely (Spiro and Spiro, 1980). Transitional phenomena may not develop or may be subverted regressively into the formation of fetishistic or even autistic objects (Greenacre, 1969; Tustin, 1980).

The critical juncture, one that brings with it the rapprochement crisis, is the switch from the narcissistic enhancement of the practicing period to the vulnerable dependence and impotence of the little child. This switch brings with it the intense anxiety of the threat of the potential loss of the needed object, or more particularly, of the love of that object. Along with this transition comes the sense of shame and helplessness that corresponds to the loss of the illusory perfection. This illusory omnipotence provides the nucleus of the grandiose self, and the transition, endured in the course of rapprochement, to a helpless dependency on a powerful and idealized other, is an important shift in narcissistic positions. These narcissistic configurations, usually embroiled in pathogenic conflicts, are markedly characteristic of borderline patients and serve as the basis for many of their difficulties in the area of object-relations (Horner, 1979).

The borderline patient, by and large, becomes impaled on the horns of this dilemma; in a sense, he is caught between the grandiose self and the idealized object. One device for dealing with the vicissitudes of narcissism and the accompanying intense conflicts over ambivalence is to split both the object and the self. The splitting-off of the good and bad parts of the object is an attempt to preserve the good, idealized object; by the same token, the internal split in the organization of the self, into good and bad parts of the self, is similarly an attempt to preserve the narcissistic omnipotence and grandiosity that has been threatened and partially lost.

As the child emerges into the oedipal configuration, the splitting and the narcissistic alternatives may effect a triangular involvement between the self and a good externalized object and a bad externalized object. The dynamics involved with such split and narcissistically invested objects may play themselves out in the oedipal situation or may be expressed in any triangular involvement in which the good object-image can be projected onto one individual and the bad object-image onto another. As Horner (1979) points out, this gives rise not so much to the classical oedipal configuration involving rivalry and the fear of punishment, but rather has the quality of a masochistic relationship involving a bad persecuting and frustrating object along with an idealized relationship with the good rescuing object. Thus, the preoedipal involvements contaminate the oedipal situation, and both contaminate and impede the oedipal resolution. Although the oedipal involvement may be sexualized, it is essentially based on preoedipal narcissistic investments in objects that act against a truly oedipal constellation and prevent authentically triangular involvements.

Confrontation with intense separation anxiety and depression due to the loss of object or the loss of the love of the object may induce a defensive retreat on the part of the ego to the earlier, more primitive posture of the grandiose self. This represents a retreat from the threats involved in the rapprochement crisis to the safer confines of the earlier practicing period. The resort to such infantile omnipotence short-circuits and inhibits the development of an authentic sense of autonomy and competence. Our borderline patients often alternate between the sense of illusory omnipotence and perfection and feelings of helplessness and shame. Such individuals are extremely vulnerable to the loss of self-esteem when faced with the demands and limitations of reality. For many highly narcissistic borderline patients, particularly those in the more primitive range, the implictions are severe insofar as any inroads on the sense of narcissistic invulnerability carry the threat not only of the loss of self-esteem or humiliation, but also of a dissolution and loss of self (Horner, 1979).

As the developments of the rapprochement phase are gradually realized, the child then passes into the final stage of separation and individuation, the phase in which the consolidation of individuality and the sense of self begin to be effected and the beginnings of emotional object-constancy are established. At this stage, the structuralization and integration of the ego develop significantly, and there are definite signs of internalization of parental demands and ideals reflecting the development of superego precursors.

The development of emotional object-constancy depends on the gradual internalization of a constant, well-integrated, positive inner image of the mother. This constancy involves more than the ability to maintain a representation of the mother in her absence. Such a cognitive acquisition contributes significantly to the child's ability to function separately from the mother, despite the attendant anxiety and discomfort of such a separation. It also involves the unification of partial good and bad aspects of significant objects, particularly the mother, into a whole and integrated representation. The achievement of such an emotional object-constancy implies the adequate resolution of preoedipal ambivalence, the modification of aggressive and hostile drives by fusion with libidinal elements, and the unification of good and bad partial object-representations into a whole object-representation that is both good and bad. Thus, the achievement of object-constancy establishes the basis for greater stability and definition in object-relationships and prepares for the transition to the oedipal configuration.

In the state of object-constancy, the love object continues to be valued and desired, even though it no longer satisfies the subject's needs and even though it may have become an object of hostile or aggressive drives. As Mahler et al. (1975) put it:

> But the constancy of the object implies more than the maintenance of the representation of the absent love object. It also implies the unifying of the "good" and "bad" object into one whole representation. This fosters the fusion of the aggressive and libidinal drives and tempers the hatred for the object when aggression is intense. . . . It has a special bearing on the fate of the aggressive and hostile drives. In the state of object constancy, the love object will not be rejected or exchanged for another if it can no longer provide satisfactions; and in that state, the object is still longed for and not rejected (hated) as unsatisfactory simply because it is absent. (p. 110)

From this review of the process of separation-individuation and its implications for later psychopathology, we would argue, along with others who have studied the process more intensely, that the pathology found within the borderline spectrum reflects the residual stigmata derived from various levels of developmental difficulty experienced during the course of separation-individuation. As conceived in the present study, however, the pathology represented by the borderline spectrum does not derive exclusively from any single phase of this process as, for example, the rapprochement phase, but rather reflects a combination of difficulties arising with varying degrees of emphasis and intensity from all the phases of this developmental process, and in the more severe levels of borderline psychopathology, reflects the residues of unresolved conflicts at an even earlier level, for example, infantile symbiosis.

In epigenetic terms, we need to remind ourselves that in the developmental process critical difficulties may be highlighted in one or other phase, but that these difficulties have their precursors and their sequelae that are also affected by and influence other phases of the developmental process. By the same token, one of the most important sequelae of the distortion of the separation-individuation experience occurs in the oedipal configuration when the residues of distorted object-relations and self-integration, particularly, play themselves out within the oedipal context and thus subvert or distort the oedipal experience and change its effect on personality growth.

These underlying deficits, in turn, can re-emerge to be reprocessed and reintegrated through the second individuation process that occurs in the adolescent period. To the extent that unresolved oedipal issues are reactivated in adolescent recapitulation, the inherent developmental defects and fixations that derive from the inadequate working-through of the separation-individuation process once again plays a determining, inevitably pathogenic role. We have already discussed some of these outcomes in Chapter 8.

DEVELOPMENTAL INFLUENCES: NARCISSISTIC PERSONALITIES VERSUS BORDERLINES

In company with a number of observers (Settlage, 1977; Bursten, 1973, 1978), I have tried to articulate the diagnostic differences between these respective areas of psychopathology in the discussion of their differential diagnosis in Chapter 5. The diagnostic differentiation of these levels of psychopathology, by implication, involves genetic differentiation as well. Although the issues are relatively obscure and poorly understood, it may help, at this juncture, to focus on some of the developmental parameters that may influence the final pathogenic outcome and determine whether or not the adult patient can function at the level of narcissistic personality organization or that of one of the borderline entities. One could presume, from the tenor of our previous discussion, particularly with regard to the vicissitudes of the development of narcissism as they emerge in the separation-individuation process, that both borderline psychopathology and the pathology of the narcissistic personalities have their roots, one way or another, in the separation-individuation process. The questions we need to address, therefore, are to what extent the characteristics of that process impinge differentially to effect these respective patterns of personality organization, and what differential influences may come to play on the developmental process to influence this outcome in one or the other direction.

We have already discussed some aspects of the differential development of narcissistic parameters, particularly in terms of the formation and emergence of pathological archaic narcissistic structures. For example, Horner (1975) argues that the grandiose self is essentially a derivative of the enhanced narcissistic omnipotence of the practicing period, whereas the idealized object derives from the rapprochement phase in which the child is becoming cognizant of the separateness of the mother, and begins to experience a sense of relative helplessness and impotence, himself. The sense of helplessness forces the child into a position of idealizing dependence on the object. This is necessarily seen at this point in development as the retention of qualities of protective omnipotence. A clinging to the practicing phase grandiose self is a development derailment of the normal narcissistic progression toward more realistic narcissistic attainments and integration and the evolution toward a more mature capacity for object love. It is at this juncture that pathological narcissism becomes separated from object love. As Horner (1975) expresses it:

> The assimilation of the power of the object, the mother of symbiosis, into the self-separating-from-object takes place during the practicing period after the first level of differentiation of self from object. The self-object representation, or schema, becomes differentiated in a distorted manner, with the power of the object "adhering" to the self. With this faulty differentiation the grandiose self as a pathological structure comes into being. (p. 103)

In fact, the residues of both the grandiose self and the idealized objects are found throughout the spectrum of borderline and narcissistic disorders. The level of pathological organization in these entities is not clear in terms of these pathological narcissistic organizations. However, there are several discriminating factors. Within the borderline spectrum, these archaic narcissistic residues are often found to operate in an alternating or oscillating pattern, which is much more pronounced than is usually found in narcissistic personalities. The narcissistic personality will generally hold to one or other of these narcissistic positions, integrate a sense of self, and maintain a relative degree of self-cohesion and stability in terms of one or the other of these pathological configurations.

In the borderline, however, shifts from the adherence to the posture of the grandiose self, with its elements of self-enhancement, specialness, entitlement, and even grandiosity, to the idealizing posture in which the object is seen as omnipotent, perfect, and otherwise idealized, are more likely to occur. In the shift to the idealizing posture, the patient's narcissism is secured by attachment to the idealized object; in the former instance, the inherent narcissism of the grandiose self preserves a tenuous narcissistic equilibrium. In both narcissistic and borderline personalities, either posture tends to carry with it its correlative opposite, which affects the individual's relationship to important objects. When the grandiose self is operative, the object is correspondingly devalued and diminished in importance; when the idealizing configuration is at work, the object is enhanced and highly valued, while the self is correspondingly devalued and depleted.

Although this dynamic configuration plays itself out at the level of narcissistic personality organization, its intensity and disruptive power is even more expressive and dramatic in the functioning of borderline personalities. The more primitive the organization of the borderline personality, the more extreme, dramatic, and pervasive are these patterns. At the further reaches of a lower-order borderline psychopathology, which approaches the psychotic, these extremes can reach almost psychotic proportions; the grandiosity verges on psychotic delusional grandiosity, and the idealization produces a corresponding state of utter humiliation, degradation, narcissistic depletion, and emptiness that verges on the delusional and usually is accompanied by a dissolution or a loss of a sense of self.

Undoubtedly, the vicissitudes of separation-individuation differentially influence these respective personality configurations strongly. Some of the possible areas of differential impact have been suggested by Settlage (1977). He comments:

> The distinction between narcissistic and borderline disorders in terms of differences in their specific determinants and psychopathologies has not yet been adequately drawn. As one possibility, these differences may prove to be due to a difference in the timing of traumatic experience in the developmental sequence. The generally-held clinical impression that borderline disorders are more severe than narcissistic disorders may be accounted for by a developmentally earlier, and therefore more devastating, trauma in the borderline disorder. A second possibility is that the difference between these two conditions will be explained by the degree of traumatic impact and the extremity of defensive response. And thirdly, the difference may come to be understood in terms of the area of the personality involved in developmental arrest and pathologic formation, for example, involvement of the sense of self and identity as these can be distinguished from ego capacities and functions per se. (pp. 810–811)

An important variable in this process is the parental matrix within which the developmental process takes place. Modell (1980), for example, has tried to pinpoint some of these differences in the familial environment. His attempt to understand some of the differences between narcissistic and borderline development overlaps with the present consideration, but with some diagnostic differences. Modell describes narcissistic personalities in terms of the affective isolation and narcissistic self-sufficiency that would bring them into a near congruence with our description of schizoid personalities. Similarly, his description of borderline personalities, in terms of their needy, clinging, intense, and distorting involvement with the therapist, would bring them more into line with the description (see Chapter 7) of the hysterical continuum within the borderline spectrum as defined here, particularly the lower-order forms.

Nonetheless, the observations are relevant. Modell observes that in the development of narcissistic personalities one of the parents is characteristically found to be emotionally absent, or distant and unrelated, whereas the other is found to be overinvolved and intrusive. These intrusions often seem to override the child's emerging need for autonomy and separateness and imply a lack of sensitivity or responsiveness to the child's inner needs and individuality. In some cases, phases of emotional absence alternate with intense intrusiveness on the part of one and the same parent. It can easily be seen that such parental behavior can force the inherent dimensions of the separation-individuation process in one or the other direction, toward excessive separation or toward excessive dependence, and thus can distort and impair the normal developmental progression of this phase.

Consequently, Modell argues that the narcissistic-schizoid patient seems to have achieved a precocious closure with respect to his involvement with significant objects, whereas the borderline patient seems to remain relatively open. The premature and fragile closure of the schizoid contrasts dramatically with the intense affect hunger and need for a sustaining object so often seen in more open and hysterical presentations of the borderline condition. Modell (1980) comments:

> We believe, along with Winnicott, that the borderline state may result from a failure of the maternal environment in the first or second years of life and that this relative failure of an object relationship results in the miscarriage of the normal process of identification, a failure to take something in, leading to a relative absence of structuralization. The environmental disturbances in the borderline case may be more massive and gross as compared to the subtle disturbances in the holding environment described in the narcissistic character. In contrast to the borderline patient, something *is* taken in by the narcissistic character. In our patients' lives, in contrast to the borderline, there was a parent who was intensively and intrusively involved. (p. 375)

Much may depend on the quality of the mother-child interaction and, particularly, the set of psychological attitudes the mother brings to that interaction. Kernberg (1977) postulates that the mother-child interaction in both narcissistic and borderline cases is essentially pathogenic and double-binding, similar to the same pattern of double-binding interaction found in the genesis of schizophrenia (Bateson et al., 1956). In this context, the mother of the narcissistic personality may reinforce the child's developmental progression in separation and individuation, but under the condition that that development take place exclusively in relationship to herself in terms that fulfill her inner need for narcissistic enhancement. The child's emerging infantile grandiosity would tend then to fixate at a level in which achievements are still connected with the partial fusion of self- and object-images and in which the child's growing autonomy and competence cannot be disengaged from the admiring involvement with the mother's narcissistic input (Rinsley, 1980a).

Along this same line, Masterson and Rinsley have moved in the direction of identifying the differential impact of various mothering patterns. They describe mothers of schizophrenic children, for example, as finding little or no gratification in the experience of motherhood or in mothering activities (Rinsley, 1980b). This experience is contaminated by an initial perplexity, and a view of the newborn infant as confusing, strange, even dangerous, and persecutory is present from very nearly the beginning of their experience with the child. By contrast, the mother of the borderline can experience gratification and pleasure in the infant's dependency during most of the first year of life; but as the child becomes increasingly separate and individuated, these mothers experience increasing anxiety, frustration, and finally hostility toward the individuating infant.

Rinsley (1980b) describes several patterns of mother-child interaction in which the mother's interaction with the child is discolored by her own internal psychological needs and the projections she brings to the interaction. These patterns of "depersonification" take the following forms:

> In the psychotic and severe borderline patterns (lower-order borderline pathology) the child may be perceived as:
> (1) an inanimate object: the child is perceived and dealt with as though it were a thing rather than another human being. The possibilities here include dealing with the child as if it were a doll, a toy, some sort of machine (the influencing machine), or even a robot, an android, and even a clone.
> (2) a part of or an excretion of one's own body: here the child is experienced as an extension of the parent's own body-self, which may be particularized in terms of specific body organs or organ systems. This might include eyes or ears, muscular apparatus, genital apparatus, or even excretory products and secretions.
> (3) a subhuman animal or monster: the child is perceived in an illusory fashion as if it were a pet animal, or even a dangerous animal or fictional being like a wolf, vampire, zombie, etc. In such cases, the child clearly becomes the bearer of the paternal projection of the parent's evil, hostile and destructive sense of himself as organized around an aggressive introject.

(4) non-existent: an extreme pattern but not infrequently found in postpartum psychotic reactions as a form of negative hallucination. It reflects the parent's need to deny the existence of the child and can take the form of not only equivalent abandonment and neglect, but may be more subtly expressed, even at later phases of development, in terms of the implicit message that the child's existence is an offense to the parents, or that it would be better if he did not exist and were in fact dead.

In cases of less severe borderline pathology (higher-order borderlines) and relatively and narcissistic personalities, the following patterns are found: the child is perceived and experienced as:

(1) a parental surrogate figure: in this instance the child becomes invested with a parental conscience or is looked to by the parent as a powerful figure who can provide guidance, control and limits for the parent. This reversal of roles reflects a re-externalization through projection of poorly integrated and pathogenic introjects within the parent.

(2) a spouse: in this instance the parent-child relationship is sexualized and becomes pervertedly seductive and incestuous.

(3) a sibling: in this context the child is experienced as a brother or sister and this distortion carries with it the features of sibling rivalry and competition, which often can be sadistic and destructive.

(4) an endlessly infantile or dependent baby: in contrast to previous patterns, which reflect the distortion of the parent-child relationship in the direction of seeing the child as more capable, responsible and adult than he really is, this pattern reflects the parent's need to infantilize the child and to keep him from growing up and achieving greater levels of separateness and independence.

One could undoubtedly articulate other meaningful patterns of interaction with a possible pathogenic outcome. But it should be noted that, in all these instances, what is occurring is a pathogenic projection on the part of the parent, which impinges on the child and forces the child into a corresponding pattern of behavior in response to the implicit parental need. Accompanying the child's adaptation in behavioral terms, there must take place significant internalizations, specifically introjections, that assimilate and internalize the often-implicit and unexpressed dimensions of the parental expectations and projective distortions. Thus, the patterns of parental projection and infantile introjection may powerfully influence the patterns of separation-individuation and the extent to which the child can internalize positive and constructive elements that become the building blocks of an emerging, healthy, functional, and adaptive personality structure (Meissner, to be published).

Consequently, we would have to regard the nature of the parent-child interaction and the quality of parental projections as they impinge on borderline development as being considerably more severe, more pathogenic, and more disruptive of the process of separation-individuation and as creating greater and more disruptive impediments to the integration of the self and the achievement of object-constancy than would be the case in narcissistic development. The patterns of interaction in narcissistic development allow for sufficient integration of a cohesive sense of self and for the development of relatively autonomous functioning, but these developments seem to take place in a context of interaction that does not allow the archaic narcissistic issues to emerge and to be resolved. We would argue that it is specifically the narcissistic aspects of the parent-child interaction that fix the developmental process in terms of these issues, although the interaction is not sufficiently pathogenic in other respects to interfere with other emerging patterns of development.

Chapter 13

The Role of
Family Dynamics

Development does not take place in a vacuum, nor does it take place in relation to a single caretaker. Much of the developmental literature sounds as though the early development of the child was a matter of his interaction with the mother—to the exclusion of other influences. This is particularly the case in regard to descriptions and analyses of the child's developmental experience in the earliest phases of development up through the end of the separation-individuation process. When the child enters the oedipal period, the father is then added to the cast of characters.

Common sense suggests that this is not at all the case. Development takes place within a family context—from the very beginning. Separation and individuation evolve within a matrix of family emotional relationships that not only shape the course of development, but are also powerfully impacted by the developmental process. Our task is to bring this broader familial context into focus as it comes to bear on borderline and narcissistic development and as it interacts with developmental vicissitudes. This chapter, therefore, complements the preceding chapter on development—they are two sides of a coin.

When two individuals meet, fall in love, and decide to marry, they enter into a process of establishing and defining an interpersonal dyadic relationship that will have certain specifiable and enduring characteristics. In entering into this process, each of the individuals brings a heritage that characterizes his or her unique psychological development so that each contributes to the composition of the marital dyad, in respective and proportional ways, elements of his or her own inner psychic constitution. The chemistry of composition will involve a substantially different quality of dyadic interaction depending on the composite elements that are brought to it. The interaction that takes place between two relatively defined and securely differentiated and individuated selves has a quite different quality and a quite different implication from the interaction between two relatively un-differentiated selves.

The relative success the marital partners experience and the manner in which these developmental tasks are approached and accomplished are determined, to a large extent, by the residues of internalized objects and the organization of introjects that form the core of the sense of their selves and contribute, in significant ways, to the integration of their respective identities. The extent to which spouses are unsuccessful in merging their individual identities into a constructive and productive shared marital experience depends, in important ways, on the extent to which that experience is contaminated by pathogenic introjects they each may bring to it.

INDIVIDUAL PERSONALITY DEVELOPMENT

The development of the human personality is a complex process which follows a sequence of phases. The process and its vicissitudes have been described in considerable detail in the work of Margaret Mahler (Mahler et al., 1975). The infant begins life in a state of symbiotic unity with the significant mothering figure, and through a progression of developmental steps, gradually is able to separate himself from this symbiotic dependency and to establish an independent, relatively autonomous separate psychic existence. The successful negotiation of this process of separation and individuation leads in the direction of a progressively more differentiated and internally integrated organization of the sense of self and the gradual establishment of an identity that reflects the unique psychological organization of that growing individual and provides the bulwark for the working-through and successful resolution of developmental crises and life's inevitable complexities and conflicts.

The successful accomplishment of this developmental sequence has been specified and discussed by psychoanalytic thinkers in a variety of terms. Successful outcome depends on the establishment of libidinal object-constancy, which implies not merely the capacity for relationship, but more specifically, the maintenance of attachment to and regard for the object through all the vicissitudes of affective change—in the face of gratifications, frustrations, libidinal wishes, aggressive assaults, disappointments, and disillusionments. It also implies the capacity to delay gratification, to tolerate frustration, and to enjoy the capacity for ego-functioning.

In more contemporary terms, the successful outcome of separation and individuation leads to the establishment of a coherent and cohesive sense of self, which is the basis for a sense of continuity and sameness within one's own experience of one's own inner psychic processes. By the same token, self-cohesion provides the basis by which one not only achieves initially, but is also able to firmly establish, and maintain, a sense of difference and of separation between self and others. One of the marks of a mature personality is the capacity to tolerate separateness and differentness of important, emotionally involved objects. We have come to recognize all of these elements as contributing to and sustaining a mature sense of personal identity and personality integration. It is known from experience that the successful negotiation of this complex developmental sequence is fraught with peril. Very few are able to negotiate it successfully, and most of us settle for a more or less successful or unsuccessful developmental career. Some, indeed, fail in this process quite miserably.

We can ask ourselves at this juncture what the implications of the relatively successful or unsuccessful achievement of a sense of identity may be for the functioning of the individual personality, as well as for his involvement in the family in which he grows up. The failure to achieve a differentiated sense of identity means that the developing individual remains intensely emotionally attached to his family. All his energy and emotional concern is focused on the welfare and well-being of his parents and family rather than on his own well-being. Because of his dependence on and attachment to his family, he does not have an individuated sense of self that is separate and independent from them. To the extent that this differentiation fails, he implies that he cannot exist without his parents, since his own existence and well-being are so intimately tied up with theirs.

This attachment and the conflicts related to it reach a crisis in adolescence when the child is caught up in the dilemma of opposing developmental pressures and infantile attachments. He cannot differentiate or separate his own sense of self from that of his parents, nor is he able to direct in any meaningful way his energies toward the development of his own life and interests and to meeting the demands of the environment. Caught in this wrenching and tormenting conflict, these children either keep themselves in a position of more or less infantile dependence or resolve the dilemma by denying their dependency and rebelliously adopting a facade of exaggerated adequacy and independence. Even when such children violently rebel or run away from home, they have not successfully resolved the issues of differentiation and detachment from their families, but rather carry the inner dependency and the related conflicts with them.

The regressive disorganization and subsequent reorganization of the adolescent ego requires a facilitating family environment for its accomplishment. The capacity of family members, both individually and as a unit, to provide an emotional context that facilitates the adolescent's integration of divergent and conflicting views of himself into a consolidated identity is impeded by the operation of shared unconscious fantasies within the family system (E. Shapiro, 1978). The borderline adolescent does not receive the necessary support from his family system to allow him to accomplish these phase-appropriate developmental tasks. Rather, the onset of adolescence provokes a response characterized by increased levels of anxiety and the need to counter any change in the relationship between the emerging adolescent and his parents.

The adolescent's progressive individuation, therefore, elicits characteristic behaviors in the parents that both distort their perceptions of him and powerfully influence their responses to him. In this view, the adolescent developmental spurt provokes a regressive reaction in the family system, which elicits defensive parental behavior that reflects the mobilization of underlying unconscious fantasies regarding the child (R. Shapiro, 1979). In such regressive phases, both the characteristics of the adolescent's behavior and of the parents' responses to him tend to repeat the parent-child interactions of earlier periods in the child's developmental history (E. Shapiro, 1982).

Borderline adolescents who have an impoverished or deficient identity never really develop their own values or beliefs. Rather, they adopt the values derived from their immediate family or adapt themselves to the strengths they find in other people and thus come to operate with a borrowed identity. The personality organization takes on the "as-if" quality so frequently found in borderline patients. Similar phenomena can be recognized in a variety of character pathologies as reflecting the relative failure of effective internalizations (Meissner, 1974b, 1980a). Not infrequently, such individuals become excessively involved and often fanatical in adherence to causes, beliefs, leaders, ideologies—anything that provides a sense of stability and direction for their faltering, fragile identity.

The most severe cases of lack of differentiation are, of course, psychotic. In psychotic patients, we find little or no motivation toward establishing their own individuality or identity or of moving ahead with a life that is their own, independent of their parents or their families. The schizophrenic child is one who has failed in the process of growing away from and separating from his parents in order to establish his own individuality. The individual with a poor sense of identity tends to accept the views of others blindly, or works at attributing views to them, which he then feels he must submit to.

It is equally true that the stance of rebellious opposition reflects the defectiveness of identity just as much as a stance of compliance. The rebel can only define his faulty identity in terms of opposition to the other, and he can only take that stand after the other has made his position known. In fact, however, the rebel has no greater autonomy or independence than his compliant and submissive peer, but rather presents a facade of adequacy and independence. Such individuals, on the surface, may appear to have clear values, strong beliefs and a well-defined sense of identity, but their beliefs are often rigid, biased, and dogmatic. They cannot change their position easily, nor can they allow themselves to listen to alternate or different points of view. They are so caught up in defending their own views that they cannot hear what anyone else is saying; their sense of identity is so fragile and embattled that they cannot afford to open themselves up to the views of others.

When their sense of identity is poorly developed, these individuals are constantly in need of praise and have a poor tolerance for criticism. They constantly look to others to build up their fragile sense of self-esteem and take any criticism as rejection or a hostile assault. The person with a mature sense of identity can take it or leave it, can accept praise, with circumspection and perspective, and can tolerate criticism and even benefit from it. He does not depend on either praise or blame to maintain his own inner self-regard. The person with a poor self, however, is hurt, demoralized, and depleted by any rejection or criticism. The major goal of their lives seems to be being liked by others or being accepted by them. The more intensely they seek to please others and gain acceptance from them, the more any rejection is regarded as a catastrophe. Such individuals who orient their motivation around being the way others in their lives want them to be, or toward pleasing those others, is precisely the one who feels angry or resentfully hurt in the face of failure to gain such approval and who will turn to the willful hurting of others in retaliation. The more maturely individuated personality with a secure sense of self is not concerned about such rejection or whether or not he is loved and approved. Others are important and valued in his life experience, but his life-course and his attitudes toward himself are not determined by the attitudes of those others.

One of the most important features of the functioning of the mature and individuated personality is the fact that his emotional functioning tends to be contained within the boundaries of his own self. He is not only able to maintain his own emotional functioning within his own boundaries, but is also able to buffer himself against the hurts, pain, and suffering of others around him. Conversely, one of the most striking features of families composed of poorly differentiated individuals is the extent to which an emotional disruption in one family member plays upon the emotional functioning of other family members. If there is an emotional upheaval, there tends to be a communication of emotion that influences the functioning and autonomy of every involved family member. The communication of emotion in such family systems is accompanied by and partially governed by shared unconscious fantasies and unconscious emotional assumptions that relate to unresolved instinctual needs and defenses that characterize the family system and the interactions that take place within it. Within the family group, these shared fantasies can be acted out by the respective members who are assigned roles and functions in an ongoing unconscious family drama (Zinner and R. Shapiro, 1974). The individual who achieves a more consolidated sense of identity can live within the field of overflowing emotions, yet maintain his own sense of individuality, separateness, and identity. This particular feature of the integrated personality, and the relative inability of less differentiated personalities to contain the flow and communication of feeling, is of the utmost importance in understanding the dynamics of family systems. We shall return to this point later in our discussion.

Consequently, a crucial issue in such family systems is the role of separation and individuation, along with their correlative elements of autonomy and dependence. There must be a capacity in the mother both to tolerate this separation and withdrawal on the part of the child, as well as the capacity to acknowledge, accept, and respond to the child's emerging individuality in meaningful and supportive ways. Where this process fails, whether it be on account of the difficulties on the part of the child—excessive infantile dependence or clinging, fear of separation with its inherent loss and risk, excessive anxiety in pulling away from the protective symbiotic orbit— or from the side of the mother—her excessive anxiety or vulnerability in the loss of symbiotic closeness, her overprotectiveness, or her excessive rejecting and thrusting away of the child's dependence—an imbalance is introduced into the process through which the child should separate and gradually individuate himself.

The process of introjection is then caught up in the vicissitudes of drives and defensive needs, so that, let us say because of maternal overprotectiveness or rejection, in order to preserve a sense of security in facing the risks of separation, the child must carry with him more than he needs of the residues of symbiotic attachment. What he takes in, then, from the mother is excessively colored by infantile dependence on or defenses against the attachment, excessively colored with infantile narcissistic needs and its attendant vicissitudes, whether of narcissistic grandiosity or devaluation or narcissistic rage; the attachment thus becomes contaminated by the intense ambivalence of the tension between the need for increasing autonomy and independence and the impediment of continuing dependence, the failure to achieve a sense of differentiated self.

One result of these developmental vicissitudes is that there is a failure to mobilize positive, constructive, relatively autonomous and differentiating forms of identification, which would allow the child to establish a sense of inner cohesiveness and of adequate differentiation from the important objects of his dependency. Rather, the child's emerging sense of self is organized around the pathogenic introjects with their embedded residues of narcissistic need, defensive conflict, infantile dependence, and associated conflicts. These introjects then contribute to a sense of inadequacy or a reactive hyperadequacy, the related ambivalence-embedded conflicts that reflect themselves in the polarities of victimization and aggression, and along with these, the failures of differentiation of self and of the stabilization of inner structures and their related functions (both of ego and superego) that ultimately compromise adult functioning and impede establishing and maintaining a secure sense of identity.

In such cases, there is an involvement with and a dependent attachment to an object, but the relationship to the object is not predicated on the basis of one independent and differentiated and relatively autonomous self relating to another independent differentiated and autonomous self. Rather, because of the lack of differentiation, there is an element of unintegrated and relatively primitive and unstructured emotional energy that permeates the organization of the self, yet is not contained within, differentiated, and integrated with the structure of the self, but rather diffuses beyond it, in a sense, to contaminate the attachment in an uncontrolled, undisciplined, unorganized, and relatively primary process manner. Thus, the object-relationships of such individuals tend to be perfused, in varying degrees, with this kind of primitive psychic energy, which is communicated in subtle and predominantly unconscious ways within the object-relationship and which comes to affect the functioning and responsiveness of the object as well as the operations of the subject.

A second important point must be made in regard to the functioning of such poorly differentiated selves. To the extent that the pathogenic introjects form the core of the self, there is a high propensity for projection, particularly into significant object-relationships. In terms of the organization of the paranoid process (Meissner, 1978), the projections represent externalized displacements of aspects of the pathogenic organization of the self, usually deriving from the repressed or split-off dimensions of the introjective configuration, and are then attributed to external objects and result in the coloring, distorting, modifying, and influencing of the character and quality of object-relationships.

THE MARITAL RELATIONSHIP

When two individuals decide to marry and form a family, their complementary and neurotic needs interact. One view of this complex emotional interaction is that there is a tendency for partners of relatively equivalent degrees of immaturity and self-differentiation to be attracted to each other. This phenomenon has not been well documented or studied, but it has a certain clinical validity. The tendency for marital partners to be operating at equivalent levels of immaturity or to manifest similar degrees of lack of self-differentiation is sufficiently general to put us on guard; when we find signs of such pathology in one marital partner, we keep an eye open for indications of a similar level of personality organization in the other partner.

In reporting on the results of early studies of family dynamics at the NIMH, Bowen (1960, 1961) remarks that clinical experience seems to suggest that individuals tend to choose marital partners who have achieved an equivalent level of immaturity, but who have adopted opposite patterns of defensive organization. In the schizophrenic families he studied, both marital partners appeared to be equally immature, but their relationships tended to fall into reciprocal patterns of overadequacy and inadequacy. Consequently, the hypothesis of complementarity of needs in marital partners seems to concern not only the type of need, but also the level of intensity and developmental immaturity of the need. These complementary patterns have also been related to the need of each marital partner to choose an object who will complement and reinforce unconscious assumptions and fantasies (Dicks, 1963; Zinner and R. Shapiro, 1972). The perception of one prospective marital partner of the other prior to marriage seems to reflect the operation of these needs, so that the respective perceptions are governed by projections reflecting the operation of these needs in the introjective economy. When Bowen (1960) asked about conscious reasons for choice of mate, the partners replied that they admired and were attracted to qualities in the other that reflected their respective facades of overadequacy. These qualities are idealized and seem to fit the narcissistic-needs one responds to the other. The idealization reflects an idealizing projection by which elements of the ego-ideal become translated into object qualities.

Among the significant developmental tasks of marriage, there is the necessity of establishing and maintaining a new level of object-relationship. If the initial engagement in the love relationship is significantly determined by the underlying needs and the seeking of complementarity in the love object, the progression in the development of the marital relationship must lead beyond the level of need-gratification to a point where the relationship is based less on the satisfaction of such needs than on a reciprocal and mutually gratifying basis of object love. Rapoport (1963) regards the degree to which there is a shift from self-orientation to mutuality as a measure of the extent to which the essential tasks of the engagement period, both for men and women, have been accomplished. The normal postadolescent young adult has generally reached a point in the development of his object-relations where he has grown out of the infantile level of need-satisfaction to the point of being able to recognize, acknowledge, and respond to the needs of others. The marriage contract, however, makes him more responsible for maintaining the relative independence of his own needs and for responding to the needs of the marriage partner than he has ever been in any other time of his life, or in any other relationship.

The need for marital partners to disengage themselves from old attachments and relationships that may interfere with the marital commitment introduces a new cycle of psychological separation, particularly from parental attachments. The developmental course itself, from the earliest stages of separation-individuation, involves repeated and progressive separations— perhaps the most critical and most significant, in terms of their impact of personality organization, being those that take place in the resolution of oedipal attachments and at adolescence. Entering into the marital relationship calls for a new phase in the process of the ultimate separation from parental figures, although in some basic sense that separation is never complete or total.

But this new phase of separation is an inevitable consequence of the need to establish a new, permanent relationship with a nonincestuous object, a relationship that carries with it its own distinctive qualities of intimacy and dependence. The ultimate question for the resolution of this crisis is whether or not this separation can be achieved and an intimate involvement in the new relationship established without the sacrifice of hard-won individuation. The success of previous phases of separation and individuation sets the stage and determines the quality of the resolution of this new separation. To the extent that a relatively autonomous and individuated sense of self has already been established, the capacity is inherently available for entering the new relationship and maintaining that individuation intact. Where separation has been less than successful, so that the individuation and differentiation of self remains fragile and susceptible to regressive pulls, the entrance into a new relationship will carry with it the residues of old attachments and will introduce into the new relationship the unresolved residues that are carried over from old relationships. This means that the separation vicissitudes are not resolved and the level of individuation attained in the new relationship will correspond to and reflect the level of individuation characteristic of those older involvements.

As a result of these patterns of interaction, the new relationship can be contaminated by the effects of the pathogenic introjects inherent in the personality organization of each partner, and their intermeshing. If the personalities that enter the marital relationship are relatively individuated and differentiated, the potentiality exists, as we have suggested, for positive and constructive identifications that enhance and enrich the personality structure of each partner. If the personalities are dominated by pathogenic configurations, however, the intermeshing internalizations in such a couple will take place in terms of the organization of such pathological introjects, as we have already suggested.

What, then, is the quality of the interpersonal experience when it is based on such pathogenic introjects or the correlatively poorly differentiated sense of self? The poorly defined self establishes a relationship of dependence upon the other that tends to have a life or death quality. It is as though life and existence depend on the attachment to the important other. Often this attachment has a quality of hostile dependence, the "can't live with you; can't live without you" syndrome, which is so familiar to clinicians. The most intense form of such a relationship is found in the symbiotic relationship of mother and child, but is often seen in its most pathological form in the symbiotic relatedness of a schizophrenic child to a symbiotically involved parent, who is usually the mother. But the same phenomenon can be observed in relatively less intense and mitigated forms whenever there is a defect in the integration or differentiation of the self. It is a characteristic of borderline families as well.

As the person with a well-differentiated and individuated identity enters into a relationship as close and intimately interdependent as the marital relationship, he or she is able to enter into, share, and participate freely in the emotional life that takes place between and around the marital partners. The less the degree of individuation or of differentiation of self, however, the more emotion tends to spill over and is communicated to the other member of the dyad in a way that influences the functioning of the other member. Within this complex of implicit and relatively unconscious emotional influences, a pattern develops, in which one of the partners begins to function with a facade of exaggerated strength and assertion, while the other partner shifts to a position of compliance, submissiveness, and giving-in to the influence and domination of the more adequate partner. Within this emotional matrix, a phenomenological shift takes place, in which one partner seems to attain a degree of hyperadequacy and the confirming of a pseudo-identity, while the other partner seems to lose identity and to become a relative nonentity. One seems to gain "self" at the expense of the other.

This pattern can be quite pathogenic. Lidz and his coworkers (1965), for example, have described the effects of this dynamic and skewed marital relationships. There are also a significant number of marriages in which neither partner will "give in" to the pressure of this dynamic process, however, and the result is a constantly conflictual and divisive marital relationship—the schismatic marriage. When this kind of unexplicit and unconscious emotional communication takes place, the ready spilling over of feelings between the partners and the susceptibility one feels to the level of expressed or unexpressed feelings in the other prevents communication and the sharing of true feelings. The greater the lack of differentiation in the partners, the greater the tendency of each to react to the other with feelings of "hurt" and despair, the more true communication is inhibited, and the greater the degree of isolation the partners feel. In such a communicative and emotionally embedded context, interchange of feelings is dominated by processes of projection and by the pervasive confusion of fact and feelings.

When identities are more stable and defined, strong emotion can be experienced without a sense of a flooding of the self or of peril to the sense of identity. Situations of intense emotional involvement are inherently difficult for individuals with poor individuation. They tend to avoid such emotional situations by forms of distancing or schizoid withdrawal or by a relative diffusion of a sense of identity, which may result in depersonalization phcnomcna or overwhelming anxiety. The well-differentiated identity, on the other hand, can operate relatively comfortably in situations of intense emotional involvement with the confidence that such involvement does not impair their ability to remain in contact with reality and to discern objectively that reality over against the fantasies and feelings that may be stirred up by the emotional involvement.

They can allow themselves, therefore, to be in contact with human misery and suffering without being emotionally overwhelmed by it or over-identifying themselves with the suffering of the other. Consequently, they can freely and spontaneously respond in supportive and helpful ways to such suffering of the other. The poorly differentiated individual, however, is easily subject to feelings of pity, remorse, guilt, and shame in the face of emotional turmoil or distress in a significant other. The impulses to help the suffering one come out of feelings of pity or guilt, so that the individual's capacity to address his helping efforts to the reality of actual needs is correspondingly compromised.

On the other hand, individuals with a poorly defined self remain extremely vulnerable to such sympathetic and pitying feelings coming from others in their environment. In the face of such pity and guilt-engendered sympathy, their needs to be taken care of and to resort to modalities of infantile dependence actually become more intense so that they tend to move to a position of increasing inferiority and inadequacy as a way of eliciting greater help and caretaking from others and as a way of intensifying the feelings of pity and guilt. The demands for care and help can increase to the point of exasperation and exhaustion of the resources of the helper. The helper inevitably becomes motivated by anger and the wish to hurt and destroy the one who is helpless, becoming punitive, rejecting, and hurtful. It should be pointed out that the intricacies of these dynamic interactions are quite familiar to experienced clinicians, both in the contexts of psycho-analytic practice and of intensive psychotherapy, in terms of transference distortions, transference needs, and the corresponding countertransference reactions. This is particularly the case in the treatment of borderline patients.

In the kinds of infantile and mutually dependent relationships within which these patterns of emotional reaction take place, it is relatively impossible for the poorly differentiated individual to take responsibility for his own functioning and feelings without blaming the other for his unhappiness and suffering. It is a fairly common experience that one member of the marital couple will blame the other for his own failure or suffering—even as he may have, at some other point in the history of the relationship, credited that other as the source of his happiness and success. There is an implicit demand that the partner become different somehow in order to respond to and alleviate this suffering. Any attempt on the part of the partner to establish a clear and well-differentiated identity threatens this underlying need and is interpreted as an attack, a rejection, a betrayal, and a disillusioning disappointment.

In such a situation, one member of the pair ends up making impossible demands on the other member, yet at the same time is caught up in the impossible process of trying to meet the demands placed upon him by the other. Such interacting demands, counterdemands, compliance, and responsiveness may achieve a sort of functional equilibrium as long as each of the partners can maintain themselves in the position of trying to be for the other what the other seems to demand. But such a system of interaction is perilously fragile and subject to the regressive pulls and vicissitudes of the neurotic needs that drive and determine it. If either partner decides to assert his or her own needs in the face of the demands of the other, to establish and differentiate his or her own self in the face of these regressive pulls and neurotic needs, that partner can expect the other to use every resource of manipulation, exploitation, pressure, rejection, and force to keep the partner in the position of compliant dependence and emotional involvement.

To focus these phenomena in terms of the paranoid process (Meissner, 1978), we can say that the emotional matrix that emerges within the marital dyad is contributed to and shaped by the interacting patterns of projection and introjection between the marital partners. To the extent that each partner brings to the marital interaction a relatively undifferentiated self based on pathogenic introjects, there is a residue of unintegrated, relatively unconscious emotion, which suffuses the organization of the respective selves and which consequently contaminates and pervades the projective and introjective processes as they play themselves out in the interaction. It is important to remember, in this context, that the individual mechanisms of projection and introjection are being played out on both sides of the marital interaction and have a powerful reciprocal influence on how the interaction is experienced and how its configuration is shaped.

To the extent that the partners are deeply involved in this emotional interaction, that is to say, to the extent that each of them enters the interaction in terms of a relatively undifferentiated self, the emotional currents have a definite interpersonal effect. Such currents of emotion may, for example, be conveyed through the projection of one partner onto the other. To the extent that the second partner is enmeshed in the underlying emotional matrix, the projective elements tend to be internalized and introjected by the second partner. Correspondingly, the projective elements of the second partner will tend to be internalized and introjected by the first. Thus, through the reciprocal interaction of interlocking projections and introjections, the internal conflicts of each of the marital partners are translated into concrete modes of perceiving and behaving within the marital relationship. Mannino and Greenspan (1976) describe the process in the following terms:

One of the partners (the subject) projects certain aspects of himself onto the other (the object), and thus views the other as an embodiment of this characteristic or set of conflicts. Through that process one or both partners misperceive important aspects of the other's character. The object of the misperception is expected to conform to the image projected by the subject through his or her behavior and covertly to gratify certain denied needs of the subject. . . . Whether or not the second partner so acknowledges the other's perception (or misperception) and behaves in a certain manner is not crucial, since the subject will deny or not attend to aspects of reality which do not fit his or her perceptual distortion . . . because the misperceptions serve to meet certain denied needs of the subject, he or she is very strongly motivated to sustain them regardless of the object's behavior or verbalizations. Some amount of collusion also may keep the process operative. When the process functions in both partners, each misperceives the other and each acts reciprocally to the other. As a result, both partners become locked into a discordant relationship pattern which is perpetuated by a defensive pseudo-realistic quality. (pp. 139–140)

Since the content of the projections ultimately derives from earlier object-relations, both in the context of therapy and in the marital relationship, these older object-relationships are equivalently reactivated and become available either for pathological expression or for possible reworking in ways that may allow for therapeutic change or psychological growth. To the extent that one approaches the marital relationship with a poorly developed and relatively undifferentiated self, one recreates a pattern of relationships that obtains between one's self and one's parents in different stages of the developmental experience. Consequently, a man can look for a substitute mother in his prospective wife and recreate with her the same pattern of conflicts and tensions that were inherent in the maternal relationship. What becomes injected into the marital relationship as a result of this projective process may not simply relate to the opposite-sex parent, but may also reflect crucial introjections of a pathological sort that derive from both parents in one of the almost infinite variety of patterns of combination of such internalizations. They are different for every individual and reflect the almost infinite variety of each individual's developmental vicissitudes.

THE FAMILY EMOTIONAL SYSTEM

The transition from the view of the family in terms of complex interactions between individual members to the focusing of the family process as derived from and functioning in terms of a single organic unit particularly characterizes and marks as distinctive the more contemporary approaches to the understanding of the family (Bowen, 1960, 1961). The implications of this view are multiple. From this perspective, the breakdown or illness of one member of the family reflects the operation of emotional processes within the entire family itself. The member who is first referred for psychiatric assistance may be the family scapegoat or may be a substitute for other disturbed family members or for the disturbance of the family itself. Pathogenic conflicts and their associated defenses may be passed contagiously from generation to generation. In severely disturbed families, and often in even not so severely disturbed families, more than one member is emotionally disabled (Ackerman, 1962).

One important aspect of the unitary organization of the family system is the flow of emotion that takes place within it and the intimate exchange of emotional influences that forms a sort of emotional contagion (Ackerman, 1958). There are countless examples of the ways in which one family member will manage to be preserved from the pathogenic effects of emotional involvements, but at the expense of one or other members of the family. The outbreak of symptoms in one or other member may serve to protect other members in the family and allow them to maintain an adequate level of functioning. There are family systems in which, when stress impinges on the family system from certain directions, there is an outbreak or exacerbation of pathology in one or another of the members or in the whole family itself. Each family system manifests different patterns of vulnerability and expresses the infinite variety of ways in which, when the family system is put under severe regressive strain, the individual members react—some by developing psychological symptoms, others by developing physical symptoms or illnesses, and still others by various forms of self-destructive or self-defeating behavior. Moreover, such currents of emotional upheaval can be translated across generational boundaries. I have seen any number of cases in which the death of a significant figure in the grandparental generation will set up shock waves that reverberate throughout the whole family system and precipitate pathological reactivity and deviant expressions in many members of the family system.

These patterns of communication of symptoms in pathological family systems are frequently seen in cases of adolescent delinquency and acting-out. The adolescent patients will often accuse the family of being sick, and victimizing or rejecting them as a way of dealing with their own problems. Undoubtedly, the complaint is self-serving in that it allows the disturbed adolescent to deny his own conflicts and pathology, but nonetheless there often is a kernel of truth in it. When such disruptive and disturbed adolescents are either hospitalized or otherwise ejected from the family, the deep conflicts that permeate the family relationships may be successfully suppressed or repressed by reason of the separation, temporarily, but they continue to exert their destructive influence at a deeper level. During therapy with such families, these conflicts may erupt with considerable disruptive force, or alternatively, they may be driven even more deeply into the recesses of the family unconscious.

From this perspective, the adolescent's delinquent symptoms can be seen as a reaction to the patterning of relationships within the family, reflecting areas of unconscious conflict within the family system. The adolescent is involved in the responding to the unconscious demands of the family's emotional system, which requires such disruptive and rebellious symptoms in order to maintain its inner equilibrium. As Mandelbaum (1977a) comments:

> A child's personality may be shaped in countless ways to incorporate the rage and frustration of several generations concerning deprivation, loss, or abandonment. Still another child may be the only link between enraged and competitive parents, required by them to hold their marriage together. A third patient may be informed that growth and changes toward maturity would be viewed as an act of abandonment by a mother who would be left alone with an alcoholic, depressed, and passive marital partner. (p. 29)

To focus first on the role of the father of a borderline patient, we can ask how his participation in the emotional matrix of the family affects his behavior and functioning. Such fathers have been generally found to be domineering, authoritarian, hypercritical, or conversely, passive, ineffectual, unable to cope with family responsibility, and often engaged in a passive-aggressive undercutting of the mother's authority. In the families of school phobics, the father was often found to be weak, ineffectual, and passive; similarly in the families of drug addicts, the father is little more than a shadowy background figure in contrast to the domineering and influential mother. This constellation has also been observed in families of manic-depressives. The effective absence and emotional unavailability of the father has been noted in a variety of contexts (Meissner, 1964; Waring and Ricks, 1965). In these cases, Bowen (Bowen et al., 1959) has indicated that the pattern of withdrawal of the father is a function of his exclusion from the intense mother-child relationship. His attempts to intervene and strengthen his own relationship with the child require that he set himself in opposition to the mother by a more or less cruel, dominating approach.

There may be interesting differences between the experience of the borderline child in relationship to each of the parental figures. A comparison of female borderline patients with normal and neurotic control groups suggested that the control groups generally recalled more approving and less disinterested and critical responses from parents than did the borderline group. But the female borderlines did not differ from the control groups in their recollections of their relationships to their mothers. By way of contrast, these patients remembered their fathers as having been significantly less approving and more disinterested than did the controls (Frank and Paris, 1981). The finding is of interest, in that it suggests that a child's relationship to the father may contribute to the genesis of borderline psychopathology in females, to a much greater extent than the relationship to the mother. The added fact that females tend to predominate in the borderline group, particularly in the hysterical-depressive continuum, lends added significance to this suggestion.

The role of the father in an often severe psychopathology of the child was underlined in the studies of the Lidz group of schizophrenic families (Lidz et al., 1965). They noted the importance of the father's impact on the child's development, since he is usually the first intruder into the symbiotic mother-child mutuality. The child needs to develop a sense of mutuality with both mother and father as a unit, rather than with just the mother. Moreover, the mother's ability to be maternal and secure in her mothering activity depends, in large measure, on the support she feels coming from the father and his ability to share her with the child. The child's estimation of the mother as a love object similarly is influenced by the degree of the father's esteem of or enmity toward the mother. This aspect of the relationship between the parents plays a critical role in the developing identifications for both male and female children. As Lidz and Fleck (1959) comment:

> This development will be difficult if the father despises the mother or is so inconsistent that no behavioral pattern appears to satisfy him. The fathers studied were very often insecure in their masculinity, needing constant admiration and attention to bolster their self-esteem. Even the domineering and more tyrannical whom neither wife nor child could satisfy could be recognized as being basically weak and ineffectual by the members of the family. (p. 335)

We see in these configurations the familiar landmarks of overadequacy and inadequacy that seem to characterize the involvement in the family emotional matrix. But the evolution of such patterns does not reflect the operation of intrapsychic or intrafamilial dynamics exclusively. The family is, in fact, a channel through which the impact of cultural influences comes to bear on its members, and particularly on the development of children. As Ackerman (1958) suggested some years ago, cultural patterns operate to create a sense of isolation and alienation in men and women, but they particularly seem to move in the direction of undermining the sense of masculine identity. One can include here the increasing demands of women for a power status along with increasing levels of assertion of aggressiveness and mastery. One can also include the social forces that continually threaten the average man and leave him with a feeling of inadequacy and insecurity in the face of the increasingly ruthless, competitive struggle that characterizes the fabric of our society. In such an arena, the contemporary male is continually threatened with defeat and failure so that the only viable criterion of achieving manhood and masculine identity is a kind of superman achievement or competence. The aspirations become such that they can never be achieved.

Only recently has the specific impact of the father on the child's developmental experience been studied. Abelin (1975) attempted to delineate the role of the father in facilitating the phases of separation and individuation. In the practicing subphase, the father plays an important part in facilitating the development of the child's exploratory and early phallic attitudes, and in the subsequent rapprochement subphase, he may play a crucial role in supporting the disengagement of the child's ego from the regressive pulls toward symbiosis with the mother. The intrusion of the father into the mother-child symbiosis sets in play a process that leads gradually to a "triangulation," which requires that the toddler both apprehend and internalize not only aspects of his relationship to his father and his mother separately, but also the relationship between the two intensely cathected objects. Using the parental objects as points of reference, the child gradually evolves an image of himself. The child's image of himself as participating in the mother-father-child triad helps establish his own emerging sense of identity and contributes particularly to the shaping of the child's emerging gender identity.

Although the experience of fatherhood fulfills a natural biological aspiration and provides a medium of psychological development, this experience is not necessarily free from conflict. As Benedek (1970) has pointed out, there is a tendency for both men and women to identify with the child of the same sex. The relationship with that child tends to reactivate conflictual aspects of the relationship of the parent to his own same-sex parent (Mandelbaum, 1977b). Thus, the introjection of aspects of the conflicted and hostile relationship of the parent with his or her parent can serve as the basis of projections of hostility toward the child and interfere with the exercise of parental love. Benedek even suggests that the desire for children of the opposite sex can be motivated by an intuitive realization that conflicts derived from developmental interactions with one's own same-sex parent may serve as the basis for re-experiencing these conflicts with the child.

Family interactions may also reflect the origins of narcissistic vulnerability in the parents. This configuration is frequently seen in the genesis of narcissistic and borderline disorders. Often, relationships between the parents themselves and the aspects that they project into the family system, and consequently, onto the child are reactivations of elements from the parents' own family of origin that had been internalized during the course of their development. The original dependence on the parents' own primary objects that was internalized in the course of their development led to relatively early narcissistic fixations that are brought to life in the context of the system of the nuclear family. Consequently, the basic function of the child in such family systems comes to be the maintenance of parental self-esteem by way of an re-enactment with the parent of the unresolved relationship from the conflicted aspects of the parent's own family of origin, which played a central role in the development of the parents' self-esteem (Berkowitz et al., 1974b).

The emotional relationship of father and child thus derives from both the father's identification with the child and his identification with his own father. Normally, these two levels of internalization are complementary and are integrated into the fathering experience. Identification with the child serves as a basis for paternal empathy, while identification with the father's own father shapes the internalized norms both culturally and personally of what it means to be a father. As Benedek notes, when cultural changes are slow paced and family structures relatively stable, fathers are less vulnerable to the fears of competitiveness from their sons and the sons find less necessity to struggle against their fathers to establish their own identities. Benedek (1970) notes:

> Just as it is normal for parents to enjoy the manifestations of the constructive aspects of their personalities in their children, it is also normal, in the sense of the psychodynamics of parent-child interaction, that fathers watch with anxious anticipation for signs which indicate that the child might have conflicts and develop problems similar to those they had to struggle against. In either case, the constructive as well as the pathognomic results of the parents' identification with the child are more direct and effective with the child of their own sex. (p. 174)

What is particularly noteworthy in these patterns is the transmission and interplay, from generation to generation, of the patterns of projection and introjection (Zinner and R. Shapiro, 1972). Not only constructive aspects are passed on, but destructive aspects as well. Fathers who take pride in defying the social order or outwitting authority figures may implant a similar criminal tendency in their children. Fathers may find themselves, with considerable surprise and even a sense of shame and remorse, acting toward their sons with the same angry and punitive attitudes that their fathers had toward them. These imitative patterns of behavior reflect the underlying configuration of the introjects that link father and son in the emotional matrix of the family.

Such patterns of intergeneration conflict may lay the basis for paternal rejection of the child. As Ackerman (1958) has observed, paternal rejection may stem from psychologically specific or relatively nonspecific causes. Interference with his role as a father, and his capacity to relate to his child, may stem from physical illness, emotional illness, alcoholism, demands of work, etc. Some fathers are largely absent due to the nature of their work, but others may be so engrossed in the demands of work that they find little time to spend with their children or what little time they do spend with them is filled with distractions that prevent real involvement or meaningful communication with their children. If a father brings his work home with him or spends his time with the family worried and preoccupied by his workday concerns, he becomes a relatively inaccessible parent.

Often enough, the father's own needs to be taken care of, mothered, and supported place him in the position of competing with his child in having these needs satisfied by the mother. Or if the sexual and emotional relationship with the wife is unsatisfactory, such a father may displace his feelings of resentment to the child and reject both wife and child. Such men frequently escape to harbors of male security—clubs, taverns, and other meeting places —or they may seek sexual gratification in extramarital affairs.

In other cases, the rejection of the child may be highly specific and can be based on projections by which the child is identified with some critical figure or figures in the father's own life with whom he had highly conflicted and emotionally intense relationships. Thus the child may be identified with the father's own father or a brother of whom he was intensely jealous. The child may even become the projective bearer of the aggressive and competitive urges of the father himself, thus intensifying and revivifying the father's own sense of masculine inadequacy and deficiency. The connection of such projective phenomena with the father's own introjective economy can often be particularly striking. The father's own inner sense of inadequacy and deficiency may be transferred to the son, who then becomes an object of disgust and rejection; the father's self-hate is translated into hatred of the child. The son will carry the guilt for the father's evil. The son will grow up seeing himself and feeling himself to be the unloved, unwanted, and rejected son because he is inferior and unworthy. Similarly a father who rejects or keeps a guarded distance from a daughter leaves her with a sense of feminine inferiority and lack of worth. These affects play a considerable role in the shaping of introjects in such children and lead to the pathological sense of self they carry into their adult lives. Such fathers may often project on their children aspects of themselves that have been repressed or have never been accepted or integrated as a functional part of their own selves. The father who was never able to break out of his dependence on his own parents may thus see his own children as rebellious, and flouting parental and societal demands—so that the child's living out these patterns of behavior becomes an unconscious source of gratification to his father.

Similarly, where the emotional relationship with the mother has broken down, the father may seek to get from the children what he has not been able to get from his wife. This may result in exaggerated demonstrations of affection and the demand for love from the child that was not forthcoming from the wife. Such fathers may become actively seductive so that the child is subjected to the father's need, and the price of acceptance and love from the father is precisely such submission. The child's own self-esteem and independent needs to be acknowledged and valued in his own right are thus violated. These complex interactions may frequently intensify and bring to a pathological pitch the oedipal involvement. As Ackerman (1958) notes:

> The child is then neither respected nor valued as a separate being but becomes the object of the father's unsatisfied love needs. Such situations often involve triangular relationships in which tremendous tension is aroused because of the patterns of jealousy and competitiveness. In all this the issue is whether the child fortifies and enhances the father's self-esteem, whether the child adds to the father's feeling of being loved or detracts from it, and whether the father's alliance with the child arouses the mother's jealousy or the mother's alliance with the child mobilizes the father's rivalry and rage. (p. 185)

In families of disturbed adolescents who have significant degrees of narcissistic pathology, the parents themselves seem not to have developed adequate inner resources for the relatively independent regulation of their own self-esteem. They frequently demonstrate the typical vacillation between narcissistic extremes: from haughty, entitled grandiosity and inflated self-concepts, even to the point of omnipotence, on the one hand, to a sense of inferiority, inadequacy, worthlessness, and shamefulness, on the other. Nor have the parents in such narcissistically disturbed families achieved any substantial autonomy from their dependence on infantile objects. They tend to turn that dependence toward their offspring, who then come to represent the earlier objects of dependence and sources of narcissistic supplies needed to maintain the parents precarious narcissistic balance.

This situation reaches a crisis at the time of adolescence, when the demand for adolescent separation can become particularly threatening. The adolescent reassesses his previous idealized view of the parents and begins to question their values and life-style as a part of his own need to separate from them and to begin to establish his own life pattern. To the narcissistically vulnerable parent, this seriously challenges his narcissistic omnipotence. In consequence, adolescent growth, separation, and emerging autonomy are no longer experienced by the parents as desirable, but take the form of a narcissistic injury. The result is often, particularly in borderline families, parental anger and anxiety, with a devaluation of the adolescent and an attempt to restore narcissistic equilibrium by projecting the parents' own negative self-valuations onto the adolescent (Berkowitz et al., 1974 a,b).

The father who brings to the family interaction such a poorly defined and insecurely established sense of self is a defective model for identification for children of either sex. He is a poor model of masculine identity for his sons and an inadequate love object for his daughters. It should not be forgotten that important components of a little girl's personality also are derived by way of critical internalizations from the father. In both sexes, the patterning of internalizations through the developmental sequence takes place in relationship to both parents so that elements from both parents ultimately blend in the child's emerging personality. The most flagrant examples of inadequate fathering and of the turning of rejection and hostility against the child are found in the families of schizophrenic children (Lidz et al., 1965). In these families, the disturbed patterns we have been discussing are writ large, but it must also be remembered that they reflect the dynamics that are operative within the family system and that characterize a particular emotional matrix.

The role of the mother in the family system that produces pathology in its children has been closely scrutinized for many years. It was long felt that the pathogenic influence of disturbed mothers in such family systems was even greater than that of the fathers, although that perception has been increasingly balanced by the patterns of paternal influence we have been describing. A good deal of attention has been focused on attempts to define the personality characteristics of mothers with children having various forms of pathology. The mothers of school-phobic children, for example, are described as anxious, ambivalent, hostile, immature, insecure in their mothering function, and demanding. Children with adjustment problems have mothers who are ineffective, irresponsible, weak, self-critical, competitive for authority, rejecting, and hostile. Children with ulcerative colitis have mothers who are insecure, inadequate in their maternal role, and ambivalent. Young addicts have mothers who tend to be controlling, overpowering, guilt-ridden, narcissistic, hostile, inconsistent, and seductive. Manic-depressives have dominant and ambivalent mothers, and the classic profile of the schizophrenogenic mother describes her as dominant, rigidly perfectionistic, lacking in confidence, distrusting, cold, masochistic, low in self-esteem, inconsistent, rejecting, and dependent (Meissner, 1964). The lack of a consistent pattern in the mothers of schizophrenic children has been noted (Fleck et al., 1963; Bowen et al., 1959).

The mothers of borderline patients have been described as falling into two separate categories, namely, the classic matriarch, on the one hand, who is unable to allow her child to separate effectively and become relatively autonomous, and the "child-wife," on the other hand. The women in this latter category tend to be relatively child-like, naive, and dependent and often ineffectual and basically hysterical. In contrast to the matriarch who disrupts the process of separation-individuation by an unwillingness to surrender her smothering domination over the child, the child-wife cannot break off her symbiotic clinging to the child. As Greenacre (1947) noted, this child-wife ideal received considerable cultural reinforcement and was brought into the service of maintaining the husband's narcissistic equilibrium. The male's own narcissistic needs were supported by a relationship to his wife in which he could be the idealized protector and patriarch, and she could occupy the position of the helpless, dependent child. Undoubtedly, an important variable in such considerations is the extent to which such culturally imposed roles and functions are effectively integrated on a psychological level, as opposed to the degree such culturally reinforced demands create an internal psychic conflict between the pressures toward conformity and the urge toward self-assertion and independence. For some women, at least, the cultural pattern might be a convenient vehicle for the expression of covert dependency needs related to their own inability to separate effectively from their own parents and to recreate a marital relationship of child-like dependency (MacMurray, 1976).

The mother's influence on the child and the general characteristic of the mother-child relation have been intensively studied. Pathology in the child has generally been found associated with maternal conflict and a tendency for mothers to keep the child in a relatively dependent position. The overprotective attitude of mothers of school-phobic children is typical: these mothers have a close emotional relationship with the child, which reinforces the child's dependence on the mother and concurrently seems to gratify the mother emotionally. A similar pattern is often found in delinquent children, with the added element that these mothers seem incapable of establishing a middle ground in dealing with their children: giving is equivalent to limitless surrender and indulgence, discipline means total deprivation and hostile, repressive control. The mothers of addicts were similarly found to be overprotective and unable to allow their children to be independent. The powerful need to infantilize in such mothers has a profound impact on the children that is reflected in the intense and binding pattern of identification characteristic of this relationship; this may relate to the frequency of homosexual conflicts in addicts. Similar patterns of symbiotic infantilization can be found in psychosomatic disorders and may even reflect a more seriously disturbed mother-child relationship than that found in schizophrenia. In ulcerative colitis, for example, the conflict between the mother's need to keep the child dependent and her own unconscious destructive impulses may be central (Meissner, 1964).

A critical issue in borderline families is the role of conflicts over autonomy and dependency. The conflicts stem from the psychic contributions of both parents, generally in pathologically reinforcing patterns. MacMurray (1976) has described several patterns in which these conflicts express themselves in the mother-child interaction. In one pattern, the mother may tend to ignore the child's emotional needs, while imposing strict controls. The infant is either kept at a distance, or the mother may vacillate between showing affection and keeping aloof. This combination of maternal detachment and control intensifies the infant's separation anxieties, which can be managed only by strict conformity with the mother's policies, thus ensuring that she will not withdraw her love. This tends to keep the child enmeshed in the maternal symbiotic orbit.

A second pattern involves the mother's need for nurturance or to maintain narcissistic equilibrium. Such mothers overwhelm and engulf the child with nurturant attention, which tends to reinforce the mother's own sense of omnipotence and relieves her anxiety by the projection of abandonment fears. Such mothers become addicted to the infant's dependence and continuing need for her. In such interactions, the father is often kept at a distance or exiled to the periphery of the mother-child unit. Weaning and toilet-training often tend to be postponed for such children. Again, the child's opportunity to separate effectively from the mother and gain greater autonomy is frustrated.

Although these differences in pathogenic mothering patterns can be observed at the level of preoedipal development, at the beginning of the oedipal period these patterns seem to follow a common pathway. The detached, controlling mother tends to continue this pattern of interaction, but the overwhelming, engulfing mother tends to more more in the direction of detachment. The love of mothers of this kind remains contingent on the infant's continuing helplessness and dependence.

A critical issue in such pathological relationships is the extent to which the child is drawn into the service of neurotic maternal needs. Neurotic mothers commonly present themselves as the self-sacrificial victims who bear the loving burden of having and raising the children. The willingness to sacrifice and suffer pain and sorrow thus becomes the hallmark of her mother's love. However this puts a terrible burden of guilt on the child who is the object of such loving sacrifice. Ackerman (1958) has commented in this regard:

> Neurotic mothers are notorious for their martyred agonies, their self-pitying dramatic displays, their exploitation of the theme of sacrifice. In actuality, however, martyred mothers make no sacrifice. If anything, they do precisely the opposite. They exploit their children. They exact an emotional sacrifice. They press upon the children with their imagined wounds, with constant reminders of all they have done for them. Neurotic children take this maternal display seriously; they are mowed down by guilt and seek penance in propitiatory behavior. They attempt in a futile way to make up to their mothers for the presumed sacrifice. Such patterns of neurotic interaction bind the child to mother, deform the quality of togetherness, and sharply restrict the range of development toward a mature autonomy. (p. 76)

In borderline cases, the mother-child interaction results in a manipulation of the child in the service of the mother's emotional needs, in which the child is gradually drawn into the position of being the caretaker of maternal emotions. The mother thus becomes emotionally dependent on the child, and as she does, she allows him to retain his sense of omnipotence insofar as he possesses the power to make her happy or sad. These processes have an enduring impact on the child as he grows up. Such patients often assume that they bear the sole responsibility for the happiness or sadness of others, thus feeding their own sense of narcissistic omnipotence. They often feel that they have great power over the emotions of others.

A number of patterns of maternal overprotection have been described (Levy, 1970). Most frequently, in clinical terms, maternal overprotection masks or compensates a strong rejection of the child. Such motives may be initiated by severe illness, accident, or deformity in the child, so that such mothers tend to favor these weaker, more sickly, generally more dependent children. Such maternal overprotection is manifested in excessive mother-child contact, infantilization, and the prevention of independent behavior in the child. There may also be a lack or an excess of control over the child's behavior—the former suggesting a deficiency in the mother's capacity to modify the child's behavior so that the child's demands continue to control the relationship, the latter a pattern of maternal domination. In the one case, the child's power is exercised in having his own way and in dominating every situation so that he becomes the central figure. Thus, the infantile power expands into a monstrous hold that subjugates the parents. In the latter case, the child's dependency on the mother is fostered, so that there is a failure of development and less growth of aggressive tendencies. The mothers of dominating child are indulgent, the mothers of submissive children dominating.

The role of overprotectiveness in the genesis of borderline disorders has been challenged by some empirical findings. Comparison of families with borderline offspring with families of both paranoid-schizophrenic and neurotic patients (Gunderson et al., 1980) suggested that both the mothers and the fathers of these borderline families were relatively sicker and less functional than the comparison group, and that their marriages were marked by a relative absence of overt hostility and conflict. The authors comment:

> Their attachment to each other seems to be at the expense of their children, either as regulators and monitors of their behavior or as sources of gratification and support, or even as clear role models. In short, these families were best characterized by the rigid tightness of the marital bond to the exclusion of the attention, support, or protection of the children. (p. 31)

Similar findings, based on the recollections of family experience by borderline patients, suggest that such patients do not remember their families as being overprotective. Although the hypothesis of overprotection was not supported, these patients recalled an attitude of neglect only in relationship to their fathers (Frank and Paris, 1981). These findings would seem to be somewhat at variance with clinical experience, in which patterns of overprotection are found frequently enough. There may be relevant issues of patient selection, methodology, or small sample size that would tend to qualify the results of these studies. The patients in these studies were selected primarily by the Gunderson criteria, which tend to lean in the direction of more primitive or disturbed borderline functioning. My own experience would suggest, within limitations, that there is a tendency for parental neglect, abuse, and hostilely depriving relationships to obtain in families of lower-order borderline pathology rather than patterns of overinvolvement or overprotectiveness. These latter patterns tend to be found more characteristically in the higher-order forms of borderline disturbance. These remain merely clinical impressions, however, and leave us with the hypothesis that more than one pattern of parent-child interaction can contribute to borderline pathological development.

The pattern of maternal overprotectiveness must be matched by the pattern of maternal rejection. Anna Freud (1970) has commented on this subject:

> There is, of course, no lack of evidence for the occurrence of rejection of infants. Many infants, instead of being kept as near to the mother as possible, spend many hours of the day in isolation; many are subjected to traumatic separations from their mothers; many, at the end of infancy, have good reason to feel deserted when another child is born; many are, indeed, unwanted. Nevertheless, there is behind these happenings a variety of determinants which decide their outcome. There is not one type of rejecting mother, there are many. There are those who are responsible for their rejecting attitude, who can be exhorted, advised, and helped toward a better adjustment to their children; there are also those for whom rejecting is beyond their control. (p. 378)

Thus the determinants of maternal rejection may be quite diverse and relatively specific or nonspecific. The child may be rejected because of certain characteristics that remind the mother of others in her experience with whom she had had hateful or ambivalent relations. Or the mother may associate threat or pain with the child, such that the rejection of the child reflects experiences or associations that threaten the mother's idealized self-image or her own personal goals or values.

Frequently enough, the child may become the inheritor of displaced hostilities from other relationships. The mother may thus displace the conflicted hostility from her own relationship to her mother to her daughter; or, as in a striking instance in my own clinical experience, the mother of an adolescent preschizophrenic boy, with whom she maintained a highly ambivalent, conflictual, and mutually rejecting attitude, recalled that when he was born and first placed in her arms she was struck with how angry he looked. She has always regarded him as an angry and unmanageable explosive child. So he has become. This reflected her own hostile, conflicted, intensely ambivalent relationship with her father who was a violent, alcoholic, frequently paranoid man, subject to outbursts of temper and violent and destructive behavior.

To keep the lines of connection clear, it was not simply that this infant became the object of a displaced perception on the part of the mother, but that, more accurately, he was the object of the projection of her own aggressive and violent impulses that had been internalized, that is to say, introjected from her violent and abusive father. Thus, it is frequently the case that the rejection of the child can mirror the parents' own sense of rejection by their parents. Frequently enough, in the context of adolescent development, the adolescent's attempt to separate, which may be reflected in unresponsiveness or rejecting behavior, are experienced by the parents precisely in these terms, so that the child becomes, projectively, a reincarnation of the rejecting parent (E. Shapiro, 1982).

Maternal rejection, however, may also be influenced by accidental factors. The pregnancy itself may have been accidental and the child unwanted. Or the pregnancy may have come at an unfortunate time in terms of the family finances or the death of significant figures in the family structure, or at a time when the mother is left particularly vulnerable in the exercise of her mothering capacities, as for example, when the father is to be drafted into the army or has suffered a serious accident or a severe illness.

Basic to the issues of overprotection and rejection is the question of the extent to which the mother herself has achieved a stable and adequate self-image and the degree to which she has been successful in establishing a cohesive differentiated self and a stable identity. To the degree she has achieved this, she can accept the independence and growth potential of her child and fulfill her mothering function without excessive rejection, on the one hand, or draw the child into the service of neurotic needs, on the other. To be a good mother, a woman must accept her own anatomy and physiology and value its biological potentialities and implications. She must be able to accept herself as fundamentally feminine and as fulfilling the role of wife before she can comfortably accept the functions and responsibilities of motherhood. Too often women who become mothers fundamentally deny and devalue their femininity; they are caught in the unfortunate torment of penis envy, they do not value their mothering and nurturing functions, and they tend to relate to their children either as narcissistically compensating or as intolerably burdensome reinforcers of their self-hate and own sense of worthlessness. It will be of great interest to see what changes in the patterning of such maternal responsiveness are wrought by the currently changing status of women in society. One would hope that meaningful change could be achieved without severe psychic cost, but the evidence of the bitterness and competitiveness and hostility of the "liberated" woman does not make one optimistic.

The marital relationship places an important stamp on the developing personalities of the children. The mother's capacity to fulfill her role as wife and to enter into a mutually satisfying and constructive relationship with her husband provides important elements in the family system. When husband and wife have not developed such mutually supportive roles and a reciprocally reinforcing relationship, they deprive the child of those critical models of adult behavior and functioning, particularly in the context of the relationship between the sexes, that are essential for the child's development. If a mother is continually expressing her dissatisfaction with her husband and devaluing him, she undercuts his value as an object for the son's identification or his value to a daughter as a model of masculinity and an object for suitable love and esteem. If her own inadequacies, or an inability to meet her husband's expectations, make her an object of her husband's devaluation and criticism, her own worth as an object for identification for both of her children, but particularly for her daughter, is undercut.

If a mother turns from her husband to her son as her major source of emotional support and reinforcement, this will only confuse and intensify the oedipal involvement of the child and make his successful resolution of oedipal conflicts more questionable. The mother who assumes the dominant or domineering position in the family and begins to take on masculine functions and roles within the family offers a disturbed apprehension in the child of masculinity and femininity and jeopardizes his own achievement of a secure sexual identity. Thus, the mother profoundly influences the child's development by the extent to which she can meaningfully and effectively fulfill her functions in the family as wife and mother. But beyond this, as the Lidz group (1965) has pointed out, the mother is the primary teacher and model from whom the child acquires a number of the basic skills of socialization and the capacity to relate to others.

We can remind ourselves, at this point, that these interactions take place in connection with an emotional matrix or shared emotional process that seems to characterize the family system. This aspect of family dynamics was noted some years ago by Bowen (1960), who described it in the following terms:

> I have used the term "emotional demand" and "emotional process" to describe the emotional responsiveness by which one family member responds automatically to the emotional state of another, without either being consciously aware of the process . . . it runs silently underneath the surface between people who have very close relationships. It operates during periods of conflict and periods of calm harmony. In most of our families there is much conflict and open disagreement and many stories of injustices and misdeeds between family members. (p. 368)

When such an emotional matrix can be identified, it implies that the processes of individuation within the family system have been defeated. A study of the patterns of interaction among family members gives some indication of how many of the family members are affected, and to what degree, and to what extent the unconscious emotional system influences the manner of interaction and transaction among the family members. In such family systems, self- and object-representations tend to be partial and poorly differentiated, reality-testing tends to be defined in terms of the demands of the family system, and mechanisms of defense, e.g., projection, become shared processes.

Such families lack a sense of the family as a whole or as a unit, just as they seem to lack a sense of the individuality of their members. Members are overresponsive, or overinvolved, longing for closeness and intimacy, but living in dreadful fear of these same emotional needs. Such pathogenic systems are the common fabric of borderline families. Although family members often seem to retain a capacity to recognize and to deal with reality outside of the family system, even to the point of maintaining successful careers and professions, their functioning within the family leaves much to be desired (Mandelbaum, 1977b).

Shapiro and his group (Zinner and R. Shapiro, 1972; Zinner and R. Shapiro, 1974; Berkowitz et al., 1974a,b; E. Shapiro et al., 1975; E. Shapiro, 1978, 1982; R. Shapiro, 1979) have described the family emotional matrix in terms of shared and unconscious assumptions or fantasies on the part of its members. These unconscious fantasies and assumptions in borderline families relate particularly to conflicts over autonomy and dependency, matters of particular importance and relevance in adolescent development. These unconscious assumptions operating within the family system work to impede and to disrupt the accomplishment of developmental tasks, stemming, as we have seen, from the earliest infantile levels through the adolescent's struggle for separation and autonomy.

When these unconscious assumptions are operating within the family system, the behavior of family members reveals the pathogenic influence. Family members manifest conflicting patterns of motivation, anxiety, and mobilization of pathological defenses, along with obvious ego regression. The family's behavior seems to be determined more by unconscious motivations and fantasies than by purposeful intentions or reality. The family begins to fail in its attempt to solve problems in the family context effectively, and confused and distorted thinking, failure in understanding otherwise clear and adequate communications, and a general breakdown in the family's capacity to work cooperatively or creatively in accomplishing its functions emerge. The same family system, however, operating in a context in which unconscious assumptions and fantasies are not in effect, or in which they are operating at a minimally disruptive level, can function realistically and effectively, particularly in regard to facilitating the development of children (Shapiro, 1979).

Recently, approaching the same set of issues, Mandelbaum (1980) has catalogued the patterns and characteristics commonly found in the families of borderline or narcissistic patients. As in other instances of the delineation of such characteristics, they are by no means exclusively found in borderline and/or narcissistic family systems, but they are sufficiently common to provide a fairly consistent family picture.

1. Marital relationships tend to be troubled and volatile and inhibit the exercise of effective parental leadership by both parents. The children frequently become targets for parental projections, which defend against the acknowledgment of deeper disappointments in the relationship between the parents.
2. The parents often have considerable difficulty agreeing over parental discipline and often engage in competitive struggles for control of the family. An interactional pattern of hyperadequacy/inadequacy is adopted between the parents, and any deviation of this pattern is resisted by family mechanisms calculated to reinstate the former homeostasis.
3. Both parents are deeply enmeshed emotionally with their families of origin. When relationships with the families of origin seem distant, this does not reflect real differentiation and autonomy. Emotional entanglements are seemingly maintained, despite the apparent separation of time and geographic distance.
4. There is often a high incidence of infantile trauma in these families. The trauma may be related to the early death or loss of the parent, divorce, suicide, alcoholism, inconstant parenting or the frequent substitution of parenting figures. Separations are experienced as abandonments and rejections and are reacted to by rage, which is repressed and projected into other family members. Primitive expressions of aggression are handled by splitting of good from bad objects; this constitutes a major defense in borderline conditions against intolerable anxiety and guilt.
5. The boundaries between the parents in their functions as husband and wife, and as parents, are easily blurred and easily trespassed. Mutual accusations and recriminations are frequent.
6. Boundaries between the parents and the children tend to be blurred. Parental invasion of the children's privacy, and incursion of the children on parental functions, is commonly observed, resulting in confusions regarding sexual identity and authority. In some families, incestuous interactions bring about intense primitive aggressive responses and a premature heightening of oedipal struggles in the parents. This results in increasing ineffectiveness in parenting functions, particularly in the accomplishment of crucial developmental tasks.
7. Such families may be characterized by a history of several generations of family emotional systems in which serious difficulties in interpersonal rela-

tionships, failures to achieve separation and autonomy, high levels of marital conflict and tension, and unresolved issues concerning separation and individuation are observed.

A concept similar to that of the family emotional system has been elaborated by Slipp (1973), who describes a pattern of interaction identifiable in families of various forms of pathology, but to the most extreme degree, in families with a schizophrenic member. He describes this "symbiotic survival pattern" as follows:

> The essential characteristics of this pattern were that each person's self-esteem and ego identity were felt to be dependent upon the other's behavior. Thus, each member felt controlled by his overwhelming sense of *responsibility* and guilt for the self-esteem and ego identity of the others, and at the same time each needed to *control* the other's behavior. (pp. 377–378)

This pattern derives from the need of the parents to act out their own intrapsychic conflicts in the interpersonal sphere of interaction. This pathological pattern exercises enormous control over the personality and functioning of the child so that he does not learn to integrate sexual and aggressive impulses or to experience a sense of himself as differentiated and independent apart from his involvement with the family. Thus as the child grows to maturity, he fails to establish a stable and autonomous sense of himself and continues to be excessively involved and influenced by the ongoing current of emotion in the family system. The identified patient in such a family is unable to be spontaneous and assertive, although he remains constantly reactive to emotional pressures deriving from others in the family system and from the family system as a whole. Conversely, the patient is strongly motivated to perpetuate this mutually controlling and symbiotic involvement, since the alternative is the fear of abandonment, or in the most severely disturbed cases, annihilation.

Insofar as the survival pattern and its related emotional closeness is required to maintain whatever level of personality integration has been achieved by these individuals, including particularly the parents, the patient's participation and continuing involvement in this emotional process is partly motivated by the need to sustain his own and his parent's personality integration. The child will unconsciously attempt to modify his own subjective self-experience in order to meet and alleviate parental needs and thus to maintain the integrity and equilibrium of the parents. The mechanism of this adaptation is realized in the process of projection and introjection by which the child comes to live out and experience himself in terms of his introjection of parental projections.

For narcissistic parents, the child's participation in this relationship carries with it a strong titer of narcissistic gratification. The child, on his part, is the object of particular narcissistic investment from the parents and becomes so vital to the parents' existence and figures so prominently in the maintenance of their self-esteem that his involvement in this emotional system tends to maintain and reinforce his sense of omnipotent grandiosity. This becomes a dilemma for the adolescent, who finds himself, by virtue of developmental urges, wanting to separate himself from this role, but feeling imperiled by his wish to do so by the implicit threat of parental abandonment and the certain loss of narcissistic grandiosity. His alternatives, consequently, are stark: either to continue to be a narcissistic object for the parents or to risk alienation from the family and loss of parental investment (Berkowitz et al., 1974a).

In families in which the symbiotic survival pattern has had a pathogenic impact, the psychotic reaction is most often found to be precipitated by a threat to the patient's participation in this family system. Slipp (1973) describes this reaction in schizophrenic families as follows:

> Disruption of the symbiotic relationship was experienced as a loss of the self, of not being capable of surviving intact alone, as well as an act of destruction of one or both of the parents. Thus, his *self-definition* continued to remain *reactive* and *relational*, i.e. he continued to remain excessively dependent upon his family relationships for his self-esteem and ego identity. In summary, the symbiotic survival pattern appeared to prevent the differentiation in the child of mental images of self and others, of mental images from external objects, of what is inside and outside (ego boundaries), and hampered the general transition from primary to secondary process cognition in certain areas. (pp. 378–379)

This pattern of emotional interaction within the family establishes a kind of emotional sink or swamp, which draws the patient into it and impedes his capacities for development and growth to maturity, leaving him with a variety of developmental impediments. Slipp (1973) described this:

> The symbiotic survival pattern in the family is characterized as follows: Each person's self-esteem and psychological survival (ego identity) is felt to be dependent on the other's behavior. Each member, therefore, needs to control the other's behavior and feels controlled by his overwhelming sense of responsibility for the self-esteem and survival of the other. Because this system of interaction itself uses magical, infantile, omnipotent techniques to achieve control over past and present object relations, it reinforces magical, primary-process thinking that the child brings to the system innately. The child, thus, continues to use preoperational, primary-process thinking to an abnormal degree in certain areas of personal relationships because: (a) the child's development is fixated at the symbiotic level of infantile functioning; (b) the fixation makes him pathologically dependent upon the family relations for his ego identity and susceptible to continuing influence by this system (this gives the appearance that the pathology resides solely in the system); and (c) it is reinforced by the ongoing, pathological family pattern of interaction. (pp. 394–395)

Although the existence of such an emotional matrix or symbiotic survival pattern can be found in its most dramatic and pathological form in families with a schizophrenic member, the same pattern, operating at lesser degrees of intensity and pathological impact, can be found in families with less marked degrees of pathology. It is a marked feature in the families within which borderline psychopathology develops, and its pathogenicity is directly proportional to the severity and intensity of the patient's involvement in the family system. That involvement is more intense and more pathogenic for the lower-order forms of borderline pathology than for the higher-order forms. Moreover, as we have already suggested, the degree of involvement and pathogenic influence exercised by this system is related to the degree of lack of differentiation of self brought to the system by the respective parents, since it is through their emotional interaction that the system is constituted.

The interlocking of personalities and their functioning in this sort of emotional process has also been described in transactional terms (Boszormenyi-Nagy, 1965). In this view, the family system is composed of the introjective aspects of individual personalities in transaction with object-relational aspects. Thus more than one individual can be involved in the operation of an action system in which they either complement each other or create a detrimental emotional feedback system. The precocious child can complement a narcissistically demanding parent, or more negatively, control of impulses in one member of the system may be achieved through the acting-out of the same impulses by others. Consequently, the other member of the system may be regarded as a constitutive agent of the action rather than merely as a participant in an indifferent social reality.

Similarly, the fragile autonomy of one family member may be reinforced at the expense of the autonomy of another member. Clinically, improvement in one family member may be accompanied by the movement of another member into the sick role. This has been described in terms of family homeostasis. The interchange of adequate and inadequate roles can thus take place not only in terms of psychological functioning, but also between the psychological and the physical realms. The achievement of greater functional autonomy in one family member who had been previously impaired may be followed by a psychological or physical impairment in some other family member or members. In this sense, it is as though certain families can tolerate an autonomous role in one family member only if it is balanced by a relatively nonautonomous functioning of another family member or members.

In family systems in which the achievement of autonomy is jeopardized, the system tends to be characterized by a sort of symbiotic involvement that exempts the involved members from the necessity of becoming separate individuals. The members seem to engulf one another, which gives the impression of sharing each other's feelings and motivations rather than gaining any mutual recognition and acceptance of differences and divergences. Such intersubjective fusion cannot tolerate autonomous change on the part of its involved members (Zinner and R. Shapiro, 1972; Berkowitz et al., 1974a; E. Shapiro et al., 1975; E. Shapiro, 1978; R. Shapiro, 1979). The unity of the system requires predictability in the action patterns of all its members. As long as all the members are intensely involved and responsive to the demands of the system, the sense of satisfaction and security of its members is guaranteed.

In extreme examples of such systems, there is no room for individual choice or spontaneous individuality. In less extreme systems, some freedom can be permitted to family members, but at certain critical points the demands of the system must predominate, and the call for the characteristic and expected involvement in the system must be responded to by all its participants or else the system is severely threatened. Particularly threatening to the maintenance of the equilibrium of the system is the movement toward autonomy and independence on the part of any of its members (E. Shapiro et al., 1975; Mandelbaum, 1977b). When the participating selves enjoy a greater degree of differentiation and individuation, the possibility exists of a dialogue in which differences can be clarified and acknowledged. In pathological families, however, relatedness is maintained in a fragile and inauthentic form by the avoidance of differences or by desperate attempts to convince the other of one's point of view or to justify oneself in the other's eyes. This pattern of interaction has been described as "pseudomutuality" (Wynne et al., 1958). Real mutuality, however, is based on the clear differentiation of self and the acceptance of differences, rather than merely on the avoidance of conflict. Frequently enough, any movement in the direction of individuation or of the acknowledgment of differences or any attempt at confrontation and authentic conflict may be labeled as betrayal of the inherent values of the family system— a radical form of treason the proper punishment of which can only be isolation and abandonment.

The family emotional system that functions in this way is organized around and functions in terms of the interlocking patterns of introjections and projections that take place between and among the family members (Zinner and R. Shapiro, 1972). On the part of the parents, such interactions are manifested in their relative insensitivity and inability to respond appropriately to the needs of their children as independent and autonomous persons. The child is seen and reacted to in terms of the parents' own intrapsychic needs, rather than in terms of the child's needs. Thus, the child is drawn into the emotional interaction in such a way as to sustain the precarious psychic equilibrium of the parents and to subordinate the child's own personality needs and growth potentials in the process.

When family interaction depends on such an introjective-projective basis, each member of the family tends to represent parts of the other individual's unacceptable self-images, so that any mobilization in the direction of separation and individuation becomes a threat to the inner psychic economy of other family members. When the participants have not achieved self- and object-constancy, there is a tendency to split off unacceptable aspects of the self and project them onto others, thus setting up the interlocking and emotionally entrapping system (Zinner and R. Shapiro, 1972; E. Shapiro, 1982). Slipp (1973) describes this very well in the following terms:

> Without a stable, integrated, and internalized system of introjects, the parents remained stimulus-bound and needed external objects upon whom to project certain split introjects. In turn, other family members were required to introject, incorporate, and act out these split introjects. However, in order to stabilize the *internal* system of the parents, the entire family became locked into a rigid, mutually controlling *external* system of interaction in which each one's self-esteem and survival was dependent upon the other member's participation. (pp. 384–385)

The implicit demand, therefore, is that other members of the system think and act and feel according to a projected image, rather than as separately motivated individuals. Differentiation of the respective selves is thus impeded and, when needs are not reciprocally met, the subjects feel rejected, worthless, furious, and enraged, and they see the nonresponding other as depriving, controlling, or generally evil. As Slipp noted, projective elements may include relatively good and benign aspects, as for example, to compensate for the lack of a stable, nonambivalent, good object; this may serve to compensate for feelings of past or present deprivation or to counter destructive and enraged feelings, and thus reestablish a sense of internal balance. Or the projective elements may involve displacement of destructive feelings onto another member of the family system who then serves as a scapegoat. Although scapegoating is only one example of the displacement of destructive feelings to other members, this is a fairly typical pattern. Other members, however, may also be seen as powerful, intrusive, controlling, domineering, and punitive and as holding a variety of other hostilely destructive attitudes.

In this fashion, the interaction between the parents and the affected child or the designated patient comes to fulfill, in the external realm of the family interaction, important psychological needs of the participants. The pressures in the system induce the affected member to introject the projective elements that are put on him either separately or collusively by the parents. The patient's participation in this triadic interaction functions to help maintain the psychic equilibrium of the parents. The power of these needs and the forces that are brought to bear to control and keep the patient in this position vis-à-vis the family are considerable. Slipp (1973) has noted in this regard:

Since intrapsychic conflicts are acted out in the interpersonal sphere, the parents continuously need the patient to stabilize their own personality. Thus, the identified patient cannot achieve his own separate identity with adequate ego control. He requires a symbiotic relation to sustain his *relational* ego identity and acts to perpetuate the system. To break from the symbiotic survival pattern is fraught with the fear of being destroyed, of not surviving intact alone, as well as the fear of loss of control and destruction of the parents. When the individual's adaptational needs are disjunctive with the family system, as a result of developmental growth or outside stress, he may be precipitated into an overt psychosis. (p. 395)

It is within this context, then, that the important patterns of internalization that determine and shape the child's development take place. When the projective elements are particularly destructive or negative, as they often are in pathological family systems, one or other of the parental figures is forced into an inadequate or inferior role and is treated in a belittling or contemptuous or undercutting manner by the other parent or other family members. As Lidz and his coworkers have noted repeatedly (1965), the function of the parents is to provide adequate models of identification for children of both sexes. Such internalizations can be harmoniously integrated only when the models are not conflicting and mutually exclusive. The maintaining of an adequate model depends not only on the inherent qualities of that particular parent, but also upon the esteem and value placed upon that parent as a love object by the spouse. When the parents are, in fact, mutually supportive and valued, the potentiality exists for relatively nonconflictual internalizations and constructive identifications. As Singer (1975) noted, this is one of the central failures in the families of borderline and delinquent adolescents.

One of the most typical and pathological patterns that evolves in deficient family systems derives from the fact that the parents come to the experience of marriage with unresolved oedipal conflicts and needs and that they seek fulfillment of these in the marital relationship. These needs, in fact, usually dictate the choice of marital partner. But when the needs and wishes are frustrated and unfulfilled, there is a regressive retreat, a heightened vulnerability, and an intensification of narcissistic needs that is only aggravated and reinforced by the advent of children. The children are drawn into the service of these consuming and unsatisfied needs, which remain largely unconscious on the part of the parents. The child is then drawn into the projective and introjective interaction with the result that his own personality development proceeds on the basis of pathological introjects, particularly of the undeveloped narcissistic residues in the parents, rather than on the basis of differentiated and integrated parental models. Often the neurotic needs of the parents are collusively coordinated, but frequently they are cast in conflictual opposition; in such cases, the child is caught between the parents, so that his response to the needs of one parent means a disloyalty and betrayal of the other. Consequently his response to the needs of one parent means antagonism and rejection from the other.

Although the operation of such projective and introjective mechanisms is most blatant and most easily observed in families with schizophrenic children, it has also been observed as a predominant mode of preceptual and behavioral interaction in families with disturbed adolescents. The normal adolescent pull in the direction of increasing autonomy and individuation is jeopardized by implicit demands placed on the child to collude with the unconscious emotional assumptions of the family system. These children, from birth, are drawn into the emotional interaction and come to play a specific role relative to parental fantasies. From birth onward, these parentally derived pressures play upon the child's own instinctual needs to embed him in the family system as a collusive participant in the process of responding to the fulfilling unconscious parental needs. Zinner and R. Shapiro (1972) have delineated the common threads of this interaction as follows:

> The common threads are: (1) that the subject perceives the object *as if* the object contained elements of the subject's personality, (2) that the subject can evoke behaviours or feelings in the objects that conform with the subject's perceptions, (3) that the subject can experience vicariously the activity and feelings of the object, (4) that participants in close relationship are often in collusion with one another to sustain mutual projections, i.e. to support one another's defensive operations and to provide experiences through which the other can participate vicariously. (p. 525)

It can be presumed that such projective-introjective interactions are to be found in all family systems, but that the outcome in terms of degrees of pathological impact is determined by a variety of factors, including the intensity and the level of primitive organization of parental defenses, the degree of differentiation and individuation of parental selves, and the corresponding content and level of pathological need embedded in parental projections.

Part IV
Epilogue

Chapter 14

Toward a Theory
of Borderline Psychopathology

This chapter culminates and, in a way, synthesizes, in theoretical terms, the considerable amounts of descriptive and empirical data in this monograph. The purpose is to pull together the various fragments, the bits and pieces of explanation, that have been focused on in discussing aspects of the overall problem of borderline psychopathology and to integrate them into a theoretical account. This will, it is hoped, lend not only consistency, but also coherence to our overall understanding of borderline conditions and serve as the basis for a more specific, articulated therapeutic rationale. Such a therapeutic rationale requires that the various elements be integrated into an overall account that brings together considerations regarding diagnoses, etiological components, and developmental issues.

If we refer back to the starting point of our discussion, particularly the conceptual and theoretical ambiguities that seem to inhere in the discussion of borderline conditions (see Chapter 2), it can be seen that the emphasis was on the fragmented attempts to conceptualize and provide a theoretical basis for the understanding of borderline psychopathology and the theoretical lines, each of which seemed to capture some part of the problem while it either ignored or dealt ineffectively with other aspects.

But the task of providing a coherent theoretical account is indeed formidable. To begin with, the theory must cover a considerable amount of ground. If we were to categorize some of the dimensions of borderline psychopathology, we might create a catalogue of aspects of the borderline syndromes that such a fledgling theory might attempt to explain. Such a topical catalogue might take the following shape:

The Vicissitudes of Drive Components and Derivatives: This might include such aspects as the role of aggression, particularly, primitive oral aggression; the predominance of oral drives generally; the lack of libidinal phase dominance; the tendency to affective lability, instability, and volatility; the tendency toward polymorphous perverse sexuality; the frequency of hypomanic and depressive behavior patterns; and the frequently noted condensation of pregenital and genital drive derivatives.

The Vicissitudes of Narcissism: This includes the frequently noted dissociation between narcissistic superiority with its connotations of entitlement, specialness, manic enhancement, superiority, and grandiosity and the corresponding configuration of narcissistic inferiority, marked by feelings of worthlessness, inadequacy, inferiority, emptiness, and shame.

Ego Capacities and Functions: This category covers a variety of ego functions and defensive organization, including aspects of ego weakness, the intolerance of frustration and delay, the vulnerability to traumatic catastrophic anxiety, the failure of inner regulatory controls, the tendency to regress, the tendency to act-out, the predominance of relatively primitive or narcissistic defensive organizations, and finally, the marked propensity for projection as a defensive vehicle.

Self-organization: This includes aspects of defects in the formation and maintenance of identity, including identity diffusion, the vulnerability and tenuousness of self-cohesion, the susceptibility to loss of self-cohesion or self-fragmentation, the often marked dissociation of ego states, the frequently intense feelings of vulnerability, the failures in the sense of autonomy and the incapacity for autonomous relating and functioning, and finally, the issues of borderline compliance.

The catalogue is formidable, if not intimidating. Each of the areas in question has been discussed in relatively meaningful terms in one or another theoretical perspective. In each area, the theory in question has had relative success and achieved a reasonable degree of explanatory power with respect to that given area, but is less applicable in other areas. In this sense, theories that deal with drive components and drive derivatives, both libidinal and aggressive drives and their derivatives, have been fairly successful in conceptualizing issues related to the area of drive vicissitudes; the same theories, however, have been quite unsuccessful in providing a coherent account of the remaining areas. By the same token, considerations based on the understanding of narcissism have contributed to our understanding of narcissistic vicissitudes, but to little else. The theory of ego functions and the defensive organization has shed considerable light on difficulties in that particular area, but again has contributed little to other perspectives. And finally, considerations of self-organization and functioning have addressed with relative success aspects of that particular area, but tell us little or nothing about other areas. Is it possible to provide a theoretical orientation that might meaningfully combine these various perspectives into a more embracing and coherent account?

The prudent answer is that, given the current state of our knowledge and of our theoretical sophistication, it is probably not possible. We may have to settle more modestly for an overriding frame of reference or explanatory framework that will allow us to integrate findings and formulations meaningfully from each of these areas, to provide a relatively consistent account, which, however, may not be a unified and unitary theory. The material we deal with, and the level of conceptual organization it allows, remains inherently inductive, so that the conceptual leap to the theory level, which would allow deduction, verification, and systematic hypothesis testing, is beyond our reach.

THE EXPLANATORY FRAMEWORK

But for all that, we need to remain at the level of empirical data or even of low-level clinical generalizations (Meissner, 1981c). We can expand an explanatory framework to provide a context in which the various perspectives and component elements of a more general understanding can be meaningfully combined.

Such an explanatory frame of reference must take into account the constitutional factors as they come to play on and interact with developmental processes. Thus in certain forms of borderline disturbance, genetic and organic factors may play an influential role in the developmental outcome. We would have to think in terms of a continuum of influences, covering a range from a possible genetic diathesis that might express itself in the form of a borderline disturbance, regardless of what kind of environmental or developmental experience the child might have had, to the form of borderline pathology that reflects only environmental influences of one kind or another without any apparent genetic input.

Similarly, a continuum of organic influences might extend from cases in which the organic component, particularly in terms of central nervous system deficits, might play a predominant role in the etiology of the borderline disturbance to cases in which such organic factors play no significant part. Nonetheless, when either genetic or organic factors do play a role, they must inevitably interact with the ongoing flow of developmental experiences.

The specific effects of a given genetic diathesis are not always clear. If schizophrenic-spectrum genetic influences are in question, they might create, for example, an inherent incapacity to process and integrate perceptual and conceptual material or they might affect the capacity of the individual to integrate conceptual and affective parts of his experience. Such a genetically determined incapacity would inevitably affect the manner in which the child would be able to participate in the developmental process and would strongly limit his capacity for successfully integrating experience with caretaking figures. The outcome would reveal itself not only in the distortion of the child's emerging capacity for cognitive processing or for the integration of cognitive and affective experience, but would inevitably also influence important processes of structure formation and internalization as derived from the child's experience with significant objects.

By the same token, when organic factors play a significant role, the inherent deficits associated with the organic impairment, as in the case of minimal brain dysfunction with its associated stigmata of irritability, impulsiveness, distractibility, emotional lability, etc., would inevitably come to play an important role in determining the quality of the child's interaction with caretaking figures. Thus, the course of the complex parent-child interaction, which so profoundly influences the course of development, would be altered. The child who has difficulties in attention, learning deficits, emotional lability, irritability, and impulsive behavior, due to organic factors, obviously makes it difficult for his parents to deal constructively and positively with such behaviors.

If such a child has a parent who also has difficulty in maintaining his own inner controls, who has difficulties dealing with aggressive conflicts, or who is narcissistically insulted by the child's disability, obviously, reverberations will be set up that will inevitably affect the pattern of development and easily lay the groundwork for pathological disturbances. Even without specific organic difficulties, children come into the world with varying genetic endowments, which express themselves in a broad range of variations in temperament and activity levels. These native endowments have important consequences for the quality of the child's interaction with the mother, in the first instance, and with other caretakers also.

A sluggish, slowly reacting infant in the arms of a hesitant, constricted, or withdrawn mother may not be sufficiently stimulated to promote an adequate developmental experience and to achieve optimal developmental milestones. By the same token, an irritable, hyperactive, hyperresponsive, or finicky child in the arms of a tense, hyperreactive, anxious, and smothering mother might be overstimulated to the extent that the child's inherent developmental potentials are overwhelmed and frustrated, to the ultimate detriment of the child's developmental progress. The possible combinations and permutations of these variables is almost limitless, but such factors must play a significant role in any developmental process.

In addition, the child's development, as we have already discussed in our consideration of family dynamics (Chapter 13), normally takes place in the contexts of a family structure, which constantly and continuously interacts with the child's developmental process. The nature and quality of the mother's interaction with the child reflect not only of aspects of her own personality organization and her capacity to enter the mothering relationship in meaningful and productive ways, but also the broader contexts of her involvement in the family, the nature and quality of her relationship with her husband, and the complex of relationships and involvements that constitute the inner life of the family and embrace not only her husband, but other children.

In our conceptualization, this complex of etiological factors comes to a focus within the developmental process itself. Thus, the core elements we will be considering are the significant internalizations that shape and provide the basis for the gradual integration of the child's personality organization and, particularly, the self-organization, which plays the central, most significant role. The account we will develop here will focus these critical internalizations through a developmental lens, as it were. An attempt will be made to articulate the aspects of the developmental process that impinge on the core internalizations and determine their character and outcome. Next, we will describe, in theoretical terms, the structural organization of these critical internalizations and the role they play in determining the pathological structure of borderline conditions.

The model is essentially concentric, then, with an outer shell that expresses the influence of extrinsic factors deriving from genetic components, from possible organic factors, and from the dynamic processes operative within the family context, most especially, but not exclusively, the elements of the family emotional system. At the center of these converging influences lies the developmental process in which not only extrinsic factors, but also interactional and internal factors, converge. It is in this context that the structural rudiments of the emerging personality organization are laid down. These inherent structural dimensions will lay the groundwork for normal, healthy personality development or deviant, pathological development.

And finally, at the core of the developmental process lie the elements of internalization that are the building blocks for the child's emerging self- and personality organization. These elements provide the focus for the series of concentric influences and provide the structure on which personality organization and functioning is built. When such internalizations reflect developmental arrests, fixations, and impairments, they become the basis for pathological personality functioning. Our task will be to delineate the nature of the developmental impediments and the defects in internalizations that lead to borderline psychopathology.

Introjection is the form of internalization that lies at the heart of the borderline structure (Meissner, 1971, 1979, 1980b, 1981b). The notion of introjection relates to Freud's original formulation of narcissistic identification, which arose in his analysis of melancholy and was later applied as the essential mechanism of internalization in the formation of the superego. The mechanism implies abandonment of an object-relationship and the preservation of the object intrapsychically by its introjective internalization.

If the process of introjection is cast in terms of the paranoid process (Meissner, 1978), the meaning of introjection is considerably broadened from the relatively narrow focus of Freud's original formulations. Introjection comes to refer to that process of internalization by which aspects of objects or object-relationships are taken in to form part of the subject's inner world. Illumination of how this process works is difficult. Jacobson (1964) sees it in terms of the merging of object-images with self-images and regards this merger as more or less psychotic. I think the process is more complex. Although there is little question that the process of introjection interacts with and influences the organization of self-representation, this seems to be a secondary phenomenon. To envision the organization of the self simply in representational terms bypasses the obvious structural referents of the self along with the structuralizing aspects of introjection (Meissner, 1971, 1972). Rather, in terms of the paranoid process, introjection gives rise to the inner organization of the core experiences around which the sense of self is shaped. The process of introjection, and the formation of the introjective configuration, plays itself out in the developmental process and is expressed in an increasingly individuated and integrated sense of self.

The process is, of course, subject to all the vicissitudes of development. We shall return to this subject shortly, but the point to be emphasized here is that the organization of the introjects and their economy is progressively differentiated. At the earliest levels of development, the introjective configuration is relatively primitive, undifferentiated, and global. At progressive stages of development, it becomes more delineated, more specifically differentiated, and increasingly structuralized.

Although the developmental aspects of introjection are of major significance, it should not be lost sight of that introjection functions basically in defensive terms—that is, broadly speaking, introjection occurs when there is a defensive need to salvage and preserve the residues of narcissism that are jeopardized by the developmental progression. The intimate involvement of introjection and the introjective organization with issues of narcissism and defense gives a characteristic stamp to the introjective organization. The introjects, thus, become the vehicle for the organization of drive derivatives and defensive configurations within the intrapsychic organization (Meissner, 1978).

The critical notion here is that intrapsychic development involves a progressive modification of infantile narcissism at sequential stages of the developmental process. At each stage, further modification of the original narcissism takes place so as to protect and preserve the emerging sense of self. Only gradually is the early infantile omnipotence and grandiosity modified and integrated. Kohut (1971) has described an early stage of this introjective organization in terms of the grandiose self. The preservation of such narcissistic remnants gives the introjective process, through which emergent self-components are formed, a defensive character. Later, introjection evolves in the direction of minimizing separation anxiety (loss of significant objects) or of defending against intolerable ambivalence.

The psychoanalytic literature has carved out certain introjective configurations and described them in terms of the aggressor-introject [Anna Freud's (1936) "identification with the aggressor"], the victim-introject (Meissner, 1978), or even the grandiose self (Kohut, 1971). Developmentally, later and more structuralized introjective configurations have been traditionally described in terms of the ego-ideal or the superego. Clearly, the limited classical description of introjective processes has not exhausted the understanding of this component of the paranoid process.

The introjective organization, however, must be regarded as organizing and expressing a specific configuration of drive derivatives, as well as serving specific defensive functions. By implication, the drive-and-defense organization of the introjects leaves them relatively susceptible to the regressive pulls of drive influences and also allows them to serve as the point of origin for further defensive operations, specifically, of projection. Consequently, in a clinical frame of reference, it is the inherent relationship of the introjective organization to drive derivatives—whether libidinal, aggressive, or narcissistic—its susceptibility to regressive pulls, and its propensity to projection that allow us to delineate and identify it (Meissner, 1971).

The question inevitably arises as to the location of this internalized, introjective organization. Is it inside or is it outside? Is it internal or is it external? Is it in the mind? In the self? In the ego? The answers do not come easily, nor can the questions themselves be unambiguously posed.

The critical questions have to do with the relationships between such introjective formations and the structure of the self and, consequently, the relationship of the self to the traditional structural components of the tripartite psychic apparatus—the id, ego, and superego. In regard to the interiority versus exteriority of the introjective organization, the answer must be neither yes nor no, but rather, more or less. The notion of "degrees of internalization" was introduced by Loewald (1962). Referring to superego introjects, he described them as being "on the periphery of the ego system" (p. 483)—that is, the introjective formations have a more peripheral character as opposed to the more central character of components of the ego system. Schafer's (1968b) clarification in terms of activity and passivity bears on the same issue. In these terms, the introjects are conceived as imaginary, "felt" presences—Schafer elsewhere calls them "primary process presences" (1968a)—by which the patient feels himself assaulted or gratified and through which he feels himself to be relatively passive. This passivity is a matter of degree and stands in contrast to the degree of activity, particularly the more purely self-originative and active quality of ego activities. Schafer (1968a) describes the peripheral quality of the existence of introjects in the following terms:

> An introjection is an inner presence with which one feels in a continuous or intermittent dynamic relationship. The subject conceives of this presence as a

person, a physical or psychological part of a person (e.g., a breast, a voice, a look, an affect), or a person-like thing or creature. He experiences it as existing within the confines of his body or mind or both, but not as an aspect or expression of his subjective self. (p. 72)

Both Loewald and Schafer are careful to avoid connecting the introjective formation with the ego, and there are good metapsychological reasons for doing so. Attempts to dissociate the introjective organization and isolate introjects within the psychic realm do not meet with much success, nor do such attempts find good theoretical support. The tension between the subjective and objective is reflected in Schafer's (1968a) further description of the introject:

The internal object seems to be located within the subjective self. And yet it is not part of that self, just as food may be experienced as being inside the mouth and stomach and yet not part of either. In subjective experience, the person aware of his engagement with internal objects or introjects feels himself to be engaged with something other than himself; yet he will acknowledge that the object is within him and thus within his subjective self. This observation seems not to fit the usual conception of the self as all that is not object and vice versa. (p. 80)

In the light of these difficulties—namely, in conceptualizing degrees of internalization and in formulating the relationship between introjective formations as self-modifications and as influencing correlative ego structures —it would seem to make greater sense to regard introjective organization as part of the self-system. The degrees of internalization within the self-system, then, would reflect the extent to which a particular introjective configuration has been successfully integrated and harmonized with other components of the self-system. The "primary process presences," to which Schafer gives such a discriminated, quasi-externalized status, reflect the separation of such introjective material from the rest of the self-content, against which it stands in relative opposition. Such primary process presences would have to be regarded as occupying a position on the periphery of the self-system.

At the same time, it has been my clinical experience that such primary process presences often evolve only as a result of extensive therapeutic clarification and delineation. Patients, more often than not, begin the therapeutic process in a condition in which the introjective formations are more or less undifferentiated from the main mass of the subjective sense of self. It is, in fact, only to the degree to which such patients are able to begin to put some distance between particular introjective formations and the rest of the subjective sense of self that therapeutic progress is made and the ground is laid for eliminating or revising such introjective configurations (Meissner, 1976b, 1977b).

DEVELOPMENTAL ASPECTS

The role of introjection, therefore, in the developmental process becomes a central issue both for the understanding of normal psychological development and of pathological deviation—particularly here, of the various degrees of borderline dysfunction. Through the operation and interplay of the mechanisms of introjection and projection, the intrapsychic components around which the sense of self emerges are gradually established. The commerce of these processes, in other words, contributes both to the organization of object-representations and to the gradual internalization of object-representational elements to compose the core elements of an intrapsychic substructural organization (Meissner, 1979, 1980a).

These inner structural modifications and the organization of object-representations are, in the beginning, primitive, undifferentiated, and global. Only gradually does the process build up the residues, both internally and objectively, and increase the degree of differentiation between these elements so that the critical developmental step of differentiation between self and object can begin to take place. Thus, it is the operation of these processes in the earliest stages of psychic development that lays the ground for the distinction between what is internal and what is external.

We can translate this process into the more familiar terms established by Margaret Mahler (Mahler et al., 1975) in her research into the separation-individuation process (see Chapter 12). In Mahler's terms, the newborn infant begins life in a state of autistic immersion within the mother-child unit. Within this normal autistic unity there is not differentiation, but rather a state of absolute merging, a condition of primitive hallucinatory disorientation in which need-satisfaction belongs to the child's own global sense of omnipotent and primary narcissism. In this phase, there is no distinction in the child's experience between internal and external stimuli.

Within this omnipotent autistic orbit, the infant's waking experience centers around the continuing efforts to achieve physiological homeostasis. The mother's ministrations are not distinguishable from the infant's own tension-reducing processes—including urination, defecation, coughing, and spitting. Little by little, however, the infant begins to differentiate between the pleasurable and the less pleasurable or painful qualities of his experience. Differentiation is achieved only in terms of levels of tension. Gradually, there is a dim awareness of the mother as a need-satisfying object in the child's experience, but the child still functions as though he and the mother form an omnipotent system, within which the duality is contained in a common boundary. Distancing emerges without separation. Gratification is sought from an emerging and distancing configuration ("nipple") that is not yet perceived as an object. This marks the transition to a more symbiotic phase of the child's development, of which the essential feature is a delusional omnipotent fusion with the representation of the mother, as well as the delusional maintenance of a sense of common boundary between these two physically separate individuals.

It is in terms of these primitive physiological affect states, governed by the experiences of pleasure and unpleasure, that the first differentiations begin. The cathectic attachment to the mother and the response to her ministrations is governed by the pressure of physiological needs. In the symbiotic phase, primary narcissism still prevails, but in a less absolute form than in the first few weeks of life. The perception dawns ever so dimly that need-satisfaction derives from a need-satisfying object—even though that object is still retained within the orbit of the omnipotent symbiotic unity. Only to the extent that separation begins to take place does the infant experience receiving milk that is not his own narcissistic (omnipotent) creation.

As these developments continue, there is a critical shift of cathexis from a predominantly proprioceptive-enteroceptive focus toward the sensory perceptive and peripheral aspects of the infant's body. This is a major shift of cathexis and is essential for the development of a body-ego. At this juncture, projective mechanisms come into play, not merely to contribute to the construction of a more or less separate need-satisfying object, but also to begin to serve the specific defensive functions of deflecting more destructive unneutralized aggressive impulses beyond the gradually emerging body-self boundaries.

As Robbins (1981b) has commented, the achievement of diacritic functioning and the capacity for perceptual recognition, even in the context of an undifferentiated self-object relationship, marks the point at which structuralizing internalizations can be identified. As will be argued, meaningful internalizations may also take place even earlier in development. The problem is how to describe them and determine their nature and contribution to psychic growth. The danger lies in including later developmental outcomes with earlier forming processes. Later identifiable forms of internalization may have a different form and function than earlier processes that operate in a less differentiated fashion as precursors.

Robbins (1981a) has proposed a biphasic view of symbiosis. The earlier unconditional symbiosis precedes the capacity to represent unpleasure and is reflected in the infant's smiling response to the mother. Here the maternal stimulus evokes an undifferentiated, pleasurable self-object representation. The second phase of territorial symbiosis reflects the onset of stranger anxiety at about eight months of age. At this point, the inner realm of pleasurable symbiotic self-object representation begins to be discriminated from the external territory of a self-object representation involving unfamiliarity or strangeness. If the prior phase of unconditional symbiosis has been relatively secure and satisfactory, the external realm can be met with curiosity and fascination. If the titration of frustration and separation has been premature or excessive, it may be met with increased anxiety and fearfulness.

This first differentiation within the symbiotic experience may provide the initial emergence of the context and the capacity to inaugurate, in relatively undifferentiated terms, the lifelong dialogue between the internal and the external. These processes point in the direction of what we later recognize as projection and introjection. As Robbins (1981b) observes, consequent to stranger prehension, these processes

> involve the function of projection and introjection in primitive structuring or representing of quantities of unpleasure. Normally projection and introjection probably differentiate after sensorimotor-affective recognition, which I refer to as perceptual recognition, and assist the formation of aggressively endowed self-object representations. This process is most readily observed in the "no" phase in response to maternal attempts to curb the infant's unbridled behavioural expressions of symbiotic expansiveness (e.g., habit training). The component of projection may be observed in the infant's mirrored perceptual awareness of negation, displeasure, even anger in relation to mother. The component of identification may be seen in the progressive internalization of the "no" experience in the form of growing awareness of anger, or recognition of an unpleasure self. The component of introjection leads to the development of self-regulation, first seen when the infant borrows the maternal "no" and directs it toward his current or prospective activities. In this way painful aspects of the self-object relationship which are at first distance-perceptual and undifferentiated are selectively internalized, allowing a positive relationship which is progressively more realistic to continue. (pp. 373–374)

As this developmental process works itself out, the organization of object-representations not only is influenced by external inputs, derived from external reality and, particularly and most significantly, from the primary objects of the infant's experience, but also is modified in some degree by the interplay between such inputs and projective elements. The organization of object-representations becomes increasingly differentiated as the child's cognitive capacities become more developed and articulated. Thus, the capacity for the development of sensory and perceptual images, the gradual emergence of more complex forms of memory organization— shifting from more immediate and stimulus-bound forms of memory processing to the gradual emergence of more sophisticated and persistent forms of recognition and finally evocative memory—the emergence of object constancies, and a variety of important influences from various forms of developmental learning, all contribute to the gradual building-up, differentiation, and organization of object-representations (Meissner, 1974a).

As the object-representation is increasingly elaborated, elements of the object-representation are correlatively internalized and introjected as parts of the infant's globally emerging and relatively undifferentiated sense of self. Even in the earliest phases of the symbiotic matrix, these internalizations are taking place so that critical elements of the inchoate core of the child's self are being shaped. At this point, we can only guess at the significance of the balance of pleasurable versus unpleasurable components and the significance of the contribution of maternal attitudes to these nascent stirrings within the child. Winnicott (1960a,b) has stressed the importance of "good-enough mothering" and a "holding" environment in the laying down of these primitive, yet crucial, early internalizations.

As these processes interplay, the organization of elements of the self becomes more decisive and is more clearly and definitively separated from representations of the object. This process has been described by Mahler and her coworkers (1975) in terms of separation and individuation. In the view proposed here, projection and introjection are the inner mechanisms that subserve the overriding process of separation-individuation. At each step of the separation-individuation process, there is a critical reworking of internalized elements that gradually allows the child to establish a more autonomous sense of self and to separate himself from dependency on the parental object. In this sense, the individuation would seem to be related to the building-up of an articulated sense of self through progressively differentiated introjections, whereas the gradual separation from the matrix of parental dependence is accomplished through the progressive projective modification and delineation of object-representations.

The process is even more complex. The building-up and integration of introjective components sets into operation critical identificatory processes that extend the processes of internalization and structuralization at a metapsychologically distinct level. These identifications have to do with the structural integration of the ego and with the transformation of superego (introjective) elements in terms of their integration with ego structures (Meissner, 1972). Reflexively, this further order of structural integration sustains and consolidates the organization and experience of the self. The degree to which such structuralizing identifications are brought into play is a function of the degree to which introjective formations are conflict-free, unambivalent, and not caught up in the pressures of drive and defense.

The threat to the separation-individuation process is particularly that of separation anxiety. Mahler has described the various forms in which separation anxiety expresses itself and the distortion that can work in the normal progression of separation and individuation. Separation as an inherent threat to development not only arises from the natural developmental impulse in the child and his burgeoning wishes and autonomous self-determination and expression, but it can also be reinforced and intensified by the reactions of the mother. If the mother reacts to the child's bids for autonomy by excessive rejection and precipitant pushing of the child away from the comforting support of his dependence on her, the child is forced into a premature posture of self-sufficiency, on one hand. If the mother is excessively threatened by the loss of the child as a dependent appendage, her efforts will be directed toward stalling his bids for relative autonomy and a prolongation of symbiotic dependence, on the other.

These varieties of maladaptive emergence from the state of maternal dependence can play upon the interaction of projection and introjection in a variety of ways. These distortions create defensive pressures that make it necessary for the child to rely excessively on the utilization of these mechanisms in ways that are specifically and excessively caught up in defensive patterns. Thus, an excess of separation anxiety can lead the child to an excessively regressive and global introjection of the parental image as a defensive means of preserving the contact with the need-satisfying, dependency-gratifying object and of maintaining narcissistic integrity. The basic threat, after all, of separation anxiety at this level is the loss of the object. That object, in turn, is essential to the preservation of the child's sense of narcissistic integrity and omnipotence. If the child is allowed to separate from the maternal orbit without excessive stirring of separation anxiety, introjection will, in fact, take place, but not under the intense pressures of narcissistic need and defensive exigency.

As the developmental process advances, there is a progressive modification of infantile narcissism and an increasing differentiation of the sense of self, which affects the quality and nature of the introjections involved at each phase and correspondingly changes the quality of defensive organization. At each phase of the separation-individuation process, there is an increasing capacity for autonomous existence and a diminishing intensity of the child's dependence on need-satisfying objects. As the respective differentiation of object- and self-representations and their inherent stability is gradually increased, there emerges an enlarging capacity for tolerating the separateness of objects.

The capacity to tolerate the separateness of objects is perhaps one of the primary goals of the development in object-relationships. It implies that the object-representation has been sufficiently developed so that the realistic qualities of the object are recognized and acknowledged, with a minimal complement of projective distortion. Thus, the discrimination between one's self and the object is clearly established and maintained. In fact, the capacity to relate to the object in relatively realistic terms and to tolerate the separateness and autonomous independence of such objects is intimately related to the stability and cohesiveness of the self. The capacity for realistic object-relationships depends upon the organization of a sense of self that has, at its core, the internalization of a good and loving parent, serving as the focal point for the integration of successively positive introjective elements. Modell (1968) has expressed this relationship succinctly in the following terms:

The cohesive sense of identity in the adult is a sign that there has been a "good enough" object relationship in the earliest period of life. Something has been taken in from the environment that has led to the core of the earliest sense of identity, a core which permits further ego maturation . . . it is a fact that these individuals who have the capacity to accept the separateness of objects are those who have a distinct, at least in part, beloved sense of self. If one can be a loving parent to oneself, one can more readily accept the separateness of objects. This is a momentous step in psychic development. (p. 59)

At the same time, correlative to the emergence and integration of increasing self-cohesion and identity, a process of integration and consolidation is taking place in the organization of object-representations that leads in the direction of object-constancy (McDevitt, 1975; Meissner, 1974a). This process involves not only the perceptual object-constancy, which allows for the consistency and persistence of perceptual experience under the constant variation of stimulus conditions, but also the more complex forms of libidinal object-constancy, which contribute to and form the basis of stable, relatively consistent, and mature object-relationships. Thus, the differentiation and consolidation of object-representations play their parts, along with the development of self-cohesiveness, in the articulation of important capacities to know and to respond to external reality.

We are left, then, with a momentous conclusion—namely, that the capacity to know, recognize, and accept reality is a critical developmental achievement, and not a given or presumable quality of human cognition. Moreover, the attainment of the capacity depends upon the critical working-through of developmental issues and the gradual consolidation of a cohesive sense of self, along with a differentiated and objectively articulated capacity for object-representations. To the extent that object-representations are contaminated by defensive needs, which motivate the coloring and modification of object-representations by projective determinants, the capacity to know and understand reality is, in that degree, impaired.

THE ROLE OF INTERNALIZATIONS

The inner impulsion of the argument drives us theoretically back to the earliest strata of experience. Here the issue of internalization is put at the heart of the debate. If, at the point at which stranger prehension begins to emerge, we can argue that the earliest rudiments of projection-like activity are expressed, we can also conclude that we are correspondingly and correlatively at a point where we can also meaningfully speak of introjective processes. But how are we to characterize these early, pre-introjective internalizing processes that shape and constitute the earliest rudiments of inner structural organization?

Internalization reflects and touches most of the important aspects of the developmental process. What aspects of internalization, then, can we specify amid the complexities of developmental progression? The infant is embedded in a matrix of object-relations (object-related) from the very moment of birth, if not before (Graves, 1980). From the very beginning, then, internalization processes are taking place and result in the laying down of building-blocks of structural aspects of the infant psyche and components of the emerging self.

If we return for a moment to our working definition, our focus here is on those specific processes by which the infant transforms the regulatory interactions with his environment and particularly with the caregivers in his environment into inner regulations and characteristics. From the very beginning of this process, the infant is interacting with his environment and assimilating from it as well as accommodating to it. In the earliest interchanges with the mother, when the first regulatory patterns are being established and the infant is finding his "ecological niche," the patterning of communications between mother and child is intense and complex and has profound effects. Our current understanding of the complexity of this interaction makes it clear that considerably more is at stake and more is involved than issues of mere homeostatic regulation.

The basis of the process, even at this most primitive level, is by no means reductively physiological, but rather involves important communications of affect that intermesh with physiological variables, and also have a considerable impact on the infant's evolving sense of well-being and security (Pine, 1981). When the good-enough mother responds sensitively and comfortingly to her infant's distress, she is not simply restoring a physiological state of homeostasis and relieving the tension related to the infant's distress, but she is, by the same actions, also communicating a set of affects and attitudes to the infant that qualify the infant's experience in the interaction.

The issues, then, are not simply quantitative (economic), but also involve important, meaning-impregnated affective experiences within the fusion of the mother-child unity that the infant somehow relates to himself. In other words, hand in hand with the physiological replacement, there is an affective infusion from the mother within the complex mother-child interaction that the infant experiences, however globally and indistinctly, as somehow his own. This is the "mirroring function" Winnicott (1967) has described so well, in which the child experiences himself as he is experienced by the mother. In this sense, then, the importance of all the parameters of early management of the cycle of waking-sleeping and feeding-eliminating and the patterns of regulatory exchange that evolve in connection with them, as well as the issues of optimal levels of stimulation in all the sensory modalities, carry with them the added impact of this sensori-affective level of communication and include, as one important aspect of their developmental significance, the dimension of internalization. Thus, these early affective components, which arise within the context of the interaction and relatedness to the mother, become a part of the infant's emerging inner world and are gradually consolidated, along with other aspects of his emerging psychic structure.

Lichtenstein (1977) has focused on the mirroring aspect of this primitive relatedness. What emerges dimly in the mirror is not so much a primary love object (mother) as the child's own image as reflected in the mother's own needs vis-à-vis the child. What is internalized is a sense of primary identity that becomes a basic organizing principle for further emerging patterns of internalization. The child begins to experience his own existence as it is reflected in and through the mother's responsive libidinal cathexis of the child.

With regard to the infant's earliest self-experiences, Dare and Holder (1981) have recently provided the following summary:

> We believe that under normal conditions the earliest self-experiences are almost totally determined by the nature of the mother/infant relationship. It is a necessity that the mother and newborn baby adapt to each other. Different babies have different "personalities" and temperaments, as well as varying adaptive capacities. The infant's adaptive capacities are, of course, considerably more limited than those of the mother. Winnicott (1965) has remarked that the infant's first view of himself is the reflection of what he sees in his mother's eyes. In other words, the mother can be understood as acting like a mirror, reflecting the first qualities of the infant's self onto the infant. When she smiles and cuddles the infant closely, the emergent self-image will be associated with feelings of warmth, safety and of being cherished. When the mother is withdrawn, depressed or angry, the emergent self is experienced as fragile, unloved and unvalued. Later, of course, the child whose mother is consistently negative towards him may come to regard himself as the cause and source of the mother's unhappiness or hostility.
>
> We would speculate that the first disjointed experiences of that which is later to become the "self" are essentially affective, deriving from bodily sensations and the interactions with the mother. At this early point in development, such experiences lack the degree of organization with regard to time and space as well as the cognitive elements which will eventually accrue to a cohesive self-representation. (p. 327)

The importance of this dimension of the infant's early experience is amply underlined by studies of the effects of object loss or deprivation at this level. These effects have been amply documented in studies of anaclitic depression, hospitalism, and even the effects of transient separation.

This pattern of communication and interaction becomes increasingly more complex and evolves in the direction of increasing activity and initiative on the part of the infant. The earliest internalized components derive from the state of the infant's object-relatedness, particularly with primary care-givers, but this gradually evolves in the direction of an increasing sense of interaction with and relation to a separate object. As the infant's experience of the object becomes increasingly distanced and gradually separate (Brodey, 1965), the experience of feeding or being fed or not being fed is gradually disengaged and connected with the presence or the absence of a feeder, so that only gradually are certain regulatory functions connected with the presence or absence of the object.

As the infant's capacity to differentiate the significant others who are interacting with him enlarges, there is a corresponding increase in the complexity and differentiation of internalizations. At this point, the infant tends to show an increase in initiatives and an increasing organization and differentiation of emotional components, such as affiliation, fear, curiosity, and exploration. By the same token, this burgeoning capacity to take initia-tive and to organize behavioral and feeling states is simultaneously enriched by and facilitates his capacity to internalize (Greenspan and Lieberman, 1980). It is at this point that the capacity to imitate and to bring imitation the service of increasing intentionality becomes important.

Imitation plays a particularly important role in the infant's emerging capacity to internalize. Imitative behaviors can be observed even in the earliest weeks of life. These primarily involve movements of the mouth, tongue, and head and have a quality of mimicry, which seems to facilitate the pleasureful interaction between child and adult. At this earliest level, such behavior undoubtedly reflects an inherent capacity for mimicry and seems to serve important uses in the maintenance and eliciting of certain kinds of pleasureful adult response (Abravanel et al., 1976), reflecting part of the infant's preadaptive repertoire of behaviors that elicit and reinforce his interaction with adults. Moreover, the infant's tendency and apparent capacity for imitative behavior can be facilitated or hindered by the pattern of response from the parent (Call and Marschak, 1966). When the interaction with the parent or caregiver is mutually pleasureful and optimally arousing, the tendency for such imitative responses is facilitated and encouraged. This also begins to take place in the evolving pattern of playfulness between child and caregiver and can be clearly identified as an evolving pattern in such early childhood games as peek-a-boo (Kleeman, 1967). These imitative behaviors are quickly brought to the service of the child's increasing initiative and the urge to mastery.

It is important, however, to realize, as Spitz (1958) has noted in con-nection with the mirroring of prohibitive gestures in connection with super-ego development, that true imitation of parental gestures begins to occur in the second half of the first year, but that these have a mimicking quality as echo-like reproductions of the adult gesture. They tend to be immediate responses, and mirror a gesture initiated by the adult. The pattern of such imitative behaviors, however, rapidly shifts from mirroring or mimicry to increasingly reflect the infant's growing initiative; it is rapidly placed in the service of his capacity to elicit responses from his environment and thus to gain increasing competence and mastery.

It is useful to remember that imitation itself is not a form of internalization, but rather a complex form of learning based on modeling (Meissner, 1972). Consequently, imitations in the developmental context may serve as inducements to or precursors of internalizations that both accompany and follow as a natural consequence the imitative behavior, although they are not the same. By the same token, imitative behaviors may reflect underlying patterns of internalization or may serve defensive functions as a vehicle for inhibiting or preventing further identification (Meissner, 1974b).

In the normal course of events, when the affective experience with the object is predominantly positive and constructive, the conditions prevail for eliciting and facilitating the infant's capacity to imitate and internalize constructively. The patterns of emerging initiative and competence that the infant develops, often in rapid and remarkable fashion toward the end of the first year, are the basis for an increasing capacity for positive and constructive identifications with loved and admired adult objects. Imitation plays a transitional role insofar as it is a vehicle through which external capacities or characteristics of significant objects can become a functional part of the infant's own capacity. But although imitation remains a matter of behavioral patterns, identification reaches beyond to include qualities and characteristics of the object itself or the object-relationship. Consequently, the behavioral modifications of imitation imply no enduring structural change in self-organization (Meissner, 1972)

Even in the first year of life, and possibly quite early in the first year, the infant has the capacity for internal psychic organization and synthesis based on the modeling of an external object. This capacity for identification emerges simultaneously with the capacity for differentiation between self- and object-images and is rapidly brought into the service of developing competence and mastery. The infant's emerging capacity for initiative and autonomous behavior provides another facilitating basis for this identificatory capacity.

However, the emergence of this capacity can be short-circuited or diverted by those vicissitudes in the infant's object-relationships that introduce excessive frustration, heightened anxiety, insecurity, loss, abandonment, or other growth-inhibiting or growth-frustrating determinants. Such vicissitudes can subvert the infant's inherent identificatory potential, with the result that forming structures are organized in terms of defensive needs or are overly influenced by and vulnerable to drive derivatives. Consequently, internalizations that occur in these defensively overburdened contexts tend to underlie pathological personality configurations and remain susceptible to degrees of drive-determined dysfunction and vulnerable to regressive pulls and defensive distortions (Meissner, 1971).

The earliest levels of affective interaction in the mother-child dyad influence inchoate and emerging patterns of internalization. The predominance of harmonious, adaptive, and mutually reinforcing interactions between mother and infant, particularly having to do with affective communications, although not exclusively, allows for a relatively unincumbered assimilation of elements from the object-related sphere to the infant's emerging sense of self. The "primary identity" has embedded in it affective reverberations of comfort, security, well-being, and positive anticipation and expectation as the infant begins to approach the external world. The effects of such "good-enough mothering," or perhaps more precisely "good-enough mother-child interacting," is to stimulate, optimally, the child's growing capacity to assimilate, imitate, take the initiative, and achieve increasing degrees of mastery and competence in responding to and engaging his environment. The inherent capacity for self-actualization and for integrating aspects of given objects in the process of selectively and adaptively shaping a sense of self receives optimal stimulus and support. These aspects of early internalization point in the direction of an emerging capacity for positive and constructive identifications.

In regard to this level of the earliest organization of structural elements in borderline personalities, Kernberg (1966) argued that the so-called internalized object-relations were split along the lines of predominant drive organizations, that is, libidinal or aggressive. He also argued that the same split occurred along the lines determined by the titration of pleasure-unpleasure in the affective experience. Beyond the confusion in the alternation between drives and affects, there is considerable question whether, outside the Kleinian world of life and death instincts, the drives can be considered as being so differentiated and specific. In addition, as Robbins (1976) pointed out, the notion of internal object-relations at a stage of development prior to the differentiation and separation of self and non-self is more confusing than clarifying. Other concepts are needed to formulate the earliest internalizations.

When the process falters, the ground is laid for a gradual accretion of impediments to the capacity to internalize aspects of objects and object-relations as an expression of initiative, adaptive selectivity, and creative integration in the formation of the self. Even the earliest elements of disquiet, disequilibrium, excessive frustration, or significant failures of the mother to respond in need-satisfying and adaptive ways to the child's distress leave a sense of lack, discomfort, and dis-ease within the infant's rudimentary experience of himself. The affective tone is negative rather than positive. The sense of trust is shifted in the direction of mistrust, insecurity, and uncertainty. The emerging capacity for dealing with the environment is cast in doubt and is unreliable, halting, and uncertain. The progression toward an increasing sense of mastery and competence falters. The affective coloration to the emerging sense of primary identity is negative and insecure. In this sense, the basis is laid for the tendency in the later course of development toward introjection as the predominant modality of internalization, rather than identification.

A crucial point in the development of internalization comes with the infant's "hatching" from the symbiotic orbit. At this juncture, the element of loss becomes an operative part of the developmental process. The diminishing of symbiotic dependence and the gradual course of separation and individuation call into play compensatory internalization processes that enable the child to assimilate aspects and functions of the caretaking objects. Continuing internalization provides the internal components for increasing individuation and serves basic needs for a sense of inner competence and capacity and for the maintenance of narcissistic equilibrium. At this point, the form of internalization we later recognize as introjection (especially in the rapprochement and oedipal phases) begins to emerge. To the extent that earlier affective assimilations have left a core of positive residues, the introjective components will build on a relatively positive base. When the residues are excessively negative or ambivalent, the quality of emerging introjects tends toward increased aggression, poorer integration, faulty internalization, permeation with unintegrated drive-derivatives, greater degrees of conflict, and the need for defensive maintenance. Such introjects are more poorly structuralized and their regressive potential is increased. They are also more susceptible to externalization and can function as core elements of pathological personality organization (Meissner, 1978).

The emergence of transitional objects and related transitional phenomena depend on the availability of processes of introjection and, correspondingly, projection. These are the intrapsychic processes by which transitional objects are created, transformed, and gradually internalized. When negative or conflictual elements, even from the earliest levels of infantile experience, contaminate these processes, the child's capacity to form and utilize transitional objects in the service of optimal psychic growth, effective separation-individuation, and increasing autonomy can be compromised—sometimes severely. Transitional phenomena may not develop or they may be subverted into the formation of fetishistic (Greenacre, 1969) or even autistic objects (Tustin, 1980).

My conclusion is that, in the first year of life, and even in the very first object-related experiences of the newborn infant, internalizing processes constitute the heart of the developmental progression. Moreover, specifiable internalizing processes function at a more primitive level, in the form of precursors, than their more evolved and differentiated counterparts in later stages of development. At the most primitive level, the process is incorporative, particularly because it predominates in the period in which mother and child are fused in a dyadic unity in which there is neither self nor object. The mother's affective relation to the child is at the same moment his own, and is gradually assimilated into the islands of experience that becomes increasingly organized and stable and form the first rudiments of the self-organization.

As these affectively colored rudiments are extended to later forms of internalization, they are progressively integrated with the continual flow of internalizations. The balance of libidinal, narcissistic, and aggressive components influences the pattern of subsequent internalizations and determines the extent to which positive or negative (pathogenic) introjections occur and come to dominate the organization of the self or the extent to which positive patterns of identification will provide the basis for more positive, autonomous, adaptive, and cohesive elements as the essential building blocks of a healthy, mature self-organization and personality structure (Meissner, 1971, 1972, 1981b).

A central construction in this theoretical perspective, one that is closely and inextricably linked to the notion of internalization, is the concept of the self. The point of view that I am proposing is that the psychoanalytic notion of the self is a theoretical construct that is both supraordinate and integrative in nature. As with all such higher-order integrating concepts, the basic intelligibility of the self cannot be reduced to its component parts. The whole, in this case, is to some extent greater than the sum of its parts. Thus, the formulation of the concept of the self adds a significant new dimension to psychoanalytic thinking, providing a basis for a more concise, effective explanation of phenomena not adequately embraced in pre-existing theory. The result of this approach is that the concept of the self in psychoanalysis is precisely a theoretical construction that serves important functions in the integration of other theoretical concepts, provides a frame of reference for the linking and coordinating of a variety of important data, and can be analyzed in terms of its own inner organization and functioning.

Thus, the concept of self is not synonymous with that of the person, despite the lingering uncertainty in this usage of the concept of the self in the earlier works of Hartmann (1964), Jacobson (1964), and Sandler and Rosenblatt (1962), whose contributions provided the originating impulse for the articulation of the psychology of the self. This emphasis on the theoretical intelligibility of the concept of the self is quite similar to the relatively common usage that evolved around the concept of ego, mistaking its technical and theoretical conceptualization for a more broadly based common-sense usage that made it equivalent to the acting person. One of the difficulties that often afflicts psychoanalytic conceptualizations is that they suffer a certain slippage from their theoretical moorings and connections and undergo a more common-sense transformation, which substantially alters their basic meaning.

It must be emphasized that the theoretical concept of the self, insofar as it serves as a supraordinate and integrating concept, does not provide the basis for a new scientific paradigm. The claim that such is the case would seem to be motivated either by a misunderstanding of the nature of the concept or by a need to strike new theoretical ground and to establish one's independence and autonomy from pre-existing theoretical formulations. As I see it, however, the concept of self is simply an advancement and a development that completes and extends certain aspects of structural theory. Insofar as it is a development of that structural theory, it requires that the earlier theory be rethought in terms of an enlarged, more meaningful articulation. Such a reprocessing of technical theoretical terms comes as no surprise to psychoanalytic theorists, since that has been the essential nature of conceptual development in the field from the very beginning.

In these specifically structural terms, the self is a supraordinate concept that includes and integrates the pre-existing elements of the tripartite theory —id, ego, and superego—in a higher-order formulation. Each of these pre-existing structural entities expresses and brings coherence and order to some subsegment of the functions of the self. It can be seen, from this perspective, that explanations couched in terms of the component psychic entities or agencies have a relatively limited and focused range, which may contribute to or explain some part of the further-reaching conceptualization provided by the self-organization, but nonetheless they have explicit validity within their appropriate explanatory range. By the same token, explanations that arise in terms of the conflicting operations of these component agencies have validity within the specific range of issues having to do with intrapsychic conflict and defense, but they begin to lose applicability in other realms of psychic experience, particularly those having to do with self-other interactions that pertain to the realm of object-relations or problems of preconflictual, preambivalent development. In other words, if one accepts the notion of a supraordinate self, the component aspect, designated as superego, for example, can be used to articulate certain functional aspects of the self in its specific involvements in relationships; it may, however, also function in a more delimited frame of reference to express specific intrapsychic dynamics, effects, or interactions and be conceived as interacting with other functional aspects of the intrapsychic organization to effect certain intrapsychic results. These variant frames of reference and levels of explanation are by no means divorced, but rather the respective explanations maintain a relative autonomy of significance and relevance.

The relationship between the concept of the self and traditional notions of narcissism raises a number of complex and extremely difficult issues. It seems clear, however, at this juncture that the concept of the self is by no means limited or confined to its connection with narcissism (Meissner, 1981d).

If we accept the concept of the self-organization as a supraordinate and integrating addition to psychoanalytic theory, it may be useful to add some greater specificity to particular areas in which the addition of the self concept better explains or increases the explanatory range of the theory. Such a theoretical gain can be illuminated in at least three areas:

1. The self as a theoretical construct provides a focus for formulating and understanding the complex integrations of functional processes that involve combinations of functions of the respective component agencies. This would have specific application to such complex activities as affects, in which all the psychic systems seem, in one way or other, to be represented: complex superego-ego integrations reflected in such formations as value systems and other complex interactions of psychic systems that involve fantasy production, drive-motor integration, cognitive-affective processes, etc. There is room here for considerable reworking and refocusing of traditional psychoanalytic ways of looking at and understanding psychic phenomena in terms of the self as a reference system.
2. The self concept provides a more specific and less ambiguous frame of reference for the articulation of self-object interrelationships and interactions, including the complex area of object-relations and internalizations.
3. The self concept provides a locus in the theory for articulating the experience of the personal self, either as grasped introspectively and reflectively or as experienced as the originating source of personal activity. This would provide a place for an account of subjectivity and subjective meaning within the theory.

This approach raises an important metapsychological issue, namely, the relationship between the experiential organization of the self and the tripartite entities. The organization of the self and the organization of structural tripartite entities cannot be simply identified. The self-organization operates at a different level of psychic organization than do the structural entities. Moreover, the structural entities, in the strict theoretical sense, are understood to be organizations of specific functions. This concept applies not only to the ego as such, but also to the superego and the id. Even though the theory at various points attributes more or less personalized, anthropomorphized metaphors to the operation of these structures, their strict theoretical intelligibility is nonetheless given in terms of the organization of specific functions attributed to the respective structures.

A defect in the structural theory and a source of considerable confusion in psychoanalytic thinking is that it is difficult to integrate and to account for complex experiential states. One of the major difficulties in the structural concept is that there is no room for the experience of one's own self as an integrated and relatively autonomous self-originating focus of action. If the realm of subjective experience can be specifically related to the cognition of and organization of the self, then there would be room for a subjective experience of self as an active and organizing principle within the intrapsychic apparatus.

A STRUCTURAL PERSPECTIVE

I would like to turn, at this juncture, to a structural formulation that may provide a template for therapeutic understanding and may, it is hoped, offer a frame of reference for the development of a meaningful therapeutic rationale.

In his illuminating criticism of extant theories of borderline psychopathology, Robbins (1976) observed that no theory of borderline personality satisfactorily encompassed the issues of borderline aggressiveness and control, on the one hand, and the issues of borderline compliance and victimization, on the other. He suggested that an understanding of the roles of both introjection and projection in borderline functioning might provide a vehicle for resolving this theoretical split. In my own work, I have attempted to develop a conceptual approach to these problems in terms of the paranoid process (Meissner, 1978). I will try to formulate this understanding in regard to the borderline spectrum.

The introjects represent those basic internalizations that form the core elements around which the individual's sense of self is constructed (Meissner, 1971, 1979). The introjects reflect the defensive and developmental vicissitudes that arise in the experience of object-relations, particularly, but not exclusively in those relationships that pertain to primary objects. The organization of the introjects takes place along two primary dimensions, the narcissistic and the aggressive. Consequently, the intrapsychic organization of these introjective configurations can take place along primarily narcissistic lines or along aggressive lines, or some combination of both.

Each of these dimensions tends to be organized in terms of a polar distribution, which is extreme or absolute in proportion to the degree of psychopathology. Thus in the narcissistic dimension, the introjective configuration can take on the aspect of superiority and grandiosity in one direction, but can also take on the aspect of inferiority and shame-filled insignificance and worthlessness in the other. Similarly along the aggressive dimension, the introjective configuration expresses itself in terms of polar attributes of hateful, evil, and powerful destructiveness, on the one hand, and impotent, helpless, weak vulnerability, on the other. I have used the terms "aggressor-introject" and "victim-introject" to express these polar coordinates of the aggressive dimension in the organization of pathogenic introjects. By the same token, the polar distribution in the narcissistic dimension can be described in terms of the "superior-introject" and the correlative "inferior-introject."

It should be noted that these polar coordinates always occur together and express correlated and reciprocally linked aspects of the patient's psychopathology. For example, where one finds evidence of the victim-introject, as it might find expression in the patient's sense of vulnerability, helplessness, weakness, or impotence, we can be sure that careful exploration will also turn up evidence of the aggressor-introject—a side of the patient that feels itself to be powerful, destructive, and perhaps even evil and dangerous. Correspondingly, the narcissistic organization of the introjects also has this same reciprocal dimension between the superior and the inferior introject. When we find evidence of a narcissistic impoverishment and a sense of shameful insignificance and worthlessness, we may be sure that lurking in the background of the patient's unconscious mind is a corresponding configuration in which part of the patient's mind sees itself as special, privileged, and entitled to admiration and special consideration. Behind the sense of shame there lurks an exhibitionistic wish, just as behind a sense of inferiority and worthlessness there lurks the residues of the grandiose self that Kohut (1971) has so aptly described. Correspondingly, when the patient's narcissistic self-aggrandizement and self-inflation is the more apparent part of the clinical picture, it can be presumed that the inferior introject is playing itself out in less apparent and often unconscious ways.

In better-organized personalities, there is a tendency for the pathological aspects of the organization of the patient's self to cluster around one or the other of these introjective configurations, with the corresponding repression of the others. Thus, in the depressive neurotic, the components of the inferior-introject reflecting the patient's inherent narcissistic vulnerability and sense of inferiority and worthlessness are easily identifiable, but it is usually only after long and often arduous therapeutic work that the more hidden and repressed elements of the patient's narcissism become evident, particularly in terms of the patient's inherent sense of narcissistic entitlement and residual grandiosity.

In the somewhat more primitive forms of personality organization we are discussing here, the various aspects of the introjective organization are a much more dominant aspect of the organization of the patient's self. Not only does the introjective configuration dominate the patient's sense of self, but it is relatively more likely that the various polar aspects of the introjective configuration will come to play a more prominent part in the patient's pathology, often being much more intrusive on the patient's self-awareness or much more expressive in various aspects of his pathology than in better-organized personalities. This is quite strikingly seen in various forms of borderline pathology, in which the aspects of the introjective configuration are never far from consciousness and are often intrusive, either in the form of determinations of the patient's own sense of self or in the form of projective distortions of significant objects. Thus, we are familiar with the characteristic picture of the somewhat regressed borderline patient who plays out the role of helpless and impotent victim, while at the same time projecting elements of aggressive destructiveness and powerful persecutory threat onto the therapist. Both these aspects of the patient's pathology reflect the organization of the introjects in terms of the aggressive polarities implied in the victim- and aggressor-introjects.

Not only is the ready availability of one polar dimension to be attributed to the self and the other projectively to the object a characteristic of borderline functioning, there can also be a ready alternation between these introjective characterizations within the subject himself. Thus, it is not at all unusual for the borderline to feel himself the helpless and impotently vulnerable victim at one point and to shift into the opposite introjective posture, that of a powerful agent of hostility, at another. Thus, the victim-introject or the aggressor-introject may come to dominate the patient's sense of himself, and in the less stable and labile forms of regressive expression, the patient may alternate between them, often quite rapidly and dramatically.

The mechanisms of introjection and projection are closely linked as functional aspects of the paranoid process. The mechanism of projection is both correlative to and derived from the introjective organization. In terms of the representational economy, following Jacobson's (1964) formula, projection can be described in terms of a transferral of elements from self-representation to object-representation. Consequently, the externalization involved in projection is an intrapsychic process—external objects are not changed or modified by the projection itself.[1] The role of projection in modifying object-representations gives it a critical function relative to object-relationships. The correlative interaction of projection and introjection plays itself out throughout the whole of the developmental course, as we shall see later. Thus, projection is a central dimension of the process by which the

---

[1]External objects may be modified secondary to the projection from the subject's inner world, but the modification is not a direct causal effect of the projection process. The modification of the object may occur as a response to the subject's expectations or as corresponding internalizations (Meissner, 1977a). Brodey (1965), in fact, describes externalization in the following terms: "1. Projection is combined with the manipulation of reality selected for the purpose of verifying the projection. 2.The reality that cannot be used to verify the projection is not perceived. 3. When this mechanism is prominent in a stable group where people are learning from each other (as in a family), information known by the externalizing person but beyond the *Umwelt* of the others is not transmitted to these others except as it is useful to train or manipulate them into validating what will then become the realization of the projection. Reality testing is subverted in this process. Interlocking systems of externalization shared in a family potentiate disturbed ego development" (pp. 167–68).

differentiation of objects is established and in terms of which the quality of object-relationships is continually being shaped and reworked.

Insofar as the projections serve to externalize elements of the introjective configuration, they bear the characteristic stamp of introjective components. Thus, the projective derivatives reflect the organization of drives and defenses inherent in the introjects. Projection deals in the commerce between self-images and object-images and is characterized by the quality of differentiation and complex organization that is inherent in such representational organizations. Consequently, projection does not exhaust the limits of externalization. Externalization, in its turn, may also function in terms of relatively dissociated and depersonalized elements of the intrapsychic frame of reference. Thus, in certain phobias, the aggressive components may be externalized and experienced as external threats without the particular configuration of more personalized and organized qualities characteristic of projections as such. More often than not, however, when such externalizations take place, they bear the stamp of introjective organization. Thus, the analysis of phobic contents can be made through the externalized elements to their introjective derivatives and, in the therapeutic work, can be traced back to the generative and pathogenic object-relationships. The classical paradigm for this process was established by Freud in his case studies of Little Hans (1909) and the Wolf Man (1918).

Consequently, the effects of projection are experienced particularly in terms of object-relationships. This is the primary focus and area of expression of the projective function. However, the projective operation may play itself out in other nonhuman contexts. The mechanism may operate in any context in which human qualities can be attributed to external realities. This may take place in primitive animistic or magically superstitious interactions with the environment, but it also takes place in more mundane contexts of interaction with pets, or other forms of animal interaction, or even in determining the quality of interaction between the individual and his social environment—social organizations, institutions, businesses, government, and so forth.

It should be noted that the operation of the paranoid mechanism of projection may be accompanied by denial, or it may not. If the projection is motivated by a defensive need to dissociate oneself from an intolerable or somehow noxious self-element, the projection will usually be accompanied by a denial. Thus, in the classical form of the persecutory paranoid projection, hostile and destructive intent is attributed to the object and, at the same time, denied the subject. Rather, the introjective components of helplessness and vulnerability serve to defend against the more destructive and threatening aggressive components. When such defensive need does not operate, however, projection may take place without denial. This is most usually the case in the projection of more benign and tolerable or acceptable attributes. A similar set of circumstances would seem to operate in the context in which the combined functioning of introjection and projection subserves certain forms of empathic responsiveness.

It can be seen that projection is a highly complex phenomenon with many gradations and variations. Moreover, it can be readily seen that projection plays a critical part in the working-through of the gradual elaboration of forms of introjection. The modification of object-representations by projective components sets the stage for subsequent reinternalizations, which serve to modify the introjective organization. Thus, the interplay of introjection and projection is a form of feedback that allows for the progressive modification and differentiation of introjective organizations and their correlative projections.

The progressive interlocking of introjective and projective mechanisms, and their correlative and mutual influence, provides the central mechanism for intrapsychic development, as well as the medium through which various forms of psychopathology are expressed. It is when these processes are somehow cut off from the main forces of synthetic integration operating within the psyche and become contaminated by regressive drive influences or external reality-based distortions that pathological influences are effected.

It may be possible to understand the differences in the organization of the pathological aspects of the narcissistic personalities in contrast to that of the borderline personalities in terms of the organization of their respective introjects. From this point of view, it seems reasonable to say that the narcissistic personality has organized itself around the narcissistically impregnated introjects and that the narcissistic aspects of these internal structures dominate the organization and functioning of the personality. The major preoccupations, therefore, of the narcissistic personality are directed toward the maintenance of the sense of self, which requires that the corresponding narcissistic integrity of these introjective configurations be preserved. Thus, the major effort in the narcissistic personality is directed toward maintaining the necessary narcissistic equilibrium entailed in this effort toward the preservation of self.

Since the predominant introjective configuration is organized around issues of narcissism, it has its own inherent characteristics of vulnerability that have to do with the maintenance of narcissistic supplies and supports. Even so, to the extent that the individual is able to maintain these necessary supplies and supports, he is also able to maintain a relatively high degree of self-integration and cohesiveness. In moderate degrees of narcissistic impairment, and in circumstances in which the individual's ability to gain the necessary narcissistic input is adequate, he runs little risk of severe psychological impairment and is correspondingly reasonably well protected against the threats of regressive disorganization or impairment in self-cohesiveness or even any sense of loss of self or diffusion of identity.

The picture is quite different in the borderline patient. Here the introjective configuration does not center specifically or solely around issues of narcissism, but rather around a more pathogenic, combined complex of issues having to do with both narcissism and aggression. Whereas the narcissistic personality primarily dealt with the vicissitudes of the superior and inferior introjects and with the corresponding narcissistic vulnerabilities, the borderline patient must deal not only with these narcissistic configurations, but also with the added burden of the aggressor- and victim-introjective configurations. Thus, although the pathology of the narcissistic personality is more or less confined to the narcissistic sector of the personality, as it affects the integration and functioning of the patient's self, for the borderline personality, the more prominent intrusion of issues having to do with vicissitudes of aggression make the picture considerably more complex, and because of the disruptive influence of unresolved aggressive elements, which often stem from relatively primitive and even oral aggressive-sadistic levels, contributes an additional burden and an additional set of vulnerabilities to the borderline personality.

The issues of victimization and victimizing in the borderline personalities play a prominent role, not only in their pathology, but also in their therapy. Thus, the maintenance of a sense of self and of inner organization is made more difficult for the borderline, since he must deal not only with the narcissistic issues and the narcissistic vulnerabilities that characterize the narcissistic personality, but in addition, with the vicissitudes imposed by unresolved and relatively primitive aggressive components. These aggressive components, in terms of their motifs of victimization and threatening destructiveness, therefore play themselves out in much more dramatic and apparent ways in the psychotherapy of the borderline patient than in the psychotherapy of the narcissistic patient. The difficulties with aggression in narcissistic patients remain relatively secondary and arise usually in the form of narcissistic rage secondary to narcissistic insult or as a vehicle for redressing narcissistic wrongs.

The vicissitudes of aggression in the borderline patient, however, play a much more primary role and contribute significantly to his inability to establish and maintain a coherent sense of self around any of the available introjective configurations. Consequently, the borderline patient has greater difficulty in establishing or maintaining a sense of object-constancy, is only capable of maintaining a sense of inner cohesiveness in relatively partial and unstable ways, and is considerably more vulnerable to regressive pressures and stresses. Although these vicissitudes may be seen most dramatically and clearly in the lower order of borderline pathology and in regressive borderline states, these same parameters play themselves out in more modulated and often more subtle ways through the whole range of borderline pathology. Thus, even in the higher-order, better-functioning borderline patient, who might be suitable for analysis, the personality may be relatively consistently organized around an integrated self-concept that allows for a considerable degree of autonomous functioning. However, under the stress induced by an analytic regression or by a severe narcissistic insult or disappointment, that relatively vulnerable cohesiveness may begin to deteriorate so that the component introjective configurations come to dominate the functioning of the personality and begin to express themselves in a variety of pathological forms.

The same structural and dynamic differentiations suggest that, developmentally, the borderline patient has not been able to integrate partial good/bad, giving/denying, satisfying/frustrating images of both self and objects. The hostile and loving parts of parental imagos have failed to achieve a satisfactory integration due to unresolved aggressive components derived from hostile or ambivalent relations with the significant caretaking objects. The unresolved aggression derives, in some sense, from drive sources, but remains unresolved because of aggressively contaminated internalizations (introjections) from external objects. The result is a form of impaired synthesis of introjective components (splitting) and the tendency to project hostility. The organization of object-representations fails to achieve a reliable constancy and self-cohesion remains precarious and vulnerable to regressive strain.

The narcissistic personality has been shaped by different developmental experiences. The passage through separation and individuation has not been contaminated to the same degree by aggressive derivatives. The narcissistic child does not meet the same degree of parental rejection, disapproval, hostility, or destructiveness. The relationship with both parents is not excessively ambivalent, so that the resolution and integration of aggression is a less pressing developmental issue. Rather, the problems for the narcissistic child lie more specifically in the narcissistic sector. The problem in separation and individuation concern the loss, potential or actual, of the narcissistic communion or narcissistic availability of the parent as separation and the establishment of autonomy assert themselves. The narcissistic personality is left with a greater sense of individuation and correlative self-cohesion, but with a pervasive sense of narcissistic need and a sense of narcissistic vulnerability from the potential or actual loss of narcissistically invested objects.

This theoretical framework provides a context within which the degrees of pathological expression of the borderline spectrum can be understood. In both the hysterical and schizoid continua, we are dealing with grades of pathological disturbance and deviation. Within the hysterical continuum, the *pseudoschizophrenics* represent the group closest to the border of psychosis, in whom the structural elements are most poorly differentiated and maintained. The introjects at this level are poorly differentiated, and their structure is easily susceptible to regressive pulls and contaminations. It is difficult for these patients even to maintain the coherence and integrity of the respective narcissistic configurations.

The clinical picture presented by such patients reflects not only a rapid and often easily influenced vacillation between various introjective configurations, but also a marked, diffuse, and at times chaotic tendency to project introjective derivatives in a manner that reflects little in the way of stability or perdurance. The lack of structure not only makes these patients easily vulnerable to regression, but also leaves them susceptible to instinctual currents, particularly those of an aggressive nature that manifest themselves in poor ego capacity and a vulnerability to overwhelming anxiety.

From a developmental perspective, such patients have clearly not accomplished the tasks of separation and individuation, and their inner lives are contaminated by the persistence of symbiotic needs and fantasies. Their pathological organization is such that they are left with relatively severe deficits in the capacity for adaptive ego-functioning and autonomy. These deficits are of such an order that their capacity for maintaining an integrated and cohesive sense of self is severely impaired and their self-organization is readily vulnerable to regressive fragmentation and disorganization.

The *psychotic character* has a somewhat more developed and consistent introjective organization, so that the introjective configurations are better defined and differentiated. The degree of distortion inherent in them is not quite as extreme as in the pseudoschizophrenic, and the ease with which alternation between introjective configurations takes place is somewhat less. The same introjective organizations are evident, but the rapidity and ease of alternation among them reflects the somewhat greater capacity of these patients to regulate their inner psychic processes so that they are not quite as susceptible to drive-determined regressive influences. The level of ego weakness remains relatively high in these patients, so that the propensity for regressive primitive defenses and for ego disorganization remains part of the clinical picture.

The emotional lability and vulnerability to severe anxiety, particularly separation anxiety, is severely troublesome. Nonetheless, the capacity for integrating a functional self in terms of one or other of the introjective configurations is somewhat greater, so that in nonregressive periods these patients can function on a much better adaptive level. Here, as in the case of the pseudoschizophrenics, the conflict between the aggressor- and victim-introjects dominates the clinical picture, not, as we have noted, to the exclusion of narcissistic components. Although the psychotic character may flee defensively to one or other of the introjective configurations, his capacity to stay in that configuration is somewhat greater than the pseudoschizophrenic.

The *dysphoric personality*, in contrast to these earlier forms of border-line psychopathology, has a more functional, greater ego capacity, which is usually operating in effective control during nonregressive phases. Only during periods of regressive crisis do the inherent ego vulnerabilities of these patients become manifest, so that the full severity of the pathology can be appreciated. At other times, these patients may function reasonably well and may even look relatively normal. At this level, the introject organization has a greater degree of stability and integration, which allows these patients to function for greater periods of time and in the face of greater degrees of regressive strain or stress than patients in the preceding categories. Because of the inherent nature of conflicts over aggression, it is more often the case that these patients will assume the victim position, so that the functional organization of their sense of self centers around aspects of the victim-introject. These patients often must endure severe conflicts over aggression, and many of their deepest pathological concerns have to do with the inherent sense of themselves as potentially and dangerously aggressive and destructive. Assuming the victim position in such cases serves clearly defensive needs.

In these patients, the core of the pathology has less to do with issues of ego weakness, although the ego remains vulnerable to regression and the capacity for primitive defenses is obviously still present. Even so, the patients are able to maintain relatively high levels of ego-functioning for most of their lives and throughout the general course of their everyday experience. It is only under special circumstances, at certain periods of regressive stress, that the capacity of the ego is undermined. Thus, the introjective configurations for these patients are much less contaminated with aggressive and narcissistic derivatives and consequently reflect both a higher degree of developmental achievement and a lesser of expression of aggression and narcissism within the patient's protective family system. Thus, the inner lives of these patients are dominated less by symbiotic needs than by the developmental failure to successfully negotiate the rigors of separation and individuation. It is these patients who more characteristically than others can be thought of as running into difficulties in the rapprochement crisis.

Although the issues of ego weakness and dysfunction rarely trouble these patients, the difficulties in the quality of their self-organization, based on the underlying introjective configurations and the correlative chronic difficulties in object-relations, suggest that the locus of pathology in these patients can be much more meaningfully sought in the self-organization than in the ego integration, as such. These aspects clearly are not so easily separable or dichotomous, but there may be questions of degree and emphasis in attempting to understand such conditions. The quality of the introjective organization is such that the development of specific ego capacities and functions is not, at least grossly, interfered with. At the same time, the patient's self-organization has a pathological quality that both distorts and discolors his inner experience of himself and tends to spill over, in the form of projective derivatives and other transactions with the patient's social environment.

At the higher end of the hysterical continuum, the *primitive hysterics* represent a level of development in which the introjective configurations have achieved an even greater degree of consistency and meaningful integration. These patients' most typical pattern is the domination of the intrapsychic economy by the victim-introject and its attendant conflicts over aggression and the tendency to depression. Such patients often manifest oedipal features, but not the authentically triangular conflicts we might expect in the neurotic. The oedipal situation for such patients might better be described as pseudo-oedipal, insofar as the oedipal involvements are contaminated by a variety of preoedipal conflicts and fixations. In these patients, the issues of orality often play a highly significant role in their inner dynamics, along with unresolved issues related to separation and individuation. Thus, regression in such patients is never as severe or as frequent as in patients in the preceding categories, but tends rather to express itself in hysterical symptom formation, in phobic or depressive anxieties, and regressively, in emotional turmoil and lability. These patients, at the same time, maintain a significantly greater capacity for inner psychic conflict and have less tendency or need for externalization of such conflicts, and correspondingly, to a lesser extent, projective distortion of external relationships.

For these patients, as has already been suggested, the victim-introject plays the dominant role in the inner psychic realm, but often with significant narcissistic components. When the narcissistic elements are in full play, these patients can often look and function like narcissistic personalities. In such cases, the patient's borderline qualities may remain relatively sequestered and only emerge at times of regressive strain when the aspects of the victim-introject, particularly, become more manifest. It is in such patients that the combination of the impulse and need to comply with and to please the therapist becomes a central issue.

When we turn to the *schizoid continuum*, all these patients share, in varying degrees, the underlying schizoid dilemma between the intense need for and concomitant fear of involvement with objects. In the more seriously disturbed patients, the schizoid dilemma reflects the failure to resolve basic symbiotic needs, so that the symbiotic wish for union with the object carries with it the implication of symbiotic engulfment. Consequently, the introjective organization of these patients is permeated by these basic infantile needs and fears. These affect, particularly, the organization of the victim-introject in which the extreme vulnerability is related to fears of engulfment and destruction. Correspondingly, there is the correlative fear of destroying the object, which relates to the intensity of inherent destructiveness in the aggressor-introject.

Thus, the inner life of the schizoid individual tends to be dominated by the conflicts between these two introjective configurations operating at a relatively primitive level. In most schizoid patients, however, the pathogenic influence of these introjects is such as to maintain a reasonable degree of structural organization that can be described in ego and superego terms. The ego-functioning in such individuals often allows for effective life involvements, a minimum of emotional turmoil and lability, and a relative absence of anxiety. There is also resistance to regression. But occasionally, where the inherent organization of these introjects, derived in substantial part from developmental vicissitudes, remains vulnerable to regressive strain, under certain stressful circumstances, a precipitous and dangerous regression and fragmentation can occur.

However, in such schizoid individuals the ego is usually capable of a better level of functioning and of maintaining psychic integrity, so that the underlying conflicts are dealt with by a combination of obsessional and emotionally distancing techniques. The object-relations dilemma is solved, in these cases, by maintaining an affective distance and uninvolvement with objects. Often in such patients the titer of narcissism is significant and may reflect itself in the sense of cold grandiose isolation and self-sufficiency that is frequently seen in such patients.

Similar issues are at play in the *false-self organization*, but here the capacity for the subject to adopt the false-self facade in the inerest of a compromise connection with and involvement with the world around him indicates a somewhat different level of underlying needs. The essential compliance of the false-self relates to the victim-introject and serves as a defensive barrier to the associated aggressor-introject. In these terms, the patient is often capable of maintaining a relatively high and consistent degree of ego-functioning. The locus of the pathology is predominantly in the self-organization in these cases. Often, the internal split in the personality is experienced in terms of the false-self configuration, and serves as a socially acceptable facade behind which the subject conceals what he may feel to be more representative of his own sense of his true self, that is, the sense of himself structured in terms of both the aggressive and the narcissistically superior introject. It is often difficult for such patients to appreciate the discrimination between autonomous self-reliance, self-assertion and independence, and the elements of narcissistic superiority and aggressive destructiveness inherent in the pathogenic introjects. In the view proposed, the patient's true self lies in none of these pathogenic configurations, but rather in the realm of his autonomous and conflict-free ego-functioning and arrested self-integration that has been subverted and impeded by the introjective organization. Underlying their clinging to the introjective alignment, there is the fear of separation and abandonment that is associated in their minds with the repressed and defended-against aggressor and narcissistically superior introjects, but involves conflicts over autonomy or independence. These patients avoid both of these alternatives by clinging to the victim position and its implicit passivity and compliance.

The situation in the organization of the *"as-if" personalities* is quite similar, both dynamically and in terms of the introjective organization. Rather than the more consistent and enduring false-self configuration, the "as-if" personality substitutes a more transient and both time- and situation-limited compliant facade, which adapts, in chameleon-like fashion, to the demands and expectations of the immediate social context. The "as-if" compromise is another way of dealing with the underlying schizoid dilemma, focusing particularly on the inherent risks of autonomy and separation. These patients have failed to negotiate successfully the separation-individuation process and avoid the establishing and maintaining of a consistent and coherent sense of self, with its attendant risks of separation and abandonment, which they see as the necessary correlates of autonomy and independence.

At the highest level of organization and functioning within the schizoid continuum, I have placed the condition of the *identity-stasis*, so-called. Patients reflect many of the same issues, but in a muted, displaced fashion. Although inherent conflicts over aggression and victimization remain significant in their intrapsychic difficulties, these patients often manifest narcissistic dimensions that can make them look very much like narcissistic personalities. Their inability to establish themselves along a decisive life-course, leading to a definite and authentic sense of identity and self-organization, can reflect not only the impediments inherent in conflicts over aggression and victimization, but can also carry the burden of signficant narcissistic inputs.

For many of these patients, for example, the choosing of a career line involves a narcissistic compromise of their underlying pathological sense of omnipotence, which does not allow them to surrender alternatives or other options in the interest of pursuing a single course. It is not infrequently the case, therefore, that the residues of the grandiose self reflecting the narcissistically superior introject play a significant role in the difficulties these patients encounter.

To round out this theoretical perspective, I would like to return briefly to the earlier question regarding the issues to which a meaningful theory of borderline personality functioning ought to address itself (see pp. 423–424). The degree to which this theory has successfully addressed these issues, I leave to my readers to judge. The first area was the vicissitudes of drives and drive derivatives. This aspect of the theory is more implicit than explicit in the presentation here, but obviously the organization and nature of the introjective configurations is strongly related to underlying drive components.

We have focused, particularly, on the aggressive and narcissistic aspects of this integration, since these elements are particularly relevant to self-organization. Libidinal drives and external aggressive elements are not irrelevant to these considerations, but they are not directly and immediately involved in the organization of the introjective components. Libido is equivalently object-libido, just as externally directed aggression is also object-directed.

The structural integration of drive components into the introjects is a matter of quality and degree. The less structured this integration is, the less well integrated and organized the introjective configuration, the more likely it is that the drives will exercise their disorganizing and relatively volatile influence independently of a capacity for intrinsic regulation and modulation. Similarly, the lack of libidinal phase dominance reflects the failure of the developmental integration of the introjective components, so as to allow this developmental progression. At the same time, the patterning of the organization of drive components in the introjective configurations has a role in the patterns of clinical symptomatology, particularly those having to do with depressive, manic, or paranoid tendencies.

The second area of concern is that of narcissism. Here, the theory is explicit and detailed, regarding the development and integration of narcissistic components, in terms of the narcissistic superior-introject and its correlative narcissistic inferior-introject.

The third area has to do with ego capacities and ego-functions, particularly in the matter of defensive organization and ego weakness. The pattern of introjective organization plays a crucial role in determining the organization of ego-functions, particularly in regard to the manner in which critical internalizations affect the organization and development of the ego as well as the superego. When pathogenic introjects dominate the developmental experience, the opportunity and the capacity for meaningful, constructive identifications is mitigated and impeded. When the introjects are sufficiently pathogenic to interfere with aspects of ego development, the pathological picture reflects the corresponding ego weakness and the primitiveness of the defensive organization and functioning.

As we have indicated, this is a matter of degree, such that at the lower levels of borderline personality functioning ego weakness plays a dominant role in the pathological picture. But as we progress toward the higher levels, ego impediments and ego weakness play a diminishing role, and the core of the pathology seems to shift more toward the organization and integration of the self and its critical role in personality functioning. A particular focus of the theory with regard to the capacity of the ego has to do with the degrees of propensity to projection.

The final area of theoretical interest is that of the self-organization. The theory addresses itself directly and immediately to this aspect of the personality functioning, insofar as self-organization takes place in terms of the core introjective configurations. These introjective elements become the central building blocks around which self organization takes place, in terms of which the individual's sense of himself is experienced and lived. It is in terms of the inherent qualities of the introjective organization that the tendencies to loss of self-cohesion, identity diffusion, and the dissociation of ego states takes place. Moreover, the quality of the experience of the self is directly related to the patterning and organization of the introjects, specifically, in terms of the delineated patterns of aggression, victimization, and narcissistic enhancement or depletion.

It would perhaps be presumptuous at this point to try to claim a more or less comprehensive theory of borderline personality organization and functioning. But at least we can suggest that the theoretical framework suggested by the paranoid process and focused around the organization and functioning of the critical introjects provides a context within which the multiple currents of etiological influences and developmental vicissitudes can be focused, so as to provide a more flexible and differentiated account of the levels of personality integration and functioning that can be identified in the borderline spectrum.

The purpose of this summary is not only to propose a point of articulation for the extensive background material provided in this volume, but also to serve as a theoretical framework within which it might be possible to articulate a more consistent and meaningful therapeutic approach to the borderline conditions. Obviously, the implications and the implementations of this approach, at the various levels of borderline integration and functioning we have been describing in terms of the borderline spectrum, must be correspondingly modified in terms of the theoretical understanding provided here. But that effort, for the moment more a promise than a fulfillment, must lie in the future. However, if the data and the integration provided in these pages have served their purpose, it may well stimulate some readers to undertake that journey for themselves.

References

Aarkrog, T. (1977). Borderline and psychotic adolescents: borderline sympto-matology from childhood—actual therapeutic approach. *Journal of Youth and Adolescence* 6:187–197.

Abelin, E. L. (1975). Some further observations and comments on the earliest role of the father. *International Journal of Psychoanalysis* 56:293–302.

Abravanel, E., Levan-Goldschmidt, E., and Stevenson, M. B. (1976). Action imitation: the earliest phase of infancy. *Child Development* 47:1032–1044.

Ackerman, N. W. (1958). *The Psychodynamics of Family Life.* New York: Basic Books.

——— (1962). Family psychotherapy and psychoanalysis: the implications of difference. In *Family Process*, ed. N. W. Ackerman, pp. 317–336. New York: Basic Books, 1970.

Adler, G. (1970). Valuing and devaluing in the psychotherapeutic process. *Archives of General Psychiatry* 22:454–461.

——— (1973). Hospital treatment of borderline patients. *American Journal of Psychiatry* 130:32–35.

——— (1974). Regression in psychotherapy: disruptive or therapeutic? *International Journal of Psycho-Analytic Psychotherapy* 3:252–264.

——— (1975). The usefulness of the "borderline" concept in psychotherapy. In *Borderline States in Psychiatry*, ed. J. E. Mack, pp. 29–40. New York: Grune & Stratton.

——— (1979). The myth of the alliance with borderline patients. *American Journal of Psychiatry* 136:642–645.

——— (1981). The borderline-narcissistic personality disorder continuum. *American Journal of Psychiatry* 138:46–50.

Adler, G., and Buie, D. H. (1979). Aloneness and borderline psychopathology: the possible relevance of child development issues. *International Journal of Psychoanalysis* 60:83–96.

Alexander, F. (1930). The neurotic character. *International Journal of Psychoanalysis* 11:293–302.

Anderson, C., and Playmate, H. (1962). Management of the brain damaged adolescent. *American Journal of Orthopsychiatry* 32:492–500.

Andrulonis, P. A., Donnelly, J., Glueck, B. C., Stroebel, C. F., and Szarek, B. L. (1980a). Preliminary data on ethosuximide and the episodic dyscontrol syndrome. *American Journal of Psychiatry* 137:1455–1456.

Andrulonis, P. A., Glueck, B. C., Stroebel, C. F., Vogel, N. G., Shapiro, A. L., and Aldridge, D. M. (1980b). Organic brain dysfunction and the borderline syndrome. *Psychiatric Clinics of North America* 4:47–66.

Angel, K. (1965). Loss of identity and acting out. *Journal of the American Psychoanalytic Association* 13:79–84.

Apfelbaum, B. (1966). Ego psychology: a critique of the structural approach to psychoanalytic theory. *International Journal of Psycho-Analysis* 47:451–475.

Arlow, J. A. (1966). Depersonalization and derealization. In *Psychoanalysis —A General Psychology*, ed. R. M. Loewenstein, L. Newman, M. Schur, and A. J. Solnit, pp. 456–478. New York: International Universities Press.

Asch, S. S. (1976). Varieties of negative therapeutic reaction and problems of technique. *Journal of the American Psychoanalytic Association* 24:383–407.

Atkin, S. (1974). A borderline case: ego synthesis and cognition. *International Journal of Psycho-Analysis* 55:13–19.

Atkins, N. B. (1967). Comments on severe and psychotic regressions in analysis. *Journal of the American Psychoanalytic Association* 15:584–605.

Bateson, G., Jackson, D. D., Haley, J., and Weakland, J. H. (1956). Toward a theory of schizophrenia. *Behavioral Science* 1:251–264.

Bauer, S. F., Hunt, H. F., Gould, M., and Goldstein, E. G. (1980). Borderline personality organization, structural diagnosis and the structural interview. *Psychiatry* 43:224–233.

Bean, M. H., and Zinberg, N. E. (1981). *Dynamic Approaches to the Understanding and Treatment of Alcoholism*. New York: Free Press.

Bellak, L. P. (ed.) (1979). *Psychiatric Aspects of Minimal Brain Dysfunction in Adults*. New York: Grune & Stratton.

Bemporad, J. R., Smith, H. F., Hanson, G., and Chicetti, D. (1982). Borderline syndromes in childhood: criteria for diagnosis. *American Journal of Psychiatry* 139:596–602.

Benedek, T. (1970). Fatherhood and providing. In *Parenthood: Its Psychology and Psychopathology*, ed. E. J. Anthony and T. Benedek, pp. 167–183. Boston: Little, Brown.

Benjamin, L. S. (1976). A reconsideration of the Kety and associates study of genetic factors in the transmission of schizophrenia. *American Journal of Psychiatry* 133:1129–1133.

Berkowitz, D. A., Shapiro, R. L., Zinner, J., and Shapiro, E. A. (1974a). Concurrent family treatment of narcissistic disorders in adolescence. *International Journal of Psychoanalytic Psychotherapy* 3:379–396.

—— (1974b). Family contributions to narcissistic disturbances in adolescents. *International Review of Psychoanalysis* 1:353–362.

Blos, P. (1962). *On Adolescence*. Glencoe, Ill.: Free Press.

—— (1967). The second individuation process of adolescence. *Psychoanalytic Study of the Child* 22:162–186.

Blum, H. (1972). Psychoanalytic understanding and psychotherapy of borderline regression. *International Journal of Psychoanalytic Psychotherapy* 1:46–60.

—— (1974). The borderline childhood of the Wolf-Man. *Journal of the American Psychoanalytic Association* 22:721–742.

Boelhouwer, C., Henry, C. E., and Glueck, B. C. (1968). Positive spiking: a double-blind control study of its significance in behavior disorders, both diagnostically and therapeutically. *American Journal of Psychiatry* 125:473–481.

Boszormenyi-Nagy, I. (1965). A theory of relationships: experience and transaction. In *Intensive Family Therapy: Theoretical and Practical Aspects*, ed. I. Boszormenyi-Nagy and J. L. Framo, pp. 33–86. New York: Harper & Row.

Bowen, M. (1960). A family concept of schizophrenia. In *The Etiology of Schizophrenia*, ed. D. D. Jackson, pp. 346–372. New York: Basic Books.

—— (1961). The family as the unit of study and treatment. I. Family psychotherapy. *American Journal of Orthopsychiatry* 31:40–60.

Bowen, M., Dysinger, R. H., and Basamania, B. (1959). The role of the father in families with a schizophrenic patient. *American Journal of Psychiatry* 115:1017–1020.

Bowlby, J. (1973). *Attachment and Loss*. vol. II. *Separation: Anxiety and Anger*. New York: Basic Books.

Breuer, J., and Freud, S. (1893–5). Studies on hysteria. *Standard Edition*, 2.

Brodey, W. M. (1965). On the dynamics of narcissism. I. Externalization and early ego development. *Psychoanalytic Study of the Child* 20:165–193.

Brody, E. B. (1960). Borderline state, character disorder, and psychotic manifestations—some conceptual formulations. *Psychiatry* 23:75–80.

Buie, D., and Adler, G. (1972). The uses of confrontation with borderline patients. *International Journal of Psychoanalytic Psychotherapy* 1:90–108.

Burnham, D. L., Gladstone, A. I., and Gibson, R. W. (1969). *Schizophrenia and the Need-Fear Dilemma*. New York: International Universities Press.

Bursten, B. (1973). Some narcissistic personality types. *International Journal of Psychoanalysis* 54:287–300.

―――― (1978). A diagnostic framework. *International Review of Psycho-Analysis* 5:15–31.

Bychowski, G. (1953). The problem of latent psychosis. *Journal of the American Psychoanalytic Association* 1:484–503.

Call, J. D., and Marschak, M. (1976). Styles and games in infancy. In *Infant Psychiatry: A New Synthesis*, eds. E. N. Rexford, L. W. Sander, and T. Shapiro, pp. 104–112. New Haven: Yale University Press.

Carpenter, W. T., Gunderson, J. G., and Strauss, J. S. (1977). Considerations of the borderline syndrome: a longitudinal comparative study of borderline and schizophrenic patients. In *Borderline Personality Disorders*, ed. P. Hartocollis, pp. 231–253. New York: International Universities Press.

Carpenter, W., Strauss, J., and Bartkow, J. (1973). Flexible system for the diagnosis of schizophrenia. *Science* 182:1275–1278.

Chessick, R. D. (1966). The psychotherapy of borderline patients. *American Journal of Psychotherapy* 20:600–614.

―――― (1974). Defective ego feeling and the quest for being in the borderline patient. *International Journal of Psychoanalytic Psychotherapy* 3:73–89.

Chwast, J. (1977). Psychotherapy of disadvantaged acting-out adolescents. *American Journal of Psychotherapy* 31:216–226.

Collum, J. M. (1972). Identity diffusion and the borderline maneuver. *Comprehensive Psychiatry* 13:179–184.

Coppolillo, H. P. (1967). Maturational aspects of the transitional phenomenon. *International Journal of Psycho-Analysis* 48:237–246.

Corwin, H. A. (1974). The narcissistic alliance and the progressive transference neurosis in serious regressive states. *International Journal of Psychoanalytic Psychotherapy* 3:299–316.

Dare, C., and Holder, A. (1981). Developmental aspects of the interaction between narcissism, self-esteem and object relations. *International Journal of Psycho-Analysis* 62:323–337.

Deniker, P., and Quintart, J. C. (1961). Les signes pseudo-névretiques dans les formes limites de la schizophrénie. *Encéphale* 50:307–323.

De Saussure, J. (1974). Discussion of the paper by Samuel Atkin. *International Journal of Psycho-Analysis* 55:21–23.

Deutsch, H. (1942). Some forms of emotional disturbance and their relationship to schizophrenia. *Psychoanalytic Quarterly* 11:301–321.

Diatkine, R. (1968). Indications and contraindications for psychoanalytic treatment. *International Journal of Psycho-Analysis* 49:266–270.

Dickes, R. (1974). The concepts of borderline states: an alternative proposal. *International Journal of Psychoanalytic Psychotherapy* 3:1–27.

Dicks, H. V. (1963). Object relations theory and marital studies. *British Journal of Medical Psychology* 36:125–129.

Dorpat, T. L. (1979a). A developmental perspective on character pathology. *Comprehensive Psychiatry* 20:548–559.

———(1979b). Is splitting a defense? *International Review of Psycho-Analysis* 6:105–113.

Easser, R., and Lesser, S. (1965). Hysterical personality: a re-evaluation. *Psychoanalytic Quarterly* 34:390–402.

Edgcumbe, R., and Burgner, M. (1972). Some problems in the conceptualization of early object relationships. I. The concepts of need-satisfaction and need-satisfying relationships. *Psychoanalytic Study of the Child* 27:283–314.

Ekstein, R., and Wallerstein, J. (1954). Observations on the psychology of borderline and psychotic children. *Psychoanalytic Study of the Child* 9:344–369.

——— (1956). Observations on the psychotherapy of borderline and psychotic children. *Psychoanalytic Study of the Child* 11:303–311.

Erikson, E. H. (1956). The problem of ego identity. *Journal of the American Psychoanalytic Association* 4:56–121.

——— (1959). *Identity and the Life Cycle*. New York: International Universities Press. [Psychological Issues, Monograh 1].

Escalona, S. K. (1963). Patterns of infantile experience and the developmental process. *Psychoanalytic Study of the Child* 18:197–244.

Fast, I. (1974). Multiple identities in the borderline personality organization. *British Journal of Medical Psychology* 47:291–300.

———(1975). Aspects of work style and work difficulty in borderline personalities. *International Journal of Psycho-Analysis* 56:397–403.

Fast, I., and Chethik, M. (1972). Some aspects of object relationships in borderline children. *International Journal of Psycho-Analysis* 53:479–485.

Fenichel, O. (1945). *The Psychoanalytic Theory of Neurosis*. New York: W. W. Norton.

Fields, W. S., and Sweet, W. H. (eds.) (1975). *Neural Bases of Violence and Aggression*. St. Louis: Warren H. Green.

Fintzy, R. T. (1971). Vicissitudes of the transitional object in borderline children. *International Journal of Psycho-Analysis* 52:107–114.

Fisher, C. (1965). Psychoanalytic implications of recent research on sleep and dreaming. *Journal of the American Psychoanalytic Association* 13:197–303.

Fleck, S., Lidz, T., and Cornelison, A. (1963). Comparison of parent–child relationships of male and female schizophrenic patients. *Archives of General Psychiatry* 8:1–7.

Flor-Henry, P. (1969). Psychosis and temporal lobe epilepsy. *Epilepsia* 10:363–395.

———(1972). Total and interictal psychiatric manifestations in epilepsy: specific or nonspecific? *Epilepsia* 13:773–783.

Frances, A., and Cooper, A. M. (1981). Descriptive and dynamic psychiatry: a perspective on DSM III. *American Journal of Psychiatry* 138:1198–1202.

Frances, A., Sacks, M., and Aronoff, M. S. (1977). Depersonalization: a self-relations perspective. *International Journal of Psychoanalysis* 58:325–351.

Frank, H., and Paris, J. (1981). Recollections of family experience in borderline patients. *Archives of General Psychiatry* 38:1031–1034.

Freud, A. (1936). *The Ego and the Mechanisms of Defense*. New York: International Universities Press, 1966.

———(1952). The mutual influences in the development of ego and id: introduction to the discussion. *Psychoanalytic Study of the Child* 7:42–50.

———(1953). Some remarks on infant observation. *Psychoanalytic Study of the Child* 8:9–19.

———(1965). *Normality and Pathology in Childhood: Assessments of Development*. New York: International Universities Press.

———(1969). Adolescence as a developmental disturbance. In *Adolescence: Psychosocial Perspectives*, ed. G. Caplan and S. Lebovici. New York: Basic Books.

———(1970). The concept of the rejecting mother. In *Parenthood: Its Psychology and Psychopathology*, ed. E. J. Anthony and T. Benedek, pp. 376–386. Boston: Little, Brown.

———(1980). Child analysis as the study of mental growth. In *The Course of Life: Psychoanalytic Contributions toward Understanding Personality Development*. vol. I. *Infancy and Early Childhood*, ed. S. I. Greenspan and G. H. Pollock, pp. 1–10. Adelphi, Md.: Mental Health Study Center, NIMH.

Freud, S. (1905). Three essays on the theory of sexuality. *Standard Edition* 7:123–245.

———(1909). Analysis of a phobia in a five-year-old boy. *Standard Edition* 10:1–149.

———(1916). Some analytic character-types met in psychoanalytic work. *Standard Edition* 14:309–333.

———(1918). From the history of an infantile neurosis. *Standard Edition* 17:1–122.

———(1937). Analysis terminable and interminable. *Standard Edition* 23: 209–253.

Friedman, H. J. (1969). Some problems of inpatient management with borderline patients. *American Journal of Psychiatry* 126:299–304.

———(1970). Dr. Friedman replies (Correspondence). *American Journal of Psychiatry* 126:1677.

———(1979). Exaggerated transference conflict as a criterion for the diagnosis of borderline personality. *Hillside Journal of Clinical Psychiatry* 1(2):123–142.

Frijling-Schreuder, E. C. M. (1969). Borderline states in children. *Psychoanalytic Study of the Child* 24:307–327.

Frosch, J. (1964). The psychotic character: clinical psychiatric considerations. *Psychoanalytic Quarterly* 38:81–96.

——— (1966). A note on reality constancy. In *Psychoanalysis—A General Psychology*, ed. R. M. Loewenstein et al., pp. 349–376. New York: International Universities Press.

——— (1967a). Severe regressive states during analysis: introduction. *Journal of the American Psychoanalytic Association* 15:491–507.

——— (1967b). Severe regressive states during analysis: summary. *Journal of the American Psychoanalytic Association* 15:606–625.

——— (1970). Psychoanalytic considerations of the psychotic character. *Journal of the American Psychoanalytic Association* 18:24–50.

——— (1982). Limitations of the concept borderline. Unpublished manuscript.

Gedo, J. E., and Goldberg, A. (1973). *Models of the Mind: A Psychoanalytic Theory.* Chicago: University of Chicago Press.

Gelcerd, E. (1958). Borderline states in childhood and adolescence. *Psychoanalytic Study of the Child* 13:279–295.

——— (1964). Child analysis: research, treatment and prophylaxis. *Journal of the American Psychoanalytic Association* 12:242–258.

Gershon, E. S., Baron, M., and Leckman, F. (1975). Genetic models of the transmission of affective disorders. *Journal of Psychiatric Research* 12:301–317.

Gill, M. M. (1963). *Topography and Systems in Psychoanalytic Theory.* New York: International Universities Press. [*Psychological Issues*, Monograph 10].

Giovacchini, P. L. (1965). Transference, incorporation and synthesis. *International Journal of Psychoanalysis* 46:287–296.

——— (1972). Technical difficulties in treating some characterological disorders: countertransference problems. *International Journal of Psychoanalytic Psychotherapy* 1:112–128.

——— (1973). Character disorders: with special reference to the borderline state. *International Journal of Psychoanalytic Psychotherapy* 2: 7–36.

Glaser, G. H., Newman, R. J., and Schafer, R. (1963). Interictal psychosis in psychomotor temporal lobe epilepsy: an EEG-psychological study. In *EEG and Behavior*, ed. G. H. Glaser. New York: Basic Books.

Glover, E. (1955). *The Technique of Psychoanalysis.* New York: International Universities Press.

——— (1956). *On the Early Development of the Mind.* New York: International Universities Press.

Goldberg, A. I. (1974). On the prognosis and treatment of narcissism. *Journal of the American Psychoanalytic Association* 22:243–254.

Goldensohn, E. S., and Gold, A. P. (1960). Prolonged behavioral disturbances as ictal phenomena. *Neurology* 10:1–9.

Goldstein, M. J., and Jones, J. E. (1977). Adolescent and family precursors of borderline and schizophrenic conditions. In *Borderline Personality Disorder: The Concept, the Syndrome, the Patient*, ed. P. Hartocollis, pp. 213–229. New York: International Universities Press.

Gottesman, I. I., and Shields, J. (1972). *Schizophrenia and Genetics: A Twin Study Vantage Point*. New York: Academic Press.

Graves, P. L. (1980). The functioning fetus. In *The Course of Life*, vol.I, *Infancy and Early Childhood*, ed. S. I. Greenspan and G. H. Pollock, pp. 235–236. Adelphi, Md.: Mental Health Study Center, NIMH.

Greenacre, P. (1947). Child wife as ideal: sociological considerations. In *Emotional Growth*, vol. I, pp. 3–8. New York: International Universities Press, 1971.

——— (1969). The fetish and the transitional object. *Psychoanalytic Study of the Child* 24:144–164.

Greenson, R. R. (1958). On screen defenses, screen hunger and screen identity. *Journal of the American Psychoanalytic Association* 6:242–262.

——— (1967). *The Technique and Practice of Psychoanalysis*. New York: International Universities Press.

Greenspan, S. I., and Cullander, C. C. H. (1973). A systematic metapsychological assessment of the personality: its application to the problem of analyzability. *Journal of the American Psychoanalytic Association* 21:303–327.

——— (1975). A systematic metapsychological assessment of the course of an analysis. *Journal of the American Psychoanalytic Association* 23:107–138.

Greenspan, S. I., Hatleberg, J. L., and Cullander, C. C. H. (1976). A systematic metapsychological assessment of the personality in childhood. *Journal of the American Psychoanalytic Association* 24:875–903.

Greenspan, S. I., and Lieberman, A. F. (1980). Infants, mothers and their interaction: a quantitative clinical approach to developmental assessment. In *The Course of Life*, vol. I. *Infancy and Early Childhood*, ed. S. I. Greenspan and G. H. Pollock, pp. 271–312. Adelphi, Md.: Mental Health Study Center, NIMH.

Grinberg, L., and Grinberg, R. (1974). Pathological aspects of identity in adolescence. *Contemporary Psychoanalysis* 10:27–40.

Grinker, R. R. (1977). The borderline syndrome: a phenomenological view. In *Borderline Personality Disorder: The Concept, the Syndrome, the Patient*, ed. P. Hartocollis, pp. 159–172. New York: International Universities Press.

Grinker, R. R., and Holzman, P. S. (1973). Schizophrenic pathology in young adults: a clinical study. *Archives of General Psychiatry* 28:168–175.

Grinker, R. R., Werble, B., and Drye, R. C. (1968). *The Borderline Syndrome: A Behavioral Study of Ego Functions.* New York: Basic Books.

Gunderson, J. G. (1977). Characteristics of borderlines. In *Borderline Personality Disorders: The Concept, the Syndrome, the Patient,* ed. P. Hartocollis, pp. 173–192. New York: International Universities Press.

Gunderson, J. G., Carpenter, W. T., and Strauss, J. S. (1975). Borderline and schizophrenic patients: a comparative study. *American Journal of Psychiatry* 132:1257–1264.

Gunderson, J. G., Kerr, J., and Eglund, D. W. (1980). The families of borderlines: a comparative study. *Archives of General Psychiatry* 37:27–33.

Gunderson, J. G., and Kolb, J. E. (1978). Discriminating features of borderline patients. *American Journal of Psychiatry* 135:792–796.

Gunderson, J. G., and Singer, M. T. (1975). Defining borderline patients: an overview. *American Journal of Psychiatry* 132:1–10.

Guntrip, H. (1969). *Schizoid Phenomena, Object Relations and the Self.* New York: International Universities Press.

Guttman, S. A. (1960). Criteria for analyzability (Panel report). *Journal of the American Psychoanalytic Association* 8:141–151.

Guze, S. B. (1975). Differential diagnosis of the borderline personality syndrome. In *Borderline States in Psychiatry,* ed. J. E. Mack, pp. 69–74. New York: Grune & Stratton.

Hartmann, H. (1939). *Ego Psychology and the Problem of Adaptation.* New York: International Universities Press.

——— (1952). The mutual influences in the development of ego and id. *Psychoanalytic Study of the Child* 7:9–30.

——— (1964). *Essays on Ego Psychology.* New York: International Universities Press.

Hartocollis, P. (1968). The syndrome of minimal brain dysfunction in young adult patients. *Bulletin of the Menninger Clinic* 32:102–114.

Havens, L. L. (1968). Some difficulties in giving schizophrenic and borderline patients medication. *Psychiatry* 31:44–50.

Hellman, J. M. (1981). Alcohol abuse and the borderline patient. *Psychiatry* 44:307–317.

Hersey, J. (1959). *The War Lover.* New York: Knopf.

Heston, L. L. (1966). Psychiatric disorders in foster home reared children of schizophrenic mothers. *British Journal of Psychiatry* 112:819–825.

——— (1970). The genetics of schizophrenic and schizoid disease. *Science* 167:249–256.

Hill, D., and Wetterson, D. (1942). Electro-encephalographic studies of psychopathic personalities. *Journal of Neurology and Psychiatry* 5:47–65.

Hoch, P. H., and Cattell, J. P. (1959). The diagnosis of pseudoneurotic schizophrenia. *Psychiatric Quarterly* 33:17–43.

Hoch, P. H., Cattell, J. P., Strahl, M. O., and Pennes, H. (1962). The course and outcome of pseudoneurotic schizophrenia. *American Journal of Psychiatry* 119:106–115.

Hoch, P. H., and Polatin, P. (1949). Pseudoneurotic forms of schizophrenia. *Psychiatric Quarterly* 23:248–276.

Hoffer, W. (1952). The mutual influences in the development of ego and id: earliest stages. *Psychoanalytic Study of the Child* 7:31–41.

Horner, A. J. (1975). Stages and processes in the development of early object relations and their associated pathologies. *International Review of Psychoanalysis* 2:95–105.

————(1979). *Object Relations and the Developing Ego in Therapy*. New York: Aronson.

Hubel, D. H., and Wiesel, T. N. (1965). Binocular interaction in striate cortex of kittens reared with artificial squint. *Journal of Neurophysiology* 28:1041–1059.

————(1970). The period of susceptibility to the physiological effects of unilateral eye closure in kittens. *Journal of Physiology* 206:419–436.

Huessy, H. R., Metoyer, M., and Townsend, M. (1974). Eight–ten year follow-up of 84 children treated for behavioral disturbance in rural Vermont. *Acta Paedopsychiatrica* 40:230–235.

Hunter, R. C. A. (1966). The analysis of episodes of depersonalization in a borderline patient. *International Journal of Psychoanalysis* 47:32–41.

Jacobs, D. (1975). The borderline or psychotic character in the prison setting. In *Borderline States in Psychiatry*, ed. J. E. Mack, pp. 63–74. New York: Grune & Stratton.

Jacobson, E. (1964). *The Self and the Object World*. New York: International Universities Press.

Jenkins, R. L., and Pacella, B. L. (1943). Electroencephalographic studies of delinquent boys. *American Journal of Orthopsychiatry* 13:107–120.

Joffee, W. G., and Sandler, J. (1965). Notes on pain, depression and individuation. *Psychoanalytic Study of the Child* 20:394–424.

Kallmann, F. J. (1938). *The Genetics of Schizophrenia*. New York: Augustin.

Karlsson, J. L. (1966). *The Biological Basis of Schizophrenia*. Springfield, Ill.: Thomas.

Katan, M. (1959). Comments on "ego distortion." *International Journal of Psychoanalysis* 40:297–303.

Keiser, S. (1958). Disturbances in abstract thinking and body-image formation. *Journal of the American Psychoanalytic Association* 6:628–652.

Kernberg, O. F. (1966). Structural derivatives of object relationships. *International Journal of Psychoanalysis* 47:236–253.

—— (1967). Borderline personality organization. *Journal of the American Psychoanalytic Association* 15:641–685.

—— (1968). The treatment of patients with borderline personality organization. *International Journal of Psychoanalysis* 49:600–619.

—— (1970a). Factors in the psychoanalytic treatment of narcissistic personalities. *Journal of the American Psychoanalytic Association* 18: 51–85.

—— (1970b). A psychoanalytic classification of character pathology. *Journal of the American Psychoanalytic Association* 18:800–822.

—— (1971). Prognostic considerations regarding borderline personality organization. *Journal of the American Psychoanalytic Association* 19: 595–635.

—— (1973). Psychoanalytic object-relations theory, group processes, and administration: toward an integrative theory of hospital treatment. *Annual of Psychoanalysis* 1:363–388.

—— (1974). Contrasting viewpoints regarding the nature and psychoanalytic treatment of narcissistic personalities: a preliminary communication. *Journal of the American Psychoanalytic Association* 22:255–267.

—— (1975). *Borderline Conditions and Pathological Narcissism.* New York: Aronson.

—— (1976a). *Object-Relations Theory and Clinical Psychoanalysis.* New York: Aronson.

—— (1976b). Technical considerations in the treatment of borderline personality organization. *Journal of the American Psychoanalytic Association* 24:795–829.

—— (1977). The structural diagnosis of borderline personality organization. In *Borderline Personality Disorder: The Concept, the Syndrome, the Patient,* ed. P. Hartocollis, pp. 87–121. New York: International Universities Press.

—— (1978). The diagnosis of borderline conditions in adolescence. *Adolescent Psychiatry* 6:298–320.

—— (1979). Psychoanalytic psychotherapy with borderline adolescents. *Adolescent Psychiatry* 7:294–321.

Kernberg, O. F., Burstein, E. D., Coyne, L., Applebaum, A., Horwitz, L., and Voth, H. (1972). Psychotherapy and psychoanalysis: final report of the Menninger Foundation's Psychotherapy Research Project. *Bulletin of the Menninger Clinic* 36:1–277.

Kety, S. S. (1976a). Genetic aspects of schizophrenia. *Psychiatric Annals* 6:6–15.

—— (1976b). Studies designed to disentangle genetic and environmental variables in schizophrenia: some epistemological questions and answers. *American Journal of Psychiatry* 133:1134–1137.

Kety, S. S., Rosenthal, D., Wender, P. H., and Schulsinger, F. (1968). The types and prevalence of mental illness in the biological and adoptive families of adopted schizophrenics. In *The Transmission of Schizophrenia*, ed. D. Rosenthal and S. S. Kety, pp. 345–362. Oxford: Pergamon Press.

———(1971). Mental illness in the biological and adoptive families of adopted schizophrenics. *American Journal of Psychiatry* 18:302–306.

Khan, M. M. (1960). Clinical aspects of the schizoid personality: affects and technique. *International Journal of Psychoanalysis* 41:430–437.

King, S. H. (1971). Coping mechanisms in adolescents. *Psychiatric Annals* 1:10–46.

Kleeman, J. A. (1967). The peek-a-boo game. I. Its origins, meanings, and related phenomena in the first year. *Psychoanalytic Study of the Child* 22:239–273.

Klein, D. F. (1975). Psychopharmacology and the borderline patient. In *Borderline States in Psychiatry*, ed. J. E. Mack, pp. 75–91. New York: Grune & Stratton.

———(1977). Psychopharmacological treatment and delineation of borderline disorders. In *Borderline Personality Disorder: The Concept, the Syndrome, the Patient*, ed. P. Hartocollis, pp. 365–383. New York: International Universities Press.

Knapp, P. H., Levin, S., McCarter, R. H., Wermer, H., and Zetzel, E. R. (1960). Suitability for psychoanalysis: A review of one hundred supervised analytic cases. *The Psychoanalytic Quarterly*, 29:459–477.

Knight, R. P. (1953). Borderline states. In *Psychoanalytic Psychiatry and Psychology*, pp. 97–109. New York: International Universities Press.

Koenigsberg, H. W. (1982). A comparison of hospitalized and nonhospitalized borderline patients. *American Journal of Psychiatry* 139:1292–1297.

Kohut, H. (1971). *The Analysis of the Self*. New York: International Universities Press.

———(1972). Thoughts on narcissism and narcissistic rage. *Psychoanalytic Study of the Child* 27:360–400.

Kolb, J. E., and Gunderson, J. G. (1980). Diagnosing borderline patients with a semistructured interview. *Archives of General Psychiatry* 37:37–41.

Kramer, P. (1958). Note on one of the preoedipal roots of the superego. *Journal of the American Psychoanalytic Association* 6:38–46.

Kringlen, E. (1964). *Schizophrenia in Male Monozygotic Twins*. Oslo: Universitetsforlaget.

Krohn, A. (1974). Borderline "empathy" and differentiation of object representations: a contribution to the psychology of object relations. *International Journal of Psychoanalytic Psychotherapy* 3:142–165.

Kuiper, P. C. (1968). Indications and contraindications for psychoanalytic treatment. *International Journal of Psychoanalysis* 49:261–264.

Levine, H. B. (1979). The sustaining object relationship. *Annual of Psychoanalysis* 7:203–231.

Levy, D. M. (1970). The concept of maternal overprotection. In *Parenthood: Its Psychology and Psychopathology*, ed. E. J. Anthony and T. Benedek, pp. 387–409. Boston: Little, Brown.

Lewis, D. O., Pincus, J. H., Shanok, S. S., and Glaser, G. H. (1982). Psychomotor epilepsy and violence in a group of incarcerated delinquent boys. *American Journal of Psychiatry* 139:882–887.

Lichtenstein, H. (1964). The role of narcissism in the emergence and maintenance of a primary identity. *International Journal of Psychoanalysis* 45:49–56.

——— (1965). Towards a metapsychological definition of the concept of self. *International Journal of Psychoanalysis* 46:117–128.

——— (1977). *The Dilemma of Human Identity*. New York: Aronson.

Lidz, T., and Fleck, S. (1959). Schizophrenia, human integration, and the role of the family. In *The Etiology of Schizophrenia*, ed. D. Jackson, pp. 323–345. New York: Basic Books.

Lidz, T., Fleck, S., and Cornelison, A. R. (1965). *Schizophrenia and the Family*. New York: International Universities Press.

Liebowitz, M. R., and Klein, D. F. (1981). Interrelationship of hysteroid dysphoria and borderline personality disorder. *Psychiatric Clinics of North America* 4:67–87.

Little, M. (1958). On delusional transference (transference psychosis). *International Journal of Psychoanalysis* 39:143–148.

——— (1966). Transference in borderline states. *International Journal of Psychoanalysis* 47:476–485.

Loewald, H. W. (1962). Internalization, separation, mourning and the superego. *Psychoanalytic Quarterly* 31:483–504.

——— (1971). On motivation and instinct theory. *Psychoanalytic Study of the Child* 26:91–128.

Lower, R. B., Escoll, P. J., and Huxster, H. K. (1972). Bases for judgments of analyzability. *Journal of the American Psychoanalytic Association* 20:610–621.

Luchins, D. J., Weinberger, D. R., and Wyatt, R. J. (1982). Schizophrenia and cerebral asymmetry detected by computed tomography. *American Journal of Psychiatry* 139:753–757.

Mack, J. E. (1975). Borderline states: an historical perspective. In *Borderline States in Psychiatry*, ed. J. E. Mack, pp. 1–27. New York: Grune & Stratton.

MacMurray, J. (1976). Mothering and the borderline patient. *Psychiatric Annals* 6:91–100.

Maenchen, A. (1968). Object cathexis in a borderline twin. *Psychoanalytic Study of the Child* 23:438-456.

Mahler, M. S. (1963). Thoughts about development and individuation. *Psychoanalytic Study of the Child* 18:307-324.

——— (1968). *On Human Symbiosis and the Vicissitudes of Individuation.* vol. 1. *Infantile Psychosis.* New York: International Universities Press.

——— (1971). A study of the separation-individuation process and its possible application to borderline phenomena in the psychoanalytic situation. *Psychoanalytic Study of the Child* 26:403-424.

——— (1972). The rapprochement subphase of the separation-individuation process. *Psychoanalytic Quarterly* 41:487-506.

Mahler, M. S., and Kaplan, L. (1977). Developmental aspects in the assessment of narcissistic and so-called borderline personalities. In *Borderline Personality Disorder: The Concept, the Syndrome, the Patient,* ed. P. Hartocollis, pp. 71-85. New York: International Universities Press.

Mahler, M. S., Pine, F., and Bergman, A. (1975). *The Psychological Birth of the Human Infant.* New York: Basic Books.

Mandelbaum, A. (1977a). A family centered approach to residential treatment. *Bulletin of the Menninger Clinic* 41:27-39.

——— (1977b). The family treatment of the borderline patient. In *Borderline Personality Disorder: The Concept, the Syndrome, the Patient,* ed. P. Hartocollis, pp. 423-438. New York: International Universities Press.

——— (1980). Family characteristics of patients with borderline and narcissistic disorders. *Bulletin of the Menninger Clinic* 44:201-211.

Mannino, F. V., and Greenspan, S. I. (1976). Projection and misperception in couples treatment. *Journal of Marriage and Family Counseling* 2:139-143.

Mark, V. H., and Ervin, F. R. (1980). *Violence and the Brain.* New York: Harper and Row.

Marmor, J. (1953). Orality in the hysterical personality. *Journal of the American Psychoanalytic Association* 1:656-671.

Masterson, J. F. (1972). *Treatment of the Borderline Adolescent: A Developmental Approach.* New York: Wiley.

——— (1976). *Psychotherapy of the Borderline Adult.* New York: Brunner/Mazel.

Masterson, J. F., and Rinsley, D. B. (1975). The borderline syndrome: the role of the mother in the genesis and psychic structure of the borderline personality. *International Journal of Psychoanalysis* 56:163-177.

Matthysse, S. W., and Kidd, K. K. (1976). Estimating the genetic contribution to schizophrenia. *American Journal of Psychiatry* 133:185-191.

McDevitt, J. B. (1975). Separation-individuation and object constancy. *Journal of the American Psychoanalytic Association* 23:713-742.

Meissner, S. J., W. W. (1964). Thinking about the family—psychiatric aspects. In *Family Process*, ed. N. W. Ackerman, pp. 131–170. New York: Basic Books.

—— (1971). Notes on identification. II. Clarification of related concepts. *Psychoanalytic Quarterly* 40:277–302.

—— (1972). Notes on identification. III. The concept of identification. *Psychoanalytic Quarterly* 41:224–260.

—— (1974a). Differentiation and integration of learning and identification in the developmental process. *Annual of Psychoanalysis* 2:181–196.

—— (1974b). The role of imitative social learning in identificatory processes. *Journal of the American Psychoanalytic Association* 22:512–536.

—— (1976a). New horizons in metapsychology: view and review (panel report). *Journal of the American Psychoanalytic Association* 24:161–180.

—— (1976b). Psychotherapeutic schema based on the paranoid process. *International Journal of Psychoanalytic Psychotherapy* 5:87–114.

—— (1977a). Cognitive aspects of the paranoid process—prospectus. In *Psychiatry and the Humanities*. vol. II. *Thought, Consciousness, and Reality*, ed. J. H. Smith, pp. 159–216. New Haven: Yale University Press.

—— (1977b). Psychoanalytic notes on suicide. *International Journal of Psychoanalytic Psychotherapy* 6:415–447.

—— (1978). *The Paranoid Process*. New York: Aronson.

—— (1979). Internalization and object relations. *Journal of the American Psychoanalytic Association* 27:345–360.

—— (1980a). The problem of internalization and structure formation. *International Journal of Psychoanalysis* 61:237–248.

—— (1980b). Theories of personality and psychopathology: classical psychoanalysis. In *Comprehensive Textbook of Psychiatry*, vol. III, eds. H. I. Kaplan, A. M. Friedman, and B. J. Sadock, pp. 631–728. Baltimore: Williams & Wilkins.

—— (1981a). Addiction and the paranoid process; psychoanalytic perspectives. *International Journal of Psychoanalytic Psychotherapy* 8:273–310.

—— (1981b). *Internalization in Psychoanalysis*. New York: International Universities Press. [Psychological Issues, Monograph 50].

—— (1981c). Metapsychology—who needs it? *Journal of the American Psychoanalytic Association* 29:921–938.

—— (1981d). A note on narcissism. *Psychoanalytic Quarterly* 50:77–89.

—— (to be published). The earliest internalizations. In *Self and Object Constancy*, eds. R. F. Lax, S. Bach, and J. A. Burland. New York: Guilford.

Mendelson, W., Johnson, N., and Stewart, M. A. (1971). Hyperactive children as teenagers: a follow-up. *Journal of Nervous and Mental Disease* 153:273–279.

Meyer, J. K. (1982). The theory of gender identity disorders. *Journal of the American Psychoanalytic Association* 30:381–418.

Meza, C. (1970). Anger—a key to the borderline patient. (Correspondence). *American Journal of Psychiatry* 126:1676–1677.

Modell, A. H. (1961). Denial and the sense of separateness. *Journal of the American Psychoanalytic Association* 9:533–547.

—— (1963). Primitive object-relationships and the predisposition to schizophrenia. *International Journal of Psychoanalysis* 44:282–292.

—— (1968). *Object Love and Reality*. New York: International Universities Press.

—— (1973). Affects and psychoanalytic knowledge. *Annual of Psychoanalysis* 1:117–124.

—— (1975). A narcissistic defense against affects and the illusion of self-sufficiency. *International Journal of Psychoanalysis* 56:275–282.

—— (1980). The narcissistic character and disturbances in the "holding environment." In *The Course of Life*, vol. 3, Adulthood and the Aging Process, eds. S. H. Greenspan and G. H. Pollock, pp. 367–379. Adelphi, Md.: Mental Health Study Center, NIMH.

Monroe, R. R. (1970). *Episodic Behavioral Disorders: A Psychodynamic and Neurophysiologic Analysis*. Cambridge: Harvard University Press.

—— (1978). *Brain Dysfunction in Aggressive Criminals*. Lexington, Mass.: D. C. Heath.

Moore, B. E. (1975). Toward a clarification of the concept of narcissism. *Psychoanalytic Study of the Child* 30:243–276.

Morris, H. H., Escoll, P. J., and Wexler, R. (1956). Aggressive behaviors of childhood: a follow-up study. *American Journal of Psychiatry* 112: 991–997.

Morrison, J. R., and Minkoff, K. (1975). Explosive personality as a sequel to the hyperactive-child syndrome. *Comprehensive Psychiatry* 16: 343–348.

Murray, G. B. (1981). Complex partial seizures. In *Psychiatric Medicine Update: Massachusetts General Hospital Reviews for Physicians*, ed. T. C. Manschreck, pp. 103–118. New York: Elsevier.

Murray, J. M. (1964). Narcissism and the ego ideal. *Journal of the American Psychoanalytic Association* 12:477–528.

Murray, M. E. (1979). Minimal brain dysfunction and borderline personality adjustment. *American Journal of Psychotherapy* 33:391–403.

Offer, D. (1969). *The Psychological World of the Teenager*. New York: Basic Books.

Offer, D., and Offer, J. L. (1969). Growing up: a follow-up study of normal adolescents. *Seminars in Psychiatry* 1:46–56.

O'Neal, P., and Robbins, L. M. (1958). The relation of childhood behavior problems to adult psychiatric status: a 30-year follow-up of 150 patients. *American Journal of Psychiatry* 114:961–969.

Ornstein, P. (1974). On narcissism: beyond the introduction, highlights of

Heinz Kohut's contributions to the psychoanalytic treatment of narcissistic personality disorders. *Annual of Psychoanalysis* 2:127–149.

Perry, J. C., and Klerman, G. L. (1978). The borderline patient: a comparative analysis of four sets of diagnostic criteria. *Archives of General Psychiatry* 35:141–150.

Pine, F. (1974). On the concept of "borderline" in children: a clinical essay. *Psychoanalytic Study of the Child* 29:341–368.

———(1981). In the beginning: Contributions to a psychoanalytic developmental psychology. *International Review of Psycho-Analysis* 8:15–33.

Pollin, W., Stabenau, J. R., and Tupin, J. (1965). Family studies with identical twins discordant for schizophrenia. *Psychiatry* 28:60–78.

Pruyser, P. W. (1975). What splits in "splitting"? *Bulletin of the Menninger Clinic* 39:1–46.

Quitkin, F., and Klein, D. F. (1969). Two behavioral syndromes in young adults related to possible minimal brain dysfunction. *Journal of Psychiatric Research* 7:131–142.

Rangell, L. (1955). The borderline case (panel report). *Journal of the American Psychoanalytic Association* 3:285–298.

Rapaport, D. (1958). *The Structure of Psychoanalytic Theory: A Systematizing Attempt.* New York: International Universities Press, 1960. [Psychological Issues, Monograph 6].

———(1967). *The Collected Papers of David Rapaport.* New York: Basic Books.

Rapoport, R. (1963). Normal crises, family structure, and mental health. In *Family Process*, ed. N. W. Ackerman, pp. 343–355. New York: Basic Books.

Reich, A. (1953). Narcissistic object choice in women. *Journal of the American Psychoanalytic Association* 1:22–44.

Reich, W. (1933). *Character Analysis*, 3rd ed. New York: Farrar, Straus and Giroux, 1949.

———(1974). *The Impulsive Character and Other Writings.* New York: New American Library.

Reich, W. (1975). The spectrum concept of schizophrenia: problems for diagnostic practice. *Archives of General Psychiatry* 32:489–498.

———(1976). The schizophrenia spectrum: a genetic concept. *Journal of Nervous and Mental Disease* 162:3–12.

Rifkin, A., Quitkin, F., Carrillo, C., Blumberg, A., and Klein, D. (1972). Lithium carbonate in emotionally unstable character disorder. *Archives of General Psychiatry* 27:519–523.

Rinsley, D. B. (1971). The adolescent inpatient: patterns of depersonification. *Psychiatric Quarterly* 45:3–22.

———(1980a). The developmental etiology of borderline and narcissistic disorders. *Bulletin of the Menninger Clinic* 44:127–134.

——(1980b). Diagnosis and treatment of borderline and narcissistic children and adolescents. *Bulletin of the Menninger Clinic* 44:147–170.

——(1980c). A thought experiment in psychiatric genetics. *Bulletin of the Menninger Clinic* 44:628–638.

—— (1981). Dynamic and developmental issues in borderline and related "spectrum" disorders. *Psychiatric Clinics of North America* 4: 117–132.

Robbins, L. L. (1956). The borderline case (panel report). *Journal of the American Psychoanalytic Association* 4:550–562.

Robbins, M. D. (1976). Borderline personality organization: the need for a new theory. *Journal of the American Psychoanalytic Association* 24: 831–853.

——(1981a). The symbiosis concept and the commencement of normal and pathological ego functioning and object relations: II. Developments subsequent to infancy and pathological processes. *International Review of Psychoanalysis* 8:379–391.

——(1981b). The symbiosis concept and the commencement of normal and pathological ego functioning and object relations: I. Infancy. *International Review of Psychoanalysis* 8:365–377.

Rochlin, G. (1973). *Man's Aggression: The Defense of the Self.* Boston: Gambit.

Rosenbaum, C. P. (1968). Metabolic, physiological, anatomic and genetic studies in the schizophrenias: a review and analysis. *Journal of Nervous and Mental Disease* 146:103–126.

Rosenfeld, S. K., and Sprince, M. P. (1963). An attempt to formulate the meaning of the concept "borderline." *Psychoanalytic Study of the Child* 18:603–635.

——(1965). Some thoughts on the technical handling of borderline children. *Psychoanalytic Study of the Child* 20:495–517.

Rosenthal, D. (1963). Theoretical overview: a suggested conceptual framework. In *The Genain Quadruplets*, ed. D. Rosenthal, pp. 505–511. New York: Basic Books.

——(1970). *Genetic Theory and Abnormal Behavior.* New York: McGraw-Hill.

——(1971). *The Genetics of Psychopathology.* New York: McGraw-Hill.

——(1975). The concept of subschizophrenic disorders. In *Genetic Research in Psychiatry.* eds. R. R. Fieve, D. Rosenthal, and H. Brill, pp. 199–215. Baltimore: John Hopkins University Press.

Rosenthal, D., and Kety, S. (eds.)(1968). *The Transmission of Schizophrenia.* Oxford: Pergamon.

Rosenthal, D., Wender, P. H., Kety, S. S., Welner, J., and Schulsinger, F. (1971). The adopted-away offspring of schizophrenics. *American Journal of Psychiatry* 128:307–311.

Ross, M. (1976). The borderline diathesis. *International Review of Psychoanalysis* 3:305 321.

Ross, N. (1967). The "as-if" personality. *Journal of the American Psychoanalytic Association* 15:59–82.

Rubenfine, D. L. (1962). Maternal stimulation, psychic structure, and early object relations: with special reference to aggression and denial. *Psychoanalytic Study of the Child* 17:265–282.

Sander, L. W., Stechler, G., Julia, H., and Burns, P. (1971). Primary prevention and some aspects of temporal organization in early infant-caretaker interaction. In *Infant Psychiatry: A New Synthesis*, ed. E. N. Rexford et al., pp. 187–204. New Haven: Yale University Press.

Sandler, J., and Rosenblatt, B. (1962). The concept of the representational world. *Psychoanalytic Study of the Child* 17:128–148.

Sarnoff, C. A. (1972). The vicissitudes of projection during an analysis encompassing late latency to early adolescence. *International Journal of Psychoanalysis* 53:515–522.

Schafer, R. (1968a). *Aspects of Internalization*. New York: International Universities Press.

—— (1968b). On the theoretical and technical conceptualization of activity and passivity. *Psychoanalytic Quarterly* 37:173–198.

Settlage, C. F. (1977). The psychoanalytic understanding of narcissistic and borderline personality disorders: advances in developmental theory. *Journal of the American Psychoanalytic Association* 25:805–833.

Shapiro, E. (1978). Research on family dynamics: clinical implications for the family of the borderline adolescent. *Adolescent Psychiatry* 6:360–376.

—— (1982). The holding environment and family therapy with acting out adolescents. *International Journal of Psychoanalytic Psychotherapy* 9: 209–231.

Shapiro, E. R., Zinner, J., Shapiro, R. L., and Berkowitz, D. A. (1975). The influence of family experience on borderline personality development. *International Review of Psychoanalysis* 2:399–411.

Shapiro, R. L. (1979). Family dynamics and object-relations theory: an analytic group-interpretive approach to family therapy. *Adolescent Psychiatry* 7:118–135.

Siever, L. J., and Gunderson, J. G. (1979). Genetic determinants of borderline conditions. *Schizophrenia Bulletin* 5:59–86.

Singer, M. (1975). The borderline delinquent: the interlocking of intrapsychic and interactional determinants. *International Review of Psychoanalysis* 2:429–440.

—— (1977). The experience of emptiness in narcissistic and borderline states. I. Deficiency and ego-defect versus dynamic-defensive models. *International Review of Psychoanalysis* 4:459–469.

Singer, M. T. (1977). The borderline diagnosis and psychological tests: review and research. In *Borderline Personality Disorder: The Concept, the Syndrome, the Patient*, ed. P. Hartocollis, pp. 193–212. New York: International Universities Press.

Slater, E., and Beard, A. W. (1963). Schizophrenia-like psychoses of epilepsy. *British Journal of Psychiatry* 109:95–150.

Slipp, S. (1973). The symbiotic survival pattern: a relational theory of schizophrenia. *Family Process* 12:377–398.

Socarides, C. W. (1968). *The Overt Homosexual*. New York: Aronson.

——— (1980). Homosexuality and the rapprochement subphase. In *Rapprochement: The Critical Subphase of Separation-Individuation*, ed. R. F. Lax et al., pp. 331–352. New York: Aronson.

Soloff, P. H. (1981). Concurrent validation of a diagnostic interview for borderline patients. *American Journal of Psychiatry* 138:691–693.

Spiro, R. H., and Spiro, T. W. (1980). Transitional phenomena and developmental issues in borderline Rorschachs. In *Borderline Phenomena and the Rorschach Test*, ed. J. Kawer et al., pp. 189–202. New York: International Universities Press.

Spitz, R. A. (1945). Hospitalism: an inquiry into the genesis of psychiatric conditions in early childhood. *Psychoanalytic Study of the Child* 1:53–74.

——— (1946). Anaclitic depression: an inquiry into the genesis of psychiatric conditions in early childhood, II. *Psychoanalytic Study of the Child* 2:313–342.

——— (1958). On the genesis of superego components. *Psychoanalytic Study of the Child* 13:375–404.

——— (1965). *The First Year of Life*. New York: International Universities Press.

Spitzer, R. L., and Endicott, J. (1979). Justification for separating schizotypal and borderline personality disorders. *Schizophrenia Bulletin* 5(1):95–104.

Spitzer, R. L., Endicott, J., and Gibbon, M. (1979). Crossing the border into borderline personality and borderline schizophrenia. *Archives of General Psychiatry* 36:17–24.

Spitzer, R. L., Williams, J. B. W., and Skodol, A. E. (1980). DSM III: the major achievements and an overview. *American Journal of Psychiatry* 137:151–164.

Stern, A. (1938). Psychoanalytic investigation of therapy in the borderline neuroses. *Psychoanalytic Quarterly* 7:467–489.

Stolorow, R. D., and Lachmann, F. M. (1978). The developmental presages of defenses: diagnostic and therapeutic implications. *Psychoanalytic Quarterly* 47:73–102.

Stone, L. (1954). The widening scope of indications for psychoanalysis. *Journal of the American Psychoanalytic Association* 2:567–594.

Stone, M. H. (1976). Manic depression found in subtle symptoms. *Psychiatric News* Dec. 3, pp. 23–29.

——— (1977). The borderline syndrome: evolution of the term, genetic aspects, and prognosis. *American Journal of Psychotherapy* 31:345–365.

——— (1978). Toward an early detection of manic-depressive illness in psychoanalytic patients. 1. Patients who later develop a manic illness. *American Journal of Psychotherapy* 32:427–439.

——— (1979). Psychodiagnosis and psychoanalytic psychotherapy. *Journal of the American Academy of Psychoanalysis* 7:79–100.

——— (1980). *The Borderline Syndromes: Constitution, Personality, and Adaptation.* New York: McGraw-Hill.

Tartakoff, H. H. (1966). The normal personality in our culture and the Nobel Prize complex. In *Psychoanalysis—A General Psychology*, ed. R. M. Lowenstein et al., pp. 222–252. New York: International Universities Press.

Thomas, A., and Chess, S. (1976). Evolution of behavior disorders in adolescence. *American Journal of Psychiatry* 133:539–542.

Tolpin, M. (1971). On the beginnings of a cohesive self: an application of the concept of transmuting internalization to the study of the transitional object and signal anxiety. *Psychoanalytic Study of the Child* 26:316–352.

Tunks, E. R., and Dermer, S. W. (1977). Carbamazepzine in the dyscontrol syndrome associated with limebic system dysfunction. *Journal of Nervous and Mental Disease* 164:56–63.

Tustin, F. (1980). Autistic objects. *International Review of Psychoanalysis* 7:27–39.

Vaillant, G. E. (1971). Theoretical hierarchy of adaptive ego mechanism. *Archives of General Psychiatry* 24:107–118.

——— (1975). Sociopathy as a human process. *Archives of General Psychiatry* 32:178–183.

Waldhorn, H. F. (1960). Assessment of analyzability: technical and theoretical observations. *Psychoanalytic Quarterly* 39:478–506.

Waring, M., and Ricks, D. (1965). Family patterns of children who become adult schizophrenics. *Journal of Nervous and Mental Diseases* 140:351–364.

Weingarten, L. L., and Korn, S. (1967). Pseudoneurotic schizophrenia: psychological test findings. *Archives of General Psychiatry* 17:448–453.

Weiss, G., Hechtman, L., Perlman, T. et al. (1979). Hyperactives as young adults. *Archives of General Psychiatry* 36:675–681.

Wender, P. H. (1969). The role of genetics in the etiology of the schizophrenias. *American Journal of Orthopsychiatry* 39:447–458.

────── (1977). The contribution of the adoption studies to an understanding of the phenomenology and etiology of the borderline schizophrenic. In *Borderline Personality Disorder: The Concept, the Syndrome, the Patient*, ed. P. Hartocollis, pp. 255–269. New York: International Universities Press.

Wender, P. H., Rosenthal, D., Kety, S. S., Schulsinger, F., and Welner, J. (1974). Crossfostering: a research strategy for clarifying the role of genetic and experiential factors in the etiology of schizohrenia. *Archives of General Psychiatry* 30:121–128.

Wender, P. H. et al. (1976). Borderline schizophrenia. *Medical World News* May 17, pp. 23–24.

Werble, B. (1970). Second follow-up study of borderline patients. *Archives of General Psychiatry* 23:3–7.

Wilson, C. P. (1971). On the limits of the effectiveness of psychoanalysis: Early ego and somatic disturbances. *Journal of the American Psychoanalytic Association* 19:552–564.

Winnicott, D. W. (1953). Transitional objects and transitional phenomena. In *Playing and Reality*, pp. 1–25. New York: Basic Books, 1971.

────── (1960a). Ego distortion in terms of true and false self. In *The Maturational Processes and the Facilitating Environment*, pp. 140–152. New York: International Universities Press.

────── (1960b). The theory of the parent–infant relationship. In *The Maturational Processes and the Facilitating Environment*, pp. 37–55. New York: International Universities Press, 1965.

────── (1967). Mirror-role of mother and family in child development. In *Playing and Reality*, pp. 111–118. New York: Basic Books, 1971.

Wolff, P. H. (1963). Developmental motivational concepts in Piaget's sensorimotor theory of intelligence. In *Infant Psychiatry: A New Synthesis*, eds. E. N. Rexford, L. W. Sander, and T. Shapiro, pp. 172–186. New Haven: Yale University Press.

Wolff, P. H., Waber, D., Bauermeister, M., Cohen, C., and Ferber, R. (1982). The neuropsychological status of adolescent delinquent boys. *Journal of Child Psychology and Psychiatry* 23:267–279.

Worden, F. G. (1955). A problem in psychoanalytic technique. *Journal of the American Psychoanalytic Association* 3:255–279.

Wurmser, L. (1978). *The Hidden Dimension: Psychodynamics in Compulsive Drug Use*. New York: Aronson.

Wynne, L., Ryckoff, I., Day, J., and Hirsch, S. (1958). Pseudomutuality in the family relations of schizophrenics. *Psychiatry* 21:205–220.

Zellermeyer, I. (1974). Reflections on adolescence. *Israel Annals of Psychiatry and Related Disciplines* 12:261–274.

Zetzel, E. R. (1968). The so-called good hysteric. *International Journal of Psycho-Analysis* 49:256–260.

———(1971). A developmental approach to the borderline patient. *American Journal of Psychiatry* 127:867–871.

Zetzel, E. R., and Meissner, W. W. (1973). *Basic Concepts of Psychoanalytic Psychiatry*. New York: Basic Books.

Zilboorg, G. (1941). Ambulatory schizophrenias. *Psychiatry* 4:149–155.

———(1956). The problem of ambulatory schizophrenias. *American Journal of Psychiatry* 113:519–525.

———(1957). Further observations on ambulatory schizophrenias. *American Journal of Orthopsychiatry* 27:677–682.

Zinberg, N. E. (1974). *"High" States: A Beginning Study*. Washington: Drug Abuse Council.

———(1975). Addiction and ego function. *Psychoanalytic Study of the Child* 30:567–588.

Zinner, J., and Shapiro, R. (1972). Projective identification as a mode of perception and behaviour in families of adolescents. *International Journal of Psycho-Analysis* 53:523–530.

———(1974). The family group as a single psychic entity: implications for acting out in adolescence. *International Review of Psychoanalysis* 1:179–186.

Zinner, J., and Shapiro, E. R. (1975). Splitting in families of borderline adolescents. In *Borderline States in Psychiatry*, ed. J. E. Mack, pp. 103–122. New York: Grune & Stratton.

Name Index

Subject Index

SEP 1 2 1985

DATE DUE

PRINTED IN U.S.A.

HIGHSMITH 45-102